INTERNATIONAL PERSPECTIVES ON FAMILY VIOLENCE AND ABUSE

A Cognitive Ecological Approach

INTERNATIONAL PERSPECTIVES ON FAMILY VIOLENCE AND ABUSE

A Cognitive Ecological Approach

Edited by

Kathleen Malley-Morrison

Psychology Press
Taylor & Francis Group

New York London

First published by Lawrence Erlbaum Associates, Inc., Publishers
10 Industrial Avenue
Mahwah, New Jersey 07430

Reprinted 2008 by Psychology Press

Psychology Press
Taylor & Francis Group
27 Church Road
Hove, East Sussex BN3 2FA

| Cover design by Sean Sciarrone |

Library of Congress Cataloging-in-Publication Data

International Perspectives on Family Violence and Abuse: A Cognitive Ecological Approach,
  edited by Kathleen Malley-Morrison.
     p. cm.
  Includes bibliographical references and indexes.
  ISBN 0-8058-4245-4 (cloth : alk. paper) — ISBN 0-8058-4246-2 (pbk. : alk. paper)

Copyright information for this volume can be obtained by contacting the Library of Congress.

Printed in the United States of America
10 9 8 7 6 5 4 3 2

To nonviolence in human relationships.
We are all one family.

Contents

Preface   xi

PART I: CONTEXT

1   Introduction   3
    Kathleen Malley-Morrison

PART II: WESTERN EUROPE

2   Iceland   17
    Anna María Hauksdóttir & Steinunn Gestsdóttir

3   England   33
    Elizabeth Donovan

4   Portugal   51
    Melanie T. Santos & Andrea E. Mercurio

5   Italy   69
    Scott Borrelli & Tommaso Palumbo

6   Germany   89
    Elisabeth Leembruggen-Kallberg, Silke Rupprecht, & Diane Cadmus

PART III: CENTRAL AND SOUTHERN EUROPE

7   Russia   111
    Anna Fastenko & Irini Timofeeva

8   Greece   131
    Georgia Stathopoulou

9   Turkey   151
    Alev Yalçinkaya

PART IV: THE MIDDLE EAST

10 Saudi Arabia   167
    Majed A. Ashy

11 Israel   187
    Odelya Pagovich

12 Lebanon   205
    Laura Sheridan & Ghassan Ghorayeb

PART V: AFRICA

13 Somalia   223
    Natoschia Scruggs

14 South Africa   245
    Ronel Fourie

PART VI: ASIA AND THE PACIFIC

15 India   265
    Sonia Chawla

16 Japan   283
    Mizuho Arai

17   Korea   301
     Mikyung Jang & Mi-Sung Kim

18   Taiwan   321
     Huei-Ping Liu

19   Republika ng pilipinas, the Philippines   339
     Nyryan E-V. Nolido

20   Australia   361
     Doe West

PART VII: LATIN AMERICA

21   Nicaragua   381
     Kevin Powell

22   Brazil   397
     Wilson Bezerra-Flanders

23   Colombia   415
     Sharon Abramzon

PART VIII: NORTH AMERICA

24   Canada   429
     Indrani J. Dookie

25   United States   451
     Kimberly A. Rapoza

PART IX: CONCLUSION

26   Human Rights   473
     Marcus D. Patterson

Author Index   501

Subject Index   513

Preface

Suppose someone asked you to give your definition of abuse as it occurs within the context of the family. What would you say? Would you define abuse as beating a child, raping a wife, or neglecting an elderly parent? Or would your definition focus on making a child work, telling your wife you are having an affair, embarrassing your husband in public, or expecting your parents to take care of their grandchildren? Whatever your definition is, it reflects your *implicit theory* concerning the nature of abuse. That is, it reflects your informal set of assumptions about who is abusive, why somebody maltreats a family member, and what behaviors within the family deserve the label *abuse*. Although many assumptions about family violence are shared by individuals from very diverse cultures, it is also true that implicit theories as to the behaviors that constitute abuse, and the causes of those behaviors, show considerable variation across cultures. There is also variation across cultures in the assumptions about the roles that are appropriate for men, women, children, and older family members, and variation in the extent to which governments are seen as having any sort of regulatory function with regard to family interactions.

In this book, authors with very divergent national origins discuss what is known about family violence and abuse in countries from every continent. Our focus is both cognitive and ecological. That is, we consider *conceptions* of abusive family interactions and the *major cultural contexts* in which family violence and abuse occur. The two primary contexts discussed in each chapter are the *macrosystem*, representing cultural and historical values and traditions relevant to family interactions, and the family *microsystems* in which these macrosystem forces play themselves out. The countries we present differ greatly among themselves in the availability of official documents and research findings; however, in each chapter, we attempt to provide a concise overview of the information available concerning child, spousal, and elder maltreatment, as well as efforts to deal with family violence and abuse. Enriching all of this material are the "voices" of ordinary citizens from these countries who responded to our survey on "Cross-Cultural Definitions of Abuse in Families."

One warning—much of the material presented in this book can only be described as heartrending. We expect and hope that all readers will be moved by the plight of the millions of people in this world who suffer abuse at the hands of family members, and we seriously address the questions of how best to end violence in the environments that are so inextricably linked—the struggling family microsystems within the macrosystem of each country, and the global macrosystem in which all nations are embedded. We suggest that violence can never be successfully ended by violence.

P A R T

I

CONTEXT

1

Introduction

Kathleen Malley-Morrison

In recent years, the United States has seen a proliferation in the number of family and intimate relationships to which the label of abuse is often applied, such as child abuse, wife abuse, spouse abuse, husband abuse, partner abuse, elder abuse, dating abuse, and sibling abuse. But what does that term *abuse* mean? How much consensus is there about the types of behavior that should be labeled abusive?

We believe that most people have an implicit theory about what abuse means. For example, when asked for her definition of abuse within the context of the family, Melissa, an American college student, said "Abuse would be any physical, verbal, or emotional action which is unwanted, uncalled for, and inappropriate that harms another person." When asked to indicate what types of family interactions should be considered severely, moderately, and mildly abusive, Melissa said that an interaction is extremely abusive "when extreme harm is inflicted—life is threatened, health is threatened—the more permanent the injury, the more extreme it is." Her view of a moderately abusive interaction is one in which "harm is inflicted that is not as permanent as extreme," and a mildly abusive interaction is one where "pain is only very temporary." When we consider this young woman's theory as to what constitutes abuse, we see that she has emphasized three dimensions—"appropriateness" of the behavior, extent of harm, and degree of permanence of harm/pain. It is also clear from her definition that the harmful behaviors may be verbal or emotional as well as physical.

A second question that we can ask about this young woman's theory of abuse is whether it has different premises for different family relationships.

When asked about extreme abuse within the married couple, Melissa said that from a husband to a wife, extreme abuse is "beating, murdering, etc." and that from a wife to a husband, extreme abuse is "using a weapon to harm or kill." Thus, she projects a similar outcome for the two forms of spousal abuse, but adds the component of "weapon" to her example of extreme abuse by a wife. Perhaps one of the premises of her theory is that wives need weapons to severely harm or kill their spouses whereas husbands do not. In husbands, she continues, a moderately abusive interaction is "forcing sex upon a wife, pushing, slapping"; in wives, a moderately abusive interaction is "hitting him with an object." We can now see that her theory of abusive family interactions does not include wives forcing sex on husbands, and that she is reiterating the theme that wives need to use weapons to cause the same degree of harm that a husband can cause simply by pushing and slapping. Finally, she holds that mild abuse by a husband is "verbal, emotional abuse" whereas mild abuse by a wife is "pushing, hitting"—suggesting again that wives are somehow more vulnerable than are husbands to lower levels of aversive behavior.

Additional elements to Melissa's theory of intrafamilial abuse become apparent as we look at her descriptions of abuse in other family relationships. With regard to child abuse, she said that extreme abuse from parent to child is "any sex on any sex; starving, beating, denying love, burning, attempting or succeeding in murder, shaking—many others." This list is longer than the list of extremely abusive interactions in marital couples, and introduces some new behaviors—starving, denying love, burning, and shaking. Her expanded list suggests that she views children's dependency on their parents as making them vulnerable to forms of abuse to which adults—particularly fathers—are not vulnerable. Although she did not make any suggestions as to moderately abusive behaviors from parents to children, she said that "spanking on the backside, mild slap on hand" were mildly abusive. This response is interesting in light of the fact that corporal punishment is still widely accepted in the United States, despite recommendations from professional groups such as the American Psychological Association and American Academy of Pediatrics that spanking not be used to discipline children.

As forms of extreme abuse against elderly parents, Melissa listed "neglect, starving, emotional and verbal abuse, physical violence." As examples of extreme abuse in sibling relationships, she listed "use of weapons, aggravated assault, murder." Here we see that, in contrast to her examples of child, sibling, and spousal abuse, Melissa did not explicitly include murder as a form of elder abuse, but did include neglect. Her inclusion of starving suggests that in her theory of abuse, elders, like children, are considered dependent on the middle generation for satisfaction of survival needs. And just as she characterized denial of love as severely abusive to children, she viewed psychological abuse as severely abusive of elders. It is only husbands whom she seems to consider as relatively invulnerable to the withholding of love and psychological abuse.

What do we mean by calling Melissa's definitions and examples of various kinds of abuse an implicit theory? The notion of implicit theories has roots in Kelly's (1955) theory of personal constructs, in which he argued that the human mind has a fundamental tendency to form dimensions of meaning, or personal constructs, and to use these constructs to make sense of experience. In his view, we all actively construct understandings of ourselves, others, and relationships; we are not just passive learners of facts about the social world. More recently, Sternberg (1985) described implicit theories as constructions that exist in people's minds in relation to a particular construct—for example, creativity, wisdom, love, success. How do these implicit theories arise? In describing laypeople's implicit theories of "success," Sternberg (2000) argued that in the process of growing up, young people observe "stories" of success in their environment and identify people who serve as role models of success. Based on these observations, they develop what may be fairly complex implicit theories of what leads people to success. These implicit theories are important because they are not just abstract ideas, but may include dispositions, actions, emotional states, and interrelationships among all these components. Sternberg noted that while implicit theories of success can be prosocial, they can also be antisocial—as when ghetto children, for example, define success as running potentially illegal street businesses.

We believe that implicit theories of abuse, like implicit theories of success, develop through young people's experiences within their environments and the stories they see unfolding there. The implicit theory that evolved in Melissa's mind appears to include the following premises: Abuse involves unwarranted injury; some acts are more injurious when done by a man than by a woman or a child; abuse of children and the elderly can involve neglect; and even a common act like hitting is abusive (presumably because it can produce pain). What other forms might an implicit theory of abuse take?

Consider the definitions provided by Makoto, a 20-year-old college student from Japan. His general definition of abuse was "not following family roles, not taking care of children or family to raise them properly, misrepresenting the family, violence." How interesting it is that the first example Makoto gives of abuse is "not following family roles" and the last is "violence." We cannot assume he views not following family roles as more abusive than violence, but neither can we assume the sequence is irrelevant.

Makoto's example of an extremely abusive interaction is one which "seriously harms physically or emotionally" and a mildly abusive interaction is "inappropriate but tolerated acts." Although he includes the idea of harm in his example of an extremely abusive interaction, in general, his theory of abuse is quite different from Melissa's, particularly in his concerns with following family roles and with not misrepresenting the family. The nature of these differences becomes clearer in his examples of abuse in particular family dyads. He told us that extreme abuse is "violence to the point of serious injury" when done by husbands against wives and parents against children. It is "adultery, squandering money, violence" when done by wives against husbands. It is "not taking care of them, violence, not following lines of respect" when done by adults against elderly parents. These specific examples of extreme abuse indicate that Makoto's theory identifies not just physically injurious violence but also violation of roles and lack of respect for elders as extremely abusive.

This interpretation of Makoto's theory is reinforced by his examples of moderate and mild abuse. For example, both moderate and mild forms of abuse by wives are "failing to perform duties," and moderate and mild forms of abuse from adults to elderly parents are "complacency." Here again, we note the emphasis in his theory on respect for roles. Finally, mild abuse from a husband to a wife, he told us, is "too much drinking, being unsuccessful, adultery." It is noteworthy that husbands' sexual misconduct and failure in a role ("being unsuccessful") are seen as only mildly abusive behaviors.

Clearly, Makoto, with his emphasis on conforming to roles and respect, has a very different implicit theory of familial abuse than does Melissa. Although we would not stereotype Melissa as a prototypical American and Makoto as a prototypical Japanese, we agree with Sternberg that people derive their implicit theories at least in part from the "stories" to which they are exposed in the environments in which they mature. We would also argue that Melissa's strong emphasis on physical and psychological aggression and Makoto's emphasis on roles and respect reflect strong cultural traditions. Finally, it is important to remember that Melissa and Makoto differ in gender as well as nationality, and that people's gender can play a powerful role in the experiences they have, the stories they're told, and the interpretations they make of personal and cultural events.

CULTURAL CONTEXTS: INDIVIDUALISM AND COLLECTIVISM

In recent decades, a popular social science approach to cross-cultural comparisons of behavior and values has focused on the constructs of individualism and collectivism. In general, according to Triandis (1995), collectivists (typically from Eastern societies) define themselves as part of a group whereas individualists (typically from Western societies) define themselves more in terms of autonomy from groups; thus, collectivists tend to have more *interdependent* views of self, whereas individualists tend to have more *independent* self-views. Moreover, the social behavior of collectivists is best predicted from group social norms and perceived duties and obligations, whereas the social behavior of individualists is best predicted from their own attitudes and values, as well as from contracts they have entered into. In addition, relationships are of supreme importance to collectivists, even when the costs of these relationships exceed the benefits.

Although strong arguments have been made that collectivism and individualism should not be treated as monolithic constructs (e.g., Stephan, Stephan, Saito, & Barnett, 1998), they continue to be used as a conceptual framework in many cross-cultural studies—particularly those comparing participants from selected Eastern countries such as Korea or Japan, with selected Western countries such as the United States or the United Kingdom. We believe that not only is it important to attend to differences in experiences and judgments within and between different Eastern and Western countries, but it is also crucial to seek out information on experiences and judgments from the Southern hemisphere. In this book, we present the perspectives from several different countries commonly considered to have collectivistic values (e.g., Korea, Japan, the Philippines), as well as from several different countries commonly considered to have individualistic values (e.g., the United States, the United Kingdom, Germany). In addition, although this chapter begins with Melissa, from a presumably individualistic country, and Makoto, from a presumably collectivistic country, we include rich information from areas of the world likely to have strong cultural traditions not lumped easily into either of these categories—the Middle East, Brazil, South Africa.

IMPLICIT THEORIES AND CULTURE

A number of investigators have argued that implicit theories vary as a function of cultural heritage. For example, Chiu, Morris, Menon, and Hong (2000) suggested that the tendency of North Americans to conceive of individuals as autonomous agents and of Chinese to conceive of groups as autonomous units reflects different culturally based implicit theories. They also suggested that reliance on these theories is most likely to occur when individuals are required to provide reasons for a judgment concerning somebody's behavior in an ambiguous situation. In our view, making judgments as to the extent to which a particular behavior (e.g., hitting) is abusive is likely to activate such culturally based implicit theories. Thus, for example, a child's asserting his or her own views in the face of opposing views from parents may be seen as healthy autonomy in cultures with an implicit theory valuing individualism but as disrespectful in a culture with an implicit theory valuing the group over the individual.

An Ecologic Perspective

Evidence concerning the role of cultural values in influencing individual definitions and perceptions of abuse supports the value of an ecological approach to implicit theories. Expanding on early work by Bronfenbrenner (1979), Belsky (1993) applied a developmental-ecological perspective to the etiology of child abuse. In his analysis of levels of "contexts of maltreatment," Belsky identified first the "developmental-psychological context," which includes attributes of both parents (e.g., their own disciplinary history) and children (e.g., age) that play a role in child maltreatment. The next level is the "immediate interactional context" (the "microsystem"), which includes both specific parenting behaviors and parent–child interactions. According to Belsky, the developmental and interactional contexts are embedded in broader social contexts that are also relevant to child maltreatment. These broader contexts include the particular community in which the family lives, and the broader societal-cultural context.

Obviously countries have different histories and different cultural contexts, which are likely to give rise to different implicit theories concerning the acceptability of aggression in close relationships and to different "stories" concerning the effects and the justifiability of such aggression. Although there may be some basic commonalities to human development around the globe, we believe that there are also important differences between and within countries in the types of social environmental contexts in which attitudes, values, and behaviors develop. Each author in this book provides a description of important aspects of the social, political, and economic contexts of development in his or her country. What is the status of women? Of children? To what extent is that country beset with internal or external violence? Also in each chapter, in defining and giving examples of abuse, respondents to our cross-cultural survey give more personal glimpses at the ecological niches in which they developed their theories concerning the abusiveness of violence in close relationships. Thus, the underlying conceptual framework for the book combines a focus on individual implicit theories with an emphasis on the broader ecological framework within which these theories develop.

Implicit Theories and Judgments of Abuse

There is substantial research literature in the United States on individual and group differences in judgments concerning potentially abusive behaviors in families and other close relationships. It is our view that these differences in judgment reflect differences in implicit theories. Although this literature is too extensive to be reviewed exhaustively here, we consider some examples from research on attitudes toward child discipline from the perspective of implicit theory.

Judgments Concerning Punishment of Children. Implicit theories of child abuse must account somehow for parental disciplinary practices. Much of the relevant literature in this domain has focused on both lay and professional judgments of spanking and other forms of corporal punishment. Is hitting or spanking a child sometimes abusive? Always abusive? Never abusive? The research reveals a broad range of views (implicit theories) on these issues. For example, Flynn (1996) found that approximately half of his sample of never-married, nonparenting American college students agreed with two statements: "It is sometimes necessary to discipline a child with a good hard spanking," and "Spanking a child usually works to correct misbehavior." Agreement with the items suggests that spanking does not fit the criteria for child abuse in the implicit theories of those students. Flynn also found that endorsement of the need for spanking was stronger in the northeastern United States as compared to the southern United States, in men compared with women, and in Blacks compared with Whites—supporting the view that different experiences in different contexts lead to different implicit theories of abuse. Other research indicates that support for corporal punishment characterizes the implicit theories of political conservatives more than of liberals (Furnham, 1995) and of literal believers in the Bible more than of nonliteralists (Grasmick, Bursik, & Kimpel, 1991).

It is not just among laypeople that differences in implicit theories of appropriate (and inappropriate) disciplinary practices can be found. In a study of social workers, Ashton (2001) found that the greater their approval of corporal punishment, the lower their likelihood of perceiving and reporting child maltreatment. Her findings provide support for the view expressed here that implicit theories of abusiveness are linked in meaningful ways with important behaviors (e.g., reporting maltreatment).

Given that implicit theories evolve during socialization experiences, we should not be surprised to find that the implicit theories of individuals who have experienced corporal punishment tend to condone corporal punishment. In one study of U.S. college students, Graziano and Namaste (1990) found that students who had been spanked (the great majority of their sample) were significantly more likely than students who had not been spanked to hold that parents have the right to spank children, that spanking is an effective disciplinary procedure, and that children need to be spanked. In an earlier study designed to test the assumption that child abuse is transmitted intergenerationally, Herzberger and Tennen (1985) found that college students recalling moderate and severe physical and emotional punishments (e.g., being spanked, hit with a belt, insulted and rejected) in their own childhoods rated those behaviors as less severe, more appropriate, and less abusive than did students not recalling such punishments.

As implied by the ecological model, the environment in which individuals develop—and modify—their implicit theories concerning the world, other people, and appropriate behavior is not limited to the environment of childhood experience. Churches, schools, and colleges are major social institutions within the ecological system with the power to affect the formulation of implicit theories. Evans and Fargason (1998) conducted an important study in which they examined educational materials for pediatricians produced throughout the 20th century. They demonstrated how, over the course of the century, the professional stance of pediatricians moved from viewing corporal punishment as morally sanctioned behavior, to viewing it as a way to control behavior, to viewing it as abusive.

Implicit Theories in Laws and Human Rights Documents

Although Sternberg (1985) differentiated between implicit theories (lacking in scientific validation) and explicit theories (constructions of scientists derived from or at least tested through empirical research), he also noted that scientists, like laypeople, have implicit theories. Such differences in implicit theories may account for many of the controversies that can be found internationally concerning what constitutes abuse. In many cultures for much of human history, women and children have been considered the "possessions" of men, and there was little interference in men's treatment (and maltreatment) of women and children. However, the evolution of countervailing points of view also has a long history. In recent decades, a number of international and regional human rights organizations have formulated principles concerning the rights of women, children, the elderly, and the disabled that have implications for interactions within domestic situations. As shown in subsequent chapters, laws and practices throughout the world have been influenced by implicit theories promulgated in such documents as the United Nations Convention on the Rights of the Child, and the United Nations document on the rights of women to freedom from violence. Although more local changes in implicit theories do not take place overnight, we provide evidence concerning the extent to which such changes are occurring in nations from many different parts of the world with very different histories and cultures.

OVERVIEW OF THE BOOK

This book was developed by an international group of psychological researchers (pre and postdoctoral from the United States, Europe, the Middle East, Asia, Africa, Latin America, Australia), most of whom have been working together for several years. As a group, we have had a number of reservations about available cross-cultural research on family violence and domestic abuse, including the tendency of many researchers to take a survey that has been developed and normed in the United States, translate it into other languages, administer it in other countries, and then make "cross-cultural" comparisons. We have been working for over 2 years to develop a survey reflective of all our international perspectives. It is an open-ended measure in which we ask respondents first to give us their definition of abuse within the context of the family, including examples of severe, moderate, and mild abuse. We then ask them to give examples of severe, moderate, and mild abuse within the context of parent–child, husband–wife, wife–husband, adult–elderly parent, sibling, and "other" family/domestic relationships. Our discussions always took place in our shared language—English—but an enormous amount of time was devoted to issues of translation. Many of our group members came from countries where there was no comparable term for abuse as applied by English speakers to various forms of aggression and neglect within family relationships. Finding appropriate synonyms and providing a participant-focused frame of reference were often challenging. To make access to our survey "easy," we posted it on the Web in 20 different languages; however, because millions of people throughout the world have no access to the Web, we also made strenuous efforts to recruit participants for face-to-face interviews, or self-administered surveys, in every country from which our authors come and/or in which they have helpful connections. In developing our survey, all translations underwent a rigorous process of discussion as well as back-translation and/or decision by multiple native speakers of the language as to the most appropriate translation of key terms. Professor Malley-Morrison and several of the other authors have had extensive experience in working with qualitative data.

One primary purpose of this book is to provide an overview of what is known about family violence and abuse in selected countries from every continent—starting with Iceland, and then moving through the continents and major subcontinental regions, roughly from east to west, and north to south, with a focus on a minimum of two countries from each major geographical area. Each chapter begins with a sort of preview, consisting of a "capsule" summarizing the major issues relating to violence, particularly family violence, in that country. The capsule is followed by a description of the individuals whose voices illustrate the points in the chapter, and a few examples of their implicit theories of abuse in families. Throughout the chapters, the more formal and academic material is supplemented and enriched by the "voices" of respondents from each country, revealing, in their own words, their implicit theories concerning abusive family interactions.

Another purpose of the book is to help readers understand the complexities of defining, measuring, treating, and preventing family violence in a global society composed of diverse cultures with diverse macro and micro-system norms underlying patterns of family interaction. In addition, because most nations are characterized by at least some cultural diversity within their boundaries, related to such variables as religion, education, and geography (rural–urban), the book addresses divergent themes within as well as across the selected nations. Moreover, we consider not just data on the prevalence of and attitudes toward family violence, but also the steps being taken in each country to address the problems. No country has a "clean record" when it comes to abuse within the family, and efforts toward change in very diverse cultural settings in very different parts of the world are worthy of consideration.

ACKNOWLEDGMENTS

Many thanks to our respondents from all over the world for sharing their views with us. Thanks also to the staff at Lawrence Erlbaum Associates, to Stan Wakefield, to all my great research assistants, to Eli H. Newberger for bringing me into this field, to Marcia Johnston for years of wonderful assistance, and to my loving and extended family.

REFERENCES

Ashton, V. (2001). The relationship between attitudes toward corporal punishment and the perception and reporting of child maltreatment. *Child Abuse & Neglect, 25*, 389–399.

Belsky, J. (1993). Etiology of child maltreatment: A developmental-ecological approach. *Psychological Bulletin, 114*, 413–434.

Bronfenbrenner, U. (1979). *The ecology of human development: Experiments by nature and design.* Cambridge, MA: Harvard University Press.

Chiu, C., Morris, M. W., Menon, T., & Hong, Y. (2000). Motivated cultural cognition: The impact of implicit cultural theories on dispositional attribution varies as a function of need for closure. *Journal of Personality and Social Psychology, 78*, 247–259.

Evans, H. H., & Fargason, C. A., Jr. (1998). Pediatric discourse on corporal punishment: A historical review. *Aggression & Violent Behavior, 3*, 357–436.

Flynn, C. P. (1996). Regional differences in spanking experiences and attitudes: A comparison of Northeastern and Southern college students. *Journal of Family Violence, 11*, 59–80.

Furnham, A. (1995). Attitudes to spanking children. *Personality & Individual Differences, 19*, 397–439.

Grasmick, H. G., Bursik, R. J., & Kimpel, M. (1991). Protestant fundamentalism and attitudes toward corporal punishment of children. *Violence & Victims, 6*, 283–298.

Graziano, A. M., & Namaste, K. A. (1990). Parental use of physical force in child discipline: A survey of 679 college students. *Journal of Interpersonal Violence, 5*, 449–463.

Herzberger, S. D., & Tennen, H. (1985). The effect of self-relevance on judgments of moderate and severe disciplinary encounters. *Journal of Marriage and the Family, 47*, 311–318.

Kelly, G. A. (1955). *The psychology of personal constructs.* New York: Norton.

Stephan, C. W., Stephan, W. G., Saito, I., & Morrison Barnett, S. (1998). Emotional expression in Japan and the United States: The nonmonolithic nature of individualism and collectivism. *Journal of Cross-Cultural Psychology, 29,* 728–748.

Sternberg, R. J. (1985). Implicit theories of intelligence, creativity, and wisdom. *Journal of Personality and Social Psychology, 49,* 607–627.

Sternberg, R. J. (2000). Implicit theories of intelligence as exemplar stories of success. *Psychology, Public Policy, and Law, 6*(1), 159–167.

Triandis, H. C. (1995). *Individualism and collectivism.* Boulder, CO: Westview.

WESTERN EUROPE

2

Iceland

Anna María Hauksdóttir
Steinunn Gestsdóttir

CAPSULE

Human rights in Iceland are strong in many respects and much has been accomplished. The status of women is (relatively) good, the rights of children are well established, and the country is small with a rather extensive social security system. Violent crime in the society seems to be less than in many other places, but both the children and the elderly are vulnerable to neglect.

One of the strongest values in Iceland's cultural heritage is personal independence. In spite of the many favorable qualities that fostering independence can bring, in the context of family violence, it can lead to an overemphasis on the role that a victim should play to resolve the abuse, and even to victim blaming. This is one of the most serious problems in addressing family violence in Iceland; in such a small, relatively safe society, where living conditions are good, people may refuse to acknowledge the problem that abuse in close relationships presents, and believe that those who experience such abuse should have the means and opportunities to avoid being abused, regardless of whether they actually can or not.

THE ICELANDIC SAMPLE

The Icelandic sample consisted of 14 males and 23 females, ranging in age from 18 to 51 years ($M = 31$). More than half had a college or graduate degree, 8 had finished some college, 11 had finished the University Entrance

Exam, 2 had technical education, and the remaining 3 had finished compulsory education. All were Icelandic and lived in Iceland, except for 5 people who had lived in another country for the past 2 to 4 years. Occupations were varied, and included students, office workers, designers, teachers, and university professors, also an engineer, a housewife, a therapist, and a fisherman.

Icelandic Participants' General Definitions of Abuse

All respondents named physical violence when they gave a general definition of abuse in the home; physical violence was not seen as justifiable under any circumstances. When asked to give examples of extreme abuse, participants frequently specified *physical violence*, but also mentioned *sexual abuse*, *dishonesty or lack of respect*, controlling (e.g., *harassment, threats*), and emotional neglect (e.g., *disregard, indifference*). Implicit theories of abuse also revealed a strong concern with individual rights; many of the respondents expressed the belief that people have a right to dignity and independence and that hindering that right is abusive. For example, a 21-year-old woman provided this general definition of abuse, "Everything that reduces [a person's] independence and freedom." Another young female student said, "[Abuse is] to not listen to the other person and not to value him or her as an equal . . ."

THE ICELANDIC MACROSYSTEM

Iceland's population lives primarily in urban areas, particularly in the capital, Reykjavík, and in surrounding areas (City of Reykjavík, 2000). First settled in 874 A.D. by Norwegian and Celtic immigrants, Iceland was independent for 300 years. The parliament, Althingi, was established in 930, making it the oldest functioning parliament in the world. Several hundred years ago, Iceland came under the rule first of Norway and then of Denmark. Much of the 19th and 20th centuries saw a struggle for independence, which was finally achieved in 1944. Although it took considerable effort for Icelanders to regain independence, the struggle was essentially peaceful. Iceland has no armed forces of its own but is a member of NATO (Thorsteinsson & Jónsson, 1991). The 1944 Constitution prohibits capital punishment. Iceland changed dramatically during the 20th century from a very poor country to a very modern, westernized country (Ólafsson, 1993). Currently, it has a mixed, open economy, and a high standard of living. Fish and other marine products account for about 70% of export revenues. Employment is high, but most families seem to need two incomes.

The Icelandic population is homogenous in ethnicity and religion. Although the Constitution provides for freedom of religion, the majority of citizens belong to the Lutheran state church, which is financially supported by the state (Statistics Iceland, 2001). Although most do not practice their faith actively, it is an important part of the country's cultural identity (U.S. Department of State, 2001).

In Iceland, as in the other Nordic nations, the state generally plays a greater role in an individual's life than it does in other western countries (Gaunt & Nyström, 1996/1984). The general opinion in Nordic nations is that governments "should use their taxes and security programmes to remove existing inequalities" (Gaunt & Nyström, 1996/1984, p. 480). The social security system includes pension insurance, occupational injury insurance, health insurance, and maternity (and recently paternity) insurance. School attendance is compulsory from the age of 6 through 15, and everyone is entitled by law to a free education, from primary through college/university level (Government of Iceland, 2000).

Although violence and abuse is a problem in Iceland as in other countries, Icelandic society is a small and relatively safe one in which to live. Firearms are illegal, with certain exceptions. Nonetheless, in recent years, serious violent crime has increased (Reykjavík Police Department, 2001). Also of growing concern has been the link between prostitution and some of the strip clubs operated in Reykjavík (Ásgeirsdóttir, Ellertsdóttir, & Sigfúsdóttir, 2001).

THE ICELANDIC MICROSYSTEM

The nuclear family is an important unit in the eyes of Icelanders, and the sanctity of the home is protected in the Constitution (Friðriksdóttir, 1995). Over the last 30 years, the proportion of families consisting of couples with children has decreased from just under 60% to 43% (Júlíusdóttir, 1995a), and single-parent households are increasingly common. Frequency of marriages has decreased during the last 20 years, and divorce has increased (Children's Ombudsman, 1998). Consequently, the proportion of children born within marriages has gone from 70% in the 1970s to under 40% in the 1990s (Children's Ombudsman, 1998). Icelanders are more likely than many other westerners to start their families relatively young (Children's Ombudsman, 1998). Birth rates among teenage girls are twice as high as in the other Scandinavian countries; the most common age for women to have their first child is around 23 years old. Twenty-five percent of the population is below 14 years old (Júlíusdóttir, 1995b). Because young couples often start their families in the home of a parent or in-laws, an unusually high proportion of households have three generations living together (Children's Ombudsman, 1998). Grandparents often bear a heavy responsibility for bringing up the youngest generation.

Although being a single parent is common and acceptable in Icelandic culture, it has several complications. One study (Júlíusdóttir, 1995b) showed that divorced parents seemed to put more responsibility on their children than did married parents, and the children frequently cooked, cleaned, and looked after younger siblings. Moreover, 31% of the children in single-parent households had no contact with their father, and divorced fathers without custody tended to be very dissatisfied with their position. In recent years, it has been suggested that this infrequent contact between fathers and children violates the premise of the UN Convention on the Rights of the Child, which states that children have the right to have regular contact with both their parents (Aðalsteinsson, 1995).

CHILDREN AND CHILD ABUSE

Various things come to mind from my childhood. Still, nothing is as memorable as the spanking and the punches. The oversights certainly did not need to be considerable nor great, for the wand to be pulled out and made visible, and it was more than just to show it, or to gesture, or to threat. The most important thing seemed to cause as much pain and to make the punishment as unforgettable as possible to those that had done wrong. Worst of all, was to have to pull down my own trousers in order to receive my punishment, and when it was over, to kiss the wand. It was made very clear that this had to be done, and until then, the punishment was not complete. (Guttormsson, 1983, p. 181)

This excerpt from a 19th century memoir does not describe common childrearing practices in Iceland today. However, life in general and childhood in particular used to be very harsh. In 1746, laws were issued as a guide for rearing children, and were enforced until the 19th century (Guttormsson, 1995). According to these laws, parents, priests, and officials were supposed to work together to promote faith and fear of God, obedience, and hard labor. Parents were warned against spoiling their children and instructed to punish them with words, hands, or rods, depending on the severity of the offense, although blows to the head and hitting as a result of anger were forbidden (Guttormsson, 1995).

In present day Iceland, childrearing practices are fairly compatible with the "Scandinavian method," which emphasizes discussion between parents and children about parental limits, and treating children as equals of adults. Spanking and using physical force are no longer seen as acceptable. Caretakers are prohibited by law from administering physically or emotionally abusive punishments to children. It is illegal to use corporal punishment in Icelandic schools, but, unlike in Sweden, Icelandic child protection laws do not make it illegal for parents to spank their children (Svavarsdóttir, 1999).

A 1994 study showed that 7% of parents had used physical force in raising their children, but most said this rarely happened (Júlíusdóttir, 1995a). Júlíusdóttir (1993) found that around 90% of Icelandic parents considered physical punishments to be unacceptable, and would rather use reasoning or positive reinforcement with their children. In spite of this, 45% said they had, seldom or occasionally, used physical punishments ranging from grabbing, shaking, or giving the child a light slap, which were the most common, to spanking, which was next in frequency. Although the women took a clearer stand than the men against physical punishments, they used them more often—perhaps because of more time with the children. When women used physical punishments, it was usually when they got angry and lost control whereas men used them more as a conscious method of upbringing.

Historically, children in Iceland learned to be hardworking, both to keep the household running, and to survive later in life (Björnsdóttir, 1995). From around the age of 7, most children had household duties similar to those of adults, differing only in magnitude. Expectations often exceeded the children's competence, and there were cases of what would be called child slavery today, especially among orphans and children of parents who could not support them (Guttormsson, 1995). Today, there is considerable social assistance available, but an antiassistance attitude persists.

Although child labor has decreased drastically, many Icelanders feel it is beneficial for children to work hard, and view academic education as overemphasized (Children's Ombudsman, 1998). Children are still an active part of the Icelandic workforce, far more so than in other European countries. Although there are laws protecting children from hard labor, and one can hire a child under the age of 13 to only do light work, older children, especially in rural areas, are known to do arduous work. Until recently, in small communities heavily dependent on fishery, schools closed temporarily when extra hands were needed in the fish factories (Guttormsson, 1995).

Independence is a strong ideal in Iceland and a theme in many of the country's most cherished literary works. Although ideas about children's independence are rarely stated verbally, the concept of "the freedom of children" is an important component of Icelandic childrearing practices (Children's Ombudsman, 1998). Children are expected to become independent and able to take care of themselves from early on. Icelandic parents give their children less guidance and protection than do parents in the other Scandinavian countries. For example, it is common for children under the age of 12 to look after younger siblings or to stay home alone, which may be why, although Iceland has one of the lowest infant mortality rates in the world, it has one of the highest child accident rates in Europe ("Slys á börnum," 2001). The notion of "freedom" for children is found among authorities as well as parents; however, some studies suggest that the conditions needed for children to prosper and be safe are sometimes neglected, at least in part because Icelanders do not want to overprotect their children (Björnsdóttir, 1995; Kristinsdóttir, 1995). As with many other aspects of Icelandic family life, this pattern may be changing.

Icelandic Participants' Perspectives on Child Abuse

In our sample, opposition to the use of physical force was apparent. Most examples of child abuse identified physical force, such as *slapping* and *hitting*, as a form of extreme abuse from parent to child. Three participants named *sexual abuse* only. Although many respondents simply defined abuse in terms of specific kinds of behaviors (such as *rejection* or *use of physical force*), others specified circumstances for the abusive behavior. A 26-year-old female systems analyst gave this example of extreme abuse, "To lock a young child in a closet because he/she cries too much." Similarly, a 25-year-old fisherman said extreme abuse was, "When a child refuses to clean up his room, he receives physical punishment, whether it is a slap across the face or something more severe."

Although not frequently cited as extreme abuse, neglect was often specified as moderate or mild abuse. A 26-year-old said "not letting a child into the home while parents are working" was moderately abusive. A male in his 30s described "a parent leaving an 8-year-old child home alone for a whole evening" as mild abuse. A young woman explained, "When I was 9 years old, I was left alone to care for my siblings, age 6 and 1, while one parent was in the hospital and the other was on a drinking binge. I consider this an example of extreme abuse."

The first child protection laws in Iceland were issued in 1932 (Kristinsdóttir, 1995). Since then, there has been considerable improvement in the legal status of children, most noticeably with the acceptance of the UN Convention on the Rights of the Child in 1996 (Government of Iceland, 2000). A Child Welfare Act was issued and the position of Children's Ombudsman created in 1995 to ensure that children's rights, needs, and welfare are respected throughout society (Children's Ombudsman, 1998). However, there is still an extreme discrepancy between services in Reykjavík and those in rural areas. Moreover, both the public and the authorities have been criticized for doing too little to protect children. Legally, everybody—especially, day-care workers, teachers, church ministers, physicians, nurses, midwifes, psychologists, and social workers—is supposed to report child abuse, but reports by many professions—especially health care workers—appear to be rare (Sigfússon, 1995).

Child Abuse

Discussion of child abuse has largely concentrated on child sexual abuse, especially on prosecution of offenders, with less attention paid to other forms of abuse. A shelter for victims of sexual abuse (Stígamót) was founded in Reykjavík in 1990, but there are no shelters outside the capital, and it is hard for people in rural areas to find assistance (Jónsdóttir, 1999). During the first 7 years that the shelter was open, 2,420 individuals sought help. In the first 4 years, 66% of the people sought help because of childhood sexual abuse. Over 90% of the victims were women or girls; most offenders were men. An examination of the victims' and offenders' backgrounds showed that they were representative of the nation with respect to marital status, education, employment status, and residence.

Although child sexual abuse has received increased attention, there is limited research on the subject (Jónsdóttir, 1995, 1999). The first relevant study, in September 2002, sampled 1,500 people aged 18 to 60; about 50% answered. According to the survey, 8% of boys and 23% of girls are sexually abused at age 18 or younger. Where the same methods were used, the number in Norway was 14%, and in Denmark 11% (Jónsdóttir, 2002).

Icelandic law treats child sexual abuse as one of the most serious crimes committed, with no crime except murder receiving heavier sentences (Jónsdóttir, 1995, 1999). These laws are very similar to those in the other Scandinavian countries (Ólafsdóttir, 1997), but while they portray child sexual abuse as extremely serious, they impose no minimal sentence for the crime, in contrast to penalties for crimes such as arson and burglary. Even when severe sexual abuse has been prosecuted, the sentences are far from stringent (Ólafsdóttir, 1997). This legal response has led to public outrage but not to heavier sentencing. Our survey participants clearly viewed sexual abuse as very serious. About one-third of our survey answers for parent to child abuse included sexual abuse. In every instance, it was named as extreme abuse, and two participants commented that this would be the most serious act a parent could do to a child.

Another criticism of the child welfare system is that there is insufficient help for children who have been victims of sexual abuse (Ólafsdóttir, 1997). Both immediate and long-term treatments have been found to be either inadequate or nonexistent. However, some improvement has taken place. As a result of recent attention, a Children's Assessment Center was founded in Reykjavík in 1997. Its aim is to improve the services given to children who are victims of sexual abuse, and to coordinate the work of the professionals who are involved in helping victims of child sexual abuse (Erlendsdóttir, 1999).

WOMEN AND SPOUSAL ABUSE

Gender Equality

Women in Iceland, as compared to women in many other countries, were never considered the property of men; husbands were never granted the right to chastise their women, nor did men have the legal right to administer physical punishments to their wives (Smearman, 1996). However, attitudes about heads of households have long placed greater authority in the hands of men than of women and, for much of Iceland's history, women did not have political equality with men (Ministry of Justice, 1997). Icelandic women began their organized fight for equal rights toward the end of the 19th century. In 1915, Iceland became one of the first western countries to grant women the right to vote and to stand in parliamentary elections (Smearman, 1996). In present day elections, women's participation is among the highest in the world (Equal Status Council, 1998). Although full gender equality has not yet been achieved, Icelanders are probably closer to this goal than most nations. The effort to rid Icelandic society of institutionalized processes contributing to gender inequalities is reflected in developing laws and policies. For example, the Act on the Equal Status and Equal Rights of Women and Men (2000) includes an article requiring employers to make arrangements to enable both men and women to reconcile family life and work.

Iceland has a traditional patriarchal family structure. Domestic responsibilities, household chores, and ultimate responsibility for children are still tasks more of women than of men, but this is changing slowly (Statistical Bureau of Iceland, 1994). One factor making it possible for both women and men to combine family life and career are paid parental leaves. Substantial changes were made to existing benefits by the government in the spring of 2000 when the Act on Maternity/Paternity Leave and Parental Leave was passed. Parental leave was introduced in the form of 9 months of paid leave wherein each parent is eligible for 3 months and the remaining 3 are to be divided according to their wishes. It remains to be seen, however, how this will work out in practice. Although fathers are becoming more involved with their children, women generally are the ones to adapt their paid work to family needs—for example, by taking maternity leaves, working part time, and taking a day off when a child is ill (Einarsdóttir & Kristjánsdóttir, 2002; Ministry of Social Affairs, 1993).

Spousal Abuse

From *Njal's Saga* (trans. 1960), written in the 13th century:

> By that time, Gunnar had wounded eight men and killed two. Now he received two wounds himself, but everyone is agreed that he flinched neither at wounds nor death itself.
>
> He said to Hallgerd [his wife], "Let me have two locks of your hair, and help my mother plait them into a bow-string for me." "Does anything depend on it?" asked Hallgerd. "My life depends on it," replied Gunnar, "for they will never overcome me as long as I can use my bow." "In that case," said Hallgerd, "I shall now remind you of the slap you once gave me [several years

earlier]. I do not care in the least whether you hold out a long time or not."
"To each his own way of earning fame," said Gunnar. "You shall not be asked
again."
    ... Gunnar defended himself with great courage ... But in the end they
killed him. (pp. 170–171)

Prevalence. The women's movement brought the issue of family violence to the public's attention around 1980. In the first Icelandic study on
domestic abuse (Ólafsdóttir, Júlíusdóttir, & Benediktsdóttir, 1982), the investigators looked at hospital records from the emergency ward at the
Reykjavík Municipal Hospital, dating from 1979, which revealed that women
were being abused within their homes (Ministry of Justice, 1997). Records
kept in the same ward from 1974 to 1991 indicated that between 6 and 9 of
every 1,000 women were injured through violence each year. In 1991, 41% of
the women had been injured in their homes (the study did not include information on who was responsible for the injuries; Zöega, Sigvaldason, & Mogensen, 1994).
    A study of Reykjavík police records from the years 1992 to 1993 showed
that close to 200 cases of spousal abuse were reported annually (Gíslason,
Thorgeirsdóttir, & Gíslason, 1995). Men were perpetrators in around 86% of
the incidents. Almost two-thirds of the cases involved abuse of a current or
former spouse. These numbers are probably much lower than the actual
occurrence; from 1992 to 2000, only 5% to 12% of women who stayed at the
battered women's shelter in Reykjavík reported their assaults to the police
(Women's Shelter, 1993, 2000). The Women's Shelter in Reykjavík (*Kvennaathvarfið*), opened in 1982, serves the whole country. For the past few
years, the number of women staying at the shelter has ranged from 95 to
120 per year, and 61 to 131 children. In 2000, 69% of the women in the shelter
named psychological abuse as a reason for their presence, 38% named
physical abuse, and less than 10% named sexual abuse. Over 70% of the
women reported a current or a former partner as the perpetrator (Women's
Shelter, 2000).
    Little was known about prevalence and nature of family violence until
the Ministry of Justice published the first systematic study of the problem
in 1997. The findings, based on a telephone poll, indicated that 1.3% of the
women surveyed had experienced domestic violence (by a current or former spouse) in the 12 months prior to the survey (Ministry of Justice, 1997).
Most had experienced more than one incident of domestic violence. The
percentage of men reporting domestic violence victimization in the past 12
months was 0.8%. Almost 14% of the women had been physically abused by
their current or former spouse (5% by a current spouse, and 9% by a former
spouse). Four percent of the men reported having been physically abused
by a current or former spouse.

Perceptions of Spousal Abuse. In Iceland, as in many other countries, family privacy is cherished and constitutionally protected. According to Smearman (1996), the attitude of the Icelandic justice system is reflected in a comment from the Police Investigative Branch (RLR) to the Icelandic Parliament in 1991: "Domestic violence is a social issue, not a matter of criminal justice" (p. 277). From the perspective of the police, a domestic violence situation can be very difficult. Victims often view the police as violating the sanctity of their home. Although domestic violence calls are given priority, the police do not have protocols for these calls, and for the most part, each situation is regarded as a special case requiring its own solution (Ministry of Justice, 1998b). The lack of anonymity that results from living in a small country, and especially in rural areas, can be a problem. Police officers and judges may know the victim and abuser personally, and perpetrators may even be respected people in the area.

There are several stereotypes about domestic violence in Iceland. In general, people think that abuse in families is rare and doesn't involve people like themselves—people of their own class or nationality (Gestsdóttir, Björnsson, & Malley-Morrison, 2000). As a student of psychology at the University of Iceland put it: "In Iceland our idea of a batterer is a drunk, lower class, uneducated man out of control, beating up his wife, who is also drunk, lower class and uneducated" (Smearman, 1996, p. 285). The title of one of the first newspaper articles about domestic violence as a social problem, "Does It Not Happen Here?" (*Gerist þetta ekki hér?*), shows the author's appreciation of her audience's view that violence happens only in other societies (Ingadóttir, as cited in Gurdin, 1996).

In the implicit theories of Nordic peoples, alcohol use and violence seem to be closely related (Ministry of Justice, 1997). When women in the Ministry of Justice survey were asked for their explanation of abuse, they most often mentioned alcohol (another common reason was jealousy). Blaming alcohol is an easy explanation for the abuser's behavior, both for victim and abuser, and perhaps there is a risk of too much being made of the relationship (Ministry of Justice, 1997). The Women's Shelter in Reykjavík maintains that the police are more likely to intervene by arresting the batterer if he appears to be drunk (Gurdin, 1996).

Icelandic Participants' Perspectives on Domestic Violence

In responses to our survey, alcohol was mentioned sometimes, but less than we had expected. A 40-year-old male gave this example of abuse in a close relationship, "I knew a couple that drank much, and the husband had a tendency to get violent when they were drinking. One time he tried to push his wife down the garbage chute. They lived on the fourth floor. This is an example of extreme abuse." A young fisherman gave this example of mild abuse in family relationships, "Children witnessing parents drinking alcohol."

There is some evidence that men and women in Iceland differ in their understanding of abuse. In the Ministry of Justice report, 5% of women said they had been abused by their current spouse, but only 2% of men said they had abused their wife. Similarly, 1.5% of the men said they had been abused by their current spouse, whereas 4% of women said they had abused their husband (Ministry of Justice, 1997). As pointed out in the report, this could mean that men do not see mild physical violence as abuse, whether they are the victims or the perpetrator. It could also mean that men and women have different standards; injury could be a criterion for the men but not for the women. Men may also have more difficulty in admitting that violence took place.

In responding to our survey, about two-thirds defined abuse differently depending on which spouse was the perpetrator. One male and one female said that "extreme wife–husband abuse does not exist." The female (a 47-year-old financial director) named "beating and rape" as forms of extreme husband–wife abuse. Psychological abuse was considered somewhat more typical of wives than of husbands, whereas the opposite was true for physical abuse. There were also differences related to gender of perpetrator regarding sexual abuse. Six respondents specified sexual abuse as extreme abuse from husband to wife, whereas two specified sexual abuse as extreme abuse from wife to husband, and both noted that this form of abuse is not common. A woman in her 40s explained, "Extreme physical violence is less common by wives than husbands, both because men usually are physically stronger than women and also because women use physical violence less often than men. It is also less common that women use sexual abuse against men." There were more similarities between answers for husband–wife and wife–husband abuse when respondents suggested sex could be used to inflict emotional pain upon the spouse (e.g., flirting with others, affairs, withdrawal of sex).

Spousal Abuse and the Law. Iceland is a signatory party to international human rights agreements and to agreements and declarations specifically addressing abuse against women (Ministry of Justice, 1997). However, domestic violence is not a distinct legal issue anywhere in Icelandic law (Ministry of Justice, 1998b). As a crime, it is not distinguished from common assault and battery under the general penal code, although several articles in the penal code and law of procedures apply to domestic violence (Ministry of Justice, 1998a). In the General Penal Code (1940), Articles 217 through 218a address violent physical assaults that are common in battering relationships, but also list exceptions to the application of these articles. Punishment for minor physical assault can be negated if the victim has "consented" (Article 218a), including situations where the victim places himself or herself willingly at risk of bodily injury. In addition, punishment may be decreased or omitted if the assault takes place during a physical fight or struggle. According to Smearman (1996), "If Article 218a could be construed to make legally cognizable the common misperception that battered women 'consent' to their abuse by 'staying' with the abuser, then the myth becomes reality in the operation of the law" (p. 302). Prosecutions for marital rape are uncommon, perhaps because of the importance given to Article 205 of the penal code (Smearman, 1996). This article provides that if the victim and rapist are married, or cohabiting at the time of the rape, and continue or resume cohabitating after the rape (or later marry or cohabitate), the penalties may be dropped. This seems to imply that violence between people in close relationships is somehow not a crime but rather a personal problem, and ignores the fact that violence often increases when women leave an abusive spouse (Smearman, 1996).

THE ELDERLY AND ELDER ABUSE

Due to increased longevity, the proportion of the elderly in the Icelandic population is growing. Changes in economic conditions, education, and government have been accompanied by changes in attitudes toward the elderly. Until recently, civil laws imposed a responsibility on adult children to care for economic, health, and social needs of elderly parents. This responsibility has now been shifted over to the state, which is appointed to care for the elderly without reference to financial status (Snævarr, 1990).

Whereas the proportion of elderly people in Iceland living below the poverty line used to be among the highest in western nations, recent data (Social Science Institute of the University of Iceland, 1999) indicate that the prevalence of poverty among the elderly has declined—from 12% in 1988 to 4% in 1999—bringing the financial status of Icelandic elderly to one of the highest in the Scandinavian countries. In spite of these seemingly good economic conditions, over 25% of elderly respondents to a national poll reported that they frequently worried about their financial standing (Gallup, 1999).

Discussion of elder abuse in Iceland has been rare. For example, in an extensive report on family violence by the Icelandic Ministry of Justice in 1997, elder abuse is never addressed as a distinct form of abuse, whereas wife and child abuse are both addressed (Ministry of Justice, 1997). In fact, the oldest participant in that study was 65 years old, limiting the conclusions that can be drawn. Still, of the people who reported having been abused, 16% said they had been physically abused by an adult child, which suggests that elder abuse is a problem in Iceland as elsewhere.

Although the incidence of elder abuse in Iceland has not been assessed, a study from 1999 compared attitudes toward elder abuse in Iceland and the United States (Gestsdóttir, Björnsson, & Malley-Morrison, 2000). Participants were asked to give their judgments of the abusiveness and typicality of various forms of elder abuse by an adult caretaker, such as, "When an elderly father complains, his son shakes him by the arm." Results showed that Icelandic participants viewed such behaviors as more abusive and less typical of their society than did American participants. Thus, Icelanders seem to judge elder abuse very harshly. It may be both less tolerated and less common in Icelandic society than in the United States. On the other hand, because of the limited research and discussion on elder abuse, people in Iceland may be less aware of the extent of the problem.

Icelandic Participants' Perspectives on Elderly Abuse

It was obvious from the answers to our survey that the potential dependence of elders on other family members influences perceptions of abuse. Neglect from children or relatives (e.g., *not visiting, ignoring*) was often listed as a mild or moderate form of abuse, and sometimes as extremely abusive. "Taking advantage of an elderly person's fragile health" was mentioned often; *physical abuse* was listed less frequently. The following example of extreme abuse illustrates the problems associated with dependency, "because of old age and fragility the elderly person is often dependent on his or her children. The children can abuse this situation by threatening and behaving in such a way that is harmful to the older person."

Our respondents were more likely to refer to financial maltreatment when giving examples of elder abuse than of abuse in other relationships. *Financial abuse* was named as extreme abuse in four cases and as moderate abuse in three. Extreme examples included this response from a young professional woman, "having elderly parents liable for a loan, which they end up paying," and this response from a college professor in her 40s, "financial abuse, e.g. steal [elderly parents'] apartment by using deceit."

CONCLUSION

When comparing studies of prevalence of abuse between nations, generations, genders, or other groups, it is important to know whether they perceive and define abuse the same way. The frequency of spousal abuse in Iceland appears to be similar to what it is in Denmark, but lower than in many other western countries, including the United States (Gíslason, 1998; Ministry of Justice, 1997). Whatever its relative frequency, Iceland has taken many steps to combat the problem and has set up institutions to deal directly with abuse, both to achieve long-term solutions, and to meet immediate needs of those trying to get out of abusive situations. Such institutions include the Agency for Child Protection, which runs Children's House: Center for Child Sexual Abuse (Barnaverndarstofa and Barnahús), the Social Welfare Office (Félagsmálastofnun), the Women's Shelter (Kvennaathvarfið), the Sexual Abuse Shelter (Stígamót), and the Emergency Sexual Assault Ward at Reykjavík Municipal Hospital (Neyðarmóttaka í nauðgunarmálum).

There has been some reluctance on the part of Icelanders, in part due to the emphasis on independence and self-reliance, to accept that Iceland, like other countries, has a problem with family violence. In recent decades, the discussion has become much more open both in media and among policymakers. More thorough studies would be of great benefit in setting laws and refining processes and protocols to deal with abuse. To be most effective, family violence in Iceland may need to be addressed by taking into account more strongly the specific characteristics of this particular society.

REFERENCES

Aðalsteinsson, R. (1995). Barnasáttmáli sameinuðu þjóðanna: Hver er þýðing hans fyrir íslensk börn? [United Nations convention on the rights of the child: Relevance for Icelandic children]. In *Ritröð Barnaheilla: Staða barna á Íslandi* (pp. 23–30). Reykjavík, Iceland: Barnaheill.

Ásgeirsdóttir, B., Ellertsdóttir, H., & Sigfúsdóttir, I. (2001). *Vændi á Íslandi og félagslegt umhverfi þess* [Prostitution in Iceland and its social context]. Reykjavík, Iceland: Rannsókn & Greining.

Björnsdóttir, L. (1995). Hækkun sjálfræðisaldurs í 18 ár og afleiðingar þess [The consequences of increasing the personal competence age to 18 years]. In *Ritröð Barnaheilla: Hækkun sjálfræðisaldurs* (pp. 15–20). Reykjavík, Iceland: Barnaheill.

Children's Ombudsman. (1998). *Mannabörn eru merkileg* [Children are remarkable]. Reykjavík, Iceland: Author.

City of Reykjavík. (2000). *Latest facts and figures from Reykjavik*. Reykjavík, Iceland: Author.

Einarsdóttir, T., & Kristjánsdóttir, G. (2002). *Towards a closing of the gender pay gap. Country report on pay differentials between men and women. Iceland*. Reykjavík, Iceland: Center for Women's Studies.

Equal Status Council. (1998). *Women and power*. Reykjavík, Iceland: Author.

Erlendsdóttir, V. (1999). Barnahús: Hlutverk þess og starfsemi [Children's House: Its purpose and operation]. In *Ritröð Barnaheilla: Kynferðislegt ofbeldi gegn börnum* (pp. 63–68). Reykjavík, Iceland: Barnaheill.

Friðriksdóttir, H. (1995). Börn og réttarkerfið: viðhorf og staða barna [Children and the justice system: Attitudes and the status of children]. In *Ritröð Barnaheilla: Mannréttindi barna* (pp. 55–59). Reykjavík, Iceland: Barnaheill.

Gallup. (1999). *Viðhorfskönnun meðal aldraðra* [Survey of attitudes among the elderly]. Reykjavík, Iceland: Author.

Gaunt, D., & Nyström, L. (1996). The Scandinavian model (S. H. Tenison, R. Morris, & A. Wilson, Trans.). In A. Burguiere, C. Klapisch-Zuber, M. Segalen, & F. Zonabend (Eds.), *A history of the family: The impact of modernity* (Vol. 2, pp. 476–501). Cambridge, MA: Belknap Press. (Original work published 1986)

Gestsdóttir, S., Björnsson, B., & Malley-Morrison, K. (2000, August). *Perceptions of elder abuse in Iceland and the US*. Poster session presented at the annual meeting of the American Psychological Association, Washington, DC.

Gíslason, I. V. (1998). Dregur úr ofbeldi gegn konum? [Is violence against women decreasing?]. In *Ársskýrsla lögreglustjórans í Reykjavík 1998* [Electronic version]. Reykjavík, Iceland: Reykjavík Police Department.

Gíslason, G., Thorgeirsdóttir, H., & Gíslason, I. V. (1995). *Ofbeldi* [Violence]. Reykjavík, Iceland: Skrifstofa jafnréttismála.

Government of Iceland. (2000). *Iceland's second periodic report on the implementation of the United Nations convention of 20 November 1989 on the rights of the child*. Reykjavík, Iceland: Author.

Gurdin, J. E. (1996). Motherhood, patriarchy, and the nation. In G. Pálsson & E. P. Durrenberger (Eds.), *Images of contemporary Iceland: Everyday lives and global contexts* (pp. 126–145). Iowa City: University of Iowa Press.

Guttormsson, L. (1983). *Bernska, ungdómur og uppeldi á einveldisöld* [Childhood, youth and education in the age of absolutism]. In *Ritröð Sagnfræðistofnunar*, 10. Reykjavík, Iceland: Sagnfræðistofnun.

Guttormsson, L. (1995). Viðhorf til barna í sögulegu ljósi [Attitudes toward children in historical perspective]. In *Ritröð Barnaheilla: Mannréttindi barna* (pp. 19–24). Reykjavík, Iceland: Barnaheill.

Jónsdóttir, G. (1995). Kynferðislegt ofbeldi gegn börnum [Sexual abuse against children]. In *Ritröð Barnaheilla: Mannréttindi barna* (pp. 49–54). Reykjavík, Iceland: Barnaheill.

Jónsdóttir, G. (1999). Hvað vitum við um kynferðislegt ofbeldi gegn börnum hér á landi? [What do we know about sexual abuse against children in our country?]. In *Ritröð Barnaheilla: Kynferðislegt ofbeldi gegn börnum* (pp. 17–26). Reykjavík, Iceland: Barnaheill.

Jónsdóttir, N. B. (2002, September 17). Fimmta hver stúlka misnotuð og tíundi hver drengur [One in five girls sexually abused and one in ten boys]. *Morgunblaðið*. Available: http://www.mbl.is/mm/frettir/show_framed_news?nid=836167&cid=1

Júlíusdóttir, J. (1993). *Den kapabla familjen i det isländska samhället. En studie om lojalitet, äktenskapsdynamik och psykosocial anpassning* [The capable family in Icelandic society: A study on loyalties, marital dynamics and psychosocial adaptation]. Sweden: Department of Social Work, University of Göteborg.

Júlíusdóttir, S. (1995a). (Ed.). *Barnafjölskyldur. Samfélag–lífsgildi–mótun* [Families with children: Society–values–socialization]. Reykjavík, Iceland: Ministry of Social Affairs.

Júlíusdóttir, S. (1995b). Hamingja foreldra er heill barna [Happy parents, healthy children]. In *Ritröð Barnaheilla: Staða barna á Íslandi* (pp. 8–22). Reykjavík, Iceland: Barnaheill.

Kristinsdóttir, G. (1995). Barnavernd og sálfræðiþróun á Íslandi: Hvert stefnir? [The future of child protection and development of psychology in Iceland]. In *Ritröð Barnaheilla: Mannréttindi barna* (pp. 25–33). Reykjavík, Iceland: Barnaheill.

Ministry of Justice. (1997). *Skýrsla dómsmálaráðherra um orsakir, umfang og afleiðingar heimilisofbeldis og annars ofbeldis gegn konum og börnum* [Ministry of Justice report on the causes, prevalence and consequences of domestic violence and other violence against women and children]. Reykjavík, Iceland: Author.

Ministry of Justice. (1998a). *Skýrsla dómsmálaráðherra til Alþingis um meðferð heimilisofbeldismála í dómskerfinu* [Ministry of Justice report to Althingi on the treatment of domestic violence cases in the justice system]. Reykjavík, Iceland: Author.

Ministry of Justice. (1998b). *Skýrsla dómsmálaráðherra til Alþingis um meðferð heimilisofbeldismála hjá lögreglu* [Ministry of Justice report to Althingi on the treatment of domestic violence cases by the police]. Reykjavík, Iceland: Author.

Ministry of Social Affairs. (1993). *Skýrsla nefndar félagsmálaráðuneytis og erindi flutt á málþingi í maí 1992 um breytta stöðu karla og leiðir til að auka ábyrgð þeirra á fjölskyldulífi og börnum* [Ministry of Social Affairs report, and papers presented on a conference in May, 1992 on the changed status of men and ways to increase their responsibility for family and children]. Reykjavík, Iceland: Author.

Njal's Saga. (1960). (M. Magnússon & H. Pálsson, Trans.). Harmondsworth, Middlesex, England: Penguin Books.

Ólafsdóttir, H. (1997). Heggur sá er hlífa skyldi. Kynferðisafbrot gegn börnum og ungmennum [Sexual abuse against children and adolescents]. Reykjavík, Iceland: Children's Ombudsman.

Ólafsdóttir, H., Júlíusdóttir, S., & Benediktsdóttir, Th. (1982). Ofbeldi í íslenskum fjölskyldum [Abuse in Icelandic families]. Geðvernd, 17, 7–31.

Ólafsson, S. (1993). Þróun velferðarríkisins [Development of the welfare state]. In G. Hálfdánarson & S. Kristjánsson (Eds.), Íslensk þjóðfélagsþróun 1880–1990 (pp. 59–74). Reykjavík: University of Iceland.

Reykjavík Police Department. (2001). Ársskýrsla lögreglustjórans í Reykjavík fyrir árið 2000 [Annual report of Reykjavík Police Department for the year 2000]. Reykjavík, Iceland: Author.

Sigfússon, A. (1995). Barnavernd og kynferðislegt ofbeldi [Child protection and sexual abuse]. In Ritröð Barnaheilla: Mannréttindi barna (pp. 44–48). Reykjavík, Iceland: Barnaheill.

Slys á börnum algengari hér en á Norðurlöndum [Accidents in children more common here than in Nordic nations]. (2001, September 4). Morgunblaðið. Available: http://www.mbl.is/mm/frettir/show_framed news?nid=737946&cid=1

Smearman, C. A. (1996). At the crossroads: Domestic violence and legal reform in Iceland. Úlfljótur, 49, 275–377.

Snævarr, A. (1990). Sifjaréttur [Family right] (4th ed.). Reykjavík: Social Science Institute, University of Iceland.

Social Science Institute of the University of Iceland. (1999). Lífshættir, lífskjör og lífsskoðun eldri borgara [Ways of living, financial standing, and attitudes of senior citizens]. Reykjavík: Author.

Statistical Bureau of Iceland. (1994). Women and men in Iceland 1994. Reykjavík, Iceland: Author.

Statistics Iceland. (2001). Statistical yearbook of Iceland 2001. Reykjavík, Iceland, Iceland: Author.

Svavarsdóttir, E. K. (1999). Að búa við vanlíðan af hendi sinna nánustu: Ofbeldi í fjölskyldum [Abuse in families]. Tímarit hjúkrunarfræðinga, 75(3), 153–157.

Thorsteinsson, B., & Jónsson, B. (1991). Íslandssaga til vorra daga [History of Iceland to the present day]. Reykjavík, Iceland: Sögufélag.

U.S. Department of State. (2001, October 26). Iceland: International religious freedom report. Available: http://www.state.gov/g/drl/rls/irf/2001/5682.htm

Women's Shelter. (1993). Ársskýrsla Samtaka um kvennaathvarf 1991 og 1992 [Annual report of Association for Women's Shelter 1991 and 1992]. Reykjavík, Iceland: Author.

Women's Shelter. (2000). Ársskýrsla Samtaka um kvennaathvarf 2000 [Annual report of Association for Women's Shelter 2000]. Reykjavík, Iceland: Author.

Zöega, B., Sigvaldason, H., & Mogensen, B. (1994). Ofbeldisáverkar: Faraldsfræðileg athugun í Reykjavík 1974–1991 [Injuries caused by violence in Reykjavík 1974–1991]. Læknablaðið, 80, 531–535.

3

England

Elizabeth Donovan

CAPSULE

Over the last century, England has made significant advances in recognizing the rights of children, women, and the elderly. Laws have been implemented to help identify and protect against abuse, and a growing body of research helps identify risk factors for maltreatment. The focus of this chapter is England, although some statistics are available only for England as a whole, or England in combination with Wales. Wherever possible, empirical research conducted in England is cited. All of the qualitative data are from English participants.

THE ENGLISH SAMPLE

The English sample consisted of 60 participants (47 females, 13 males), ranging in age from 20 to 73 years old, with an average age of 42 years. Many participants (45%) had a postgraduate degree, many others (35%) had a first degree, and 20% were high school graduates. Of the 80% of respondents who were employed, almost all identified themselves as full-time professionals; the other 20% were either retired, unemployed, or working in the home.

English Respondents' General Definitions of Abuse

Among our English participants, implicit theories of abuse within the family put a strong emphasis on psychological abuse; almost all of the English respondents (95%) defined abuse in terms of psychological abuse—for example, "lack of nurturance, acceptance, understanding, psychological manipulation" (female, 29 years old) and "verbal abuse—shouting at other family members. Psychological abuse by undermining self-esteem, breaking promises . . ." (female, 57). Physical abuse was included in 80% of the general definitions—for example, "physical or verbal attack intended to hurt. An assault such as a punch or hitting with a slap" (female, 36), and "physical or verbal attack intended to hurt" (female, 36). Sexual abuse accounted for only 40% of the definitions—generally, listed simply as "sexual abuse" (female, 57) or "rape" (female, 22).

Examples of extreme abuse generally emphasized dominance and the breaking of trust—for example, "an assertion of power or dominance over another—may be physical, emotional, verbal" (female, 55), "where one tries to dominate the other, to have more authority" (female, 21), and "exploiting position of authority to boost one's own ego at the expense of another's peace and happiness. Not giving the nurture the family member needs and deserves" (female, 29), and ". . . where trust is broken, where the abused is made to feel the guilty one when the abuser plays power games . . ." (female, 30).

THE ENGLISH MACROSYSTEM

Low infant mortality rates and high life expectancies are general indicators of the overall good health of the English population. Unemployment is fairly low, although 17% of the population lives under the poverty line (Central Intelligence Agency, 2002). Health care is government funded. In 1998, 83% of total health care expenditure was publicly funded, drawn mostly from taxes, then from social security (World Health Organization, 2002).

There were only 761 homicides in Britain in 1999/2000, a relatively low rate, due in part to the fact that it is illegal to own a firearm in England. In 1999/2000, the proportion of all notifiable offenses in which firearms were used, excluding air weapons, was only 1% (Home Office, 2000a). Gun control laws have been made tougher over the past few years, mainly in response to specific, devastating incidents of gun violence. For example, in 1996, 17 people, many of whom were children, were killed by an armed man in Dunblane, Scotland; the government responded by banning handguns ("Aiming High," 2003).

The Role of Women

The last century saw many changes in men and women's relative status. Most saliently, women now make up almost half of the labor force, although gender gaps exist at every stage in women's and men's lives—in political and public life, in education, and in the workplace. Women have been eligible to vote since 1928 and eligible to stand for election to Parliament since 1918; however, they are still vastly underrepresented in political life. Women comprise 52% of full-time undergraduates in British universities, but women make up over 70% of the students in education, languages, and subjects allied to medicine, whereas men make up over 80% of students in engineering and technology, and computer science (Equal Opportunities Commission [EOC], 2001). Despite the fact that the Equal Pay and Sex Discrimination Act was introduced in 1975, sex stereotyping persists in the workplace. For example, over twice as many men as women are managers and administrators. Gross individual income of women is 51% of men's (EOC, 2001).

The Status of Children

The UN Convention on the Rights of the Child was ratified by England in 1991. It is not part of English law, but England has laws specifically for the protection of children, most significantly in the Children's Act, 1989 (National Society for the Prevention of Cruelty to Children [NSPCC], 2002). Children are entitled to a free education (EOC, 2001), and since 1987, have been free of corporal punishment in state schools. Impetus for change was provided, in part, by cases of corporal punishment, or the threat of corporal punishment, brought before the European Court on Human Rights during the late 1970s and early 1980s (Branigan, 2001). Yet, despite recent urging by the UN, England refuses to ban corporal punishment in the home, which is effectively protected by an 1860 law allowing "reasonable chastisement" ("UN attack on smacking welcomed," 2002).

Other issues facing English children are bullying and work-related accidents. The National Society for the Protection of Children estimates that 450,000 children are bullied at school each week. When asked whether they had ever been bullied, over half of 11-year-olds and a third of 13-year-olds said they had been bullied in the previous year (Church, Summerfield, & Fry, 1994). Work is also not uncommon for school-age children in England. Although it can offer benefits (for example, by giving a sense of responsibility, as well as income), work also involves risks; it was recently estimated that 44% of working children were injured on the job (NSPCC, 2001).

Risk Factors for Child Abuse

A number of risk factors for child abuse have been identified at the exosystem level—for example, factors associated with material and social deprivation. In a study of 14,256 children, 115 of whom had been placed on child protection registers, Morris, Scott, Mortimer, and Barker (1997) found that paternal unemployment, overcrowding, car ownership, and nonownership of home were all associated with registration on child protection registers. Maternal unemployment was also associated with increased risk of maltreatment, as was lower maternal social networking (e.g., seeing less of relatives, having fewer people to confide in, and fewer friends).

Gillham et al. (1998) had similar results in a study of all registered cases of child maltreatment for the years 1991 to 1993 in the 22 social work areas of Greater Glasgow. They found that rates of child physical abuse, sexual abuse, and neglect were associated with levels of male and female unemployment, single-parent density, and child poverty. The relationship was strongest between physical abuse and rates of male unemployment. Similarly, Morris et al. (1997) found a high proportion (33%) of abusers to be unemployed.

THE ENGLISH MICROSYSTEM

The typical English family consists of one or two children living with two married parents. Typically, women are 28 and men are 30 at the beginning of a first marriage. Over a third of children live with parents who have chosen not to marry. Additionally, 8% of the population is divorced, making single-parent homes quite common. Both parents are likely to work outside the home, although men are more likely to be in full-time employment. (Ninety percent of men with dependent children are fully employed compared to 65% of women with dependent children.) There is a significant lack of day-care facilities in England, and children who are not old enough to attend school are likely to be looked after by parents or other relatives (EOC, 2001).

Child Maltreatment

It is difficult to get an accurate assessment of the prevalence of child abuse occurring within the home because there are no national statistics for these rates in England. However, results of surveys do provide estimates for physical abuse (7% for boys, 6% for girls), neglect (6% for boys, 7% for girls), sexual abuse (1% of children, when perpetrated by a parent, and a further 2% by a relative or carer), emotional abuse (8% for girls, 4% for boys), and parental physical punishment (18%; NSPCC, 2001). Not surprisingly, abusers are most often people on whom children are highly dependent. In a retrospective study of all physical and sexual abusers convicted between January 1, 1988, and June 30, 1994, in the West Midlands police jurisdiction, Morris et al. (1997) found that of the 964 abusers studied, 97% were in positions of trust, usually living in the same home. Overall, most physical abusers were male (60.5%), as were most sexual abusers (97.5%). Physical abuse of young children tended to be committed by younger women against children under age 9; sexual abuse was perpetrated more often on girls ages 9 to 11. Of children under 12 months, 1.5% had been sexually abused and 8.5% had been physically abused. Interestingly, it is infants who are most at risk for certain types of abuse. Sibert et al. (2002) found that serious physical abuse is 6 times more common in babies than in children from 1 to 4, and 120 times more common than in 5- to 13-year-olds.

English Respondents' Perspectives on Child Abuse

Physical Abuse. In England, serious physical abuse has been defined as regularly experienced violent treatment of children by parents or carers, injuries resulting from such treatment, or physical effects of such treatment lasting at least until the end of the day (Cawson, Wattam, Brooker, & Kelly, 2000). Our respondents used a description of physical violence 50% of the time in their examples of abuse. The threshold for physical abuse was quite low—for example, "Mother taking a small daughter (say 5/6 years old) and 'shaking some sense into her' " (female, 40). Examples of severe physical abuse such as "beatings" (female, 49) and "torture" (male, 27) were also included in participants' implicit theories of child abuse.

Neglect. Our respondents were far less likely to list forms of neglect than of physical aggression when giving examples of maltreatment. Only 17% of our respondents made reference to child neglect, although the examples given were generally described as severely abusive. These ranged from "Neglect—leaving children at home while parents are at the pub" (73-year-old female) to "Locking a child in a room and feeding it only enough to keep it alive" (57-year-old female).

Sexual Abuse. Cawson et al. (2000) defined child sexual abuse as involving sexual acts with nonconsenting children and children age 12 or less. Only 20% of our respondents listed a sexual act as an example of abuse, although one 44-year-old woman described her own experience of abuse, "being sexually abused by my mother's boyfriend. Being bathed in bleach at age 5 by my mother who insisted that I was a 'whore and a slut.' " About half of the respondents mentioning sexual abuse specified that father to daughter sexual activity was severely abusive—for example, "Father coercing daughter to have sex with him" (40-year-old female); however, several respondents acknowledged that sexual abuse can be perpetrated by either parent, against either a son or a daughter: "Sexual interference . . . I think mother to son/father to daughter would be equally abusive" (37-year-old female).

Emotional Abuse. Emotional abuse has been defined as experiences of psychological control and domination, physical control and domination, humiliation, withdrawal, antipathy, terrorizing or proxy attacks (Cawson et al., 2000). In their examples of abuse, 42% of our respondents listed a form of emotional abuse—generally as mild abuse, rarely as severe abuse. Examples of mild child abuse were "Verbal abuse such as 'haranguing' the child" (male, 54) or "Parents being irritable and cross with child because of their own problems" (female, 45). Interestingly, some respondents gave examples of favoring one child over the other as a form of emotional abuse, "elder child obliged to go to bed early and younger one allowed to stay up, causing resentment" (female, 73).

It seems that our respondents' implicit theories of severe child abuse conceptualized it as physical assault. Neglect was recognized less often, despite the fact that in 1999, of the 34,600 names added to child protection registers in England, the most common reason was neglect alone, accounting for 35% of cases. (Physical abuse accounted for 23%; emotional abuse for 16%; sexual abuse 12%; multiple abuse 12%; and 2% were classified as other; NSPCC, 2002). The implicit theories revealed in our data did not include infants (never mentioned by our respondents) as potential victims of child abuse, despite the research findings already cited (Sibert et al., 2002) indicating that infants are at the highest level of risk for physical abuse.

Corporal Punishment. The use of physical force to discipline children in Great Britain is widespread. In 2000, 71% of parents said they had physically disciplined their child (The ESRC Violence Research Programme, 2001). Thirty percent of our respondents spontaneously reported that physical punishment is abusive. For instance, "Hitting a child of either sex with a belt or other object for disobeying the parent. Tying or locking a child of either sex in a room for answering back" (female, 32) was an example of extreme abuse. "Slaps" and "smacks," which connote punishment, were classified as moderately abusive, "Slap round the legs (mother to son) for being naughty/cheeky" (female, 40). Overall, although many of our respondents considered physical punishment to be unacceptable, it is apparently viewed as more justifiable than physical force used for "no reason."

SPOUSAL ABUSE

In 1999, a precise definition of domestic violence was created, specifying that domestic violence is usually perpetrated by former or current partners and may include physical, sexual, emotional, or financial abuse (Home Office, n.d.). However, the exact prevalence and incidence of domestic violence is unknown. In 1996, the British Crime Survey included questions about violent incidents not reported to the police, or reported to the police but not recorded. Responses indicated that about 4% of both men and women had been physically assaulted by a current or former partner in the last year. Women were twice as likely to say they had been injured (2.2% compared to 1.1%), more than 3 times as likely to say they had suffered from frightening threats, and more likely to have suffered repeated assaults during the year. Lifetime estimates of at least one physical assault were 23% for women and 15% for men (Mirrlees-Black & Byron, 2001).

The Domestic Violence Data Source (2001) indicates that lifetime prevalence of abuse by a partner or ex-partner tends to cluster at around 1 in 4 women, which is consistent with the BCS findings. Domestic violence is the most common form of violence that women in England face. Every week, two women are killed by their current or former partners (Home Office, 1998).

Mooney (1993) found that, in a random sample of 1,000 men and women in north London, 30% of the women had suffered physical violence "more severe" than being grabbed, pushed, or shaken, by a current or former partner or boyfriend. Thirty-seven percent had suffered mental cruelty. Furthermore, a 1989 survey in England suggested that 1 in 7 wives had been raped by their husbands, and two-fifths of these had been raped violently (Painter & Farrington, 1998).

Risk Factors

Women most at risk for domestic violence are those who are separated from a partner they have been living with. Data from the 1999 British Crime Survey revealed that these women were by far the most likely victims of domestic assault, with 22% reporting being assaulted at least once during the previous year. Younger women (those under age 25), women who do not work outside the home, women whose household income is below 5,000 pounds, and women with children at home are all at heightened risk. Ethnicity is not a risk factor (Home Office, 2002b). Microsystem conflicts over children are often associated with abusive situations. The London Metropolitan Police found that in 1 in 8 cases of domestic violence, there were issues of child contact or child custody. They also found that alcohol plays a role, as around 45% of victims of domestic violence thought that the assailant was under the influence of alcohol (Home Office Targeted Policing Initiative, 2001).

Attitudes Toward Domestic Violence

A recent survey of more than 2,000 young people, ages 14 to 21, suggests that domestic abuse is far from being seen as unacceptable. One in 2 young men and 1 in 3 young women thought there were some circumstances where it might be acceptable to hit a woman or force her to have sex. One in 5 young men thought forcing their wives to have sex would be acceptable and 1 in 7 thought it would be justifiable in a long-term relationship. One in 6 of the boys said they might personally force a woman to have sex, whereas 1 in 10 would rape a woman if nobody would find out. As for justifications, 1 in 10 thought there was nothing wrong with raping a woman if "the man was so turned on he can't stop," whereas 1 in 6 said it was ok "if she'd slept with loads of men" (Zerotolerance website, 2001). One might expect that implicit theories such as these about circumstances legitimizing violence might discourage victims from reporting incidents of domestic violence. Indeed, of the 1 in 7 wives who reported having been raped by their husbands, 91% told no one at the time (Painter & Farrington, 1998). Of the 48,000 women who contacted rape crisis centers in 1998, only 12% reported the incident to the police (Home Office, 1999).

Other research suggests that women would be willing to discuss domestic violence under the right circumstances. Richardson et al. (2002) found that 85% of women said it would be acceptable for a GP to ask if they had been abused, yet only 5% had been asked. Sturman (2000) found that 38% of victims of drug-assisted rape wanted police to be sympathetic, 29% wanted them to be believing, and 24% wanted them to be nonjudgmental.

English Participants' Perspectives on Wife Abuse

Two-thirds of our respondents listed a form of emotional abuse when asked for examples of wife abuse. Physical abuse was mentioned 40% of the time and sexual abuse only 18% of the time. When asked for an example of mildly abusive behavior from a husband to a wife, it was almost always (92% of the time) a form of emotional abuse. These examples were usually forms of ignoring, "withdrawing affection, sulking for long periods, refusing to communicate or compromise, lying" (female, 52) or verbal put-downs, "husband verbally puts wife down; makes her feel small and worthless, or his intent is to diminish her sense of self . . ." (female, 43), especially in public; "criticism of partner in front of a third party" (female, 73). Emotionally abusive acts considered moderately abusive were behaviors designed to humiliate the wife: "Husband throws dinner at wife because it is not to his liking and shouts at her" (40-year-old female); "Putting wife's opinions, beliefs, down in front of others. Open sneering. Not allowing the wife financial autonomy" (female, 59). Also emphasized were controlling behaviors, such as "Bullying, possessiveness and controlling attitudes of husband not wanting wife to have social life" (female, 41). When emotional abuse was given as an example of severe abuse, it was usually chronic, "Persistent verbal attacks" (male, 27) or "having an affair" (female, 26).

Physical abuse, mentioned in 40% of cases, was rarely seen as mild or moderate. Examples of physical abuse considered mild or moderate were "a husband slapping his wife" (female, 36) or "hitting out at the wife: a punch, slap or kick ..." (female, 21) or, "Thump or slap" (female, 36). Several of these respondents suggested that alcohol might provoke a husband to violence; "a drunken outburst of violence every so often ... monthly" (female, 21). For a physical act to be judged as severely abusive, it was usually described as persistent; "daily events where the husband beats up his wife" or "torturous" (female, 21), "extreme physical violence ... leading to physical injury which demand hospitalization" (male, 54). It was also often characterized as involving alcohol; "husband's alcohol-fueled aggression leads him to physical attack of wife" (female, 59); "Frequent beatings of wife by the husband on his return intoxicated from a night out" (female, 32). Finally, sexual violence accounted for 17% of total possible answers. Sexual abuse from a man to a woman was never judged to be mildly abusive. Only one respondent described sexual abuse as moderate; "sexual bullying" (male, 48). Severely abusive sexual acts were "rape" or "marital rape."

Our participants' implicit theories frequently included the assumption that alcohol use is associated with wife abuse. This is reflected by national statistics indicating that in cases of domestic violence in 2000, in England and Wales, 44% of offenders were thought to be under the influence of drink (British Crime Survey, 2000). Similarly, the Home Office Targeted Policing Initiative (2001) found that 45% of victims of domestic violence thought their assailants were under the influence.

Male Victims of Domestic Abuse

Although domestic violence accounts for only 8% of assaults against men, this is still a significant minority of cases. The BCS found that estimates of physical violence experienced in the previous year were the same (4.2%) for men and women, although women were more likely to be the victims of repeated violence and were more likely to sustain injuries. One interesting discrepancy that the BSC discovered was that over 1 in 10 young men (aged 16–29) with a long-standing illness or disability had been assaulted in the previous year. Among women, only limiting disabilities seemed to increase the likelihood of assault.

English Respondents' Perspectives on Husband Abuse

About 60% of the participants' examples of husband abuse involved emotional abuse and about 40% were physical acts. As with wife abuse, the majority of emotional abuse examples were clustered in descriptions of mild and moderate abuse. "Withholding sex" was mentioned fairly frequently as a form of husband abuse—much more commonly than in descriptions of wife abuse. For example, a 20-year-old man judged that "withdrawal of sex by wife" would be severely abusive. (The same respondent said that a severely abusive act from a husband to a wife would be "physical beating of wife by drunken husband.")

Examples of abuse by a wife were often qualitatively different from examples of abuse by a husband. Weapons were mentioned in 17% of descriptions of severe female to male abuse. For example, "Wife stabbing husband with a knife in a rage" (female, 40) and "wife throws boiling water on husband during a row in kitchen" (female, 38). Weapons were never mentioned in descriptions of husband to wife abuse. In several cases, we found that the same description of abuse was judged to be severe if perpetrated by a wife, and moderate if perpetrated by a husband. A 45-year-old man described mild abuse from a husband as "Grabbing wife or verbally abusing her," moderate as "Thump or slap, ... Verbal aggressive comments," and severe as "Rape, beating, imprisoning." This man said that a mildly abusive act from a wife to a husband would be "Shouting," a moderately abusive physical act would be "Verbal insults, slapping face," and a severely abusive physical act would be "Physical assault, poisoning."

Thus, many participants seem to have implicit theories of spousal abuse with different standards for abuse depending on whether it is perpetrated by a husband or a wife. Possible explanations are that women are perceived to be less abusive, so the threshold, according to implicit ideas of what women are "capable of" start at a lower level, or, conversely, that there is less tolerance for abuse perpetrated by a woman.

ELDER ABUSE

Adults over age 65 currently make up 15 to 16% of the English population. The vast majority (95%) live in private housing, either on their own (39%), with a partner (48%), or with other relatives (13%; Help the Aged, 2001). Although most are healthy enough to stay out of residential facilities, unpaid family and friends are often involved in caring for them. These "carers" number 5.7 million in Great Britain and are often themselves older adults; in fact, 14% of men and 11% of women over 65 are carers. Of those who care for someone in their own household, 45% spend 50 hours or more a week caring and 77% spend more than 20 hours a week (Help the Aged, 2001).

References to "granny battering" appeared in the 1970s, but didn't adequately describe the problem of elderly people being maltreated in their homes. In 1988, the British Geriatric Society held a conference to identify types of elder abuse and characteristics of victims (Ogg & Munn-Giddings, 1993). One conclusion of the conference is that there may be no "typical victim." An elderly woman still being abused by her husband after 40 years of marriage is very different from a confused and disabled woman experiencing violence from a caregiving son. Furthermore, confused, elderly persons may also be aggressive toward carers, who may themselves be old. Still, some consensus has been reached. Action on Elder Abuse (n.d.) broadly defines elder abuse as "a single act or lack of appropriate action, occurring within any relationship where there is an expectation of trust, which causes harm or distress to an older person."

The prevalence of elder abuse was systematically estimated for the first time in 1992. Victims of verbal abuse included 7% of those ages 60–64, 6% of those ages 65–74, and 3% of those over 74. Physical abuse was reported by 3% of those between 60 and 64, 2% of those ages 65 to 74, and 1% of those over 74. Three percent of individuals ages 60 to 64, 1% of those ages 65 to 74, and 1% of those over 74 reported financial abuses (Ogg & Bennett, 1992). Most often, elder abuse victims are female, over age 75, physically dependent, mentally impaired, and often socially disruptive. The typical abuser tends to be an elderly child living in the same household. Many of the abusers are male, with mental health problems (Ogg & Munn-Giddings, 1993). Reay and Browne (2001) found that risk factors for physical abuse were carers' alcohol consumption and past abuse by fathers. Homer and Gilleard (1990) found that among patients receiving respite care, the strongest predictors of abuse were the carer's alcohol consumption and the disruptive behavior by the patient. A poor relationship prior to need of care, and previous abuse over many years, were characteristic of many of the abusive relationships.

Our Respondents' Perspectives on Elder Abuse

Overall, our respondents mentioned emotional abuse (48%) and neglect (41%) most often as examples of mild, moderate, or severe abusive acts from an adult child to an elderly parent. Judgments of mild abuse typically described pettiness, "deliberately forgetting to fetch a requested item that the elderly person needs if the elderly person has been asking for lots of things to be fetched that day"; thoughtlessness, "speaking about parents as if they cannot hear or understand"; and lack of respect, "Adult answering questions on the elderly parent's behalf in a shop." Examples of moderate abuse focused more on vulnerabilities associated with age—for example, "lack of sensitivity to health concerns that don't affect younger people," "shouting, causing deliberate confusion." A 55-year-old man said "reminding the elderly person of a past event (e.g., death of a loved one) which they find extremely upsetting" would be moderately abusive. Mental cruelty, described as "psychological attacks" and "humiliation" were typical examples of severe abuse. One 40-year-old woman responded that "persuading a parent to sign a euthanasia form against his/her will" would be severely abusive.

Examples of neglect were given at every level of abuse severity. Mildly abusive examples of neglect were likely to center on thoughtlessness, "not respecting that person, not listening," "lack of attention," and "failing to bother to find out what the elderly person needs." Moderately abusive examples of neglect tended to focus on restricted communication or involvement—for example, "arrange for elderly person to go into a residential home and never visit even when promising to do so." Forms of neglect considered severely abusive were typically willful acts endangering the life of the older person—for example, "deprivation of food over a long period of time, or heat, in order to encourage the death of an older person" and "denial to the parent of decent humane treatment, food and warmth."

Physical abuse was also frequently mentioned (30%). Implicit theories of elder abuse revealed little tolerance for physical aggression, which was viewed, almost exclusively, to be severely abusive. These severely abusive physical assaults often depicted a parent who was in some way incapacitated, and therefore an easy target, "daughter or son physically assaulting . . . granny because she is demented or confused," "son hitting father because son is having difficulty helping father to get dressed in the morning." Although sexual assault and financial exploitation have been recognized as ways in which an elderly person might be abused (e.g., McCreadie & Tinker, 1993), our respondents almost never mentioned these types of abuse. On the rare occasion that sexual abuse was mentioned, it was seen as severe, and usually perpetrated by a son toward his mother, "son's sexual abuse of his elder mother." Financial abuse, again mentioned rarely, was judged to be a moderate form of abuse; "taking advantage of elderly parent by persuading them to give presents of possessions and money."

INTERVENTION AND PREVENTION PROGRAMS

What is now known as the National Society for the Prevention of Cruelty to Children (NSPCC; then known as The London Society for the Prevention of Cruelty to Children) was founded in 1884. The NSPCC is probably the best-known organization dedicated to protecting the rights of children. It has 180 teams and projects throughout England and Wales with the objective of preventing cruelty to children. It also operates a free, 24-hour helpline and is involved in public education and parliamentary campaigning (NSPCC, 2002).

The history of government protection for children can be traced to the first act of parliament for the prevention of cruelty to children (the "children's charter"), which was passed in 1889. This act enabled British law to intervene in relations between parents and children. It authorized police to arrest anyone found ill treating a child and to obtain a warrant to enter a home if a child was thought to be in danger. The act was amended in 1894, recognizing, among other things, mental cruelty against children ("Timeline," 2002). Early in the 20th century (1908), sexual abuse within families became a matter of state jurisdiction, rather than the clergy's. The Children Act 1948 established a children's committee and a children's officer in each local authority. The groundbreaking Children Act 1989 gave all children the right to protection from abuse and exploitation and the right to have inquiries made to safeguard their welfare ("Timeline," 2002).

Other acts and government projects include the Protection of Children Act 1999, aimed at preventing pedophiles from working with children ("Timeline," 2002). Further reform is expected shortly as a result of an inquiry into the death of Victoria Climbie—an 8-year-old girl who, after leaving the Ivory Coast in 1998, eventually ended up living in England in the care of her great-aunt Marie-Therese Kouao and her great-aunt's boyfriend, Carl Manning. In February 2000, Victoria was found dead as a result of terrible maltreatment. In January 2001, Kouao and Manning were convicted of murder and child cruelty and sentenced to life imprisonment (The Victoria Climbie Inquiry, 2002). The government report following Victoria's death, due out in 2003, is expected to recommend radical reform in child protection ("Timeline," 2002).

The Children's Act 1989 (compatible with the 1989 UN Convention on the Rights of the Child) brings together most private and public law relating to children. It considers both children's and parents' rights, and puts the responsibility for children in need in the hands of local authorities. It emphasizes that children have a right to be in an environment that facilitates development, and takes into account religious, racial, cultural, and linguistic factors. Other rights include the right to health, individuality, respect, dignity, opportunities for learning and socializing with adults and children, and freedom from discrimination such as racism or sexism. A general philosophy of the Act is that children, except in extreme circumstances, should be brought up in their own homes. Parental rights generally include the right of parents to be involved in decisions about their children and their children's care, both inside and outside the home (e.g., in daycare facilities; Department of Health, 2000).

To determine which children in a community are "in need," the Act considers whether a child requires services from the local authority in order to have the opportunity for a reasonable standard of health and development, whether the child's health or development would be impaired without such services, and whether the child is disabled. The main duties of the local authorities are identification and assessment of potential children in need, prevention of neglect and ill treatment, provision of family support for children in need who live with their families, and provision of services for disabled children (Department of Health, 2000). If children are considered to be suffering from, or likely to suffer, significant harm, they are placed on a Child Protection Register in the Social Services Department. In extremely abusive situations, a child may be removed from his or her home and may then become the responsibility of the local authority (Department of Health, 2000). Some research indicates that children being "looked after" by the local authorities form an at-risk population for maltreatment (e.g., Hobbs, Hobbs, & Wynne, 1999).

In the last decade, the English government has taken significant steps to tackle the problem of domestic violence, including setting up, in 1994, an official Interdepartmental Working Party on Domestic Violence to promote a coordinated response on local and national levels. In 1997, for the first time, the government appointed Ministers for Women, supported by a Women's Unit. The unit has been instrumental in promoting women's issues and rights. In December 2002, the Prime Minister launched a campaign to reduce the number of women and children made homeless by domestic violence (Women's Aid, 2002). There are now around 400 "safe houses" in Britain, taking in more than 55,000 women and children a year. This number of refuges represents only a third of the number of places that a landmark select committee report on domestic violence said were necessary more than 20 years ago (Women's Aid, 2002).

Protection from domestic violence has recently been modified, under both civil and criminal law. Protection from violence under the civil law falls mainly under the Family Law Act 1996, Part IV, which provides a single set of remedies, available in all family courts. The two main types of orders available under the Act are occupation orders, which regulate occupation of the family home, and nonmolestation orders (Women's Aid, 2002). Protection under criminal law has undergone recent changes in response to a growing awareness of the obstacles abused women faced in the legal process. In 1990, a Home Office Circular to Chief Constables helped put in place specific policies on domestic violence. Overall, police are required to treat domestic violence at least as seriously as other forms of violence. The policy emphasizes that in cases of suspected domestic abuse, the primary duty of officers is to protect the victim and any children, then to consider action against the offender. Police have the power to intervene, arrest, caution, or charge an abusive man. Furthermore, a policeman or policewoman does not need to witness the assault, nor does he or she need a warrant to arrest someone they think is about to commit an offense. Finally, the Protection from Harassment Act 1997 introduced new measures for protection under both criminal and civil law. Two new criminal offenses included in the Act are the offense of Criminal Harassment and the offense involving Fear of Violence (Women's Aid, 2002).

Protection for older adults comes from a variety of laws that are not necessarily specific to older adults. For example, legislation on domestic violence, including the Family Law Act 1996, is not confined to spouses. Similarly, if the abuse is of a racist nature, the Race Relations Act 1976 may be employed. Preventative statutes such as the Health Services and Public Health Act 1968 allow local authorities to promote the welfare of older people and the NHS Community Care Act 1990 requires local authorities to undertake an assessment of need (Action on Elder Abuse, n.d.).

SUMMARY

Awareness of domestic violence is increasing in England. A growing body of research has helped to highlight both the prevalence of domestic violence against children, women, elderly, and men and the specific risk factors for each of these groups. Responses from our sample of English people reveal understanding of, but also misconceptions about, the nature of domestic violence.

Rates of child abuse (physical abuse, neglect, sexual abuse, and emotional abuse) vary between 3% and 8%. The greatest risk factors for a child being abused in the home seem to be material and social deprivation, and parental unemployment. Single-parent density is also associated with abuse. Sexual abuse is far more likely to be perpetrated by men, and although physical abuse is more likely to be committed by men, physical abuse of young children tends to be committed by younger women. Infants are at the greatest risk for serious physical abuse.

Our respondents most readily associated child abuse with physical aggression, despite the fact that neglect is a more common form of child abuse. Moreover, infants were not explicitly identified as potential victims of physical abuse. Corporal punishment was spontaneously identified by our respondents as being abusive, yet it was usually specified as "moderately" abusive. It may be a component of implicit theories that it is wrong to physically discipline a child, but it's not as bad as hitting a child for other reasons.

One in four women in England experience abuse by a partner or ex-partner during a lifetime. Women most at risk for abuse are those separated from a partner they have been living with. Younger women, women with lower incomes, and women with children living at home are at a greater risk. In fact, child custody or contact is involved in a significant number of incidents of domestic violence. Alcohol consumption seems to be associated with domestic violence.

In their examples of wife abuse, our respondents were most likely to list emotionally abusive acts. The behaviors varied from "ignoring" to "controlling" and were usually considered mildly or moderately abusive. Physical and sexual abuse were seen as unacceptable, almost always judged to be severely abusive. Many respondents linked domestic abuse and alcohol consumption in their examples of abusive acts. Examples of husband abuse were quite different—typically less severe—from examples of wife abuse, perhaps indicating that women are assumed to be less abusive, or possibly that there is less tolerance for abuse from a woman to a husband.

Elder abuse has only recently been recognized in England. An estimated 1% to 7% of the elderly population are victims of verbal, physical, or financial abuse. The vast majority of older people in England live in private housing, either on their own, with a spouse, or with another relative. Abuse is perpetrated most often from an elder child living in the household, and females are at a greater risk for abuse. Some of the risk factors appear to be alcohol consumption by a carer, disruptive behavior by the victim, and a poor relationship prior to need of care. Our respondents mentioned emotional abuse and neglect most often as forms of elder abuse. There were also several examples of physical abuse, but rare mention of financial and sexual abuse.

ACKNOWLEDGMENTS

I would like to thank Judy Donovan and Jack Donovan for their invaluable help in collecting data. I would also like to thank Jerry Kennard, the staff of St. Andrew's Psychotherapy & Counselling Unit, Anna Baldwin, Marilyn Crawshaw, and Treva Broughton, as well as all the other people who were kind enough to participate in this research.

REFERENCES

Action on Elder Abuse. (n.d.). *What is elder abuse?* Available: http://www.elderabuse.org.uk/ Main%20Webpages/Questions.htm

Aiming high: The EU should act on gun crime. (2003, January 7). *Leader.* Available: http:// www.guardian.co.uk

Balding, J. (1998). *Young people in 1997: The Health Related Behavior Questionnaire results for 37,538 pupils between the ages of 9 and 16.* Exeter: Schools Health Education Unit, University of Exeter.

Blunkett confirms tough new gun penalties. (2003, January 6). *Guardian.* Available: http:// www.guardian.co.uk

Branigan, T. (2001, November 3). Christian schools ask for right to hit pupils. *Guardian.* Available: http://www.guardian.co.uk

British Crime Survey. (2000). Available: http://www.homeoffice.gov.uk/rds/pdfs/host1800.pdf

Cawson, P., Wattam, C., Brooker, S., & Kelly, G. (2000). *Child maltreatment in the United Kingdom. A study of the prevalence of child abuse and neglect.* London: NSPCC.

Central Intelligence Agency. (2002). *The world factbook 2002.* Available: http://www.cia.gov/cia/publications/factbook/geos/uk.html

Church, J., Summerfield, C., & Fry, D. (1994). *Social focus on children.* London: HMSO.

Department of Health. (2000). The Children Act Report 1995–1999. *A report by the Secretary of State for Health, the Secretary of State for Education and Employment and the Lord Chancellor on the Children Act 1989 in pursuance of the Department of Health.* London: Stationery Office.

Domestic Violence Data Source. (2001). Available: http://www.domesticviolencedata.org

Equal Opportunities Commission. (2001). *Facts about women and men in Great Britain 2001.* Available: http://www.eoc.org.uk/cseng/research/factsgreatbritain.pdf

Gillham, B., Tanner, G., Cheyne, B., Freeman, I., Rooney, M., & Lambie, A. (1998). Unemployment rates, single parent density, and indices of child poverty: Their relationship to different categories of child abuse and neglect. *Child Abuse and Neglect, 22*(2), 79–90.

Help the Aged. (2001). *The older population.* Available: http://www.helptheaged.org.ukP.pdf

Hobbs, G. F., Hobbs, C. J., & Wynne, J. M. (1999). Abuse of children in foster and residential care. *Child Abuse and Neglect, 12,* 1239–1252.

Home Office. (n.d.). *Government policy around domestic violence.* Available: http://www.homeoffice.gov.uk/cpd/cpsu/domviol98.htm

Home Office. (1998). *Living without fear.* Available: http://www.cabinet-office.gov.uk/womens-unit/archives/living_without_fear/contents.htm

Home Office. (2000a). *Intelligence and Security Committee Annual Report, 1999–2000.* Available: http://www.homeoffice.gov/uk/rds/cjschap8.html

Home Office. (2000b). *The 2000 British crime survey.* Available: http://www.homeoffice.gov.uk/rds/pdfs/hosb1800.pdf

Home Office Targeted Policing Initiative. (2001). *Understanding and responding to hate crime—Domestic violence fact sheet.* Available: http://www.met.police.uk/urhc/dv_fact4.pdf

Homer, A., & Gilleard, C. (1990). Abuse of elderly people by their carers. *British Medical Journal, 301,* 1359–1362.

House of Commons. (2001). *A century of change: Trends in UK statistics since 1900.* Available: http://www.parliament.uk/common.pdf

McCreadie, C., & Tinker, A. (1993). Abuse of elderly people in the domestic setting: A UK perspective. *Age & Ageing, 22,* 65–69.

Mezay, G., Bacchus, L., Bewley, S., & Haworth, A. (2002). *An exploration of the prevalence, nature and effects of domestic violence in pregnancy: VRP summary findings.* Available: http://www1.rhul.ac.uk/sociopolitcalscience/vrp/Findings/rfmezey.pdf

Mirrlees-Black, C., & Byron, C. (2001). *Domestic violence: Findings from the BCS Self-Completion Questionnaire.* Available: http://www.homeoffice.gov.uk/rds/pdfs/r86.pdf

Mooney, J. (1993). *The hidden figure: Domestic violence in North London.* London: Islington Council.

Morris, I. S., Scott, I., Mortimer, M., & Barker, D. (1997). Physical and sexual abuse of children in the West Midlands. *Child Abuse and Neglect, 21,* 285–293.

National Society for the Prevention of Cruelty to Children. (2001). *NSPCC Inform: The online child protection resource.* Available: http://www.nspcc.org.uk/inform/Statistics/CPStats/CP_Intro.asp

National Society for the Prevention of Cruelty to Children. (2002). *What we do.* Available: http://www.nspcc.org.uk/html/Home/Whatwedo/whatwedo.htm

Ogg, J., & Bennett, G. (1992). Elder abuse in Britain. *British Medical Journal, 305,* 998–999.

Ogg, J., & Munn-Giddings, C. (1993). Researching elder abuse. *Aging and Society, 13,* 389–413.

Painter, K., & Farrington, D. (1998). Marital violence in Great Britain and its relationship to marital and non-marital rape. *International Review of Victimology, 5,* 257–276.

Reay, A., & Browne, K. (2001). Risk factor characteristics in carers who physically abuse or neglect their elderly dependants. *Aging and Mental Health, 5,* 56–62.

Richardson, J., Coid, J., Petruckevitch, A., Chung, W., Moorey, S., & Feder, G. (2002). Identifying domestic violence: Cross sectional study in primary care. *British Medical Journal, 324*, 274.

Sibert, J. R., Payne, E. H., Kemp, A. M., Barber, M., Rolfe, K., Morgan, R. J. H., Lyons, R. A., & Butler, I. (2002). The incidence of severe physical abuse in Wales. *Child Abuse and Neglect, 26*, 267–276.

Sturman, P. (2000). *Drug-assisted sexual assault: A study for the Home Office under the Police Research Award Scheme.* London: Home Office.

The ESRC Violence Research Programme. (2001). *Taking stock.* Available: http://www.health. qld.gov.au/violence/domestic/dvi/news20.pdf

The Victoria Climbie Inquiry. (2002). Available: http://www.victoria-climbie-inquiry.org.uk/Background/back_chron.htm

Timeline: The history of child protection. (2002, October 10). *Guardian.* Available: http://www. guardian.co.uk

UN attack on smacking welcomed. (2002, October 4). *Guardian.* Available: http://www.guardian.co.uk

Women's Aid. (2002). *Policy and practice.* Available: http://www.womensaid.org.uk/policy

World Health Organization. (2002). Available: http://www.who.int/country/gbr/en/

Zerotolerance. (2001). Available: www.zerotolerance.org.uk

4

Portugal

Melanie T. Santos
Andrea E. Mercurio

CAPSULE

Although Portugal has undergone social and economic changes creating a more modern country, it is still, to some extent, a largely patriarchal society, dominated by male-oriented values and male privilege. Females have traditionally been viewed as subservient and inferior to men. Social norms like these, which are difficult to alter, can foster attitudes and beliefs that perpetuate violence against women, who are frequently victims of their husbands' aggression. Although recent legislative initiatives have increased women's safety and rights, those rights are often not exercised due to cultural norms discouraging women from seeking legal action.

Similar to women, Portuguese children have historically possessed few rights guaranteeing their health and welfare. Despite current governmental efforts to afford children greater protection in society, Portugal has had to wrestle with issues related to child abuse and exploitation, particularly child labor. Despite reverence for the elderly in Portugal, many elderly face dire poverty, but there has been some recognition of maltreatment of Portuguese elderly.

THE PORTUGUESE SAMPLE

We were able to assess implicit theories of family violence and abuse through survey responses from 53 participants from Portugal, including the islands of the Azores and Madeira. These respondents ranged in age from

15 to 59, with a mean age of 25. Although "student" was the most common occupation reported, other occupations included teacher, mechanic, plumber, construction worker, factory employee, psychologist, and homemaker. Most participants (80%) indicated that they were in high school at the time of data collection. The remaining participants reported either having a college degree (15%) or currently attending college (5%). Ninety-eight percent of the sample said their current religion was Catholicism.

Portuguese Participants' General Definitions of Abuse

In giving a general definition of abuse, about half of the Portuguese participants made reference to "physical and psychological abuse" or to "physical and verbal aggression." Several participants defined abuse in fairly general moral terms—for example, "Not respecting one another," "Treating people badly," "Doing things that aren't right," and "It's when behaviour between a couple isn't the most correct, depending on what they agreed on and their culture established in society." Among the other definitions were "Giving someone too much confidence. They may abuse the confidence you give them"; "Not taking care of the family"; "Making other people do things that we can do instead"; and "Abuse is not respecting each other physically and mentally. It's not just beating a child or anybody else, it's also not trusting somebody in your own family or not being fair with them."

THE PORTUGUESE MACROSYSTEM

Historical Context

The Republic of Portugal was established by the Lusitanians in 1249, making it one of Europe's oldest states. In the 15th century, armed with great scientific and nautical knowledge, Portugal established colonies in South America, Africa, and Asia and developed a formidable world empire (Marques, 1975). This period was known as the Era of Discoveries, a golden age of exploration and imperialism (Bradford, 1973). In the early 1900s, civil uprisings between monarchists and republicans caused the monarchy to fall and Portugal fell under fascist control in 1925. In 1974, the fascist regime was overthrown, and liberation from the dictatorship represented a new beginning for Portuguese society. The new government restored fundamental rights and freedoms, establishing a sense of hope within the people; however, in the years immediately following the establishment of the democratic regime, the Portuguese government faced political, economic, and social challenges (Manuel, 1996). The transition to democracy was arduous and citizens grew increasingly dissatisfied with issues related to health care, education, and the economy. In 1986, Portugal joined the European Economic Community (EEC), a strategic step helping to integrate the Republic culturally and economically with the rest of Europe. Portugal became a full member of the European Monetary Union (EU) in 1999, further strengthening the process of democratization and assisting progress toward a free-market society. Today, the Republic of Portugal is a constitutional democracy with a market-based economy (U.S. Department of State, 1999), and is led by a President, a Prime Minister, and a Parliament freely elected by the people.

Cultural Context of the Portuguese Family

Four key cultural values that help define the Portuguese family include *honra* (honor), *respeito* (respect), *bondade* (goodness), and *confiança* (trust; Araújo, 1996). The family is of supreme value and often remains together for the sake of honor. Family honor is a moral code (Loizos, 1978). Honra, however, can sometimes be as disabling as it is strengthening. Portuguese families adhering rigidly to principles like honra may unwittingly foster familial dysfunction, including abusive relationships between husbands and wives and parents and children. Family values within the Portuguese culture also emphasize secrecy and confidentiality, discouraging members from disclosing private matters to outside parties. It appears that in the face of a cultural proclivity for gossip, Portuguese families would rather suffer in silence than expose themselves to potential public embarrassment (McIntyre, 1999).

Confiança is another formative family value. Within the Portuguese culture, the family is often viewed as sacred, to be protected at all costs (Costa-Crowell & Oliveira, 1999). According to Araújo (1996), 80% of her Portuguese participants considered family to be the best thing in the world. But when questioned about violence in the family, many of those respondents said it occurs frequently and is generally directed against women and children. Trust and confidence were frequent themes in the implicit theories of our Portuguese respondents—including a concern that too much trust could be dangerous if taken advantage of. For example, one 18-year-old man defined severe abuse as "abuse of excessive confidence."

Respeito is also highly idealized within Portuguese culture. The familial structure is patriarchal, with authority and respect passing from father to mother to eldest child (McIntyre, 1999). In some cases, if the eldest child is a female with a brother close in age, he will have status over her. For example, a 12-year-old male may have more authority and power than his 14-year-old sister. Respeito is generally a unilateral trait. The young respect the old, and the meek respect the strong (Araújo, 1996). A 28-year-old woman illustrates the importance of respeito when she states "severe

abuse" is "when you don't respect somebody or something. It's only thinking of yourself and not thinking of the others. In some ways it can be considered a mental problem."

Respondents from our survey suggest, however, that the unilateral nature of respeito may be changing. An 18-year-old student said moderate
abuse from a husband to a wife was "the wife having to obey the husband's
rules." A 46-year-old woman defined abuse as "not respecting each other
physically and mentally. It's not just beating a child or anyone else. It's also
not trusting somebody in your own family or not being fair with them." This
same woman also reported, "I knew someone that whenever he had too
much to drink he would disrespect everybody by name-calling or even picking a fight."

Araújo (1996, p. 588) defined bondade as "[acting] generously, sacrificing
the self for another." This value is greatly inspired by Catholic doctrine and
the ability to forgive others no matter what malice they have demonstrated.
A 30-year-old female respondent defined moderate abuse from a parent to a
child as "the parent not doing everything he can so that the son can have a
good future"—and that is considered worse than "giving the child a bad
punishment."

The Status of Portuguese Children

Today, children in Portugal enjoy a more protected status than in the past
(Wall, 2000). The perception of a child largely as an additional financial contributor to the family income and eventual caretaker for the elderly is
slowly being replaced by a new ideal—one that offers children better educational opportunities, more legal rights, and the chance to achieve a higher
social and financial position in society. Children now have more freedom
and a greater ability to make their own choices. Nevertheless, they are still
expected to obey and respect their parents.

Some research suggests that Portuguese children recognize that they
have rights at home as well as at school and that these rights are valuable
and important (Veiga, 2001). However, Veiga (2001, p. 187) also found that
"the importance of rights appeared to be greater than its existence" in either the school or the home. In addition, children who perceived a low degree of parental support, or whose parents had limited education or were
divorced, indicated that their rights existed to a lesser extent than for other
children.

Portugal's educational system lags behind that of other European nations. It was not until 1986 that children were required to attend 9 years of
school. Once the 9 years of schooling have been completed, children can
pursue various areas of study or vocational training. Unfortunately, fairly
high dropout rates and high rates of illiteracy pose problems (International

Women's Rights Action Watch, 2001). It has been reported that 46% of Portuguese children drop out of school early, a percentage that places Portugal among the worst within the European Union in educating their young people (Systems, n.d.). Although females elect to pursue further education after secondary school more than males, the number of children opting to continue their education after age 15 is relatively low (Portugal: Reports to Treaty Bodies, 2001). School facilities are also disappointing, often with outdated materials and little access to computers and the internet. A study by the Central Region Teachers' Union found that 48.3% of the schools sampled had no library, 69% did not have computers, 87% were without a cafeteria, and unbelievably 27% did not even have telephones (Systems, n.d.).

Portugal has recently made efforts to promote preschool education (U.S. Department of State, 2000). According to a 1996 study by the European Commission, only 50% of children between the ages of 3 and 5 years were attending preschool. To address this problem, the Ministry of Education hired new teachers and increased the number of preschool programs. Preschool is now reportedly free for all 3- to 5-year-olds, and the number of children attending preschool has been increasing annually (U.S. Department of State, 2002). A child's educational rights were a concern to our participants. One respondent noted that "making a school-age child work rather than fulfill his educational obligations" was a moderate form of abuse. At the mild level, this participant said that "making older siblings care for their younger siblings when the elder child has schoolwork" is a form of maltreatment. Another respondent said that "making a child do work that affects schoolwork and performance" is an extreme form of abuse.

The Status of Portuguese Women

The traditional patriarchal family was formalized in the country's legal code until 1976, when the downfall of fascism occurred. Today, Articles 13 and 36 of the Portuguese Constitution establish equality between the sexes and within the family. Under the Portuguese Constitution, Article 13 states that "all citizens have the same social rank and are equal before the law" (Assembleia da República, 1997). Article 36 further delineates that "spouses have equal rights in relation to both their civil and political capacity and to the education and maintenance of their children" (Assembleia da República, 1997).

CHILD ABUSE IN PORTUGAL

Not until the early 1980s did the rights and welfare of children become an issue of national importance for the Portuguese government (Consideration of Reports, 2001). The right to exercise parental authority in any way seen fit was historically neither questioned nor challenged by outside parties. Gross cases of child maltreatment by parents went unpunished because legislation did not permit the intrusion of law enforcement and the court systems into the family domain. As human rights issues came to the fore in Portugal, perspectives began to change about the role the government should play in protecting children and in fostering development.

The Portuguese government has made progress in raising awareness of children's issues, aligning legislation with provisions of the Convention, and creating programs aimed at improving childhood development. For example, the government implemented the "National Programme against Poverty" and the "Minimum Guaranteed Income" to assist underprivileged families and children achieve more economically independent lives. This is important because sources indicate that 20% of the Portuguese population live below the poverty line (Press Release, 2001). The role of poverty in child maltreatment was a concern of one of our respondents, who gave the following example of extreme child abuse, "parents making their child beg on the streets and taking the earnings for themselves as well as punishing the child if significant earnings were not brought back."

There have been substantial modifications to welfare and security systems geared toward children living in poverty or at risk for abuse (Portugal: Reports to Treaty Bodies, 2001). In 1996, the government also launched an emergency family service system (the Family and Child Support Project; PAFAC) in response to the maltreatment of children within the family. This program was designed to provide dysfunctional families with medical, psychological, and educational services, and to create a systematic, objective means of assessing and verifying cases of family violence and child abuse (Consideration of Reports, 2001).

Concern over sexual abuse of children has prompted the legislature to initiate stringent penalties and to establish better laws for victims. Among our respondents, sexual abuse was always regarded as extreme child abuse, most often in the context of "a father sexually molesting his daughter." A law enacted in 1999 provided medical professionals and teachers with the responsibility of alerting appropriate authorities in cases of possible sexual abuse or exploitation. Moreover, Portugal has signed and ratified the Optional Protocol to the Convention on the Rights of the Child on the Sale of Children, Child Prostitution, and Child Pornography, which provides rules against the sexual exploitation of children.

Despite efforts by governmental and nongovernmental organizations (NGOs) to promote children's rights and to create a safer, healthier environment for child development and growth, the Committee on the Rights of the Child has criticized Portugal for failing to provide adequate information on violations of children's rights. The Committee specifically advised the Portuguese government to improve and expand its data collection procedures on child abuse and neglect as well as on sexual abuse and exploitation (Portugal: Report to Treaty Bodies, 2001). Unfortunately, with the exception of child labor, there appears to be very little published empirical evidence on the extent of these social problems in Portugal.

Although no statistics were found on how many children are abused each year, a study of 334 school children ages 9 to 15, conducted in 1984 and 1985, confirmed considerable physical violence (Ferreira da Silva, 1991): Only 11% of participants reported never being physically punished. Data from our own study, in which the predominant examples of child abuse were physical in nature, is consistent with the findings of Ferreira da Silva. In addition to asking questions involving child maltreatment, Ferreira da Silva also inquired about spousal abuse within the family. She concluded that in families where children reported physical abuse between their parents (19%), physical punishment of the children occurred more frequently than in families where spousal aggression was not reported.

Child Labor

There has been considerable attention to the issue of child labor in Portugal. Among the examples of child abuse recorded by our respondents were "making a child do work that one would not want to do oneself," "having a child do work that is not appropriate for his age," and "making a small child work." In recent years, the Portuguese government has been striving to correct, through legislation, the child labor problem, but it continues to be a subject of concern to both NGOs and public authorities. Much of the debate has focused on the definition of child labor, an issue that has proved difficult to resolve.

Another problem concerns the prevalence of child labor in Portugal and the sources used to assess it. Whereas past estimates by national organizations and NGOs ranged from 40,000 children (Report for the WTO General Council, 2000 as cited in Worst Forms of Child Labour Data, n.d.) to 200,000 children (Child Labor in Portugal, 1999), the Inspectorate General of Labour reported a decrease in detected cases of child labor from 300 cases in 1990 to 121 cases in 1996. According to a government survey conducted in 1999, approximately 10,000 children were being exploited in work situations. Critics of the sources used to measure child labor suggest that data collected by inspectors or government-related agencies are limited by the restrictions of legal and technical definitions of child labor that make it virtually impossible to consider all forms of child labor or to elaborate on related aspects of the problem. In other words, it has been suggested that previous studies and methods of data collection have been inadequate and have, therefore, left interested parties with an unclear and possibly inaccurate picture of the true nature and scope of the child labor problem (Child Labor in Portugal, 1999).

The issue of child labor is further complicated by the fact that it arises out of a complex mix of economic, cultural, social, and educational factors that combine to foster conditions encouraging and sustaining this type of abuse. One investigator argued that "the use of child labour in agricultural and domestic work is part of a strategy of socio-economic continuity in rural families in the north of Portugal" and that "the work plays an important role in socializing minors into rural economics mentality" (Cristovam, 1999, para. 2). This type of labor is not always viewed as work because it is not always visible to the public, making it more difficult to detect and report. A 1998 investigation cited poor job skills, weaknesses in the educational system, high failure and dropout rates in school, jobs requiring few specialized skills, traditions, and poverty as among the variables involved in perpetuating the problem (Cristovam, 1999).

An in-depth study addressing child labor in Portugal was launched in 1998 as a collaborative effort by a number of organizations, research institutions, and government-related bodies, including the International Labor Organization (ILO), the International Programme on Elimination of Child Labour (IPEC), the Statistic Department of Labour, and the Universities of Coimbra and Minho. Approximately 26,000 families with children between the ages of 6 and 15 were recruited and interviewed in mainland Portugal in October, 1998 (Child Labor in Portugal, 1999). Questionnaires were administered to both adults and children to determine the number of children working in Portugal and the factors associated with child labor. The findings revealed that although most of the children studied did not appear to be working unreasonably long hours and seemed to be attending school, there were some who were subjected to lengthy work days and were therefore unable to maintain their schoolwork. At one end of the spectrum, 4.7% of economically active children reported working 7 days a week for 7 or more hours per day. Although this is a small percentage, it remains troubling nonetheless that any child would be placed in such a circumstance. The study also revealed that children working outside the home came from lower income families, lived in poorer housing conditions, and had parents who had completed a lower level of education, compared with children who performed no activities. In addition, when asked why they engaged in work-related activities, most children referred to the financial needs of the family (Child Labor in Portugal, 1999).

The government acknowledges that child labor cannot be eliminated through inspectors and law enforcement alone, and that energetic steps to address the root causes facilitating its existence are essential. Attention must be focused on creating economic opportunities for adults, and moving toward a "higher technology industrial base with a corresponding need for better-educated and skilled labor" (U.S. Department of State, 2001, p. 7). This may help prevent third parties from employing children as a cheap form of labor. Greater resources to fight child labor must also be redirected toward family run farms and family businesses, where the government now finds the problem most concentrated. This is taking place more readily in northern and central regions where farming predominates. Child labor in the home, where inspections without a warrant are illegal, diminishes governmental power to protect children from exploitation (U.S. Department of State, 2000). Indeed, unpaid family work may be the hardest form of child labor to detect and reduce, as it is easier to hide from the public eye. More importantly, unpaid family work is not technically covered under the law as a form of child labor even though it has the potential to prejudice a child's development in the same way as do other forms child labor (Child Labor in Portugal, 1999). Further progress may require extended public education campaigns by the government as well as fundamental social changes within the country.

SPOUSE ABUSE IN PORTUGAL

In Mediterranean cultures such as Portugal, Greece, Cyprus, and Sicily, the use of violence by the male head of the household has historically been considered an appropriate means of maintaining society's moral code (Gelles & Cornell, 1983). Cultural attitudes permeating these societies have traditionally sanctioned men's aggression against their wives, and women often reinforced these actions by taking submissive roles and by remaining loyal to their husbands. A Portuguese participant in our study recalled that "My neighbor would utilize his wife rather than a work animal to plow his land. In addition, he would use a long stick with a nail protruding from the end to whip his wife to force her to maintain her pace." Although incidents such as this are not commonplace, when they do occur, they are rarely reported to authorities.

Violence and aggression have been considered appropriate means of punishment for women who infringe on familial cultural norms and rules (Gelles & Cornell, 1983). Although these values may be undergoing some change in Portugal today, several of our respondents considered it abusive for a wife "to neglect her chores," "be a bad housekeeper," or "fail to prepare a dessert for every meal." Interestingly, although many examples of moderate abuse focused on a wife not doing her chores, it was sometimes considered mildly abusive for husbands "not to help with chores"—a somewhat more tolerant standard for the exact same transgressions.

Araújo (1996) maintains that some Americans perceive Portuguese men to be more macho than non-Latino men. Machismo, or compulsive masculinity, is a cultural ideal in which a man is aggressive, sexually active, violently jealous, and nonexpressive of emotions, except for anger. Those with a macho image often value dominance and power, and this dominance can frequently lead to violence. A young female participant commented on this issue, stating that male domination and machismo are harbingers of abuse: "In whatever culture, group, or ethnicity, there exists abuse that can be attributed to male dominant societies." Within the Portuguese community, providing physical security and financial stability for the family is a way for men to display their authority. Women have traditionally held the more subservient role of providing care to their husbands by performing household duties such as cooking, cleaning, and even sometimes laying out their spouses' clothing for the following day (Araújo, 1996).

A concern with machismo was seen in several of our participants' examples of abuse listing husbands as being jealous and as wanting their spouses to obey unconditionally. Next to physical abuse, the violation of gender roles (e.g., "making a husband iron his own clothing") was most often perceived as abusive when committed by a female—again, evidence of unequal treatment, driven by cultural norms, holding men and women to different standards.

Regarding sexual activity, Araújo (1996) found that a wife's promiscuous behavior was more likely to be perceived as abusive than was her counterpart's. The ethnic tolerance of male promiscuity appears to be established through social learning and cultural sanctions (Campbell, 1985; Loizos, 1978), and continues today. In our sample, the Portuguese respondents on average perceived a woman cheating on her spouse as a more grave offense than a man being unfaithful to his wife. According to our respondents, it is somewhat acceptable for a man to cheat on his wife because he is virile or simply because he is a man, whereas a female would shame and disgrace the family if she were to act in a similar manner.

A study by Figueiredo and Silva (1988) found that 3% of college students and 11% of their parents agreed that a husband has the right to hit his wife. A previous study indicated that only 18% of the general population approved of a husband hitting his wife (Comissão da Condição Feminina, 1982). Although the findings of these studies indicate relatively low rates of tolerance toward spousal abuse, subsequent studies have not provided encouraging results. Vaz (1988), who measured actual experiences of domestic violence rather than perceptions, found that 61% of elementary school children, 13% of college students, and 25% of adults sampled had seen their fathers hit their mothers. More recent statistics have not improved either. Of all acts of maltreatment reported in 1999, 67% were acts of violence directed against a spouse or significant other (Apoio a Vítima, 1999). In 2000, 95% of the 11,765 reported cases of domestic violence were perpetrated against women (U.S. Department of State, 2002).

Ferreira da Silva (1991) surveyed married adults from the general population as well as school-aged children on their experiences with spousal abuse. Twenty-seven percent of the married individuals had been involved in a domestic altercation. Not surprisingly, those identifying themselves as a victim of spousal aggression were predominately female (94%). All males in the sample identified themselves as the aggressor with one stating that he was victimized as well. On the other hand, all females in the sample identified themselves as victims, with 10% stating that they were aggressors also. A dramatic 90% of the children reported that they had seen their father hit their mother.

Traditionally, women in Portugal have been denied protection by cultural norms and laws excusing men who beat their wives. Before the rise of democracy, women were afraid to report conjugal violence due to fear of the secret police (Costa-Crowell & Oliveira, 1999). Although laws have changed, and new initiatives addressing spousal abuse have been put in place, it appears that fear still looms. Although Portuguese men and women are technically afforded the same legal protection, the law and society do not always hold them equally accountable. In addition, women subjected to marital violence often do not acknowledge their legal rights because they are inhibited by social norms and attitudes discouraging them from seeking legal recourse (U.S. Department of State, 2000). It seems that in many ways, the old tradition and culture still prevail.

ELDER ABUSE IN PORTUGAL

A strong social norm of honoring and respecting elders dominates the Portuguese culture. The extended family is close knit and grandparents are often involved in childrearing duties, particularly now that more women are entering the labor force. When elders are in need of care, it is considered unusual or improper to place them in an outside facility. They are normally taken in and cared for by one of their children, often daughters or even daughters-in-law. In fact, an overwhelming 41% of our sample gave examples of elder abuse that mentioned "improper care" of elderly parents as well as other forms of neglect (e.g., "not giving them any attention").

Due to a decrease in birthrates and increase in life expectancies, the elderly population has grown progressively in Portugal. The average life expectancy is now around 79 years for women and 73 years for men (Senior Citizens News, 1999). The aging population (i.e., individuals over the age of 65) grew from 11% in 1981 to 15% in 1999. Lisbon has undergone a particularly sharp rise in its elderly population; this has been attributed to the relocation of many young people out of Lisbon to areas where there are cheaper, more affordable housing options.

The elderly in Portugal are protected under Article 72 of the Constitution, which guarantees "the right to economic security and to conditions of housing and of family and community life that respect their personal autonomy" (Assembleia da República, 1997, Article 72). Economic security was a concern of some of our respondents. One respondent reported personal knowledge of a case where a son of an elderly gentleman put all of his father's assets under his name, claiming it was for his father's protection. He then kept it all for himself.

The constitution also stipulates that economic, social, and cultural measures for the elderly be established to provide older men and women with the opportunity to lead active, self-fulfilling lives in their communities. Unfortunately, many elderly people lacking help from their extended family face conditions of poverty. Comparative studies conducted on European nations indicate that Portugal has one of the highest rates of poverty for the elderly at 70.4% (Netherlands Interdisciplinary Demographic Institute, n.d.). Older women are especially vulnerable to poverty, particularly when they have little educational background or few job skills. Elderly people living alone also risk social exclusion and can suffer isolation from the larger community.

Elder Abuse in Portugal

The topic of elder abuse in Portugal is relatively new. Consequently, very little research regarding rates of abuse toward the aging population can be found. A number of different factors may be contributing to this gap in information. First, awareness of elder abuse did not gain international attention until the early 1980s. The first World Assembly on Aging took place in Vienna in 1982. International efforts to address the concern over abuse toward the elderly seemed to develop more slowly than in the case of child or spousal abuse. Second, Portugal was undergoing difficult economic and social changes throughout the years following its transition to democracy; thus, the government was less able to direct sufficient resources toward issues of family violence and abuse during this time. The country's financial instability forced the government to focus on restoring economic harmony and social order to all sectors of society before turning to other areas of concern. Finally, and perhaps most importantly, in a country in which the elderly are presumably honored and respected, a false reality may prevail in which society believes such abuse to be unthinkable and therefore not in need of study. Thus, it is not surprising that research regarding various forms of elder abuse is especially lacking in Portugal.

Within our sample, many respondents who had given examples of child, wife, and husband abuse provided no examples of elder abuse—perhaps because it was a less familiar concept. Of those respondents who did give examples, they rarely listed any form of physical aggression. Instead their examples of abuse focused on more psychological and material issues—such as "abandoning" elders, "disrespecting them," "forgetting they were your parents," "forgetting everything they had done for you," "not giving them a hand when they need it," and "forgetting that once they took care of you and not being there now that they need you."

INTERVENTION AND PREVENTION PROGRAMS

Under Article 69 of the Portuguese Constitution, children are now guaranteed the right to "their full development" and are protected "against all forms of abandonment, discrimination and oppression and against the abuse of authority in the family or other institutions" (Assembleia da República, 1997, Article 69). The constitution further stipulates that "special protection" will be afforded to children who are "orphaned, abandoned, or in any way deprived of a normal family environment" (Assembleia da República, 1997, Article 69). Extending protection for children lacking a "normal family environment" had a significant impact on legislation addressing children at risk for sexual abuse, neglect, or maltreatment (Consideration of Reports, 2001).

In 1990, Portugal ratified the United Nations Convention on the Rights of the Child [United Nations International Children's Emergency Fund (UNICEF), 2002]. Ratification has, in large part, been the catalyst behind numerous legislative initiatives aimed at establishing and increasing children's rights. The National Children's Rights Commission, a government organization operating under the direction of the High Commissioner for the Promotion of Equality and of the Family, oversees the implementation of the principles of the Convention into Portuguese policies and laws (U.S. Department of State, 2002). It is also responsible for submitting a report to the Committee on the Rights of the Child every 5 years, enumerating the steps taken to address deficiencies with respect to child rights and welfare, thereby helping to ensure that the government remains vigilant in the prevention of child abuse (UNICEF, 2002).

Among the steps taken by the government to address problems related to child labor was the creation of the National Commission to Combat Child Labour (CNCTI) in 1996 (U.S. Department of State, 2000). The CNCTI has worked in collaboration with the National Confederation of Action on Child Labour (CNASTI) and the Institute of Support for Children (IAC) to form regional and local intervention teams that work with school dropouts and minors with jobs to encourage school attendance and to help ensure they are not being economically exploited. The Ministry of Education has also directed efforts at children at risk for dropping out of school by allocating more funds for alternative education plans. In 1998, the government established the Plan on the Elimination of Exploitation of Child Labour (PEETI; U.S. Department of State, 2001), which developed programs in which trained teams of social workers assist families with children who have dropped out of school or who are working. The teams provide educational and vocational programs tailored to individual children and their particular needs. They also offer "scholarships" to assist families with financial difficulties. Proponents of PEETI are advocating for a change in the language of laws related to the minimum age for working so that the safety and health of children performing unpaid family work are protected.

In sum, a great deal more progress can be made toward protecting the youth of Portugal. As Portugal continues to emerge from its previous state of political unrest and economic instability, the government should be able to shift more resources toward advancing children's rights. Coordinated efforts at the national level must be accomplished in collaboration with efforts at regional and local levels. Moreover, as is also true of child labor, additional research is needed to clarify the ways in which the problems of child abuse, neglect, and sexual exploitation are influencing the welfare of the children of Portugal. Without more precise information about what types of abuse are most prevalent, where the greatest problems lie, and under what circumstances they are most likely to emerge, it is challenging for the Portuguese government to implement and execute more effective prevention and intervention programs for children.

Portugal has gradually become conscious of spousal abuse, and there has been a growing formal recognition of the problem, its effects on members of society, and the need for reform. Under Portuguese law, domestic violence is now a public crime (U.S. Department of State, 2002). The legal definition of domestic violence has outfitted police with substantially more authority and power to investigate and prosecute cases of spousal abuse than in the past, potentially providing victims with greater protection from aggressors. In 1998, amendments to the penal code provided prosecutors with the legal power to file charges against alleged perpetrators of domestic violence without the consent of the victim if it was deemed "in the victim's interest" (U.S. Department of State, 2000). A woman can now also have her husband arrested if there is physical evidence of abuse. Punishment is even more rigorous than in the United States, with the sentence for a first time conviction being up to 8 years of incarceration.

Additional mandates by Parliament have called for the creation of domestic violence units within police departments and for the Attorney General to incorporate a section on "domestic violence" within the annual report on crime; however, as of 2001, these particular changes had not been instituted. The government has taken steps to increase public education campaigns and has provided specialized training for police to strengthen their effectiveness in dealing with domestic violence (U.S. Department of State, 2002). A 24-hour, toll-free hotline for victims to report cases of domestic abuse has been in place since 1998. The hotline has reportedly been successful, assisting female victims who are illiterate and increasing public awareness of family violence. Unfortunately, though, legal changes and public initiatives have mostly affected only ideals, with familial power often still lying with the male. Female victims of abuse are still reluctant to report perpetrators to the authorities (U.S. Department of State, 2000).

Because the number of elderly people in Portugal is steadily rising, it is more important than ever for Portugal to study issues related to aging. The country must adopt and revise policies geared toward the needs of a growing elderly population. In cases where a family is not capable of assisting elderly relatives, where the family is not serving a protective function (i.e., the family is abusive), or where there is no extended family, home-based care services and long-term care facilities may be essential ingredients for improving the quality of life for older individuals.

CONCLUSION

Portugal today is vastly different from 20 years ago. Democratization and gradual modernization have fueled changes in Portuguese culture and the nature of the family. Although significant inequality between men and women remains, the traditional subservient role of females is slowly being challenged as more women work outside the home, attain higher levels of education, and enter professions once dominated by males. Children's status in society is also undergoing substantial modifications in light of heightened public awareness campaigns and legislative measures directed toward child health and development.

Notwithstanding all the positive strides Portugal has made in advancing the basic rights of its citizens, spousal abuse, child abuse, and abuse toward the elderly are not simple issues that can be approached from a single perspective or solved through any one intervention or law. Family violence is fostered on societal, cultural, familial, and individual levels. The Portuguese government must target the causes of domestic abuse at all levels in order to effectively combat it. They must increase job training and work opportunities for women, strengthen the educational system, improve elderly services, and promote the rights of women, children, and the elderly through educational campaigns.

Unfortunately, fundamental social and cultural changes may be required before there can be substantial reductions in family violence. Portugal remains, to a large extent, a patriarchal society in which males are expected to display dominance and control over women. Attitudes and beliefs like machismo, driven by social and cultural norms that have existed for centuries, are often resistant to change. Social structures that reach back centuries form a barrier to changes in customs that may be necessary to advance the status of the weaker members of society.

There are encouraging signs, however, that the Portuguese government recognizes the problems within the familial sphere that need to be addressed to ensure the health and happiness of all members of its society. Due to the political and economic upheaval caused by years of harsh rule under a dictatorship, Portugal has trailed behind other European nations in the process of modernization. It will take time for the nation to reap the benefits of reform efforts such as mandatory schooling of children through nine grades, and other adjustments initiated to benefit the Portuguese people. With an increasingly strong economy, the Portuguese government and relevant NGOs will be better equipped to combat domestic violence. In the years to come, Portugal will undoubtedly continue to promote change that allows all its citizens—men, women, and children alike—to enjoy a safe and secure life, free from fear of abuse and family violence.

REFERENCES

Apoio a Vítima. (1999). *Manuel alcipe para o atendimento de mulheres vítimas de violência*. Available: http://www.apav.pt

Araújo, Z. A. (1996). Portuguese families. In M. McGoldrick, J. Giordano, & J. K. Pearce (Eds.), *Ethnicity and family therapy* (pp. 583–594). New York: Guilford.

Assembleia da República. (1997, September). Constitution of the Portuguese Republic (4th rev.). Available: http://www.parlamento.pt

Bradford, S. (1973). *Portugal*. New York: Walker.

Campbell, J. C. (1985). Beating wives: A cross-cultural perspective. *Victimology: An International Journal, 10*, 174–185.

Child labor in Portugal: Social characterization of school age children and their families. (1999). Available: http://www.ilo.org/public/english/standards/ipec/simpoc/portugal/report/english/indexpr.htm

Comissão da Condição Feminina. (1982). Violência na família, alguns números para pensar. *Boletim da CFF, 4*, 43–47.

Consideration of reports submitted by state parties under Article 44 of the Convention. (2001). Available: http://www.unhchr.ch/tbs/doc.nsf/(Symbol)/CRC.C.65.Add.11.En

Costa-Crowell, C. L., & Oliveira, R. (1999). The "old ways" have changed in the old country. *Standard-Times*. Available: http://www.s-t.com

Cristovam, M. L. (1999). *Report examines child labor situation*. Available: http://www.eiro.eurofound.ie/1999/02/Feature/PT990218F.html

Ferreira da Silva, L. (1991). O direito de batar na mulher: Violencia interconjugal na sociedade portuguesa. *Analise Social, 26*, 385–397.

Figueiredo, E., & Silva, L. (1988). *Portugal—os próximos 20 anos—conflicto de gerações e de valores*. Fundacao Calouste Gulbenkian.

Gelles, R. J., & Cornell, C. P. (1983). Introduction: An international perspective on family violence. In R. J. Gelles & C. P. Cornell (Eds.), *International perspectives on family violence* (pp. 1–22). Lexington, MA: Lexington Books.

International Women's Rights Action Watch. (2001). *IWRAW Publications*. Available: http://www. igc.org/iwra/publications/countries/portugal.html

Loizos, P. (1978). Violence and the family: Some Mediterranean examples. In J. P. Martin (Ed.), *Violence and the family* (pp. 183–196). Chichester, England: Wiley.

Manuel, P. C. (1996). *The challenges of democratic consolidation in Portugal: Political economic, and military issues 1976–1991*. Westport, CT: Praeger.

Marques, O. A. (1975). *Historia de Portugal* (Vol. 3). Lisbon, Portugal: Editora Palas.

McIntyre, T. M. (1999). Family therapy in Portugal and the U.S.: A culturally sensitive approach. In U. P. Gielen & A. L. Comunian (Eds.), *International approaches to the family and family therapy. Series on international and cross-cultural psychology* (pp. 87–115). Padua, Italy: Unipress.

Netherlands Interdisciplinary Demographic Institute. (n.d.). *Economic status of elderly: Strong differences by gender, age, and household status*. Available: http://www.nidi.nl/research/prj20103.html

Portugal: Reports to Treaty Bodies. (2001). Available: http://www.hri.ca/fortherecord2001/vol16/portugaltb.htm

Press release: Committee on Rights of Child concludes consideration of Portugal's Report on Compliance with Convention. (2001). Available: http://www.unog.ch/news2/documents/newsen/crc0154e.html

Senior Citizens News. (1999). *Healthy aging*. Available: http://www.tiesweb.org/senior/news archives4.htm

Systems. (n.d.). Available: http://www.geocities.com/tpilomia/Portugal.14.systems.htm

United Nations International Children's Emergency Fund. (2002). *Convention on the Rights of the Child*. Available: http://www.unicef.org/crc/introduction.htm

U.S. Department of State, Bureau of Democracy, Human Rights, and Labor. (1999). *Human rights practices for 1998*. Available: http://www.usis.usemb.se/human/human1998/portugal.html

U.S. Department of State, Bureau of Democracy, Human Rights, and Labor. (2000). *1999 country reports on human rights practices*. Available: http://www.state.gov/www/global/human_rights/1999_hrp_report/portugal.html

U.S. Department of State, Bureau of Democracy, Human Rights, and Labor. (2001). *Country reports on human rights practices for 2000*. Available: http://www.usis.usemb.se/human/2000/europe/portugal.html

U.S. Department of State, Bureau of Democracy, Human Rights, and Labor. (2002). *Country reports on human rights practices—2001*. Available: http://www.state.gov/g/drl/rls/hrrpt/2001/eur/8324pf.htm

Vaz, J. G. M. (1998). *O ensino da sexologia—relato de uma experiênca*. Porto, Portugal.

Veiga, F. H. (2001). Students' perceptions of their rights in Portugal. *School Psychology International, 22*(2), 174–189.

Wall, K. (2000). *Portugal: Low fertility*. Available: http://europa.eu.int/comm/employment_social/eoss/downloads/portugal_2000_fertil_en.pdf

Worst forms of child labour data. (n.d.). Available: http://www.globalmarch.org/worstforms report/world/portugal.html

5

Italy

Scott Borrelli
Tommaso Palumbo

The harmonious development of a child's personality, which insures that he/she embraces the values of peace, tolerance and co-existence, cannot be achieved by using violent means which contradict these goals.
—Judge Francesco Ippolito (1996, decision of
The Supreme Court of Cassation in Rome)

CAPSULE

Today's Italy is a dynamic and quickly changing society, and the Italian zest for life, la dolce vita, is envied by more reserved cultures. The country is also the Italy of the old ways (la via vecchia), reflecting an enduring value system organized to protect the family. Suspicion of the unknown and preference for control means that consultation with agencies outside of the family is discouraged; consequently, domestic violence tends to be shrouded in secrecy. The perception that Italian government is corrupt, neglectful, and untrustworthy promotes a bribery and kickback culture, la bustarella ("the envelope"), which is a central and accepted way of life. Our respondents often referred to "blackmail" to describe various domestic abuses, including financial, emotional, and psychological maltreatment.

Family (la famiglia) is the center of Italian life. The principles of family loyalty and honor are omnipresent, fortified by a historically rooted mistrust of government and outsiders. The Italian family is rooted in enduring patriarchal and hierarchal traditions that continue to restrict the freedoms of women and children, compromising attempts to address problems of domestic violence. Such traditions maintain the relatively wide gap dividing the male population from women and children, shaping differences in the ways in which Italian men and women perceive domestic violence. Because exclusion from the family remains the most powerful retribution against disloyal members, individuals are reluctant to betray family secrets, and reporting rates of family violence remain low (Adami, 1996).

Sweeping changes in European and Italian law, promoting services for victimized children and women, and innovations in socialized health care, offer new hope for troubled families (Ahmad, Lopez, & Inoue, 2000). As Italian society modernizes and families evolve into less insular and more egalitarian entities with broader social accountability, the traditional family unit is likely to become less stable. On the other hand, changes toward more exchange and openness are already empowering Italy's victims, opening up new avenues of support, and improving research into the problems and solutions of domestic violence.

THE ITALIAN SAMPLE

The Italian sample consisted of 100 participants (39 male and 61 female) ranging in age from 19 to 69 years. Data were collected from online and paper–pencil versions of the cross-cultural survey. The majority of respondents were Italian residents of northern, central, and southern Italy. Others were Italian nationals residing in London and recruited at Italian cultural centers. The participants represent a broad range of social backgrounds, education, and occupations, including students, retirees, professionals, blue-collar workers, teachers, artists, managers, and housewives.

Italian Participants' General Definitions of Abuse

While often defining abuse in terms of physical or sexual violence, our respondents also emphasized abuses of power and disrespect for individual rights. Some examples include "imposition of own will," "every behavior that reduces the dignity of the individual," and "use of power to damage others." Forms of physical violence were particularly common as examples of extreme abuse toward women (61%), but also fairly frequent as examples of extreme child abuse (51%), elder abuse (41%), and abuse of males (46%—equal with psychological abuse). Among the examples of extreme abuse were "beating," "burning," "father hitting mother and/or children," "hitting someone to the degree of injury," and "harming someone above what they can tolerate." Men listed forms of physical abuse at a much higher rate than did women (64% vs. 44%), who gave examples of sexual abuse (32%) twice as often as did men (14%). Overall, the results suggested that women, children, and the elderly remain vulnerable members of Italian society. Men's roles as primary perpetrators of violence probably reflect the authoritarian and machismo attitudes that Italian males are socialized to demonstrate, and that may go awry under stress.

General examples of moderate abuse included "slapping," "forcing child labor," "abuses of power," "insulting," and "stealing," whereas examples of mild abuse included "deprivation," "sarcasm," "swearing," "invasion of privacy," "withholding of sex," and "absence of dialogue." About one-third of the responders omitted any general examples of mild abuse. One respondent commented: "I don't believe in moderate or mild abuse; abuse is abuse."

THE ITALIAN MACROSYSTEM

Culture and Lifestyle

Italy has been subjected to major cultural and political influences throughout its long and turbulent history—in part because of its strategic position on the Mediterranean Sea, offering an historically envied transit between western and eastern Europe. Italy's expansive European peninsula shares its northern borders with France, Switzerland, and Austria, and its heritage with northern European, classical Greek, African, Asian, and Arab-Islamic cultures. Major cultural differences also exist among its 20 separate regions and, especially, between northern/central (more industrial) and southern (more agrarian) Italy (Bull, 1996).

Italians have learned to rely on their extended families and close friends, and on internal resources for security and protection, rather than on typically undependable governments and their local representatives (e.g., the police and the judicial system). In one study, the significance of family as a value far outweighed job (62.5%), leisure time (53.6%), religion (13.6%), and politics (4.7%; Buzzi, Cavalli, & Lillo, 1997). According to one study, 50% of Italians view their government with disgust, mistrust, or anger (Schwartz, 2001). Consequently, emphasis on family allegiance tends to undermine the influence of law and of civic mindedness, and makes collecting data on domestic violence difficult (Bruno, 2002).

The Church and the Mafia

The Roman Catholic Church and the Mafia, two of Italy's defining institutions, remain persistent influences on the family, as well as on government and public life. Traditional family values are maintained by the pervasiveness of Catholic morality and by socioeconomic factors contributing to Italy's relatively low rank among industrialized societies on the United Nations Human Development Index (which combines indicators of national income, life expectancy, and educational attainment; Houseknecht & Sastry, 1996). Both the Mafia and the Church embody authoritarian and patriarchal principles. Both reinforce strict hierarchies, group harmony and agreement, the maintenance of rigid sex roles, and, consequently, a range of inequities based on sex and age (Trompenaars & Hampden-Turner, 1998). Under these systems, the aged, women, and children, and other more silent minorities such as lesbians, gay men, and bisexual women and men, are victims of discrimination and abuse.

Efforts to increase the visibility of less powerful groups such as women and gays in the Catholic hierarchy continue to raise strong opposition from Church authorities. Following World Gay Pride celebrations in 2000, Pope John Paul II reasserted the Church's traditional stand on homosexuality as "contrary to natural law" and "intrinsically disordered" (Willey, 2000, p. 16). Violence against gay men is frequent but, as with other minority groups, reporting is extremely low given the likely scandal. Rome has the highest percentage of gay men murdered, usually by male prostitutes (Biagini, Bertozzo, & Ravaioli, 1998). Incidents of violence against lesbians, typically within their own families, are also on the increase. Although the Italian penal code contains laws protecting individuals against gender, race, and religious discrimination, no laws include sexual orientation as a nondiscrimination category (Biagini et al., 1998).

Status of Women

Major chinks appear to be occurring in the patriarchal armor shielding Italy's institutions. Since World War II, Italian women have rallied successfully for positive social change. Rights to full-time motherhood at home (e.g., liberal maternity leave) and in the workplace (e.g., equal employment opportunities) have been acknowledged (Saraceno, 1998). Nonetheless, although Italian women have the highest proportion of self-employment in the European Union, they remain significantly underrepresented in political, governmental, professional, and management positions (U.S. Department of State, 1998). On the other hand, incidents in the Camorra (the Neapolitan Mafia) show women inheriting status and power from incarcerated or murdered husbands, and perpetrating similar levels of violence and crime (DiGiovanni, 2002).

Recent changes in the Italian family have included fundamental alterations in the role of women in the family and in society as a whole, and women have emerged "as the most significant agents of change in the struggle against gender-based violence" (Kapoor, 2000, p. 14). Marriage is on the decline, and Italy has the lowest birthrate in its history, down from 2.2 to

1.22 children per woman between 1975 and 1994 (Astolfi, Ulizzi, & Zonta, 2002). Acknowledging that Italy's population is likely to decline by 25% in the next two generations, Pope John Paul II urged Italian families to have more children (Washington Times, 2002).

Inequities in the workplace are a continuous reminder of the resistance that this predominantly patriarchal society shows to women leaving the home. A recent United Nations study of Italian women workers demonstrated that they work 28% longer hours than men, and 9% longer than any other cohort of women in twelve OECD nations (Sgritta, 1997). Working women also have weak economic support from the government. Only 1% of Italy's GDP is dedicated to family support subsidies, compared to the average of over 6% of other European Union members (Sgritta, 1997). One result is what one woman called moderate wife abuse; "asking her to take care of all the domestic chores, even when she works."

In Italy, individual problems, including mental health issues, are sometimes seen in the community as a "blot on the family honor; a sign of bad blood lines" (Spiegel, 1971, p. 45). Family honor is a dominant theme in Italian culture, and the basis for development of personal identity (Storti, 2001). Consequently, it is expected that individual problems will be resolved within the established family unit. In cases of domestic violence, individual freedom to access social supports and interventions remains severely hampered by cultural traditions. However, such traditions are increasingly challenged by the demands of modern times, including the drive toward individuation promoted by ease of international exchange, the omnipresence of the media (dominated by American individualistic values), and the lure of a seemingly infinite range of opportunities for motivated individuals (Sant Cassia, 1991).

THE ITALIAN MICROSYSTEM

Italian interactions have been characterized as affective, relational, and highly contextual (Trompenaars & Hampden-Turner, 1998). Italian males who control Italy and its governmental and corporate activities are strong on building alliances, negotiating, and exploiting personal and political relationships. Organizational structures tend to look somewhat disorganized and informal, due to the predominance of interpersonal involvements where emotions are exchanged freely (Tung, 1998). Words and verbal agreements are sacred, and betrayals are anathema. In our sample, the most common examples of abuse were forms of psychological abuse (53% men and 52% women), including "limiting other people's freedom," "verbal abuse," "emotional blackmail," "imposing own will on others," "lack of respect," "taking advantage of others," "using the vulnerability of others," and "breach of privacy." Generating embarrassment seems to be a common power tool used by both Italian men and women to control behavior. For example, one young woman respondent identified "embarrassment in public" as mildly *and* moderately abusive of husbands, "embarrassment in public" as moderately abusive of wives, and "embarrassment in private" as mildly abusive of wives—with the implication that men are less capable than women of being embarrassed "in private" with no observers present.

Italian families tend to be extended rather than nuclear, with individual identity depending on family stability (Trompenaars & Hampden-Turner, 1998). Families represent a fortified cross-generational network, including grandparents, aunts, uncles, cousins, close friends, and godparents (Giordano & McGoldrick, 1996). Individuals who are not blood relatives are kept at a distance and viewed in terms of the degree to which they are able to contribute to the family's interests (Trompenaars & Hampden-Turner, 1998). Although divorce and separation are on the rise, most remarry, contributing to the low percentage of single-parent families. Statistics show that approximately 97% of Italian couples are legally married, which is far more than in most other European countries, and reflects the influence of religious practice on the family (ISTAT, 2002). In 1999, a high court ruled that even platonic extramarital relationships are adulterous, as they betray "the mutual trust at the heart of the marriage" (Owen, 2003, p. 23).

Responsibility to the extended family has traditionally overridden marital intimacy (Arenson, 1979). One-third of Italian adults ages 30 to 34 still live with their parents, demonstrating a level of intrafamily dependence more typical of Mediterranean cultures such as Greece and Italy than of other Western European countries. Moreover, as recently as 2002, Italy's highest appeals court declared that fathers must support their adult children until they find a suitable job (Reuters, Rome, April 5, 2002)! Also characteristic of Italian families is a life-long bond between mothers and sons (sometimes referred to as mammoni, "mama's boys"). The loyalty (and submission) required of Italian sons by their mothers reflects a strong matriarchal undercurrent in society. While asserting dominance in their marriages, men characteristically continue throughout life to submit to their parents. In 2003, Italy's highest appeal court set a precedent by ruling that interference in a marriage by an "overbearing and intrusive mother-in-law" is grounds for divorce (Owen, 2003, p. 23). In another case, custody of an 11-year-old boy was given to his father on the grounds that his mother was "overprotective" (Owen, 2003, p. 23).

Patriarchy Under Fire

The Italian patriarchal system is "derived from Greek and Roman law, in which the male head of the household had absolute legal and economic power over his dependent female and male family members" (Lerner, 1986,

p. 238). Giordano and Riotta-Sirey (1981) suggested that, because of this tradition, Italian women expected violence under certain circumstances, even if they had not yet experienced it from their husbands. However, in recent decades, the media, economic influences, and educational and career opportunities have encouraged the emergence of more assertive wives and children. Such forces have created increasing difficulties for Italian men, who may still need the traditional submission of their families to ensure identity and status. It is likely that the destabilization of the patriarchal role contributes to family violence because it is one main way men attempt to control their partners (Walker, 1999).

THE INDIVIDUAL/DEVELOPMENTAL CONTEXT

Alcohol Consumption

Alcohol consumption, especially from local wineries, is a traditional Italian family institution. Adolescents and even children are allowed to imbibe at dinner under adult supervision. Although per capita consumption of alcohol is high, alcohol abuse in Italy is relatively low as compared to France and Germany (Hanson, 2003). However, drinking has recently been identified as contributing to domestic violence in Italy (Terragni, 1999), and substance abuse may play a particularly significant role in more severe forms of physical abuse in families (Bardi & Borgognoni-Tarli, 2001), as well as in other forms of violence. By one estimate, nearly 18% of violent acts in Italy are committed by individuals (mostly men) affected by alcohol and/or drugs (Fuchs, 1998). The greater constraints on women's use of alcohol is reflected in this example of moderate husband-to-wife abuse offered by a 39-year-old male: "Allowing her to get drunk and make a fool of herself in public." A 30-year-old female respondent identified "drunkenness" along with "physical violence" and "cheating" as extreme forms of wife abuse.

VIOLENCE AGAINST CHILDREN

According to the Italian Ministry of Justice, there are about 5,000 cases of child abuse and/or neglect per year, and an incidence of severe violence of about 0.3% (ISTAT, 2002). In 1996, in a stunning move toward child protection, Italy's highest court, the Supreme Court of Cassation in Rome, issued a decision prohibiting corporal punishment (Global Initiative to End All Corporal Punishment of Children, 2002). This decision noted that the common justification of corporal punishment, that it is done for the "correction" of children, expresses a view of childrearing that is culturally anachronistic and historically outdated, and that should be replaced with a less hierarchical and authoritarian orientation. In line with the Supreme Court ruling, our survey respondents gave examples of physical punishment across all three levels of mild (e.g., "slapping"), moderate (e.g., "physical punishment"), and severe ("beating") abuse.

The lack of public funding for research and programs makes it difficult to fully understand the magnitude of the child abuse problem, but two recent studies shed some light. In a study by the Center for Europe's Children (1999), over 9,000 children from 19 hospital Child Emergency Units were assessed for abuse. Doctors suspected abuse in over 7% of these cases (primarily serious neglect, but also cases of physical and sexual abuse), were certain of abuse in over 2%, yet were able to confirm abuse in only .8%. Projecting the confirmed abuse numbers from these studies on a national scale suggests a disturbing 50,000 cases of actual child abuse and neglect per year, rather than the official figure of 5,000 cases annually. These projected figures are more reflective of the nearly 500,000 calls related to child abuse made to the hotline Telefono Azzurro in a recent 12-month period (Center for Europe's Children, 1999).

In the second study (Bardi & Borgognini-Tarli, 2001), a survey on parent–child conflict resolution with over 2,000 families in Tuscany revealed that physical punishment was common, with the incidence of minor violence (e.g., pushing, slapping) at 77%, and severe violence (e.g., kick, bite, hit with fist) at 8%. Risk factors for abuse were found at both exosystem and microsystem levels, including low-income; stressed caretakers; and "problematic" children. The likelihood of violence increased with the number of problems in the family.

Disturbingly, in a comparative study of Italian women victims of violence, it was found that all children who had witnessed marital violence exhibited clinical symptoms, and women victims were more likely to abuse their own children (McClosky, Treviso, Scionti, & dal Pozzo, 2002). Other ways domestic violence can hurt children is reflected in this male respondent's foiled attempt to protect his mother from his father's violence: "My father threw me out of the house—figuratively not literally—for keeping him from hurting my mother."

Italian Participants' Perspectives on Child Abuse

Implicit theories of child abuse appeared to have specific tenets related to gender of parents. One 23-year-old male illustrated this point well by listing "father beats his daughter" as an example of extreme child abuse, "father beats his son" as an example of moderate abuse, and "mother beats her son" as an example of mild abuse. There were also some sex differences in perceptions of child abuse. For example, male respondents identified physical abuse nearly twice as often as sexual abuse as an extreme form of abuse (61% vs. 32%), whereas women identified physical and sexual abuse at approximately equal rates (45% and 47%). These results suggest that Italian men may be less aware of or less willing to identify child sexual abuse, perhaps because they are in many cases the perpetrators. Examples of adults' abuse of power were common and included "physical and sexual violence," "battering," and "forcing children to work."

VIOLENCE AGAINST WOMEN

Research on domestic violence in Italy indicates that it is widespread, underreported, and often blamed on the victim. One sample (Bruno, 2002) of thousands of women from 28 antiviolence centers, mainly in northern and central Italy, reported many types of physical aggression (e.g., pushing hard, throwing on the bed) and psychological aggression (e.g., being told you are stupid, fat, a whore, a bad mother, and provocative). The majority of perpetrators were partners (79–93%). In most cases (65–78%), perpetrators had no criminal or psychological history, and were employed and well integrated into society.

Romito and Gerin (2002) evaluated the feasibility of asking all women attending a health care service about violence. They found that no woman made negative comments or stopped the interview when the issue of violence was broached. Moreover, a large minority revealed present or past abuse for the first time. The more violence the woman had experienced, the more eager she was to talk about it. Unfortunately, health professionals are prey to many common biases toward women victims—including beliefs that the woman provoked the man, or is unbalanced or even masochistic—that represent de facto collusion with male violence (Gonzo, 2000).

Despite the frequency of violence and its health consequences, a common response of health services and professionals has been to deny the problem (Romito, 2000). Among emergency department physicians interviewed in one Italian city, 45% claimed never to have had any professional contact with female victims of abuse, even though the "Casa delle Donne" (a Women's Center) in the same city had been contacted by nearly 1,300 new cases over a 4-year span (Gonzo, 2000). Battered women in another Italian study (Romito, 2000) said they had often sought care after an incident of partner violence. Many of them, out of fear or discouragement, had told health care workers they had "fallen down the stairs." Despite signs like black eyes and bruises around the neck, physicians had often accepted the women's versions of events.

In 1997, the Italian Institute of Statistics (ISTAT) surveyed a sample of 20,064 women, ages 14 to 59, on experiences of sexual abuse in the forms of molestation and rape, exposure to violence, and obscene phone contacts (Sabbadini, 1998). The investigators concluded that 50% of the women had experienced at least one type of abuse. Based on a review of other studies with patient samples, Gonzo (2000) reported that separated/divorced women were in all cases more likely to have suffered physical/sexual aggression by their former partners.

Family traditions are clearly colliding with modern realities. Studies show that as women reach more egalitarian status in Italy, they also become more vulnerable to male abuse (Dall'Aria, 1999). They tend not to report episodes of domestic violence for a variety of reasons, including lack of safe alternative housing, fears of disrupting family routine, the cultural emphasis on family privacy, and a cumbersome judicial process that discourages victims from pursuing prosecution (Ville, 2002). Embarrassment, fear, shame and ignorance of the law also continue to prevent Italian women from reporting incidents (U.S. Department of State, 2002).

Social welfare programs remain relatively weak in Italy, more so for women than for children. Women continue to seek help in family networks, but are increasingly finding this traditional support threatened by the breakdown of families through separation and divorce (Tosi, 2000). In response to increasing pressures, several safe housing options have been established, some judicial processes have been streamlined, and legal restraining orders were introduced in 2001 (Gazzetta Ufficiale, 2001). Still, old systems continue to sabotage women's rights. These include court rulings in 1998 and in 2001 that kissing a woman on the cheek (not considered an erogenous zone) and patting a woman colleague on the bottom, if "fleeting and [with] no sexual connotation," are not sexual harassment (Owen, 2003, p. 23).

Italian Participants' Views of Wife Abuse

Examples of wife abuse given by our women respondents often revealed discontent with sex-role inequities—for example, "limiting freedom/ choices," "bossing around the wife," "refusing to have sexual intercourse," "imposing his will," and "financial constraints." Many women identified "emotional blackmail" as a form of abuse across different relationships (e.g., parent–child, husband–wife, adult–elderly parent). In addition to physical and sexual abuse, other common examples of wife abuse identified by both male and female respondents included "financial exploitation," "insulting," and negative comparisons between the daughter-in-law and the husband's mother: "Telling his spouse his mom still cooks better than she does." Signs of changing norms came from several female respondents, who identified "not helping out" and "not sharing in everyday domestic chores" as mild or even moderate wife abuse.

Italian Participants' Perspectives on Husband Abuse

There is little discussion or research on female-to-male abuse in Italy, and it is not yet considered an important problem (T. Bruno, personal communication, July 26, 2002). This reflects the nature of relationships between the sexes, where female aggression is strongly prohibited. However, one source reveals that of 25,000 contacts with a victim help line, 30% were men, although only 2% of men admitted to being victims of female spousal abuse (Sicilian Culture, 2002). Moreover, our survey results indicate that abused Italian men are a troubled and relatively unidentified minority group subjected to restrictive gender roles and pressures.

In our sample, descriptions of psychological abuse were the most common examples of husband abuse given by both men and women (46%)—suggesting that women may exhibit aggressive inclinations and attempts at control primarily in psychological ways. These include the withholding of role-expected behaviors such as domestic care, affection, nurturance, and sex, "not looking after husband and home" and even "making husband die due to lack of care." As examples of extreme husband abuse, nearly 60% of male and 39% of female respondents listed types of physical aggression, 38% of the men and 51% of the women listed types of psychological aggression, and 3% of the men and 10% of the women made references to sexual abuse. Sexual abuse, other than "withholding sex," was never mentioned as a form of moderate or mild abuse of husbands. Other examples of husband abuse implied threats to family hierarchy and male status, gender roles, and distribution of power; "enslave the husband—like a puppet" (extreme abuse); "making the husband feel inadequate" (moderate abuse); and "using/turning children against him" (extreme abuse). Threats by wives to the special relationship between the Italian father and his son(s) were viewed as very abusive. For example, one 32-year-old female career journalist described "diminishing the father's role" as an example of moderate abuse, and "obstructing father–son interactions" as extreme abuse.

ABUSE OF THE ELDERLY

Italy is growing smaller and older, second only to Japan as the most rapidly aging society in the world (Theil, Nadeau, Pepper, & Takayama, 2002). The aging rate of the Italian population, life expectancy, and overall health care expenditure (7.7% of the GDP) are similar to other European countries, but are also inadequate, especially as the numbers of elderly grow (Lori, Golini, & Cantalini, 1995). Italian respect for authority and responsibility toward older family members is a powerful norm. These values usually mean keeping elderly parents in the family home rather than placing them in nursing homes, which tend to offer low-quality care (Carbonin, Bernabei, Zuccala, & Gambassi, 1997). Social legislation has lagged considerably behind the needs of this population, and family carers suffer the stresses of modern demands, especially as more woman carers choose or are required to work to keep up the household finances.

Modern life in Italy has made the elderly a more vulnerable and alienated group. The elderly may be less safe in the hands of their families, as family members become more diverse, transitional, and increasingly less home centered. As the majority of women outlive their partners, they are more likely to live alone, which adds to women's risk factors (United Nations, 2002). In the city of Milan alone, of 270,000 elderly, one-third live alone, and 3.2% are at risk of dying in a situation of extreme neglect due to a substantial lack of public services (Tosi, 2000). Additionally, increasing incidents of poverty result in more elderly becoming homeless, and elderly suicides are on the rise (Mingione & Zajczyk, 1992).

Although elder abuse has been recognized as a social problem of increasing proportion in Italy, it has not yet received adequate attention, and there is little research on this issue. Unlike the organizations slowly but significantly springing up to support women and children, and despite the influence of the United Nations and the European Union, there is still no major national organization dedicated to the prevention of elder abuse in Italy (T. Bruno, personal communication, July 26, 2002).

Italian Respondents' Perspectives on Elder Abuse

Respondents generally provided a different perspective on elder abuse than on child and spouse abuse. For example, neglect and abandonment outweighed the other types of elder abuse as most common (66% of examples); "not taking care of basic necessities for parents"; "lack of care/support"; "not visiting parents." Several respondents considered placing aging parents into a residential home as acts of mild abuse (e.g., "delegate their care to a third party") and even severe abuse ("abandon/left in a residential home"). Nearly one-third of our respondents identified "financial exploitation" as an example of either severe or moderate abuse. This may well reflect the tradition of power and authority (partly financially based) of the family elders and the blurred line between traditional financial collaboration between young and old generations and financial abuse. Clearly, strong cultural traditions proscribing the institutionalization of the elderly, especially in the south, along with social structures allowing the elderly to stay in the home, play a role in the reluctance of families to reach out to social and health care systems (Carbonin et al., 1997).

The emphasis on neglect and abandonment as forms of elder abuse contrasts strikingly with, for example, wife abuse, where the most common examples were of physical abuse. Psychological abuse, mostly in the forms of "insults" and "verbal disrespect," was described by 53% of our respondents—primarily as forms of mild (57%), and moderate abuse (34%)—highlighting the importance of respect toward elders in Italian society. Physical violence, occasionally listed as an example of extreme abuse, was mentioned least often—in stark contrast to wife and child abuse, where it was considered the main and most extreme type of problem.

INTERVENTION AND PREVENTION

Cultural traditions hindering the recognition of family violence in Italy (Terragni, 1999) have also limited the development of research, especially with regard to intervention into and prevention of family violence (Bruno, 2002). However, it is clear that progress is being made. The first broad "action plan" for children and youth, which took into account the importance of collaboration between government and family, was drawn up by Prime Minister Prodi's government in 1996 (Law No. 285/1997). Sadly, 1998 saw the collapse of Prodi's 28-month-long center–left government, and progress in social programs was interrupted. One major practical achievement over the first 4 years of the plan was serious investment in laws to support family life. These laws included acts designed to reduce poverty, reform social services, provide allowances for motherhood, and improve the care and rights of foreign children. For example, the enactment of Law No. 451, 1997 gave a clear mandate to investigate children's issues in Italy and to develop relevant programs to support child and adolescent personal and social development. Law No. 457 further catapulted child rights into broad public view with its emphasis on the principles of responsibility, respect, and consideration for children (ASEM, 2000), and its recognition of the increasing problems of child abuse. This decree highlighted the distinctive types of both prevention and intervention necessary to end child abuse, and promoted a diversified set of strategies to combat child labor and other practices violating children's rights and welfare. Among its recommendations were a draft law ratifying and implementing the European Convention of Strasbourg on the exercise of children's rights and the implementation of the National Health Plan and the Mother and Child Project. Recommendations were also made for improving community spaces, educating and training adolescents, integrating the school/vocational training/work program sequence, and developing protective measures and actions in favor of juvenile victims of abuse and sexual exploitation. Additional advances included the incorporation of sex education in the schools in 1998, after 30 years of debate and opposition from Italian Catholic authorities, and the significant stiffening of prison sentences for child sexual abuse, including the possession of child pornography (Pina, 1997a, 1997b).

Italy's membership in the European Union has been a powerful catalyst toward addressing the problem of domestic violence. Similarly, CEDAW, the Committee on the Elimination of Discrimination Against Women (United Nations, 1996) has played a pivotal role in publicizing the status of women in Italy, and in identifying the need for programs addressing domestic violence. A major milestone was achieved in 1999 when Italy ratified the United Nations' "Optional Protocol," providing a route for women to bring complaints to CEDAW once all national remedies were exhausted (United Nations, 1999).

Trends in the European Community have also resulted in the establishment of Geriatrics as a medical specialty in Italy, and the introduction of an act promoting and providing guidelines to local health care agencies for the long-term care of older persons. The POSA (Progetto Obiettivo Salute dell'Anziano), distributed in 1992, also emphasized multidisciplinary care and the integration of informal support networks such as not-for-profit and volunteer agencies.

To reduce skyrocketing costs, the Italian National Health Service, which has provided free health care to Italian citizens since 1979, was remodeled in the 1990s. Influenced by the United Kingdom model, the revised model transferred considerable health care services to more autonomous, private-like companies (Carbonin et al., 1997). Still, there remains a significant lack of elderly services compared to need, and there has been little research addressing the effectiveness of Italian health care models. Advances in geriatric care are still improving on recent attempts to provide more comprehensive care (De Leo, Carollo, & Dello, 1995).

CHALLENGES AND HOPES

Many experts operating daily in the field, such as judges working in both criminal and civil courts, have openly acknowledged that domestic violence is a phenomenon of dramatic proportions that affects all social classes (Kapoor, 2000). In response, in 2001, Italy passed the "Measures against domestic violence" legislation (Act n. 154), which offers a comprehensive collection of interventions at penal and civic levels. This law allows, when appropriate, removal of abusers rather than victims from families, and promotes ways to protect the welfare of the child by keeping the family relatively intact. Unfortunately, the current inefficacy of the judicial system functions as a powerful deterrent for anybody who contemplates reporting a case of abuse. Further barriers to reporting include distrust in the civil and penal codes, disorganized procedures, and a chronic lack of structural and human resources. Victims of domestic abuse, therefore, often find it easier to retreat back to the very culture of silence and suffering that generated their abuse than to ask for institutional help (Impallomeni, 2002).

Signs of noteworthy social awareness arrived with the establishment of two victim support services in the late 1980s. Reflecting an ongoing hesitation to bring the problems of domestic violence to full light, neither of the two services has received public funding. They are staffed primarily with volunteers managing the busy phone lines. The first, Telefono Azzurro, was established in 1987 to offer research and assistance to child victims of abuse. The hotline, Telefono Rosa, was established in 1988 to provide legal, medical, and other types of support to women victims of abuse. The development of these prototypes of service and the fact that their help lines receive thousands of calls every day has drawn considerable attention to the scale of the problem, and they provide excellent models for the prevention and care of victims of abuse.

Ineffective institutional response and time-honored reluctance to "betray" family secrets may explain the discrepancy between the number of abuses reported to the police and those reported to voluntary support services such as the Telefono Rosa in Rome, and the Artemisia in Florence (Bruno, 2002). According to the Italian Ministry of Justice, about 2,000 cases of domestic violence were reported in 1992 and in 1995. However, between 1988 and 1999, the Telefono Rosa's help line reported receiving over 350,000 calls on abuse of women, perpetrated primarily by husbands and ex-husbands. Telefono Rosa reported that 3 out of 4 Italian women victims decline to report it to the authorities (Center for Europe's Children, 1999).

Given the rules of family privacy, mental health services are also perceived as potential intruders into the family unit. However, these services are continuing to find unique ways to promote utilization and to address domestic violence issues (Bruno, 2002). In extreme circumstances, when families finally yield to the need for help, the primary goal is to restore a fractured family structure rather than attend to individual emotional issues. A study by Fara and Caffo (2001) revealed that Italian youths perceived family violence as both rare and mild, suggesting a dangerous minimization of the actual problem. Programs to increase awareness, open communication, and to provide safe reporting protocols are essential components of solutions.

As marital separations and family breakdowns challenge Italian family traditions, one institutional response has been the Tribunale per i minorenni, a child advocate court empowered to remove children from broken families, and to place them with grandparents, foster parents, or social services (Fara & Caffo, 2001). In spite of the obvious advantage of safeguarding the child, it is possible that such intrusions might further destabilize other family members left behind, and generate additional mental health problems and even abuse. Important research showing that children who experience abuse are more likely to perpetrate and/or become victims of violence as adults (Romito, Saurel-Cubizolles, & Crisina, 2001) must continue to inform social policies.

CONCLUSION

There are a number of major clashes with tradition as Italy drives toward modernization, reestablishing its influence internationally. One issue involves the mixed messages inherent in the contradictions between religious rules, individual choices (for example, on sexual behavior and abortion), and the reality of pervasive Italian criminality and low accountability to governmental authority. There is also the potential confusion that the coexistence of patriarchal and matriarchal roles induces in men and women, accompanied by the dramatic surge of women in power, and the increasing expectation that Italy, characteristically suspicious of outsiders, collaborate with them.

Such monumental changes are likely to increase the incidence of violence for men, women, children, and the elderly, as well as the steps to address it. Maverick and self-regulatory changes in family relationships, perhaps the most significant of societal changes, are already helping to increase awareness and to shape newer approaches to domestic violence. In closer collaboration with all members of the global community concerned about and acting to eliminate violence of all kinds, Italy's problems with violence will necessarily be addressed vigorously. The historic resilience and creativity of the Italian people will help win the war on domestic violence.

ACKNOWLEDGMENTS

Dr. Borrelli would like to thank his colleagues at Boston University, Walden University, and the University of Maryland (European Division) for their great support, including Kenneth J. Kovach, EdD, and Carol Ann Dolan, PhD. Special thanks to Gerrit C. Verduijn, and to Jason S. Zack, PhD. Both authors would like to thank Dr. Teresa Bruno at the Antiviolence Centre Artemisia in Florence and Ornella Tarantola. Dr. Borrelli may be contacted at: DrBorrelli@e-psychonline.com. Dr. Palumbo may be contacted at: info@phemiology.org.

REFERENCES

Adami, C. (1996, January–March). Female hardship and violence against women. The Anti-violence Center of Venice. *Inchiesta, 26*, 94–95.

Ahmad, O. B., Lopez, A. D., & Inoue, M. (2000). The decline in child mortality: A reappraisal. *Bulletin of the World Health Organization, 78*(10), 1175–1191.

Arenson, S. (1979). Rankings of intimacy of social behaviors by Italians and Americans. *Psychological Reports, 44*, 1149–1150.

ASEM Resource Centre Child Welfare Initiative. (2000). Official Gazette of the Italian Republic, Decree of the President of the Republic. No. 194. Available: http://www.asem.org/documents/Italy/actionplan2000.htm

Astolfi, P., Ulizzi, L., & Zonta, L. (2002). Trends in childbearing and stillbirth risk: Heterogeneity among Italian regions. *Human Biology, 74*, 185–196.

Bardi, M., & Borgognoni-Tarli, S. M. (2001). A survey on parent–child conflict resolution: Intrafamily violence in Italy. *Child Abuse and Neglect, 25*, 839–853.

Biagini, E., Bertozzo, G., & Ravaioli, M. (1998). *The European Region of the International Lesbian and Gay Association*. Available: http://www.ilga-europe.org/

Bruno, T. (2002). *Il lavoro dei Centri Antiviolenza in Italia: Dati statistici sulla violenza domestica* [The activity of Antiviolence Centres in Italy: Statistics on domestic violence]. Florence, Italy: Artemisia.

Bull, A. (1996). Regionalism in Italy. *Europa, 2*(4). Available: www.intellectbooks.com/europa/number2/bull.htm

Buzzi, C., Cavalli, A., & Lillo, A. (1997). *Giovani verso il 2000* [Youth towards the year 2000]. Bologna: Il Mulino.

Carbonin, P., Bernabei, R., Zuccala, G., & Gambassi, G. (1997). Health care for older persons—a country profile: Italy. *Journal of the American Geriatric Society, 45*, 1520–1522.

Center for Europe's Children. (1999, June 14–16). *Towards a child friendly society*. Conference of European Ministers Responsible for Family Affairs. National Report. XXVI Session, 1999. Stockholm.

Dall'Aria, E. (1999). Study of sexual harassment in the laboratory: Are egalitarian women at higher risk? *Sex Roles, 41*, 681–704.

De Leo, D., Carollo, G., & Dello, B. M. (1995). Lower suicide rates associated with a tele-help/tele-check service for the elderly at home. *American Journal of Psychiatry, 152*, 632–634.

DiGiovanni, J. (2002, July 6). Blood sisters. *London Times*, pp. 24–30.

Fara, G. M., & Caffo, E. (2001). *2° Rapporto Nazionale sulla condizione dell'infanzia, della pre-adolescenza e dell'adolescenza* [2nd National Report on infancy, pre-adolescence and adolescence]. Rome: EURISPES. Available: http://www.eurispes.it/Eurispes/2rappinfanzia/2rn_infanzia.htm

Fuchs, D. (1998). *Unveiling the hidden data on domestic violence in the European Union*. European Women's Lobby. Available: http://www.womenlobby.org/oldsite/en/themes/violence/dossier-en.html

Gazzetta Ufficiale della Repubblica Italiana. (2001, April 28). *Misure contro la violenza nelle relazioni familiari* [Official publication of the Italian Republic: Legislative measures against domestic violence, N. 98]. Rome: Ministry of Economy and Finance, Istituto Poligrafico e Zecca Dello Stato.

Giordano, J., & McGoldrick, M. (1996). Italian families. In M. McGoldrick, J. Giordano, & J. K. Pearce (Eds.), *Ethnicity and family therapy* (2nd ed., pp. 567–582). New York: Guilford.

Giordano, J., & Riotta-Sirey, A. (1981). *An Italian-American identity*. Unpublished manuscript, Institute for American Pluralism, American Jewish Community, New York.

Global Initiative to End All Corporal Punishment of Children. (2002). *Supreme Court of Italy declares all corporal punishment unlawful—1996*. Available: http://www. endcorporalpunishment. org/pages/hrlaw/judgments.html#italy

Gonzo, L. (2000). I servizi sociosanitari a Bologna: dai risultati di una ricerca a un progetto di formazione [Socio-sanitary services in Bologna: From research outcomes to training project]. In P. Romito (Ed.), *Violenze alle donne e risposte delle istituzioni. Prospettive internazionali* (pp. 153–165). Milan: Angeli.

Hanson, D. (2003). *Alcohol: Problems and solutions.* Available: http://www2.potsdam.edu/alcoholinfo/

Houseknecht, S. K., & Sastry, J. (1996). Family "decline" and child well-being: A comparative assessment. *Journal of Marriage and the Family, 58,* 726–739.

Impallomeni, M. (2002). *Violenza Domestica. Un Incontro—Dibattito* [Domestic violence: A public debate]. Available: www.mclink.it/n/dwpress/dww6/art1.htm

ISTAT. (2002). *National Institute of Statistics.* Available: http://www.istat.it/English/The-Instit/index.htm

Kapoor, S. (2000). *Domestic violence against women and girls.* UNICEF [Innocenti Research Center No. 6, 1–22]. Available: http://www.unicef.org/vaw/domestic.pdf

Lerner, G. (1986). *The creation of patriarchy.* New York: Oxford University Press.

Lori, A., Golini, A., & Cantalini, B. (1995). *Atlante dell'invecchiamento della Popolazione* [Atlas on the aging of population]. Rome: CNR.

McClosky, L. A., Treviso, M., Scionti, T., & dal Pozzo, G. (2002). A comparative study of battered women and their children in Italy and the United States. *Journal of Family Violence, 17*(1), 53–74.

Mingione, E., & Zajczyk, F. (1992). The new urban poverty in Italy: Risk models for the metropolitan area of Milan. *Inchiesta, 97–98,* 63–79.

Owen, R. (2003, March 15). Divorce Italian style? Blame it on mama-in-law. *The London Times,* p. 23.

Pina, J. (1997a). Italy—Children: New law to put paedophiles in the slammer. *Interpress Service.* Available from the Contemporary Women's Issues database.

Pina, J. (1997b). Italy—Rights: Sexual violence against children increasing. *Interpress Service.* Available from the Contemporary Women's Issues database.

Reuters, Rome. (2002, April 5). *Mamma mia, what big babies!* Available: http://www.cbsnews.com/stories/2002/04/05/world/main505524.shtml

Romito, P. (2000). *La violenza di genere contro donne e minori—Un introduzione* [Gender violence against women and minors—An introduction]. Milan: Angeli.

Romito, P., & Gerin, D. (2002). Asking patients about violence: A survey of 510 women attending social and health services in Trieste, Italy. *Social Science Medicine, 54,* 1813–1824.

Romito, P., Saurel-Cubizolles, M.-J., & Crisina, M. (2001). The relationship between parent's violence against daughters and violence by other perpetrators: An Italian study. *Social Science Medicine, 7,* 1429–1463.

Sabbadini, L. L. (1998). *La sicurezza dei cittadini. Molestie e violenze sessuali.* Versione provvisoria [Citizens' safety. Sexual harassment and violence. Provisional version]. Rome: ISTAT.

Sant Cassia, P. (1991). Authors in search of a character: Personhood, agency and identity in the Mediterranean. *Journal of Mediterranean Studies, 1*(1), 1–17.

Saraceno, C. (1998). *Mutamenti della famiglia e politiche sociali in Italia* [Family change and social policies in Italy]. Bologna: Il Mulino.

Schwartz, P. (2001). *Italy's Berlusconi and his "House of Freedoms"—a new dimension in the development of the right wing in Europe.* Available: http://www.wsws.org

Sgritta, G. (1997). Il sostegno economico ai figli: un quadro europeo [Financial support to minors: A European overview]. In M. Barbagli & C. Saraceno (Eds.), *Lo stato della famiglia in Italia* (pp. 328–343). Bologna: Il Mulino.

Sicilian Culture-News and Views. (2002). *Female spousal abuse up according to survey.* Available: http://www.sicilianculture.com/index.htm

Spiegel, J. (1971). *Transactions: The interplay between individual, family, and society.* New York: Science House.

Storti, C. (2001). *The art of crossing cultures* (2nd ed.). Yarmouth, ME: Intercultural Press.

Terragni, L. (1999). Sexual violence in Italy: Processes of social definitions and characteristics of the phenomenon in diverse Italian contexts. *Polis, 13*, 255–270.

Theil, S., Nadeau, B., Pepper, T., & Takayama, H. (2002). Young at heart. *Newsweek* (Atlantic Edition), 140(12/13), 70–73.

Tosi, A. (2000, May). *European observatory on homelessness: Women, exclusion and homelessness in Italy* (Italian National Report, 1999. Dipartimento di Scienze del Territorio. Politecnico di Milano). Available: http://www.feantsa.org/obs/italy_1999.pdf

Trompenaars, F., & Hampden-Turner, C. (1998). *Riding the waves of culture* (2nd ed.). New York: McGraw-Hill.

Tung, R. L. (1998). *The IEBM handbook of international business*. London: International Thompson Business Press.

United Nations. (1996). *Italy report. Convention on the Elimination of all Forms of Discrimination against Women*. Available: http://www.un.org/esa/gopher-data/ga/cedaw/17/country/Italy/C-ITA2P1.EN

United Nations. (1999). *An optional protocol to CEDAW*. Available: http://www.un.org/womenwatch/daw/cedaw/protocol/optional.htm

United Nations Department of Public Information. (2002, March). *Population ageing: Facts and figures*. Second World Assembly on Ageing, Madrid, Spain. Available: http://seniors.tcnet.org/articles/article%20population_ageing.htm

U.S. Department of State, Bureau of Democracy. (1998). *Italy country report on human rights practices for 1997*. Available: http://www.usis.usemb.se/human/human1998/italy.html

U.S. Department of State, Bureau of Democracy. (2002, May). *Country reports on human rights practices for 2001*. Available: http://www.usis.usemb.se/human/2001/europe/italy. html

Ville, R. (2002). *Child abuse: Some reflections based on the situation in six European countries*. Available: http://www.unicri.it/documentation/Issues&reports/I_R6.htm

Walker, L. E. (1999). Psychology and domestic violence across the world. *American Psychologist, 54*, 21–29.

Washington Times. (2002, November). *Italy, the UN report: Order to procreate*. Available: http://www.overpopulation.org

Willey, D. (2000, July 9). Pope condemns gay rights march. *BBC News Online*. Available: www.bbc.co.uk

6

Germany

Elisabeth Leembruggen-Kallberg
Silke Rupprecht
Diane Cadmus

CAPSULE

Germany has a highly structured social system that has experienced great stress and pressure since reunification in 1990. Like many other postmodern western societies, the Federal Republic of Germany is afflicted with abuse and violence— both within the family, and in other societal institutions, including geriatric care and the workplace. It takes the form of verbal, physical, sexual, and psychological abuse and is manifested in adult–child relationships, spousal relationships, and the treatment of elderly members of German society. What is encouraging is the response of the German government to this issue. A concerted effort on the part of the government and social services is being made to combat this abuse. Together with EU and UN legislation, Germany-wide campaigns via multimedia, professional training and specific legislation are in place to combat abuse on all levels, in all walks of life and in every part of the family unit. The German Ministry for Family, Seniors, Women and Youth has the overarching responsibility for implementing these governmental policies.

THE GERMAN RESPONDENTS

Our respondents included residents from Northern, Middle, Southern, and Eastern Germany, as well as Germans living outside Germany. There were roughly equal numbers of males and females, ranging in age from 20 to 57 years. These respondents represented a broad educational range, including postgraduates from university, advanced vocational training, and technical schools, and students from Hauptschule, a 5-year program of basic skills and vocational training. Occupations included technical specialists, housewives, professional business people, students, psychotherapists, and several unemployed respondents.

It was difficult to recruit participants from East Germany. They were unwilling to fill out the survey, especially those 30 years or older, the generation that grew up under the communist regime. Most said they didn't know what to write or thought the survey would be multiple choice. All of the men who agreed to fill out the survey stopped after the definition of abuse question. A 54-year-old former East German woman took days to complete the survey and constantly asked for clarification. Apparently, people who grew up under communism never thought much about abuse, except that sexual abuse is bad. Such an interpretation is supported by research findings indicating that violence was not a topic for public discussion in the former East Germany and that the family was a possible retreat from the communist state (Hagemann-White & Gardlo, 1997).

General Definitions of Abuse

A working definition of domestic violence in the German literature focuses on behaviors among family and household members that can threaten or cause serious physical harm, including abusive mental, emotional, or psychological treatment, and verbal or nonverbal threats of abuse. The victims can be children, wives, husbands, and grandparents (Hafte & Frandsen, 1985). This broad description finds resonance in the responses of our German respondents, who agreed that abuse can be expressed via verbal and nonverbal behaviors ranging from "physical or mental abuse" to "having fights and yelling at each other," to "daily torture including sexual abuse." As a female respondent stated: "In my opinion, there is no such thing as mild abuse. It usually escalates from a little slap (with assurances it will never happen again) to a push and shove, with assurances of no repeats, and it only goes from bad to worse." A 43-year-old German male respondent shared the following experience of abuse to someone he knew: "The person was yelled at and ridiculed by x on a daily basis. The consciousness of the person was almost destroyed. There were also beatings, even though all was kept secret from the mother—under threat of more beatings."

One East German respondent emphasized a broad understanding of the overall family environment in the child's psychosocial development in her definition of abuse in the family: "Parents should do everything to help raise their children in a happy and secure environment. Abuse means to enforce their own advantages in an egotistical way at the disadvantage of children or weaker persons." A second East German respondent indicated that it was moderately abusive "If a child/adolescent is forced to follow a certain path of education or profession to fulfill the expectation/standard of the family." A German woman who did not identify her origins defined abuse as "any kind of verbal or physical mistreatment not happening in good intention of a parent or significant other, which negatively affects a child's or spouse's psychological or physical well-being. This ranges from destructively insulting remarks like 'you are just too stupid to cook' to beating a child as punishment." A West German woman expressed dismay that verbal acts are not recognized as abusive in Germany: "What I find very sad, is verbal abuse is not recognized legally in Germany . . . Verbal abuse is accepted in the culture. But they don't realize the damage. It's only recognized when it turns into physical abuse."

THE GERMAN MACROSYSTEM

Historical Context

In May 1949, two different constitutions were drawn up, creating two Germanys: East Germany agreed upon the "Verfassung," the German Democratic Republic's (GDR) constitution based on communist philosophy. West Germany, the Federal Republic of Germany (FRG), accepted the 1896 "Grundgesetz," known as the Basic Law, based on capitalistic principles. Although based on different philosophies, both constitutions incorporated equal rights provisions. The Federal Republic of Germany, a member of the United Nations since 1973, is a signer of the Declaration to the Rights of Man, the Rights of Women, the Convention on the Rights of the Child, and the Rights of the Elderly. Basic rights are protected under Federal and State constitutions. Article 3 of the Basic Law affirms the equality of men and women and provides protection for the family, the elderly, the weak, and those at risk in the greater population (Kelling, 1974).

In 1989, social changes began occurring when refugees from East Germany escaped to West Germany via Hungary and Czechoslovakia. Demonstrations in Leipzig and Berlin led to the eventual collapse of the Berlin Wall, and on October 3, 1990, Germany became a unified nation once again, and the Basic Law became the Constitution. Different social and economic systems in the two Germanys had major and continuing implications for family life, the roles of women, and the causes and correlates of violence in contemporary German families.

German Government

The German Ministry of Families is responsible for protecting the rights and interests of the family, senior citizens, women, and youth. Under the leadership of Dr. Christine Bergmann and Renate Schmidt, great strides have been made in promoting research, providing guidelines, and, in cooperation with the parliament, changing laws governing domestic violence (*haeusliche Gewalt*) and the care of senior citizens (*Altenpflege Reform*). Other accomplishments include expanding the laws protecting children, women, and the elderly against physical and sexual violence and pornography. New laws protecting foreign women (*Frauen und Auslaender Recht*), particularly when brought to Germany under false pretenses, have been set in place (Bergmann, 2001).

Germany has long been a highly socialistic country. The foundations of social legislation were established at the time of Otto von Bismarck (1815–1898; Kelling, 1974) and include health insurance, worker compensation, and pensions. The government supports the German family in many practical ways, including rent subsidies and social benefits (Moeller & Liedloff, 1988). Since 1955, in West Germany, each family receives a monthly financial stipend for the support of children, known as *Kindergeld* (Kindergeld, 2002). In 2002, Germany became the "second highest child benefit payer in Europe" ("Since taking office," 2002, p. 1). A generous policy of "childraising leave" allows both parents to take employment leave at the same time ("Family policy objectives," 2002).

The Role of Women in Germany

There are formal milestones in the progress of women toward equality in Germany. They were admitted to university in 1901 and received the right to vote in 1919. Equality of role in marriage and property rights was introduced in 1958. In 1977, the Reform in Marriage and Family Law introduced the "partnership principle in marriage." In divorce, the principle of guilt was replaced by "irretrievable breakdown" (German Information Center, 2002, pp. 1–3). In 1979, women in the workforce gained the right to leave for 6 months to care for newborn children. In 1986, childraising years were included in the calculation for retirement pensions, and financially supported childrearing leaves were introduced for both women and men (German Information Center, 2002). The Basic Law, *Grundgesetz*, was broadened in 1994 to include state commitment to "foster equal rights" and work toward "eliminating existing disadvantages" between men and women (German Information Center, 2002, p. 1).

Prior to unification, equality of the sexes was a core element of the socialist way of life in East Germany. Marxist philosophy stresses that there cannot be freedom and independence as long as the sexes are not equal (Lenin, as cited in Plat, 1972, p. 113). Consequently, the East German government introduced laws making it possible for women to reach beyond home and family. The first stage of GDR women's policy was the integration of women into employment (1946–1965), and by the late 1980s, women were fully integrated into the labor market. The second stage brought about an educational initiative mandating comprehensive schooling for both sexes until the age of 16, and special programs aimed at increasing the number of women entering higher education. By 1980, women had closed the gender gap in higher education. They also made gains in traditionally "male" subjects such as mathematics, natural sciences, engineering, and agriculture (Kolinsky, 1998). To help women combine family life and professional life, day-care facilities for children were expanded, and a campaign was launched against the traditional division of roles in the organization of housework.

The third stage of GDR's women's policy (1971–1989) focused on measures to reduce the conflict between career and family. Among these changes was the "baby year," which provided up to 3 years of fully paid leave for either parent after the birth of a child. However, whereas the notion of an equitable division of housework and childrearing enjoyed widespread support among both men and women in former East Germany, reality was much different (Gysi & Meyer, 1993, p. 159). The 1973 and 1988 studies of the Central Institute for Youth Research on "Young Marriage" revealed that despite the greater involvement of men in raising children and in helping out in the kitchen, young women still had a much greater household burden and enjoyed much less free time (Pinther, 1991). As Helwig (Kolinsky, 1998) described it: "GDR women's policies, it seems, . . . transformed women but had little effect on men" (p. 27). Because of the double burden, East German women showed more symptoms of stress. Schmidt (1999) described them as a Dra-dra: "The *drahtige Drachen* (wiry dragon) is a woman of any age, of delicate figure, but incredibly tense, bitter, irritable, and authoritarian. She embodies a mixture of motherliness and strictness, out of which a full exhaustion always speaks, because life takes from her" (p. 175).

After the Wall—Die Wende

When one of our respondents, a former resident of East Germany, was asked how things had changed for her after the Wende, the 50-year-old mother replied: "These days here in the East we don't ask anymore, 'How are you?' We ask, 'Have you got a job? Where? How much money do you make? How long do you have to work?' and so on . . . Usually the topic of work and health (if you are sick you cannot work, therefore no money, lower standard of life) comes first." Such a perspective is common among former East Germans (Nauck, Schneider, & Tölke, 1995).

After reunification, women were affected by dramatic cutbacks in social programs pertaining to maternity leave, day care, and bonus pay. As a result, many East German women had difficulty coping in a radically different, capitalist system for which they were little prepared (Golz, 1996, p. 6). As another respondent, a former university student reflected: "Much has changed. A few streets down western investors such as Christ, Wempe, Hollywood Planet, and others built monuments to capitalism. I remember a more drab, gray and lifeless quarter as I walked these very streets in 1984 . . . But that doesn't mean the change was necessarily good."

Macrosystem and exosystem factors contributing to stress since the Wende include not just the unemployment rate, but also a declining birthrate, an increase in violence, racism, and substance abuse, and an increase in fear and psychological disorders. Only 1 in 5 East German employee continues to hold a job, an experience very different from the era before reunification. The GDR guaranteed employment for its citizens and had the highest labor market activity rate in the world, although disguised unemployment was widespread. In 1989, 91% of East Germany's women were employed whereas currently only one-third have regular employment. Women with young children face a particularly hard time as they can no longer rely on kindergarten and crèche (day-nursery) places, and employers are often unwilling to hire women with children. Some writers have speculated that as a result of such dramatic social changes there has been a corresponding rise in domestic violence (Cooper, 1997; Jung-joo, n.d.).

The distinction between "Ossis and Wessis" is dwindling, but remains at the heart of tensions between East and West German citizens. A 1989–1990 survey of women in Bavaria (FRG) and Eastern Germany revealed greatly differing ideas about professional life and the role of the housewife. Only 29% of Bavarian women agreed with the statement: "Only a professionally active women is truly independent in marriage and partnership," whereas 72% of East German women agreed with it. Similarly, only 34% of East German women agreed that "To be housewife and mother fulfills a women completely" as compared to 64% of West German women (Dannenbeck, Keiser, & Rosendorfer, 1995, p. 115). In spite of the many crises and tensions, the family was highly valued in East Germany and has been a source of physical and emotional support for its members during the radical and painful transformation of East German society (Kolinsky, 1998).

THE GERMAN MICROSYSTEM

Family forms have undergone considerable change in both East and West Germany. In East Germany, a Family Code was promulgated in April 1966, with the goal of establishing norms for the family in a socialist society. The family model, *Leitbild*, had four main elements: 1) marriage as a lifelong union, 2) compatibility between the family and wider societal interests, 3) the formal equality of men and women, and 4) relations of a qualitatively new kind between family members (Kolinsky, 1998). The family, defined in the Code as the smallest cell in society, was deemed irreplaceable for rearing and socializing children. However, raising children was not regarded as the responsibility solely of parents; instead, the kindergarten, school, and mass organizations such as "Thaelmann Pioneers" (an organization that practically all children joined in 5th grade as part of their initiation into the communist society) were to collaborate in childrearing.

In comparison with the United States, social regulations and social benefits were, and are, extremely high in both German states. For example, in the East, every citizen had the right to work, and a duty to work was mandated for either spouse. Although family life was not shadowed by the worry of parents losing their jobs, life may have been very stressful with both parents working full-time (Kolinsky, 1998). In postwar West Germany, the family was esteemed as a source of stability and order. The model of the man as breadwinner and the woman as housewife, along with adherence to wedding vows, was typical. In the postwar years, divorce rates were low, as were illegitimacy rates (Guist, 2002). Currently, the German family is no longer primarily a *Kernfamilie* characterized by the father–mother–child triad. One finds, as in most postmodern societies, new familial norms including nuclear families, single-parent families, adoptive families, stepfamilies, blended families, multi/intergenerational families, and unmarried partners with children.

CHILD ABUSE

Historical Perspectives on Child Abuse

In the former East Germany, child abuse was considered a typical sign of bourgeois criminality that could not find a breeding ground or room for development in a socialist state (Gries & Voigt, 1989). In 1973, a renowned criminologist (Kaiser, 1973) wrote: "The appearance of child abuse in socialist societies is controversial" (p. 296). It cannot be denied that children were abused, neglected, injured, and killed in the former East Germany; however, the few case studies that are available deal only with extreme cases (such as child homicide) and completely disregard emotional abuse and less severe physical abuse, such as beatings. Further, these few case studies appeared only in scientific papers, and were rarely reported in the censored public media. Therefore, the general public did not have exposure to the topic of abuse. If mentioned, it was usually in connection with capitalist societies and was attributed to their inherent inequalities.

Gries and Voigt (1989) found that abusing parents in the GDR tended to be uneducated and without a high school degree, thus of a lower social class; however, because socialist ideology denied the existence of classes, it had to deny any causes presumed to be associated only with capitalism. GDR officials emphasized the supposedly low prevalence of abuse in their country using two arguments: First, the socialist system does not condone abuse. Secondly, the GDR had laws to find and punish cases of abuse. In 1967, the GDR was one of the first countries to implement the mandatory reporting of signs of abuse for medical professionals. However, the jurisdictional conditions for judging child abuse were only vaguely mentioned.

Thus, GDR literature does not give any credible child abuse statistics. Some researchers reported only 32 cases in 8 years (Müeller, 1976) and compared those numbers to extremely high numbers in West Germany. The reason for the disparity, however, was in the differing definitions of abuse. Whereas West German reports included cases of beating and emotional abuse, East German authors reported only extreme cases of abuse. By trying to make reality fit with the postulated ideology, East Germany had to disguise and deny abuse, and abusing parents were portrayed as people who commit crimes cold heartedly and deserve to be punished. For example, Wallrabe (1968) observed: "If we have a look at the offenders, we find that most of them stem from a disrupted, asocial and deficient background. . . . For the most part they are unstable, instinctive and strongly seedy offenders . . . In their cruelty they go as far as harming their children deadly. Their low character equals the character of a murderer" (p. 69).

Harsh corporal punishment was a widely accepted practice in Germany until the 1960s (Wolff, 1997). Because corporal punishment was not considered abusive, there were no efforts to protect children from it. In the late 1960s and early 1970s, however, the New Child Protection Movement (NCPM) developed, modeled after programs in the Netherlands, Scandinavia, and the United States (Wolff, 1997). As a result of the NCPM, child maltreatment is now understood as a broad problem involving sociopsychological, cultural, political, and gender spheres.

Physical and Emotional Child Abuse

Use of physical violence within the family is reported in both East and West Germany. In a 1992 study, 81% of youth claimed to have been slapped, 43% severely. In a 1994 study of 3,000 parents, 61% confirmed using corporal punishment, either lightly or severely, with 20% administering beatings ("Gewaltfreie Erziehung," 2002). The real number of maltreated children is unknown, particularly as incidents of maltreatment may fall under the guise of childrearing practices (Huxoll, 2002; Stimmer, 2000). The best data come from the *Bundeskriminalamt* (the German equivalent of the U.S. Federal Bureau of Investigation). According to available data, cases of the most severe child abuse and neglect have been relatively stable since 1990 and range from 25,000 to 33,000 cases per year (approximately 2 children per 1,000 minors under the age of 18; Wolff, 1997). However, if information from child welfare statistics are added in, Germany has a child abuse rate of approximately 15 children per 1,000 children under 18 years (Wolff, 1997).

Child Sexual Abuse

The prevalence of child sexual abuse (*sexueller Missbrauch*) in Germany is also difficult to determine. Rates tend to differ because of varying definitions of child sexual abuse, age designations, and other factors (Hermann, 2002). Additionally, there are no mandatory reporting laws or systems (Wolff, 1997). Based on data from the Bundeskriminalamt, nearly half of all cases of offenses against children known to the police represent sexual abuse cases. In the late 1990s, reported cases of child sexual abuse ranged from a low of 11,098 in 1985 to a high of 16,381 in 1992 (Wolff, 1997). The sexual abuse cases take many forms, including talking about sex; making sexual gestures inappropriate to children; fondling; vaginal or anal intercourse; cunnilingus and fellatio; pornography; masturbation; and perversions (Schotensack, Elliger, Gross, & Nissen, 1992). The profile is as follows: 1) 30% to 40% of victims are preschool age; 2) child sexual abuse is rarely a single occurrence and may last up to 5 years; 3) it is perpetrated on both girls (6–10%) and boys (8–15%); and, 4) it has long-term effects on child development, affecting personality, sexuality, and interpersonal relationships (Hermann, 2002).

Although child sexual abuse is illegal, the legal definition of child sexual abuse varies, depending on the form of abuse. For example, dissemination of pornographic writings is forbidden to children 18 years and younger ("Facts about Germany," 2002). Committing sex acts on a person less than 14 years of age is forbidden ("Sexual Offense Laws-Germany," 2002); promoting the "engagement of minors in sex on or before a third person on a person less than 16 years" is a punishable offense ("Sexual Offense Laws-Germany," 2002, p. 5). Legal age of consent is thus 14, 16, and 18, depending "on the circumstances" ("Germany: Age of Sexual Consent," 2002, p. 10). As Helga, housewife and mother of four teenagers, noted:

> Sexual abuse ranges from very mild to very aggressive and brutal behaviors. Whether ... the abuse is touching, fondling or the act of rape itself, all are equally detrimental. I think sexual abuse can be verbal—one can actually be raped by words. We think of rape as a physical thing, but it can be mental,

too. The end effect is the same. One lives with the mental effects the rest of one's life. It's a hurt that's just there. Full stop. One carries the scar for life.

German Participants' Perspectives on Child Abuse

In our German sample, abuse against children was frequently seen to be primarily physical or sexual. According to one East German respondent, "sexual abuse of a child by a parent" is an extreme form of abuse, whereas "beating the child or withholding dinner because of poor grades" is moderately abusive, and "locking a child in a room for bringing home poor grades or depriving the child of love by giving him or her 'the silent treatment' " is mildly abusive. Considering that both locking a child in a room and withholding dinner were considered abusive, this respondent clearly sees the need for further alternatives to physical punishment.

Conceptions of child abuse sometimes included "verbal abuse" and "psychological abuse." One respondent noted:

> Psychological abuse is as extreme as any other kind of abuse, especially when verbal or other psychological cruelty is involved. . It can be equally long lasting and destructive on comfort and quality of life. This form of abuse might even be considered worse than the others, as it can be suppressed, talked down, ignored or interpreted as an insufficiency of the victim.

Another respondent said child abuse was: "If a parent comes to the child and says, 'you damn shit-head, why did you do this?' " Further, she wrote, "I don't know what is worse, verbal or physical. I think verbal can be worse than physical, in some instances. Even the intonation of the voice can be abusive."

Several responses revealed the growing concern with issues related to child abuse. One respondent commented, "there is a general fear of expanding the definition of abuse too broadly" (interview, March 22, 2002). A 45-year-old psychologist respondent observed:

> We didn't think about such fine discriminations before the survey. We had to stop and think: What does it mean to be abused? We had to think about gradations of abuse. We were probably verbally abused often—for example, in school. But as we grew up with it, we didn't notice it and thought it normal. (interview, April 2002)

DOMESTIC VIOLENCE AND ABUSE IN GERMANY

Most empirical research in the area of domestic violence in Germany, similarly to the United States, has been fueled by feminist concerns for the victims. The German Parliamentary Act, Action Plan 1, passed in December

1999, stipulated that violence against women and children must be banned. A broader understanding of domestic violence is developing, though; in March 2002, a Berlin group announced intentions to raise public awareness concerning partner abuse by women by opening the country's first shelter for battered men. Available data indicate that in Germany, every third relationship is characterized by battering ("Gewalt gegen Frauen," 2002). It is estimated that 46,000 German women spend some time at women's refuges every year because of domestic violence ("Germany gets tough," 2002). The Men's Advisory Service indicates that approximately 5 to 10% of domestic violence in Germany consists of women acting against men ("Berlin to open," 2002).

German Participants' Perspectives on Domestic Violence

When asked to define an extreme form of wife abuse, the respondents to our survey were quick to mention a husband "beating" or "sexually abusing" his wife. On the other hand, when asked to give examples of husband abuse, they mentioned issues like a wife "beating her husband with household items" or "getting pregnant to force him to stay with her even though he doesn't love her anymore." Differences in the examples may reflect physical differences between the genders. Thus, although a man may use his fists or greater size and power when aggressing, a woman may use household items or completely different methods against her husband.

A difference between wives and husbands is also seen in the examples of moderately abusive acts; "ignoring his wife," "cheating," and "looking down on her" were examples of wife abuse, whereas "withholding sex," and "belittling the husband's financial and/or sexual competence" were examples of husband abuse. Examples of mild wife abuse included "yelling," "using his wife as a house slave," and "having her do all the housework," whereas mild husband abuse was: "ridiculing," "getting him to pay for everything," "getting him to perform housework," and "not giving him freedom to meet others."

THE ELDERLY IN GERMANY

The Ministry for Family, Seniors, Women and Youth has three main goals; to support older citizens in their activities, to protect the aged and help them remain viable, independent citizens, and to provide assistance and help to elderly who are sick and need of care. However, as in other countries, problems in caring for an aging population exist (Bundesministerium-Dritter Bericht zur Lage der aelteren Generation, 2001, p. 1). In particular, recent studies indicate a twofold problem; a declining birthrate and an aging population. It is estimated that by the year 2020, approximately a third of the German workforce will be retired (Guist, 2002, p. 2).

As in other societies, awareness of senior rights is growing. The Graue Panther association, established in the Federal Republic in 1975, is modeled on the Grey Panther movement in the United States and is devoted to actively promoting the rights of senior citizens. The overarching goals of both the Grey Panther movement and other state and local initiatives, *Laender und Kommune*, include helping seniors break through the isolation that they experience (Senioren-Schtuz-Bund, 2000, p. 601).

Elder Abuse in Germany

Elder abuse exists in Germany as it does elsewhere in the world (Swagerty, 1999). The perpetrators of abuse range from institutional caregivers to spouses, significant others, family, and nonfamily members who become caregivers (Marshall, 2000). It is estimated that yearly, 340,000 60- to 75-year-olds are victims of "violent acts by family and household members" in Germany (Wetzels & Greve, 1996, p. 1). However, for every case of elder abuse and neglect reported to authorities, experts estimate that there may be as many as five unreported cases. Recent research suggests that elders who have been abused tend to die earlier than those who are not abused, even in the absence of chronic conditions or life threatening disease. Elderly abuse and neglect, as well as the care given elderly in nursing homes, has become the subject of public and media debate (Goergen, 2001). Despite heightened awareness in the last 3 years (Goergen, 2001), abuse still goes unreported. Abuse in the private lives of the elderly, within close social circles, is rarely discussed (Landeshauptstadt Hannover, 1999). Factors contributing to elder abuse include the "spiraling burdens" of financial difficulties, inadequate living conditions, and the pressures of day-to-day elderly care. Often elder abuse occurs because the abuser is ignorant concerning care for the elderly person or is uninitiated and untrained in "treating dementia or other disabilities requiring continual supervision from the caregiver" (Marshall, 2000, p. 2).

German Respondents' Perspectives on Elder Abuse

Common types of elder maltreatment observed in Germany include physical, emotional, and psychological abuse, caregiver and self-neglect, and financial exploitation (Goergen, 2001). Our respondents provided examples of each type. A respondent from the former East Germany gave this example of extreme elder abuse: "If the elder is sick and cannot help him or herself anymore and nobody takes care of him or her." A similar example was: "The elder is left alone and neglected without being able to help him/herself." Examples of moderate abuse were: "If the elder has to give all his money to the adults or is put into a home for elders against his will." "Oppression of elders. Help and support given only when he/she gives financial support." A typical example of mild abuse was: "Elder is not taken seriously in conversations."

As one respondent said,

[Mild abuse] begins with emotional destruction by constantly belittling the person rather than building up the person, focusing on what he or she can no longer do rather than encouraging the person. The destruction of their soul begins with screaming at the elderly person. [Moderate abuse is] giving an elderly person food he or she cannot eat because the food has not been cut up; or the elderly person is not fed, even though the person is in no position to feed him or herself. [Extreme forms] of elderly abuse . . . are tying the elderly to their beds; [often] they are left to die in their own feces.

Other examples included "making fun" of the elderly, and in extreme cases, "rape and severe beatings."

Institutional abuse and violence exist as well. One respondent observed:

In the city, the elderly are put into old person homes. In some of them, there is a lock up section. The residents take off because they don't want to be in the home, and then they lock them up. Even the windows are locked. The people are pushed aside from society. . . . There's a split in Germany. In the country, you'll have 3 generations with one family all living in one house. But in larger cities, they are in old folks home.

INTERVENTION AND PREVENTION

Current Approaches to Child Abuse

Currently, the goal of government policy in Germany is to change abusive childrearing practices. Two tactics have been used: First, according to legislation, children have the right to an upbringing free of violence. Physical punishment, "injury to the soul," and other acts violating a child are illegal (paragraph 1631, Section 2 of the German Penal Code). This law was not designed to "criminalize" parents, but to initiate a change in social consciousness and childrearing practices, similar to what was done in Sweden (Arbeitskreis Neue Erziehung, 2000). Second, efforts at "prevention" have focused on public awareness and education, as well as on intervention programs. The intent is reduction in violence within society as well as in the home (Thyen, Thiessen, & Heinsohn-Krug, 1995). The law addresses all forms of maltreatment, including parental coldness, withdrawal of emotional support, humiliation, and belittling. The difficulty lies in how to rear children with acceptable discipline and limits (*Grenzsetzung*), without resorting to verbal, emotional, and physical abuse ("Mehr Respekt vor Kindern," 2002).

In conjunction with the new law, handbooks, pamphlets, and *Elternbriefe* have been written to provide parents with new coping techniques, skills, and ideas for age appropriate discipline without violence (Arbeitskreis Neue Erziehung, 2000). Courses such as "Strong Parents—Strong Children" are conducted throughout Germany by the German Children Protection League ("Recht auf eine gewaltfreie Erziehung," 2002). Trends indicate that intrafamily violence is falling. Since the introduction of the law on child punishment, "the use of corporal punishment in child-raising has declined by about 10% in comparison with earlier studies" (Mehr Respekt vor Kindern, 2002, p. 3). A recent study, commissioned by the government, reveals a "significant decline" in the use of the silent treatment, yelling, corporal punishment, and other forms of violence as disciplinary measures for children ("More respect for children," 2002, p. 1). Such steps are important because, as noted by Barnow, Lucht, and Frebyberger (2001, p. 171), even though the "mechanism explaining the link between negative parenting and later aggression" is at issue, it appears that "punishment and emotional rejection increase the risk of maladaptive developmental outcomes."

Combating Domestic Violence

During the past 25 years, Germany has taken a very progressive approach to fighting domestic violence. For example, the term originally utilized by the police, which seemed to trivialize the problem, was *Familienstreitigkeiten* or family conflict. More recently, that term has been replaced with *haeusliche Gewalt*, referring to the more socially contextual construct, domestic violence (Hagemann-White & Gardlo, 1997). The field has expanded from a focus primarily on violence in marriage and partnership to include child abuse and the abuse that women can inflict on male partners. This evolution reflects the principle of equality for men and women, the dignity of the individual, and the right to freedom from physical and mental harm (Baer & Schweikert, 2001). Public attempts to raise awareness of domestic violence go back at least to 1977, when 3,000 women marched in West Germany to protest domestic violence. Despite such efforts, it was only in 1997 that Germany finally declared rape within marriage a criminal offense.

Most empirical research in the area of domestic violence in Germany, as in the United States, has been fueled by feminist concerns for the victims. In 1995, for example, a program specifically designed to assist women was developed—the "Berlin Intervention Project Against Domestic Violence," based on the "Domestic Violence Intervention Project" of Duluth, Minnesota. Recently, "perpetrator-orientation" intervention efforts have materialized, in conjunction with more traditional victim-oriented intervention efforts (Kavemann, Beckmann, & Rabe, 2001).

Since the mid-1970s, with impetus from the women's movement, Germany has moved toward significant social change in dealing with violence against women—including the creation of Frauenhaeusern, shelters for battered women and their children. The first women's shelters in West Germany were established in Berlin and Cologne in 1976 (Bundesministerium- Bekaempfung von Gewalt, 1999). Currently, there are 200 to 400 houses providing emergency care, shelter, legal advice, and assistance (Brueckner, 2000; "Gewalt gegen Frauen," 2002). The first emergency helplines for victims of sexual assault and rape were established in 1977. Wildwasser Groups, established in 1983, offer assistance to sexually abused women and girls (Brueckner, 2000).

The government's position on violence against women is spelled out in the Action Plan of the Federal Government to combat violence against women (Bundesministerium-Bekaempfung von Gewalt, 1999). This plan addresses several limitations to earlier protections. Until 1997, rape was defined in the German penal code as "the use or threat of violence against a woman to force her into extramarital sexual intercourse" (Krahe, Schutze, Fritsche, & Waizenhofer, 2000, p. 142). Clearly, this definition was severely limited as it focused narrowly on married women experiencing extramarital forced sex. Since the law was revised in July 1997, the definition of rape is no longer restricted to vaginal intercourse but refers more generally to the penetration of the victim's body—male or female. As a result of this revised law, a greater number of sexually abused individuals, both males and females, can legally qualify as having been raped and press charges accordingly.

Combating Elder Abuse

In a concerted effort to face the challenges of institutional and private elderly abuse, working groups for the prevention of violence against the elderly have been created. Specialized "senior advice boards" (*Seniorenbueros*) provide information, coordinate educational programs for seniors, and provide a host of community services ("Die BaS stellt sich vor," 2002). Information evenings and specialized training for caregivers, as well as brochures and telephone crisis lines for elder abuse, are part of an expanded program of information, prevention, and intervention (Bundesministerium fuer Familie, Senioren, Frauen und Jugend, 2001, pp. 6–51). New legislation governing elderly care took effect August 1, 2003, intended to establish a new professionalism and profile for caregivers (Schmidt, 2002).

THE FUTURE

The very recent history of how the German government and its citizens have confronted social issues indicates promise for the future. The opening in 2002 of the first shelter for battered men and Germany's recent legislation declaring rape within marriage a criminal offense is clear indication of responsiveness to the needs of its citizens. Although such efforts to combat violence may not be implemented as quickly as some would like, the country has shown itself to be progressive. Hopefully such efforts, along with an increase in the public's awareness of the devastating effects of domestic violence, will lead to its reduction.

REFERENCES

Arbeitskreis Neue Erziehung, e.V. (2000, November). *Kinder gewaltfrei erziehen* [Raising children without violence]. Available: http://www.bmfsfj.de/Gewalt.pdf
Baer, S., & Schweikert, B. (2001). *Berliner Interventionsprojekt gegen haeusliche Gewalt* [Berlin intervention projects against domestic violence] (3rd ed.). Available: http://www.bmfsfj.de/Anlage15389/Text.pdf
Barnow, S., Lucht, M., & Frebyberger, H. J. (2001). Influence of punishment, emotional rejection, child abuse, and broken home on aggression in adolescence: An examination of aggressive adolescents in Germany. *Psychopathology, 34,* 167–173.
Bergmann, C. (2001). *Frauenrechte* [Women's rights]. Available: http://www.bmfsfj.de/top/dokumente/Rede/ix_60134.htm
Berlin to Open First Refuge for Battered Men. (2002). Available: http://www.dadi.org/berlnbtr.htm
Brueckner, M. (2000). Feministische Soziale Arbeit [Feminist social work]. In F. Stimmer (Ed.), *Lexikon der Sozialpaedagogik und der Sozialarbeit* (pp. 236–241). Muenchen: Oldenbourg.
Bundesministerium fuer Familie, Senioren, Frauen und Jugend. (1999). *Bekaempfung von Gewalt gegen Frauen* [Fighting violence against women]. Available: http://www.bmfsfj.de/Anlage2998/AktionsplanderBundesregierung.pdf
Bundesministerium fuer Familie, Senioren, Frauen und Jugend. (2001). *Dritter Bericht der lager der aelteren Generation in der Bundesrepublik Deutschland: Alter und Gesellschaft und Stellungnahme der Bundesregierung* [The third report on the situation of the elderly in Germany: The position of the federal government vis-à-vis ageing and society]. Available: http://www.bmfsfj.de/Altenbericht_Teil_1.pdf
Cooper, B. (1997). *Building feminism from the ground up.* Available: http://www.civnet.org/journal/issue3/cfbeco.htm

Dannenbeck, C., Keiser, S., & Rosendorfer, T. (1995). Familienalltag in den alten und neuen Bundesländern Aspekte der Vereinbarkeit von Beruf und Familie [Family life in the old and new German states: Aspects of compatibility from work and family]. In B. Nauck (Ed.), *Familie und Lebensverlauf im gesellschaftlichen Umbruch* (pp. 103–118). Stuttgart: Enke.

Die BaS stellt sich vor [BaS introduces itself]. (2002). Available: http://www.seniorenbueros.org/

Facts about Germany: Legal overview. (2002). Available: http://www.inhope.org/english/facts/germany/overview.htm

Family policy objectives. (2002). Available: http://text.bundesregierung.de

German Information Center. (2002). *Facts about Germany: Life in society.* Available: http://www.germany-info.org

Germany: Age of sexual consent. (2000). Available: http://www.ageofconsent.com/germany.htm

Germany gets tough on domestic violence. (2002). Available: http://news.bbc.co.uk/hi/english/world/europe/newsid_354000/354288.stm

Gewalt gegen Frauen [Violence against women]. (2002, May 17). *WDR.* Available: http://www.wdr.de/tv/recht/sendung/beitrag/rs1999_090_504.html

Gewaltfreie Erziehung [Violence-free upbringing]. (2002). Available: http://www.karlsruhe.de/Jugend/Kinderbuero/Fambild/gewaltfr.htm

Goergen, T. (2001). Stress, conflict, elder abuse and neglect in German nursing homes: A pilot study among professional caregivers. *Journal of Elder abuse & Neglect, 13*(1), 1–26.

Golz, P. (1996, November 19). *My second life: East German women in a changed world: An interview with Simone Shoemaker.* Available: http://web.uvic.ca/german/444/review.html

Gries, S., & Voigt, D. (1989). Kindesmisshandlung in Deutschland. Geht die DDR einen Sonderweg? [Child abuse in Germany: Is East Germany going a special way?]. In D. Voigt (Ed.), *Qualifikationsprozesse und Arbeitssituation von Frauen in der BRD und in der DDR* (p. 42). Berlin: Duncker & Humblot.

Guist, C. (2002). *People in Germany are growing older and older.* Available: http://www.goethe.de/kug/ges/soz/thm/en22907.htm

Gysi, J., & Meyer, D. (1993). Leitbild: berufstätige Mutter DDR-Frauen in Familie, Partnerschaft und Ehe [Model: The working mother in East Germany-Women in family, partnership and marriage]. In G. Helwig & H. M. Nickel (Eds.), *Frauen in Deutschland 45–92* (pp. 139–165). Berlin: Akad. Verlag.

Hafte, B., & Frandsen, K. J. (1985). *Psychological emergencies and crisis intervention.* Englewood, CO: Morton.

Hagemann-White, C., & Gardlo, S. (1997, August 24–27). *Interdisciplinary European workshop: Family conflict and domestic violence.* Loccum, Germany. Available: http://www.umaine.edu/conflict/LoccumReport.htm

Hermann, B. (2002). *Kindesmisshandlung* [Child abuse]. Available: http://home.t-online.de/home/B.Herrmann

Huxoll, M. (2002). Kindesmisshandlung und sexueller Missbrauch [Child maltreatment and sexual abuse]. In W. Fthenakis & M. Textor (Eds.), *Das Online-Familienhandbuch.* Available: http://www.familienhandbuch.de/cmain/f_Aktuelles/a_Haeufige_Probleme/s_442

Jung-joo, Lee. (n.d.). *Reunification won't produce results without women's participation.* Available: www.womennews.co.kr/ewnews/enews42.htm

Kaiser, G. (1973). Soziale Merkmale junger Opfer [Social characteristics in young victims]. In G. Kaiser (Ed.), *Jugendrecht und Jugendkriminalitaet* (p. 296). Basel: Weinheim.

Kavemann, B., Beckmann, S., & Rabe, H. (2001). *An overview of work with perpetrators of domestic violence in Germany.* Available: http://www.wibig.uni-osnabrueck.de/download/tatereng.doc

Kelling, H. W. (1974). *Deutsche Kulturgeschichte* [German cultural history]. New York: Holt, Rinehart & Winston.

Kindergeld. (2002). In W. Fthenakis & M. Textor (Eds.), *Das Online-Familienhandbuch* [The on-line family manual]. Available: http://www.familienhandbuch.de/cmain/f_Programme/a_Leistungen_fuer_Familien/s_102.html

Kolinksy, E. (1998). *Social transformation and the family in post communist Germany.* London: Macmillan.

Krahe, B., Schutze, S., Fritsche, I., & Waizenhofer, E. (2000). The prevalence of sexual aggression and victimization among homosexual men. *Journal of Sex Research, 37,* 142–150.

Landeshauptstadt Hannover. (1999). *Modellprojekt Hannover: Gewalt gegen aeltere Menschen in persoenlichen Nahraum* [Model project Hannover: Violence against elderly persons in their personal sphere]. Available: http://www.hannover.de/deutsch/buerger/lhh/lhh_verw/ueb_ag/mo_aelte/gew_aelt.htm

Marshall, C. (2000, February). Elder abuse: Using clinical tools to identify clues of mistreatment. *Geriatrics.* Available: http://www.findarticles.com/cf_0/m2578/2_55/59247241

Mehr Respekt vor Kindern [More respect for children]. (2002, February 8). Available: http://www.bmfsfj.de/dokumente/Pressemitteilung/ix_69088_4751.htm

Mueller, E. P. (1976). *Demokratischer Sozialismus und reale Politik* [Democratic socialism and material policy]. Koeln (Cologne): Dt. Inst.-Verlag.

Moeller, J., & Liedloff, H. (1988). *Deutsch heute* [German today] (2nd ed.). Boston: Houghton Mifflin.

More respect for children. (2002, February 13). Available: http://eng.bundesregierung.de/dokumente/Artikel/ix 69213.htm

Nauck, B., Schneider, N. F., & Tölke, A. (Eds.). (1995). *Familie und Lebensverlauf im gesellschaftlichen Umbruch* [Family and life course in societal change]. Stuttgart: Enke.

Pinther, A. (1991). Junge Ehen in den 70ern und 80ern Jahren [Recent marriages in the 70th and 80th years]. In W. Hennig & W. Friedrichs (Eds.), *Jugend in der DDR. Daten und Ergebnisse der Jugendforschung vor der Wende.* Weinheim: Juventa Verlag.

Plat, W. (1972). *Die Familie in der DDR* [The family in the GDR]. Frankfurt am Main: Fischer.

Recht auf eine gewaltfreie Erziehung [The right to a violence free upbringing]. (2002). Available: http://www.sw.fh.-koeln.de/sp/personen/scheffler/evaluation/scheffler_rechte.html

Schmidt, M. G. (1999). *Grundzuege der Sozialpolitik in der DDR* [Fundamentals of the social politics in the GDR]. Bremen: Zentrum fuer Sozialpolitik.

Schmidt, R. (2002). *Neue Qualitaetsmassstaebe in der Altenpflege* [New quality standards in elderly care]. Available: http://www.bmfsfj.de/dokumente/Pressemitteilung/ix_91026_4924.htm

Schotensack, K., Elliger, T., Gross, A., & Nissen, G. (1992). Prevalence of sexual abuse of children in Germany. *Acta Paedopsychiatrica, 55,* 211–216.

Senioren-Schutz-Bund 'Graue Panther', e.V. [The Gray Panthers]. (2000). In F. Stimmer (Ed.), *Lexikon der Sozialpaedagogik und der Sozialarbeit* (p. 601). Muenchen: Oldenbourg.

Sexual Offence Laws, Germany. (2002). Available: http://www.interpol.int/Public/Children/SexualAbuse/NationalLaws/csaGermany.asp

Since taking office. (2002). Available: http://eng.bundesregierung.de/frameset/index.jsp

Stimmer, F. (2000). Lexikon der Sozialpädagogik und der Sozialarbeit [Lexicon for social pedagogy and social work] (4th ed.). München: Oldenbourg.

Swagerty, D. (1999, May 15). Elder mistreatment. *American Family Physician.* Available: http://www.findarticles.com/cf 0/m3225/1059/5494206

Thyen, U., Thiessen, R., & Heinsohn-Krug, M. (1995). Secondary prevention—serving families at risk. *Child Abuse & Neglect, 19,* 1337–1347.

Wallrabe, D. (1968). *Zur forensisch-psychiatrischen Begutachtung des Taeters bei Kindestoetung, Kindesmord und Kindesmisshandlung unter besonderer Beruecksichtigung des sozialen Milieus und der Persoenlichkeitsentwicklung* [Forensic-psychiatric assessment of offenders in child murders, child deaths and child abuse with special consideration of the social environment and personality development]. Unpublished doctoral dissertation, Berlin.

Wetzels, P., & Greve, W. (1996). Alte Menschen als Opfer innerfamiliaerer Gewalt - Ergebnisse einer kriminologischen Dunkelfeldstudie [Elderly people as victim inner family violence - the results of a German victimization survey]. *Zeitschrift für Gerontologie und Geriatrie, 29*, 191–200.

Wolff, R. (1997). Germany: A nonpunitive model. In N. Gilbert (Ed.), *Combating child abuse: International perspectives and trends* (pp. 212–231). New York: Oxford University Press.

III

CENTRAL AND SOUTHERN EUROPE

7

Russia

Anna Fastenko
Irini Timofeeva

CAPSULE

During the past two decades, Russia has been undergoing a crucial transition from a soviet system to a pro-Western type of country, a transition affecting all levels of Russian society economically, politically, and culturally. A recent report on Russia's economy in National Geographic magazine (November, 2001) shows a monthly per capita income of approximately $200–300, with pensioners subsisting on far less. Financial hardships and poverty probably have become the most interfering and destabilizing factors for the vast majority of the population, and have contributed to an elevation of violence on both the family and macrosystem level.

In general, problems of family violence were not a topic of public discussion in the former USSR. Under the Communist system, the prevailing ideology was characterized by purposeful neglect of negative aspects of people's lives, although some kinds of misbehavior in families (e.g., alcoholism, physical abuse, cheating) were profoundly and officially criticized by various state organizations and local work committees. Only since the beginning of Perestroika has the hidden problem of fairly widespread family abuse and neglect emerged as a point of public and political attention. Such evidence as is available makes it clear that it is typically the weakest family members who are most vulnerable. Women and children compose the vast majority of cases of domestic violence. The tradition of filial piety provides a moderate degree of protection of elders, although they often suffer greatly from poverty. Discussions of family violence generally make no reference to men, who have much more social, financial, and authoritarian power in the male dominant Russian society. Scientific research on family violence and abuse is still somewhat limited because of the unavailability of funding, so most of the statistics in this chapter are derived from mass media, and internet sources rather than from published formal scientific reports.

THE RUSSIAN RESPONDENTS

The Russian survey was filled out by 102 participants (65 female, 37 male) of different ages (18–77 years old) with a median age of 33 years, predominantly from metropolitan Moscow and St. Petersburg areas. Religious affiliation was 78% Orthodox Christian and 22% atheists. Educational level varied from high school or associate degree to college and an advanced degree, the most representative group consisting of current college students (51) or professionals with a degree (36). The participants mostly described their socioeconomic status as low (14), low medium (57), or medium (28). More than a third of the people who filled out the survey wrote that they live in a three-generational family—parents, children, and grandparents.

Russian Participants' General Definitions of Abuse

Nearly every Russian respondent mentioned some form of physical aggression as an example of severe abuse, and 84% of the respondents made reference to verbal aggression. Also, people from different ages, education, and SES groups gave examples of behaviors such as "being dishonest," "telling lies," "cheating," "being unfaithful," "taking advantage of another person," which could be considered as forms of psychological abuse. "Being disrespectful" was mentioned by almost all participants as an example of family abuse at one level or another.

When asked to give an example of a severe form of abuse in the family, 77% of the respondents mentioned "wife battering," and the other 21% mentioned "child battering." This emphasis on physical abuse of women and children indicates a general attention to and intolerance of the harshest form of mistreatment of the weakest in the family. Also, 29 people listed "alcohol abuse and drunken behavior" as examples of severe abuse in families. Extremely negative attitudes toward substance abuse in both men and women were shown, despite the fact that alcoholism in Russia primarily hits men. "Alcoholism" was mentioned as either a severe or moderate form of abuse toward women by more than 80% of the respondents.

THE RUSSIAN MACROSYSTEM

Many current implicit theories about family violence in Russia originated in the historical set of beliefs known as *Domostroi*, which dictated that women were to devote themselves solely to domestic duties, and men were responsible for physically disciplining wives who disregarded their duties. For example, in the mid-17th century, there was no penalty for the husband's murder of his wife, but a wife who killed her husband was to be buried up to her neck and left to perish (Horne, 1999).

Following the 1917 Socialist Revolution, there was some change in attitudes toward women. An important principle of communist theory was that the status of women defines a country's cultural and economic progress. The Soviet constitution declared women and men legally and politically equal, providing full financing of maternity care, legalized abortion, state-supported child care, and the right of married women to live separately from their husbands with full rights to divorce. Surprisingly, such "freedom" tended to become a double burden for women, who began working full-time jobs, as well as continuing to be responsible for practically all household and childrearing duties. This double burden was reflected in the findings of a recent study by Arai, Perlitsh, and Erdyneev (2000), which addressed concepts of female gender roles in Russian women in Buryatia (South Siberia). This study of 102 female college students revealed idealistically high expectations of women as good mothers, wives, housekeepers, and dedicated professionals, and an assumption that it was necessary for women to fulfill those expectations in order to consider themselves potent and successful women.

At the same time, widespread sexual harassment and age discrimination in the workplace make it very difficult for many women to find and maintain employment, even with high educational level and work experience. During the last two decades, due to ongoing employment discrimination and the renewed emphasis on traditional family roles advocated by a resurgent Russian Orthodox Church, Russian women are again being forced to depend economically on men (Horne, 1999). Some social scientists (www.projectharmony.ru) believe that this dependence contributes to the occurrence of violent behavior in families, and supports and nurtures typical Russian stereotypes of appropriate gender roles. These roles, in turn, foster myths about the nature of violence in families. According to the reports of the program of cooperation of local communities against family violence in Russia, "Project Harmony" (www.projectharmony.ru/chto/mifi.html), among the most common misbeliefs are the following: 1) Women provoke violent behavior against themselves and deserve it; 2) Women can always avoid abusive situations; 3) Once he has started behaving violently, a perpetrator cannot prevent the reoccurrence of such behavior; 4) Male perpetrators are aggressive with everybody, regardless of the person or situation; 5) Children need their father, even if he is extremely aggressive; 6) Arguments between husbands and wives have always existed; they should be considered natural and not implying any serious consequences; 7) Alcohol is a major stimulus of violence; 8) Family violence is a newly originated phenomenon, caused by current economic hardships, speeding of life timing, and related stress; 9) Women who are abused by their partners enjoy being a victim and get sexual masochistic satisfaction from situations involving violence; and 10) Male abusers usually are not fortunate in life, and cannot deal with the stress and problems they have.

In a sociological survey in the small Russian town of Rybinsk, Klimenkova (1998) provided some statistical evidence for the strength of such myths. For example, 99% of the respondents believed that male aggressiveness and rudeness were natural accompaniments of masculinity, and even approved of men who "had a relationship on the side." Various excuses offered for such behavior included "negative influence of school and street," "tough times while serving in the army," and "unbearable stress of economic burden." A common bias among respondents of both genders was an underestimation of the active, independent, and creative role of women in Russian society. Moreover, despite general acceptance of a patriarchic norm, many respondents expressed opinions incompatible with the traditional scheme of gender roles. One of the respondents, a 28-year-old male actor, noted that "Men are now weaker than women, they lack flexibility and sober-mind to resist hardships of the crisis in the country."

Another issue is that domestic violence is considered a private family matter in Russian society, an assumption reflected in the proverb "dirty laundry is not to be washed in public." Although this norm has been changing slightly during the past decade, Russians generally maintain close friendships with only a few people throughout their lifetimes; disclosing personal information to others outside of the circle of friends and family is not typical (Horne, 1999).

THE RUSSIAN MICROSYSTEM

Family Structure

Two major characteristics of both urban and rural Russian families are, on the one hand, westernized nuclear families consisting primarily of parents and their children, and, on the other hand, the common "vertical" expansion of the family, which means at least three generations living in the same home. The second practice has its roots not only in Russia's historical legacy of multigenerational households with an older member at its head, but also in the consistent lack of housing, especially in cities, after the Communist Revolution (1917). Ninety-one out of 102 participants in our survey lived either with their parents and grandparents, or with their children and parents/parents-in-law, depending on the age of respondents.

Russian childrearing practices are similar to those in the United States and Europe, with parents taking full responsibility for their children's health, and intellectual and social development. Still, many people in Russia view grandparents as caregivers as well. For example, one of the participants in our survey stated that if a grandmother neglects her responsibilities of taking care of a grandchild, it might be considered a moderately abusive type of behavior. Such grandparenting responsibilities are feasible due to an early retirement age (55 years for women and 60 years for men), which is not mandatory, but useful in taking pressure off young parents, and giving them opportunities for professional development and personal growth.

Nonetheless, it is quite possible for a nuclear family to raise a child without any help from other relatives; maternal leave in Russia is very liberal (a one-year fully paid leave of absence, and an additional 3-year partly paid leave, with full preservation of her position until the woman returns to work). There is also a wide net of day-care centers and preschool institutions. Schooling is free and mandatory for all children from age 7 to 15; another 2 years of high school is free for adolescents who pass required exams. New times have produced new services from nannies and babysitters, so both parents have an opportunity to work full-time.

Childrearing practices vary as a function of socioeconomic status, education, nationality, area (urban/rural), and cultural background. Still, there are some common notions concerning what kinds of behaviors toward children are unacceptable, and neglect and corporal punishment are viewed as the most severe forms of child maltreatment. Corporal punishment has been prohibited in schools since 1917, and was criticized and even prosecuted by the communist society if it happened in the family. In our sample, physical punishment, including "spanking," was identified as abusive by the vast majority (93%) of respondents.

There is a high rate of divorce in Russia—an average of 59% from 1993 through 1999 (Russian Annual Statistical Report, 2000). Usually single mothers take full responsibility for raising their children, whereas divorced fathers tend to provide substantial financial assistance. In general, although women in Russia are as educated as men, their social and family status is lower. There are many housewives and stay-at-home moms, and for employed women (still the majority of the population), their expertise other than work is typically restricted to housekeeping and childrearing—in contrast to men's extensive leisure interests and socializing.

FAMILY VIOLENCE

According to Horne (1999), the rates of reported cases of family violence in Russia exceed Western figures by 4 or 5 times; however, actual incidence and prevalence rates are generally underestimated and unstudied. The number of women killed by their partners generally provides the only rough estimate of ongoing violent family abuse; an average of 14,000 murdered women was reported by the president's advisor on women's issues (Human Rights Watch Report, 1997). Although there is evidence that violence has always been present in Russian culture, it also appears that there has been an increase in domestic violence since the breakup of the Soviet Union (Horne, 1999). This increase appears to be related to the general escalation of aggression in Russian society during the transition from a communist to a more democratic and capitalistic form of society.

Official reports of some forms of family violence in Russia are actually quite low; for example, between 1993 and 1999, not a single sexual harassment or elder abuse case went to the court of the Russian Federation. The number of rapes reported during this postcommunist period was 10,000 cases per year, which is almost nothing compared to nearly 100,000 rapes reported in the United States yearly. Such figures are virtually meaningless, however; victims very seldom go to the police, knowing in advance they cannot count on a sympathetic hearing and effective help. The overall image of the police was so low during the last decade that it was reflected in a common saying: "Police don't do anything—one should deal with the situation on one's own."

People's implicit theories of domestic violence are at the same time a cause and a reflection of mistreatment in families; old traditional views on gender roles and childrearing are sometimes used to justify abuse, whereas general awareness of the family violence problem indicates some evolution in people's stereotypes and judgments.

Violence Against Women

According to information from the Russian Ministry of Internal Affairs (1998), violence against women occurs in 1 out of every 4 families, which is an average of 610,000 thousand cases of family abuse per year (Kuznetsov, 1999). In 1996, the president's advisor on women's issues announced that an average of 14,000 women in Russia are killed each year by male partners. Kuznetsov (1999) reported that the incidence of women murdered per capita in the Russian Federation surpasses the rate in all other countries and exceeds the rate in the United States by several times. According to a survey of 3,900 women in three major cities, every seventh woman reported being moderately or severely physically abused by her husband (Kuznetsov, 1999). Making the picture even worse, data from sociological studies show that more than 40% of the victims do not report violent behavior in their families, due to complete economic and social dependency on their partners and disbelief in the possibility of prosecution and punishment of perpetrators. Moreover, domestic violence in Russia remains a low priority in both governmental and private sectors. Recently, the issue has received increasing attention in the popular media; however, the approach is a highly conservative one, in which "misbehavior" of the victims is often identified as the cause of the violence, and various myths about domestic violence are promulgated.

Interestingly enough, a 1995 study by the Russian Association of Crisis Centers for Women revealed that although many Russians believed that violence in general is not a norm in Russian society, 81% of the women and 33% of the men thought that domestic violence was a common occurrence. The majority of both men and women believed that a husband who beats his wife is guilty and should be punished, but half of the respondents believed that women provoke violent behavior from their husbands.

Russian Participants' Perspectives on Wife Abuse

In spite of all the disturbing statistics, many Russians have implicit theories indicating a general intolerance of violence and the awareness needed to build healthy abuse-free relationships within the family, as indicated by respondents to our survey from Moscow and St. Petersburg. For example, "battering" and "hitting with objects" were considered the most severe types of abuse by about 60% of the participants. The other 40% mentioned various kinds of psychological abuse and neglect, which were viewed even more negatively than physical abuse by many respondents. Women considered "cheating" and "lying" to wives to be as abusive as battering. Also, many respondents considered it abusive if husbands did "not help wives in housekeeping and childrearing," were "unreliable in times of trouble," did "not take financial responsibility for the family," "refused to provide moral support," were "selfish and egoistic," and so forth. An answer given by a 33-year-old worker is representative of many similar points of view: "A husband must give his wife money for decent housekeeping, protect her from harshness of life, be handy and do some work around the house, console her if she is upset—otherwise the husband is neglecting his immediate duties and therefore is abusing his wife." Four other female respondents underlined the importance of making serious decisions and taking responsibility for the family during hard times, describing "indifference and carelessness" as a significant (moderate) form of abuse by a husband. "Blaming a wife for not being a good housekeeper/mother," in other words denying her the most vital expressions of female gender role, was also considered by a significant portion of participants (20), regardless of their gender, as a pretty serious (moderate) form of family abuse.

"Being unfaithful" to a wife was viewed as abusive by only 18 respondents (11 women and 7 men); moreover, some respondents asserted that "having an adulterous affair and failing to hide it from a wife" was as abusive as the affair itself. A 33-year-old woman with two children stated that the worst torture for a wife is when she learns about her husband's cheating. Because this respondent believes that all men are naturally polygamous (seeking many partners), her implicit theory is that men are abusive when they don't succeed at hiding adultery from their lawful wives.

From the perspective of our respondents, the content of verbal mistreatment was not as important as the fact of saying something humiliating or aggressive in front of other people. For instance, two men and three women ages 19–43 indicated that saying something like "that woman is so much prettier than you" is an insult if other people could hear it. Two people wrote that saying "she is a lousy housekeeper" is a model of public humiliation; seven respondents described a situation of "criticizing a wife in front of her step-parents" as very embarrassing.

Husband Abuse

Husband abuse is not recognized as a problem in Russian society. Despite the fact that relevant amendments and laws of constitution are gender unspecific, and a person may be subject to legal responsibility regardless of his or her sex, not a single male abuse case has been reported to state officials, whereas many women abuse reports are stacked in every police department (general figures not available). The proportion of men to women killed by a family member is 1 to 7 (Timofeeva, 2002), and is not necessarily linked to severe physical abuse cases only.

On the other hand, there is a wide public awareness of multiple cases of families where women abuse their husbands verbally, psychologically, and even physically. Such situations are usually considered to be a man's own fault. The general attitude is reflected in the question: "Why do you let her do this to you?" This question is directly linked to a prevailing notion of male dominance, self-respect for "being strong," and social image, which is completely incompatible with the role of abused husband. So, even if fairly severe cases of husband abuse are occurring, they will never be reported to the public, to relatives, or even to close friends. Maintaining a masculine image is critically higher in the motivational hierarchy than is suffering from some mistreatment behind closed doors. Besides, due to financial independence and freedom from childrearing, it is always assumed that men are "free to go" when the relationship goes wrong.

Russian Participants' Perspectives on Husband Abuse

Although abuse of men is infrequent compared to abuse of women, some wives try to get back at their husbands in quite an aggressive way. All 102 participants of our survey were able to think about a few situations of wives abusing their husbands. Only rarely were examples given of physical aggression ("a wife hits a husband with a frying pan"). More typically (67 responses), reference was made to verbal aggression, which appears to be considered a leading form of abuse toward men in the family. "Acting in a way to diminish a man's masculinity" was viewed as the most severe form of husband abuse by both male and female respondents. Also, 63% of the respondents mentioned a wife "being unfaithful" as another kind of severe husband abuse. The most unexpected common answers were examples of moderate abuse involving wives' failures to feed, take care, and even groom their husbands properly. For example, a 48-year-old woman said it would be moderately abusive if "a woman, in order to get back at her husband, washed his clothes and did not rinse them well enough, so that the man's skin gets irritated and he feels uncomfortable." Interestingly enough, a wife "spending a lot of money for pleasure," "being idle," and "financially 'milking' a husband" were described by 13 respondents as being mildly abusive. "Inability to run the house sparingly, clean, and cook well" was listed by 9 people as the same level of husband abuse as "cheating," "shouting," or "lying" by another 41 respondents.

One of the typical scenarios given as an example of moderate abuse of both wives and husbands by more than 70% of the participants, both male and female, was "revealing mistakes," "revealing private or sexual secrets of the partner," or just "blaming and badmouthing him or her in public." This emphasis reflects well the strength of the already mentioned proverb that "dirty laundry not to be washed in public," and the validity of the saying for both genders.

In defining and providing examples of abuse in families, none of the respondents mentioned any kind of sexual violence against a partner. This does not mean sexual violence does not occur in Russian families, but reflects a general unwillingness to discuss the problem. References to all sexual matters were strictly avoided during the soviet period, which originated from a commonly known official position that "there is no sex in the Soviet Union" (a real citation from a few government leaders of the 1970s–1980s). Massive moralistic propaganda resulted in public suppression and avoidance of the issue, and discomfort in talking about sex-related matters. It is almost impossible to get a clear picture of a problem people were taught not to think about, even though current times have significantly opened up the topic, and recently gained freedom of the press supports the dissemination of proper information and education.

Child Abuse

Russia's current social, political, and economic upheaval, and the diminishing availability of human services, combined with a high incidence of alcoholism and high frequency of single parenting, are contributing to a high frequency of child abuse in Russia (Berrien, Aprelkov, Ivanova, Zhmurov, & Buzhicheeva, 1995). Still, neither the general population nor professionals acknowledge the magnitude of the problem. Clear enough is the public awareness of homeless and orphaned children, but there is no specific term in the Russian language to describe abused children. Russians have long believed that parents need to provide food, clothing, and shelter for their children; however, only within the last decade has the state recognized "social orphanhood" (defined as "orphans with living parents") and "child maltreatment" (defined as "neglect, physical, emotional, or sexual maltreatment").

Child and elder abuse have generally been considered as less significant types of abuse by the general public, the media, and officials, reflecting a traditional tolerance for these forms of mistreatment. People are usually compassionate to the victims, but have regular excuses for the abusers (the majority of whom are men). Despite such downplaying of the problem, statistics of reported cases of child abuse reveal its magnitude: More than 2 million children below the age of 14 are battered by their parents every year; for some children, those beatings are fatal (Ogorodnikova, 1995). More than 50,000 children a year run away from their homes to escape parental violence.

The welfare of children is also affected by a macrosystem-level socioeconomic crisis. There is a skyrocketing number of neglected children (several million, according to some estimates), whose living and even survival became purely a matter of their own personal concern. Unfortunately, it is impossible to collect exact statistical data due to the complex characteristics of such children. They may have parents, a formal home, and even be enrolled in a local school, but their parents are either alcoholics, or leave their children unattended for days and even weeks, or don't provide enough food and clothing so that such children have to steal or beg for money. Not unique among this group of neglecting families are cases where parents expel their children from home as a form of punishment or just in angry outbursts.

Overall, there has been very little research on the issue of child abuse in Russia. Even the most noticeable forms of abuse—physical and sexual—are minimally studied (Berrien, Safonova, & Tsimbal, 2000). One of the few direct studies was conducted in Siberia (Berrien et al., 1995) with 412 students from a school for intellectually gifted children; this study revealed that 28% of the children had experienced physical abuse, with 4% abused seriously enough to require medical attention. In total, 46.7% of the respondents had experienced or witnessed various forms of child abuse. Despite the fairly high rates reported by children in this and several other studies, only 3% of 2,060 adults surveyed from different regions of Russia acknowledged severely beating their children within the past year (Achildieva, 1997).

One possible explanation for the underreporting of child abuse might be cultural characteristics of the population in the Russian Federation, which espouses high ethical norms of Christian and Soviet morality, but is almost uneducated in terms of family values and matters. Parents autonomously raise their children as they determine, and corporal punishment is an accepted form of discipline. A 33-year-old female journalist from Rybinsk, who was a respondent in a sociological study (Klimenkova, 1998), commented, "Of course they (parents) often beat their children, sometimes quite hard. People get very tired and exhausted after work, and breakdown at their children." Another respondent from Klimenkova's study, a 54-year-old female teacher, said, "Nowadays battering and punching are the most frequent ways of childrearing."

According to the Russian Department of Internal Affairs (2000), there are about 625,000 orphans in Russia, only 10% of whom are real parentless children. Others are "social orphans" who became victims of the widespread "child protecting" practice of taking abused children to orphanages rather than allowing them to be adopted. In addition, parents of handicapped or seriously ill children are forced to place them in social institutions or orphanages where the children typically are deprived of any contact with the outer world and cannot develop and have normal lives. Growth of social orphanhood and child neglect has been attributed to institutional forces, sometimes called "Violence with Inaction," by responsible State officials. Altshuler, Kushnir, and Severny (2000) describe several cases of children who were victims of institutional neglect. One 7-year-old boy from Moscow, Sasha Belyakov, asked different state agents "Please take me from my mother" for almost 2 months. (His mother was an alcoholic and totally neglected him.) The boy was ignored by authorities, although not by the neighbors who fed him. None of the authorities even visited the apartment where he lived under terrible conditions. In the end, Sasha burned to death in a fire in the apartment. In another case, Petr Kalinin, a 15-year-old boy from a rural settlement in the Krasnodarsky region (North Caucasus), hanged himself after a year of vain requests to be rescued from an alcoholic father who tortured and beat him. Petr was the eldest of nine children in that family. After Petr's suicide, his two alcoholic parents continued to abuse the other eight children, despite coverage of the tragedy in the local newspapers. In Moscow, a random police raid (Altshuler & Severny, 2000), revealed 225 homeless children, 189 of whom were sent back to the streets without any assistance.

Although many children are taken from abusive families and placed in orphanages, those children often do not fare well when they finally leave the institutional setting. There is evidence (Ogorodnikova, 1995) that out of 15,000 children leaving orphanages every year, 5,000 become criminals, 3,000 add to the ranks of the homeless, and 1,500 commit suicide. The fact that there are significantly more international than domestic adoptions of Russian children suggests questionable social welfare practices, because there are always enough Russian families seeking to adopt a child. This situation is remarkable given the tendency of legislative institutions to ban all laws favoring international adoption in order to stop "child trade and slavery." These restrictive policies, designed to protect children from exploitation, become another force contributing to an expanding pool of hundreds of thousands of Russian orphans.

According to some independent researchers (www.owl.ru/syostri/world), about 40% of Russian families (totally 23 million) tolerate some form of child abuse. Moreover, there is hardly any information children can receive, from school or other institutions, about protective services or even hot-line numbers for victims of child abuse. Only recently, one TV channel and some radio stations started advocating advertisement of noncommercial organizations where children can get help. Russian children get passports and become lawful members of the society at age 16, but may be heavily beaten throughout childhood and not even be aware that help officially exists. Moreover, many aspects of child abuse have not yet been addressed by the state, and are acknowledged by only a few child-protection organizations maintained by dedicated volunteers.

Local newspapers reported the following cases of child abuse, which took place in different regions of Russia, but are similar in their desperation and lack of social support: Dima K. is a 10-year-old boy who lives in Novosibirsk with his 84-year-old grandmother without any resources, because they are not eligible for financial support. Dima's mother, although a heavy alcoholic, is alive, so the boy is not formally an orphan. If his grandmother dies, Dima will be sent to an orphanage, in which he has already had a brief experience. He promises that if sent there, he will run away. Where? Twelve-year-old Masha from Moscow was adopted into a new family when she was 4, but when her adoptive mother died, the child and her grandmother were evicted from their apartment by her adoptive father, an alcoholic. Police were not of much help in the situation, and only a representative of protective services for children prevented Masha's suicide. (She was about to jump from a window on the 14th floor.) Sonya, from a town of Penza, was not even 5 years old when brought to an emergency room with severe bleeding and bruises after spending a few hours with father. The girl was heavily beaten for not keeping an eye on her younger 2-year-old brother, who smudged his clothing. Before hitting his daughter, the man slapped his wife so that she had to hide herself at the neighbors.

All these stories, and thousands of others still awaiting public or official attention, speak to the urgent necessity of real action in order to begin a long fight for children's rights and against family abuse and neglect. This fight begins in people's minds when old implicit theories of acceptable behavior give way to modern understanding, and general awareness becomes the main force of change. Evidence of these changes can be found in the implicit theories of child abuse derived from the responses of participants in our study.

Russian Participants' Perspectives on Child Abuse

Overall, total neglect of parenting duties (e.g., "the child is not fed regularly or is locked in the house for days") was considered to be the most severe type of child abuse, followed by physical punishment. Verbal aggression scenarios ("shouting and calling names") were the vast majority (over 80%) of descriptions of moderate types of abuse. Typical examples of verbal abuse were "calling a child stupid, thick, lazy, and unable to achieve anything"; pointing out mistakes and making comparisons to other relatives or friends' negative personality traits (e.g., "you are as awkward as your cousin"); making references to a child's lack of age-appropriate skills, misunderstanding, or physical incompetence (e.g., "saying 'you always spill something when cooking' when talking angrily to a 9-year-old daughter," an example given by a 24-year-old female teacher). As mild forms of abuse, participants mentioned such behaviors as "not considering a child's interests or preferences," "blaming the child for poor school performance," and "not keeping promises for rewards," and so forth, which may be considered forms of psychological abuse. "Not buying a toy for a kid when he or she earned it by good behavior is not severely abusive, but is very wounding for a trusting child," said a 53-year-old nurse.

Many respondents in the age group between 18 and 25 years old gave examples of parents verbally and psychologically abusing their adolescent children. Some form of the phrase "parents stick their noses in lives of teenagers, which is none of their business" was mentioned by 28 young people. Girls wrote a lot about overprotection by parents, "checking on where and with whom daughters spend their time," and considered such supervision embarrassing. Boys were more concerned with "excessively high expectations" of future professional or work growth parents put on their children's shoulders. Such conflicts of interest between generations, which often lead to abusive words and behavior, may be typical internationally, but may also illustrate a specific burden for Russian teenagers and young people who have to live with their parents at least until college graduation because of limited housing and income problems.

Our survey finding that "slapping" and other kinds of corporal punishment was totally unacceptable differs significantly from estimates of an Institute of Childhood study (Ogorodnikova, 1995), which reported that only 25% of parents believe that physical punishment is an unacceptable form of treating a child; about 75% of parents in the Institute study acknowledged and justified some corporal punishment of their children. Such discrepancy leaves room for more thorough investigation and interpretation of people's attitudes and perceptions in the area of childrearing practices.

Comparing results from our survey with similar research in the area, we noticed that none of our participants mentioned sexual abuse in their responses, avoiding one of the most significant areas of child mistreatment. This fact again probably reflects the taboo nature of sex as a topic for Russian people, because a rough prevalence of 8,000 sexually abused children per year is considered a drastic underestimation (Ogorodnikova, 1995). Tsimbal (1997) estimated that there are at least 26,000 cases of sexual crimes against children each year, but the actual figure may be even higher.

Elder Abuse

Elder abuse is generally not recognized as a problem in Russian society. During the preparation of this chapter, not a single publication could be found concerning this form of family violence. Why is public attention to issues of family violence so selective? One of the reasons is obviously a low life expectancy in Russia, which minimizes the number of old citizens, especially in the age group of 75 and over. Another explanation is that harsh economic problems shifted public as well as individual attention from the area of psychological and even physical comfort of senior citizens to issues of mere survival. Because poor nutrition, limited medical care, and unavailability of social services are major problems for the majority of elders, verbal, psychological, and even moderate physical abuse are not given serious attention at any level of Russian society. The only support system old people can rely on is their family, which in many cases is a source of ongoing mistreatment; thus, many elders cannot escape abuse.

One significant aspect of the changed economic situation in Russia is a drastic impoverishment of 99% of senior citizens, who lost all their savings during financial perturbations. These senior citizens can barely survive on the state pensions provided. Being old and faced with both ageism and poverty, elderly people experience a double disrespect from the majority of younger people, who spurn them both for their age-related weakness and unattractiveness, and for not having any social significance. Lubov Shtyleva's (2000) description of common patterns of elder mistreatment in Murmansk, a midsize town in the north of the Russian Federation, is quite representative of the situation in hundreds of similar cities and towns all over the country, although the term "elder abuse" has never been used in any reports or articles related to the issue. Shtyleva noted that every fifth citizen of the Murmansk region is retired, with an average of 22$ of pension per month as a major source of income. Because a pension is paid on a fairly regular basis, it can become the only income not only for a retired person, but also for other unemployed members of the family. Such a devastating situation often leads to high levels of distress. People fail to cope with the poverty and find the only solution in suicides. In 2000, the vast majority (78%) of people committing suicides were elders. Another new and significant sociological problem is represented by the growing number of homicides committed to get rid of sick, helpless, and dependent members of the family, especially in order to obtain their property.

Battering of older people is rarely reported. According to a 54-year-old nurse in a Rybinsk sociological study reported by Klimenkova (1998), "Mothers will never complain on their sons, tolerating any abuse and cruelty. Even if police persuade her to submit a claim and at least have some rest while her son is arrested for 2 weeks, the elder mother would always say: 'Don't touch him—he is my son.' " Such tolerant attitudes may be an indication of the eastern cultural influence on Russian mentality, where patience and family solidarity are viewed as the most valuable dignities of older people. One should also take into consideration the fact that in the former Soviet Union, family violence research focused predominantly on physical abuse, which legitimately fell under the jurisdiction of the Constitution, whereas all other forms of abuse were mentioned only as accompanying physical violence. Thus, the commonly occurring financial or psychological abuse of old people still remains unrecognized by media and public organizations.

Russian Participants' Perspectives on Elder Abuse

Results from our survey are consistent with the situation just described. Taking care (financially, physically, and socially) of older parents was a crucial factor in all the judgments about various forms of elder mistreatment. "Total lack of care" was viewed as extremely abusive by the vast majority of participants, whereas "disagreeing with older parents and grandparents" and "being disrespectful to their judgment" fell in the next category of moderate abuse. Verbal abuse composed a solid 82% of all examples of moderate abuse. More than half of the respondents stated that "being rude and arguing" with elders is quite offensive, whereas another 16% mentioned that even "raising one's voice" when talking with elders is abusive.

Mildly abusive scenarios showed the most diversity of judgments of what should and should not be present in everyday relationships with older members of the family. A large portion of respondents (64) emphasized that any kind of neglect, especially psychological, is abusive, even though mild. Examples included "lack of attention to worries and interests of aged parents," "little time spent with them," not showing respect (e.g., "not inviting old parents to dinner"), and "denying them the opportunity of learning some details about their children's and especially grandchildren's lives." Active mild psychological abuse was described in terms of "denying grandparents contacts with their grandchildren," "not taking their opinion into consideration," "being skeptical about their life experiences," and so forth. The statement "not showing respect" was given in 77 examples of mild or moderate abuse. Also, 12 respondents indicated that it would be abusive if "children, following a mutual argument or fight with elderly parents, delayed restoring peaceful relationships in order to make their older parents feel dependent on their good will."

Interestingly, 12 respondents indicated that "neglect or mistreatment of parents-in-law" was just as abusive as mistreating one's own parents. This response reflects a common notion that "marrying a person means marrying his/her parents," and the assumption that spouses are supposed to help their partners take care of the parents-in-law. Such practices are not typically followed, but the ideal stereotype still exists.

Financial forms of elder abuse were mentioned by 22% of all participants and included not only "expropriation of money or property" from older parents, but also, and even more commonly, "purposeful neglect and abuse," "pursuing a sooner death of the elderly in order to take advantage of their apartment or house." "Some people just can't wait for their parents to die, so they passively omit any help or support elders may need"—a 57-year-old businessman commented on a question about severe elder abuse.

In regard to elder mistreatment in general, it is important to stress that it is considered a matter of public pity and compassion, but not a reason for any sort of legal or public action. An explanation can be based again on the grounds of overall poverty, decline of living standards, and inability of the state to provide necessary services and financial support for senior citizens. These problems are seen as justifying elder neglect on the governmental level; consequently, neglect is also accepted on a family level, when people simply cannot "beat the system."

INTERVENTION AND PREVENTION

Although much of the material in this chapter might seem a bit depressing, there are many changes occurring in legal, community, financial, informative, and other aspects of the long-term fight for human's rights and peaceful living in all families in the country. New funds are available to women's and children's organizations every year, and shelters, protective agencies, and support groups become more accessible for victimized members of a family. The most important factor is a faster spreading of information about such services and organizations, as new computer and mass media technologies grow and expand, with the goal of reaching every home in urban and rural Russia. For instance, 3 years ago, children even in large cities had no idea where to go or whom to call to avoid parental abuse. In 2002, almost every child who watches main TV channels and goes to school is not only aware of hot lines for troubled children, but can very clearly state that every child has his or her own rights and there is such a thing as child abuse, and it may be prevented or stopped. This is an enormous achievement for today's children compared to the previous generation of youngsters, who never talked or even heard about possibilities of legally protecting themselves or claiming their own rights before age 18.

Women, even if they are pretty desperate about their family situations with abusive husbands, are no longer restricted to blaming fate or going to church asking for patience and endurance. They can now also weigh all the pros and cons of various women's support organizations or even shelters. Even if a woman doesn't know an exact name and address of such a place or institution, she knows that it exists in her town or in the nearest larger city, and can find information about it much more easily than in the mid-1990s.

Advertising has started to play its role not only in selling goods, but also for the benefit of nonprofit organizations. It took about 15 years after the beginning of Perestroika, but now nonprofit commercials and wall posters are the same reality as are educational hours in schools and various talks about human rights and their protection on the radio and TV.

Ongoing westernization of Russia brings western way of thinking to various spheres of life, slowly changing old stereotypes to modernized perceptions of career building, childrearing, gender roles, protection of personal interests. Growth of individual-oriented resources, services, and institutions, openness of information on a much higher level all across the country contribute significantly to a revised understanding of one's opportunities in life, human rights in general, and their realization in a given situation, place, and time. Taking into consideration all the devastating numbers and stories described in this chapter, it's too early to report a radical improvement in the area of family violence in Russia yet, but one can definitely see a hopeful perspective in the dynamic of governmental policies, efforts of domestic, world and European committees and organizations, some signs of life stabilization and gradual economic and industrial restoration, information boom, and many other factors.

Also there are many changes happening to people's implicit theories of violence in families, which was reflected in many answers to our survey. People's everyday judgments influence their everyday behavior, and even a slight liberalization and modernization of old conservative attitudes toward family life has an enormous effect on hundreds of thousand of men, women, children, and elders. Moreover, acceptance of changes is the first step toward letting change happen in one's life, so that knowing about people's new attitudes toward and perceptions of family violence in a particular country may make a contribution to a global fight for human's rights. We are very grateful to all participants of our survey for sharing their opinion and for providing a detailed illustration of current thoughts in Russian society.

ACKNOWLEDGMENTS

We would like to express our gratitude to Elena Zaretsky and the Gaynulliny family for their assistance in recruiting participants for our study.

REFERENCES

Achildieva, Y. F. (1997). Atypical family: Research conventionality or objective reality? In Y. F. Achildieva (Ed.), *Atypical family: The standard of living and social status* (pp. 5–8). Moscow: Idz-vo "Stankin."

Adamushkina, M. (1995, October 31). Domestic violence? There is no such a problem. *Nezavisimaia Gazeta*, p. 6.

Altshuler, B., Kushnir, L., & Severny, A. (2000, September). A statement by the human rights program "Right of Child." *Press conference at the National Institute of Press*, Moscow, Russia.

Altshuler, B., & Severny, A. (2000, September). *Russia: State violence against children*. Russian NGOs' Written Contribution to the UN Committee on the Rights of the Child Day of General Discussion.

Arai, M., Perlitsh, H. D., & Erdyneev, A. (2000, August). *Career development issues among Siberian and American women college students*. Poster session presented at annual meeting of the American Psychological Association, Washington, DC.

Berrien, F., Aprelkov, G., Ivanova, T., Zhmurov, V., & Buzhicheeva, V. (1995). Child abuse prevalence in Russian urban population: A preliminary report. *Child Abuse & Neglect, 19*, 261–264.

Berrien, F. B., Safonova, T. Y., & Tsimbal, E. I. (2000). Russia. In B. M. Schwartz-Kenney, M. McCauley, & M. A. Epstein (Eds.), *Child abuse: A global view* (pp. 195–207). Westport, CT: Greenwood Press.

Horne, S. (1999). Domestic violence in Russia. *American Psychologist, 54*, 55–61.

Human Rights Watch Report. (1997). *Russia: Too little, too late: State response to violence against women in Russia* (No. 7, p. 5).

Klimenkova, T. (1998). Realization of civil rights of freedom from violence. In *Women's rights in Russia: Research of real practices and public awareness* (pp. 1–391). Moscow: MFF.

Kuznetsov, B. (1999). Report of the Petrozavodsk city police department on the changes to constitution. Article #6 on stopping family violence. Available: www.projectharmony.ru/chto/statistics.html

Ogorodnikova, O. (1995). *Children are weeds on the Russian flower bed*. Available: www.ug.ru/95.24/240201.html

Russian Annual Statistical Report. (2000). *Goskomstat Rossii* [State Bureau of Statistics], p. 99.

The Russian Association of Crisis Centers for Women. (1995). *Report for the nongovernmental forum of the United Nation's fourth world conference on the status of women: Violence against women in Russia*. Moscow.

Shtyleva, L. (2000). *Report at the Kola Peninsula congress of women*. Available: www.wcons.org.ru

Tsimbal, E. I. (1997, March). *Extrafamilial and intrafamilial sexual abuse in children*. Paper presented at the National Conference on children in Russia: Violence and Defense, Moscow.

Timofeeva, I. (2002). *Sotsial'no-psykhologicheskie faktory zhestokogo obraschenija s zhenschinami v sem'e*. Doctoral dissertation. UDK 159.9:316.356.2

8

Greece

Georgia Stathopoulou

CAPSULE

Research on family violence in Greece has been so limited that it is difficult to determine the extent of its prevalence, its nature, and its consequences. However, there are several indications that family violence is a significant problem for Greek society. According to a 1999 survey in European Union countries, Greece had the highest level of domestic abuse. This high incidence of domestic abuse is most often attributed to the lower status of women in Greek society. Among the main reasons for the lack of sufficient information is the very limited reporting of family abuse. Greek victims are often reluctant to report abuse because of the social emphasis on the close-knit structure of the family and the subsequent need to preserve family ties as well as insufficient protection of the victims by the law enforcement and legal authorities.

Child abuse and neglect have been addressed only in the last 15 years. Much of the research has approached child maltreatment from a cultural perspective, emphasizing Greece's transition from a traditional society to an industrialized member of the European Community. Some of the factors reported by Nakou, Stathacopoulos, and Agathonos (1987) include the value of sons and high expectations of their behavior, sexual tension between the sexes promoted by cultural codes of conduct, and life-long obligations of children toward their parents. It is estimated that only a very small percentage of child abuse and neglect cases are reported to the legal system, although reporting has increased, probably due to increased public awareness. Sexual child abuse remains a strongly taboo issue in contemporary Greek society. As a result, it has neither been ad-dressed in the literature nor provided for by the Greek legal system.

Elder abuse is the least studied form of family violence in Greece, but the ex-tant studies indicate that abuse of older family members is not an unknown phe-nomenon in Greek society. According to a recent study (Pitsiou-Darrough & Spinellis, 1995), the elderly are at risk for multiple forms of family abuse, the most prevalent of which is verbal assault; women and the younger elderly (be-low 70 years old) are the most frequent victims.

THE GREEK SAMPLE

Our Greek sample consisted of 79 participants (29 men and 50 women) from urban centers as well as 31 participants (18 men and 13 men) from a small village on the island of Crete. The urban sample, recruited mainly from Ath-ens, represented a wide range of ages (16 to 83 years old), as well as socio-economic status and education (ranging from 6 to 20 years of education). The rural sample was recruited from Malaxa, a small mountain village on Crete with a population of around 80 people. The income of the inhabitants is derived from small-scale farming, wage labor, and pensions. In Malaxa, the nuclear and extended family households are the basic units of social re-lations and personal loyalty. Participants ranged in age from 25 to 84 years and were very homogeneous in social class and education. The rural sam-ple provided data only on domestic abuse (from wife to husband as well as from husband to wife).

Greek Participants' Definitions of Abuse

Greek respondents frequently defined abuse as the violation of human rights; [abuse is] "any violation of human rights as well as any form of vio-lence among people" (female, 28 years old); "when you treat somebody in the worst possible way without acknowledging the fact that he is a human being with exactly the same rights as you" (male, 30); and "lack of respect towards an individual's emotional and physical well-being, as well as any action that purposefully violates the individual rights of the person" (fe-male, 29). Related to this theme was a definition of abuse as inequality among humans; "when people treat each other badly, when they don't ac-knowledge the equality among people, and in extreme cases any kind of vi-olation, either physical or emotional, from the stronger to the weaker one" (female, 44).

Another common theme was abuse as an assault on someone's personal-ity; [abuse is] "to impose things on others, to harm others either physically or emotionally, to destroy somebody's personality" (female, 26); "abuse can take many forms: assault on somebody's personality (profession, appearance, mental capacity, etc.) as well as emotional and physical violence" (female, 30); "any form of oppression of somebody's will, thinking, and emotions; the oppression of a human soul by different means such as guilt, emotional burdening, that others might impose on an individual's personality" (male, 25); and "any kind of behavior (physical and emotional abuse) that assaults the individual's personality and undermines his self-esteem" (female, 34). These responses reflect the political and ideological background of Greek people. Additional definitions of abuse included the "dehumanizing treatment of other people" (female, 21); "any kind of coercion" (male, 59); "any kind of oppression" (male, 42); as well as "financial exploitation," "sexual violence," "lack of respect," "violation of boundaries," and "criticism."

THE GREEK MACROSYSTEM

Violence in the Media

As in many countries, the Greek media portrays considerable violence, including domestic violence. A 1998 study of eight TV programs revealed 390 scenes of violence against adults. In 83% of the domestic abuse scenes, women were the victims, whereas men were the "victims" (usually in comic scenes) in only 17% of those scenes. The programs reinforced Greek cultural gender stereotypes of submissive women tolerating the abusive behavior of strong and authoritative men (Papamichael, 1999). A second study (Koronaiou, 2000) revealed that 60% of reality TV shows present themes of violence against women and portray the victims as masochistic women who consciously or unconsciously desire their own victimization. Koronaiou (2000) concluded that these shows further victimize female victims of violence by portraying them as responsible for their abuse.

The Status of Women

Although the Greek legal system is considered to be one of the most feminist ones in Europe, gender inequality is prevalent in every domain of social, economic, and political life. Out of the 300 Parliament members elected in 2000, only 31 were women. Despite the fact that Greek law requires equal pay for equal work, recent data (1998) from the National Statistical Service show that women's salaries in manufacturing were 71% of men's in comparable positions; in retail, women's salaries were 88% of men's.

The National Report of Greece provides data from the Ministry of Justice on the judicial approach to rape for the years 1986, 1987, and 1992 (Republic of Greece, 1996). The data indicated that a) the number of people convicted for rape is very small and b) the Courts impose more lenient sentences in crimes of violence against women than indicated by law. Factors appearing to discourage rape victims from seeking justice include lengthy procedures, difficulty finding witnesses, and forensic reports referring to the victims' previous sexual life, including whether or not they were virgins. Moreover, rape in marriage does not constitute a separate crime.

The general provisions of the Civil Law penalize physical violence against women in the family, as well as insult of personality. There is no separate provision for psychological abuse, although it can be considered an injury against an individual's personality and therefore covered by the general provisions of the Civil and Penal Code. However, the data indicate that battered women almost never take their cases to the courts, probably discouraged both by the legal procedures and by Greek culture's emphasis on the integrity of the family and woman's role as all enduring, self-sacrificing primary caretaker.

Police practices also contribute to underreporting of violence against women. The official data of the Ministry of Public Order and statistics from Police Precincts throughout Greece show that only a small percentage of abused women (0.06%) go to the police. The National Report of Greece (1996) concluded that the number of women who complain to the police but who do not press charges is probably large, but no exact estimate is possible because these cases are not recorded. Since 1999, GSES, in cooperation with the Ministry of Public Order, has undertaken training programs on how to treat domestic abuse victims.

The Status of Children

The Greek Civil Code provides that adulthood is reached at 18 years, at which age the individual can engage in all legal transactions without a legal representative. Upon the completion of the 15th year of age, children can participate in a labor contract with parental consent. The legal age of consent is 15 years for sexual activity and 18 years for marriage. The Court can allow marriage even before the age of 18 if the wedding is imperative.

Parental care is defined in the Greek Civil Code as the care of underage children, which is considered both a parental privilege and a duty, and is mutually exercised by both parents. It involves caretaking of the underage child, managing the child's property, and legally representing the child. Greek law has directly or indirectly provided the following criteria for determining the child's interest: a) the child's attachment bonds to his/her parents and siblings, b) the child's capabilities and personal tendencies, c) the child's own opinion, depending on age and maturity, d) factors allowing the child to develop as a responsible, socially conscientious individual, without any discrimination on the basis of gender, e) the stability of the child's developmental conditions, and f) the child's attachment to people outside his or her immediate family.

The Elderly in Greek Society and Family

Greek culture is defined by interdependence among its members, and co-residence of the elderly with their children is one expression of this interdependence. Thirty-nine percent of the elderly (in rural areas the percentage rises to 40%) live with their children, 25% live with their children and their children's families, 10% live with their single/widowed/divorced children, and 4% live with their grandchildren (Georgoule, Kondlyle, Chandanos, & Chatzevarnava, 1996). The institutionalization of the elderly carries social stigma for the whole family and is extremely limited: 0.8% of the elderly Greek population lives in nursing homes, whereas in Western Europe, elderly who live in nursing homes represent 8–11% of the total population (Symeonidou, 1996).

THE GREEK MICROSYSTEM

It is difficult to describe the Greek family microsystem without attending to differences between urban and rural families. According to Agathonos-Georgopoulou and Tsangari (1999):

1. In traditional rural families, family members are closely connected and collectivistic, forming well-organized, protective webs of cooperative interdependent functions and roles. By contrast, urban families are isolated and lacking in supportive networks.

2. In rural families, family roles are predetermined, attachment bonds are unbreakable, and life is quite predictable. In urban families, communication is more limited, family roles are less clear, and life is hard and unpredictable.

3. In rural families, there is intense communication between children and their parents, without many outbursts of anger and agitation. In urban families, children grow up in a context of social loneliness, alienation, confrontation, and desperation. Parents, overwhelmed by their own struggles for survival, often ignore the child's need for encouragement, support, and role models.

DOMESTIC VIOLENCE

According to the National Report of Greece to the UN Commission for the Elimination of All Forms of Discrimination Against Women (1996), there have been unsurpassed difficulties in establishing the extent, nature, seriousness, and consequences of domestic violence in Greece. A 1999 survey of European Union countries showed that 1 in 5 Greek women had been physically abused at least once by a husband or partner. Even this figure is likely to be an underestimate due to the Greek view that "domestic affairs should never become public." It is estimated that only 1 in every 20 cases of battered women report their case to the legal system.

Data from the Center for Abused Women in Greece show that from 1990 to 2000, 3,000 women sought assistance from the Center. The majority of these women had been in an abusive situation for 3 to 4 years, and had exhausted all other means of improving the relationship with their partners. A significant number visited the Center to request assistance for their batterers, who in most cases were unaware of the woman's actions. At the Shelter for Abused Women, 200 women with 250 children sought protection from 1993 to 2000. The women's ages were from 16 to 75 years old, and the children were from 30 days to 19 years old. The women had been maltreated in a variety of ways; 80% reported both physical and sexual abuse. Fifteen percent of the women who sought shelter eventually returned to their abusive husbands.

In a survey of 100 battered wives, Epivatianos and Vasileiadis (1981) found that the vast majority had been subjected to long-term physical abuse. The women attributed the battering primarily to their partners' irritability, infidelity, alcoholism, mother, gambling, and jealousy, although a few women also mentioned their partner's laziness, financial disputes, issues of dowry, and their own infidelity. Epivatianos and Vasileiadis concluded that although Greek husbands are considered both more authoritative and more repressive than husbands from other European countries, they do not hit their wives "all that much"; moreover, they concluded, Greek wives are more accepting, and "do not go to extremes" like reporting or divorcing their husbands.

In a recent study of 676 women (Antonopoulou, 1999), 230 (34%) reported being either exposed to or victims of domestic abuse in their childhood. Twelve women (2%) reported sexual violence. Of the women victimized by domestic violence, 66% had been battered by their spouse and 33% by their father. Approximately half of the respondents believed that women's demands for equality and access to employment provoke violence. One third of the men, and 10% of the women, endorsed an item that women should be obedient at home. Antonopoulou concluded that partner violence occurs within a context of social attitudes stressing the inequality of women.

Greek Participants' Perspectives on Wife Abuse

In our sample, implicit theories of abuse—particularly judgments of extreme abuse—varied depending on sex of perpetrator. All or the urban participants and nearly 90% of the rural participants referred to some form of physical aggression in giving an example of extreme wife abuse—but over 30% of the rural respondents indicated that physical aggression was severe only when it was unjustifiable. A 40-year-old Athenian woman said extreme wife abuse is "when the husband beats his wife to the point he leaves physical marks on her," and a 24-year-old Athenian man said extreme abuse is "severe physical abuse for an unjustified reason." In the rural sample, the only circumstance specified as justifying physical violence against a wife was her "sexual infidelity": 28% of the rural males and 15% of the rural females indicated that physical abuse would be justifiable in that situation. Only 1 man and 2 women cited the husband's sexual infidelity as extreme abuse toward the wife. The data reflect the implicit theory, still prevalent in rural Greece, that men's honor depends on the behavior of the women of their family.

Sexual abuse in the form of *rape* was a common example of wife abuse in the urban sample (approximately 30%). It was most often considered extremely abusive (25 cases), but also as moderate (5 cases), and mild (4 cases). According to a 56-year-old woman "[extreme wife abuse is] when the husband coerces the wife into unnatural sexual acts," whereas according to a 26-year-old man "[moderate wife abuse is] when the husband rapes his wife." The same man's example of extreme wife abuse was "when the husband is sexually unfaithful to his wife." The husband's sexual infidelity was often reported as either the cause of some form of abuse or as a form of abuse itself. An example of extreme wife abuse from a 26-year-old woman was "when he openly demands to have an extramarital affair." Another 26-year-old female said that extreme wife abuse was "like when a male member of my extended family beat his wife when she threatened him that she would reveal his extramarital affair to their relatives." The frequent mention of sexual abuse in our respondents' answers is a significant finding because sexual abuse, although suspected as a frequent form of women's domestic abuse, is neither mentioned frequently in the literature nor addressed by the Greek legal system.

Although our participants' definitions of domestic abuse emphasized physical aggression, their implicit theories of abuse also encompassed psychological aggression. A 26-year-old male gave, as an example of wife abuse, "when the husband puts psychological pressure on his wife, especially when he is the only one who works outside the house, she has no income and therefore, is dependent on him." Emotional abuse in the form of restraining a wife's personal freedom or choices was frequently listed as either moderate or mild abuse—for example, "when he doesn't allow her any individual rights, doesn't allow her to hold her personal opinion" (female, 30); "when the husband imposes his opinion on his wife, without taking into consideration her own" (female, 46); "when the husband does not allow his wife to take any initiatives" (female, 19); and "when, during an argument over a financial household situation, the husband insults the intellectual abilities of his wife" (female, 30).

Greek Participants' Perspectives on Husband Abuse

Implicit theories of husband abuse conceptualized it primarily as nonphysical aggression. Across all the levels of abuse, the most frequent example of husband abuse was verbal abuse. A common example was to "talk back to him," and nearly a third of both male and female respondents indicated that it was moderately abusive for a wife to "insult her husband in public." (Only 2 participants, both women, cited being insulted in public as a moderate form of wife abuse.) Physical aggression was listed as a form of husband abuse by only 24 participants (16 defined it as extreme and the other 8 as moderate).

The wife's sexual infidelity was a common example of extreme abuse (cited by 20% of respondents). Additional forms of extreme husband abuse were "emotional abuse," "financial exploitation," "neglect," "indifference for his preferences," and "divorce." Some respondents perceived it as extremely abusive for a wife to challenge her husband's traditional patriarchal authority. For example, a 19-year-old female said it was extremely abusive "when she doesn't fulfill his needs—cooking, housekeeping, social needs, etc.," and a 46-year-old woman said it was abusive "when the wife has her own separate bank account." A 16-year-old girl said moderate husband abuse was "when she doesn't let him watch TV" and a 64-year-old woman said it was abusive "when she goes to visit her girlfriends in the neighborhood." A 34-year-old woman said it was mildly abusive "when the wife does not allow him to participate in childrearing."

The "failure of a wife to take care of her husband" was given as an example of abuse by over half of both the male and female respondents. These findings are relevant to an ongoing debate among sociologists on the significance of gender-specific power in Greek social life. Some sociologists argue against the notion of gender inequality in rural Greece, asserting instead that women control the domestic area, whereas men dominate in the public domain (Dubisch, 1986).

CHILD ABUSE AND NEGLECT

Research on Child Abuse and Neglect in Greece

Greece started to address the issue of child abuse and neglect in the late 1980s, when two professionals, a social worker and a pediatrician, first brought attention to the issue in the biggest children's hospital in Athens.

For years "culturally defined attitudes towards parental roles contributed to the strong resistance, not only of the general public but of the professionals as well, in recognizing that appropriate parenting is not an infallible innate attribute of the parent" (Kokkevi & Agathonos, 1987, p. 94). Early research was directed at the identification of specific risk factors in child-abusing families. For example, Kokkevi and Agathonos (1987) found that abusive mothers were characterized by lower intellectual functioning, seclusiveness, and lower self-control than were nonabusive mothers. Interestingly, though, abusive fathers did not seem to differ in either intellectual functioning or psychological profile from nonabusive fathers.

Kokkevi and Agathonos (1987) attributed their finding that more child abusers were mothers than fathers to the sociocultural context of parental roles in Greece:

> It is too easy for the young, socially isolated Greek mother to turn to her children seeking the satisfaction that her husband cannot grant. A young, needy baby can never satisfy such needs. Disappointment, emotional deprivation, role reversal, and unrealistic expectations lead to violence vented on a child rather than to dialogue: an alternative reaction may be total resignation from the mothering role which leads to neglect. (p. 98)

Among the social characteristics found in child-abusing families are early marriage (85%), low educational level (76%), and unemployment or unsteady employment (41%) (Agathonos, Stathakopoulou, Adam, & Nakou, 1982). In a study of 197 physically abused children and their families, and a control group of 163 nonabusing families, Agathonos-Georgopoulou and Browne (1997) identified the following microsystem and exosystem predictors of child maltreatment: parental mental health problems, poor relationship between parents, parents with adverse life experiences, mothers' strict discipline by their own parents, frequent life events for the parents in the previous year, lack of social support for the mother, and unsteady employment of the father.

A study in the semiurban town of Volos showed that among the children who visited the town's Center of Mental Health in a 3-year period, 32 (8%) were victims of abuse (Zoumbou, 1993). Of these, 53% had been physically abused, 25% neglected, and 22% sexually abused. Boys were much more frequently victims of physical abuse than were girls (78% boys and 31% girls), girls were more often victims of sexual violence than were boys (33% girls and 7% boys), and girls were more often victims of neglect than were boys (33% girls, 14% boys). Only the victims of child sexual abuse visited the Center explicitly because of abuse, whereas children subjected to physical abuse or neglect had sought help for psychosomatic or psychological symptoms.

Child-abusing parents often use violence and/or neglect of the child as a disciplinary action. Potamianou and Safilios-Rothschild (1970) found that in a sample of healthy children, mothers as often as fathers were the disciplinary agents. By contrast, in a sample of retarded or emotionally disturbed children, the mother, presumably overstressed and impatient, most often punished the child. Most Greek mothers punish most often for inappropriate behavior and poor school performance. By contrast, fathers tend to punish more often for immoral behavior (e.g., stealing, associating with bad peers), in accordance with the cultural stereotype identifying the father as the primary protector of family honor. Physical punishment is used most often in cases of disobedience and poor academic performance (Potamianou & Safilios-Rothschild, 1970, p. 390).

There are also interesting discrepancies between parents regarding the combination of discipline and affection. Greek mothers appear to maintain a balance of punishment and love, permitting them to be severe when it seems necessary and affectionate at other times. However, once Greek fathers assume a disciplinarian role, they appear unable to also assume a warm, supportive role; therefore, their relationship with their children tends to be one of authority–submission in which love and affection have little place on either side (Doumanis, 1983; Potamianou & Safilios-Rothschild, 1970).

Anthropological research has shown similar findings regarding the parent's gender and child discipline in rural Greece. Iossifides (1991) asserted that:

> It is agreed among all the villagers that there is no love like that of a mother for her child ... A father is also said to love his children, but his love is generally not considered to be as "deep" (*vathia*) or "great" (*megali*) as the mother's ... He is the final arbitrator, naughty children being threatened that their father will be told if they do not stop misbehaving. (p. 142)

Iossifides found that the most frequent discipline method, alone or in combination, was physical punishment, most often combined with reprimanding and physical isolation (such as locking up in the basement).

A study by Zarnari (1979) on children's socialization patterns in Greek families revealed that parental discipline of 8-year-old children is influenced by social class and gender. In general, childrearing patterns tended to encourage children's dependency, although low social class families showed stronger support for children's dependence whereas middle and upper class families exhibited more liberal attitudes. The majority of the mothers (82%) reported punishing their children for misbehaving: 52% did not allow their children to engage in activities they enjoyed, 49% used physical punishment, and 28% reprimanded their children. Working-class mothers re-

ported physical punishment more often than did members of the other social classes.

Doumanis (1983), who conducted an observational study of rural Greek
mothers and their children, reported that only rarely did she see rural
mothers spanking their children. In cases when the mother seemed likely to
spank her child harshly, women in her extended family intervened and actively protected both the mother and the child from the mother's anger.
The following excerpt illustrates very vividly how the extended family and
the rest of the community would intervene in such a case:

> When Kostas, who was ten years old, [returned home late for lunch one
> day] . . . [his mother's] anxiety turned to anger for the unnecessary torment
> she had endured and she began shouting, calling him names and threatening
> to beat him to death. In a moment several women and children had gathered
> around her to soothe her, telling her both how justified her anger was and
> how usual is for children that age to forget themselves. While this was going
> on at Kostas' house, an elderly aunt living next door took the child, who had
> just got [sic] back and was in a state of panic, to her own house to spend the
> night. Knowing that this was the best solution for all concerned, the mother
> and father did not argue with the person who informed them about the aunt's
> intervention and only repeated their threats to the child for all to hear. In this
> way the child was made fully aware of the seriousness of his misbehavior hav-
> ing indirectly received the harshest of sanctions, being kept away from his
> home, and this without direct punishment from his mother and without cause
> for bitterness. (pp. 65–66)

A more recent attitude study of mothers of 1- to 14-year-old children
(Stathacopoulos & Agathonos, 1987) revealed that children's harsh discipline seems to be the norm in Greece. According to the findings, 10% of the
study mothers reported that they spank their children, 14% shut them in
dark rooms or shout at them, whereas 26% use other kinds of verbal punishment—yet almost all the mothers suggested that dialogue is the best way of
educating children.

A study by Agathonos et al. (1982) on sociomedical outcomes in a sample of 54 abused and/or neglected children ages 0 to 10 years old (mainly
from one children's hospital in Athens) provided the following findings:
bruises and lacerations (42.5%), head injuries (including fractures; 35%),
fractures of long bones (15%), burns and scalds (13%), injuries from a sharp
instrument (9%), and failure to thrive (28%). Twice as many boys as girls
had been either injured or neglected—perhaps because of the greater expectations that Greek parents, especially mothers, have of their sons. The
perpetrator of the abuse and/or neglect was the mother in 39% of the cases,
the father in 26%, both parents in 24%, and others in 11%.

The Secretariat General of the European Commission (1999) recently conducted a study of attitudes toward child abuse among the countries members of the European Union. According to their findings, 68% of Greek people believe that violence against children is either very or fairly common in their country. The Greek respondents considered the following behaviors to be abusive to children: physical punishment by parents (84%), physical punishment by teachers or other "child-minders" (85%), psychological punishment (87%), sexual abuse by parents/relatives (99%). Nearly all of the Greek respondents thought the European Union should be involved in combating child abuse.

The European Commission study also examined people's attitudes regarding potential causes of child abuse. These findings showed that Greeks placed great emphasis on alcohol/drug abuse, unemployment, poverty, low education, personal experiences of abuse in childhood, genetics, the media, and the decline of morality in modern society as potential causes. Regarding the social acceptability of child abuse in Greece, more than 4% found it acceptable in certain circumstances, 60% found it unacceptable in all circumstances but not always punishable by law, and 32% found it unacceptable in all circumstances and always punishable by law. Greek respondents clearly took the lead among all the participant countries in considering child abuse as unacceptable under any circumstances but still not always punishable by law (60% vs. 30% mean average among the European Union countries). Regarding the legal system's efficacy in combating child abuse, 72% of Greeks (compared to 64% mean average of EU countries) reported they do not think their country's laws can be effective in preventing child sexual abuse.

Greek Respondents' Perspectives on Child Abuse

Many of the findings from the Greek and European Union studies are consistent with our own data. The majority of the respondents (81%) listed some form of physical abuse in their examples of extreme child abuse. Among the 28 respondents who gave gender-specific examples of child abuse, 24 identified the father and 4 the mother as the perpetrator. A distinctive characteristic of some examples of extreme physical abuse is their tremendous cruelty—for example, a 68-year-old female wrote "to burn the child with a cigarette or to kill him," a 52-year-old male wrote "to cut the child's head off." Other examples of extreme abuse were "to hit the child with an object or a belt on the head," "to verbally abuse the child to the point that the kid believes he/she will die," "when the child is subjected to frequent and unjustified violence," "to hit the child with either the hand or an object to the point that the child gets bruises," and "severe hitting to the point that the child needs hospitalization."

Sexual abuse was the second most common example of extreme child abuse provided by our respondents (27% of the total sample). Other examples of extreme child abuse included emotional abuse, verbal abuse, neglect, and financial exploitation. The most common examples of moderate and mild child abuse were forms of verbal abuse, but other examples included "physical abuse," "emotional abuse," "neglect," "financial exploitation," "time-out," "withholding of allowance," "lack of respect," and "not providing help with homework."

Although child sexual abuse has been identified by both the European Union and our survey as a major concern, it has not been adequately addressed. This lack of attention may reflect the fact that sexual abuse is a socially taboo topic in Greece. In a recent press release, the Helsinski Monitor expressed concern over the high prevalence and underreporting of child sexual abuse. According to the press release, Tsigris, a criminologist, identified two major reasons for underreporting:

> One is that the interrogating authorities, the prosecutors and the police, dissuade victims of sexual abuse from pressing charges for the violence they suffered because instead of discretely investigating the problem, they essentially treat the victims themselves in an abusive manner. Second is the fact that certain vehicles of the press . . . use the victims to satisfy sensationalist desires, which does everything to discourage the victim from going public in these cases. (Available: www.greekhelsinki.gr/bhr/greek/articles/pr 20 11 01.html)

ELDERLY ABUSE

Coresidence of adult children and their elderly parents, despite its beneficial aspects for both generations, can be a cause of conflict (Symeonides, 1996). Over 91% of one sample of Greek elderly and young people considered it the children's obligation to take care of elderly parents, regardless of the amount of sacrifice required (Georgoule et al., 1996). Nevertheless, Greek elderly report the highest levels of loneliness among the European countries, perhaps because of failed high expectations (Georgoule et al., 1996). Greek culture, with its stress on interdependence, is characterized by a mutual exchange of services and resources; however, the lack of precise rules controlling this exchange, and discrepancies in perceptions of received/provided support, can produce conflict and abuse among the involved parties.

Georgoule et al. (1996) found that among the elders in their sample, 56% were very satisfied with the support they received from their children and/or grandchildren, 22% were relatively satisfied, 11% not very satisfied, and 11% completely unsatisfied. The rank ordering of major causes of conflict between the generations was, according to the elderly: differences in opinion over behavior issues, disagreements over property, disagreements over the caretaking of family members, and ideological–political differences.

Elderly Abuse in Greece

In 1987, the Greek Ministry of Health and Social Welfare, Department of Aging, collected data from Athens hospitals to determine the prevalence of elderly abuse and neglect in Greece. Data from the Principal Orthopedic Hospital in Athens indicated that out of 16,000 patients brought to the hospital for injuries, only 33 cases were diagnosed as beatings (2%). Of these cases, only six (18%) were 65 years old or older. The other hospitals surveyed also revealed few cases of physical abuse against the elderly—an average of about six cases per month. The major problem for the elderly was neglect or abandonment (Pitsiou-Darrough & Spinellis, 1995).

The realization of the limited information available on elderly abuse and neglect, the need to establish national policy on the issue, and the need to inform various international organizations led to the first major study on elderly abuse and neglect in the late 1980s (Spinellis & Pitsiou-Darrough, 1991). The findings indicate that out of 757 respondents, 117 (15%) had suffered some type of abuse within the previous year. Another 109 (14%) knew at least one case of elderly abuse. No examples of major criminal abuse were reported, but a few of the physical abuse cases required hospitalization. The most prevalent form of maltreatment was verbal assault. The service providers reported 131 cases of elderly abuse, including 81 cases of physical abuse and 106 cases of neglect. Twenty-two of the elders reported enduring more than three types of abuse, 10 elderly suffered between 5 and 11 types, and 13 had been subjected to 2 types.

Spinellis and Pitsiou-Darrough (1991) reported the following characteristics of the abused respondents: Women were victimized more often than men, and individuals under the age of 70 suffered more abuse than did persons over the age of 70. Lower percentages of abuse were found among the elderly who lived alone. Most abused elderly lived with relatives (67%), and in many cases (51%), the abuser was a family member. Most abused respondents stated that their health status was not very good. The majority also reported very poor self-concept and life satisfaction. The authors concluded that "recognizing their predicament and unable to find a solution to their problem, these abused elders continue to live in an unhealthy environment" (Pitsiou-Darrough & Spinellis, 1995, p. 57). Fifteen percent of the abused elderly blamed themselves for their condition. In the control group, 16% of the respondents said they had been abused by a family member, 16% had been abused by a perpetrator who was not a family member, and 60% said they did not know their abuser.

The police records of the same period (September 1988–February 1989) revealed that 65 cases of elderly abuse were recorded, among which 54% were cases of male victimization and the rest were cases of female victimization. Most of the victims recorded in the police records were victims of theft or of some other kind of material abuse. Only four records alluded to either verbal or physical abuse. Based on Greek social and legal conditions, we can draw a few conclusions about the findings: Because violence against women is very underreported despite its high prevalence, elderly women are probably less inclined to report their victimization than are men. Because men are most often the owners of the family property, they are more often subjected to material abuse than are women. The socially prescribed gender role of masculinity probably makes cases of material abuse much easier to report by male victims than any other form of either physical or emotional abuse.

Greek Respondents' Perspectives on Elder Abuse

The majority of our participants (56%) listed forms of physical abuse when giving examples of extreme abuse against an elderly parent. The most frequently mentioned reasons were financial disputes or the elder's intrusion into their children's lives. A 43-year-old woman said "[extreme elderly abuse is] when the unemployed son hits his father to take his money." "Neglect" was listed as an extreme form of elderly abuse by 14% of our participants. Other examples of extreme elder abuse included "lack of respect," "indifference to the parents' needs," "verbal abuse," "lack of communication," "financial exploitation," and "placing the parents in nursing homes." According to a 39-year-old male participant, "[extreme elderly abuse] is when the son has left his village and since the time he left he doesn't communicate with his parents."

Nearly 25% of the participants listed some form of verbal abuse as the most common example of moderate elderly abuse, the second most common form being neglect (17%). As a 24-year-old woman indicated "[moderate elderly abuse] is when the adult child yells at his parents and insults them because they don't like the child's friends." A 30-year-old man reported that "[moderate elderly abuse] can be either physical or verbal abuse caused by parental intrusion in the child's personal life." Other forms of moderate elderly abuse include physical abuse, psychological abuse, lack of communication, financial exploitation, strained relationships, and disregard of parental advice. According to a 26-year-old man "[moderate elderly abuse] is when the child doesn't respect the parent, ignores the parent's advice, insults and puts him down in any given opportunity." A 35-year-old woman said "[moderate elderly abuse is] when the adult child is indifferent towards the parents' entertainment and socialization needs."

Frequent examples of mild elderly abuse were "indifference towards the parents' needs," "verbal abuse," and "social isolation." For example, according to a 59-year-old man, mild elderly abuse is "when the child visits the parent and doesn't stay for long enough." A 20-year-old man said "[mild elderly abuse is] when the child gets bored when he spends time with his parent and leaves the parent alone when he needs company." Additional forms of mild elderly abuse included "lack of financial support," "neglect," "lack of communication," "financial exploitation," and "disrespectful behavior." A 24-year-old man said "[mild abuse is] the child's denigration of the parent and to make him believe that he is not useful."

Although "placing the elderly in nursing homes" was given as an example of both extreme and moderate elder abuse, other participants said it was moderately abusive "when the children cohabitate with their parents in order to get their assistance and support." A 39-year-old man said "[moderate abuse is] when the son or daughter make the parent live with them so that they can have their pension money or any other kind of income." Another 39-year-old man said "[mild abuse is] when the elderly parents live with their child and the child's family and they are isolated and their only duty is to take care of their grandchildren."

INTERVENTION AND PREVENTION

Recently, the Greek Government, through the Secretariat for Equality, has launched multimedia campaigns to raise public awareness concerning family violence. It has also established services to provide support to victims of domestic abuse.

In the Greek Penal Code, there is no provision regarding the protection of childhood or youth as independent legal entity. Disciplinary acts that do not violate current social values do not constitute violations of the Penal Code. Socially accepted disciplinary methods include reprimands, the restriction of recreational and entertaining activities, restriction of personal freedom, and corporal punishment. The most recent revision of Family Law (Article 1329/83 in the Penal Code) provides that such disciplinary action is permitted if it is necessary for the child's development and does not assault the child's personality. It is clear that this provision leaves considerable room for a judge's interpretation. If the Court decides that a parent has abused the social limits, it can subject him or her to at least a 3-month sentence or to a tougher sentence if the parent has committed additional illegal acts against the child.

In Civil Law, the term *child maltreatment* refers to all cases of child abuse and neglect. The term is useful because it covers cases not addressed by the Penal Code, such as emotional abuse or neglect of the child's emotional growth and educational advancement. In these cases, although the perpetrator cannot be legally prosecuted by the Penal Code, the child's interests are protected by the Civil Code. In cases of mismanagement of parental care, the Civil Code provides for either partial or whole removal of parental care from either one or both of the parents.

It is estimated that only a very small percentage of cases of child abuse and neglect are reported to the legal system, as is true of other forms of family violence. However, in recent years, this percentage has been growing, probably due to increased public awareness. The Penal Code (Article 40) provides that every citizen who becomes aware of a child abuse and/or neglect case has the obligation to report it orally or in writing to the Federal Prosecutor or to Police. However, failure to comply does not entail any legal consequences. Regarding sexual abuse, Article 336 of the Greek Penal Code can be applied, if physical force is involved—that is, if physical force or the threat of serious and immediate danger is used to force someone into extramarital intercourse or an indecent act. If two or more perpetrators act jointly to perpetrate a rape, or if an act of rape causes the death of the victim, the punishment is imprisonment for at least 10 years.

The Greek Penal Law distinguishes between the following kinds of child sexual abuse: seduction of minors, abduction with consent, abuse of minors, incest and indecency between relatives, insult of sexual dignity, sodomy. Regarding incest, Article 345 of the Penal Code provides that sexual intercourse with blood relatives is punishable for up to 10 years, depending on the exact relationship of perpetrator and victim (e.g., parent vs. sibling). Indecency between relatives (Article 346) is punished with imprisonment of up to one year. "Insult of sexual dignity" (Article 337), including "unchaste gesticulations or ... proposals regarding unchaste acts," is punishable by imprisonment of not more than a year or a fine. It is also a criminal offense for a caretaker to fail to prevent a minor from committing a criminal offense or engaging in prostitution.

Legal Protection of the Elderly

The Greek social and legal systems currently offer little protection and assistance to elderly victims of family violence and neglect (Pitsiou-Darrough & Spinellis, 1995), although the Greek Criminal Code provides some limited direct or indirect protection of the elderly. For example, the Penal Code provides that an elderly person can file a complaint against his abuser with the assistance of a legal representative. Furthermore, elderly people can give a deposition at home in cases when they are either too old or too sick to appear to Court, and their testimony can be used as evidence by the Court (Article 215). However, according to Pitsiou-Darrough and Spinellis (1995), the Penal Code does not provide for elderly victims who, because of diminished mental or physical capacity, become victims of such crimes as illicit appropriation, theft or even extortion, fraud, or sexual abuse or rape.

CONCLUSION

Although it is difficult to estimate the prevalence of family abuse in Greece, there is evidence that it is a social phenomenon of considerable dimension. Recently, there has been an increased awareness of the seriousness of the situation. More research is needed to elucidate the incidence as well as the causes and multiple dimension of family violence. The Greek legal and social services system needs to be reformed in order to address the issue more efficiently.

REFERENCES

Agathonos, H. (1988). Report of Meeting: First European Congress on Child Abuse and Neglect, Rhodes, Greece, April 6–10, 1987. *Child Abuse and Neglect, 12*, 123–128.

Agathonos, H., Stathakopoulou, G., Adam, H., & Nakou, S. (1982). Child abuse and neglect in Greece: Sociomedical aspects. *Child Abuse and Neglect, 6*, 307–311.

Agathonos-Georgopoulou, H., & Browne, K. D. (1997). The prediction of child maltreatment in Greek families. *Child Abuse and Neglect, 21*, 721–735.

Agathonos-Georgopoulou, H., & Tsangari, M. (1999). Εγχειρίδιο για τα δικαιωματα του παιδιου [A manual for children's rights]. Athens: Child Health Institute.

Antonopoulou, C. (1999). Domestic violence in Greece. *American Psychologist, 54*(1), 63–64.

Creatsas, G., Panagiotopoulou, V., Mortzou, M., & Euthymiou, G. (1987, April 6–10). *Factors affecting the punishment of children by their mothers*. Paper presented in the First European Congress on Child Abuse and Neglect, Rhodes, Greece.

Doumanis, M. (1983). *Mothering in Greece: From collectivism to individualism*. London: Academic Press.

Dubisch, J. (Ed.). (1986). *Gender and power in rural Greece*. Princeton: Princeton University Press.

Epivatianos, P., & Vasileiadis, A. (1981). The battered wife syndrome in Greece. *Galinos, 23*, 1047–1052.

General Secretariat for the Equality of the Sexes. (2003). Σπαστε την σιωπη [Break the silence]. Available: http://www.isotita.gr/flash/spaste/spaste1.html

Georgoule, I., Kondlyle, D., Chandanos, G., & Chatzevarnava, E. (1996). Αλληλεγγυη αναμεσα στις γενεες σχεσεις και αλληλουποστηριξη μεταξυ ηλικιωμενων και νεοτερων μελων της ελληνικης οικογενειας [Mutual aid among the generations: Relationships and support between older and younger members of the Greek family]. In National Center for Social Research (Ed.), *Aging and society, Minutes of the Panhellenic Conference EKKE* (pp. 401–429). Athens: National Center of Social Research.

Iossifides, M. (1991). Sisters in Christ: Metaphors of kinship among Greek nuns. In P. Loizos & E. Papataxarchis (Eds.), *Contested identities: Gender and kinship in modern Greece* (pp. 135–155). Princeton: Princeton University Press.

Kokkevi, A., & Agathonos, H. (1987). Intelligence and personality profile of battering parents in Greece: A comparative study. *Child Abuse and Neglect, 11*, 93–99.

Koronaiou, A. (2000). Η θεματικοποιηση του πονου [The portrayal of pain]. In Center for Research of Gender Equality (Ed.), *Breaking the silence: Family violence: A crime behind closed windows* (pp. 80–83). Athens: Kethi Publications.

Kostavara, K. (2000). Αντιμετωπιση των δραστων βασικη προυποθεση για την εξαλειψη της βιας κατα των γυναικων μεσα στην οικογενεια [The confrontation of the perpetrators: Main presupposition for the erasure of violence against women in the family]. In Center for Research of Gender Equality (Ed)., *Breaking the silence: Family violence: A crime behind closed windows* (pp. 32–36). Athens: Kethi Publications.

Papamichael, S. (1999). Η βια στην ελληνικη τηλεοραση και τα τηλεο πτικα προτυπα που συνδεονται με τα δυο φυλα: Τα αποτελεσματα μιας ερευνας [Violence in Greek TV and gender models: The findings of a study]. Ο *Αγωνας της γυναικας, 66/67*, 27–32.

Pitsiou-Darrough, E., & Spinellis, C. D. (1995). Mistreatment of the elderly in Greece. In J. I. Kosberg & J. L. Garcia (Eds.), *Elder abuse: International and cross-cultural perspectives* (pp. 45–64). Binghamton, NY: Haworth.

Potamianou, A., & Safilios-Rothschild, C. (1970). Trends of discipline in the Greek family. *Human Relations, 24*, 387–393.

Republic of Greece, Ministry of the Interior, Public Administration and Decentralization, General Secretariat for Equality. (1996). *National report of Greece to the UN Commission for the Elimination of All Forms of Discrimination Against Women.* Athens: National Printhouse.

Republic of Greece, Ministry of the Interior, Public Administration and Decentralization, General Secretariat for Equality. (2000). *National report of Greece to the UN Commission for the Elimination of All Forms of Discrimination Against Women.* Athens: National Printhouse.

Secretariat General of the European Commission. (1999). Eurobarometer 51.0. *Europeans and their views on domestic violence against children.* Available: http://europa.en.int/comm/public-opinion

Spinellis, C. D., & Pitsiou-Darrough, E. (1991). Elder abuse in Greece: A descriptive study. In G. Kaiser, H. Kurry, & H. J. Albrech (Eds.), *Victims and criminal justice* (pp. 311–338). Freiburg: Eigenverlag Max-Planck-Institute.

Stathacopoulos, N., & Agathonos, H. (1987, April 6–10). *Relationships, expectations and attitudes towards discipline in abusive Greek parents.* Paper presented in the First European Congress on Child Abuse and Neglect, Rhodes, Greece.

Symeonides, C. (1996). Δημογραφικη γηρανση και φροντιδα για τους ηλικιωμενους στην Ελλαδα και στις χωρες της ΕΟΚ [Demographic aging and elderly care in Greece and the countries of European Communion]. In National Center of Social Research (Ed.), *Aging and society: Minutes of the Panhellenic Conference of EKKE* (pp. 93–107). Athens: National Center for Social Research.

Zarnari, O. (1979). Patterns of socialization in the Greek urban family. *Eklogi, D,* 3–11.

Zoumbou, V. (1993). Κακοποιηση–παραμεληση παιδιων στο Βολο. Προβληματα–προοπτικες [Child abuse–neglect in Volos. Problems–prospects]. In H. Agathonos-Georgopoulou (Ed.), *Family, child protection, social policy* (pp. 165–168). Athens: Child Health Institute.

9

Turkey

Alev Yalçınkaya

CAPSULE

Geographically Turkey is in both Asia and Europe. Turkish society values its traditions while adapting to modern living conditions. In the traditional Turkish family, the father is the head of the household and the mother is the caretaker of the children, although this structure varies according to the education of the spouses, urban versus rural origins of the family, working status of the spouses and economic conditions. There are no direct translations of the terms "abuse" and "abusive" in the Turkish language. Harassment (taciz) and misuse (istismar) would be the closest in meaning.

Turkish culture is a culture of relatedness rather than separateness. Parents are expected to support their children in every way, including financially, during their school years and as they begin their family life. Furthermore, parents expect their adult children, especially their sons, to take care of them in old age. Children who do not fulfill these expectations might be considered to be mistreating their parents. Research in the area of abuse toward women, children, and especially the elderly is relatively new. Violence and abuse in the family exist, but relatively little is known about the form it takes or how extensive it is.

Violence toward women, which can occur at all socioeconomic levels, usually takes the form of physical abuse. However, emotional abuse, such as control, belittlement, unequal division of labor, and restriction of freedom, is also very common. There has been scant attention to sexual abuse of women but some evidence suggests that people believe a husband owns his wife sexually.

Protection of women against family violence comes from strong networking of women. In addition, government and nongovernment organizations are taking new steps toward giving women equal rights.

Child physical abuse for disciplining purposes is common—especially for sons. Strict obedience is expected of children, who are also expected to work at an early age. Although female infanticide is not common, sons are valued more than daughters and given more opportunities, such as education. Sexual possessiveness toward females starts at an early age, virginity being valued for daughters. Fathers and other male members of the extended family feel it is their right to protect the daughter's "honor." Child sexual abuse exists, but little is known about it due to the small amount of research and the taboo nature of the subject.

The least studied area is elder abuse. Mostly, adult sons are expected to take care of their elderly parents. This can create a potential for elder abuse, especially of a financial nature. However, in general, the elders of the family are very respected.

THE TURKISH SAMPLE

The Turkish sample consisted of 37 women and 21 men, ranging in age from 20 to 64 years, with a mean of 32. Sixty-eight percent of the respondents were college graduates, 15% high school graduates, 9% college students, and 7% had master's or doctoral degrees. Fifty-one percent of the women and 85% of the men were employed. Forty-nine percent of the women were single, 38% were married, and 13% were divorced. Thirty-eight percent of the men were single, 57% were married, and 5% were divorced. Twenty-three percent of the respondents were living in Istanbul, 45% lived in other areas of Turkey, and 32% were Turks living abroad. Occupations included engineer, government officer, storeowner, lawyer, stockbroker, business, teacher, nurse, researcher, and college professor. All of the respondents grew up in nuclear families.

Turkish Participants' Definitions of Abuse

When asked if they or someone they knew had experienced a situation they considered abusive, 50% of the sample described instances of abusive behavior. Thirteen out of 58 respondents reported that they experienced an abusive situation themselves, and 16 reported that someone they knew had experienced abuse. Most of these experiences were forms of physical abuse, either from a husband to his wife, from parents to children, to the respondents themselves when they were children, or sometimes from other parental figures—for example, "It hurt me very much that my elementary school teacher slapped my face. I think this is moderately or extremely abusive." A large number of respondents also indicated that they or someone they knew had been sexually abused. Two participants reported knowing someone sexually abused by family members—for example, "One of my female friends told me that she has been raped by her brother. I got very angry when I heard that. I still doubt the truth in that story." Fewer people reported emotional abuse. Among the reports of those who did were descriptions of "a controlling father," "a mother's preferential treatment towards her son over her daughter," and "cheating" of the spouses.

When asked to define abuse within family relationships, one of our Turkish respondents, a 46-year-old woman, provided a nice summary of her implicit theory of abuse:

> In our society, patriarchal—in other words male-dominated—culture and family types are still dominating. In their everyday lives, children, young people, and some women are recommended to behave in prescribed forms consisting of duties, as if they don't have any rights to live. This fact is interfering with people's basic human rights, rights of freedom and rights of living freely, and it restricts the life of members of a family. Within such a structure, abuse being at the roots of such thinking exists with all of its dimensions.

THE TURKISH MACROSYSTEM

Turkish History

Turkey has been home to a rich variety of cultures since 6500 B.C., including Hittites, Persians, Macedonians, Romans, Byzantines, and Ottomans. The Turks became fully Muslim by the 10th century. The Ottoman Empire, established in the 11th century, was the last of the Turkish states in the region before Mustafa Kemal Atatürk established today's Turkish Republic in 1923. Among his many reforms was making the new republic a secular state.

Atatürk is admired in Turkey today, not just as a great leader, but also for his big steps toward women's and children's rights. Before 1923, women did not have many rights under family law. For example, there was no lower age limit for marriage, and the husband had the right to divorce his wife, but the wife did not have such a right. If the couple divorced, the husband automatically took all custodial rights of any children. Female children could inherit only half of what male children inherited. In the court, two female witnesses were considered to be equal to one male witness (Çakır, 1994). Under Atatürk's leadership, the 1926 Turkish Civil Code banned polygamy. Women were granted equal rights in divorce and child custody, and in 1934, women were given the vote (İlkkaracan, 1997). As a symbolic sign of the protection of children's rights, Atatürk declared the 23rd of April as National Sovereignty and Children's Day—based on the Grand National Assembly's first meeting on that day in 1920. Every year, Turkey celebrates this day as a national holiday, during which the President and Prime Minister turn over their positions to children who sign executive orders relating to educational and environmental policies, and parliamentarians in the Grand National Assembly are replaced by children who convene a session to discuss children's issues.

Contemporary Turkey

Turkey has a young population, with more than 50% age 30 years and younger, and only 2.3 million out of 56.5 million age 65 years and older. Sixty-five percent of the Turkish population (41 million) live in urban areas, whereas the remainder live in villages (SIS Report, 1990). Urban regions, including big cities like Istanbul (population of 10 million) are industrialized, modern, and cosmopolitan, home to people from all parts of Turkey. Rural regions are traditional and agricultural, providing the entire nation's food, including wheat, vegetables, and fruit. Although there is a blend of subcultures through constant migration, urban areas tend to be more developed and modern than rural ones, with more access to education and technology.

The Turkish Family

The Turkish family is nuclear, authoritarian, and patriarchal. In general, husbands have higher value, prestige, and power than do wives, and older generations have higher status than do younger generations. The role of the extended family is still important (Fişek, 1993). Both husband's and wife's relatives are visited often. These dynamics are important to an understanding of family violence and abuse, because visiting parents and relatives can be a source of conflict and can give rise to husband–wife or wife–husband abuse. Two of our respondents defined the following behavior as abusive: "if a husband or wife speaks badly about the other one to his or her relatives and gossips." Close networking among relatives is associated with social control and feelings of shame and embarrassment, which can have both positive and negative consequences. The positive aspect is the protective value of shame. Perpetrators may fear the shame they face, and reduce the frequency and degree of abuse as a result of being confronted by relatives. However, the negative aspect of shame occurs when the victim does not talk to relatives about being abused. Shaming can also be a form of abuse. Among our participants' examples of abuse were: "to belittle the wife in front of others," "to hit the child in front of others," and "to scold the child in front of other people."

Status of Women

According to 1990 Census of Population Report (SIS Report, 1990), 28% of Turkish women, as compared to 10% of Turkish men, are illiterate. Although the illiteracy rate is still very high for women, there has been a large increase in literacy since 1980, when the rate was 56% for women and 24% for men.

As part of Atatürk's reforms, the marriage age was set at 17 for men and 15 for women. In some cases—for example, pregnancy—a judge can permit the marriage of a woman as young as 14, but only if she is psychologically and physically mature enough to marry (Arın, 1997). Even today, Turkish family law is going through substantial positive changes. In 1996, the adultery law changed in favor of women. Women can no longer be imprisoned for adultery, and they, as well as men, can now use adultery as a basis for divorce. For the first time in the history of the Turkish parliament, a commission was established in 1998 to research gender inequality, and a new law to protect the family was accepted. According to this law, women or children who experience violence can personally apply to the court and ask for a protection order against the perpetrator. If the order is violated, the perpetrator can be arrested and go to jail. In addition, not only the women and children themselves but also any third party can apply to the court directly—without having to go through the police and the state doctor first—for the immediate action of a protection order against the perpetrator (Gülçür, 1999). In 2002, the law defining the husband as the head of the family changed, and husbands no longer have a legal right to final say over the choice of domicile or decisions concerning children.

Other recent laws include a 1998 statute banning virginity tests. Traditionally, in large parts of Turkish society, virginity has been considered a reflection on the honor of a girl and her family, and males consider themselves as guardians of the honor of the young girls in their family. In some cases, girls were forced to have tests proving they were still virgins. The 1998 law says that neither parents nor government officials can force a girl to have a virginity test without her consent.

Status of Children

Children are considered a valuable asset in the Turkish family. Rather than sources of emotional satisfaction, the importance of children is considered to lie in their potential for providing economic assistance in the future, and to ensure the continuance of the family name. Parents typically want their sons to get educated, work, and become successful, whereas they want their daughters to be good wives and have happy marriages (Kağıtçıbaşı, 1981). Middle and upper class families living in urban regions tend to favor a democratic and egalitarian approach to discipline and avoid corporal punishment. However, in the rural regions of Turkey, discipline is often inconsistent, not based on verbal reasoning, and dependent on adult moods. A common pattern in both urban and rural families is to reward compliance, meekness, respect, and quietness in their children, and punish curiosity, talk, and initiative (Fişek, 1993). Although children are valued, so is their respect and obedience, sometimes to an extreme. In our study, one 46-year-old male respondent defined "too much oppression" as an extreme form of abuse from a parent to a child and "making the child obey" as a mild form of abuse.

Because children are typically expected to conform to their parents' daily routines, young children in some families tend to go to bed at the same time as adults, thus staying up until midnight. It is also a common problem to make use of children in the labor force, and there may be a thin line here between what is culturally acceptable and what would be considered abusive. Children can be sent to the field to help the family with agricultural work and sons can be sent to work as apprentices. The lucky ones might end up learning new skills and open their own businesses at an older age. But in the hands of an abusive master, children can face a lot of maltreatment, including physical abuse. Some parents might accept the beating of their children by the master in the name of discipline. According to an old Turkish saying, a parent sending his child to a master, adds, "his flesh is yours, his bones are mine." Girls are lucky not to be sent out to apprenticeships, but are usually apprentices to their mothers at home, learning to cook and clean the house at an early age—to become good candidates for future marriages.

Since 1998, education has been compulsory up to the age of 14 and according to the Human Rights Reports (2000), "the Turkish government is committed to furthering children's welfare and works to expand opportunities in education and health, including a further reduction in the infant mortality rate."

VIOLENCE TOWARD WOMEN

Rates of Physical Violence Against Women

In recent years, Turkey has seen an increasing interest in and effort against violence toward women. Among the few studies in the area of family violence, a significant number have focused on physical abuse of women. In

Esmer's (1991) study, 116 couples in Istanbul were interviewed. Forty-four percent of the respondent women reported having been beaten by their husbands at least once and 54% of the husbands admitted to having battered their wives. For husbands who beat their wives, the major reason seemed to be that the wives "did not do as they were told." In another survey (PIAR, 1992), out of 1,181 women, 22% reported having been physically abused by their husbands. Forty-five percent of these women felt helpless in this situation; only 25% could develop a strategy to defend themselves from the beatings. In a nationwide survey of 2,479 women, 30% of the respondents reported having been physically abused by their husbands (AAK, 1995; Gülçür, 1999). In a study of 140 abused and nonabused women, Yüksel (1985) found that 62% of the domestic violence that was reported started during the first year of marriage. Forty-one percent of the abused women, and 44% of the abusing husbands had a high school education and higher (Yıldırım, 1998).

Turkish Participants' Judgments Concerning Violence Against Women

Despite these high prevalence rates, the KAMAR survey (1990; Yıldırım, 1998) in 23 cities with 2,007 people revealed that 64% of their respondents did not approve of husbands beating their wives—but 27% did. In our study, qualitative analysis of Turkish respondents' answers to how they define abuse from a husband toward his wife revealed beating as the most frequent response. Specifically, 23 people gave "beating" as an example of abuse from a husband toward his wife, whereas only 6 people said that beating was a type of abuse from a wife to a husband. One of our female participants described her experience:

> 25 years ago my family did not accept my current husband whom I wanted to marry on the basis of mutual love, common worldview and common hearts. As a result of my resistance and my decisiveness, I was being beaten by my father, who has feudal values, and by my two uncles (I was 21 years old), when my brother who is 4 years younger than me and who was 17 at the time, coincidentally came home. Being a witness to this scene, he went to the kitchen, grabbed a knife, and attacked my father and uncles, took me out of their hands, and took me out of the house with his hands which were cut with broken glass during all that struggle.

As in several other cultures, implicit theories of spousal abuse seemed to vary depending on the gender of the perpetrator. Examples that came up as a form of abuse from a wife toward her husband, but not from a husband toward his wife were as follows: "disobedience," "doing things without permission from husband," "flirting with other men," "not being understanding and supporting," "not taking his feelings seriously," "asking for equality," "doing what she wants," "turning everything into a problem and causing tension," "lying," and "criticizing husband through jokes." These findings parallel those of the Hacettepe University's Consensus Survey (1988), which found that 45% of men believed that a husband has the right to beat his wife if she does not obey him. Sixty-six percent of the men believed that the husband was the sole authority at home and that wives had to obey their husbands. According to the results of the AAK study (1995), the wives' disobedience was the major reason reported by all respondents in 525 families in which the wives were abused. Other reasons were economic (28%) and alcohol (15%). In Yüksel's study (1985), women stated that beating occurs when women raise their voice because of their husband's drinking or gambling (Yıldırım, 1998). Three of our respondents also reported that a wife's "raising her voice or shouting at her husband" was abusive.

Gülçür (1999) asked 155 women in Ankara how often they argued with their husbands. Twenty-two percent reported that they argued with their husbands very frequently, 69% said they argued rarely, and 9% said they never argued with their husbands. More than half of the women said they did not believe their husbands had the right to use violence, 37% said their husbands had the right to use it some of the time, while 6% said they believed their husbands usually or always had that right.

Outcomes of Violence Toward Women

According to Gülçür (1999), only half of her respondents subjected to violence took some countermeasures. Twenty-eight percent did not talk to her husband for some period of time, 23% temporarily left home; and 7% asked for help from friends, family, or neighbors and left home permanently. Only 6% went to a doctor or hospital, called the police, applied to a social service worker or institution, or went to a women's shelter. No respondent reported having filed a legal complaint. Abused women who stayed in their marriages gave as reasons protection of children (40%), economic constraints, and not having anywhere else to go (33%; AAK, 1995; Yıldırım, 1998).

Other Types of Abuse Toward Women

In spite of the law describing marriage as "an institution which provides people with a means to fulfill their sexual needs in accordance with the law and for this reason, the issue of rape should not appear in a marriage," marital rape is a problem in Turkey (Arın, 1997). In Gülçür's study (1999), in addition to the 39% of women who had experienced physical violence, 89% had been subjected to one or more forms of psychological violence, and

16% had been forced to have sex by their husbands. While 5% had been threatened with economic restrictions, 3% had been locked inside the home, 6% had been forced to remain at home due to threats involving the children, and 3% had been subjected to other categories of violence. We had parallel results in our study. Our participants reported the following abusive behaviors from a husband to his wife: "expect her to work hard," "cheat," "control her life and restrict her freedom," "belittle in company," "forced sex," "neglect," "threat," "shout, curse," "insult," "not giving her any choice," "not letting her work," "telling her that something she buys was not necessary," "jealousy," and "financial exploitation."

Abuse Against Husbands

Although there appears to be little attention to the issue of husband abuse in the public and scholarly literature in Turkey, our respondents provided evidence that their implicit theories of spousal abuse did include a conceptualization of abuse by wives—a conceptualization that emphasized psychological aggression. Their examples included "cheat," "restrict freedom," "belittle in company," "neglect," "raise her voice," "scold, insult," "use finances without responsibility," and "do not do her duties."

CHILD ABUSE

Child abuse and neglect is a new topic for Turkish society. Turkish researchers began focusing on child abuse and neglect in late 1980s. Little research has been published in international journals (Baral, Kora, Yüksel, & Sezgin, 1998; Oral et al., 2001). It is mostly pediatricians, psychiatrists, and psychologists who bring public, professional, and governmental awareness to child abuse and neglect in the Turkish society (Baral et al., 1998; Oral et al., 2001).

In one of the few studies, Bilir, Arı, and Dönmez (1986; Oral et al., 2001) evaluated 5,000 children. Their study revealed that 36% of the children less than 5 years of age reported that they had been physically abused at some point in their lives. Within another clinical population Oral et al. (2001) found that 60% of 50 psychiatric patients (23 males and 27 females), ranging in age from 1 month to 25 years, had been physically abused; 26% had been sexually abused; 20% had been severely neglected; and 18% had been emotionally abused. In most cases, different types of abuse existed together. The offender was the father in 34 cases, the mother in 22 cases, stepfather in four cases, stepmother and aunt in two cases each, a relative, an older sibling, and a neighbor in one case each. Multiple offenders were involved in 17 cases, both parents being the perpetrators in 11.

Among our respondents, nearly half made reference to physical aggression by parents. For example, one 37-year-old woman identified "beating" as an extreme form of child abuse. A 22-year-old man identified "beating to the point of hospitalization" as extreme, "beating badly" as moderate, and "beating" as mild child abuse. More than half of the respondents mentioned some form of emotional abuse. One 36-year-old woman said that "a parent who scolds, beats and belittles their child, especially in front of other people" is an example of an extreme abuse. Her example of moderate abuse was "not appreciating a child who is trying to please his/her parent" and mild abuse was "not loving the child ... and having a military type of discipline."

In a review of child sexual abuse research, Baral et al. (1998) found that all of the offenders were male and most of the victims were girls. Most of the abusers were fathers, and the oldest daughters were most severely abused. The main differences between Turkey and Western countries were that in Turkey, there was a smaller proportion of stepfathers among the abusers in Turkey and a lower number of occurrences of vaginal penetration. Few of our respondents mentioned sexual abuse when giving examples of child abuse. One 37-year-old female reported that "leading a daughter towards prostitution giving poverty as an excuse" was an extreme form of abuse from a parent to a child.

Another problem concerning children is child labor. In our sample, one 26-year-old female respondent reported that "to give a child too much responsibility, such as making a 10-year-old child do things like picking the sibling up from school, doing shopping and cooking" would be a moderate form of abuse, whereas "constantly insulting a child" would be a moderate form of abuse. The same respondent reported that "locking the child in a small room" would be an extreme form of abuse.

According to Oral et al. (2001) "it is not mandatory to report abuse cases to child protection agencies and there is no distinct child protection agency in Turkey. Physicians treat only the presenting symptoms with limited legal and social intervention on cases of injuries, unless there is a third party asking for legal intervention, or mass media involvement."

ELDER ABUSE

There appears to have been little public attention to the issue of elder abuse in Turkey. As Turkish society values respect toward elders, elderly people are turned to for their wisdom and highly respected. In fact, the custom of kissing the hand of elderly people and putting it to one's forehead as a symbol of respect is still common in Turkey. There is a mutuality between children being taken care of and valued at an early age and elders being taken care of and respected at later years of life. In fact, Kağıtçıbaşı (1981) found that security in old age as a reason for childbearing was considered very important. Young adults, especially the son rather than the son-in-law, are expected to provide financial assistance to their elderly parents when they need it. Yalçınkaya, Turan, and Rapoza (2000) had parallel findings when they compared 61 Turkish and 68 Caucasian American college students' attitudes toward elder abuse. Turkish participants rated an elderly man's financial exploitation by his son as more abusive than did Caucasian American participants. Indeed, echoing these results, one of our respondents in this study, a 34-year-old woman described her experiences:

> A male acquaintance of mine has four daughters and a son. He lost his wife 5 years ago. He had his own house and his pension. While he was living with his divorced son in that house, the son took advantage of his father's soft spot for him, had him sell the house and then spent all the money. In addition to that he asked his father to get credit from the bank, took that money also and disappeared. Now the father on the one hand is paying off his debts from his pension, and on the other hand, he lives with one of his daughters as he has no house to live in. Meanwhile he has to bear with verbal insults from his son. I think this is an extreme case of abuse.

Other examples of elder abuse from our participants included "not taking care of them," "not responding to their needs," "sending them to elder homes," "not listening to them," and "not obeying them."

Implicit theories of abuse in families in many countries may embrace a wider set of relationships than seem typical in the United States. In Turkey, one area of conflict is between mothers- and daughters-in-law. For example, in a hypothetical scenario in the Yalçınkaya, Turan, and Rapoza (2000) study, an elderly mother-in-law who is giving a hard time to her daughter-in-law ends up being given tranquilizers by the daughter-in-law. Turkish college students rated the conflict as more likely to occur in their culture and rated the mother-in-law's behavior as being more abusive than did the American participants (Yalçınkaya et al., 2000). This might reflect the fact that a mother-in-law has higher status than her daughter-in-law, as traditionally a woman's status increases after she gives birth, especially to a son, and then again when she becomes a mother-in-law (Kağıtçıbaşı, 1981). A daughter-in-law has less status than her mother-in-law, and therefore is seen as less privileged—a situation with a potential for elder abuse.

INTERVENTION AND PREVENTION

According to Yıldırım (1998), violence against women started to get media attention in the 1980s. The first important date for this movement was a walk in May 17, 1987—the so-called "No-to-Beating Walk." Twenty-five years later, independent women's groups and women's rights associations, such as Women for Women's Human Rights (WWHR), the Association to Support Women Candidates (Kader), "The Flying Broom" women's advocacy group, the Turkish Women's Union, and the Foundation for the Evaluation of Women's Labor are growing in number and becoming active. Arın (1997) wrote that "since its beginnings in 1980, the greatest achievements of the Turkish women's movement have been that they influenced changes in the Turkish civil and criminal codes." Some of the changes that the Turkish government has enacted in response to the growing awareness of women's rights in Turkey have included the "protection of the family" law which allows women or children who experience violence to apply to the court and ask for a protection order, as well as a change in the law defining the husband as the head of the family to mean that husbands no longer have a legal right to final say over the choice of domicile or decisions concerning children.

In addition to the Turkish government's, NGOs', and activist groups' efforts, the strength of women's networking in Turkey is a cultural fact that might be seen as important in helping to empower women.

The Turkish government has also made important progress in terms of children's rights. Turkey is one of the six original countries to participate in IPEC (International Programme on the Elimination of Child Labor) in 1992 (www.ilo.org), and it ratified the UN Convention on the Rights of Children in 1994. The Turkish government works together with UNICEF and NGOs to protect children's rights in Turkey.

CONCLUSION

Turkish society has started recently—in the last 20 years—to become familiar with the concept of abuse, through the media, the government's progressive changes in family law, nongovernmental organizations' active work, and research in the area of abuse toward women, children, and the elderly. The research indicates that violence toward women and children exists, mostly in the form of physical abuse. Emotional abuse, such as controlling, unequal division of labor, rigid expectations for strict obedience, and restriction of freedom is common, but is culturally accepted and generally not recognized as abusive. Protection of women and children against family violence comes from strong networking of women. Government and nongovernment organizations are taking progressive steps toward giving women and children equal rights. Although in general the elders of the family are very respected, this is an area that needs further study.

ACKNOWLEDGMENTS

Deepest thanks to my cousins Gülnur and Ahmet for their valuable support with the data collection and to all the respondents for sharing their ideas and experiences with us.

REFERENCES

Aile Araştırma Kurulu Genel Müdürlüğü (AAK). (1995). *Aile içi şiddetin sebep ve sonuçları* [Reasons and consequences of violence within families]. Zet Nielsen Research Company, Ankara: Bizim Büro Basımevi.

Arın, C. (1997). The legal status of women in Turkey. *Women for Women's Human Rights Reports*, No. 1. Istanbul, Turkey: Author.

Baral, I., Kora, K., Yüksel, S., & Sezgin, U. (1998). Self-mutilating behavior of sexually abused female adults in Turkey. *Journal of Interpersonal Violence, 13*, 427–437.

Bilir, S., Arı, M., & Dönmez, N. B. (1986). Physical abuse in 16,000 children with 2–4 years of age. *Journal of Child Development and Education, 1*, 7–14.

Çakır, S. (1994). *Osmanlı kadın hareketi* [Ottoman women's movement]. İstanbul: Metis Yayın - ları.

Esmer, Y. (1991). Algılama ve anlatımda eşler arası farklılıklar [Perception and communication differences among couples]. In N. Arat (Ed.), *Kadın ve cinsellik* [Women and sexuality] (pp. 97–119). Istanbul: Say Yayınları.

Fişek, G. (1993). Life in Turkey. In L. L. Adler (Ed.), *International handbook on gender roles* (pp. 438–451). Westport, CT: Greenwood.

Gülçür, L. (1999). A study on domestic violence and sexual abuse in Ankara, Turkey. *Women for Women's Human Rights Reports*, No. 4. Istanbul, Turkey: Author.

Hacettepe University Consensus Survey. (1988). Ankara, Turkey.

İlkkaracan, P. (1997). A brief overview of women's movement(s) in Turkey (and the influence of political discourses). *Women for Women's Human Rights Reports*, No. 2. Istanbul, Turkey: Author.

Kağıtçıbaşı, Ç. (1981). Value of children, women's role and fertility in Turkey. In N. Abadan-Unat, *Women in Turkish society* (pp. 74–95). Leiden: E. J. Brill.

KAMAR-Gallup. (1990). *Kadına yönelik şiddet araştırması* [Research on violence towards women]. İstanbul: Kamar Araştırma.

Oral, R., Can, D., Kaplan, S., Polat, S., Ateş, N., Çetin, G., Miral, S., Hancı, H., Erşahin, Y., Tepeli, N., Bulguç, A. G., & Tıras, B. (2001). Child abuse in Turkey: An experience in overcoming denial and a description of 50 cases. *Child Abuse and Neglect, 25*, 279–290.

PIAR-Gallup. (1992). Türk kadınının gündemi araştırması [Research on status of Turkish women]. *Research report for the Directorate General on the status and problems of women*. Ankara: Turkish Prime Ministry.

State Institute of Statistics (SIS). (1990). *Census of Population Report*. Ankara: Republic of Turkey, Prime Ministry.

Yalçınkaya, A., Turan, F., & Rapoza, K. (2000, August). *North American and Turkish young adults' attitudes toward elder abuse*. Poster session presented at the annual meeting of the American Psychological Association, Washington, DC.

Yıldırım, A. (1998). *Sıradan Şiddet* [Ordinary violence]. Boyut Kitapları.

Yüksel, Ş. (1985). *Comparison of violent and non-violent families*. İstanbul: İstanbul Tıp Fakültesi Psikiyatri Kliniği Anabilim Dalı.

THE MIDDLE EAST

10

Saudi Arabia

Majed A. Ashy

CAPSULE

Over the centuries, Saudi Arabia, the land of several prophets, and the birth-place of Islam and Arabic civilizations, has developed protective mechanisms for the weak and the vulnerable. Each system and society has built-in protective mechanisms as well as risk factors. Saudi Arabia, as an Islamic and Arabic culture, has been dealing with ways to counter family maltreatment for centuries. The problem has been viewed within a larger context of moral and spiritual development. Treating family members with compassion, justice, and mercy is seen as a product of personality and moral qualities of fear of God, humbleness, fairness, mercy, compassion, and wisdom that should be nurtured in people from birth. Islam and many traditions aim at cultivating these qualities.

In recent years, reports coming from Saudi Arabia's medical, health, and security communities demonstrate an increasing awareness of the incidence and social implications of various forms of domestic violence (Aba-Alrgosh, Almaghloth, Albishr, Almokaid, & Alenezi, 2002). Because it has been observed that violence at home produces violence in society, there are calls upon the security and health communities to consider family violence a national security issue (Aba-Alrgosh et al., 2002). Others have called for establishing national guidelines to assist medical personnel in dealing with child abuse cases (Kattan, 1998).

National statistics regarding the extent of these problems are limited for many reasons: the relative recency of professional and community attention to these issues, the relatively small numbers of professionals working in these areas, and the cultural valuing of family and national privacy. In addition, some physicians resist diagnosing child abuse or neglect because of lack of belief that

parents can maltreat their children, inadequate training, problems in establish-
ing the diagnosis with certainty, the risk of stigmatizing the family, personal and
legal risks, and the potential effect on their practice. Others are reluctant to be-
come involved in social or legal bureaucracy (Al-Eissa, 1998; Kattan, 1998). All
of this appears to be changing in Saudi Arabia today.

THE SAUDI SAMPLE

Our sample consisted of 40 participants (33 females, 7 males) ranging in age
from 18 to over 60 years old. Most of them filled out a survey through the
research web page. The minimum education level was high school, and 25
participants responded in English.

Saudi Respondents' Definitions of Abuse

When asked about their definition of abuse, some participants defined
abuse in general terms as any behavior that violates Islam, "Abuse is any
behavior that violates the teachings of Islam" (female, 19 years old), or violates cultural expectations "any inappropriate behavior" (female, 30). These
definitions seem to use the religious teachings or moral and cultural manners and rules as the points of reference. On the other hand, some participants chose to define abuse by giving specific examples such as "physical
Abuse! Like hitting the partner or children severely."

When asked to give examples of mild, moderate, and extreme abuse,
most participants seemed to use a continuum with emotional abuse on the
mild end, physical abuse without "signs" at the moderate level, and physical abuse "with signs" on the extreme end of abusiveness. Some participants used the impact of the abuse and the perspective of the abused as
criteria for judging the severity of the abuse—for example, "Extreme abuse
is when the person loses her identity and self-esteem, and becomes totally
subservient; at the same time she is not aware of what is happening. Moderate: No moderate. Mild: if the woman is aware of the abuse but still chooses
to not to seek help" (female, 44). Some considered the role of the abused as
a factor in determining how abusive a behavior was—for example, "Mild
abuse: occasional verbal abuse that may be provoked by the person being
abused" (female, 29).

THE SAUDI ARABIAN MACROSYSTEM

The Saudi Arabian state was first established in the center of the Arabian
Peninsula in the early 18th century. Modern Saudi Arabia was founded in
1932 by King Abdul Aziz Bin Abdul Rahman Al-Saud. The nation experienced

remarkable growth over a short period, spurred by the discovery of oil in the 1930s. The people of Saudi Arabia enjoy a high standard of living based on an increasingly diversified economy, and have access to the most modern amenities and services (Saudi Arabia Profile, n.d.).

The Middle East, of which Saudi Arabia is an integral part, has been considered the birthplace of civilization, the area where humans first developed agriculture, domesticated livestock, perfected trade, invented writing, and set the stage for the rise of civilizations such as Babylon, Nineveh, Phoenicia, and Egypt. Islam, one of the world's great monotheistic religions, has Saudi Arabia as its heartland. The followers of Islam, called Muslims, believe in God—in Arabic, Allah—and that Muhammad is His Prophet. Today, the worldwide community of Muslims, which embraces the people of many races and cultures, numbers approximately one billion (Saudi Arabia Profile, n.d.).

The Kingdom of Saudi Arabia is a monarchy with a political system rooted in Islam's cherished traditions and culture. Its rules are governed by the Holy Qur'an and the *Sunnah* (teachings and sayings of the Prophet Muhammad), which call for peace, justice, equality, consultation, and respect for the rights of the individual. During the 1950s and 1960s, 20 government ministries were founded—a first step taken toward formalizing the long-established Islamic system of popular consultation. In the *Majlis*, weekly meetings open to all, members of the general public can approach the King and leaders at local, provincial, and national levels to discuss issues and raise grievances.

The rapid modernization of Saudi Arabia has led to a reevaluation of the country's political and administrative system, and to changes made in total adherence to the Islamic religion. In 1992, King Fahd introduced a new Basic Law for the System of Government, *Majlis Al-Shura* (Consultative Council), and the Provincial System. The following year, he announced bylaws for the Council of Ministers System. These new bylaws emphasize the importance of the family as the nucleus of Saudi society, with the vital role of teaching its members to adhere to Islamic values. In defining the relationship between the ruler and the people, the system emphasizes the equality of all Saudi citizens before God and the law in their concern for the well-being, security, dignity, and progress of their nation (Saudi Arabia Profile, n.d.).

THE SAUDI ARABIAN MICROSYSTEM

Generally, the family structure in Saudi Arabia is made up of the husband, the wife, and the children, living in an apartment or a separate home from their extended families. Sometimes other family members might live with the nuclear family, such as an elderly parent, and a single or divorced sister or daughter. Most families include maids from Asian or Arabic countries, who take care of the home and sometimes the children. They often live with the family for decades, becoming an integral part of the family. In addition, some homes include a car driver, a gardener, a cook, and possibly others, living outside the home in an attached apartment. In recent years, more official and public attention has been directed toward domestic help abuse. New labor regulations are enforced and more cases are investigated (Aba-Alrgosh et al., 2002). In addition to the pain experienced by abused domestic help, it has been reported in the media that some maids have physically, emotionally, and sexually abused the children for whom they are supposed to care (Al Jazeerah, 2002). Most children, males and females, stay with their families until they marry. Few people live alone, doing so only for purposes of work or study if they have to move to another city. If the son or daughter does not marry, he or she stays in the family home.

Gender Roles

Women's position in Saudi Arabia is shrouded in stereotypes and myths and few facts. This is due mainly to the private nature of Saudi society, lack of statistics about wife abuse, the politicization of this issue, and the uniqueness of Saudi dress style. This is not to say that wife abuse does not exist in Saudi society, or that it is not a problem that should be examined and given serious and urgent attention, however, to characterize the whole culture, system, or religion as abusive to women misrepresents the situation. Women in Saudi Arabia have rights that Islam, traditions, and the system grant them. As in other countries, work is needed to enforce these rights. It is also important, as Prince Abdullah bin Abdul Aziz, the Crown Prince of Saudi Arabia, has emphasized, to develop legal, educational, and health systems that will provide more opportunities for women. and protect them from abusive family members. Wife maltreatment has serious consequences on women's well-being, on children, and on society at large.

Culturally, the father is expected to be the head of the family. He is considered responsible in front of God and in front of the government for the religious, moral, financial, and physical well-being of the family. The home and the children's immediate physical and emotional needs are considered the wife's responsibilities, but it is the husband's responsibility to provide his wife with the facilities that can help her meet her duties. Such support may include hiring domestic help, as long as it is within his financial ability. Within the culture, this system is seen as a useful division of labor rather than as a hierarchal structure. It is believed that women are more equipped emotionally and physically to take care of the family and that men are more equipped to be the providers.

With the rapid cultural and economical changes in the Saudi society, more women are pursuing education and developing careers of their own, ranging from becoming nurses, social workers, and teachers to business-women, religious scholars, university professors, and physicians. As a result, the expectations of women in Saudi Arabia regarding marriage and work have been changing. Many young Saudi women prefer to marry Saudi men who will support them in their education and career goals, in addition to being loving, respectable men on whom they can depend when they need to. Similarly, many young Saudi men prefer to marry working Saudi women who can share in the financial responsibilities of the family and who have a variety of interests.

Saudi men and women are diverse in their values and attitudes, and attempts to mold them into fixed stereotypes will not contribute to understanding this society. It is simplistic to try to classify Saudi women as either traditional, oppressed, and weak housewives or as progressive, enlightened, and strong working women. First, in Arabic, there is no equivalent for the word "housewife." The man is called "Rab Albait" or the god of the house, and the woman is called "Rabat Albait" or the goddess of the house, because they both take care of the home and the family. If she works, then she will be called "almarat alamilah," "Al zawja alamilah," or "Al om Al amilah," or working woman, working wife, or working mother.

Many working Saudi women have to work hard to balance the demands of their careers and their families. The system tries to support women in their efforts by providing various possible paid leaves from work, and by reducing the time of work for men from 8 a.m. to 2 or 3 p.m. for most government offices. Nevertheless, it is still difficult for some working wives to achieve this balance and for some Saudi men to adjust to these changes. In fact, several media reports argue that this conflict is a major contributor to the rising rate of divorce in Saudi Arabia (Alnaeem, 2002). A 29-year-old woman in our sample gave as an example of mild wife abuse "not helping the wife in anything, especially dealing with kids, and no emotional encouragement."

There are many professional and independent women in Saudi Arabia who adhere strongly to traditions and the Islamic code of dress and behaviors, including "obeying" the husband. There are also many Saudi housewives who cherish raising their children, while doing volunteer work to help other young women have careers. For decades, many Saudi housewives have volunteered in a nongovernmental national organization for women called Alfaisaliyah, where housewives who know how to read and write teach those who do not, women who have skills in making things such as clothing or decorative items teach those who do not, and so on. Alfaisaliyah would give the women certificates of skill to take to the government to get loans and support to start their own small private businesses. The housewives would get social recognition for their efforts in addition to possible intrinsic rewards.

The family can be a protective factor in Saudi society from domestic violence. Most Saudi extended families live in the same city for generations and family members visit each other frequently. This frequent extended family contact prevents the social isolation that can put wives or children or elderly at increased risks of abuse in many societies. Extended family members tend to share intimate information about their lives, "unhappiness" can be detected easily, and family members can intervene if they see that a child or a female relative is abused. Grandparents might intervene to protect a child from an angry father, or to protect a sister from an abusing brother. They might send an elderly and respected person in the family to talk with the husband and wife, and to try to address any marital problems in a group setting in front of the elderly from the families involved.

Even though some families might accept violent behaviors as "normal" parts of marriage, and as a private issue between the husband and wife or parents and children, many families in Saudi Arabia now have members who consider abuse as unacceptable and degrading, and who would encourage serious interventions against the abuser. The family might put new conditions on the abuser and provide shelter for the abused. Of course, the educational and economical levels of family members play important roles in their methods and extent of intervention. On the other hand, there are circumstances where a family, through neglect, lack of support, or even pressure on the wife or the husband to stay in a dysfunctional situation, might increase the risk of abuse and its escalation. Some wives or children might attempt to seek help from other family members only to be told to go back to an abusive situation. This reality underlines the need for programs educating the public about domestic abuse. Programs geared especially toward respected elderly, who are most likely to intervene in domestic issues, can be of great value in protecting family members. These elderly may also belong to government bodies that can provide professional help through the elderly person or directly if needed. This approach might help society benefit from the wisdom and compassion of the elderly in combating an important social challenge.

Culture and traditions play a very important role in Saudi society. Most of the traditions teach respect of the elderly, mercy on the young, and compassion between men and women. These cultural values come from a long history of chivalry, poetry, and religion. According to the traditions of chivalry dominating various aspects of the culture, "real" men do not hit a woman, a child, an elderly person, or anyone who is weaker than themselves. I would suggest that integrating the positive aspects of chivalry into prevention programs might work especially well with any young men who might feel a need to act violently in the home in order to "prove" their manhood.

There are some persistent traditions from early Saudi society that can increase the risk of domestic violence. Many of these traditions were largely modified or eliminated by Islam, but some have survived among some people. Some men might use these ancient traditions to disrespect women, to act rough with women or children in the name of "manhood," or to justify the argument that a "real man" would not allow his wife to argue with him, or work, and so on. Such traditions are deeply rooted in pre-Islamic history, and show strong resistance to efforts by the government, scholars, and the media to change them. Traditions that are thousands of years old do not change in a decade or two, and do not change by force. Long-term efforts are needed.

The traditional segregation of men and women in schools, social gatherings, and work places in Saudi Arabia is seen traditionally as a mechanism to protect women from men, and to encourage marriage. According to the Islamic law, sexual activity outside marriage is forbidden. Women also have their gatherings that are closed to men where they feel free to discuss various issues without the continuous presence of men. The same applies to men's gathering.

Saudi society is trying to solve some other problems that Saudi women might encounter such as Al-Moakasat and Al-Onosa. Some men engage in following women in the markets or malls, Moakasat, in a way that is viewed by many Saudi women as harassment and dangerous. Security officials, the media, and the public are seriously concerned about this phenomenon, which can make public places unsafe for the woman or her family. Severe punishments are enforced on these men; nonetheless, this phenomenon is showing resistance. In addition, many Saudi women and families are concerned that many Saudi women are remaining single until they enter their 40s and beyond, Al Onosa, even though they would like to marry. The reasons are not clear, but may include families asking for high dowry, men delaying marriage for economic or other reasons, women refusing to marry eligible men due to education involvement, and men preferring to marry younger and nonprofessional women.

The Role of Children

Seventy percent of the Saudi population is under the age of 18 years (Al Jazeerah, 2002), and Saudi Arabia has one of the highest population growth rates in the world. Some Saudi families have more than 10 children even though birth control methods are permitted in Islam, and are available in all pharmacies in the country without a prescription. There are several factors contributing to this high birth rate. Saudis, based on Islam, consider money and children to be the beauty of life, and traditionally, Saudis find it a source of pride to have a lot of children. In addition, Saudis tend to marry young, in their early 20s, which gives them many years of fertility and opportunities to have children. Even though some Saudis now prefer to limit the number of children, especially now that more Saudi women work and seek education, the concept of having a small family is not a Saudi ideal (Dahlan, personal communication, 2003).

Families are usually very involved in the rearing of children, from birth right through marriage. Family involvement in mate selection is seen as protection for the young people against making choices they may regret later. Parents and other senior relatives help in the selection process, including making inquiries into the candidate's history and behavior, and potential conflict resolution efforts. Some family interventions might be counterproductive if they prevent a daughter from marrying a suitable man because they want to keep her salary, or ask for high dowry; consequently, Islam forbids preventing a woman from marrying a suitable man who has proposed to her, and the government has put a cap on the dowry that a family can ask.

FAMILY VIOLENCE AND ABUSE

Dr. Aba Alrogosh, a professor of psychology and vice president at Naif Arabic Academy of Security Studies in Ryadth, defines family violence as "any behavior that aims at harming a family member or a group of members or relatives in the horizontal level (such as brother to sister) or ventricular level (such as parent to child) and it can range from being directed towards the mind or the top of personality such as through criticism or sarcasm or insults, to physical harm that can lead even to death" (Aba-Alrgosh et al., 2002, p. 1). Dr. Al Bishr, Professor of Criminal Politics in Naif Academy, adds that "family violence occurs when the mind is unable to persuade" (Aba-Alrgosh et al., 2002, p. 1). Dr. Al Maghloth, Professor of Social Services at King Saud University, emphasizes the need to differentiate between abuse and punishment. In his view, abuse is a result of a violent personality and a certain social and family history leading the person to act violently with a wife, children, or relatives, sometimes for no apparent reason. On the other hand, he views punishment as carried out with the purpose of teaching, by a person who is not violent and has no psychological problems. From this perspective, all societies have some systems of punishment (such as prisons or financial penalties) considered essential for social health (Aba-Alrgosh et al., 2002, p. 2).

Perspectives on Men and Women in the Qur'an

A man who abuses his wife has no support in Islam. In fact he is committing a Zulm or wrongdoing, which is one of the biggest sins in Islam. Some lay Muslims misinterpret a verse in the Qur'an, saying that it allows hitting wives. Looking at the whole Qur'an, the life of the prophet (*pbh*), and the teachings of Islam, one finds no support for this interpretation. The prophet (pbh) never hit a woman, man, child, or a slave. Islamic scholars provide various interpretations for this verse, and a clear religious statement against wife's abuse might help clarify this for the general public.

Islam declared the spiritual and essential equality of men and women (Qur'an, 4:1). In addition, men and women have the same religious and moral duties and responsibilities, and face the same consequences of their deeds. "If any do deeds of righteousness be they male or female and have faith they will enter paradise and not the least injustice will be done to them" (Qur'an 4:124). "For Muslim men and women ... for men and women who are patient and constant, for men and women who humble themselves, for men and women who give in charity, for men and women who fast (and deny themselves), for men and women who guard their chastity, and for men and women who engage much in Allah's praise, for them has Allah prepared forgiveness and great reward" (Qur'an 33:35; Badawi, 1995).

According to the Qur'an, woman is not blamed for the "fall of man." In narrating the story of Adam and Eve, the Qur'an frequently refers to both of them, never singling out Eve for the blame. Islam declared that Adam and Eve decided to eat from the forbidden tree together, and that it is not Eve that seduced Adam, thus, freeing women from historical guilt. "And they both ate from the tree" (Al Bakarah). Islam stated that the creation of women and men and the love between them are signs of His existence. The Qur'an states: "And among His signs is that He created for you mates from among yourselves that you may live in tranquility with them, and He has put love and mercy between you; Verily, in that are signs for people who reflect" (30:21). In addition, Islam stated that, in the eyes of God, women's work is as appreciated as men's work, "So their Lord accepted their prayers, (saying): I will not suffer to be lost the work of any of you, whether male or female. You proceed one from another" (Qur'an 3:195). Pregnancy and childbirth are not seen as punishments for "eating from the forbidden tree." On the contrary, the Qur'an considers them grounds for love and respect due to mothers. Regarding pregnancy and childbirth, the Qur'an states: "We have enjoined on the person kindness to his/her parents: In pain did his/her mother bear him/her and in pain did she give him/her birth" (Qur'an 46:15; Badawi, 1995).

Islam forbade forcing women into marriages they do not want. According to Islamic Law, women cannot be forced to marry anyone without their consent. Ibn Abbas reported that a girl came to the Messenger of God, Muhammad (P), and said her father had forced her to marry without her consent. The Messenger of God gave her the choice (between accepting the marriage or invalidating it; Ibn Hanbal No. 2469). In another version, the girl said: "Actually I accept this marriage but I wanted to let women know that parents have no right [to force a husband on them]" (Ibn Maja, No. 1873; Badawi, 1995).

Islam encouraged the good treatment of women in general and wives specifically, "But consort with them in kindness, for if you hate them it may happen that you hate a thing wherein God has placed much good" (Qur'an 4:19). Prophet Muhammad (P) said: The best of you is the best to his family and I am the best among you to my family (Ibn-Hanbal, No. 7396). "Behold, many women came to Muhammad's wives complaining against their husbands (because they beat them)—those (husbands) are not the best of you" (see also Qur'an 2:231; Qur'an 2:229, 33:49). "It is the generous (in character) who is good to women, and it is the wicked who insults them" (the Prophet). And: "A Muslim must not hate his wife, and if he be displeased with one bad quality in her, let him be pleased with one that is good." "Nor is there a man who walks with his wife hand-in-hand, but that God sets it down as a virtue for him; and if he puts his arm round her shoulder in love, his virtue is increased tenfold" (Badawi, 1995).

The Qur'an makes it clear that the sole basis for superiority of any person over another is piety and righteousness, not gender, color, or nationality: "O mankind! We created you from a single (pair) of a male and a female and made you into nations and tribes that you may know each other. Verily the most honored of you in the sight of Allah is [one who is] the most righteous of you. And Allah has full knowledge and is well acquainted [with all things]" (Qur'an 49:13; Badawi, 1995).

Islam recognizes the full property rights of women before and after marriage. A married woman keeps her maiden name, and Islam gave women the right to divorce their husbands. Forms of marriage dissolution include mutual agreement, the husband's initiative, the wife's initiative (if part of her marital contract), court decision on the wife's initiative (for a cause), and the wife's initiative without a "cause" provided that she returns the marital gift to her husband [khul' (divestiture)]. In addition, Islam gave mothers priority for custody of young children (up to the age of about 7). A child later chooses between his mother and father (for custody purposes). Custody questions are to be settled in a manner that balances the interests of both parents with the well-being of the child (Badawi, 1995).

Saudi Participants' Perspectives on Wife Abuse

In providing examples of severe, moderate, and mild wife abuse, the Saudi respondents tended to list psychological and emotional abuse as mild, physical abuse without injuries as moderate, and physical abuse with injuries as severe. Indeed, almost all participants listed behaviors such as "beating," "choking," and "stabbing" as forms of extreme physical abuse. A 23-year-old man gave "shouting or arguments" as examples of mild abuse and "shouting or slapping" as examples of moderate abuse. Other examples of moderate abuse included various forms of public embarrassment: "shouting and cursing in public and in front of family and friends" (female, 29), "mistreating the wife in public" (female, 31). It is interesting to see here that a man marrying more than one wife is not mentioned as a form of abuse. Within the Islamic Saudi culture, a man can marry more than one wife, up to four at the same time, as long as he can treat them justly and can provide for the families. In addition to other objectives, this right stems from a concern of Islam for the well-being of widows, who were rarely permitted to remarry before Islam. The Prophet encouraged his followers to marry widows, and in fact married several himself. Even though this right is given by law, most Saudi men marry only one wife. This right is seen to be used only under certain circumstances such as if the wife is infertile.

Saudi Respondents' Perspectives on Husband Abuse

Saudi implicit theories of spousal maltreatment show somewhat different criteria for husband abuse than for wife abuse. Although a 24-year-old woman listed "throwing things" at the husband, and a 23-year-old man listed "beating with a weapon" as examples of extreme abuse, most of the examples of husband abuse focused on verbal and psychological behaviors. They considered it mild abuse if the wife "shouts or insults" the husband in private, and extreme abuse if she does it in public. A 29-year-old woman said it was abusive for a wife to nag a husband, "asking for things the husband cannot provide ... especially those needing money." This is understandable in the Saudi culture, where men derive a lot of pride from their roles as husbands and fathers providing for their families; public humiliation can hurt them deeply, psychologically and socially. In addition, it is considered abusive to ask a husband to provide for the family beyond his financial ability—for example, to satisfy luxury needs of their wives, such as a new car or home. Being in debt is seen as a huge psychological burden that can do serious damage to the emotional and social well-being of the husband; moreover, it is an Islamic value to live within means, and not to go in unnecessary debt.

Child Maltreatment

Reports of child abuse found their way into the medical literature as early as 1990 (Kattan, 1998). Dr. Kattan provides a detailed definition of child abuse:

> Child abuse can be in the form of neglect on the medical or educational levels, withholding medicine or food or appropriate supervision, neglecting protecting them from accidents, and neglect on the social or organizational levels. Child abuse can be physical in the form of hitting, cutting, bruising, imprisonment, attacks of sexual nature, or strangling and so on. Child abuse can also be emotional such as by threatening, stimulating fear, having unrealistic and high expectations from the child that disturb their emotional development, or insulting. A fourth form of child abuse is sexual abuse where a person, at least 5 years older, would use, coerce or manipulate a child to satisfy the sexual needs of the adult. (p. 2)

Within the medical community, an abused child tends to be defined as

> one whose parent or other person legally responsible for his or her care inflicts or allows to be inflicted physical injury, sexual offence, or creates or allows substantial risk to the child. A neglected child is one whose physical, mental or emotional condition has been impaired because of failure to meet the child's needs for clothing, shelter, education, medical care, proper supervision or guardianship, or one who has been abandoned. (Al-Eissa, 1998, p. 2)

Several forces operate against child maltreatment in Saudi Arabia. In addition to governmental, media, public, and professional forces discussed later, Islam is a main force that plays an important role in determining implicit theories regarding abuse, and in designing intervention programs. Before Islam, some Arabian tribes accepted the practice of female infanticide; however, Islam forbade this custom, and considered it a crime comparable any other murder (Qur'an 81:8–9). Islam also criticized the attitudes of parents who prefer having sons and feel shame if they have a female child (Qur'an 16:58–59). In addition, Islam encouraged the good treatment of girls. The prophet (pbh) said: "Whosoever has a daughter and he does not bury her alive, does not insult her, and does not favor his son over her, God will enter him into Paradise" (Ibn Hanbal, No. 1957). "Whosoever supports two daughters till they mature, he and I will come in the day of judgment as this (and he pointed with his two fingers held together)."

Saudi Respondents' Perspectives on Child Abuse

In the Saudi sample, mild maltreatment is generally seen as psychological, moderate seems to include some physical abuse without leaving marks or injuries, and extreme abuse is seen as physical abuse that can cause injury or long-term damage. For example, a 29-year-old woman said that "either a mother or father cursing either a son or daughter is mildly abusive; hitting the child in public is moderately abusive; and hitting the child severely, causing bruising and fractures, male or female, usually from the father is severely abusive." A 23-year-old man said that "shouting or punishing" was mildly abusive, "beating with hands or shouting" was moderately abusive, and "beating the child with a weapon such as metal or fire" was extremely abusive. A 24-year-old woman considered it to be both mildly and moderately abusive for a father to "interfere in daughter's decisions regarding certain aspects of her life such as place of work."

Elder Maltreatment

Islam considered kindness to parents, especially mothers, next to the worship of God and an opportunity to do good deeds so one can go to heaven. "And we have enjoined upon man (to be good) to his parents: His mother bears him in weakness upon weakness . . ." (Qur'an 31:14; see also Qur'an 46:15, 29:8). "Your Lord has decreed that you worship none save Him, and that you be kind to your parents . . ." (Qur'an 17:23). "A man came to Prophet Muhammad (P) asking: O Messenger of God, who among the people is the most worthy of my good company? The Prophet (P) said, Your mother. The man said then who else: The Prophet (P) said, Your mother. The man asked, Then who else? Only then did the Prophet (P) say, Your father" (Al-Bukhari and Muslim). In another tradition, the Prophet advised a believer not to join the war against the Quraish (i.e., the pagan disbelievers at that time) in defense of Islam, but to look after his mother, saying that his service to his mother would be a cause for his salvation. Mu'awiyah, the son of Jahimah, reported that Jahimah came to the Prophet, peace be upon him, and said: "Messenger of God! I want to join the fighting (in the path of God) and I have come to seek your advice." He said, "Then remain in your mother's service, because Paradise is under her feet."

The elderly have a special place of respect in Arabic traditions. Traditionally, they are viewed as wise, experienced, and deserving to be rewarded by love and respect for their life work in the family and society. Many Saudis believe that "parents' prayers open closed doors" for their children, and that they should do all they can to avoid having their mothers or fathers angry with them because "parents' anger comes with Allah's anger." It is expected that adult children will take care of their elderly parents. Very few nursing homes exist in Saudi Arabia, and they are mostly for elderly people who have no relatives.

Saudi Participants' Perspectives on Elder Abuse

While many Saudis adhere to these traditions, elder abuse seems to be on the rise. Several newspapers report cases where an elderly person is abandoned in a hospital or left in a mall in a strange town, or sometimes abused financially, psychologically, or even physically (Aba-Alrgosh et al., 2002). This has been reflected in some of the examples provided by our participants. For instance, a 31-year-old woman gave this example of extreme abuse, "A son leaving his old blind mother in the street for someone else to take her." Similarly, a 31-year-old woman's example of extreme abuse was, "Leaving them on the streets, in the mall, for someone to find them and send them to house for the elderly." No statistics or studies are available to examine this phenomenon, but one might suspect that rapid social, cultural, and economical changes are threatening the moral and social fabric of society.

In our sample, many Saudis listed putting an elder in a nursing home as a form of elder abuse. This can be understood in the context that within the Saudi culture, it is expected that children will return the favors of the parents by taking care of them when they are old. In addition, taking care of one's parents is a religious obligation as stated in Islam. A 29-year-old woman states "putting an elderly parent in a home is rare if the children can provide care. It causes a stigma on the children. How can they not care for an elderly parent or relative?" There was considerable emphasis on lesser forms of neglect—for example, "not visiting an elderly parent," and "not taking enough care of them."

Sibling Maltreatment

Within Saudi culture, a brother is supposed to take care of, protect, serve, and love his sisters. Unfortunately, some brothers abuse their sisters psychologically, financially, and physically. There are no statistics available about the extent of this problem. However, within our sample, psychological abuse between siblings was considered mild abuse, physical abuse without injury was considered moderate, and physical abuse with injuries was considered severely abusive. Other forms of abuse mentioned included "not helping the sisters in transportation" (because women cannot drive in Saudi Arabia), "controlling the sister's behavior," "forcing her to marry someone she does not like," and "sexual abuse." I would argue that brother to sister abuse might be the most common form of domestic violence in Saudi Arabia.

INTERVENTION AND PREVENTION

The Government

On the governmental level, Saudi Arabia is a founding member of the United Nations, the Arab League, the Organization of the Islamic Conference (OIC), the Gulf Cooperation Council (GCC), and the Organization of Petroleum Exporting Countries (OPEC). As a member in these organizations, Saudi Arabia is in continuous dialogue and cooperation with numerous governments and bodies to address various pressing international problems such as family violence. Saudi Arabia is a signatory of the Nuclear Non Proliferation Treaty, the U.N. Human Rights Declaration, the Women's Rights Declaration, and the Convention on the Rights of the Child. Further, the Saudi government has established its own governmental office for human rights watch, and an independent one has also been established. There are also plans to establish a human rights institute in Saudi Arabia (U.N., n.d.).

The government has also provided scholarships abroad for Saudis to study areas related to family violence such as psychology, criminal justice, and family medicine. In addition, the Labor and Social Issues Ministry has established a free hot line that provides counseling for families and individuals suffering from social problems including abuse, and is operated by psychologists, education specialists, and social workers of both genders[1] (Al-Gamhoor & Al-Namlah, 2002). In addition, there are discussions to establish Women Councils in districts where women of the district can meet and discuss their issues, and where social and supportive services for women and families will be provided (Alramlawi, 2002).

The government provides free health care for all, free education for both genders from preschool to postdoctorate studies, and loans, free of interest, to support young people in the costs of marriage or to own a land or home, or to start a new business. These efforts are designed to help increase family resources and to reduce stress that might be a predisposing factor in family abuse.

The Media

In the last decade, Saudi telecommunications have developed very fast. Saudi Arabia now has several satellites that provide Saudis with access to hundreds of television stations from all around the world. A Saudi today

---

[1]The toll-free number is 800-124-5005.

can watch any American, European, Russian, Chinese, Arabic, African, Latin, or other stations. While the official Saudi stations reflect the Islamic nature of the Saudi society, the government does not censor any of the international stations. This applies to written media and to radio stations as well. Family violence issues have been heavily discussed in soap operas, talk shows, experts' interviews, religious programs, health programs, family programs, and women's programs.

In addition, reports of child, wife, and elderly abuse are published in major newspapers (Algohar, 2002; Alnaeem, 2002; Al-Rashid, 2002a, 2002b). Columnists discuss these issues and introduce new ideas and solutions, and health and security professionals discuss the medical, security, and psychological implications of these problems (Alrokosh, Almaghloth, & Albishr, 2002; Kattan, 1998). Very often novelists seem to examine and reflect social issues much earlier than do other professionals. One can find many worldwide known novels, such as *Cinderella*, that focus on child abuse and its consequences. This also applies to Saudi Arabian novels. Some Saudi female and male writers have devoted entire novels to giving voice to the suffering of the victims of family violence and its long-term consequences (Al Oliyan, 2000). In her nationally acclaimed and award winning novel, *The Female Spider*, Al-Oliyan follows the story of a young woman who suffers under the oppression of her tyrannical father.

The heroine wonders: "What is freedom? I wonder about the meaning of that wonderful, burning, magical word . . . I am the one tied by shekels and restrictions that are hidden, and prison walls surround me from all sides . . . Is freedom happiness . . . openness . . . freedom from everything and anything . . . or is it freedom of opinion . . . freedom of word . . . and freedom of thinking . . . or is it the revolution against traditions and old torn rules that are inherited since thousands of years?" She goes on to describe her normal life: "There was nothing unusual, strange or special in my life . . . never . . . everything was going in its natural path . . . young and beautiful woman from a known and respected family . . . the father is a dictator, a tyrant as they say . . . the mother is kind and weak and without an opinion." Later, she describes an incident that affected her deeply: ". . . in the middle of my confusion and distraction I heard loud screams coming from the lower level in our home. I ran down the stairs and my fear was increasing . . . and I was surprised with a horrible seen in front of me . . . my father is hitting his wife with all hardness and violence and her children are holding her . . . she screams and they cry. I tried to take the stick away . . . he pushed me . . . insulted me . . . it is my duty as a human with feelings . . . with blood in her veins . . . to try to save her . . . or at least to say a word of truth . . . of faith . . . my father . . . I beg you . . . for the sake of the children . . . leave her . . . you are killing her . . ."

After the abuse, she writes: "I stood in darkness ... trying to catch my breath ... the house is empty ... and the storm was quiet ... the screams, the noise and the sounds of the stick falling on weak, soft bodies disappeared in the far ... but the smell of violence ... of harshness is filling the place ... disgusting smell ... whatever is her crime my father, this is not how she should be treated ... wild, primitive methods that make humans equal to animals without reason ... a return to the ages of ignorance and injustice when humans had nothing but their physical power ... the disaster is not just in hitting women but also in these innocent children with now torn souls ... how are they going to face the future ... with broken hearts and deep wounds that will never heal ... what condition these children will be in when they see their mother being hit by their father and both are of ultimate value to them ... what they saw will always stay in their memories ... feeding them pain ..." (Al Oliyan, 2000, pp. 1 & 21–22).

The Public

On the social level, several public figures took responsibility in leading governmental and nongovernmental efforts to improve the conditions of women, children, and the elderly. For example, in the last four decades, King Fahad Ibn Abdulaziz Al Saud, as the first minister of education in the country, has introduced major reforms into the education system to provide education for women in all levels, from preschool to doctorate and medical degrees. In addition, Crown Prince Abdullah Ibn Abdulaziz Al Saud has encouraged and invited Saudis to engage in an open dialogue about women's roles in society, how to give women more career opportunities, and how the society can benefit more from women's knowledge, education, and skills in society. Prince Sultan Ibn Abdulaziz Al Saud and his son Prince Bandar have been leading figures in the moral and financial support of humanitarian efforts to support families in need and the nongovernmental organizations that provide services to them. Prince Naif Ibn AbdulAziz's Academy for Security Studies, and with support from Princes Naif Ibn Abdulaziz and Ahmad Ibn Abdulaziz, has been conducting rigorous psychosocial research in the issues of violence and crime in general and, more specifically, domestic violence (Prince Naif Academy, 2002). Prince Sultan Ibn Salman leads a national campaign for caring for children and adults with disabilities. Princess Munera Bint Abdulrahman Ibn Saud and Dr. Aldamigh have established a nongovernmental center for social counseling and family problems.

In addition to other public figures, Dr. Kattan, a nationally known female pediatrician, has been leading the efforts with Dr. Al-Eissa to establish a national committee for child protection and to establish mechanisms for reporting abuse and enforcing laws (Al-Eissa, 1998; Kattan, 1998). On a more private level, several men and women host weekly meetings in their homes for friends and family members, where they invite professionals to discuss various issues including methods of resolving family problems and new ways of raising children.

Religion

On the religious level, many scholars regularly include in their Friday speeches (*khotba*) encouragements for treating family members with mercy and fairness, and warnings against wronging others (*zulm*). In addition, some scholars work on correcting the public misunderstanding of Islam and remind Muslims of the compassionate behavior of the prophet (pbh) toward his family. Some female Muslim scholars furthermore point out the rights Islam gave to women and oppose taking these rights away (Al Jazeerah, 2002).

Health Professionals

Several health professionals in Saudi Arabia are calling for considering violence toward children a major national problem, arguing that it should become a focal point of substantial public and governmental attention (Al-Eissa, 1998). They urge the establishment of a National Committee on Prevention and Management of Child Abuse and Neglect, with the goals of assuming an active leadership role in attacking the problem, providing a mechanism for increasing knowledge about the causes of this problem, and identifying steps that can be taken to prevent and treat abuse (Al-Eissa, 1998, p. 2).

Associated with this committee would be a professional team functioning to protect the child, and simultaneously helping the parents to understand their own problems.

> The major services of this team include identification of abused or neglected children, treatment of injuries or conditions resulting from such abuse or neglect, early intervention for psychological maladjustments, as well as rehabilitation of the child's parents and protection of the child from repetitive abuse or neglect. If the suspected incident of child abuse or neglect is substantiated, several outcomes are possible: Counseling or psychotherapy may be provided, placement of the child in a foster home of a close relative or in temporary shelter may be arranged, and/or criminal charges may be filed, depending on the circumstances. (Al-Eissa, 1998, p. 2)

The King Faisal Specialist Hospital and Research Center (KFSH&RC) is the first hospital in the Kingdom to develop a program to detect, report, and prevent child abuse. A Child Advocacy Committee was initiated in 1994, and this Committee established an internal policy and procedure for dealing with all cases of child abuse. This policy was adopted by the hospital administration and involves the hospital security department, which reports to the Riyadh legal authorities all cases of suspected or proven child abuse seen at or admitted to KFSH&RC. This is the first such policy in the Kingdom; it was modeled after the child abuse policies used in North America (Kattan, 1998). Dr. Kattan (1998) recommended that other institutions establish similar committees, and adopt and enforce similar policies for the benefit of the children of Saudi Arabia. "The establishment of these committees would be followed by other committees at the regional and national levels, aimed at promoting awareness of child neglect and abuse, identifying the incidents of child abuse and the factors related to it in this country, and establishing treatment guidelines for both the child and the abusive adults" (Kattan, 1998, p. 1).

CONCLUSION

Although there is now an increasing awareness and acknowledgment in Saudi Arabia that family violence and abuse is a serious problem, more widespread efforts are needed to prevent it, understand it, and develop legal and law enforcement mechanisms for protecting the victims and stopping the abuser. "In addition to not being soft on those who commit family violence ... there is a need to establish laws and mechanisms that determine the definitions of family violence and the various crimes that fall under them" (Aba-Alrgosh et al., 2002, p. 1).

Because we can't assume perfection in any society or system, I would argue that the first step toward reducing family abuse is to recognize the mechanisms already present within a society that can protect individuals from family abuse, and that we should work on strengthening those mechanisms rather than trying to implant systems lacking roots in the culture. In addition, we need to identify and respond to the risk factors specific to different cultures rather than assuming that the problems and solutions of one culture can be generalized to every other culture. I would argue that within the Saudi system, culture, and traditions, there are protective factors that help to reduce domestic violence.

Family violence is in violation of Islam, traditions, and humanity. Saudis, like all people around the world, love their wives and husbands, daughters and sons, parents and grandparents, and brothers and sisters, and do not accept hurting them in any way, even by a family member. Saudi Arabia, as the heart of Islam and Arabic traditions, should continue the efforts to counter family violence, and thereby be the leader and best example for all

Muslims on these issues. Saudi Arabia enters the 21st century as a country proud of its history, open to the world, and working on modernization and reform in balance with its Islamic and Arabic identity and responsibilities. It is also working with other nations to solve the problems that face the world today, including family violence.

REFERENCES

Aba-Alrgosh, G., Almaghloth, F., Albishr, K., Almokaid, S., & Alenezi, H. (2002). The increase of family violence in Saudi Arabia [online Al-Jazirah newspaper]. Available: issue # 10910: http://www.al-jazirah.com/

Al-Eissa, Y. (1998). Child abuse and neglect in Saudi Arabia: What are we doing and where do we stand? *Annals of Saudi Medicine, 38*(2), 2.

Al-Gamhoor, H., & Al-Namlah, A. (2002). Women will share in solving social problems in the counseling department [online Al-Jazirah newspaper]. Available: issue # 10862: http://www.al-jazirah.com

Algohar, H. (2002). Stories of parents' maltreatment [online Al-Riyadh newspaper]. Available: issue # 12481: http://www.alriyadh.com.sa/

Alnaeem, O. (2002). Surprises and the wife's salary [online Al-Jazirah newspaper]. Available: issue # 10925: http://www.al-jazirah.com

Al Oliyan. (2000). *The female spider*. Riyadh: Saudi Press.

Alramlawi. (2002). Women' councils [online Al-Jazirah newspaper]. Available: issue # 10862: http://www.al-jazirah.com

Al-Rashid, N. (2002a). Warnings against almisyar [online Al-Riyadh newspaper]. Available: issue # 12485: http://www.alriyadh.com.sa/

Al-Rashid, N. (2002b). Alhajr, a tribal tradition [online Al-Riyadh newspaper]. Available: issue # 12410: http://www.alriyadh.com.sa/

Badawi, J. (1995). *Gender equity in Islam*. Plainfield, IN: American Trust Publications.

Kattan, H. (1998). Child abuse and neglect: Perspective from King Faisal Specialist Hospital and Research Center. *Annals of Saudi Medicine, 38*(2), 1.

Kattan, H. (2002). Violence against children: A reality that should not be ignored [online Al-Riyadh newspaper]. Available: issue # 12281: http://www.alriyadh.com.sa/

Prince Naif Academy for Security Studies. (2002). Available: http://www.saudiembassy.net/naass/index.html

Saudi Arabia Profile. (n.d.). Available: http://www.saudiembassy.net/profile/Saudi-Profile00.htm

United Nations. (n.d.). Available: http://www.un.org

11

Israel

Odelya Pagovich

CAPSULE

The nation of Israel was born out of war and conflict, and has faced war and conflict for most of its relatively short history. Although the great majority of its citizens share a common religion (Judaism), many are refugees and immigrants from countries with diverse experiences and cultures. Despite such differences in origins, the majority of Israelis are fairly traditional in their gender roles, and women's status is not equal to that of men. Children are very important in Israeli families, and disagreements over childrearing are a major source of conflict between husbands and wives. Both child and wife abuse have been recognized as social problems, and there are mandatory reporting laws for child abuse, and shelters for battered women. There has been some acknowledgment that elder abuse can also be a problem, but as yet, there is little in the way of intervention and prevention services to address elder abuse.

THE ISRAELI SAMPLE

The Israeli sample consisted of 150 participants—79 females and 71 males from 19 to 78 years of age. A majority classified themselves as middle and upper middle class. Approximately 28% had completed high school, 12% had completed some college, 34% had graduated from college, and 28% had completed graduate school. The majority of the sample was living in Israel and Jewish; a few participants were Muslim or Christian, and a few were Arabs. Nearly half the sample was married; 47% were single, and a small portion were widowed, divorced, or separated. The majority of participants' parents were native Israelis, but other origins were Moroccan, Iranian, Lebanese, Turkish, Russian, Ethiopian, and Egyptian.

Israeli Participants' Definitions and Examples of Abuse

When defining abuse, most of the participants emphasized harm: "Abuse is anything that causes a physical wound or physical pain"; "[Abuse is] any act that forces a woman/man or child to seek medical care"; "abuse is any act which causes pain and intent does not matter." However, some participants did believe that intent was an important criterion for abuse: "An abusive act can only be considered abusive if there is intent to harm or intent to abuse."

Israeli respondents were sensitive to the psychological consequences of abuse, especially sexual abuse: "Although an individual may not be harmed physically by a slap, the emotional abuse takes its toll and the emotional scars are the ones that scar the most. Even if the physical abuse leaves no scars, the emotional abuse is eternal"; "[Abuse is] any act that causes an individual to feel threatened or scared"; "an unwanted touch can be considered abusive because many times, an individual cannot fight back or confuses respect with abuse and what is right and wrong with fear"; "[Abuse is] an act, like tickling that could potentially lead to more abusive behaviors or inappropriate touches. As we know, one thing can lead to another." Several respondents were distressed at the request for examples of different levels of abuse—for example, "There is no such a thing as moderate mild and extreme abuse—all abuse is extreme and categorizing it is wrong—some abuse may inflict more or less pain, but it is all the same and it is all wrong."

When asked if they or someone they knew had ever experienced abuse, Israeli respondents provided a number of examples of abusive experiences, with an emphasis on domestic violence. For example, a 42-year-old clerical worker stated

> not only was I burdened with physical and emotional scars from my husband, but I also had to endure the guilt of seeing my children's suffering . . . I remember one time he asked me to go to a function with him at work. I told him that under normal circumstances and with more notice I would go, but that there was nobody to take care of the kids on such short notice and that it would be better if I stayed home. Enraged, my husband bypassed me, went upstairs and swung at all of the children while simultaneously yelling at them that if they were not around, I would be able to attend the event . . . I cried and cried the entire night, but the abuse did not end.

A 21-year-old woman in the army said, "I have a friend that in my opinion experienced psychological abuse. Her husband would fight with her about ridiculous issues and would not speak to her/would ignore her for two weeks. He would also abstain from any sexual activities with her for very long periods of time (Sometimes for more than a two-month period). He did all of this in order to punish her."

THE ISRAELI MACROSYSTEM

The state of Israel was founded on May 14, 1948 (from a League of Nations mandate under British administration; www.cia.gov/cia/publications/factbook/geos/is). It is a country where immigration is the core of its existence. It is also a country that has had to fight for its existence almost without cease—and this struggle may be a contributor to domestic violence in the country. According to Ghent (1998, para. 5), "The intifada, the Gulf War, the massive influx of immigrants from the former Soviet Union and Ethiopia, and recent fears of Iraqi chemical warfare have all led to upsurges in domestic violence, social workers and physicians report." Ghent goes on to quote Rachel Bialer, director of a woman's shelter in Israel: "I think it's a very aggressive society we live in . . . Our history has a lot to do with it." Ghent also quotes Gurith Schneidman, head of social work services at Hadassah's two Jerusalem hospitals, who commented, "Whenever political tensions rise, the numbers in the emergency rooms are higher." During months that Israel has felt threatened by one of its neighbors, the number of battered women referrals increased significantly over the preceding months.

The Status of Women and Children in Israel

Avni (1991) reported that Israeli women live in a predominantly traditional society, wherein the woman is expected to abide by male authority and to be a "good wife and mother." According to Avni, women tend to work part-time, occupy lower positions, and earn less money than do men in equivalent positions. There is also evidence that in the Arab sector, the participation of women in the labor force is even lower—only 22%—and that the rate of unemployment is higher than in the Jewish population. In general, women work mostly in lower paying jobs, in services, education, health, welfare and clerical positions, and are significantly less represented in prestigious and lucrative occupations (Jewish Virtual Library, n.d.). Although service in the Israel Defense Forces is compulsory for both men and women, inequality does exist. In 2000, Israel's parliament adopted an amendment to the Security Service Law, opening all military professions to women, a change that met with strong objections from religious institutions and politicians (Jewish Virtual Library, n.d.).

The Committee for the Advancement of Women in Israel's Parliament has been active in the field of advancing women's status through legislation. In 1998, the Authority for the Advancement of Women was established to "place issues related to the status of women and gender equality on the national agenda, to create programs and policies based on gender equality, and to promote gender mainstreaming in all walks of life" (www.israel-un.org/ecosoc/women/). This law is expected to increase public awareness about the status of women through media and education. In Israel, 16% of the women live in poverty, compared to 14% of men, perhaps because most single-parent families are those of single women.

Israel views itself as a child-centered society, and parents usually have strong opinions regarding modes of childrearing. Furthermore, women are considered as the more competent spouse when dealing with childrearing (Eisikovitz, 1993). As a result, childrearing may become an arena wherein women try to assert their control over family life. This may pose a problem because men in a society such as Israel's may view themselves as being in charge of all family matters and may attempt to impose their wills in the domain of childrearing. If a woman is less willing to yield control of this domain to her partner, he may feel insecure and intimidated and utilize violence to compensate for these emotions. Consistent with this view, Eisikovitz, Guttmann, Sela-Amit, and Edleson (1993) found that physical violence against women often occurred as a result of conflicts over childrearing. Eisikovitz's finding is reflected in the responses of some of our respondents. For example, one woman described the abuse she and her children experienced at the hands of her husband, stemming from arguments over the best childrearing methods. If she did not comply with her husband's wishes regarding childrearing, then he would beat the children as a means of taking revenge on her.

Life is somewhat different for women living in a *kibbutz* (a communal settlement wherein all inhabitants have duties according to their given skills and all is shared). Families work to serve the needs of the kibbutz by performing tasks that are vital for community survival. Within the kibbutz there is equality of opportunity and responsibility. Residents are usually not given salaries but are provided with housing and other necessities, including medical care and education. Women and men both work on the kibbutz equally and share the same responsibility.

VIOLENCE IN ISRAEL

Varying cultures, religions, and ethnic differences in Israel makes treating abuse challenging. For example, in religious Arab and Jewish families, there is a strong desire to keep family matters private. The fervent religious groups often deny abuse or hide any suspected cases in an effort to protect the family name.

Two respondents in our sample demonstrated the obstacles that religious views may pose in reporting abuse. A 42-year-old male Orthodox respondent wrote that abuse does not exist in moderate and mild forms within the family. At the end of the survey, when given an opportunity to write remarks, he stated that the family is one of the most sacred groups in society, a "refuge, a place wherein individuals should feel safe and protected from any harm. The family is a unit wherein respect and structure are key elements. Therefore, family members will do anything and everything to maintain the structure and will not harm or jeopardize it at any cost or with any behavior." Likewise, a 29-year-old mother of three said "every man was created in the image of G-d and all man was intended to love thy brother as thyself . . . Abuse transgresses what G-d intended when he created mankind." This woman also wrote that it is the responsibility of the community to step in during times of abuse and to "unite as one."

CHILD MALTREATMENT

Perspectives on Child Maltreatment in Israel

In a study of 235 Israeli students, Shor and Haj-Yahia (1996) examined perceptions of psychological, physical, and sexual abuse, as well as physical, medical, and educational neglect. In general, agreement concerning the abusiveness of particular behaviors was higher with regard to cases with externalized physical (e.g., cigarette burns) or behavioral danger signs, and lower with regard to neglect. Respondents tended to recognize forms of maltreatment that were most relevant to their field of specialization. For example, individuals in the education field saw maltreatment in a situation wherein parents ignored a teacher's recommendation for helping their child to be more successful academically. The students indicated greatest willingness to report cases of child abuse falling into the categories of severe sexual and physical abuse, but displayed low willingness to report cases of neglect.

In a study of pediatricians' perceptions and reporting of child maltreatment in Israel, Shor (1998) found that 80% of her sample agreed that neglect (e.g., lack of vital health care treatment) was a form of maltreatment posing a "medium extent" of risk to the child. Not providing care of a nonmedical nature (e.g., cleanliness) was seen as a lesser form of maltreatment. The willingness of pediatricians to report cases of educational neglect and psychological abuse to either welfare agencies or the police was lower than for other categories of abuse. Sixty-six percent of the participants indicated that they had suspected cases of maltreatment (mostly physical or sexual abuse) within the previous year.

In a later study, Shor (1999) studied childrearing practices in 273 Jewish immigrant families from the European countries of the former Soviet Union. She found that when parents were presented with a scenario describing child abuse, they said they would not seek help in such a situation. Their reasons were a belief that parents can legitimately do whatever they want with their own children, lack of confidence that a request for help would be fruitful, and a desire to maintain the privacy of the family. These families associated a request for help with a fear of damaging the family name; moreover, informing others about matters within the family was something they had learned to avoid in the former Soviet Union. They also emphasized that when someone hits a child, "he/she must hit the child only on 'safe' places of the body, that is, those which will not cause damage such as the back of the head, the hands, or the buttocks" (Shor, 1999, p. 495). Several respondents noted that harsher punishments should be given to boys because harsh punishments of girls might physically harm them. Although many of the participants did not consider lack of provision of a child's needs as a form of abuse or neglect, this may reflect the fact that the participants considered a 7-year-old girl (but not a 5-year-old) to be self-sufficient. They also tended to see corporal punishment as an acceptable option for punishment, viewing it as beneficial to a child's self-sufficiency, education, and well-being.

Prevalence of Child Maltreatment

According to Lowenstein (1995), in Israel during the 1980s, an examination of child abuse and spousal abuse had just begun to emerge. In one recent study, Sternberg and Krispin (1993) studied perceptions of domestic violence in a sample of 110 Israeli children in the age range of 8 to 12 years old. Of these 110 children, 33 had been physically abused by their parents within the last 6 months. A 1994 study (Schein et al., 2000) of 1,242 participants from 48 cities across Israel revealed that 31% of the female respondents had experienced some form of childhood sexual abuse, of which fondling was the most common form. Sixteen percent of the males had also experienced some form of childhood sexual abuse, but only 1% experienced fondling. The most common perpetrators were male strangers, followed by male adult neighbors and/or family friends, and adult male relatives.

Reported cases of child maltreatment appear to have increased steadily since the passage of reporting laws. In 1996, there were a total of 3,808 youth investigations concerning child maltreatment, and nearly 300,000 of the 2 million children in Israel were considered at risk for maltreatment. In 1997, 20,989 referrals were made to child protective services. Of these referrals the breakdown of the types of abuse endured by children was as follows: physical abuse, 33%; severe neglect, 31%; emotional abuse, 29%; and sexual abuse, 7%.

Israeli Participants' Perspectives on Child Abuse

Fourteen percent of our participants viewed corporal punishment as sometimes necessary. A 35-year-old man whose parents immigrated from Russia commented: "It is okay to implement corporal punishment if its outcome is to improve and better a child, but if it has negative effects, then other means of discipline should be used." A 32-year-old woman who had emigrated from Russia a few years ago said "we try not to hit our children and if we do—we make sure to hit them lightly and softly so that we do not cause any physical bruises."

On the other hand, many participants viewed several forms of physical punishment as abusive. For example, a 26-year-old female categorized "hitting a child with a belt" as extremely abusive and slapping a child as moderately abusive. A 53-year-old male financial advisor gave an example of "hitting one's child or throwing an object at him/her" as an extreme form of abuse, and "slapping a child" as an example of moderate abuse. Another respondent stated that "strangling one's child" is considered extremely abusive. A 20-year-old man stated that "hitting a child hard" is considered an extreme form of abuse whereas "depriving a child of food or not allowing them to watch television" could be considered moderately abusive. A 31-year-old businesswoman said "slapping a child on the face or the behind" could be considered a mild form of abuse. A 65-year-old man wrote that "hitting a child with a stick" is extremely abusive, "hitting a child without objects" is moderately abusive, and "slapping a child" is mildly abusive. Finally, one respondent said the severity of abuse can be determined only after the damage is known. In his implicit theory, any abuse requiring medical attention or emotional counseling is extreme. He stated, "A child who ends up in the hospital must have been extremely abused by one of his family members, but a child who has a mild bruise or who is slapped lightly and does not receive medical care is definitely not considered an extreme form of abuse."

Although psychological abuse is generally less likely to be reported (e.g., Shor, 1999), it was among the types of abuse that respondents reported having experienced and/or observed. One 24-year-old student stated, "My friend's mother died when she was 18 years old. Her father took her and her younger sister to live in his house. He would insult them, tell them insulting and false stories about their mother after she died and would bother them on a continuous basis." The same participant also has a close friend whose father and mother tell her that she will not amount to much in life because she has yet to finish her college degree. A 40-year-old male beautician/ make-up artist stated that "any attempt to injure a child physically and emotionally" is extremely abusive, and "not considering a child's emotional and physical needs" is mildly abusive.

The implicit theories of several respondents identified pressures related to home or school work as having potential for abuse. A 20-year-old male respondent serving in the Israeli Army wrote that "making a child clean his/ her house" can be considered a mild form of abuse. A 23-year-old woman who had completed some college stated "if a child does not complete his math homework, it is abusive if his/her parents do not allow him/her to go out with friends, watch television, or attend school trips." A 30-year-old male who is in marketing stated that an extreme form of child abuse is "hitting," whereas "not letting a child speak on the phone or not letting child see friends" as a form of punishment is moderately abusive. This respondent viewed "making a child clean the house and do house chores" to be mildly abusive.

Many of our respondents listed forms of neglect—also less likely to be reported by pediatricians—as examples of severe or moderate abuse. One woman wrote "Not giving a child food or sending a child to bed without food as a form of punishment is extreme, because the child is helpless and cannot feed him/herself . . . Not feeding a child does not teach them the difference between right and wrong, it merely shows them what the meaning of cruelty is." Other forms of neglect were "not tending to a child's needs," "not helping with their homework," "not keeping the house clean," and "not doing a child's laundry."

In our sample, most of the participants who mentioned sexual abuse (e.g., "sexual relations between a parent and a child, rape, molestation, fondling and touching children in an inappropriate way/manner") as a form of child abuse identified it as extremely abusive. One of the few participants reporting a personal experience of sexual abuse stated that when her father used to lay her down to sleep at night, he would sometimes fondle her. She stated that worse than the abuse itself was the fact that she never knew on which night he would touch her and on which night he would just put her in bed and tuck her in like a "normal father should do."

A 29-year-old participant in our sample described the sexual abuse that she endured by her second cousin when she was 4, then commented,

On my way home, I told my brother what had happened and he told my parents who took immediate action. I will never forget that day until the day I die. The scariest part of it is that it all happened while the rest of my family and cousins were downstairs . . . I am so glad that Israeli society has become more aware of the fact that abuse does take place within the family and that children fall prey to sexual and physical abuse. Although I do not feel that abuse permeates our society, it is comforting to know that the society as a whole is becoming more aware that abuse can take place within the confines of ones own house, let alone by a family member.

DOMESTIC VIOLENCE

Wife Abuse

According to Yaar and Herman (2000), fear of domestic violence explains the broad support for restricting the number of gun permits for civilians. People seem to fear this more than they fear terrorist attacks. It is estimated that about 200,000 women are suffering from domestic violence in Israel (Siegel, 2003). In the year 2000, there were 13 shelters for abused women and their families, which sheltered 715 women and 882 children. There is also one hostel for battering and violent husbands. The level of domestic violence in Israel may be related to the lower status of women. In a study of 35 Israeli women in a battered women's shelter in Israel, Avni (1992) found that battering husbands often regarded their earnings as a favor to the family, entitling them to receive extra benefits from their wives, including obedience and submissiveness.

In one early study of domestic violence in Israel, Edelson and Lev (1988) found that prevalence rates of abuse were lower in Israel than in the United States, with approximately 5% of Israeli women (as compared to 33% of the American women) reporting abuse each year. On the other hand, evidence of increasing proportions of domestic violence in Israel was reported in a 1988 survey conducted by the Los Angeles/Tel-Aviv Partnership (a federation of Greater Los Angeles). Steiner and Zemach (as cited in Aushenker, 2000), who conducted anonymous interviews in 1,019 households in Tel-Aviv, found that 200,000 Israeli women (approximately 11% of the Israeli population) had been the victims of spousal abuse. In addition, approximately 67,000 women (4% of Israeli women) reported having experienced domestic violence within the previous year. Of these participants, 19% reported violent incidents occurring daily or several times in the same week, 42% reported several times a month, 14% reported several times a year, and 25% reported less frequent abuse. Nine percent of the women reported that their spouse had threatened to hit them, 7% reported having been hit by their spouse, 6% reported having had something thrown at them, 5% reported having had to have sexual relations against their own will, and 2% reported having had their spouse trying to strangle them. Twenty-six percent of the women had spoken with either their family doctor or another medical professional. In most of these cases (77%), the conversation took place at the initiative of the woman. Of those women who spoke with their physician, only 16% were referred to a police department to file a formal complaint and only 32% were referred to supportive services dealing with domestic violence. Steiner and Zemech found a significant rate of violence across all strata of Israeli society, although it was higher among those with low education.

Grynbaum (2001) distributed an anonymous questionnaire in both Hebrew and Russian in a primary care clinic in Beer Sheva to all women ages 18 to 60 years old. The response rate was 96%. The results showed that 41 women (31%) were at high risk for violence. Women over 40 who had emigrated from the former Soviet Union during the last 10 years, and were living alone or were unemployed, were at the highest risk of experiencing violence. None of the participants visited a domestic violence shelter during the study or in the subsequent 2 months even though all participants were given a sheet with contact information for local shelters; only three women even tore off the center's address and phone number.

Mesch (2000) found that women in Israel feared sexual assault and violent partners. Moreover, they also feared violent and sexual victimization of their children. The implicit theories of many of our respondents indicated that they saw sexual violence as more abusive than physical violence. Among the typical examples, a 26-year-old female classified "raping one's wife" as an extreme form of abuse, "hitting or punching one's wife" as moderate abuse, and "slapping one's wife" as mild abuse. A 53-year-old male financial advisor considered a husband "raping his wife" to be extremely abusive, "throwing objects" as moderately abusive, and "hitting" as mildly abusive.

Eisikovits and Enosh (1997) conducted an intensive analysis of the experiences of 20 couples composed of battered women and their abusers living in the same household. In order to participate, the couples had to report at least one episode of man-to-woman physical violence during the preceding 12 months. One of the wives explained her experience this way: "(after the beating) I was shocked for some time. I could not believe he did it. I wasn't feeling anything, not thinking about anything particular. . . . A bit later, I started feeling all the pain and hate and humiliation. Yes, mostly humiliation." Other women in the sample had immediately proceeded to take action following the violence, whereas the men appeared to deny or minimize the occurrence, adopting a "business as usual" stand (p. 465), and trying to keep their wives from making a fuss over the violence. Many of the women did, however, try to make the violence public as a way of getting assistance.

In a later study, Eisikovits (1997) reported on the views and experiences of 20 battered women who had reached a turning point at which they refused to continue enduring domestic violence and took active steps to stop it, even while living with the perpetrators. One woman explained what it was like to endure a battering relationship: "The violence transforms me, too: I become violent . . . it influences me. It forces me to burst out and do to the kid's things he does to me . . . it is hard for me . . . and I know it is wrong to do it." The willingness of these mothers to tolerate violence became so degrading that they put themselves in danger of becoming abusers themselves. They no longer saw themselves as warm, loving caregivers, but rather as "child abusers." All of the women except one defined the turning point as an outcome of the collapse of a system of meaning that had kept them in the violent relationships. Living in violence had been possible as long as they had a sense of mutuality, help, and common beliefs and goals shared with their partners. Although they were living in violence, they did not feel they were alone, so they could reduce violence to mere episodic events. Only when they realized that they had been perpetuating false hopes that the violence would end, despite evidence to the contrary, could they actively confront their victimization.

Rabin, Markus, and Voghera (1999) studied a sample of 292 battered women, 88 Arab and 204 Jewish. The target population was battered women over the age of 18 whose perpetrator was their husband or steady partner and who were treated in a hospital emergency department. Rabin et al. found that the Jewish perpetrators were significantly older and had had more education than had the Arab perpetrators. More of the Arab women were pregnant and more of them arrived in the emergency department with a family member. Arab women reported that the violence occurred more in the home setting whereas Jewish women reported most of the abuse occurring outside the confines of the home. Rabin et al. noted that because most Arab women live with their husband's extended family, and do not leave the home unaccompanied, there is little room for protection within the home. The peak of the inception of the abusive behaviors occurred in both groups immediately after marriage. In both groups women reported (in the following order): "hands and fists, heavy objects, sharp objects, sexual abuse, and guns." A significantly larger proportion of Jewish women began divorce proceeding as compared with Arab women.

Rabin et al. also found that among both the Arab and Jewish women, only a small number went to shelters. If a woman goes to a shelter, there is often no option for her to return to her home because her behavior is seen as betrayal of the family and of the man. Rabin et al. also found that most of the women did not end up being hospitalized, because they did not require immediate medical care, but rather required social and psychological support and somebody to talk to. Jewish women tended to use social services more than did Arab women and were more apt to file police reports and share information about abuse with social workers. This may be due in part to the fact that the Arab helping professionals themselves represent specific family clans within the culture; other reasons may include the risk of a breach of confidentiality and a fear that true assistance cannot always be assured. Furthermore, the Arab women did not feel that the police could contribute to their safety. In both groups, half the women perceived abuse as a life-threatening situation.

ELDER ABUSE

Israel tends to have a relatively low proportion of elders who live alone. Brodsky, Sobol, Naon, King, and Lifshitz (1991) found that 50% of their sample of 200 Israeli elders lived with their children, who reported that the emotional and physical burden of care was very heavy. Although the accepted norm throughout Israel's history is that elderly live with their families whenever possible, this does not mean elder abuse does not take place. In a study conducted by Lowenstein (1989, cited in Lowenstein, 1995) of 46 elderly and their caregivers, 12% of families indicated, as one of the major reasons for seeking institutionalization, their fear of becoming abusive toward their elderly parent because they felt as though they were being overburdened.

According to Lowenstein (1995), if one applies accepted prevalence rates of elder abuse (4–10%) from published studies to the Israeli population of elders, then one can estimate that 20,000 to 50,000 Israeli elders are being abused each year. Neikrug et al. (1992, cited in Lowenstein, 1995) interviewed an Israeli sample of 452 people concerning their perceptions of types of elder abuse, the severity of the problem, and their firsthand knowledge of cases of elder abuse. More than 50% of the participants thought that some problem of abuse exists, whereas 39% thought that abuse was widespread. Eleven percent of the sample knew at least one case of abuse among friend's relatives, and 7% knew about cases of elder abuse within their immediate and extended families.

A number of the participants in my sample considered intent when determining whether or not an act could be considered extremely or mildly abusive. For the most part, acts that were considered to be done purposefully were categorized as extreme whereas acts done unintentionally were considered mild. In contrast, some participants stated that "there is no such a thing as mild abuse; causing another person pain could never be considered mild." Many of the participants felt that placing a parent in a nursing home was abusive. The most common examples of physical and psychological abuse were forms of neglect—including lack of communication, lack of medical care, not visiting, not calling, institutionalizing, or ignoring a parent. One 74-year-old woman in a nursing home gave the following example of emotional abuse:

> As soon as my medical care became a bit more difficult and I required more attention and was unable to do some regular house chores on my own, my

children placed me in a nursing home. Although the nursing home is near to their homes, I still suffer from loneliness. If they don't call for a couple of hours, or if they don't come to visit me regularly, I begin feeling down. I feel like when they needed me and when they were most vulnerable, I was always there for them, but now when I need them, I feel so alone.

Another 78-year-old woman talked about how she feels like she is a burden on her children and often needs to wait around in her room for help with a shower or in order to get her sheets changed. She said, "I sometimes need help eating or I need help showering and putting my clothes on. I feel like I am such a burden to my children at times and I wish that I did not feel like I always needed them. I wish I did not feel like I was a burden, because that feeling is abusive towards myself . . . they make me feel so helpless so I start believing that I am . . . and that is abusive." Few respondents gave examples of physical abuse toward an elderly, but if they did, their responses were not much more detailed than "hitting" or "slapping" or "rough transport in a wheelchair." Most acts of psychological abuse included belittling and yelling at an elder parent.

Fleishman et al. (1999) described the role of Israel's services for the aged in identifying private institutions for the elderly operating illegally and giving poor quality. He found that although many of the centers for the elderly were deficient in care, improvements were being made. Bergman and Lowenstein (1988) stated that Israel has undoubtedly entered that "age of aging" and as the frail elders is expected to grow rapidly, it is reasonable to assume an increase in the incidents of elder abuse in the future.

SIBLING ABUSE

Another family relationship in which children suffer victimization is the sibling relationship. In this sample, hitting, slapping, pushing, punching, biting, hair pulling, and scratching were all considered extreme and moderate forms of abuse. Participants also reported being hit with objects such as broom handles, rubber hoses, belts, and sticks. Consistently, sexual acts were considered extremely abusive, whereas acts of psychological abuse were categorized as moderate or mild. Breaking a sibling's possession, stealing and snooping in private materials were common examples of sibling abuse. One 22-year-old participant wrote "I will never forget when I caught my brother looking in my diary. I felt like that was extremely abusive because he violated my privacy and I think that when one feels violated, it is abusive. I felt like I was robbed of my private thoughts and my trust as well because I always left my diary out in the open."

Another respondent stated:

My brother and sister used to break my toys on a constant basis. I felt like they did not respect my property. They would also tease me and tell me that my parents did not want to bear me as a child and that I was a mistake. I used to get so upset, but sometimes I feel like sibling abuse is just a part of growing up and I know that my brother and sister did it out of love.

INTERVENTION AND PREVENTION

Itzhacky (2000) found that community intervention in cases of sexual incest and abuse are successful in preventing the recurrence of sexual abuse within the community. When a few cases of child sexual abuse occurred in a small urban community, they were discussed openly and the acts were punished. Both individual and community-based interventions were used, and were found helpful and effective in changing community norms toward child sexual abuse.

Children Protection Laws

According to Shor and Haj-Yahia (1996), child maltreatment was recognized as a significant social problem in Israel back in the late 1970s. Sznaider and Talmud (1998) noted that in 1988, cultural attitudes toward child abuse in Israel changed, and the state became a participant in moral action. The development of child abuse legislation came about in 1989 when a 3-year-old, Moran, in Tiberias died in a hospital after being there for 5 months in a coma. Her case of abuse was a story of "poverty, bad housing, drug addiction and many other symptoms of social misery." Although she was not the first child to die as a result of abuse, her case became a huge media event that came to be known as "the eyes of Moran." Five days after Moran's death, Israeli Parliament convened its first meeting on child abuse (Kadman, 1992) and 9 months later, the Israeli Child Abuse bill was passed. This law encompassed the Israeli *obligatory reporting law*, which states that not only professionals, but also all members of the public, are required to report instances of child abuse. Since the enactment of that law, Israel has passed additional laws designed to aid maltreated children and prosecute their abusers. The Law of Evidence-Child Protection (1983) states that a child under the age of 14 believed to have been a victim of abuse shall be investigated by a special investigator and not be required to testify against the perpetrator in court. Amendment 29 (1989), The Law for the Prevention of Abuse of Minors and the Helpless, has the following stipulations:

1. It imposes mandatory reporting requirements on professionals who have either knowledge or suspicion of child abuse. This responsibility is imposed on all professionals who have contact with children as part

of their work. Failure to report child abuse is punishable by 6 months in prison.

2. It identifies sexual abuse of children as separate crime and makes sexual abuse a particularly serious felony when committed by a parent, other family member, or person responsible for the child. Penalties may run as long as 10 to 15 years in prison.

Concern with child abuse in Israel has expanded since ratification of the United Nations Convention on the Rights of the Child to include a ban on corporal punishment. On January 25, 2000, the Supreme Court in Jerusalem ruled that corporal punishment of children by their parents is never educational and always causes serious harm to the children. Yitzhak Kadman, head of the National Council for the Child, declared that the ruling established a precedent and "finally recognized the right of children not to be exposed to violence of any kind, even when those who use violence makes excuses for it, saying it is 'educational' or 'punitive' " (Izenberg, 2000, para. 2). In our sample, a 51-year-old doctor commented that the child reporting laws in Israel have made health practitioners more attentive to signs of abuse when performing routine clinical care. She says laws are essential "so that newly trained residents don't take a bruise or a cut on a child's leg or arm as a definite sign of a fall, rather they look for other signs that may indicate abuse." Another pediatrician said as a physician, it is her responsibility to go beyond her medical duties and ensure that if a child is abused, she knows about it. She stated, "I like to develop an emotional time to my patients and I always speak to them in my office for 15–20 minutes before attempting to do a physical exam; it is during this time that I search for signs of maltreatment."

Wife Protection Laws in Israel

While Israeli hospitals have been required to report suspected cases of child abuse, spousal abuse has been a grayer area. Until recently, cases were not reported unless a woman filed a complaint with the police; however, increased awareness of domestic violence in Israel has brought about the passage of a number of laws that have improved the status of women. A recent bill, which makes reporting of domestic violence mandatory, is in the process of evaluation. For example, with the passage of a new law, hospital officials can inform legal authorities of suspected abuse, have the husband placed under 24-hour police custody, and keep the woman in the hospital for 24 hours until a safe place can be found. The 1991 Domestic Violence Law empowered the family court to issue protective orders against violent spouses. In 1998, Israel adopted a comprehensive Sexual Harassment Prevention Law, which defines sexual harassment and makes it both a criminal offense and the basis for a civil suit against the perpetrator and his employer. In March, 2000, an amendment to the Equal Rights for Women Law was passed, which deals with equal social rights for women in all spheres of life; the right of women over their bodies, protection against violence and trafficking, and representation for women in the public sector. The equality proposed by this law extends to all spheres of life except family life. Issues of marriage and divorce continue to be exclusively within the jurisdiction of the religious courts—Jewish, Christian, Muslim, or Druze. These courts continue to exercise control over women's lives and their choices about their lives (http://www.hrw.org/wr2k1/women/women6. html+family+violence+laws+in+israel&hl=en).

Shelters for Women and Children

At present, Israel has 13 shelters for abused women and their families, which, during 2000, sheltered some 715 women and 882 children. There is also one hostel for battering and violent husbands. One of the facilities in Jerusalem collaborates with Hadassah Medical Organization, which forwards patients in need of housing (Werczberger, 2001).

CONCLUSION

Born out of violence, and feeling a constant threat of external violence, Israel has not been free of violence within the home. Recently, there has been increasing recognition of the problems of child and spouse abuse, and efforts to combat the problems. The major forms of child abuse are physical abuse, severe neglect, and emotional abuse, with sexual abuse being much less frequently reported. While domestic violence is fairly widespread, it is seldom reported to authorities. Most elderly Israelis live with some member of their family, which appears to put them at some risk of abuse from the overly-stressed family member. There have been strong legislative actions to protect children from abuse, and the Supreme Court passed a decision that corporal punishment is harmful to children. Efforts to provide greater protections for women from domestic violence are underway.

ACKNOWLEDGMENTS

My thanks to KMM, the group, and especially my family for seeing me through this process.

REFERENCES

Aushenker, M. (2000, March 24). Stopping the violence. *The Jewish Journal* [online]. Available: http://www.jewishjournal.com/old/domesticviolence.3.24.0.htm

Avni, N. (1991). Battered wives: Characteristics of their courtship days. *Journal of Interpersonal Violence, 6*, 232–239.

Avni, N. (1992). Economic exchange between battered wives and their husbands in Israel. *International Journal of Victimology, 2*, 127–135.

Bergman, S., & Lowenstein, A. (1988). Care of the aging in Israel: Social service delivery. *Journal of Gerontological Social Work: International Perspectives*, 97–116.

Brodsky, J., Sobol, E., Naon, D., King, Y., & Lifshitz, C. (1991). *The functional, health, and social characteristics and needs of the elderly in the community.* Jerusalem: JDC-Brookdale Institute of Gerontology.

Eisikovits, Z., & Enosh, G. (1997). Awareness of guilt and shame in intimate violence. *Violence and Victims, 12*, 307–322.

Eisikovits, Z., Guttman, E., Sela-Amit, M., & Edleson, J. (1993). Woman battering in Israel: The relative contributions of interpersonal factors. *American Journal of Orthopsychiatry, 63*, 313–317.

Fleishman, R., Holzer, I., Walk, D., Mandelson, J., Mizrahi, G., Bar-Giora, M., & Yuz, F. (1999). Institutions for the elderly operating without a license: Quality of care and the surveillance process. *Quality Managed Health Care, 8*, 1–12.

Ghent, J. S. (1998, August 7). In Israel, 200,000 women may be abused every year. *San Francisco Jewish Community Publications.* Available: www.jewishsf.com/bk980807/laisrael.htm

Grynbaum. (2001). Domestic violence: Prevalence among women in a primary care center—a pilot study. *Israel Medical Association Journal, 3*, 907–910.

Itzhaky, H., & York, A. S. (2001). Child sexual abuse and incest: Community-based intervention. *Child Abuse & Neglect, 25*, 959–972.

Izenberg, D. (2000, January 26). Supreme Court: Corporal punishment of children is indefensible. *Jerusalem Post.* Available: http://www.nospank.net/israel.htm

Jewish Virtual Library. (n.d). Available: http://www.us-israel.org/

Kadman, I. (1992). The child abuse prevention bill: A turning point in Israeli society regarding child abuse. *Social Security, 38*, 135–156.

Lowenstein, A. (1995). Elder abuse in a forming society: Israel. In J. I. Kosberg & J. L. Garcia (Eds.), *Elder abuse: International and cross-cultural perspectives* (pp. 81–100). Haworth.

Mesch, G. S. (2000). Perceptions of risk, lifestyles activities, and fear of crime. *Deviant Behavior, 21*, 47–62.

Neikrug, S., Ronen, M., Edelstein, et al. (1992). *Abuse of the elderly in Israel.* Unpublished manuscript, Bar Ilan University, Ramat Gan.

Rabin, B., Markus, B., & Voghera, N. (1999). A comparative study of Jewish and Arab battered women presenting in the emergency room of a general hospital. *Social Work in Health Care, 29*, 69–84.

Schein, M., Biderman, A., Baras, M., Bennet, L., Bisharat, B., Borkan, Y., Fogelman, Y., Gordon, L., Steinmetz, D., & Kitai, E. (2000). The prevalence of a history of child sexual abuse among adults visiting family practitioners in Israel. *Child Abuse & Neglect, 24*, 667–675.

Shor, R. (1998). Pediatricians in Israel: Factors which affect the diagnosis and reporting of maltreated children. *Child Abuse & Neglect, 22*, 143–153.

Shor, R. (1999). Inappropriate child rearing practices as perceived by Jewish immigrant parents from the former Soviet Union. *Child Abuse & Neglect, 23*, 487–499.

Shor, R., & Haj-Yahia, M. (1996). The approach of Israeli health and mental health students toward child maltreatment. *Child Abuse & Neglect, 20*, 425–435.

Siegel, J. (2003). Survey: 200,000 Israeli women have been abused. *Jewish Bulletin—News* [online]. Available: http://www.jewishsf.com/bk991105/idomesticabuse.shtml

Sternberg, K. J., & Krispin, O. (1993). Effects of domestic violence on children's behavior problems and depression. *Developmental Psychology, 29,* 44–55.

Sznaider, N., & Talmud, I. (1998). Moral sentiments and the social organization of public compassion: The case of child abuse in israel. *International Journal of Contemporary Sociology, 35,* 15–27.

Werczberger, R. (2001). The advancement of the status of women in Israel. *Jewish Virtual Library* [online].

Yaar, E., & Herman, T. (2000, April). [online]. Available: Peace Index: http://www.tau.ac.il/peace/Peace_Index/2000/English/p_april_00_e.html

12

Lebanon

Laura Sheridan
Ghassan Ghorayeb

CAPSULE

Issues central to Lebanese society, such as the predicaments of women, children, domestic keepers, the effects of the civil war, and recovery from that war are essential to the understanding of family violence in Lebanon. The ravages of the wars, beginning in 1975 and lasting to 1991, confront the government with a seemingly insurmountable reconstruction project, one that progresses slowly under the current recession. Attempting to regain their previous lives, families returned from war to vestiges of homes, no jobs, and high inflation—leading to a need for women and children to work at low-paying jobs to help their families survive.

Lebanese society tends to adhere to a patriarchal and age hierarchy: Men and elders preside over women and juniors, with few exceptions (Joseph, 1993a, 1993b). Within this tradition, men have the authority to direct the actions and behaviors of the women in their families, blood or otherwise. A woman's perceived domain is her home; to venture beyond is to encroach on the male realm, particularly in economic, military, and labor development (Holt, 1999; Shehadeh, 1999c). Efforts by women and young people to challenge this hierarchy may be a source of conflict in families today. "Honor" crimes in which women and girls can be subjected to violence for liaisons with males are not unheard of.

Domestic help, almost always women from outside Lebanon and the Arab world, find themselves in an even more vulnerable position than Lebanese

*women. Research (Abu-Habib, 1998; Haddad, 2000) has documented that for-
eign women, brought to Lebanon under work visas, can become the targets of
family violence. Many live in the same house as their employers, with room,
board, and a stipend in return for housekeeping and cooking duties. Employers
have been known to confiscate the documents of their employees, thus preventing them from returning home; physical and sexual abuse has also been documented (Abu-Habib, 1998; Haddad, 2000). Lebanon does not currently have
laws in effect to protect the rights of these women.*

THE LEBANESE RESPONDENTS

Respondents to our survey (73 females and 46 males) ranged in age from 15
to 44, and were recruited by researchers in the United States and Lebanon.
Many attended college in Lebanon, some in the United States. Others grew
up in Lebanon and were currently living abroad, but all were self-identified
as Lebanese. Although the majority were university students, other walks
of life included homemakers, young professionals in various industries, and
high school students. No participants reported participation in militias.
Nearly all participants were single; only 2 women and no men said they
were married. When they chose to report their religious affiliation, the vast
majority labeled themselves as a member of a Christian sect; 5 males and 5
females labeled themselves as members of an Islamic sect.

Lebanese Participants' Definitions of Abuse

Although large percentages of respondents mentioned types of physically
(55%) and psychological/verbally (35%) abusive behaviors when giving definitions of abuse, examples of control (36%) and a disrespectful relationship
(25%) were also mentioned. Women mentioned psychological/verbal abuse
(including "disrespect") more frequently than did men, but there were no
gender differences in the frequency with which physical or sexual aggression (19%) was listed.

In analyzing definitions of abuse, we were particularly interested in the
responses focusing on issues of respect and the use of power to dominate
and control others, as well as the more "classic" aspects of abuse (e.g.,
physical, sexual, psychological/ verbal abuse). Participants who mentioned
control in their general definition of abuse were critical of the extreme use
of control in a variety of family relationships, but particularly by husbands
against wives. Men and women did not differ in the frequency with which
they mentioned control in their definitions of abuse. However, when allusions were made to specific family relationships within the definitions, the
responses indicated considerable dissatisfaction with elements of patriarchy in the Lebanese family. The use of control by an elder (e.g., a parent,

grandparent, or older sibling) and/or by a male (e.g., husband, brother) was often mentioned. A female respondent defined abuse as "to use power we have on others." Her example was a "father's authority over his children over 21 years old." The aged and gendered hierarchy is clear in another woman's definition: "Abuse is when an older person from the same family uses his dominance for exploiting weaker members." The possibility of women being abusive to subordinate family members was not reflected in any of the participants' responses.

These responses show not only an awareness of patriarchy existing in the family, but also a judgment that imposing control over another is abusive. Based on her observations of individual families in Lebanon, Joseph (1993b) described patriarchy as the normative organization of the Lebanese family. Inherent in possessing elder or male status is the capacity to "direct others as part of the self, to expect service and compliance . . . [and] differential respect as rights due" (Joseph, 1993b, p. 470). In the current study, this "legitimatizing" of the use of control by a male and/or aged family member seems to be challenged by many participants, including several of the men. For example, one 23-year-old male stated: "Abuse is the use of power against another person's will, like from a parent to a child." Another young man said that abuse is the "erasing of one's identity by wanting his child to grow up as he sees or wants him to be—deciding what's best for him." (Clearly, the participant is referring to the power of a father to direct the life of his son, as shown in the use of masculine pronouns: "he," "his," and "him.") One young woman said abuse was "when someone forces you to act as if he owns you." A 22-year-old woman indicated that abuse refers to a situation of "girls . . . dominated by their brothers."

"Disrespectful behavior" was another major theme; over a third of the respondents gave examples of disrespectful actions in their definitions. The identification of disrespectful behaviors as abusive, however, does not show the same rejection of patriarchal/connectivity traditions implied in definitions of abuse focusing on control. That is, the implicit theories of these participants characterize all instances of disrespect in the family, regardless of relationship, as abusive. Respect, to which men and the aged are particularly entitled, seems to be the norm among family members, and to deviate from this norm is considered abusive.

THE LEBANESE MACROSYSTEM

Historical Context

At the crossroads between the Western and Arab worlds, Lebanon gained its independence in November 1943 through a League of Nations mandate. Although the mandate freed Lebanon from French administration, the French influence continues to be visible in areas such as government, language, education, and society. These effects especially hold true for the Lebanese Christian population, who tend to identify with the French (Feghali, 1997).

The "jewel of the Middle East" disintegrated into a war in 1975, first between Palestinians and Lebanese, and later between Muslims and Christians and even sects within these religions. Numerous attempts to quell the violence failed, and the war did not end until the Syrian disarmament of the various militias. Many authors have described the multiple factors contributing to the war; references can be found at the end of the chapter (e.g., Khalifah, 2001; Shehadeh, 1999a).

The very nature of wars can be a source of child maltreatment both during and after the hostilities. War created a predicament for children, albeit not official, for example, military service. The Lebanese military does not draft or accept male conscripts or volunteers under the age of 18 years. During the civil war, however, the country's military was just one of the warring groups on Lebanese soil. Palestinians, Christians, Sunni and Shi'a Muslims, and Syrians, among others, formed militias as the war progressed. As factions multiplied and conflicts spread, more families and residential areas came under the "rule" of informal militias, which governed the different sectors. As members were killed or injured, the groups conscripted the easiest available source of labor—male children (Human Rights Watch, 2001). On occasion, even female children were militarily trained and fought with male comrades. Jocelyn Khweiri (1999), who eloquently described her own experience as a front line fighter for the Phalangist party, also told of the gender prejudice and disbelief she endured from family, friends, fellow fighters, and observers.

The Economy

A major impediment to rebuilding and rebounding from the war is the economic strife prevalent in the country. Inflation of the Lebanese lire caused its value to plummet; whereas before the war 3 lire equaled the value of the U.S. dollar, now the equivalency rate is 1,500 lire to the dollar. A recent article (Assaf, 2002) in the *Daily Star* noted the current financial stress and the effects most families are experiencing. Parents are also working longer days for half the money as compared to the years before 1975 and the civil war (Assaf, 2002).

Legal and Legislative Issues

One of the pressing concerns regarding abuse in the family is the absence of a national legal policy. Marriages and personal status issues in Lebanon are presided over by religious courts; there is no civil court jurisdiction (Joseph, 1997). Complaints and procedures are presided over by religious courts, as determined by the individuals' identified religion. Gender equality, while protected by the Lebanese Constitution (1926), is not assured under the legal codes, especially in the case of married women (Shehadeh, 1998), and judgments of the respective religious court take precedence over the secular.

Aftermath of the War

The postwar reconstruction of Lebanon has entered into a second decade, with efforts focused on Beirut, other major cities, and power resources. Thus far, reconstruction efforts have proceeded slowly due to a major economic recession. The current government is in the process of paying back debts to other countries and stabilizing the employment and investment sectors. Syrian presence, which was instrumental in bringing the civil war to a halt, is still felt in both military and political arenas. The Syrian military occupation has been reduced recently, especially in Beirut and after the Israeli withdrawal from the southern parts of Lebanon; its political presence, however, continues to influence the relationship between the nations.

As in the case of other societies recovering from a long-term war, Lebanese families are confronted with many continuing problems. Kidnappings, assassinations, relocation, and interrupted education are just a few of the dilemmas faced by families today. Several authors (e.g., Assal & Farrell, 1992; Farhood, 1999; Farhood et al., 1993; Zahr, 1996) have described both immediate and prolonged impacts of the war on the Lebanese family as a whole and its individual members. Given that many of the battles occurred in residential neighborhoods, children were exposed to bombing of homes, shootings, and death of family members and friends (Farhood, 1999). Only a decade into recovery, many of our participants grew up in the midst of intense fighting.

Status of Women in Lebanon

"One of my friends got married to a person she didn't love just to satisfy her parents; this is extremely abusive" (woman, 22 years old). "A friend got married very young and her husband believes he is the boss of the family and all she has to do is cook and take care of his children and obey" (woman, 20). Such examples of cases of abuse known to our participants provide insight into the traditional status of women in Lebanon, and growing discomfort with that status. According to Keenan and colleagues (1998) and Joseph (1996), women in Lebanon face many biases against their gender, although steps toward equality are being taken. In executive and ministry positions, judgeships, and other branches of government, there are few women to be found (Shehadeh, 1999b). For those women who work, whether in a male-dominated career or simply to earn extra spending money, discrimination, explicit or implicit, is very much in operation (Shehadeh, 1999c). Most women were and are forced to find work out of necessity because of lack of sufficient income from their husbands' employment and rising costs of living (Joseph, 1997), especially in metropolitan areas. Many of these women are concurrently raising large families, and, with little or no education or training, find few jobs available to them. The jobs to be had often have poor wages, poor working conditions, and no benefits. Although wealthier families often employ housekeepers, cooks, chauffeurs, and au pairs, this source of employment has decreased for Lebanese women because of the influx of immigrant women from surrounding Arab states, Sri Lanka, Somalia, and the Philippines (Abu-Habib, 1998).

Education is another arena in which women have experienced discrimination (Joseph, 1997). In more rural regions, and with the government in a state of reconstruction, public schools are inadequately supplied and funded. Families that are financially able to enroll their children in private schools usually do. According to one perspective (Boukhari, 1997), if the costs of education become a strain on a family's resources, girls are more frequently taken out of school than boys, for three reasons: mothers get more help with household tasks, the family is able to save money, and boys continue their education with the goal of getting a higher paying job to help support the family.

THE LEBANESE MICROSYSTEM

Although Lebanese family dynamics are a cultural amalgamation of West and East, the family unit is revered and held in utmost priority, regardless of religion or cultural influence. As many expatriates return to the country to raise a family, after having survived or fled the civil war, or finished educational goals, cultural influences foreign to Lebanon have been incorporated into the newly begun families. Combined with the French and Western cultural infusion, significant variations are observed in individual families (Feghali, 1997).

Traditionally, males exerted unmitigated influence in nearly all visible spheres of Lebanese life: government, business, and family (Shehadeh, 1999c). The prevailing philosophy relating to family matters in Lebanon is what Joseph (1993a, 1993b) termed patriarchal connectivity—a synthesis of patriarchy, which is a social structure allowing males and seniors to make decisions concerning the lives of others, and connectivity, which is an aspect of the relationship between persons that allows other people to be involved in determining one's identity. According to Joseph (1993a, p. 453), patriarchal connectivity is the "production of selves with fluid boundaries organized for gendered and aged domination"—a culture in which men and the older generation have a superior status and the ability to wield power over the lives of females and young people. As Keenan et al. (1998) noted, Lebanese men reign supreme, especially when in public. It is their responsibility to preserve the family honor, make important decisions, and provide for immediate and extended family (Joseph, 1993a, 1993b; Keenan et al., 1998). Wives, on the other hand, have duties to care for husbands, children, in-laws, and finally, their own families. When a woman marries, she usually gives up her own family identity and is considered part of her husband's family (Joseph, 1993b; Keenan et al., 1998).

Status of Children

Given the cherished nature of children in a Lebanese family (Shenk, 1990), it is not surprising that Lebanon is one of the many countries that have signed and ratified the United Nations' Convention on the Rights of the Child (1/26/90). According to the Global Initiative to end all Corporal Punishment of Children (2001), Lebanon has laws forbidding the use of corporal punishment against children in schools and in the penal system; however, there are no laws addressing the use of corporal punishment in the home. Indeed, the frequency with which general definitions of abuse by Lebanese participants referred specifically to child abuse reveals considerable concern with the well-being of children in Lebanese households.

Child labor is a problem that continues to plague Lebanese society. The legal minimum age of employment is 8 years, at which age there are significant restrictions on the type of work and number of hours and shifts allowable. Several of our participants made reference to child labor when giving examples of abuse. A 22-year-old man defined extreme abuse in the family as "sending [children] to work in the street and in dangerous jobs."

Currently, the age of mandated education in Lebanon is 12 years, at which time the parent can remove a child from a public school or private school. The discrepancies between public and private schools are great, more so than in Western countries. Private schools offer education in either the Lebanese, French, or American system, are chosen and funded by the parents, and are generally seen as superior (Assal & Farrell, 1992). They are available at nearly every income bracket and many parents go to great lengths to send their children to the best school they can afford. According to a recent U.N. Committee Meeting on the Rights of the Child (2002), 2/3 of children in Lebanon currently attend some type of private school, although the lower working classes typically send their children to public schools. Participants' responses revealed the emphasis that the Lebanese place on education; "restricting a child's education" was specifically mentioned in participants' general definitions of abuse and examples of child abuse.

FAMILY VIOLENCE

Spousal Abuse

"[My own experience was] verbal, mental, physical abuse; no money, re-stricted phone calls, blackmail in every aspect of life—an extremely abusive situation" (female, 39). Acknowledgment of spousal abuse has increased in Lebanon since the end of the civil war and the emergence of worldwide awareness and rejection of violence against women. Despite this increasing awareness, going outside the extended family for aid in family matters is viewed as shameful and unacceptable (Keenan et al., 1998; Lakkis, 1999). Women who reach beyond the family for help find that resources are scarce and not easily accessible. There are few social service agencies, shelters, or hotlines to which battered women can turn. Indeed, if they ex-ist, they are poorly advertised and most women are unaware of their exis-tence. In most cases, women who attempt to contact authorities are ig-nored and sent back to their homes.

Taking into consideration that marriage and family are keystones in Leb-anese society (Joseph, 1993a; Shehadeh, 1999c), some departures from im-plicit role expectations can upset the traditional order and be perceived to be abusive. One female respondent explicitly defined abuse as "the break-ing and contradicting of our society's definition of a family."

Lebanese Participants' Perspectives on Wife Abuse

While patriarchal connectivity reflects a long cultural tradition, the implicit theories of our female participants suggest the tradition is being recon-ceptualized as embodying abusive practices. Consider these responses: "One of my friends got married to a person she didn't love just to satisfy her parents: This is extremely abusive" (female, 22). "A friend got married very young and her husband believes he is the boss of the family and all she has to do is cook and take care of his children and obey" (female, 20). "The husband thinks that he is the boss, beats his wife, doesn't give [her] the chance to express [her] opinion" (female, 20). A 39-year-old woman gave vivid descriptions of extreme abuse by a domineering husband: "physical abuse, control of finances and freedom, verbal abuse." By classifying "control," in such examples as "restriction of freedom," "financial control," "being a decision maker in marriage decisions," "control the wife's comings and goings," and "prevent the wife from going out without him" as abusive, participants provided evidence of some rejection of the traditional social hierarchy delineated by Joseph (1993a, 1993b). In some instances, the responses both supported and rejected tradition: One young man wrote "never ever hit a woman, especially yours."

Lebanese Respondents' Perspectives on Husband Abuse

Despite evidence of dissatisfaction with patriarchal connectivity, judgments concerning the abusiveness of violating traditional gender roles—especially in regard to implicit theories about a wife's duties to her husband, her family, and her household—was pervasive in our sample. Over three-quarters (78%) of the respondents mentioned some instance of breached gender roles as examples of husband abuse; only 38% listed breached gender roles when giving examples of wife abuse. One 20-year-old woman wrote that "not caring for him, not understanding his needs" was an example of moderate wife to husband abuse. Not "performing her duties and responsibilities as a normal mother" was another young woman's example of mild husband abuse, along with the wife "not taking care of her children and home." Similarly, a 22-year-old woman stated that moderately abusive behavior from a wife to a husband was "not accomplishing her home duties." A 22-year-old male indicated that a wife "go[ing] out on daily basis without taking care of the house" is moderately abusive and "having a boyfriend/affair" is extremely abusive. Only two participants mentioned a wife's use of controlling behaviors as forms of husband abuse—specifically, "possessive behavior" and "refusing to satisfy [her] husband's sexual needs." Interestingly, the view that men's controlling behaviors are abusive was found in both men and women; there was no gender difference in the frequency with which the use of control was identified as a form of abuse.

Lebanese Participants' Perceptions of Child Abuse

When asked for their general definition of abuse, 37% of our participants cited some act specifically between a parent and a child. The responses identified a range of different types of behaviors that could be considered child abuse. For instance, a 24-year-old male defined abuse in the family as "stop the kids [from doing] something, sexual abuse of kids, violence with kids." When prompted to give examples of abusive behavior between a parent and child, examples of extreme abuse involved sexual behaviors, such as "incest," "rape," and "sexual harassment." Half of the female participants included at least one sexually aggressive behavior in their definition of extremely abusive actions from a parent to a child.

Physically abusive behaviors were also frequently listed as extremely abusive, with "spanking," "beating," and "hitting" as examples from nearly half of the female participants responding to this item. One woman shared this case with us: "My friend's father used to beat her and her mother every single day for extremely trivial reasons, such as not washing the dishes . . . I consider this situation extremely abusive." Sexually aggressive actions, such as "rape" and "sexual harassment," were mentioned by 46% as extremely abusive. No behaviors of a sexual nature were included in any of the examples of moderate or mild abuse. When the gender of the parent perpetrating the abusive behavior was identified, participants almost always mentioned the father, especially when referring to sexually abusive behaviors. An example of extreme abuse was a "father sexually harassing his daughter."

Implicit theories of abuse identified not only physically and sexually aggressive actions toward children, but also the use of control over children. Controlling behaviors were identified as extremely (17%), moderately (21%), and mildly (27%) abusive when perpetrated by a parent over a child. A 20-year-old male gave, as an example of child abuse, "when parents use their level to make [the child] live the life they lived." "Preventing from getting an education," a specific type of control and evidence of the value placed on education, was identified by 3 participants as a form of child abuse. "Neglect" was mentioned by only one male participant, who included it with "child labor" as examples of extreme abuse.

ELDER ABUSE

According to Abyad (1995), the geriatric population in Lebanon is just beginning to receive much needed attention and recognition. It is possible that this traditional lack of attention is reflected in how some participants responded to the request that they give examples of abuse from a adult to an elderly parent: Eight of the participants gave a response focusing on a middle-aged parent as a perpetrator of abuse to a child who was an adolescent or young adult. It is also possible, of course, that this item may have been misunderstood or misinterpreted.

Regarding the status of elder adults in the Lebanese family, there are certain expectations as to the intergenerational relationship. Children, while prized additions in a family, are laden with expectations as to the care of their parents in old age (Shenk, 1990). As one cross-cultural study on nursing home placement noted, families of Lebanese descent were concerned with how the family would be perceived if an older member was placed in a nursing home (Fitzgerald, Mullavey-O'Bryne, & Clemson, 2001); such an act would be considered dishonorable. The expectations of the elderly and perceived obligations to one's parents are deemed central to the Lebanese family system, and disregarding these considerations would have individual, familial, and community consequences (Fitzgerald et al., 2001; Shenk, 1990). Lebanese families, in the Fitzgerald et al. study, noted that the importance of caring for the elder under the family roof is a higher priority than financial or occupational concerns. As a growing number of investigators have noted, if the family is unable to care for older members, there are no governmental programs or safety nets to provide for the elderly, and charitable organizations are left to aid as many as possible (Donati, 1999; Nasser, 2002).

Lebanese Respondents' Perspectives on Elder Abuse

In their examples of abuse between an adult and an elderly parent, three respondents specifically listed "putting an elderly parent in a nursing home or hospital." More generally, "neglect" was given as an example of elder abuse. Twenty percent of the participants indicated that they considered neglecting an elderly parent as severely abusive. Physical aggression was also frequently mentioned under the category of severe abuse, with 60% of both men and women including some physical action in their definition. When describing moderate and mild abuse, participants focused more on psychological/verbal abuse than on neglect. Psychologically and/or verbally abusive behaviors were identified in 77% of the examples of moderate aggression, and 82% of mild aggression. Examples included "shouting" or "screaming" at the elder, "insulting," "psychological oppression," "disrespect," and "ignoring." A theme of abandonment was also fairly common, as were examples of "manipulation or extortion of the elder's monetary funds, without their consent."

OTHER ABUSIVE RELATIONSHIPS IN FAMILIES

Sibling Abuse

In Lebanon, there appears to be little attention to aggression among siblings as a form of abuse. When asked for examples of sibling abuse, our participants typically focused on behaviors consistent with the "classic" definitions of aggression—such as sexual, physical, and verbal abuse—but again showed some rejection of the traditional patriarchal system values. For instance, one male participant specifically labeled "honor crimes" as extremely abusive in a sibling relationship. "Being a decision maker in marriage decisions" was this young man's definition of moderate sibling abuse. A young woman referred, in her definition of mildly abusive behavior between siblings, to "males controlling females' behavior or liberty." Another female respondent, in her example of mild sibling abuse, said "having authority over each other, like there is no equality between them. Usually the male has more rights than the female."

Seventeen respondents (45%) wrote that sexual abuse was extremely abusive in a sibling relationship; no one mentioned sexual behaviors under the categories of moderate or mild abuse. "Incest" and/or "rape" were often the only examples given. Implied, but sometimes explicitly stated, was the assumption that the sexual behavior occurred between a brother and sister. If the perpetrator was specified, the brother was deemed the instigator.

Physical aggression, such as "beating," "slapping," and "punching," were often given as examples of extreme (63%) and moderate (51%) abuse. A "brother beating his sister" was considered to be moderately abusive, clearly exemplifying a gendered theme in physical aggression: Males use physical violence against females. An age trend in responses was observed as well: Older siblings, usually a brother, were pigeon-holed as abusers of younger siblings, male or female. A 21-year-old woman didn't specify gender but specifically defined sibling abuse as "beating or bullying younger siblings." Every description of mild aggression included at least one example of psychological or verbal abuse. Examples included "yelling," "swearing," "insulting," and "humiliating" the sibling and "using "bad language" with him/her.

Abuse of Domestic Workers

In Lebanon, families with sufficient financial resources frequently employ domestic help—most frequently women from countries such as Sri Lanka, Somalia, and the Philippines. So frequent is the immigration from these three nations that they all have a specific work visa branch in Beirut International Airport. These women work as personal assistants, maids, cooks, nannies, gardeners, or chauffeurs for a family who can contract for these services for any length of time. In return, the workers receive wages and often room and board (Abu-Habib, 1998).

The pitfalls of this arrangement can be many. Employers often take away the woman's passport until her tenure is finished, thus preventing her from leaving Lebanon (Abu-Habib, 1998). Instances of severe physical, sexual, and psychological abuse have also been noted (Abu-Habib, 1998; Haddad, 2000). Help for women in these situations is difficult to find and receive. More often than not, the worker has traveled alone to Lebanon in order to make a living on her own, or to support family members in the home country. Family members from her native country, especially if dependent on the wages received from Lebanon, have little power to intervene (Abu-Habib, 1998). To further compound the situation, there are no laws in Lebanon governing the contracts with or employment of foreign domestic workers (Abu-Habib, 1998), and thus embassies can do little to aid their compatriots. Under a work visa, workers can be detained from leaving Lebanon, even with a passport, if they do not have the consent of the employer. A few participants mentioned the presence of domestic help in their family lives and described specified instances of abuse in the employer/employee relationship. For instance, a 39-year-old woman gave an example of moderate abuse of a domestic employee as "physical and verbal abuse; keeping her locked up in the house all the time." Her example of mild abuse was "lock[ing] her in the house when no one was home; not feeding her for punishment; not giving her her money." Extremely abusive was "beating her to death." Another respondent told us "[Extreme abuse is] an 18-year-old boy who rapes, beats, verbally abuse, and murders a maid about 24 years old" (male, 19).

Other Family Relationships

Twelve of the respondents (52%) who identified other family relationships in which abusive behaviors occurred described scenarios involving grandparents. The perpetrator of the abuse, however, varied from participant to participant. Several gave examples of the grandparent behaving abusively, such as "beating," "disrespecting," and "not considering the child to be a person with opinions." Others, on the other hand, stipulated that the grandchild perpetrated aggressive behaviors toward a grandparent. An 18-year-old woman indicated that "hitting a grandparent" was extremely abusive, whereas "ignoring and disrespecting" and "verbal assaults" were moderately and mildly abusive, respectively.

There were also examples portraying in-laws as behaving abusively. An example of extreme abuse in this dyad, given by a 20-year-old woman, was "she [the mother-in-law] insults the wife by cursing and swearing in front of family and friends." An example of moderate abuse by a mother-in-law was trying to "put bad ideas in her son's head." Another woman gave an opposing example of a daughter-in-law "making the mother-in-law work like a maid" as extremely abusive. This woman's definition of moderate abuse described a daughter-in-law "making the son dislike her [the mother-in-law/his own mother]."

Other identified relationships were typically within the extended family; between grandparents and grandchildren, uncles/aunts and nephews/nieces, employers and employees. One participant indicated that a child was capable of perpetrating extremely abusive behaviors, such as "complete disrespect and beating." The victim could be "anybody older." Another respondent designated the uncle as the perpetrator of abuse to "children"; her examples included "sexual," "physical," and "moral" abuse. A 22-year-old woman gave examples of "sexual behaviors" and "withholding financial help" as abusive when observed between an aunt or uncle and a niece or nephew. There was no mention of abuse in intimate same-sex relationships under the "Other Relationships" section, although the societal atmosphere in Lebanon is slowly becoming more accepting of gay and lesbian citizens.

INTERVENTION AND PREVENTION

There are a number of signs of change in Lebanon, including progress toward gender equality in the legal and judicial domains. Women's testimony in court is now equal to men's (Joseph, 1997), and both genders have the right to vote. In 1999, the section of the Penal Code previously mitigating sanctions against assaultive husbands, who could justify murdering a woman for committing an "immoral act" (honor crimes), was amended to increase the penalties (U.S. Department of State, 2001). Activists have also demanded the repeal of Article 522 of the Penal Code, which legitimizes the marriage between a rape survivor and her rapist (Oxfam, 1999, cited in Lakkis, 1999). Various organizations, such as Oxfam and UNIFEM, are currently implementing women's rights campaigns in Lebanon.

In regard to supports and protection for children, UNESCO (1994, as cited in El-Hassan, 2001, p. 121) noted that gender equality in educational achievement occurs "once girls get into schools," when "equal access is ensured." Child advocates are pushing for legislature to increase the minimum age of employment to 13 years, a year more than mandatory education limits specified by the U.N. Committee on Rights of the Child (1997, 2002).

CONCLUSIONS

Although Lebanon continues to struggle to reach its premorbid status as a cultural and recreation hot spot, strides are being made in reconstructing the government, infrastructure, education, and business. The influence of the war continues to affect, in various ways, the Lebanese people and their interactions with others and the environment. This chapter is a small step toward understanding Lebanese perceptions of the acceptability of different family interactions. The attention paid to psychology and psychological research is slowly increasing and can potentially facilitate the development of culturally appropriate therapeutic paradigms, methodologies, and treatments.

ACKNOWLEDGMENTS

The authors would personally like to express sincere thanks to Dr. Doumit Salameh and his students; only with their efforts and generosity was this chapter possible. We'd like to sincerely thank the countless family, friends, and volunteers, both in the United States and Lebanon who graciously divulged their ideas, opinions, perceptions, and critiques to us. In addition, we thank the many organizations, such as the Friends of the Disabled and Oum al Nour, who provided helpful information and further contacts to broaden our research.

REFERENCES

Abu-Habib, L. (1998). The use and abuse of female domestic workers from Sri Lanka in Lebanon. *Gender and Development, 6,* 52–56.

Abyad, A. (1995). Geriatrics in Lebanon: The beginning. *International Journal of Aging and Human Development, 41,* 299–309.

Assaf, N. (2002, January 11). Shrinking families earning less, spending more, say experts. *The Daily Star* [online]. Available: http://www.dailystar.com.lb

Assal, A., & Farrell, E. (1992). Attempts to make meaning of terror: Family, play, and school in time of civil war. *Anthropology and Education Quarterly, 23,* 275–290.

Boukhari, H. (1997). Invisible victims: Working with mothers of children with learning disabilities. In L. Abu-Habib (Ed.), *Gender and disability: Women's experiences in the Middle East* (pp. 36–45). Atlantic Highlands, NJ: Oxford.

Donati, C. (1999, January). Lebanon: There's no place like home. *The New Courier* [online]. Available: http://www.unesco.org/courier/1999_01/uk/dossier/txt23.htm

El-Hassan, K. (2001). Gender issues in achievement in Lebanon. *Social Behavior and Personality, 29*(2), 113–124.

Farhood, L. F. (1999). Testing a model of family stress and coping based on war and nonwar stressors, family resources and coping among Lebanese families. *Archives of Psychiatric Nursing, 8,* 192–203.

Farhood, L. F., Zurayk, H., Chaya, M., Saadeh, F., Meshefedjian, G., & Sidani, T. (1993). The impact of war on the physical and mental health of the family: The Lebanese experience. *Social Science and Medicine, 36,* 1555–1567.

Feghali, E. (1997). Arab cultural communication patterns. *Journal of Intercultural Relations, 21,* 345–378.

Fitzgerald, M., Mullavey-O'Bryne, C., & Clemson, L. (2001). Families and nursing home placements: A cross-cultural study. *Journal of Cross-Cultural Gerontology, 16,* 333–351.

Global Initiative to end all Corporal Punishment. (2001). *State-by-state analysis: I–L* [online]. Available: http://www.endcorporalpnishment.org/pages/frame.html

Haddad, R. (2000, July 29). Abuse maid agency suspended. *The Daily Star* [online]. Available: http://www.dailystar.com.lb

Holt, M. (1999). Lebanese Shi'a women and Islamism: A response to war. In L. Shehadeh (Ed.), *Women and war in Lebanon* (pp. 167–194). Gainesville, FL: University of Florida Press.

Human Rights Watch. (2001, June). *Lebanon: Child soldiers global report 2001* [online]. Available: http://www.hrw.org/mideast/lebanon.php

Joseph, S. (1993a). Connectivity and patriarchy among urban working-class families in Lebanon. *Ethos, 21,* 452–484.

Joseph, S. (1993b). Gender and relationality among Arab families in Lebanon. *Feminist Studies, 19*(3), 465–486.

Joseph, S. (1996). Gender and citizenship in Middle Eastern states. *Middle East Report, 26*(1), 4–10.

Joseph, S. (1997). Secularism and personal status codes in Lebanon. *Middle East Report, 27*(2), 37–39.

Keenan, C. K., El-Hadad, A., & Balian, S. A. (1998). Factors associated with domestic violence in low-income Lebanese families. *Image: Journal of Nursing Scholarship, 30*, 357–362.

Khalifah, B. (2001). *The rise and fall of Christian Lebanon* (2nd ed.). Toronto: York Press Ltd.

Khweiri, J. (1999). From gunpowder to incense. In L. Shehadeh (Ed.), *Women and war in Lebanon* (pp. 209–226). Gainesville, FL: University of Florida Press.

Lakkis, S. (1999, March). Strength in numbers. *Links* [online]. Available: http://www.oxfam. org.uk/policy/gender/99mar/399leba.htm

Lebanese Constitution. (1926). [online]. Available: http://www.uni-wuerzburg.de/law/le00000_ .html

Nasser, C. (2002). Providing shelter for the old and unwanted. *The Daily Star* [online]. Available: http://www.dailystar.com.lb

Shehadeh, L. (1999a). The war in Lebanon. In L. Shehadeh (Ed.), *Women and war in Lebanon* (pp. 7–29). Gainesville, FL: University of Florida Press.

Shehadeh, L. (1999b). Women before the war. In L. Shehadeh (Ed.), *Women and war in Lebanon* (pp. 30–42). Gainesville, FL: University of Florida Press.

Shehadeh, L. (1999c). Women in the public sphere. In L. Shehadeh (Ed.), *Women and war in Lebanon* (pp. 45–70). Gainesville, FL: University of Florida Press.

Shehadeh, L. (1998). The legal status of married women in Lebanon. *International Journal of Middle Eastern Studies, 30*, 501–519.

Shenk, D. (1990). Aging in a changing ethnic context: The Lebanese-American family. *Ethnic Groups, 8*, 147–161.

United Nations, Committee on Rights of the Child. (1997, November). *Convention on the rights of the child: Document of 406th meeting summary record (partial)* [online]. Available: http:// www.eurochild.gla.ac.uk/documents/un/rights/crc/crc-sr406.htm#top

United Nations, Committee on Rights of the Child. (2002, January). *Convention on the rights of the child: Summary record of the 751th meeting* [online]. Available: http://www.unhchr.ch

U.S. Department of State. (2001, February). *Country reports on human rights practices* [online]. Available: http://www.state.gov/g/drl/rls/hrrpt/2000/nea/800.htm

Zahr, L. K. (1996). Effects of war on the behavior of Lebanese preschool children: Influence of home environment and family functioning. *American Journal of Orthopsychiatry, 66*, 401–408.

AFRICA

13

Somalia

Natoschia Scruggs

CAPSULE

Throughout the 1990s, Somalia made international headlines due to oppressive military rule and interclan fighting. In January 1991, tensions escalated, the East African country's central government officially collapsed, and anarchy reigned. Armed clan militia and warlords filled the power vacuum left behind, raping, plundering and killing out of vengeance. Violence, unspeakable human rights atrocities, and fear of starvation either claimed the lives or prompted the flight of thousands of Somalis. Forty-five percent of the population was either displaced internally or fled Somalia (Putnam & Noor, 1993). Today, there is a huge Diaspora, with large Somali communities throughout Africa, Europe, Oceania, the Middle East, and North America. Cultural values and social norms are challenged as Somalis strive to assimilate in their host countries while simultaneously retaining what it is that defines them as Somalis.

Somali nuclear families are embedded in extended families and clans characterized by respect for traditions, valuing of independence, separate spheres of interest and power for men and women, and respect for the older generation. The eldest child, regardless of gender, is always given the utmost respect from siblings, and maternal uncles are viewed as second fathers, to be consulted when making major life decisions. Men and boys have the responsibility for looking out for girls and women, even after they have become married. Although women were granted many rights under the 1979 constitution, all progress was erased by the civil war. Reports of Somali women and girls being

*raped within their own country and in refugee camps in neighboring nations
abound.*

*Child discipline is expected to be strict and is the responsibility of the entire
family. Traditionally, children and the elderly were well protected within the
family network. However, societal disintegration has left these two groups particularly vulnerable. More than 50% of all child deaths are due to diarrheal dis-
ease-related dehydration, malaria, and respiratory infections (Asylum in the
UK, 2001), and primary school gross enrollment is less than 10% (UNICEF Somalia Survey, 2000). Many elderly are displaced as their family members scramble
to make homes abroad; some are too impoverished to afford transporting a fee-
ble elderly relative.*

THE SOMALI SAMPLE

The Somali participants, representing both genders (22 males/18 females),
were primarily residents in five countries (Somalia, Australia, England, the
Netherlands, and the United States). They ranged in age from 15 to 78 years
and have attained educational levels anywhere from no formal education
other than the Qur'an to doctoral degrees.

Somali Participants' General Definitions of Abuse

Addressing the issue of family violence with Somalis is complicated. The
majority of our respondents could not separate their feelings about abuse
from those they have for a corrupt political system, which they blamed for
the breakdown of Somali society and morals. "We did not have abuse before the civil war," was a sentiment repeatedly echoed. Several respondents
made even stronger statements, confidently asserting, "Abuse does not exist in Somali culture." One respondent gave an example of what family
abuse means to him but admitted that he "made up his definition since
coming to America" because "[there is no] word for abuse in Somali."

Overwhelmingly, survey participants associated abuse within the family
with physical aggression. Twenty-five percent specifically listed "hitting,"
"slapping," "punching," and "kicking." Fifteen percent mentioned "mental"
in their definitions of abuse, whereas 15% gave definitions focusing on not
taking care of personal responsibilities and familial obligations—such as
"disregarding the feelings of others," "not keeping one's promises," "making
excuses for the ill behavior of others and being too passive." Forms of sexual abuse were listed by only 3% of participants. Examples of extreme
abuse were generally physical acts; examples of moderate abuse usually involved disregarding the will of others; and examples of mild abuse were
most often verbal offenses (e.g., "using profanity toward an elder," "yell-

ing"). Three recurring themes were issues surrounding polygamy ("jealous wives," "abusive stepmothers"); family honor ("not teaching children to respect others," "not defending family values to the outside world," "not keeping one's word"); and respect for free will and equality of self and others ("not listening to differing opinions," "not allowing relatives to choose their marriage partner").

THE SOMALI MACROSYSTEM

Because the Somali Democratic Republic existed as a nation-state by Western standards only from 1960 to 1991, with a civil war in 1969 and intermittent violence from 1988 onward, few official statistics are available. Relevant macrosystem information is presented from the colonial periods, along with data from the Somali government (1960–1985) and international organizations operating in the Horn of Africa.

Historical Context

The earliest ancestors of present-day Somalis seem to have been hunters who lived in the Stone Age from 50,000 B.C. to 35,000 B.C. Somalia appears to have been under continuous occupation by man since the later Middle Pleistocene Age (at least 30,000 years ago). This means that Somali civilization far outdates that of ancient Egypt, which developed approximately 5000 years B.C. (Clark, 1970). At a very early date—sometime between the 11th and 12th centuries—Islam began winning converts in Somalia. The conversion was swift and nonviolent, but led to conflicts between Somali Muslims and Abyssinian Christians in what is now Ethiopia, Somalia's traditional archenemy. The Muslim Somalis suffered a tremendous blow in the 1530s when Portuguese explorers arrived in the Red Sea and lent support to the Christians. An era of invasions ensued, including sporadic attacks on Somali coastal cities, orchestrated by the Portuguese. European expansion into the Horn of Africa took place with the 1869 opening of the Suez Canal in Egypt. Somalis were divided and ruled by four foreign powers: the British in north central Somalia and northeast Kenya; the French in the northwest (present-day Djibouti); the Ethiopians in the Ogaden region; and the Italians in the south. Shifting colonial boundaries effectively placed countless ethnic Somalis outside the political boundaries of Somalia (Abdullahi, 2001). Twenty percent of our Somali respondents said they had been born in an East African regional country and not Somalia (Ethiopia, Kenya, and Tanzania).

Domination by outsiders ran counter to an ardent spirit of independence, and Somalis rebelled continuously but unsuccessfully against European colonization. During World War II, rivalry between the Allied and Axis powers in Europe engulfed the Horn of Africa when the Italians invaded Ethiopia in 1935 and British Somaliland in 1940. Just one year later, the British recaptured Somaliland, and took the Ogaden (formerly ruled by Ethiopia) and Italian Somalia (Issa-Salwe, 1994). In 1949, the United Nations made Italian Somalia a trust territory, guaranteeing its independence within 10 years. Observing this development, Somalis in British Somaliland pressed for their own independence and on July 1, 1960, both territories were united under one flag and named the Somali Republic (Putnam & Noor, 1993).

The Somali Republic. From 1960 to 1969, a parliamentary democracy and constitution fostered the peaceful settlement of clan and regional disputes. By the mid-1960s, accusations of governmental corruption were widespread, and in October 1969, the president was assassinated and the army seized power in a bloodless coup (Lewis, 1994). Believing that democracy had not suited Somalia well, the military regime closely associated itself with the Soviet Union, and developed a "pragmatic local application of Marxist–Leninism," emphasizing "*hanti-wadaagga 'ilmi ku disan*" (wealth sharing based on wisdom), "*waddajir*" (togetherness/unity), "*is ku kalsoonaan*" (self-reliance), and "*iskaa wab u qabso*" (self-help; Lewis, 1994, pp. 50–51). After the Shah of Iran fell in 1979, the United States needed a new ally in the Gulf region. A Somali–American relationship developed, based on the exchange of military equipment for American access to Somali ports and airfields (De Waal, 1993; Putnam & Noor, 1993).

State Collapse. An ill-fated coup attempt in April 1978 revealed growing dissatisfaction with the military regime, which responded by scapegoating the ethnic group of the coup organizers and encouraging clan/ethnic tension. Nepotism, corruption, and interference in all aspects of daily life did not coincide well with the strong egalitarian beliefs of the largely nomadic Somalis. Dissidents formed opposition movements, and by the mid-1980s, Somalia had become bitterly divided along clan lines. The military regime collapsed in January 1991, and its leader, Siyaad Barre, went into exile in Nigeria (Abdullahi, 2001; Issa-Salwe, 1994). The "Black Hitler," as many Somalis call him, the man who almost single-handedly tore his country apart by encouraging clan prejudice and fighting in his effort to retain dictatorial power over a freedom-loving nomadic people, died in 1995, far away on the other side of Africa.

With Siyaad Barre gone, the northwest declared itself independent as the Republic of Somaliland, and the northeast followed suit in 1998, calling itself the Republic of Puntland. Although neither is recognized as an independent state in the international community, Somaliland and Puntland have been able to maintain relative peace. Both republics established constitutions and began rebuilding infrastructure. Meanwhile, the south continued to languish. Mogadishu lay in ruins, and the combination of warfare, drought, and food shortages wrought havoc on the Somali people. In 1992, the United States endeavored to ease the effects of famine by reducing violence and delivering humanitarian assistance. The United Nations took over these efforts in 1993 but withdrew in 1995, after suffering significant casualties (Central Intelligence Agency, 2003). By late 1999, around 500,000 Somali refugees lived in nearly 24 countries, most of them regional neighbors. The internally displaced Somalis numbered about 300,000 and more than one million faced food shortages (U.S. State Department, 2002). To date, peace talk efforts to reunite Somalia have failed. There is no central government, and no end in sight to the violence and human rights abuses that have gripped the country for nearly 20 years.

Somali Cultural Context

Somalis have no history of feudalism, or of strong political and religious hierarchies, or of kings or presidents or rigid central governments uniting all Somalis. They have never had a system of institutionalized inequity of humans by birth; every man was considered equal, regardless of education, wealth, or background. Before European colonization, Somalis lived in decentralized city-states under a form of social order referred to by Western scholars as "pastoral democracy." They are patrilineal, predominantly (60%) pastoral nomads and nearly 100% Sunni Muslim. Their faith is important and, according to Abdullahi (2001), "Somali identity is intertwined with Islam" (p. 8). Over 70% of our respondents identified themselves as Muslim.

Somalis are linguistically and culturally homogenous, speaking just one language, Somali, and putting great emphasis on storytelling and poetry. Their history has traditionally been transmitted orally, and Somalis take great pride in their ability to recite genealogy. According to Lewis (1994, p. 99), "At as young an age as five or six years, children are capable of reciting their full genealogy to their clan-family ancestor and they are taught this by their mother—who may belong to another clan." During a casual conversation I had with an 8-year-old Somali boy, he recited his genealogy, going back 10 generations and thereby supporting Lewis's assertion.

Social Structure

Putnam and Noor (1993) summarize Somali social structure as follows:

Among Somalis, a primary division exists between the Samaale and the Sab. The Samaale are the majority of the Somali people and consist of four main clan families—the Dir, Isaaq, Hawiye, and Daarood (Darod)—each of which is further divided into sub-clans. The Samaale are primarily of nomadic origin and live throughout Somalia and in Ethiopia, Kenya and Djibouti. The Sab consist of two clan families, the Digil and Raxanweyn (Rahanwein), located primarily in southern Somalia, where they mix farming and herding and are more likely than the Samaale to be sedentary. (p. 13)

The *Sab* and its affiliated groups are considered minorities because they are more related to the Oromo (of Ethiopia) than to the Somali. Somalis further divide themselves into "*reer*" or "*rer*," comprised of related families functioning as a group—acting, as necessary, to fulfill obligations arising from blood feuds and other conflicts (Aidid & Ruhela, 1994). *Reer* are headed by elected or hereditary chiefs, who have nominal authority in groups that can range from hundreds to thousands of members. Essentially, *reers* are *diya*—that is, compensation-paying groups that are a fundamental aspect of traditional Somali political organization. They link patrilineal kin by way of contractual agreement [*heer (xeer)*] "to support one another, especially in regard to compensation for injuries and death against fellow members" (Putnam & Noor, 1993, p. 14).

The terms of a xeer are democratically decided by the male members of the reer at "*shir*," lineage-group councils (Aidid & Ruhela, 1994, p. 174). It is at shir that the male heads of all families collectively discuss crimes and punishments, and "decide the proportion in which they will receive compensation for external actions and amounts payable in international disputes" (Lewis, 1961, pp. 175–176). Xeer agreements, which became mixed with Islamic law called "*Shari'a*," formed the basis of the traditional Somali justice system. Sir Richard Burton (1966) described how justice was meted out to a murderer in northern Somali tribes:

... The price of blood in the Somali country is the highest sanctioned by al-Islam. ... The Somali usually demand 100 she camels, or 300 sheep and few cows; here, as in Arabia, the sum is made up by all the near relations of the slayer; 30 under age, but the rest must be sound and good. Many tribes take less from strangers—100 sheep, a cow, and a camel; but after the equivalent is paid, the murderer or one of his clan, contrary to the spirit of al-Islam, is generally slain. When blood is shed in the same tribe, the full reparation if accepted by the relatives is always expected; this serves the purpose of preventing fratricidal strife, for in such a nation of murderers, only the *Diyat* prevents taking of life. Blood money, however, is seldom accepted unless the murdered man has been slain with a lawful weapon. Those who kill with *Danakalah*, a poisonous juice rubbed upon meat, are always put to death by the members of their own tribe. (p. 174)

The administrative authorities and judicial courts of Somalia today (the Republics of Somaliland and Puntland) recognize this traditional system of justice and settle the disputes of both the pastoral and the agricultural Somalis according to traditional judicial conventions, traditions, and agreements (Aidid & Ruhela, 1994). Abdullahi (2001) gives two examples of clan usage of heer [xeer]: 1) If a family loses animals due to drought, clan members may come together and donate animals to the family at loss; 2) when a family has animals stolen from them, clan members "take action to seek restitution first by negotiation" (p. 139). In urban areas, such as Mogadishu and Hargeisa, the clan acts as an extended family providing a social network and support. Clan chiefs or tribal elders, and their deputies, are elected by the majority of the people, which illustrates the strong sense of egalitarianism, independence, and democracy for which Somalis are renowned. Clan chiefs are usually elected after each candidate presents a speech and answers questions pertaining to how he would handle matters like compensation for cases such as murder, rape, elopement, and damaging someone's reputation (Aidid & Ruhela, 1994, p. 176).

Somali Participants' Perspectives on Conflict Resolution

When asked whether they or someone they know had ever resolved an intense family conflict without abusive behavior, 67% of our respondents gave answers reflecting Somali cultural values favoring free will, consensus, majority rule, and avoidance of coercion in decision making, as well as the importance of extended family. For example, a 19-year-old woman wrote: "My cousin moved out without telling his parents. His worried parents called other relatives for advice. The final result was [they] let [him] live alone and see how long [he] could survive on his own." An 18-year-old whose father had divorced his mother and taken on another (abusive) wife wrote: "When my family found out how my father's wife treated us, they were furious with our father because he did not ask about how we felt . . . in the end, we were raised by our father's mother." A 22-year-old female wrote: "We always have family conflict. However, we always solve them by taking a vote if it concerns the whole family . . . majority rules."

Perhaps, on examining Somali cultural values, one might ask how a country made up of people with such strong roots of egalitarianism and democracy could disintegrate? Abdullahi (2001) answers this question with three explanations: 1) colonialism, 2) two decades of brutal military rule, and 3) urbanization. Differences between rural and urban Somalia were observed by many of our participants. As in most countries around the world, traditions die hard in rural Somalia and modify comparatively faster in urban areas, creating new patterns of social life.

THE SOMALI MICROSYSTEM

The Somali Family

Clan affiliation is important in Somalia, but one's immediate family serves as the ultimate source of personal security and identity. Somalis are patrilineal—they trace their lineage through the male. Upon first encountering one another, they will ask, "tol maay tahay?" which translates to, "what is your lineage?" Whom you are from is of more importance than where you are from (Putnam & Noor, 1993, p. 4). Although household structures vary between rural and urban dwellers, Somali households are typically comprised of nuclear families: mother, father, and children. It is not rare, however, to find households that include extended family members—for example, grandparents, aunts, uncles, cousins, and family friends viewed as relatives. Responses from our participants suggest that patterns of household composition have remained unchanged in the Somali Diaspora. When asked with whom they lived in childhood, and with whom they lived now, 60% indicated immediate family members, while 20% indicated extended family members.

Islam forbids the use of alcohol and drugs. Nevertheless, countless men in East Africa—many of them Muslims—engage in the practice of chewing qat, a mild narcotic stimulant. The side effects of qat are similar to those of substances banned in most Western countries. After a significant Somali community became established in Great Britain, and awareness of the importation of qat grew, authorities put the substance on the list of illegal narcotics. It appears that the United States will follow suit, as qat has been found in Somali communities in Minnesota (Haynes-Taylor, 1999). Thirteen percent of our participants listed male use of narcotics or alcohol as overall or extreme abuse. Some of our participants reported that they felt money and time used to purchase and use qat was money and time selfishly taken away from a man's family.

Somali law acknowledges the husband's authority over his family but does not permit arbitrary interference in matters falling in his wife's sphere of influence. For example, in rural areas where sheep and goats fall under the control of women and their daughters, a husband may be required to seek his wife's permission before selling or slaughtering an animal (Lewis, 1994). The husband represents the family in the outside world (i.e., community meetings and settling disputes), but the wife "assumes the governorship of a household" and has "complete freedom in the management of her household without interference from her husband's family or from anyone else except perhaps her husband" (Abdullahi, 2001, p. 120). Islam reinforces these gender roles, but there are signs of change, as exemplified by one divorced father of three who participated in our survey. During an interview, he stated that it felt only natural for the children to remain with him when his marriage ended. Raising them alone would be difficult but guaranteed that they would receive a proper education, discipline, and love. Many within the local Somali community in the suburban American city he now calls home considered it odd at first to see a man completing tasks customarily associated with women (childrearing and all of its requirements—changing diapers, cooking, etc.). However, Somali single-parent headed households, including male-headed ones, are becoming more common, particularly in the Diaspora.

Marriage, Polygamy, and Divorce

Somali marriage customs are a mixture of tribal and Islamic traditions. In accordance with Islam, Sunni Somalis have historically observed such marriage customs as *nikah, levirate* (marrying the dead brother's wife), *sororate* (marrying the wife's sister), and *polygamy* (marrying up to four wives at a time; Aidid & Ruhelia, 1994, p. 217). In addition, as with other Muslims, Somalis prefer cross-cousin marriages between, for example, a daughter and the son of two paternal uncles; a girl and her mother's sister's son; a boy and the daughter of his father's sister; and a boy and the daughter of the younger sister of his mother (Aidid & Ruhelia, 1994, p. 217).

Men marry for the first time between 18 and 25 and women between 15 and 20, although the acquisition of education has pushed these ages to as late as 30. Historically, couples did very little direct courting and a high value was placed on a woman's virginity at marriage, with the practice of female infibulation being specifically designed to ensure maidenhood (Office of the Senior Coordinator, 2001). Changing social norms both within Somalia and in the Somali Diaspora are challenging these practices. Nonetheless, it is the prospective husband's family (father and/or other senior agnates) that initiates contact with the girl's family to ask for her hand in marriage. If the girl's family accepts the offer, the prospective groom presents her family with a "*gaabaati*," a small gift of livestock or money that signifies the couple's engagement.

During the engagement, a series of gifts are exchanged between the two families: "*Yarad*" (bride-wealth) is paid to the prospective bride's family and "*dibaab*" (dowry) is paid to the prospective groom's family (Lewis, 1994, p. 36). The exact quantity of yarad is negotiated between the two families, whereas the woman's family decides the value of dibaad, which does not usually exceed two-thirds of the yarad (Lewis, 1994, p. 40). *Mehar*, roughly not in excess of one-fifth of yarad, must also be paid or promised to the woman in the presence of a *wadaad* as a sort of insurance against divorce. If the couple does divorce later, the woman must be given mehar in accordance with Islamic tradition.

Wedding ceremonies are festive, heavily attended, and last for 3 days. The various events—some strictly for the groom and other men, and some for the bride and other women—can stretch from evening into the early hours of the morning. When asked to give an example of a mild form of abuse in a wife–husband relationship, one Somali man wrote, "wife who comes home late because she went to [a] wedding." Although this response may seem humorous, some Somalis I interviewed stated that women participate in many wedding celebrations that are long in duration and costly to attend—which can cause serious strife in some marriages.

The newly married couple usually makes their home near the husband's family. The wife becomes part of her husband's family but never completely absorbed by it. She retains her maiden name, her natal lineage membership, and her own ". . . legal personality independent of her husband, which being the responsibility of her own kin provides an enduring insurance in times of difficulty, and marital discord" (Aidid & Ruhelia, 1994, p. 215). In our sample, one woman told of how her sister had married an abusive man (verbally) and eventually got away from him with the help of her brothers. It is the duty of her male relatives to protect her from domestic abuse; conversely, her relatives are held responsible for her deeds. If a wife murders her husband, her birth family is held accountable (Lewis, 1994). When children are born, they serve to bind the wife more firmly to her husband's family, giving her more status in his family as a mother and daughter-in-law. The children are legally considered to belong to their father, and the woman is always part of her birth diya-paying group.

Islam allows for a man to take on a second, third, or fourth wife when any of the following conditions apply: He has to marry his dead brother's wife in order to look after his brother's children and property according to the Islamic religion; he wants to have many children as ordained by Islam; his existing wife or wives stop bearing children; and he is not happy with his first wife, but cannot divorce her because of his concern for the children (Aidid & Ruhelia, 1994, p. 218). The Family Code of 1975 (Law 23) enacted by the Somali government January 11, 1975, puts additional stipulations on Somali nationals. The stipulation pertaining to polygamous behavior reads as follows: No man shall marry a second woman unless he is formally allowed to do so by the district court having jurisdiction.

It is officially illegal and perceived to be morally unethical for a man to take on an additional wife without the consent and knowledge of the first wife and her family. Nevertheless, laws and moral sentiments are not always mirrored in daily practices. Eighty-eight percent of our survey participants voiced disdain for men who take on additional wives either when they have not received the first wife's consent or when they lack the means to provide for all of their wives and children. Some of our participants related painful personal stories of abuse at the hands of one of their father's wives who was not their birth mother, illustrating some of the problems that arise due to jealousy between the wives and rivalry between siblings. The most dramatic story came from a 27-year-old male participant who now lives in the Netherlands:

> When I was around eight years old my father told me that I would be spending a week or so with my mother-in-law (stepmother) who was also living in Mogadishu (My father had divorced my mother. We were living with our grandmother and my mother was living alone in another district). Hearing that, I said, "That is great." The first day was great with all the fun and food but when my father went back to my grandma and I remained with my (step-mother), the real trouble began. The next day my (stepmother) did not give me anything to eat. I could see her eat breakfast in front of me and when she finished she locked me inside the house (and said), "hey, if you scream I will beat you. Just be quiet." I (cried) the whole day and (she beat me) with a stick. There (was) blood everywhere on my body. Because of hunger or some-thing else, I could not sleep that night. I remember I used my blood as ink to draw a picture on the wall. A week that was a hell passed away and my father came back at last. Hours later he asked my (stepmother) who drew the pic-ture on the wall. I said I did and he asked, "with what?" I told him my blood; then he started to check my whole body and found scars. He said, "Come on, let's go." That was the last time I visited. The great news is that my father di-vorced "my stepmother" on the spot and weeks later remarried my mother.

Children's Roles in the Family

The roles of Somali children are determined by gender. Boys are expected to learn from their fathers the duties of "*xil*" (familial responsibilities), rang-ing from how to protect women and children in their family to how to se-cure a livelihood and someday support their own wives and offspring. Boys are encouraged to be independent and courageous, to seek adventure, and to become emotionally strong. Although groomed by their fathers, it is to their mothers and uterine relatives that grown, unmarried Somali men pledge their loyalties. Sons especially represent their mothers in disputes involving their father and his other wives and children.

On the other hand, mothers groom their daughters. Girls learn how to cook, and to handle day-to-day household affairs and the expectations of a good "*xille*" (wife, from the root word *xil*, same as familial responsibilities). In rural areas, girls, along with their mothers, are responsible for caring for the sheep, but never for the camels, which are the responsibility of boys and their fathers. Girls are taught to be housebound and obedient, and "oc-cupy themselves more with their personal beauty" than with outside activi-ties (Abdullahi, 2001, p. 122).

As in many societies, Somali fathers highly prize the birth of sons. One Somali proverb explains the cultural reasons for this: "*wiil dhalaayaaba ab durug*" (it is a boy and the genealogical tree will grow; Abdullahi, 2001, p. 125; Lewis, 1994, p. 99). Viewing male offspring as culturally important should not be confused with a lack of respect or gratitude for females. The birth of any child is important and has many ceremonies associated with it. For example, 7 days after the birth of a child a "*wanqal*" is held. It is a social gathering at which Allah is thanked for blessing the family with a child, and a name is chosen and revealed to everyone in the community. Another ceremony, which is attended only by women, is known as "*afartanbah*." This is a celebration to signal the end of the 40-day housebound seclusion a new mother enters after giving birth. This tradition has proved to be difficult to maintain in urban areas where there are more pressures to go back to work and make money.

FAMILY VIOLENCE

Domestic Abuse

It is difficult to get a grasp on the prevalence of sexual and domestic abuse among Somalis because such issues are never talked about outside the family (Schuett, 2000). Moreover, "Domestic violence is not considered abnormal," according to Badawi (2000a, 2000b, 2000c). Since the civil war, cases of domestic violence have increased exponentially. Perhaps the most disturbing aspect of this increase is that Somali women in the Diaspora are not much safer than their sisters remaining in the homeland. Khadigia Ali, a community health worker in Toronto who works closely with the Somali immigrant community, has seen an increase in the number of domestic abuse cases over the past 4½ years. Ali links this increase to the rampant use of qat among Somali men. She recalls a young mother of four coming to her office in tears and severely battered. The woman was seeking help because her husband, "bit her and punched her in the mouth so hard that her teeth fell out" when she refused to give him the grocery money to buy qat (www.togdheer.com/khat/addiction.shtml). There have also been increases in domestic violence cases within the United States. Abdi Ugas, a translator for Somali and Arabic speakers in the Minnesota Hennepin County court system, says he has been called to translate in cases of spousal abuse more frequently over the years and attributes the increase in cases brought to court to the fact that Somali women are beginning to stand up for themselves (Haynes-Taylor, 1999). There are no facilities or services for battered women and children in Somalia but such facilities are springing up all over the diaspora, including in Great Britain and Ohio, USA, where an African American male, Ramadan Abdullah Badi Islam, runs a safe house for Muslim women and children fleeing from domestic abuse or searching for housing (Keyser, 2000).

Somali Participants' Perspectives on Spouse Abuse

Husbands are the public figureheads, whereas wives play crucial economic roles, with their labor being relied on heavily in both rural and urban families. Somali culture is patriarchal, and high priority is placed on a man's ability to care for his family financially and morally. Any inability to do so was defined as abusive by many of our survey participants. More than 20% of the examples of extreme abuse focused on issues of personal or financial neglect of family members: "when a husband does not defend his wife against his sisters when they are causing trouble" (female, 19 years old); "a husband who spends much of his time with friends rather than with his wife" (female, 60); "a husband who allows his wife to do everything" (18-year-old male); "a man who puts his family last" (male, 70); and—a particularly interesting response—"[a husband] who lets his wife party" (female, 28). Thirty-eight percent of the respondents considered it moderately abusive if a husband "does not help his wife with household chores" or "lets her do all the work without help." Forty-nine percent felt that a husband who is "secretive about his whereabouts" and "passive toward his wife's feelings" is being mildly abusive. Very few participants made reference to physical aggression as a form of abuse, although a 19-year-old female said "always hitting . . . even with no reason" was severely abusive, "hitting once in awhile and always yelling" was moderately abusive, and "always yelling" was mildly abusive in both the husband–wife and wife–husband relationship. Gender and age were unrelated to responses.

Abuse of Children

All Somali children are expected to obey and respect their elders, an expectation that is not taken lightly. Elder siblings, aunts and uncles, as well as other members of the extended family, play a major disciplinary role in the child's life. Traditionally, Somali families prefer to talk to their offspring, "to instruct and persuade them to become good children," instead of physically beating them (Aidid & Ruhela, 1994, p. 201). Our survey data reflect the importance of this cultural practice, as 61% of survey respondents cited verbally or physically humiliating a child in public or private ("yelling," "slapping," etc.) as extremely or moderately abusive.

Somali Participants' Perspectives on Child Abuse

Somalis have a strong belief that parents must teach children morality while simultaneously respecting each child's individual ideas and opinions. If a child misbehaves, it is acceptable for any relative to administer discipline. One respondent (female, 22) said it is extremely abusive "not to teach the child confidence, respect and hardship." A 24-year-old male said that "a parent not teaching a child the importance of caring for and respecting others" is moderately abusive. Similar examples of child abuse were "make excuses for [the] child's mistakes" (female, 22, moderate), and "defend [a] child's wrongdoing while knowing that they have done wrong" (male, 25, mild). Interestingly, examples of abuse from older participants included "disregarding children's feelings" and "infringing upon their right to choose"—in particular, their right to choose a spouse. A 66-year-old male and a 60-year-old female found this practice to be extremely abusive, but a 45-year-old woman described it as moderately abusive. This generational gap may be due to the fact that arranging marriages as a practice has become rather uncommon, according to Somalis I interviewed.

Other practices identified by participants as forms of child abuse echoed the themes of neglect and lack of respect seen in the judgments of spousal abuse. Among the examples of extreme child abuse were: "parent leaving child to be cared for by [nonrelatives]," "parents who do not feed the child because they spend their money on other things," and "parents [who] always demand respect but do not return it." Examples of moderately abusive parental behavior highlighted the cultural value of respecting children's viewpoints while reiterating the importance of being respectful of a child's dignity—for example, "not asking your child's opinion in decision-making about their lives," "people who favor one child over another," and "yelling at children in front of their peers." One of the most dramatic examples of mildly abusive parental behavior was ". . . telling [the child that] he is not yours."

Sibling Abuse. "In Somali culture, it is usually the oldest in the family who can make . . . decisions while others cannot," according to a 25-year-old male respondent, who viewed this cultural practice as abusive to younger children. In Somali families, the eldest child, regardless of gender, has authority over all other children—especially in their parents' absence. In spite of the fact that gender is not a determining factor in who exercises authority, 40% of our participants specifically accused male siblings of being the chief perpetrators of sibling abuse. The two main ways in which male siblings abuse their power are by "demanding that their sisters stay in the home" and by "choosing their husbands, not based on their sisters' feelings, but on their own feelings toward the bridegrooms." An understanding of the sibling relationship reveals why brothers can be seen as oppressive in the worst of times, and saviors and protectors in the best of times. According to Badawi (2000a, 2000b, 2000c), "a brother will often risk his life, sacrifice obligations to his wife and children" when his sister is suffering.

Brothers are expected to remain loyal to their sisters throughout their lives. If there are any signs of domestic abuse, a woman's brothers deal with her husband and assure her safety and her children's. When observed, this cultural expectation is a great tool for preventing abuse. However, the civil war and forced migration have split whole families apart and undermined implementation of this integrated familial social net.

SOMALI ELDERS

After all of their children have married and started their own families, elderly parents continue as the nucleus of the extended family. Even in their senior years, parents retain some authority to mediate disputes and manage family affairs. Both male and female children are expected to care for their aged parents when it becomes necessary. It is customary for the mother to go and live with her daughters whereas the father goes to live with his sons. Abdullahi (2001) views the traditional pattern of elderly parents residing with a same sex child as beneficial for several reasons, noting that a man whose mother-in-law resides with him is less likely to be violent with his wife. Besides preventing possible family abuse, the presence of elderly relatives in the household can also help give grandchildren and younger nieces and nephews a sense of cultural connectivity. This is particularly true in the Somali Diaspora, where elders are human personifications of a land that many young Somalis have never visited. Putting an elderly relative in a nursing home is considered not only disrespectful but also taboo. It is a practice that most Somalis view as peculiarly Western. Some of our participants described a system in which elderly parents resided with their same sex offspring on a rotational basis. One elderly man lived 6 months out of the year with one son in the United States and the remaining 6 months with another son in Canada. Respondents made it clear that Somali children believe their elderly parents should have a say about where they reside and their wishes should be considered.

Somali Participants' Perspectives on Elder Abuse

Forty-two percent of the participants who answered the elder abuse questions said that disregarding the feelings, advice, and opinions of elderly relatives is abusive. One-fourth of the respondents specifically listed "neglecting the needs of the elderly" and "never talking to them" as abusive. Examples of moderate elder abuse were "leave an elderly relative home alone without a caretaker" (66-year-old male), and "lying" (40-year-old male).

OTHER ISSUES RELATED TO INTERPERSONAL VIOLENCE AND ABUSE

After independence, Somali women were assured legal protection and rights by the state. Under the Family Law of 1975, women were given rights in divorce and property inheritance. When the Somali Democratic Republic became a one-party socialist state in 1979, a new constitution was adopted and women were granted additional rights. Constitutional articles "provided guarantees of social, cultural and political rights" and specifically promised "equality of the sexes" (Badawi, 2000, p. 2). The 1984 elections, which granted women 25 of 177 seats in parliament (the People's National Assembly), made it appear that the status of women was significantly improving. However, after the 1987 elections, all members of the executive branch (Council of Ministers) were men. Critics such as Hada Aden, director of a Somali women's organization, claim that women have been ". . . both political instruments and victims of deceit" throughout Somali history (Achieng, 1999, p. 2).

The eruption of civil war and subsequent total collapse of the Somali state redefined the role of women: They became heads of households in addition to having the responsibility of all domestic duties. Preexisting social problems, such as domestic abuse and violence, were pushed to the fore and became less easy to conceal from the outside world. Nongovernmental organizations report that they are "aware that many women hide their problems from society because of their fear of being beaten again, family pressure to present a good image, feelings of guilt, and repressive laws and attitudes" (Badawi, 2000, p. 3).

Female Circumcision

WHO estimates that 130 million women and girls ranging in age from infancy to mature adulthood have undergone "female genital mutilation" (FGM), which involves the partial or complete removal of female genitals. FGM is practiced in nearly 30 African countries and among a few minority groups in Asia. In Africa, the prevalence rate ranges from around 5% in the Democratic Republic of Congo and Uganda to 98% in Djibouti and Somalia. About 75% of all cases are found in Egypt, Ethiopia, Kenya, Nigeria, Somalia, and Sudan. Although perceived as a ritual that upholds the value of chastity and improves a girl's prospects for marriage, FGM violates the human rights of girls and women because it involves the removal of healthy sexual organs without medical necessity and has detrimental—sometimes dire or even fatal—long-term physical effects and very serious psychological consequences. The procedure also breaches the human right to health and bodily integrity (UNICEF, 2000).

In Africa, efforts to eliminate female genital mutilation range from laws criminalizing the procedure to education and outreach programs. Nine countries have banned the procedure, prosecutions have occurred in three, and three countries have proposed laws against FGM. Twenty countries conduct or support education and outreach programs. Penalties for those convicted vary from monetary fines to lifelong incarceration. Legislation specifically prohibiting FGM has also been passed in seven industrialized countries with significant populations from countries where it is practiced. The United Kingdom (1985), the United States (federal law, 1996; state laws, 1994–1998), and Canada (1997), which all have large Somali communities, have all enacted laws against FGM (UNICEF, 2000).

Officially, only one of our participants mentioned FGM; her example of moderate abuse by a parent was ". . . circumcise their children even though it is against their beliefs." In private, a 23-year-old female told me she felt FGM is a way for men to control female sexuality. She added that girls born to Somali parents in Western countries were luckily left untouched; she would not say whether she herself had undergone the procedure. A 43-year-old male told me he hated FGM and that his wife had been traumatized by the ordeal at a very young age. He attributed her coldness toward him to "that operation and the abuse suffered from her controlling parents." When I asked if he would allow his 8-year-old daughter to undergo the procedure, he said no and added that he does not allow his children to spend much time around his in-laws because of their "outdated ideas." Although many Somalis disagree with female circumcision, getting them to talk openly and publicly about it is difficult.

Rape

Rape has always been considered the gravest of offenses. Ancient Somalis considered rape to be "when girls were sexually assaulted, or when a man violently forced a woman/girl to have sex without her consent" (Badawi, 2000a, 2000b, 2000c, p. 3). A man found guilty of raping a female was punished severely and according to the age of the victim. In addition to being subjected to a public beating at the hands of men and women with sticks, a rapist was fined 15 she-camels if his victim was a girl under age 15, a maiden betrothed to a man but not yet married, a woman whose husband had died and who was still in mourning attire, or an elderly woman. A fine of 50 camels was due when the victim was a woman who nursed a boy, or when a woman was of marriageable age but unmarried or betrothed and the rapist refused to marry her and pay the full bride price she would normally have fetched (Badawi, 2000). Badawi explains, "the custom of marrying the raped girl off to her molester was to cover the disgrace and 'shame of marriage-lessness' brought to the girl and her family" (Badawi, 2000, p. 5). Unfortu-

nately, these social codes and laws are of a bygone era, as rape and violence against women are commonplace in contemporary Somali society.
Countless women and girls say they have been raped, molested, and assaulted by Somali men and even by United Nations personnel within Somalia and in refugee camps outside the country (Badawi, 2000, p. 10). As was
true in regard to female genital mutilation, very few of the Somalis I interviewed associated sex acts with abuse, and none would comment openly
about rape; but in private men and women of all ages expressed sorrow
over the fact that women and girls—their mothers, daughters, sisters, aunts,
and grandmothers—will always have to live with the horrible memories of
having been sexually assaulted.

HIV/AIDS

Along with an increase in sexual violence in a society comes increased exposure to HIV and AIDS. No one knows the prevalence of HIV/AIDS in Somalia but lack of information and low public awareness, coupled with population movement within the country and across the borders of neighboring
nations is likely to increase infection levels. A December 1999 UNICEF study
found that condom use in Somalia was under 1%, sexually transmitted disease rates were unacceptably high, and that most Somalis believe AIDS to
be a foreign or non-Muslim disease that cannot affect them ("Somalia: Urgent need for HIV/AIDS awareness," 2001). Even more alarming are the findings of a joint report issued by UNAIDS, UNICEF, and WHO: Only 26% of Somali girls have heard of AIDS and only 1% know how to avoid infection
(Zaza, 2002).

INTERVENTION AND PREVENTION

Somali women have not taken the abuse against them and their children sit-
ting down; they are fighting back in increasing numbers, both within and
outside Somalia. Ayaan Hirsi Ali, a Somali-born woman who has lived in the
Netherlands since age 9, caused a controversy in December 2002, when she
went on Dutch public television and denounced abuse against Muslim
women, claiming "orthodox Muslim men frequently indulge in domestic and
child [sexual] abuse," something she knows from having worked as an in-
terpreter for Dutch immigration and social services ("What protection for
refugee women," 2002). Ali's comments drew sharp criticism and death
threats against her life; however, they also helped make other Somali
women feel comfortable talking about issues in the Diaspora and back
home that are causing families a tremendous amount of pain (violent child
street gangs, rape, drug usage, etc.).

Ali is not the only Somali woman who is displaying such courage. There are numerous women's organizations within Somalia that are demanding to be included in the peace talks between the country's various regional leaders. Organizations in the Diaspora have also banded together to protest the condemnation of a Somali lesbian couple to death ("Kabissa-fahamu Newsletter," 2001) and to organize the first ever HIV/AIDS awareness campaign that took place in Somalia in July 2002 ("First-Ever HIV/AIDS Awareness Campaign," 2002).

CONCLUSIONS

Although the future of the nation of Somalia remains uncertain, her children have proved themselves to be survivors. Within Diaspora communities stretching around the globe, one can observe aspects of traditional Somali culture yielding to forced change due to migration. Family structure and dynamics have undergone significant transformations, as have ideas regarding gender roles and abuse among Somalis. Our survey participants gave us a glimpse into their world and access to their thoughts on social and cultural issues with which they grapple daily. We now have a better understanding of contemporary Somali attitudes toward abuse within the family, and for this, I thank them.

ACKNOWLEDGMENTS

The goal of this work is to shed light on the values and attitudes of an understudied yet wondrous group of people—the Somalis. Special thanks to everyone at the Somali Development Center (Boston, MA), and most especially Saida Mohammad for her invaluable advice and tireless efforts to recruit survey participants.

REFERENCES

Abdullahi, M. D. (2001). *Culture and customs of Somalia* (pp. 8, 58–59, 120, 122, 125, 142–145). Westport, CT: Greenwood Press.
Achieng, J. (1999, March 29). "We want rights, say Somali women." *Daily Mail and Guardian*. Johannesburg, South Africa.
Aidid, M. F., & Ruhela, S. P. (1994). *Somalia: From the dawn of civilization to the modern times* (pp. 173–218). Delhi, India: Vikas Publishing House Pvt Limited.
Asylum in the UK: Somalia assessment. (2001, October). Home Office Immigration and Nationality Directorate, Country Information and Policy Unit. Available: http://www.ind. homeoffice. gov.uk/ppage.asp?section=193

Badawi, M. (2000a). *The culture and tradition of women in Somalia. Part I: Background* (pp. 1–6). Center for the Strategic Initiatives of Women. Available: www.csiw.org/women05.htm

Badawi, M. (2000b). *The culture and tradition of women in Somalia. Part II: Violence and discrimination against women in Somalia today: Rape* (p. 3). Center for the Strategic Initiatives of Women.

Badawi, M. (2000c). *The culture and tradition of women in Somalia. Part III: The peace process: Violence against women by the UN Forces* (p. 10). Center for the Strategic Initiatives of Women.

Burton, R. F. (1966). *First footsteps in East Africa.* London: Routledge & Kegan Paul.

Central Intelligence Agency. (2003). US Central Intelligence Fact Book, Somalia, Country Report. Available: http://www.odci.gov/cia/publications/factbook/geos/so.html

Clark, J. D. (1970). *The prehistory of Africa.* London: Thames & Hudson.

DeWaal, N. (1993, December). *Violent deeds live on: Landmines in Somalia and Somaliland.* London: African Rights and Mines Advisory Group.

Ending violence against women and girls. (2000). *The state of world population 2000* [online]. Available: www.unfpa.org/swp/2000/english/ch03.html

First-Ever HIV/AIDS Awareness Campaign. (2002, July 16). Available: http://allafrica.com/stories/200207160125.html

Haynes-Taylor, K. (1999). Hennepin County court fights barriers to justice for East Africans. *Star Tribune* [online]. Available: www.startribune.com/www.members.tripod.con~Somali1/interpreter4.html

Issa-Salwe, C. M. C. (1994). *The collapse of the Somali state: The impact of the colonial legacy* (pp. 31–78). London: HAAN Associates.

Kabissa-fahumu Newsletter. (2001, February 27). *The Magnus Hirschfield Centre for Human Rights* [online]. Available: www.kabissa.org/lists/newsletter-submissions-1/0958.html

Keyser, J. (2000, November 27). Influx of Muslim immigrants, refugees attracting Americans to Islam. *Ohio News* [online]. Available: www.ohio.com

Khat: Harmless stimulant or addictive drug? (2000, May/June). *The Journal of Addiction and Mental Health.* Available: www.togdheer.com/khat/addiction.shtml

Lewis, I. M. (1961). *A pastoral democracy: A study of pastoralism and politics among the northern Somali of the Horn of Africa.* London: Oxford University Press.

Lewis, I. M. (1994). *Blood and bone: The call of kinship in Somali society* (pp. 36–40, 99–151, 175–176). Lawrenceville, NJ: The Red Sea Press, Inc.

McGowan, R. B. (2002, March 14). Muslims in the Diaspora: The Somali communities of London and Toronto. *Muslim News* [online]. Available: http://www.ualberta.ca/~cjscopy/reviews/muslims.html

Office of the Senior Coordinator for International Women's Issues. (2001, June 1). Somalia: Report on female genital mutilation (FGM) or female genital cutting. U.S. Department of State. Available: http://www.state.gov/g/wi/rls/rep/crfgm/10109.htm

Opoku-Dapaah, E. (1995). *Somali refugees in Toronto: A profile.* York, Canada: York Lanes Press.

Programme for Women and Children in Somalia: Plan of Operations, Mid 1984–1987. (1984). Government of the Somali Democratic Republic in Cooperation with the United Nations Children's Fund.

Putnam, D. B., & Noor, M. C. (1993). *The Somalis: Their history and culture, CAL Refugee Fact Sheet #9* (pp. 4–14). Washington, DC: The Refugee Service Center.

Schuett, D. (2000). Domestic violence poses cultural challenges for immigrant women. *The Post-Bulletin* [online Domestic Violence Series]. Available: www.postbulletin.com/domestic/zimmigrant.html

Somalia Country Reports on Human Rights Practices, 2000. (2001, February). United States Embassy Stockholm. Released by the Bureau of Democracy, Human Rights and Labor, U.S. Department of State. Available: www.usis.usemb.se/human/2000/africa/somalia/html

Somalia faces the future: Human rights in a fragmented society. (1995, April). *Human Rights Watch—Africa, 7*(2) [online]. Available: www.hrw.org/africa/somalia.php

Somalia: Urgent need for HIV/AIDS awareness. (2002). [online]. Available: www.unsomalia.org/media/2002/stories/20020716_1.asp

UNICEF. (2000). *The progress of nations* [online]. Available: www.unicef.org/pon00

UNICEF Somalia survey of primary schools in Somalia, 1998/99. (2000, May 20). *Somalia Watch* [online]. Available: www.somaliawatch.org/Archivemay/000520602.htm

U.S. Department of State. (2002, March 4). Somalia country reports on human rights practices—2001. Bureau of Democracy, Human Rights and Labor. Available: http://www.state.gov/g/drl/rls/hrrt/2001/af/8403.htm

What protection for refugee women at risk of domestic violence in the UK? (2002, November/December). *Women's Asylum News, 27.* Available: www.asylumaid.org.uk/Publications/women's%20Asylum%20News/Articles/refugee%20women%20&%20DV%20NovDec%202002.htm

Zaza, K. (2002, July 16). *HIV/AIDS—Reaching the youth* [online]. United Nations Integrated Regional Information Network, United Nations Office of Humanitarian Affairs. Available: www.sosafrikintl.org/hivaids/aids-reaching youth.html

14

South Africa

Ronel Fourie

It is vitally important that all the structures of Government, including the President should understand fully that freedom cannot be achieved unless women have been emancipated from all forms of oppression.
—Nelson Mandela (1994, p. 4)

CAPSULE

South Africa's previous political regime, with its racial segregation, created an environment of unequal development on all levels of society. Its control over economic power, education, housing, and employment led to poor socioeconomic conditions, especially among the Black and Colored people, who suffered poverty, homelessness, high unemployment, and other social problems such as alcoholism and drug abuse. These conditions put pressure on family life, and led to high levels of crime. The HIV/AIDS epidemic in South Africa contributes greatly to violence, especially to child rape, fueled by the myth that AIDS can be cured by having sex with a young girl who is still a virgin, or with sexually inactive persons such as elderly women. Alcohol abuse is a major health problem and plays a significant role in family conflict and violence.

THE SOUTH AFRICAN RESPONDENTS

Sixty-two South Africans (20 males and 42 females) between 14 and 60 years of age answered the survey. The sample is representative of the different racial groups in South Africa. Respondents were very frank about personal experiences of family violence, and explanations were quite explicit—perhaps because of an openness to discussing issues created during the political transitional phase since 1994. The Truth and Reconciliation Committee (TRC) was established to allow people from all backgrounds to come forward to speak about the hurts and discrepancies of the past. This policy has been found to have a healing effect on people disadvantaged by political wrongdoings.

South African General Definitions of Abuse

South Africans showed a broad variety of implicit theories concerning family abuse. The respondents mainly defined abuse in physical and psychological terms, with a few references to material/financial abuse. Among the typical definitions were "physical fighting when drunk" (female, 18 years old); "When people disrespect each other" (female, 34); "Swearing at each other and hitting each other" (male, 38); "Any situation where the freedom of a woman is in jeopardy" (female, 41); "When one man killed his wife, and his children are now suffering because they don't have a mother" (female, 58). There was also considerable variation in examples of severe moderate and mild abuse. For instance, examples of extreme abuse ranged from "usage of physical force" (male, 17) to "When a woman is hurt physically or sexually, including murder or rape" (male, 14), to "when my husband stabbed me with a broken bottle and knives several times" (female, 45).

THE SOUTH AFRICAN MACROSYSTEM

Historical Context

Tribal groups, including the SAN, Khoi-Khoi, Xhosas and Zulus, occupied the land when Dutch settlers arrived in 1652 and began colonizing. Britain took possession of the Cape Colony in 1814, ruling until South Africa became independent in 1910. Strong connections with Britain persisted through the Second World War, and a policy of racial separation called Apartheid was officially established in 1948. Racial segregation and discrimination resulted in significant disparities between Whites and Blacks. Racial tension gained momentum in the 1960s, intensifying political unrest. In 1991, Parliament scrapped the Apartheid laws, and a process of transformation started. The first multiracial democratic elections were held in 1994, after which a new Constitution was adopted.

South Africa still faces many problems. According to Statistics South Africa, the unemployment rate is currently 29.5%. Previously disadvantaged groups suffer greatly from poverty. High levels of crime, in some instances coupled with corruption, are predominant. Furthermore, South Africa has the highest number of HIV infected people in the world, with 4.2 million of its 43 million people infected. One in every four women between the ages of 20 and 29 is HIV positive (UN Aids, 2001).

Status of Children

Children form a large part of the population, with 42% of the total population under the age of 18. Traditionally, South African children are valued in all cultural groups, but approximately 40% of them grow up surrounded by poverty, neglect, crime, exploitation, assault, and fractured families. These children are at risk for infant death, stunted growth, poor adjustment, and dropping out of school ("Government Education White Paper 5," 2001). They live in overcrowded conditions, which may include sharing housing with unrelated males in order to reduce living expenses, and sharing a room with sexually active adults. Recreational activities and resources are limited, and children frequently find themselves unprotected in unsafe neighborhoods with high levels of gang activities.

With disintegration of the traditional family structure, South African teenagers are facing difficult times. South Africa has the eighth highest teenage suicide rate in the world, with approximately 6 suicides for every 100,000 young people (approximately 250 a year). Teenagers seek refuge in drugs and alcohol, with an estimated 1 out of 6 becoming dependent on drugs. Teenage pregnancies are also high, with 17,000 babies born to mothers under the age of 16 each year ("Trying times make for troubled teens," 2001).

Street children are another problem in South Africa. The disintegration of families, coupled with poverty, unemployment, overcrowding, and abuse, leads some children to abandon their homes and live in the street. They do not go to school or receive any form of education, but become incorporated into gangs who provide their only support and protection. Several social programs attempt to resettle street children, but their success rate is relatively low, partly because of the runaways' strong ties with other street children. There are no exact figures, but it is estimated that 10,000 child live on the streets, especially in metropolitan areas. Most are boys, but approximately 10% are girls, who tend to end up in prostitution networks where they can have an income (Center for Conflict Resolution, 1998).

The effect of HIV/AIDS on children is enormous. It is estimated that every year, 70,000 South African babies contract HIV. Over 90% of these infections are a result of mother-to-child transmissions (www.christian-aid.org.uk). In many cases, both parents die of HIV/AIDS, leaving the children orphaned. The most disturbing factor is the common myth that having sex with a virgin will cure AIDS. Politicians, community organizations, and news sources have condemned this belief, but girls continue to be extremely vulnerable targets of rape.

Status of Women

The status of women differs from society to society within the country and is shaped by religion, culture, and traditional values. Although gender equality is established in legal statutes, inequality between men and women prevails on social, cultural, and traditional levels. South Africa is liberal in the African context regarding the status of women, but women have a subordinate status and restricted autonomy in society. Their experiences differ according to race and grouping, with Black women the most disadvantaged by discrimination, poverty, fewer opportunities, and low literacy rates.

On certain levels of society, women are viewed as equals, but stereotypical views of women as inferior to men and belonging in domesticated role as wives and mothers, are common. The majority of African women are influenced by a system of customary law. For example, the practice of *lobola* (bridesprice) is a traditional arrangement between two families, in which the woman essentially becomes the property of her husband. The status of women is further influenced by income. Men are more likely to earn more money than their wives and have more control over the money—making women dependent on husbands and likely to stay with their husbands despite abuse. Studies on the culture of sexual violence indicated that 40% of men (N = 2,059) had the opinion that punishing their wife, through means such as physical violence, verbal abuse, controlling freedom, and withholding sex, is legitimate (The Men as Partners Program, n.d.).

Things are changing. Equal social rights for women in all spheres of life are promulgated in official documents granting women rights over their own bodies, statutory protection against violence, representation in the public sector, and full legal equality. The South African government is strongly committed to gender equality, which is a basic principle of the Constitution. Women are being appointed to the Cabinet (26.5% of politicians are women) and fill senior positions in private and public sectors.

THE SOUTH AFRICAN MICROSYSTEM

There are two major forms of South African family. The White and Indian communities are mainly nuclear families (parents and one to four children), whereas Black families tend to be extended (including grandparents, and sometimes uncles and aunts and their children)—not only because of cultural values but also because of poverty. Both family types tend to be patriarchal, with the father recognized as the head of the family and women responsible for child upbringing.

Huge social, economic, and cultural differences characterize South Africa, affecting family structure and stability. On the one hand, there are stable middle class communities in which abuse of family members is limited, and social services are well developed and organized. In the larger portion of the population, however, policies of the previous governmental system have contributed to disparities in the distribution of resources, migration, changes in the traditional roles of men and women, and a growing subculture of family violence. The majority of these families live in unsafe and unhealthy conditions with an acute shortage of housing and basic services, and inadequate resources to provide for the needs of their children. The migration of parents, who often leave children in the care of grandparents in rural areas, has led to family disorganization, with father and mother roles fading. Some migrant workers have lost contact with their families entirely. Further pressure is put on family life by problems such as alcoholism, drug abuse, parenting difficulties, and violence in the community.

FAMILY VIOLENCE IN SOUTH AFRICA

Over the last decade, legislators have drawn attention to family violence, and statistics show an ever-increasing prevalence of abusive behaviors, with rape being the most prominent form. The 1993 "Prevention of Family Violence Act" made marital rape a criminal offense (Bureau of Democracy, 2001). A Bill of Rights, part of the South African Constitution, specifies that citizens have the right to freedom from all forms of violence, including family violence, and prohibits degrading treatment of any individual. The Child Care Amendment Act arranges for the protection of children in matters such as sexual exploitation. In 1996, the South African government adopted The Hague Convention on the Civil Aspects of International Child Abduction Act, 1996. In 1998, the South African Government adopted the Domestic Violence Bill, which described domestic violence as "any controlling or abusive behavior that harms the health, safety or well-being of any person."

Social service mechanisms have been established to deal with family violence. The Domestic Violence Bill provides victims with a safe environment away from their abusers. Medical and educational practitioners are compelled to report child abuse and other forms of family abuse to the police. Any peace officer may, without a warrant, arrest any person responsible for domestic violence. The Social Welfare Department, together with an array of nongovernmental organizations (NGOs), regularly assists citizens with problems such as abuse. However, although an excellent Constitution is in place, accompanied by appropriate legislation, enforcing these laws has been a problem. The South African Police Service (SAPS) are plagued by understaffing and an overload of serious crimes such as murder, rape, and armed robbery. *Die Burger* (a South African newspaper) reports that leading NGOs responsible for matters such as family violence believe The Domestic Violence Bill is not successful because police don't have the resources to apply the laws ("Dertien sterf," 2001). Furthermore, the judiciary is overloaded with trials waiting to go through the system. Cases are often withdrawn by victims out of fear either of the abusers or of the emotional impact of prolonged trials.

Child Abuse

For many years, child abuse was an unacknowledged and taboo topic, but the severity of the problem finally forced the government, communities, NGOs, and families to recognize the need for drastic measures. Child rape and sexual assault are common, with children the victims in 41% of all rapes and attempted rapes. In the year 2000, 25,578 sexual crimes against children were reported. Most cases happened in poor areas, and were associated with alcohol abuse by the perpetrator (South African Police Statistics, 2002). A 2001/2002 survey by the South African Institute for Race Relations (SAIRR) revealed a child rape incidence rate of approximately 20,000 per year. Only 50% of the child rape cases were referred to court, and only 9% resulted in a conviction. Over 8,000 cases were withdrawn, some because of pressure and intimidation, especially when the victim knew the perpetrator (SAIRR, 2001).

Based on a study of 11,735 women between the ages of 15 and 49, it was estimated that schoolteachers commit a third of all child rapes, and school is often the place where sexual harassment and rape takes place (Medical Research Council Survey, 2002). Of the women raped before the age of 15, 33% were attacked by teachers, and 21% by relatives. This survey revealed that 1.3% of the women reported having been raped before the age of 15— sometimes as young as age 5. Although it is mandatory to report child abuse in South Africa, girls who complain of sexual abuse generally receive hostile and unsympathetic responses from school authorities (Human Rights Watch, 2000).

Sexual harassment of girls at school has complex social effects. It negatively influences their academic performance and often leads to their dropping out of school, which in turn affects their ability to earn a living. Child prostitution has become a growing problem, particularly in urban areas. According to the South African Police Statistics, 28,000 children in the Johannesburg area are engaged in prostitution, and around 15 new girls between the ages 15 and 18 are arrested every month. Poverty is one of the factors involved in this problem, and sometimes girls are urged by their own parents to go out and earn money for the family. One 18-year-old respondent described a form of abuse she called moderate: "When my mother scream at me when I don't want to be a prostitute and say I would not get food."

Although law prohibits the employment of a child under the age of 15 years, child labor is common, particularly in rural areas. To enhance family income and relieve the family's poor living conditions, children often work in the agricultural industry, in the informal market, or in family businesses. While statistics are inconsistent, it is estimated that 400,000 children are involved in child labor, with 59% in the agricultural sector ("Worst forms of child labor," 2000).

South Africa Respondents' Judgments Concerning Child Abuse

Although I have focused on very extreme forms of abuse, our respondents' implicit theories of abuse include classic forms of physical abuse, emotional abuse, verbal abuse, and neglect, and recognize alcohol as a predictive factor. Examples of abuse from a 16-year-old male respondent were "My father forced me to go with him to illegal liquor dealers. He used to hit me. And when the abuse of alcohol hampers the family affairs." Examples of extreme child abuse were "when my mother want to sell me as a prostitute for money to buy alcohol," "neglecting a child and not providing enough food and shelter," and "when a father is burning his child." Examples of moderate abuse were "when parents fight with each other in the presence of the child," and "when a child is not provided with basic needs." Examples of mild abuse included "heavy spanking," "putting a child in a dark room alone," and "not providing enough love."

Violence Against Women

Despite efforts to ensure equal rights for women, the abuse and violation of women in South Africa is reaching epidemic proportions, and the country has become a particularly risky place for them. Gender-based violence seems to be accepted as normal. Few social pressures or controls operate to deter men from violence against women. Even though the Domestic Violence Bill (1999) is a powerful tool, only a small percentage of rape cases end up in conviction. The attitudes of men, as well as of society, play an integral part in violence against women. Not only does gender discrimination occur in the family environment, but also in general customs and practices. In the male-dominated South African society, women are perceived as objects and possessions that can be controlled. This perception is further enhanced by the fact that men normally hold the financial power in the relationship. Women are subordinate to men to such an extent that they do not believe they have the right to stand up against their partner in any way, including refusal of sex.

Research on Women Abuse

Research on violence against women in South Africa is fragmented and inadequate; nevertheless, the available data make it clear that violence against women is extremely high and that rape is the major form it takes. Domestic violence and abuse generally are underreported. A woman may talk to close friends or family members about her abuse, but is either too afraid or too ashamed to talk about it to anyone else. Threatening a woman, taking control of her income, and preventing her from seeing friends are often seen as just the way it is in a marriage and are not reported or even seen as abuse.

In a study in Mitchell's Plain, Cape Town (representative of the conditions in low-income, high social problematic townships in South Africa), 48% of the sample ($n = 412$) said they had been abused in the past and/or were being abused at present. Verbal abuse was most common, followed by emotional abuse, physical abuse, isolation, sexual abuse, and lastly, economic abuse. The use of alcohol and drugs was often the contributing factor to the abuse incident (Jacobs, 1999). Data from a 1998 study of women ($N = 1,306$) from three South African provinces revealed that being beaten in childhood and witnessing a mother's abuse were important for women's perceptions and experiences of violence (Gender and Health Group of the Medical Research Council, 1998). Some women exposed to violence in childhood tended to view it as normal and thus tolerate it. Exposure to violence in childhood also influenced self-esteem, reducing the ability to leave potentially violent relationships. Although low education was not necessarily a risk factor for abuse, there were indications that women with higher education and income were less likely to be abused.

Domestic violence is also associated with lack of resources and poverty, especially when the male partner is unemployed. Bourgois (as cited in Jewkes, 2002) explained that poverty and unemployment reduce the ability of men to provide for their families, which negatively affects their sense of masculinity, leads them to lash out at women, and increases conflict over resources. Social isolation of a woman seems to be a related risk factor for domestic violence. There is also a strong correlation between conservative ideas about the status of women and the abuse of women, with both traditional men and women seeing the woman as subordinate to her male partner. Alcohol also plays a strong role; 67% of men had used alcohol before an occurrence of domestic violence. The violence may have been a by-product of either his drunken aggressiveness or of conflict sprouting from his drinking habits. The misuse of alcohol by women is also a source of conflict leading to domestic violence, as is women's infidelity (Jewkes, 2002).

South African Respondents' Judgments Concerning Spouse Abuse

In our participants' implicit theories, many forms of spousal aggression were deemed abusive. Among the examples of extreme abuse were the following: "When a man is molesting his wife sexually in the presence of their children" (male, 16); "My husband was hitting me and drag me out of the house. He attacked me with a panga (long knife)" (female, 35); and "Depriving a wife of access to financial matters, freedom of speech, decision making, frequent assault and verbal insults" (female, 41). Even the examples of moderate abuse were quite severe—such as "When a man put his wife's face in a bucket of water to learn her a lesson" (female, 30)—as were some examples of mild abuse: "Poor treatment such as swearing and to be physically assaulted" (female, 58); "When a man is involved in another sexual relationship" (female, 43); and "When a man takes off the clothes of his wife and hits her with a waistband" (male, 16).

Sexual Abuse and Rape

It is important to discuss sexual abuse and rape as forms of abuse in their own right because they are pandemic in South Africa. All women and girls are potential victims, irrespective of age, status, income, or culture. Police estimate that only 2.8% of all rape cases are reported to police. The South African Demographic and Health Survey (SADHS) showed that only 15% of women reported an incident to the police when physical force was used to make them have sex against their will (SADHS, 2000). Another study indicated that in 1998, only 25% of rapes and only 11% of attempted rapes were reported to the police (Medical Research Council, 1999).

According to the South African Police Services (SAPS), rape is significantly associated with drinking, especially drinking in the company of friends, gang members, people who have been involved in criminal activity, and at public drinking places such as *shebeens* (social drinking place), bottle stores, and clubs. Offenders serving a sentence for rape reported having alcohol/drugs immediately before or at the time they committed the offense ("SAPS Crime Report," 2000). In a study on rape victims in Cape Town and Johannesburg, Martin (1998) found that 15,342 rapes were reported in 1983 in comparison with 52,160 cases in 1997. Although several factors account for the increase, such as growing trust in the police and more openness about these crimes, it is apparent that the incidence of rape is on the rise. The brutality with which the violence is conducted—increasingly involving objects like knives and guns—is of great concern (www.speakout. org.za). Most reported cases of rape and domestic violence are withdrawn in or before they reach court, usually at the request of the complainants.

One reasons is that rape often happens within the family environment; being raped within the marriage is regularly seen as an unwanted experience, but not as true rape. Dropping cases can also occur when the judiciary system fails to deal effectively with the complainants (www.news24.com December 13, 2001).

Effect of HIV/AIDS

South Africa has an estimated 4.7 million HIV-infected people—half of them women, who have higher infection rates than men ("Parliamentary Briefing," 2001). It is estimated that only 1 out of 100 HIV positive South Africans are even aware of their condition. The rest simply don't go for testing (CBS News, June 27, 2000). Women have become particularly susceptible to HIV/AIDS for several reasons: 1) a traditional custom whereby people have more than one lover; 2) lack of education about the use of condoms to avoid spreading HIV/AIDS; 3) a patriarchic society in which men refuse to use condoms; and 4) a social taboo against discussing HIV/AIDS.

Causes for Domestic Violence/Rape in South Africa

South African society in all its heterogeneity is an extremely and increasingly violent society. Mana (2001, p. 2) concluded that "Violent societies are violent towards women, and militaristic forms of masculinity are strongly associated with rape and other manifestations of sexism." In South Africa, with its history of social and political dislocation, men's insecurity is coupled with a contracting economy, resulting in unemployment and unmet expectations. A feeling of frustration and powerlessness is translated into emasculation (Simpson, as cited in Pokroy, 1999), which then results in violence against women. Men use sex to fulfill a nonsexual need, namely the need for power, to dominate and to prove their masculinity (Mawby & Walhute, as cited in Pokroy, 1999). Aggression is not directed at the source of the problem, but at women, because in a patriarchal society, women and children are "owned" by men. In addition, because of the violent history of the nation, violence and crime have been normalized (McKendrick & Hoffman, as cited in Pokroy, 1999).

Women's Reactions

A number of organizations have put a huge effort into the problem of domestic violence against women, but the majority of abused women have limited resources and limited options. Women who speak out against domestic violence have a great deal to lose: their home, custody of their children, financial support. A strong belief in cultural, family, and religious values also make it difficult for women to report violence by a family member.

In more threatening situations, women are afraid the perpetrators will resort to even more serious acts, including murdering them. One of our respondents told us: "My father used too much alcohol. My mother was looking for love and had an affair with another man. My father heard about this and killed her."

Status of Men

In South Africa, men are expected to be masculine and strong, and are viewed as chiefly responsible for the financial welfare of the household. In the work environment, they fill most of the senior and medium- to high-income jobs. However, their role is in a period of change. With women moving into traditionally male-dominated fields of expertise, pressure is put on a society that doesn't know exactly how to respond to the phenomenon.

Forms of Abuse of Men

Due to South Africa's patriarchal society, the abuse of men is a subject not generally discussed. It is believed that men should be able to protect themselves. Male rape, for example, is seen as a problem occurring only among gay men; consequently, men fear that if they report abuse, especially sexual abuse, they will be identified as gay. South African legislators are in the forefront worldwide with proposed legislation acknowledging that male rape occurs. The law is still under development, and sexual assault and other forms of male abuse are mostly not reported to either the police or the social welfare societies. Research on the issue is inadequate because it is extremely difficult for men to talk about their victimization, and because society underestimates the problem.

South African Perspectives on Husband Abuse

Our respondents were fairly unanimous in the forms of husband abuse they identified as common within the South African society: when a woman is "slapping/hitting her husband" either in private or in public, but mostly privately ($N = 43$); "cursing and screaming at her husband"; "when a woman has an affair with another man"; "when a woman does not prepare food for her husband or do other household jobs such as cleaning the house"; "psychological infliction," "verbal abuse especially in the presence of other people"; and "withholding sex from a husband." More extreme forms of abuse against men were also identified by respondents—specifically, gang raping and "When a women throws a rock towards a man injuring his head." Nevertheless, there is still a perception that men are not abused. As one respondent said, "I don't think it exists. It is only a man who can abuse a woman." Other respondents acknowledge mild and moderate, but not extreme, forms of male abuse.

ELDER ABUSE

Status of Elderly

Elders in South Africa are traditionally highly respected, and an age-based hierarchy typifies families. Grandparents are often responsible for children when parents are at the workplace, and have a particularly important role in rearing children orphaned due to HIV/AIDS. Elders are, however, sometimes seen as a burden, and this perception can lead to abuse. Putting an elderly parent in an old age facility is often seen as a form of neglect, but when elderly people become increasingly dependent, they become targets of maltreatment. Although it is nearly impossible to quantify the extent of elder abuse and neglect, all of our respondents identified matters such as "malnutrition" and "emotional abuse and neglect" as common problems among the older society. A significant number of elderly people living alone become targets of self-neglect. They find themselves among the poorest of the nation and have difficulty sustaining an adequate lifestyle. High rent, service charges, and food prices add to this problem.

Medical and social work services aimed specifically at the elderly are insufficient. Clinics and state hospitals providing cost-effective services are in place, but transport to these facilities, long waiting times, and lack of geriatric services are problems. Not enough residential old age homes are available; consequently, elders have to be absorbed into the community, where they become more vulnerable to abuse and neglect. The few available residential homes are mostly in financial distress, with underpaid staff, few recreational activities, and sometimes substandard food and facilities.

On the governmental level, a pension program is in place whereby women at the age of 60 and men at the age of 65 years and older are eligible for a pension, as well as for reduced fees on services such as transportation and medical services. The sharing of a pension, especially in the Black communities, is the norm. This leads to certain dynamics whereby the elder person has a very important role as the source of income for the entire household. On the other hand, it leaves them vulnerable and open for abuse and exploitation by family members who want to obtain control over their money.

Forms of Elder Abuse

Although elder abuse has long been occurring in South Africa, public recognition has occurred only in the last few years. Statistics are not readily available for several reasons: the shortage of resources, the fact that cases are not reported, and the general perception that certain behaviors are not abuse, but rather the natural way to interact. Due to the poverty in South Africa and a culture of collectivism, the small social pension received by the elderly is in many cases the only income for an extended family. As a result, family members harass their elders into handing over their money, or know where their money is hidden and steal it.

In South Africa with its constitutional focus on human rights, any degrading treatment of an elder person is seen as a violation of their human rights. Nevertheless, elder maltreatment is found on all levels of society, within the family, at old-age homes and institutions, and at the governmental level (systemic abuse). Reasons found for abuse of the elderly include pathologies of the abuser (e.g., mental illness, alcoholism); learned patterns of violence and the stress of family caregiving; external stress related to income and employment status; demographic and social changes resulting in increased numbers of frail elders placing excessive demands on families; and stereotypic and prejudiced attitudes toward the elderly ("Mothers and fathers of the nation," 2001, p. 5).

For the majority of the elder population, the most apparent form of abuse involves government pensions. Because only a small percentage of elderly South Africans were enrolled in employee pension schemes over their productive years, a preponderance of elderly people depend on the government's Social Pension System, initiated in 1928 for Whites only. Pensions were not granted to African people until 1943, and even then there was a huge disparity in the amount paid to Whites in comparison to Blacks. This discrepancy was not rectified until 1994 (www.polity.org.za).

The first problem for elderly pension recipients occurs at the pay-points where they can collect their pension on a preset date once a month. Typically, at the pay-points, they stand in long queues, often for many hours, with few places to sit and little protection from harsh weather, often without food or water—a situation which itself can be considered abusive. As soon as they receive their pension, they become targets of criminals who know well when payday arrives. Burial societies, moneylenders, and people selling liquor and other goods all target the elderly person. Thirteen cases were reported of elderly people who lost their lives during 1999 and 2000 in these queues. Three were killed in armed robberies and the other 10 died of exhaustion or other medical conditions ("Dertien sterf in rye vir pensioen," 2001).

South African Perspectives on Elder Abuse

In our survey, respondents identified financial abuse—including misusing a parent's pension—as a major problem. In one example of extreme abuse, the respondent wrote: "I've seen how a child physically abused his mother to get her money. He wanted to buy marijuana." Others said, "when a man hit his parents on pension day in order to get their money," and "to steal the pension of an old person and then not provide him/her with food" were abusive.

A study conducted in four suburbs of Cape Town (Bo-Kaap, Guguletu, Kensington, and Mitchell's Plain) revealed that elder abuse in the local Muslim population is mainly perceived as disrespect and neglect of older persons, leading to abusive practices. Disrespect included verbal abuse and/or financial exploitation, even in family settings (Mosaval & Ferreira, 2000). In our survey, emotional abuse was widely recognized by respondents. Specific examples of emotional/psychological abuse of the elderly included "swearing," "ignoring," and "talking impolitely."

Systemic abuse perpetrated on elderly people by institutions is a great concern. Inadequate conditions at old-age homes, and the perception that sending an elder person to such institutions is a form of neglect, were themes in our sample. One respondent said it is moderate abuse "when personnel of the old-age home are impatient with persons who cannot walk fast." Another said it is mild form of abuse "to send an elder to an old-age home because the family of this person doesn't want to look after her." Participants saw any form of physical abuse as extreme, and made a clear association between physical abuse and financial matters (pension).

Keikelame and Ferreira (2000) reported that their respondents identified incest rape as the most common form of sexual abuse of older women. "The rape was typically preceded by physical beatings and verbal abuse, in an attempt to extort the older woman's pension money from her. If she failed to submit and to hand over the money to the son, then he would rape her and forcibly take the money" (p. 7). They added that this kind of behavior becomes repetitive, but victims are inclined to protect the abusive family member and not talk about these crimes. In our own survey, reference was also made to sexual abuse. One participant identified an extreme form of abuse as "when grandchildren rape a grandmother and steal her money." Participants in our survey also identified depriving the elder person of basic needs such as food, clothing, and shelter as forms of abuse. One respondent said abuse is "when the family members doesn't look well after an old person, giving food and love."

INTERVENTION AND PREVENTION

Programs for Abused and Neglected Children

The government places a huge emphasis on the protection of the children, which is guaranteed through the Children's Charter. However, social services are stretched, and not all children have access to them. The South African Police have a special unit, the Child Protection Unit, that concentrates on child abuse and has specially trained personnel to assist children. Trauma centers, counseling centers, and shelters focusing on the well-being of children can be found throughout the country. A 24-hour childline where children can call to seek help or report abuse operates with great success. Some of the institutions providing programs for abused children are Childline South Africa; Child Abuse Resource Center; Child Justice Alliance; Child Welfare; National Peace Accord Trust; and Helpline. These institutions and others provide crisis control, children's homes, legal representation, and counseling.

Programs for Abused Women

South Africa deserves credit for its efforts to improve the plight of women. A good (according to a developing country's standards) social welfare department is in place. The Department of Welfare provides toll free centers where persons can seek help or report family violence, and has social workers throughout the country to assist communities with social issues, including family violence. A 27-year-old woman gave us this example of mild abuse: "My father was always fighting with my mother except when the social worker came to visit them. Then he was behaving himself." Programs to help abused women include support groups with access to consultation and legal advice. Most organizations are, however, in urban areas; rural areas, where the majority of women reside, lack resources. Among the support organizations available are: LifeLine: provides a 24-hour telephone counseling and referral service; National Network on Violence Against Women: a network of domestic violence service organizations providing advice and shelter to victims; Family and Marriage Society of South Africa: providing education and support for both men and women in abusive relationships; National Institute for Crime and the Rehabilitation of Offenders: counseling with offenders as well as victims of violence; and Rape Crisis: counseling services for rape survivors, awareness training and advice to families of rape victims.

Programs for Abused Elders

Although elderly abuse is a phenomenon recognized only for the past few years, several actions are already in place to deal with this problem. The South African government, supported by church groups and by nongovernmental organizations, has a commitment to address all forms of elder abuse. In 1998, the South African Council for the Aged established a toll free line, the Halt Elder Abuse Line (HEAL). Elderly persons can phone in and report any abuse taking place. This information is forwarded for investigation to government welfare offices, the police, or nongovernmental organizations. Because of this initiative, a number of abused elderly were put in places of safety, and perpetrators were prosecuted.

Programs for Abused Men

Very little support for abused or raped men exists in South Africa. Most institutions caring for rape victims specialize in the counseling of women and children only. However, there is a growing conviction among social services, protection services, and other support groups that specialized programs for abused men need development.

CONCLUSION

Domestic violence in South Africa is not a new problem, but has attracted increasing societal and governmental attention over the past 10 years. Many people experience domestic violence, but underreporting and the desire to keep the incident domestic conceal rates of occurrence. The status of women and children has been improved dramatically and the South African Government has established new legislation in support of the protection of women, children, and elderly people.

REFERENCES

Bureau of Democracy, Human Rights and Labor. (2001, February).

CBS News Report. (2000, June 27). *60 Minutes.*

Center for Conflict Resolution. (1998, October). *Streets ahead, 7*(3). Cape Town: Author.

Dertien sterf in rye vir pensioen [Thirteen die in pension line]. (2001, August 3). *Die Burger*, p. 2.

Gender and Health Group of the Medical Research Council. (1998).

Government education white paper 5 on early childhood education. (2001, May). Available: www. gov.za

Human Rights Watch. (2000). *World Report: South Africa.* New York: Author. Available: www. hrw.org/africa/southafrica

Jacobs, T. (1999, November). *Breaking the silence.* Cape Town: Health Systems Trust.

Jewkes, R. (2002). Risk factors for domestic violence: Findings from a South African cross-sectional study. *Social Science & Medicine, 55,* 1603–1617.

Keikelame, J., & Ferreira, M. (1999). *Mpatekomi, ya bantu babadala* [Elder abuse in black townships on the Cape Flats]. Cape Town: HSRC/UCT Centre for Gerontology.

Mana, A. (2001, March). *Transformation thwarted: Gender based violence in Africa's new democracies.*

Mandela, N. (1994, May 24). *State of the nation.* Speech delivered shortly after election of first democratic government in South Africa.

Martin, A. (1998, November 27). *Combatting sexual violence in South Africa* [online]. Available: http://www.idrc.ca/reports/read_article_english.cfm?article_num=293

Medical Research Council. (1999). *Violence against women in South Africa: Rape and sexual coercion.* Cape Town: Author.

Medical Research Council Survey. (2002). *Role of teachers in abuse.* Cape Town: Author.

The Men as Partners Program. (n.d.). [online]. Available: http://www.solutions-site.org/cat4_sol118.htm

Mosaval, Y., & Ferreira, M. (2000). *Bejaarde ouers het las geword* [Elders became a burden].

Mothers and fathers of the nation: The forgotten people. (2001, February). Ministerial Report. South African Government. Cape Town.

Pokroy, J. (1999). *Police sensitivity to rape survivors.* Unpublished bachelor's dissertation, University of the Witwatersrand, Johannesburg, South Africa. Abstract from: http://www.speakout.org.za/legal/police/police_sensitivity.html

South African Demographic and Health Survey (SADHS). (2000). *Reporting of domestic violence.* South Africa: Department of Health.

South African Government Parliamentary Monitoring Group Briefing. (2000, October 2). Improvement of quality of life and status of women. Cape Town. Available: www.gov.za

South African Institute for Race Relations (SAIRR). (2001, December). *2001/2002 survey.* Cape Town.

South African Police Crime Report. (2000). [online]. Available: http://www.saps.org.za

South African Police Statistics. (2000). *Child prostitution.* Available: http://globalmarch.org/worstformsreport/world/south-africa.html

UN Aids and World Health Organization (WHO). (2001). *Report* [online]. Available: http://www.news24.com

Worst forms of child labor: South Africa. (2000). [online]. Available: http://www.globalmarch.org/worstformsreport/world/south-africa.html

ASIA AND THE PACIFIC

15

India

Sonia Chawla

CAPSULE

Indian culture is rooted in 5,000-year-old Vedic traditions. It is a patriarchal soci-
ety with a strict social and familial hierarchy. Women and children, who occupy
a lower status position within the family and society, are particularly vulnerable
to abuse. Although family life is regarded as intensely private, within the past 20
to 30 years, domestic violence has been exposed as a problem in Indian as well
as international media. For example, the world became aware of bride burning,
a rare and extreme end to the more pervasive problem of dowry abuse. Such vi-
olence, directed at a young bride in order to extort money and luxury items from
her family, captured the attention of Indian lawmakers and resulted in stronger
legislation against it; however, despite the best intentions of the lawmakers, tra-
ditions enabling abuse of women persist in India.

Children are also a vulnerable population. Because children are expected to
obey and respect their elders, and corporal punishment is often used by parents
and sanctioned by Indian society, disobedient children may be subjected to vio-
lence. Also, because boys are preferred in India, girls are subject to neglect. Al-
though illegal, prenatal sex selection is a large problem, with many couples
choosing to selectively abort female fetuses. Prenatal sex selection, along with
dowry deaths, have created the problem of more men than women in India,
which is the opposite of the biologically driven norm.

With the increasing westernization and urbanization of India, some traditions
are being replaced. The extended family, for instance, is being replaced with the

nuclear family living arrangement predominating in the West. This change is making the elderly, traditionally a segment of the population with much power in the familial hierarchy, more vulnerable to abuse. Although domestic violence has not, in the past, been considered a serious problem by much of society, the situation is beginning to change. Victims and support groups are beginning to increase pressure on society to provide for victims of domestic violence, and lawmakers have proposed more legislation detailing stricter punishments for committing acts of domestic violence. However, the traditional attitudes that prevail in India still encompass inequality among family members, thus enabling the abuse to continue.

THE INDIAN SAMPLE

The 51 Indian participants were predominantly middle to upper middle class, urban, young, educated North Indians. Although there are some voices from different generations as well as from different social classes, the sample did not have any rural participants. Survey responses were gained over the internet (which, due to the extreme privacy Indians feel toward family matters, was not very successful) and from one-on-one interviews during a visit to New Delhi. As the capital of India, New Delhi has many immigrants from all over India as its residents, and consequently, some respondents were not North Indians.

Indian Participants' Definitions of Abuse in Families

Most respondents defined domestic abuse in terms of physical violence, with a lesser number of respondents including verbal, psychological/mental, emotional, and sexual violence. Some references were also made to the "restriction of expression" of family members, "theft," and "broken relationships." A number of respondents mentioned "helplessness" and "neediness" as being abusive, reflecting the desire for all family members to contribute to the family. "Drinking" and "drug use" were often given as examples of abuse because of the violence to which they may lead. Finally, many people defined abuse as "not treating family members properly" or "neglect."

Examples of physical violence were generally characterized as extreme abuse, whereas verbal abuse was seen as a milder form of family maltreatment. Emotional, sexual, and psychological violence were less often mentioned. One possible explanation is difficulties in translation. Some of the respondents, namely those of lower socioeconomic levels, were not fluent in English and the survey had to be translated for them. The term "abuse" does not have a one-to-one translation in Hindi, so it was translated to mean "maltreatment"—a term that may have different connotations.

One common response was that level of abuse varies not by the action, but by the effect on the victim or the intention of the perpetrator. A 39-year-old female defined extreme abuse as "when the abuser behaves thus knowingly and willfully," contrasting it with mild abuse, which she defined as "when the abuser behaves thus without forethought." "Back-biting" or "gossip" appeared as examples of mild to moderate abuse. One participant, a 28-year-old maid, responded that she "minds her own business and doesn't know an example" of extreme abuse, alluding to the negative connotations in Indian society of intruding into others' lives. She also mentioned not minding one's own business in her example of mild abuse; "people talk about her personal life such as how they get their food, how they get to wear clothes, etc. (gossiping/back-biting)."

The two lower class respondents viewed violence resulting from an argument as extreme if the victim's position was the correct one (e.g., the victim's spouse should not "come home drunk" or "squander the family's money"). Another behavior characterized as extremely abusive by these respondents was "kicking or locking the victim out of the house." However, it is impossible to generalize about differences in family violence views or incidence across socioeconomic classes because of the limited data from this and other samples.

THE INDIAN MACROSYSTEM

India is currently the world's largest democracy, with a population second only to China, of over 1 billion people. It gained its independence from Britain in 1947 and, at that time, was split, based on religious majority, into the countries of India (the area with a Hindu majority population) and Pakistan (the area with a Muslim majority population).

Culture

Indian culture is patriarchal, patrilineal, and collectivistic, and Indian people are extremely emotional, especially with family and close friends. Societal ideas tend to be very traditional; however, in the past 20 years, India has seen a massive westernization, especially in urban areas. Despite this modernization, many social problems still exist—namely, ethnic disputes, overpopulation, and severe income inequality. Although India consists of many culturally distinct regions, "Indian culture" is used here to refer to practices common to most of the country.

Caste System

The caste system was probably introduced into the subcontinent during the Aryan invasion in the second millennium BC. It was apparently intended as a means of classifying occupations, but became more of a system for social stratification. According to the *Rig Veda*, a Hindu sacred text, the four original *varna* were the *Brahmans* (priests and religious leaders), the *Kshatriyas* (warriors and rulers), the *Vaishyas* (landowners and merchants), and the *Shudras* (artisans and servants). The fifth caste, the *Dalits* (untouchables), developed later, and its members were delegated the menial and dirty jobs related to human waste and decay.

At the height of the caste system, separation was maintained at all times, and members of higher castes often viewed members of lower castes as unclean or impure. These expectations evolved into abuses, such as the requirement that *Dalits* ring a bell to signal their approach to the higher castes and their prohibition from schools and places of worship. With India's independence and the ratification of her constitution in 1947, caste-based discrimination was made illegal (Federal Research Division, 1995); however, some discrimination based on caste still occurs today, especially in more rural areas of India, in the occupational arena. It is not uncommon for a man not to get a job for which he has applied due to his caste affiliation.

Media

More films are made in India than in any other country in the world, including the United States, and viewing films is a popular form of entertainment, especially among young, unmarried men (Derné, 1995). Because sex and husband–wife relations are taboo topics in Indian society, films have a great deal of power as portrayals of male–female interactions. Dasgupta and Hegde (1988) found instances of sexual harassment, physical assault, rape, and murder of women in 70% of Hindi films. Derné (1999) claimed that such mistreatment is eroticized in Indian films, where men perpetrate violence against women to woo them, typically with successful results.

THE INDIAN MICROSYSTEM

The family is the core unit of Indian society. Many families, particularly in rural areas, are extended, consisting of many generations and different degrees of blood relatives living in a single household. The head of the family is the eldest male, and his position is one of respect and authority. Familial duties and roles differ based on age and sex, with elder members of the family having authority over the younger members and men having a higher status than women. Traditionally, the occupants of an Indian home include a husband and wife, their children, and the husband's parents. Some of the husband's brothers, along with their wives and children, or uncles, with their wives and children, may live in the same house. It is rare for any of the woman's relatives to live with her, because she is considered part of her husband's family.

The role of son in Indian society is extremely important, because the society is patrilineal, and the son is responsible for caring for his parents in their old age. It is the parents' duty to raise a son as well as possible, ensuring that he receives the highest and best education available, and that he is well fed and well nourished (a concern in some of the poorer rural areas of the country). The son also inherits his parents' property because he is responsible for continuing the family line. Whereas the son is often the focus of his parents' positive attention, the daughter is seldom viewed positively. Traditionally, men are the breadwinners, and women take care of the home and children. Because women do not bring money into the home, yet require food and clothing to survive, daughters are sometimes seen as a drain on family resources, especially in lower socioeconomic families. Some parents try to marry off a daughter as soon as possible so she can join another family. Often, the daughter's new family will require her parents to provide a dowry, or a gift of cash, furniture, vehicles, jewelry, and other luxury items. While it has been hypothesized that the dowry was originally a means for a daughter to secure some of her birth family's resources (Kishwar as cited in Vindhya, 2000), it is now typically a gift to the bride's new family, often at their request, to offset the expense of their new daughter-in-law.

The most prominent members of the Indian family are the elders. In traditional Indian society, age is venerated, and the experience and wisdom of the older generation are to be respected at all times. Because it is generally the elders who own the house in which the family resides, they have a certain amount of power (e.g., they can dictate what they like and do not like happening on their property). When a family member encounters an older relative, a traditional Indian greeting is to bend down and, with one hand, touch the relative's feet.

Maintaining awareness of the proper hierarchy in the family is extremely important. Using casual or friendly language with elders and people hierarchically higher up can be viewed as an insult. Because it is the parents' responsibility to ensure that their children are raised to behave properly, they tend to be strict in their rearing practices. Children learn early on that they should behave obediently and respectfully to all relatives older than they are.

FAMILY VIOLENCE IN INDIA

The Indian Constitution outlaws discrimination based on race, caste, sex, religion, and place of birth. Additionally, it makes special provisions for women, children, and "socially and educationally backward classes of citizens or for the Scheduled Castes and the Scheduled Tribes,"[1] thereby acknowledging the potential for such populations to become subject to discrimination or other unfair treatment. Similarly, the Indian Penal Code contains laws against assault, force, causing hurt, endangerment, restraint, and confinement, which can be applied to situations within families.

Laws on Abuse Against Women[2]

In 1874, colonial India created the Married Women's Property Act, specifically stating that a woman's property remains her own, instead of becoming her husband's, when she marries. In 1961, the Indian government passed the Dowry Prohibition Act, thereby making dowries illegal and establishing a system of penalties for demanding dowry and for abusing or killing the wife for an insufficient dowry. In 1986, a specific policy was established in the penal code dealing with the problem of dowry death, providing a specific definition of the crime and establishing a mandatory minimum prison sentence for committing a dowry murder. Additionally, the 1986 law made it much easier to prosecute cases of dowry death by shifting the burden of proof from the prosecution to the defense. Thus, in the case of dowry death, the accused is "guilty until proven innocent," rather than "innocent until proven guilty."

The Indian Penal Code also contains laws against assault or using criminal force against women with "the intent to outrage her modesty," against rape, and against the husband or any of his relatives subjecting the wife to cruelty. Although there are laws against adultery, they apply to adultery committed against the husband by the wife, but not the reverse. The wording of many of these laws is vague and interpretations can vary widely (e.g., the meaning of "cruelty"). One study of domestic violence cases in the state of Andhra Pradesh, in southeast India, found that in 89% of the cases of violence against women, the husband and his family were acquitted. The acquittals were based on the individual judge's interpretation of the law, the lack of any documentation regarding a dowry (which is typically a verbal agreement), witnesses to the violence recanting when questioned in court,

---

[1]"Scheduled Tribes" is a term used by the Indian government to refer to groups or tribes of people who are officially recognized.

[2]All information on laws is from legal service india.com and "Maha Library" (2002).

and the dismissal of suicide notes as evidence of a woman being overly sensitive and prone to melodramatics, such as committing suicide (Vindhya, 2000). Ironically, suicide notes are more often used to exonerate the husband and his family than to implicate them in the woman's suicide. Additionally, because women have a predominantly social role in society, laws concerning abuse of women are viewed by the courts as social laws to be interpreted and enforced according to the judge's discretion. Consistent with mainstream Indian sentiments, many judges believe that incidents involving women and families are not within their jurisdiction. They prefer not to meddle in family affairs, a policy that results in the acquittal of accused perpetrators of domestic violence.

Laws on Abuse Against Children

In 1960, the government created the Children Act, which provides for neglected children. The punishments for neglect consist of a fine and/or 6 months of imprisonment; however, there is no requirement for mandatory reporting of suspected neglect or abuse. Instead, any officer who finds a maltreated child has the prerogative of deciding whether to take the child into custody or to file a report with the Child Welfare Board. In order to press charges officially against an abusive or neglectful parent, the prosecutor must obtain direct permission from the Governor of the State on a case-by-case basis, making it very unlikely that child abuse and neglect cases will get prosecuted.

To address the increase in sex-selective abortion in India, the Pre-Natal Diagnostic Techniques (Regulation and Prevention of Misuse) Act was created in 1994. This act made it illegal to obtain prenatal tests such as amniocentesis and ultrasound solely for the purpose of sex determination, and established punishments for attempting to find out fetal sex for the purpose of aborting female fetuses or killing female babies shortly after birth.

The strict family hierarchy in Indian society makes it quite easy for family members to abuse their power, which can lead to domestic violence. Unlike social violence, however, family violence has rarely been studied in India, especially prior to 1980. The importance of maintaining social traditions, as well as steadfast refusal of the state and academia to interfere in the home life of Indian citizens, have made studying the issue very difficult. With the women's movement in the late 1970s, researchers and lawmakers began to address issues of family violence, particularly wife and child abuse. Studies of abuse against the elderly are still extremely rare, and research on violence against men and between siblings is practically nonexistent.

VIOLENCE AGAINST CHILDREN

In India, child abuse and neglect is a very serious social problem. Corporal punishment is a legal and socially sanctioned form of discipline, both in school and in the home. Unlike child labor, which occurs predominantly among poor families, child beating is ubiquitous (Segal, 1995). The National Institute of Public Cooperation and Child Development finds that using instruments such as sticks, rulers, and/or hairbrushes is an acceptable, normal form of discipline (Segal, 1995). Because of this acceptance of corporal punishment, there are few reliable statistics on the prevalence of child abuse in India. Much of the population, including many child-care professionals such as social workers and law enforcement officials, are only just beginning to realize the extent of the problem (Chowdhury, Pattnaik, & Patro, 1994; Segal, 1999).

Because reliable birth control methods are not widely available in much of India, some families control their number of daughters by illegally practicing prenatal sex selection and female infanticide. Child marriage and selling daughters into prostitution are also common ways of getting rid of another female mouth to feed. Female infanticide is the most researched and widely known of the types of differential treatment, and the data show that among children ages 0 to 6, there are currently around 6 million more males than females in India (Census of India, 2001). However, the media attention given to female infanticide focuses mostly on the violence and inhumanity of the mothers. The Indian government has initiated a program in which women can anonymously put up their newborn girls for adoption; however, this program, although well intentioned, overlooks the major factor in infanticide; society's oppression and the inequality of females. If daughters and sons had equal opportunities and value in India, the overwhelming need and desire for sons would be lessened, and families would be less likely to kill or grossly neglect their daughters (Hegde, 1999).

Indian Respondents' Perspectives on Child Abuse

Our respondents labeled "beating" children, both with and without the aid of instruments, as at least moderately abusive, with many mentioning that "severe or repeated beatings" are extremely abusive. Comparing these responses to Indian tradition, it seems that Western ideas of corporal punishment as abusive are infiltrating at least the attitudes, if not the behavior, of adults in India. One respondent, a 39-year-old female, told the following story that she characterized as extreme child abuse:

One incident comes to mind. This was reported in the "Malayala Manorama" newspaper in the last week of July 1999. A merchant punished a boy terribly—

kneeling outside naked without food or water for an entire day—the boy was sold to him by the boys' parents. I do not know which is more extreme—the mental agony the kid felt in being thought expendable by his parents or the physical agony and humiliation of the inhumane punishment.

Many of our respondents mentioned "unequal treatment of boys and girls" as being abusive, although none specifically cited prenatal sex selection or female infanticide. One respondent, a 23-year-old female, phrased all her examples of parent–child abuse in terms of the daughter as the recipient of punishment for disobedience. A 27-year-old male called unequal treatment of boys and girls moderately abusive, and includes "denying the girl equality in the very basic necessities of life like food, health care, and education."

VIOLENCE AGAINST WOMEN

In India, the predominant form of violence against women in families is husband–wife abuse. The bride's low status increases her chances of being the target of abuse, making her five times as likely to suffer from abuse, especially dowry abuse, in the first 7 years of her marriage than after the 7-year mark (Prasad, 1994). In addition, injuries and stress brought about by marriage have been implicated in accounting for increased mortality rates in women ages 15 to 19 (Rao, 1997).

Dowry abuse is performed primarily for economic reasons: The groom and his family desire more material goods and see the bride as a means of extorting cash, property, and luxury items from her family (Vindhya, 2000). Mothers-in-law are often collaborators in the violence or encourage their son from behind the scenes to beat his wife. Kandioti (1988) explains the mother-in-law's participation in violence against her son's wife, as well as the new wife's acceptance of the violence, as a part of a patriarchal bargain. Women are willing to endure violence with the implicit knowledge that some day they will have power over their own daughters-in-law. Other researchers have similar theories concerning the often overt (and nearly always covert) participation of mothers-in-law in perpetrating violence against young women. Fernandez (1997) explains that many Western theories of domestic violence do not apply in India because the multiple social groups and hierarchies in Indian society lead some women to shift loyalty from one group to another, necessitating a multifactor model to explain dowry abuse (Natarajan, 1995). For instance, some women may show preferential loyalty to their family (one social group) over their fellow women (another social group) and thereby actively or passively influence the men in their family to abuse a new bride. Some of our survey responses showed concern over this form of abuse. For example, one respondent, a 27-year-old male, defined abuse as "constant demand for dowry or threat to harm a bride," and a 23-year-old female identified "beating a daughter-in-law" as moderately to extremely abusive.

Husband–wife violence is highly tolerated in Indian society. In many instances, police and other law enforcement officials will not intervene on behalf of the woman. As Prasad (1999) reported, one battered woman who sought legal action was told by the police that violence within a marriage was normal and that she should "go home and try to work it out" (p. 483). Rao (1997) found that many men and women freely acknowledged the occurrence of wife beating, justifying it as acceptable because the wife had not behaved herself. Justifications for wife beating can range from the wife disobeying the husband to mistreating her in-laws to not bearing any sons to not preparing food to her husband's liking. When questioned as to whether they were physically assaulted, however, only 22% of the women in Rao's sample admitted to having been victims of assault—many fewer than had acknowledged being beaten. Rao attributed this discrepancy to the possibility of women not interpreting "justifiable" beatings as assault, but rather as appropriate responses to misbehavior. Further, he found that most of the women who admitted being abused had required medical attention due to the severity of their beatings. He concluded that the husband–wife physical assault must be sufficiently severe or undeserved to be considered abusive.

Indian Participants' Perspectives on Wife Abuse

All of our respondents, when asked what constituted husband–wife abuse, gave examples of noneconomically driven wife beating. However, many respondents qualified their examples by giving reasons for the beatings. For example, one 23-year-old male stated that it is moderately abusive for "a man to beat his wife if he suspects illegal contacts," and a 60-year-old male qualified all of his definitions of husband–wife abuse with "when they are poor" and "when [the] husband comes home drunk," implying that alcohol and poverty are major factors in domestic violence in India. Another respondent, a 23-year-old female, qualified her explanations of husband–wife abuse by attributing all abusive behavior to the wife's standing up for her own beliefs. A 27-year-old male said "curbing the wife's career aspirations" was mildly abusive, and a 28-year-old male said it was moderately abusive to "order a partner around without giving her the opportunity to protest the order." Younger adults tended to provide examples of abuse that were contrary to traditional, socially accepted Indian customs. Although there were not enough respondents over age 40 to compare attitudes across generations, it is interesting to see some evidence that social attitudes toward women may be changing, with the traditional idea of women as the man's property becoming defined by young adults as a form of abuse.

Many respondents, in describing violence against women, mentioned "sexual assault" and "rape." A husband "forcing sex on his wife," or otherwise sexually abusing her, was given as an example of abuse by half of the respondents. A 25-year-old woman considered rape extremely abusive but was pessimistic about society's views, explaining, "I tend to think this is wishful." She is correct in her assumption that it is wishful thinking to imply that society would see marital rape as extremely abusive, because non-consensual sex between a husband and wife is specifically not defined as rape according to the Indian Penal Code (Maha Library, 2000), an oversight that is strongly condemned by women's groups in India.

Another behavior characteristically viewed as abusive in Indian society, and noted by several respondents, is "public humiliation" of a wife. In Indian society, honor is very important. Stripping a person of his or her dignity is considered to be severely abusive. Also, Indian society is communal; people are very dependent on one another, especially in villages. Thus, it is considered important to maintain one's propriety in society, along with the family's honor, and public humiliation is viewed as an overt act of abuse.

VIOLENCE AGAINST MEN

Men, being in the primary position of power in Indian society, are not likely to be victims of domestic violence, and there has been no real research examining family violence directed at them. If it does occur, cases are not reported, as it would bring shame and dishonor not only on the man himself, but also on his entire family. Because of their status, it is very easy for men to extract themselves from a violent situation, either by leaving the family or by casting out the offender. Unlike women, men from failed marriages who live apart from their families do not face scorn and social isolation.

Indian Participants' Perspectives on Husband Abuse

Most of our respondents, when asked to provide a general definition of abuse, included no examples of violence toward men. When asked to provide examples of severe, moderate, and mild abuse directed toward a husband, most participants either could not think of examples or answered that domestic abuse against men is "still unheard of." Some of those who did provide definitions and examples of abuse against husbands mentioned the rarity of wife–husband abuse. A 27-year-old male said that "husband beating" takes place in the "socially and economically backward section of the society." By referring to husband beating, but not wife beating, as "backward," this respondent underscores the judgment in Indian society that wife beating is somewhat socially acceptable but husband beating is not.

Another contrast in responses between wife–husband abuse and husband–wife abuse is the relative severity attributed to physical violence. Several respondents categorized physical violence against women as mild to moderately abusive or provided caveats as to when physical violence would be abusive (e.g., "when the wife is asserting her own beliefs"). However, in the few examples of wife–husband violence, all were categorized as extremely abusive. Additionally, no respondents provided caveats as to when any violence directed toward the husband would constitute abuse. The implication, then, is that all violence directed toward the husband is abusive, but not all violence directed toward the wife is abusive.

In India, it is seen as a wife's duty to have sex with her husband, which is reflected in the Indian Penal Code, which has no mention of husband–wife rape (Maha Library, 2000). Additionally, this idea is depicted in Indian films. Derné (1999) described one scene in the 1987 film *Anubhav* in which a woman refuses her husband sex. When she escapes to her mother, the mother tells her that she must sleep with him because he is her husband. One of our respondents, a 25-year-old female, said "refusing the husband sex" is moderately abusive.

VIOLENCE AGAINST THE ELDERLY

There has been very little research on domestic violence against the elderly. Because the elderly hold such a high and powerful position within the Indian family and because of the reverent attitude of Indian society toward the elderly, many Indians believe that that aggression directed toward elderly members of a family simply does not exist. This perception, however, has been shown to be incorrect. Segal (1999) explained that family structure in India is changing; instead of the adult son living in his parents' home, the elderly parents are now living in the son's home. This altered family structure means that the elderly are losing the authority they once had as owners of the home, which may make them more vulnerable to abuse.

Indian Participants' Perspectives on Elder Abuse

All of our respondents considered disrespect toward the elderly as abusive behavior. A 23-year-old female said it was abusive "to ignore the advice of the elderly when they interfere in an adult's life." A 60-year-old man viewed elder abuse strictly as "a wife mistreating her father-in-law," which in Indian culture is a relationship deserving of extreme respect on the part of the wife for the head of the household.

Interestingly, our respondents frequently gave examples of "neglect" as forms of abuse toward the elderly, but not in regard to any other familial relationship. "Failure to take care of elderly members of one's family" was an example of extreme abuse by a 27-year-old male, and "allowing the elderly to take care of themselves" was seen as extremely abusive by a 28-year-old man. Clearly, the high status of elderly family members, and the social obligation to provide and care for them, are responsibilities taken seriously in Indian society.

OTHER ABUSIVE FAMILY RELATIONSHIPS

In addition to considering abuse in the mother-in-law to daughter-in-law relationship, a number of participants discussed abuse of a domestic servant by an employer. Three upper middle class women in their late 20s listed "sexual abuse" between employers and domestic servants as an example of extreme abuse, "physical torture" as moderate abuse, and "verbal abuse" as mild. One 26-year-old male even defined abuse in terms of the domestic servant, explaining that abuse is when "a servant is treated like a servant first and a human later."

INTERVENTION AND PREVENTION

However bleak the situation may be for sufferers of family violence in India, all hope is not lost. Many scientists are bringing family violence issues to the forefront of society, providing hard evidence of the destructive consequences and making it more than simply a moral injustice. In the past 15 years, these scientists and a number of feminists and battered women's support groups have worked to educate lawmakers and the public about domestic violence.

Because the few domestic violence laws that do exist in India are rarely enforced, more efforts than simply enacting legislation are needed to combat the problem of familial abuse. The only way to completely end family violence is through changing the attitudes and dominance hierarchy of Indian society. While this promises to be an extremely gradual and difficult solution, there are women's and children's advocacy groups trying to achieve this goal. It is also becoming more and more common, at least among the middle to upper class, for women to leave and/or divorce abusive husbands. While discussing the fate of battered women in India, a lawyer related to me that she has been handling quite a few divorce cases, with the number of divorces steadily rising. In one of her cases, divorce proceedings were initiated by the woman's father against the wishes of the married couple. The husband had beaten the wife, but the couple was in love and wanted to remain together. The woman's father, however, did not approve of the violence directed toward his daughter and decided to take legal action to remove her from her abusive situation. Although this is only one example, it demonstrates that the traditional acceptance of husband–wife violence is becoming unacceptable, at least among the middle and upper classes. Hopefully this change in tradition will begin to permeate all levels of society.

As yet, there appear to be no effective provisions set up by the government or law enforcement to provide support for victims of domestic violence. However, groups of women, some of whom have been battered, have banded together to fight social inequality and to attempt to change the laws and misogynistic attitudes in Indian society. In urban areas and close, large communities, these organizations can be extremely helpful to women and girls, but in isolated rural areas, there are still no real alternatives for victims of domestic violence.

Many Indians living abroad have services available to them if they become victims of domestic violence. Many culture-specific shelters exist for South Asians in the United States, the United Kingdom, and Canada. These organizations provide the same services as general shelters (e.g., food, shelter, money, training, legal assistance), but also address some culture-specific issues, helping victims to acculturate to the dominant culture and work through the psychological distress they may experience because of Indian attitudes that they deserved to be beaten. Appendix 1 provides a list, organized by country, of several shelters designed to help South Asian victims of domestic violence. Although there are additional resources available to victims of abuse, many of them are not appropriate for Indian women. For example, there are a number of middle-aged Indian women living in the United States who, with support from American friends, have sought out therapists and counselors to help them salvage their abusive marriages. These American therapists, not fully understanding the mentality of the middle-aged Indian woman, recommend that the women divorce their husbands; yet once such a divorce is finalized, these former wives are left destitute. Moreover, because the life of an Indian woman revolves around her husband and family, once she has left her husband, the main focus of her life is missing. She may feel as though she has no purpose. Although the therapist's advice was given with good intentions, very often this advice ends up making the Indian woman's life worse instead of better. Because this is a large problem in Indian communities outside of India, increased cultural training is necessary for therapists and counselors who may work with Indian immigrants.

ACKNOWLEDGMENTS

I would like to thank the following people for providing tremendous help in the writing of this chapter: Kathie Malley-Morrison and the rest of the chapter authors in this book; my family, especially Harish C. Chawla, Barbara Chawla, Anita Chawla Narag, and Parul Chawla; Marcia Johnston; and A. Heath Finnie.

REFERENCES

Census of India. (2001). [online]. Available: http://www.censusindia.net/results/resultsmain.html.

Chowdhury, A., Pattnaik, S., & Patro, A. (1994). Psycho-social profile of abused children in India. *Early Child Development and Care, 104,* 85–93.

Dasgupta, S., & Hegde, R. (1988). The eternal receptacle: A study of mistreatment of women in Hindi films. In R. Ghadially (Ed.), *Women in Indian Society: A Reader* (pp. 209–216). New Delhi, India: Sage.

Derné, S. (1995). Market forces at work: Religious themes in commercial Hindi films. In L. Babb & S. Wadley (Eds.), *Media and the transformations of religions in South Asia* (pp. 191–216). Philadelphia: University of Pennsylvania Press.

Derné, S. (1999). Making sex violent: Love as force in recent Hindi films. *Violence Against Women, 5,* 548–575.

Federal Research Division, Library of Congress. (1995). *India: A country study* (Area Handbook Series) [online]. Available: http://lcweb2.loc.gov/frd/cs/intoc.html

Fernandez, M. (1997). Domestic violence by extended family members in India: Interplay of gender and generation. *Journal of Interpersonal Violence, 12,* 433–455.

Hegde, R. (1999). Marking bodies, reproducing violence: A feminist reading of female infanticide in South India. *Violence Against Women, 5,* 507–524.

Kandioti, D. (1988). Bargaining with patriarchy. *Gender and Society, 2,* 274–290.

Legal service India.com. (n.d.). Available: http://www.legalserviceindia.com

Maha library. (2000). Available: http://www.mahalibrary.com

Natarajan, M. (1995). Victimization of women: A theoretical perspective on dowry deaths in India. *International Review of Victimology, 3,* 297–308.

Prasad, B. (1994). Dowry-related violence: A content analysis of news in selected newspapers. *Journal of Comparative Family Studies, 25,* 71–89.

Prasad, S. (1999). Medicolegal response to violence against women in India. *Violence Against Women, 5,* 478–506.

Rao, V. (1997). Wife-beating in rural South India: A qualitative and econometric analysis. *Social Science and Medicine, 44,* 1169–1180.

Segal, U. (1995). Child abuse by the middle class? A study of professionals in India. *Child Abuse and Neglect, 19,* 217–231.

Segal, U. (1999). Family violence: A focus on India. *Aggression and Violent Behavior, 4,* 213–231.

Vindhya, U. (2000). "Dowry deaths" in Andhra Pradesh, India. *Violence Against Women, 6,* 1085–1108.

Shelters and organizations that help Indian victims of domestic violence

Organizations in India:

Sakshi	New Delhi	464-3946, 462-395
Women's Rights Initiative	New Delhi	431-6925, 431-3904
Majlis	Bombay	618-0394
Swaadhar	Bombay	872-0638
Prevention of Crime and Victim Care	Madras	044 527-9085
Sneha	Madras	827-3456
Vimochana	Bangalore	526-9307
Anweshi Women's Counselling Center	Kozhikode	Cannanore Road
Sachetna	Calcutta	31, Mahairban Road
Socio-Legal Aid Research and Training Center	Calcutta	P-112 Lake Terrace
Pragatisheel Mahila Manch	Calcutta	11 N. Ho Chi Minh Road, Sarania, Behala
Swayam	Calcutta	280-3429, 280-3688

Organizations in the United States:

Casa de Esperanza	AZ	(916) 674-5400, (916) 674-2040
Aasra	CA	(510) 505-7503, (800) 313-ASRA
Narika	CA	(800) 215-7308, (510) 540-0754
Human Options	CA	(714) 497-7017, (714) 497-5367
Asian Women's Shelter	CA	(415) 751-0880 (crisis line), (415) 751-7110
Maitri	CA	(888) 8-MAITRI
IBPW	CA	(408) 956-9115, (415) 926-6652
Indian Community Outreach	CA	(510) 648-5840
Sahara	CA	(888) 724-2722
South Asian Network	CA	(562) 403-0488, (562) 403-0487
Trikone	CA	(408) 270-8776
Sneha	CT	(800) 58-SNEHA, (860) 233-5684, (860) 272-8624
Shamokami	CT	(203) 624-8727
ASHA	DC,VA,MD	(202) 783-5102, (703) 821-3743, (301) 279-9194
Asian/Pacific Islander Domestic Violence Resource Project	MD	(202) 464-4477
Raksha	GA	(404) 841-0725
Abused Women Coalition	IL	(312) 489-9018, (312) 278-4566
Hamdard Center	IL	(708) 628-9195
Asian Human Services	IL	(773) 728-2235
Apna Ghar Inc	IL	(312) 334-4663
Club of Indian Women	IL	(708) 968-3793
Metropolitan Battered Women's Program	LA	(504) 828-2893
Center for Pacific-Asian Family Inc	LA	(213) 653-4042, (213) 653-4045, (800) 339-3950
Asian Shelter & Adv Project	MA	(617) 338-2350, (617) 338-2355
Manavi	MA	(508) 427-5700 ext. 202, (617) 497-0316
Asian Task Force	MA	(617) 739-6696, (617) 277-3648

(Continued)

Indian Subcontinent Womens Assoc for Action	MA	(617) 981-2888
South Asian Women For Action	MA	(617) 265-5405, (617) 731-3416, (617) 666-5080
Asha	MD	(301) 369-0134
Samhati	MD	(301) 229-6597
Michigan Asian Indian Family Services	MI	(888) 664-8624 (crisis line), (248) 477-4985
Asian Women United of Minnesota	MN	(651) 646-2261 (crisis line), (651) 646-2118
Resource Center for Women & Their Families	NJ	(908) 302-2545, (908) 685-1122
Women's Crisis Services	NJ	(908) 788-7666, (908) 788-4044
Manavi	NJ	(908) 687-2662
AMICAE, Inc	NY	(716) 672-8423, (800) 836-5940
Asian Indian Women's Network	NY	(714) 894-2608
Helping Prof of American Asso of Psych's from Indi	NY	(718) 353-9206
Massachusetts Area Muslim Women's Committee of NY	NY	(212) 316-6446
Nav Nirmaan Foundation	NY	(718) 441-5852, (718) 478-4588
New York Asian Women's Center	NY	(212) 732-5230
Sikh Women's Association	NY	(718) 699-1593
Sakhi for SA Women	NY	(212) 695-5447
Salga (Lesbian & Gay Association)	NY	(212) 294-2555
Sikh Women's International	NY	(212) 246-3381
South Asian AIDS Action	NY	(212) 239-1451 ext 6126
South Asian-American Women's Asso	NY	(607) 962-3277
KIRAN	NC	(919) 865-4006
Women of the Indian Subcontinent Support Group	OH	(614) 486-0650
SAWERA	OR	(503) 778-7386
SEWAA	PA	(215) 328-4772
Daya	TX	(713) 914-1333
Saheli	TX	(512) 703-8745
Samhati	VA	(301) 229-6597
Chaya	WA	(877) 922-4292, (206) 325-0325

Organizations in Canada:

SAW Community Center	Montreal	(514) 485-9192
South Asian Women's Association	Montreal	(514) 937-4714
Vancouver and LM Multicultural Family Support Center	Vancouver	(604) 436-1025
South Asian Women's Center	Vancouver	(604) 739-4505, (604) 325-6637
Punjabi Women's Association	Vancouver	(604) 581-6941
Burnaby Multicultural Society	Vancouver	(604) 299-4808

Organizations in the United Kingdom:

ASIA Women's Group	London	0171-263-3182
Nafsiyat	London	0171-263-4130
Women's therapy Center	London	0171-263-6200
Ashiana	Sheffield	0114-255-5740

16

Japan

Mizuho Arai

CAPSULE

In the early 1970s, filial violence (aggression against parents) became the first type of domestic violence to be viewed as a social problem in Japan. The use of a baseball bat to hit mothers and fathers was one of the serious physical attacks committed by children in the 1970s and 1980s. Bullying at schools has also become a national problem, particularly in the 1990s. In these cases, groups of children pick on one particular youngster and abuse him or her psychologically and physically. In some recent incidents, middle school students have attacked their teachers with pocketknives. In addition, there has been a tendency for some Japanese boys (middle and high school students) to physically attack homeless people and middle-aged men on the street.

Child abuse has been a center of attention in Japan since newborn "coin-locker babies" were found dead in coin-operated lockers in train stations in the 1970s. Physical abuse and neglect have been the most frequent forms of child abuse. Recently, child abuse issues can be seen in the newspapers and on TV news programs almost every day. For example, in January 2002, newspapers reported that a mother's boyfriend beat her 5-year-old daughter so severely she was hospitalized in critical condition.

Marriage in the Japanese family system means that a wife enters her husband's family rather than creating a new family. Fulfilling the role of bride and daughter-in-law within the family is the most important responsibility for wives, who are expected to serve their parents-in-law. The patriarchal family system, which stresses obedience of women to men, young to old, and daughter-in-law to mother-in-law, exerts strong pressure on daughters-in-law to take on the role of caregiver. Older people often refuse to do things for themselves (even when they can), while placing demands on daughters-in-law. The daughters-in-law bow to the demands because they are afraid of being criticized by their husbands' relatives and neighbors.

The typical Japanese husband is viewed as a workaholic who works long hours for large corporations, goes out drinking with fellow workers and clients after work, and plays golf on the weekends. He rarely spends time with his wife and children and provides almost no help with household tasks such as cleaning and changing diapers. However, a few men have begun to express misgivings about the kind of lives they lead. For example, some men have organized support groups to pursue goals such as pressing companies to provide childcare leaves for men as well as for women, and decrying the distinctively Japanese phenomenon of assigning married men to distant posts, entailing lengthy absences from their families.

Historically, there has been a high incidence of wife battering in Japan; however, until recently, there was a strong tendency to view this as a private matter. Pornography, readily available through various types of mass-produced visual media, has been linked to the growing rate of violence and sexual abuse against women in contemporary Japan. There have also been frequent recent reports in the Japanese news media of male teachers in middle and high schools becoming sexually involved with their female students.

Unfortunately, domestic violence is a young field in Japan and has only recently begun to draw public attention, due to the efforts of feminist groups and victims of abuse (Hada, 1995). Although there are laws against maltreatment of children, there are no specific laws preventing domestic violence, particularly spousal abuse. New laws are needed in order for the police and judiciary system to respond to the problem in an effective way, and to provide proper medical care and emergency protection by legal system (Hada, 1995).

THE JAPANESE SAMPLE

The sample from Japan consisted of 100 women and 46 men between the ages of 19 and 60; 129 respondents were students recruited from Toyo University, Chukyo University, and their families, relatives and friends, and 17 participants answered the survey from Japan over the internet. Most participants described themselves as middle class. Level of education ranged from high school to Master's degree. Occupations included accountant, businessman, university professor, housewife, and university student.

In defining abuse in families, many of our Japanese respondents referred to physical and psychological harm—for example, "violent acts by cigarette burns, metal bat" (female, 22 years old); "from victim's or third person's view point, receiving unreasonable physical or psychological damage" (male, 20); "any acts causing trauma" (male, 19). Other definitions illustrate implicit theories embedded in Japanese cultural values concerning displaying respect, suppressing negative emotions, and maintaining harmony—for example, "any acts without respecting the others" (male, 51); "hating the family that should be friendly and peaceful" (female, 37; male, 24); "violent acts and behaviors by selfish feelings" (female, 37); "whenever people feel uncomfortable" (male, 22); "causing psychological and physical damage on others by selfish acts" (female, 40). There was also some emphasis on unrealistic expectations or unjustifiable actions—"blaming a person when he/she can't perform well on the assignment" (female, 42); "any punishments without reasons" (male, 20). Perhaps the most modern perspective can be found in this definition: "any acts which violate human rights" (male, 22).

These themes were echoed in the Japanese respondents' examples of extreme abuse within the family. Among the examples emphasizing physical harm were; "using fire and tools to be violent physically and psychologically" (female, 20; female, 21); "violent acts by personal emotions other than educational purposes" (female, 22); "putting boiling water to a child" (female, 23; female, 21; female, 21); "tightening a child in a pillar all day long" (male, 19); and "using discipline as an excuse, tightening a child's legs and putting him/her upside down on a tree; putting boiling water; no food (I stated these as example because I saw them on the news)" (female, 22). Japanese respondents also emphasized psychological forms of damage in their examples of extreme abuse—"when a victim of abuse loses self-respect" (female, 42); "raising a child with saying 'hopeless' or 'stupid' on a daily basis" (female, 42); and "a mother telling a child that she didn't want to give birth to that child" (female, 21). There were also a few mentions of "hazardous neglect" and "sexual abuse" as examples of extreme abuse.

THE JAPANESE MACROSYSTEM

Japanese culture is fairly uniform throughout the country. Not only does Japan have a large population on limited land, but people have lived for centuries under centralized governments that regulated peoples' lives to a considerable extent. Primary importance has traditionally been placed on the group rather than on the individual. Groupism is deeply entrenched and the pressure to conform is described by a Japanese saying that "the nail that sticks out gets pounded down."

Japanese Media

Contemporary media in Japan reveals an obsession with sex. Funabashi (1989) noted that sexual themes such as "touching the body" and "peeking under the skirt," which used to be strictly taboo, have now been exposed to "broad daylight" (p. 257). Magazines with pictures of female bodies are widely sold in bookstores and convenience stores. According to Dussich (2001, p. 279), rape is portrayed in the Japanese media as "the unfortunate plight of women who stray from their traditional roles"—a way of punishing women who are too assertive or too modern. Rape is also pictured as an extension of normal sexual gratification, and many Japanese men consider it appropriate to rape women for sexual pleasure. In a horrible incident in 1989, several male high school students who had watched sexually violent films kept a teenage girl for 2 months, repeatedly raping and torturing her, then murdering her and hiding her body in concrete.

THE JAPANESE MICROSYSTEM

The Traditional Japanese Family

The traditional Japanese family structure, with the father as leader of a hierarchical family system, is a form of patriarchy influenced by Confucian principles. However, despite the traditional authority of the father, many Japanese fathers today are physically present in the family but unable to provide any psychological support to their spouses or to be proper male figures to their children (Kumagai, 1981). Consequently, most surveys and child abuse prevention hot lines do not report a high incidence of fathers' perpetuating child abuse (Kozu, 1999, p. 51).

In the traditional Japanese family structure, the status of women, especially married females, was inherently low. When a woman married a Japanese man, she became "yome," a bride of her husband's family. It was her responsibility to take care of her husband's parents rather than pursue any desires for a career of her own (Kozu, 1999). The ideal, and only socially acceptable role, for the Japanese woman was to be married and raise children. Moreover, marriage was often the only status offering women any financial security; thus, there was strong social pressure on all women to marry within the "marriageable age."

In recent years, marriage has become just one of many lifestyles. Although men are still socially and economically dominant, women can live fairly good lives on their own as working members of society. A survey by the Japanese Institute of Life Insurance conducted in 1986 revealed that, among women ages 25 to 29, about 50% responded, "it is natural for women to marry," whereas the other 50% responded "women do not necessarily have to marry" (Seimei Hoken Bunka Senta, 1987). Those who do marry do so at an increasingly older age. In 1972, the mean age of women's first marriage was 24.2; it rose to 25.6 by 1986, and to 25.9 by 1990. The more educated a woman, the later she marries. Some women postpone marriage, saying they want to enjoy their single lives a little more or want to establish their careers first. Others question: Is marriage really a good thing? Isn't a single life better? A career-oriented woman who wants to continue working after marriage wants a marriage partner who will understand and respect her work and share both housework and child care; however, most Japanese men still believe their wives should take care of their needs even if working full time (Yoshizumi, 1995).

Current Status of the Family in Japan

The nuclear family, consisting of the father, mother, and child(ren), has become increasingly dominant in Japanese cities, intruding on the heritage of extended families (father, mother, father's parents, children) living together. At the same time, the family structure itself has undergone a transformation in postwar society, giving rise to several variant forms. These variants include the "pseudo-single-mother family," in which the father, although legally present, is in fact too busy to spend time with his family. In these families, Japanese husbands place priority on their career as "company man," leaving their homes early in the morning and coming home late at night, and spending very little time with their wives and children. These fathers avoid matters concerning their offspring by saying, "wives are responsible for the education of the children." In another variant, the "latent-disorganization family" or "domestic divorce," the husband and wife remain legally married but have no true conjugal relationship (Yoshizumi, 1995).

For the past half century, it has been a trend in Japan to dissolve failed marriages by mutual consent, and not by government intervention (Kozu, 1999). More and more Japanese wives are beginning to question the validity of a conjugal relationship devoid of emotional and mental interaction and to seek deeper and more egalitarian relationships with their husbands. Increasingly, middle aged and elderly wives are initiating divorce in order to escape the control of tyrannical husbands or a marriage that exists only in form. The Japanese divorce rate, however, is lower than that of other developed countries—primarily because even when the conjugal relationship has not lasted, many Japanese couples maintain the outward form of marriage. This low divorce rate does not mean an absence of marital problems (Yoshizumi, 1995).

Even in the face of change, an important aspect of Japanese culture is an emphasis on avoiding situations that produce conflict for the sake of maintaining harmony and saving face. Verbal communications and expressions of feelings leading to resentment and conflict are shunned (Kozu, 1999). To maintain harmony and save face, there is a tradition of family secrecy and shame. Not mentioning family secrets or exposing the family to shame publicly has been regarded as a virtue; thus, the Japanese tend to settle family problems within the family. Divorce is one of the deviant, shameful life events; therefore, most battered wives remain in their marriages to follow the cultural norm (Kozu, 1999). Due to this long existing tradition of family privacy, it is impossible to determine the true prevalence of family violence in Japan.

Childhood in Japan

In 19th century Japan, it was impossible for overtaxed farmers to feed a large family, particularly because the weather was too severe to grow crops in northeastern Japan. Until 1867, children were traditionally considered disposable (Kouno & Johnson, 1995). Infanticide was common, culturally accepted, and not a criminal activity. Moreover, there were other ways to decrease family size under economic hardships: abandonment, child trafficking (selling children), and adoption (Kouno & Johnson, 1995). In the early 20th century, most adopted children were killed, which both the biological and foster parents understood. When a child was adopted, the biological parents paid "supporting fees" to the foster parents—a sum intended as a payment for killing and burying the child (Kitahara, 1989). Adopted children who were not killed, or who were sold into the life of courtesans, prostitutes, and textile workers, were often physically abused (Kitahara, 1989). Children in their own families were also frequently victims of physical abuse, due to financial problems, strained marital relationships, father's frequent job changes, problems with childrearing, housing problems, and other stresses (Kitamura et al., 1989). Finally, the Japanese custom of family cosleeping (all family members sleeping in the same room) and cobathing lend themselves to the possibility of incestuous relations (Kitahara, 1989); there is evidence that sexual abuse has sometimes taken place during cosleeping and cobathing.

FAMILY VIOLENCE IN JAPAN

Emergence of the Field of Family Violence in Japan

There are many features of traditional Japanese society—for example, patriarchy, hierarchical relationships, face saving, secrecy—that have promoted family violence. However, due to rapid economic and industrial change after the Second World War, people's lifestyles and values have diversified. In addition, numerous international treaties and conferences on human rights since the late 1980s, and recent feminist movements, have increased public awareness concerning family violence. Compared to other countries, Japan is still far behind in the mental health and human rights fields, yet there are many organizations from grass roots to legislative levels trying to improve the life of the Japanese today (Kozu, 1999).

In the 1970s and 1980s, the term "domestic violence" was applied to children's physical and emotional violence against family members, especially parents (Kumagai, 1981). However, for the past decade, attention and action toward other types of domestic violence has increased in the general public, particularly in regard to child abuse and spousal abuse (Kozu, 1999). Along with the public awareness, there has been a growth in grass-roots level websites in Japan supporting the victims of violence. According to the Study Group of Violence from Husbands and Partners (Gender Equality Bureau, 1998), some professionals hold that although domestic violence has been latent socially, it has come to the surface to get both academic and public attention.

Japanese Laws

Japanese society has long regarded the internal life of the family as a matter of family discretion, and authorities have been reluctant to enter into cases of family violence (Kitamura et al., 1999; Kouno & Johnson, 1995). The family court is the only authority to investigate the home and, if necessary in a case of child abuse, deprive parents of their power. The first law in Japan to deal with child abuse was the Child Abuse Prevention Act of 1933, which prohibited the abuse, desertion, abandonment, or neglect of a child by his or her parent or guardian, and made it illegal to use a child under age 14 in an acrobatic show or circus, or to employ a child as a vendor, beggar, or unusual exhibition specimen (Kitahara, 1989). Interestingly, incest was not a criminal act, and there were no criminal laws to punish parents who sexually abused their children (Kozu, 1999). Sex acts with children under 13 years old were considered "indecent assault" or rape, irrespective of the assailant's age, social status, or gender (Kouno & Johnson, 1995); however, until recently, the only laws that could be invoked in cases of incest were the ones against rape and forced obscenity (Kitahara, 1989).

On May 17th, 2000, a new Child Abuse Prevention Act was approved. According to this act, child abuse (i.e., abusive behaviors intentionally inflicted on children age 17 and under by their parents or guardians) includes;

1. intrafamilial physical violence (violence resulting in an external injury; bruises, broken bones, or burns, or violence jeopardizing a child's life;

throttling necks, drowning, hanging upside down, poisoning, not giving food, locking out in winter, or restraining in the room);

2. neglect (desertion or malnutrition, uncleanness, medical neglect, or not letting the child attend school.);

3. intrafamilial sexual abuse (sexual violence by parents or guardians, or incest by parents);

4. and intrafamilial psychological/emotional abuse (extreme behaviors other than 1, 2, and 3 that cause psychological injury—e.g., anxiety, worry, depression, apathy, no response, strong aggression, abnormal habits) (Kousei Syou, 2000).

Prevalence of Child Abuse

As already noted, prior to 1867, due to the tax collection system, children were killed to decrease family size, and child abuse and neglect were the solution for economic hardship (Kouno & Johnson, 1995). In 1933, the Child Abuse Prevention and Child Relief Act was established to protect children under 14 years old. In the following years, mother–child suicides increased; as a result, the Mother and Child Protection Act was instituted in 1937. After the Second World War, influence from the United States led to expanding the existing Child Welfare Act of 1947 to protect all children. However, the selling of children and prostitution continued to exist until passage of the Eugenic Protection Law in 1957 (Kouno & Johnson, 1995).

In the late 1900s, Japanese railway stations and airports provided coin-operated lockers for storage of luggage and packages; however, these lockers were also used to store illegal materials such as firearms, drugs, smuggled goods, and explosives (Kouno & Johnson, 1995). They also became secure hiding places for murdered infants, termed "coin-locker babies." These murdered infants became a sensational social problem and led to a government-sponsored 1973 investigation of child abuse; even this investigation was limited to abuse of children younger than 3 years old. Later, one of the national agencies of the Ministry of Health and Welfare, the Public Child Guidance Centers, undertook a study of abuse of children of all ages (Kozu, 1999). Because the study was limited to cases handled by the Public Child Guidance Centers, the findings probably reflect only a fraction of the abuse actually taking place at the time (Kozu, 1999).

Thanks to child abuse prevention hot lines in two major areas (Association for the Prevention of Child Abuse, 1996) and other grass-roots organizations, reports of abuse cases are increasing (Kouno & Johnson, 1995). Physical abuse appears to be the most prevalent form of child abuse recognized in Japan. Child sexual abuse cases appear to be less prevalent than in the United States, perhaps because the topic of sex is taboo and Japanese are reluctant to talk about it (Kouno & Johnson, 1995). Despite this reluctance, some of our respondents showed an awareness that sexual abuse occurs in Japan. One 21-year-old female gave the example of "sexual abuse in the opposite sex parent–child relationship" as an extreme form of child abuse and "sexual assault from father to daughter" as a moderate form of child abuse.

In the first investigation of child abuse in 1973, 26 cases of child abuse and 139 cases of neglect but no cases of sexual abuse were reported. In 1985, using information from public hospitals and pediatricians, a Child Abuse Investigation Committee found 173 cases of child abuse, 50 cases of psychological neglect, and three cases of other types of neglect. Over 400 cases of abuse, including 223 cases of physical abuse, 34 cases of psychological abuse, 46 cases of sexual abuse, 111 cases of neglect, and 2 cases of "other" were reported in a nationwide survey on abused children under age 18 (Kouno & Johnson, 1995). According to Kozu (1999), 1994 statistics indicate that 1,961 child abuse cases were reported by the Public Child Guidance Centers, but these numbers are only the tip of the iceberg. In 1995, another study examined the frequencies of several forms of physical abuse and one type of emotional abuse (harsh scolding) as well as of help seeking by victims of child abuse (Kitamura et al., 1999). All participants were women, ranging in age from 19 to 25. The results showed that emotional and physical abuse occurred with approximately equal frequency and that a very low rate of help seeking occurred. This study showed that in Japan, most abuse cases are unidentified, and the prevalence of child abuse is no lower than in the Western countries, even though abused children typically do not seek other people's help (Kitamura et al., 1999). Examples of child abuse from our respondents sound frighteningly real and one wonders if anything was ever done about them. For example, one respondent (female, 19) reported that "a mother put a child in a closet with his/her hands and legs tied up almost everyday when someone visited a house."

In 1997, the *Jidou Soudan* Center (Children Consulting Center) in Tokyo conducted a survey to investigate the latest prevalence of child abuse. This study showed that 2,061 cases of child abuse were reported from 175 *Jidou Soudan* Centers nationwide. In the reported cases, 48.9% were physical abuse, 40.4% were neglect, 5.9% were psychological/emotional abuse, and 4.9% were sexual abuse. Over 50.6% of the children who were victims of abuse were male; 41.5 % of them were under the age of five, and 36.4% were 6 to 11 years old. Female children were victimized through sexual abuse and psychological/emotional abuse. The perpetrators were the biological mother (50.8%), biological father (28.5%), stepfather (4.8%), adopted father (4.3%), and stepmother (3.1%). In the sexual abuse cases, over 50% of the perpetrators were the biological father; three cases in which the biological mother was the perpetrator were reported.

Japanese Participants' Perspectives on Child Abuse

In our survey, some respondents defined child abuse as "unnecessary physical punishments to infants (without reasons)" and "physical and verbal abuse toward children, ignorance, bullying." One 60-year-old female respondent described "abusive behaviors to cause life threatening situations" as an extreme form of child abuse. In her implicit theory of child abuse, "unnecessary physical punishments, causing a death of an infant, [and] believing that infants think the same as adults think" were examples of extreme forms of child abuse. She also stated that "making a child handicapped through injuries" was a moderate form of child abuse and "parents losing their temper [because] they can't make a distinction between discipline and physical punishment" was a mild form of child abuse.

Many Japanese respondents mentioned that "abuse is abuse, we can't distinguish the levels of abuse. Any abusive behavior causes psychological trauma." A 41-year-old female stated that "abuse is not happening in my neighborhood," although the Japanese media report cases of abuse frequently on TV and newspapers. Whenever she sees news about child abuse such as killing one's own child or torturing a child psychologically and physically, that participant says she feels very upset and wonders about the reasons behind the abuse. Another respondent (female, 39) stated that "I saw a mother of a child (a girl, 5 or 6 years old) keep kicking her daughter in a shopping mall. A grandmother of this child was not trying to stop the mother from kicking the child, but was smiling and supporting her daughter." A 42-year-old female indicated that she was sexually abused by her uncle. She also stated that "any behavior that takes self-respect away from a person" is abuse in any relationship and there are no different levels of abuse. In her view, "abuse must be judged case by case, and depends on the perspective of the recipient."

Many of our respondents stated that "hitting a child because she/he didn't stop crying" was a form of extreme abuse, as was "a biological or a stepfather forcing his daughter to have sex," and "leaving a child alone all night long because she/he didn't follow parents' orders." A 20-year-old female said she was shocked when her mother told her that she was not her child when she didn't clean her room. A 21-year-old woman gave as an example of moderate abuse "mother is telling a child that 'you are not worthy to live. I shouldn't have given birth to you.'" Another 21-year-old woman stated that it is abusive for "a parent to accuse a child of 'not being a smart' or say 'you are not my child' when child gets a bad score on his/her test."

Many Japanese respondents from our sample also stated that "locking a child in a closet," "leaving a child on a porch during a cold winter night," and "leaving a baby in a car during a hot summer day" is extremely abusive. Some Japanese stated "putting a cigarette or iron or hot water on a child" and/or "sexual abuse" of a child are extremely abusive, and that "giving a punishment more than discipline" is a mild form of abuse. A 40-year-old woman stated her conviction that "people who became parents must have abused their child's feelings at least once by words and it happens not only in Japan but also in the world."

SPOUSE ABUSE

Although it has long been believed that there is no spousal abuse in Japan, historically there has been a high incidence of wife battering in the country. There is still a strong tendency to view this problem as a private matter, and Japanese society, including women, has yet to grasp the severity of the problem (Hada, 1995). It was not until the 1990s that there was any kind of organized movement at the grass-roots level to deal with domestic violence (Hada, 1995). Specifically, in April 1992, the Domestic Violence Action and Research Group undertook a survey to determine the extent of domestic violence occurring in Japan (Hada, 1995). Because the questionnaires were distributed to women's groups, adult education classes, and social service agencies, the sample was not representative of Japanese society as a whole; however, the results showed that 77% of the participants had been victims of at least one form of abuse; physical (for example, getting hit, kicked, threatened or cut with a knife, or burned with lit a cigarette); emotional (including repeated ridicule, restriction of contacts with family of origin or friends, threat of divorce or harm, withholding of adequate financial provisions); or sexual (such as a forced sex, refusal in cooperating with contraceptive use, forced sex with use of physical violence, forced abortion). Forty-four percent of respondents answered that they had experienced all three kinds of abuse (Hada, 1995).

Another finding from the Japan Bar Association's hot line services for battered wives (Nihon Bengoshi Rengokai, 1994) was that battered wives tend to stay in a marriage due to their financial dependence, and that violence is often associated with the husband's drinking. If the abuser is a husband, the intervention of police is rare and the violence is not taken seriously as a crime. Additionally, at lease one out of two spousal abusers is also physically violent against his children (Kozu, 1999).

According to a recent investigation by the Japanese government (Sourifu, 1999), 90% of the victims of domestic violence are female. The survey results indicated that 2.7% of 4,500 female respondents had experienced "sufficient violence to endanger their lives" and 6.8% had experienced forced sex. Approximately 25.6% of the perpetrators were "utter strangers" and 14.9% were friends, acquaintances, or boyfriends. Over 50% of victims sought help from their family; 8.8% didn't seek any help. Over 9% of the Japanese respondents had suffered from being stroked by someone of the opposite sex; 13.6% of these victims were women and 4.8% were males. Moreover, almost half of the Japanese females had been molested in a train (Sourifu, 1999).

Japanese Participants' Perspectives on Domestic Violence

In our survey, one 39-year-old male respondent listed "violent acts, verbal abuse, forcing and refusing to have sex, cheating" as examples of wife abuse. He also mentioned that he had a friend who was arrested after his wife reported to the police that her husband kept abusing her and she couldn't take it anymore.

> He was abusive towards his wife due to the differences in their (husband and wife) opinions and his stress from his workplace. He is polite to everyone and causes no harm to people, and he rarely drinks alcohol. He is a bit argumentative and he does things at his own pace, so whenever he didn't like the things his wife said, it seems his behaviors were changed in his household.

Another respondent (female, 38) explained that her friend's husband had been abusive toward her friend and their child daily. Frequent examples of extreme wife abuse (from both males and females) were "being physically and psychologically violent after getting drunk," and/or "not contributing any salary to the house," and "cheating." Common examples (from both males and females) of ways in which wives abuse husbands were "not cooking food" or "not doing housework at all"—typically seen as either moderate or mild abuse. Some Japanese males stated that "not giving pocket money to a husband" is moderate or mild abuse, and some Japanese females stated that "comparing a husband with other husbands" is moderately abusive. Presumably based on their implicit theories of abuse, some Japanese females stated that they could not think of any abusive behaviors from a wife to a husband although they can think of many abusive behaviors from a husband to a wife.

ELDER ABUSE

Aging is one of the serious issues in Japan today. By the year 2025, the population age 65 or above will reach about 20% of the Japanese population, and 2.3 million of elderly will be bedridden (Harris, Long & Fujii, 1998). However, the number of family members who might provide care is declining; thus, who will be the caregiver is one of the biggest issues facing Japan in the future.

In Japan, women are expected to be a caregiver for their parents-in-law and their husbands and then to be cared for by their daughters-in-law (Sodei, 1995). In recent years, however, the conflict between the wife and the mother-in-law often results in elder abuse in Japan. The most common pattern in Japan, unlike the United States, is mistreatment of aged mothers by their daughters-in-law (Kaneko & Yamada, 1990). In their 1985 study, Kaneko and Yamada (1990) found the rate of occurrence of elder abuse (with self-abuse excluded) to be approximately 0.8% of persons 60 years of age and over. Also, they mentioned that the actual figure is probably more than 1.5 to 2 times higher (Kaneko & Yamada, 1990). Verbal abuse was noted by approximately one-third of the respondents, with much smaller proportions of neglect and physical abuse (Kaneko & Yamada, 1990).

According to the first national survey done by Koreisha Shogu Kenkyukai (1994), 40% of elderly victims were physically abused. Women were 2.5 times more likely to be victimized than men and more than half of the victims were above age 80. About 33% of abusers were daughters-in-law in the same household (Kozu, 1999).

Japanese Participants' Perspectives on Elder Abuse

Traditionally, a strong cultural value in Japan has been filial responsibility, assuring care for the elderly. Japanese social interaction is tied to social obligation. It is expected that Japanese parents' devotion and sacrifices for their children's educational and career achievements will be paid back in later care provision to those parents when they need assistance. If children do not provide care for their elder parents, it is considered socially unacceptable and abusive (indicating no respect). Many of our Japanese participants indicated that "not feeding" or "not helping" elderly parents is extremely abusive. One 51-year-old female respondent wrote that "forcing them to live in a nursing home" was an extreme form of elder abuse. Another respondent (female, 23) stated "distribution of property before they die" is an extreme form of elder abuse. Some Japanese female respondents indicated that "being a selfish son who makes an elderly mother follow his orders," "scolding an elderly parent," "making an elderly parent eat meals alone," or "not being a conversational partner" were types of elder abuse.

SIBLING ABUSE

Although sibling abuse is one of the more common and serious forms of abuse in family violence, research regarding abusive sibling behaviors is very limited. Arai and Shairs (1999) examined judgments of sibling abuse in college students and young workers from the United States and Japan. Results indicated that young Japanese women viewed some abusive behavior items as more acceptable than did Caucasian women. The groups did not differ in total frequency of reported sibling abuse, but young Japanese women reported experiencing more psychological abuse from siblings than did young American women.

Japanese Participants' Perspectives on Sibling Abuse

Only a few of our respondents provided examples of sibling abuse—perhaps because of a general assumption that sibling aggression is not abusive or does not occur in Japan. Generally, the examples of sibling abuse identified sexual abuse as a type of extremely abusive sibling behavior, physical abuse as moderately abusive, and psychological abuse as mildly abusive. Common examples of sibling abuse were "ridiculing differences in abilities among siblings" (female, 20), "ignoring siblings' personalities" (male, 25), "younger siblings wearing their older siblings' hand me downs" (female, 21), and "kicking and punching a middle kid by older and younger siblings" (female, 20).

OTHER RELATIONSHIPS

In-law relationships were the principal type of "other" family relationship identified by Japanese participants as one in which abuse could take place. The responses portray an implicit theory of abuse in which jealous mothers-in-law continue to mother their son and interfere in intimacy between newlyweds. The triad of mother–son–daughter-in-law can be stressful and can cause marital estrangement as the husband begins to stay away from home in avoidance of getting caught in the middle.

One of the most publicized problems of recent years in Japan is bullying. The problem is groups of school children ganging up on some poor boy or girl with physical, but more commonly mental, harassment, until the victim will no longer attend school, or in extreme cases, commits suicide. Probably because our survey emphasized abuse in families, no references were made to neighborhood bullying.

INTERVENTION AND PREVENTION

Some great improvements have been achieved by the government and grass-roots volunteer groups and organizations since the early 1990s. The Ministry of Health and Welfare began to implement a national program called "advocate activities" in 1994 (Kozu, 1999, p. 53). In the private sector, there are active and influential volunteer child abuse prevention centers in Tokyo and Osaka (Kozu, 1999). Compared with the child abuse efforts, social services for domestic violence are still quite limited; however, for spousal abuse victims, there are hot line services across the country, and lawyers are addressing the problem of spousal abuse as a human rights issue (Kozu, 1999). In the private sector, there is only one organization in Japan for battered women. In the public sector, there are public health centers, and women's centers provide a wider range of services (Kozu, 1999).

As for intervention, the role of psychologists in family violence is still rather small and clinical education and training is still young (Kozu, 1999). Training for mental health providers and further research in domestic violence intervention is needed. As Kozu (1999) suggested, the most demanding challenge for the future is funding of service organizations, and public recognition of the magnitude of the problem. Moreover, seminars and symposia not only for academic professions but also for general audiences need to be offered to provide people with adequate information concerning family violence and access to the prevention and intervention programs.

To prevent and intervene in child abuse, spousal abuse, and elder abuse at an early stage, Japan needs to improve the legal system along with a nationwide program for prevention and social services. Kitamura et al. (1999) suggested that the Child Welfare Act needs to be amended to (a) define the groups of professionals who have a duty to report suspected child abuse; (b) immunize the report of professionals from breach of confidentiality; (c) empower the head and designated staff of child guidance centers to investigate the child, parents, and other related individuals, even at home; and (d) set up legal or nonlegal advocacy groups for the protection and care of children, with power to investigate, to communicate with concerned people and groups, and to act as a guardian ad litem when necessary. Kouno and Johnson (1995) indicated that social welfare priorities need to be revised and budgets for the prevention, detection, and treatment of child abuse need to be increased. Because the number of child welfare caseworkers is inadequate, trained professionals are lacking to assess abused children and their families, and the pay and social status of social workers are extremely low in Japan (Kouno & Johnson, 1995); such problems also need to be addressed.

ACKNOWLEDGMENTS

Special thanks to Naomi Sotoo for her help at the beginning of this project; Akiko Abe, Takashi Abe, Dr. Tadashi Omori, Yoko Makino and Nami Arakawa for the data collection.

REFERENCES

Arai, M., & Shairs, M. S. (1999, August). *Acceptability and frequency of sibling violence: A cross-cultural perspective*. Poster session presented at the annual meeting of the American Psychological Association, Boston, MA.

Dussich, J. P. J. (2001). Decisions not to report sexual assault: A comparative study among women living in Japan who are Japanese, Korean, Chinese and English-speaking. *International Journal of Offender Therapy & Comparative Criminology, 45*(3), 278–301.

Funabashi, K. (1989). Pornographic culture and sexual violence. In K. Fijimura-Fanselow & A. Kameda (Eds.), *Japanese women* (pp. 255–263). New York: The Feminist Press at the City College of New York.

Gender Equality Bureau. (1998). *Report on the study group of violence from husband and partners*.

Hada, A. (1995). Domestic violence. In K. Fujimura-Fanselow & A. Kameda (Eds.), *Japanese women* (pp. 213–228). New York: The Feminist Press at the City College of New York.

Harris, P. B., Long, S. O., & Fujii, M. (1998). Men and elder care in Japan: A ripple of change? *Journal of Cross-Cultural Gerontology, 13*, 177–198.

Kaneko, Y., & Yamada, Y. (1990). Wives and mother-in-law: Potential for family conflict in postwar Japan. *Journal of Elder Abuse & Neglect, 2*(1/2), 87–99.

Kitahara, M. (1989). Childhood in Japanese culture. *The Journal of Psychohistory, 17*(1), 43–72.

Kitamura, T., Kijima, N., Iwata, N., Senda, Y., Takahashi, K., & Hayashi, I. (1999). Frequencies of child abuse in Japan: Hidden but prevalent crime. *International Journal of Offender Therapy and Comparative Criminology, 43*(1), 21–33.

Koreisha Shogu Kenkyukai [Elderly Care Research Group]. (1994). *Koreishano fukushishisetsu ni okeru ningenkankei no shosei ni kakawaru sogoteki kenkyu* [Comprehensive study on interpersonal relationships of the elderly at elderly care support centers]. Tokyo: Author.

Koseisho [Ministry of health, labour and welfare]. (2000). *Jidou gyakutai boushihou* [Child abuse prevention act]. Available: http://www.jca.ax.apc.org/~fsaito/childabuse.html

Kouno, A., & Johnson, C. F. (1995). Child abuse and neglect in Japan: Coin-operated-locker babies. *Child Abuse & Neglect, 19*(1), 25–31.

Kozu, J. (1999). Domestic violence in Japan. *American Psychologist, 54*(1), 50–54.

Kumagai, F. (1981). Filial violence: A peculiar parent–child relationship in the Japanese family today. *Journal of Comparative Family Studies, 7*(3), 337–349.

Nihon Bengoshi Rengokai, Ryoseino Byodoni Kansuru linkai [Committee on Gender Equality, Japan Bar Association]. (1994). *Fufukan Boryoku 110 ban houkokusho* [Report of material violence hotline]. Tokyo: Author.

Saiko Saibansho Jimusokyoku [General Secretariat, Supreme Court]. (1992). *1991 nen shiho tokei nenpo: 3. minjihen* [Annual report of judicial statistics for 1991: 3. Family cases]. Tokyo: Hosokai.

Seimei Hoken Bunka Senta (Japan Institute of Life Insurance). (1987). *Josei no seikatsu ishiki ni kansuru chosa* [Survey on women's attitudes toward life]. Tokyo: Seimei Hoken Bunka Senta.

Sodei, T. (1995). Care of the elderly: A women's Issue. In K. Fujimura-Fanselow & A. Kameda (Eds.), *Japanese women* (pp. 213–228). New York: The Feminist Press at the City College of New York.

Sorifu [Prime Minister's Office]. (1999). *FY 1999 Annual Report on the State of the Formation of a Gender Equal Society.*

Yoshizumi, K. (1995). Marriage and family: Past and present. In K. Fujimura-Fanselow & A. Kameda (Eds.), *Japanese women* (pp. 183–197). New York: The Feminist Press at the City College of New York.

302

THE K

Korea
older
and
law
dre
fro
in
p

CHAPTER

17

Korea

Mikyung Jang & Mi-Sung Kim

CAPSULE

Given their collectivist values, Koreans have typically been concerned with family unity, privacy, and saving face. This orientation has led to a tendency to see any behavior that is publicly embarrassing (e.g., showing disrespect of elders in front of other people) as more abusive than using physical aggression in the home. Consistent with this orientation, Koreans put considerable emphasis on emotional maltreatment, indicating that "indifference toward family members," and not treating them respectfully as human beings are very abusive. Interestingly, because of the established tradition wherein firstborn sons take care of their parents physically and financially in later years, the mother-in-law/daughter-in-law relationship has considerable significance. There has been a growing awareness of the possibility of maltreatment from mothers-in-law toward daughters-in-law in earlier years, and of daughters-in-law toward mothers-in-law in later years. In addition, a tradition of childrearing that enforces parents' values, along with a more contemporary concern about children's academic achievement, has sometimes led to child maltreatment, a problem exacerbated in recent decades by intensive economic growth. Finally, although there was traditionally no recognition of sexual violence as a potential marital problem in Korean society, progressive scholars/experts have recently proposed the concept of "marital rape."

OREAN SAMPLE

n respondents to the cross-cultural definitional survey included 74 Koreans and 102 college students. The older Koreans were 21 males 3 females ranging in age from 25 to 55, and working as housewives, ers, doctors, pharmacologists, salesmen, graduate students, and hairssers. The college students were 32 males and 70 females ranging in age m 18 to 25 years old. Data were collected from the college students during a class. The older Koreans were recruited through a convenience sampling technique.

Korean Participants' Definitions of Abuse

The implicit theories of our respondents about violence within the families showed many similarities to legal and hot line definitions of abuse. In defining abuse, both the college students and the older adults commonly referred to the infliction of force that was continuous, repeated, without a good reason, and indefensible. For example, one 18-year-old female student said "abuse is battering of wife or children without any reason when a father is soaked by alcohol and comes back home late." Consistent with collectivist values, respondents placed considerable emphasis on psychological/mental violence; indeed, the older Koreans mentioned psychological/mental forms of violence more frequently than physical violence. For example, they defined family abuse as, "to give mental anguish without understanding the other people" (28-year-old female working for an art gallery); "to scold the other's faults or mistakes with extreme disapproval, not admitting anything" (female salesperson, 46); "no conversation and not listening to the other" (female salesperson, 44); "favoritism" (male personal financial manager, 30); and "disregard" (female student, 18).

The implicit theories of abuse shared by many of our Korean respondents clearly attributed abuse to both personality and childhood family environment. According to a 19-year-old male student, "being battered or seeing a lot of violent behavior as a child makes a person extremely violent." A 46-year-old housewife said: "Children who have grown up without seeing parent's harmonious conjugal life repeat the same phenomena rather than change behavior for the better life when they married." A 25-year-old developmental therapist (female) wrote that "the abuser's false belief about humans" was a cause of abusive behavior. Students also viewed "conflicts," "conjugal problems," "mistrust," and "lack of intimacy" among family members (including stepmother/father–child relationships) as factors in abuse. One 18-year-old male student mentioned that "abnormal family structure, like Cinderella's stepmother, makes a family member's behavior extremely abusive," and a 19-year-old female student said, "parents' unrealistic expectations concerning their children make their behaviors abusive."

Despite considerable consistency in the views of Korean men and women, there were some gender differences among college students in presumed causes of abusive behaviors. For example, several male students said that the attitude of the recipient of abuse is what makes an abuser's behavior extremely abusive. According to an 18-year-old male student, "an abuser's behavior becomes more violent when the victim is resistant." Some male students reported, "a recipient of abuse's passive and unresisting attitude is a cause of mildly abusive behavior in family relationships." Thus, it is implied that the victim is at fault if an abuser becomes abusive, an assumption not shown in female students, who hold instead that patriarchy in Korea, under the influence of Confucian ideology, contributes to extremely abusive behavior. One young woman wrote, "Korean social structure, such as authoritative father and man's superior position in family and society, makes a person's behavior more extremely abusive." Several female students also said that rank in the family is associated with moderately abusive behaviors.

THE KOREAN MACROSYSTEM

Cultural Heritage of the Korean Family

The importing of Metaphysics (a branch of Confucianism) from China and Japanese legislation on "the headship of a family" has had a strong impact on Korean family life. Despite changes, the important values defining the Korean family are "filial piety to the parents (the Academy of Korean Studies, n.d.)," revealed through the ancient custom of ancestor worship, and love for children (the Society for the Study of Korean Women's Society, 2001). Family matters such as succession to property, economic rights, women's rights, sibling's rights, and kinship relationships have all been related to systems in the worship ceremony for dead parents.

Kinship relations of the Koryo dynasty (10th to 14th centuries) were bilateral, meaning that kinship relationships could be expanded variously regardless of patrilineage or matrilineage (Noh, as cited in H. J. Lee, 1990), and males and females had equal rights (Huh, as cited in H. J. Lee, 1990). Koryo marriages were generally not arranged by parents but were love marriages, and uxori-local (husbands live with wives' parents; Kim, 2000). After the mid-17th century, Confucian norms spread into the general public (Ewha Women's Studies, n.d.), "clan rules" were consolidated, and discrimination in inheritance emerged, privileging the eldest son and discriminating against females (Choi, 1983). By the end of the Chosun dynasty (14th to 19th centuries), the family system had become patrilineal (H. J. Lee, 1990), married daughters were considered no better than a stranger, and the patriarchical family was established. Following the Chosun dynasty, Korea was under Japanese colonial rule for 36 years. Japan introduced the "system of succession to the headship of a family," the traditional system disappeared, and the head of a family gained rights to all properties and decisions regarding marriage and divorce.

The basic Japanese structure of succession to the headship of a family, which grants superior rights to men and is maintained in the civil law of the ROK, has been under attack for violating constitutional protections of human rights and equity. Kim (2000) argued that the laws on the headship of a family should be abolished because they promote the view that only males can head the family. This view has led to an imbalance in the sex ratio of boys to girls, in part through an estimated abortion of over 30,000 girls a year. Boys (even in infancy) have prior rights to be head of the family over grandmothers, mothers, and other older women of the family (the Civil Law, Article 984), which can lead to a disregarding of women.

With the rapid economic growth of the 20th century, children came to be viewed as having two major roles: as the parents' vehicle to higher social positions through advanced education, and as the state's prospective labor force (Cho-Han, 1998). The autocratic military regime of the 1960s and 1970s contributed to these concepts of children's roles, envisioning Korean modernization with regard to economic development only and suppressing other aspects such as human rights. In response to this ideology, and to free future generations from poverty, most people did their best to educate their children. Today, education no longer guarantees wealth, and the nation is no longer poor, but the established mind-set is not easily changed. According to a national survey of 769 parents, 90% thought their sons had to graduate at least from college, and 89% thought their daughters had to. Of the reasons that parents gave for sending their children to college, 50% said it was for the advantage of getting socially acceptable jobs (Cha, 2002).

As distinct from the Western emphasis on independence and individualism, Korean parent–child relationships are interdependent, and might be expected to serve a protective function for family members as they age. However, unsatisfied filial piety can cause conflicts between generations (Mo, 1999), and adult children can feel economic as well as psychological burdens in supporting aged parents. Many aged parents have insufficient money for their old age because they invested too much in their children's education and marriage. In addition, public systems for supporting aged people are limited (Society for the Study of Korean Women's Society, 2001). Until recently, Korean families took full responsibility for their own well-being, such as childrearing, education, medical care, and supporting aged parents. However, recognition of a role for social welfare is now emerging.

Legislation on Domestic Violence

The ROK joined the U.N. Commission on Human Rights in 1990 and signed the U.N. Convention on the Rights of the Child in November 1991. As a result of human rights agreements and feminist activism, two provisions for combating domestic violence were enacted in July, 1997—the Act on the Punishment of Domestic Violence, and the Act for the Prevention and Protection of Victims of Domestic Violence. Before this legislation, most people, even police, seemed reluctant to intervene in domestic violence cases because family life was considered private. Moreover, prior to the enactment of this legislation, victims appeared not to recognize their aversive experiences as "abusive." Rather, abusive acts were called "something wrong" or "not being very nice." The legislation on domestic violence, however, clearly defined engaging in such activity as a criminal offense demanding state/community intervention and imposed a penal sanction or protection order against the offender.

The growing public recognition of family violence as a problem has been reflected in the news media, which have announced an increased prevalence of reported domestic violence following the legislation and the economic crisis associated with the International Monetary Fund. The data indicated that reported child maltreatment cases totaled 807 in 1997; 1,238 in 1998; 2,155 in 1999; and 1,472 in the first half of 2000—about 35% more than in the same period of 1999 (Ahn, 2000). According to the North Kyungsang-do Regional Police Headquarters, during 5 months in early 2000, 197 cases of family violence were reported to the police—an increase of 71% (i.e., 82 cases) over the same period in the previous year. All reports but one were made by victims, indicating that communities were still not intervening in cases of violence within the family (Chun, 2000).

The Act on the Punishment of Domestic Violence defines domestic violence as behavior that does physical, psychological, or economic damage to family members, including a cohabiter and relatives who live together. The offenses include criminal injury, assault, abandonment, abuse, detention, threat, libel, blackmail, robbery, and habitual criminal behavior, but they do not include marital rape or child punishment. According to the Seoul Women's Hotline (2001), a study of 140 participants in internet counseling indicated that forms of violence accompanying battering included verbal abuse (70%), economic abuse (11%), insulting behavior (8%), and marital rape (3%). In many cases, a habitually battering husband coerced sex as a reconciliation after battering (Lee, n.d.). With regards to child punishment, Ahn (1994) found that 79% of a sample of Korean parents ($n = 57$)

considered spanking or hitting to be an acceptable punishment for children. About half did not consider 9- to 15-year-old children as victims of abuse even if they sustained bruises from being disciplined. For 3-year-olds, however, almost 80% of the Koreans viewed hitting as abusive. In the first national survey on child maltreatment in 1999, 65% of Koreans held that parents had a right to batter their children ("Korean marriage and divorce," 2000). Given that marital rape often occurs on a continuum of violence and that child maltreatment is often condoned under the name of discipline, Han (1998) suggested that the legislative acts may not provide sufficient protection of the right to freedom from violence addressed in the relevant U.N. conventions. I. S. Han (1998) also noted that the Acts provide no legal formalities, such as restraining the defendant from contacting the plaintiff, restraining the defendant from exercising parental authority, ordering probation, or mandating counseling programs to deal with failures in Protection Orders.

CHILD MALTREATMENT

The Act for Prevention of Child Abuse was established in July 1997 and integrated into the Act for Child Welfare in 2000. According to the Act for Child Welfare, child abuse is defined as "physical, mental, sexual, harsh behavior condoned by adults . . . that could result in preventing children's health, well-being, or normal development, and abandonment/neglect condoned by those who are granted children's custody." Article 29 specifically describes prohibited behaviors; abuse that results in physical injury; abuse that causes the child to be humiliated sexually; emotional abuse that results in harm to the child's mental health or development; abandonment or behavior that neglects fundamental protection, nurture, and the provision of medical care; the exploitation of children through behavior forcing them into sexual activity; behavior that compels a handicapped child to be viewed by the public in order to make money; behavior that uses the child as a vehicle for begging; behavior that makes the child do stunts dangerous to the child's health and safety for the purpose of entertainment; behavior that gets money as the price of mediating children's custody outside the authorized institute; and behavior that uses money that was donated to the child for other purposes.

Most child welfare centers recognize the commonly identified four types of child maltreatment; physical abuse, emotional abuse, sexual abuse, and neglect; some centers add abandonment to these four types. However, obtaining reliable and valid data on domestic child maltreatment in Korea is difficult because some criteria for child abuse are vague and because there is no definition by common consent. Bae-keun Lee, a vice-president of the Korean Association for Preventing Child Abuse, argued that it is necessary to get social agreement on the definition of child maltreatment in order to discover, intervene, and prevent the abuse, and to define the range of child maltreatment in order to establish legal and systemic devices (as cited in Park, n.d.).

Prevalence of Child Maltreatment

According to the Korea Institute for Health and Social Affairs (Kang, 2000), the prevalence of child abuse within families in Korea reached 2.6 % (approximately 507,000 children) in late 1998. Kim and Cho's (1998a) survey of 534 parents found that 1 out of every 2 are verbally violent and 8 out of 10 are physically violent, using corporal punishment on their children. In 1999, the first national survey on child abuse was undertaken with the aim of developing policy. This parent-oriented survey gathered responses from 1,094 families from all provinces except Cheju and covered all age groups including infants, who are at high risk of abuse (Hong, 1999). The study defined corporal punishment as spanking, spanking with a rod, hitting parts of child's body with hands, pinching, and shaking. Some behaviors that could be viewed as emotional abuse (e.g., threatening to hit, shouting) were not regarded as child maltreatment but inappropriate discipline. The prevalence of child maltreatment reported for the year preceding the survey was 44%; physical abuse was 23.5%; emotional abuse, 19%; neglect, 20%; and sexual abuse, 1%. The prevalence of corporal punishment was 74%.

Tolerance of child maltreatment as a form of discipline can be explained as a product of collectivism. In many Asian cultures, parents perceived children as extensions of themselves. According to Ahn (1994), spanking is a task that results in greater pain to parents than to children, not only because they sympathize with their children, but also because any misbehavior necessitating spanking is a reminder of their failure as parents.

Kim and Ko (1990) and Doe (2000) revealed that child abuse was closely related to other forms of domestic violence. Additional battered family members were reported in 80% of the families of mildly battered children (i.e., the children who were slapped and spanked) and 75% of the seriously battered. A survey conducted by the Seoul Women's Hotline during the first quarter of 2000 revealed that 60% of the respondents (41 cases) indicated that the wife batterers also battered their children.

Korean Respondents' Perspectives on Child Maltreatment

Among the common examples of child abuse in our sample were "battering" or "corporal punishment," "verbal assault/aggression," "enforcement of the parents' values," and "not allowing a meal." Many of the definitions highlighted uniquely Korean aspects of the participants' implicit theories concerning the contexts of abusive behavior. The responses often mentioned "enforcement of parental values while ignoring the children's opinions," and academic-related maltreatment. Under the influence of Confucian ideology, even though only 3% of Koreans are Confucian, parental implicit theories consider children to be objects who must follow their parent's discipline rather than as independent beings (Kim & Cho, 1998a). Moreover, as Confucianism has been combined with the previous military culture in Korea, "discipline" and "corporal punishment"' have been confused, which has led to a social atmosphere tacitly permitting child maltreatment within the family. It is characteristic of Korean society that children are viewed more readily as students preparing for college entrance than as children or adolescents with independent characteristics and human rights.

Consistent with Ahn's (1994) findings on tolerance of corporal punishment, the National Policy Minister Office II reported that in 1996, 65.4% of Koreans thought that parents had a right to beat their children. Of adolescents who had been battered by parents, 83% thought it was caused by their own wrongdoing ("Father and family," 1999, cited in "Korean marriage and divorce," 2000). Similar views were shown by some of our respondents: "It is difficult to define corporal punishment as abuse because it comes from love" (housewife, 50). However, others disagreed, saying, "Maltreatment is produced under the cloak of love" (housewife, 33). A 20-year-old female student wrote, "To punish him physically when the child spills water is moderately abusive." Another female student said "It is abusive to punish a child when the child talks back or does not obey parent."

Many examples of abuse showed revealed reconceptualizations of traditional manifestations of parental authority; "to enforce the parent's suggestion for selecting son's marriage partner is very abusive"; "I want to do a dance major in college but my parent forced me to do a management major" (female student, 18); "to press the children for acceptance of the parent and to hit the child, arguing that the parent is always right" (housewife, 47); "to confine in a room without time limits with the reason that the children didn't obey parents, or unilateral enforcement" (female teacher, 45). Academic-related maltreatment was frequently identified as child abuse at all levels of abuse. Examples of child abuse offered by college students included "battering a child because of low academic achievement," "telling the child he/she is inferior," "withholding a meal when the child did not perform well in an exam," "depriving the child of needed sleep, insisting more time should be spent studying," and "sending to educational institutes for supplementary study."

Examples of child abuse also included sexual abuse and not talking with the child. Among college students, a typical example was "a stepfather's sexual abuse to the stepdaughter or father's sexual abuse to the daughter."

With regard to lack of communication, a 45-year-old housewife confessed, "stopping conversation and disregarding my 17-year-old boy for about two days when he did a behavior that I did not want is moderately abusive." When providing examples of extreme maltreatment, older Koreans generally linked physical maltreatment to other types of maltreatment. For example, a 28-year-old female (working in an art gallery) wrote that extreme child maltreatment was "to abuse physically and mentally as if the child is an animal reared in order to be butchered." A 25-year-old part-time worker (female) said extreme abuse was "to batter and confine children in a room."

CONJUGAL VIOLENCE

Practical resources, more than legislation, have provided advanced definitions of conjugal maltreatment that include sexual violence. For example, the Pusan Women's Hotline defines sexual violence as marital rape, coercion to engage in prostitution or other unlawful sexual activity, and an assault on a person related to sex (Pusan Women's Hotline, 2001). Using a battering survey during the first half of 2000, the Seoul Women's Hotline (2001) analyzed its counseling cases (130 responses of telephone counseling and 140 responses of internet counseling). Regarding the circumstances in which wife battering occurs, frequent responses were a husband losing his temper without reason (telephone, 41%; internet, 50%), the husband's drinking (telephone, 38%; internet, 39%), a wife talking back to the husband (telephone, 30%; internet, 1%), and a wife mentioning the husband's infidelity (telephone, 14%; internet, 6%).

Prevalence of Conjugal Maltreatment

According to a national survey by the Korean Institute for Health and Social Affairs (1998), prevalence of marital violence was 6.7% (husband-to-wife violence was 5.6%; wife-to-husband, 1.1%). It was estimated that husband-to-wife violence occurs in 728,000 families and wife-to-husband violence in 143,000 families. The Korea Legal Aid Center For Family Relations reported that husband-to-wife violence mostly begins before marriage or simultaneously with marriage (Yang & Ahn, 1996). With regard to wife–husband violence, the most frequent types were name calling and insulting (24%), followed by throwing things (19%), pinching or scratching (19%), not serving meals to husband properly (13%), and severe physical violence (10%; K. Lee, 1999). The most frequently used method of violence from husband-to-wife was battering using own body (47%), battering with objects (34%), verbal violence (10%), and throwing things and smashing (7%). A 2000 Health and Welfare Committee survey revealed that 1 out of 3 couples experienced violence; 28% were battered wives and 16% were battered husbands ("Increased prevalence of family violence," n.d.).

Korean Respondents' Perspectives on Conjugal Maltreatment

When asked to give examples of abuse in spousal relationships, our respondents generally gave the same examples for husband abuse as for wife abuse—including sexual abuse, physical violence (e.g., "battering"), and verbal aggression. The most frequent examples were physical aggression, followed by verbal aggression, indifference, economic abuse, and sexual abuse. A 20-year-old male student wrote, "It is an extreme form of verbal abuse to say that 'you don't know anything', or 'go die'." The most frequently mentioned examples of moderate and mild spousal abuse were types of verbal abuse—for both wives and husbands as perpetrators. Respondents listed "yelling," "slander," "insult," and "not talking." For example, a 19-year-old male student said that "it is moderately abusive to say that 'you always do something wrong'."

Although most of the college students and respondents in their early 30s appeared to regard the conjugal relationship as one of equal rights, and applied the same criteria to husband abuse as to wife abuse, some participants gave somewhat different examples for the two types of spousal abuse. For example, a husband's patriarchal attitude and authority was given as a form of wife abuse at all levels of abuse. A female student wrote, "To force a wife to stay at home as a housewife is very abusive, if she wants to work outside." A male student stated, "It is abusive that a husband judges and decides everything about family matters." In addition, students cited a wife's economic abuse of her husband at all levels of abusiveness. As an example, an 18-year-old male student said "it is abusive that a wife compares her husband with another man for salary and complains for less amount of income." A 19-year-old female student considered it abusive "to regard a husband as a moneymaking machine."

Examples of indifference or neglect as forms of spousal maltreatment focused largely on failure to fulfill traditional gender roles. Abusive indifference from a wife to a husband commonly included "not taking care of the husband and housework." However, abusive indifference by husbands included "not helping in the home," as well as "neglect" in general. A 50-year-old male respondent gave the following example of extreme husband abuse; "to repeatedly complain about the husband's income and not to prepare meals well."

Although sexual violence has traditionally been a taboo topic in Korean society, the issue received public attention when a husband disguised himself as a burglar and battered and raped his wife, who was suing for divorce

(H. Lee, n.d.). Recently, progressive scholars have proposed substituting the concept of "marital rape" for that of "wife rape." Among our respondents, there were differences in the views on sexual maltreatment depending on whether they were considering wife or husband abuse. Examples of sexual abuse by husbands were always referred to as extreme or moderate forms of abuse, and mainly included "unwanted sex" or "sex without a wife's agreement." Sexual abuse by wives was always seen as a moderate form of abuse and included "refusal to have sex" with a husband. The specific behavior of "unwanted sex" was regarded as a severe form of abuse when done by the husband to the wife, but as moderate when done by the wife to the husband. Most of our older respondents seemed reluctant to apply the term "sexual violence" to marriage, much less to use the term "wife rape." One possible explanation is that they tend to think of sex as a conjugal duty; however, it must be considered that marital rape often occurs on a continuum of violence and unilateral enforcement.

SIBLING MALTREATMENT

A study of sibling interactions in Korean preschool children (K. Lee, 1990) showed that patterns varied from prosocial to antagonistic behaviors, such as physical aggression, authoritarian attitudes, and showing anger. However, sibling maltreatment has not received the attention given to spousal, child, and elderly abuse. It has been mentioned only as a relationship in which domestic violence can occur, or only in reference to the relationship between abuser and victim in a survey of child maltreatment. Park's survey in 1996 (as cited in Doe, 2000) showed that 30% of battered children were punished by older siblings. In a study by K. H. Han (1998) of 1,451 middle and high school students, 23% of the respondents reported experiencing physical violence from their siblings during the past year and 17% said they had used physical violence on their siblings. The most frequent type of sibling violence was kicking or hitting with a hand. Four percent of the respondents reported throwing objects and smashing things, and 2.3% beating with a stick or a belt.

Korean Respondents' Perspectives on Sibling Maltreatment

When asked to give examples of severe sibling maltreatment, most of our respondents mentioned battering or physical violence. For example, a 19-year-old female student said that "sibling conflict like an older sibling's battering and insulting are abusive experiences." College students frequently mentioned sexual abuse and verbal aggression as severe forms of abuse, whereas older respondents more often cited psychological/mental abuse, such as "not communicating with each other," "blaming," and "rivalry" as severe forms of abuse. As an example of psychological/mental abuse, a 33-year-old saleswoman said, "breaking with each other is severely abusive." A 38-year-old male hairdresser wrote, "Discord between brothers' wives is moderately abusive." According to a 19-year-old female student, "raping or sexual abuse by an elder brother is very abusive."

The students seem to be respectful of their siblings' property and willing to do their fair share of work at home. An 18-year-old female student described as a moderate or mild form of abuse, "using sibling's things without permission" and "not sharing cleaning the room with other siblings." Older Koreans said sibling maltreatment sometimes involved "economic disputes" (housewife, 46) or "comparison of benefits from original family members" (housewife, 48). The Korea Legal Aid Center for Family Relations (2000) reported that the proportion of counseling on inheritance of property has grown, suggesting that economic factors are increasingly important in family relations. On the other hand, "extreme concern" (48-year-old housewife) and "constant material and mental dependency" (44-year-old housewife) were regarded as sibling maltreatment by older Koreans, who were perhaps concerned with the burdens that can come with sibling relationships

ELDER MALTREATMENT

Elder maltreatment is committed covertly and not discussed overtly because of the influence of a Confucian value, filial piety, rooted in Korean society. Elder abuse has received less attention than child or wife abuse (Korean Society for Study of Elder Abuse, n.d.). There have not yet been separate acts from the Act on the Punishment of Domestic Violence and the Act for the Prevention and Protection of Victims of Domestic Violence. Although an Act for Elder Welfare was established in 1980 and revised in 2000, it does not mention elder abuse.

Types of psychological abuse described by the Korean Society for Study of Elder Abuse (n.d.) include coercion of the elder who has difficulty doing housework, complaining or showing a bad temper when the elderly gives advice, and making elders feel that the person who is responsible for them wants them to disappear. The Society gives as an example of verbal abuse saying to the elderly "you are useless" and threatening to send them to an institute for the aged. As an example of material abuse, they list forgery of the elder's will or property document and failure to return borrowed money or goods.

The Caritas Nunnery Counseling Center for Elder Abuse suggests as examples of physical abuse confining the elderly in a room or a basement, tying the elderly to a chair or a bed, and leaving the elderly home alone and unable to prepare meals more than 2 to 3 days. As forms of psychological abuse, the Caritas Center includes blunt expressions of the stress of supporting the elderly, estrangement in a family meeting, reluctance to visit the elderly, and blame for mistakes such as a urinary disorder due to impaired physical function. Their examples of neglect include not assisting elders needing help in bathing or using a bathroom. Unlike other forms of domestic violence, definitions of elder abuse often include "self-neglect." For example, the Korean Society for Study of Elder Abuse defines "elder abuse" as "self-neglect or physical, emotional/psychological, sexual, financial/material abuse, and neglect that are intentionally or unintentionally condoned by a person who responsible for the elderly" (Korean Society for Study of Elder Abuse, n.d.).

Prevalence of Elder Maltreatment

The Korea Institute for Health and Social Affairs collected data from 865 elders over age 65 in 2001. Nearly 8% had experienced abuse from their children or other family members. Types of abuse were verbal and psychological (8% of respondents), economic exploitation (2%), neglect (2.5%), physical abuse (0.3%), and other abuse. Almost 43% of the elder abuse occurred "almost every day." In regard to causes, 39.5% was due to economic problems and 22% to differences in character. A study by the Korean Institute of Criminology (1995) also found psychological abuse to be the most frequent form of elder abuse. For example, the most frequently endorsed forms of psychological abuse were "I felt that the person who helps and looks after wants me to disappear (17%)," and "I had severe verbal attack and insult from the person who looks after me (17%)."

Korean Respondents' Perspectives on Elder Maltreatment

Koreans regard emotional abuse toward an elderly person as more severe than other types of abuse. In a study of American and Korean college students, the Korean students judged material and physical maltreatment of an elderly person as less abusive and psychological maltreatment as more abusive than did Caucasian American students (Jang, You, Malley-Morrison, & Mills, 1999; Malley-Morrison, You, & Mills, 2000). In our survey, both the older participants and college students mentioned "emotional abuse," "physical abuse," "abandonment," "sending to facilities," "neglect," and several types of economic abuse as forms of elder abuse. Forms of emotional abuse, such as "disregard," "verbal attack," and "indifference" or "not caring for the elderly" were the most frequently mentioned types at all levels of abuse. College student examples of economic abuse included "not giving pocket money to an elderly parent" or "not giving financial support" rather than financial exploitation.

Overall, the importance of showing filial piety toward the elder (i.e., honoring the elder as a senior) and taking care of them seemed to be the most critical factors in Koreans' implicit theories of elder abuse. Respondents appear to believe that it is a son's (especially first son's) obligation to take care of his parent both physically and financially. Sending a parent to facilities or abandoning them instead of living together was regarded as extremely abusive. Other examples of extreme elder abuse were "to avoid obligation for supporting the elder parent" (student, 19); "not to visit the parents intentionally at their birthday" (male, 38); and "to point out and talk about the parent's faults directly" (housewife, 48). As examples of mild abuse, the following behaviors were mentioned; "not to please the parents and not to make them feel comfortable" (housewife, 33), "adult children not getting along with siblings" (housewife, 50), and "a conflict of opinion due to a generational gap" (30-year-old company employee).

MALTREATMENT IN OTHER FAMILY RELATIONSHIPS

The only other potentially abusive family relationship of interest in the medical and social news is between mothers-in-law and daughters-in-law (e.g., Choi, n.d.). In our survey, in-law was the most frequently mentioned "other" abusive relationship. Examples of abuse were given from mother-in-law toward daughter-in-law, from daughter-in-law toward mother-in-law, from granddaughter-in-law toward grandmother-in-law, between sisters-in-law, and between brother's wives. In addition, abuse of adult children by elderly parents, of grandchildren by grandparents, and uncle and nephew/niece relationships were mentioned.

A concern with daughter-in-law abuse is much more characteristic of Korean than of Western countries. In our sample, the most frequently mentioned example of in-law abuse was a "disrespectful attitude from parents-in-law." Although the practice is now changing, for a long time Korean first-born sons brought their wives into their parental home where they would all live together. According to traditional norms, the son and daughter-in-law were expected to respect and be responsible for the son's parents, which is why Koreans often prefer sons to daughters. While having two generations in one household was common, it also resulted in many conflicts, especially between mother-in-law and daughter-in-law. Parents-in-law usually have more power in the home than daughters-in-law; sometimes that power differential led to abusive behavior against the daughter-in-law. The traditional authority of the husband's family due to patriarchal society enabled the son's mother to wield enormous power.

With respect to abuse from the mother-in-law toward the daughter-in-law, emotional abuse was most frequently mentioned at all levels of abuse in our survey. Consider the following responses: A 46-year-old saleswoman defined extreme abuse as "That a mother-in-law coerces the daughter-in-law with the authority of a mother-in-law, not trying to understand the daughter-in-law's stand." She defined as moderate abuse "That a mother-in-law compares a daughter-in-law with other daughters-in-law and discriminates against her with the son." A 43-year-old male said "A mother-in-law meddling in the whole life of her son's couple and making them divorce" was extreme abuse. A 47-year-old housewife's example of moderate abuse was "a mother-in-law incites her son to punish his wife." A 19-year-old student said "when a son married a girl whom parents object, mother-in-law's denial of her existence is very abusive."

Even though the large family system is ending and a nuclear family is now common in Korean culture, women still desire to have a son in order to get the right to a voice. Although women have great power as mothers, men usually have the advantage of social success. So, under the new capitalistic patriarchy, women want to achieve their ideals by having children who can succeed socially (Cho-Han, 1998). Therefore, they are reluctant to relinquish their power as a mother even when their son gets married.

INTERVENTION AND PREVENTION

Centers for consultation and reporting of child abuse have been in operation in Korea since 1995, and a 24-hour hotline system was established in 2000. The Health and Welfare Committee authorized 17 child welfare centers in conjunction with the operation of the Act for Child Welfare. A nongovernmental organization, the Women's Hotline, started counseling for battered wives in the early 1980s and now has 23 branches around the country providing phone or internet counseling and shelters. Different Women's Hotline branches provide somewhat different definitions of domestic violence, indicating that there is no single definition. Nevertheless, because their definitions include sexual violence as a subtype, these organizations have achieved more advanced definitions than can be found in the national legislation. Most typically, the hotline definitions identify four types of domestic violence; physical, psychological/emotional or mental, sexual, and economical. For example, the Pusan Women's Hotline (2001) defines domestic violence as "a planned, intended, and repeated use of physical force and mental abuse that results in a serious physical and mental injury and pain by one of family members on the other family members."

However, even though domestic violence is generally defined as violence between spouses, parents and children, or siblings, counseling settings seem to focus primarily on husband-to-wife abuse. Only one man's hotline ("go manline") has been operating since 1995, even though a number of cases of wife-to-husband violence have been reported.

CONCLUSION

In Korea, there has been substantial discussion on whether it is desirable for society to intervene in family violence. However, since the Act on the Punishment of Domestic Violence was put into operation in 1998, family violence has been acknowledged as a social problem. Domestic violence in Korea can be explained by Confucian ideology and tolerance of corporal punishment, as well as by the collectivist value of ingroup loyalty and saving face. An important Confucian principle says "cultivate one's morality first, rule the family second, govern a country third and then make all the world peaceful (*Soo-Shin Je-Ga Chi-Gook Pyoung-Chun-Ha*)." It means that improving one's virtue and managing a household take precedence over governing the universe. Although Confucian ideology emphasizes "to cultivate one's morality," abusers seem to pay more attention to "to rule the family," sometimes encouraged by the concept of the headships of a family status legitimized in civil laws. They use violence toward the spouse and children as a means of solving family disputes and keeping order. According to a recent survey, 20% of Koreans regard the Confucian concept of "predominance of men over women" as a cause of domestic violence ("Korean marriage and divorce," 2000). In our cross-cultural survey, patriarchal thinking and authority based on Confucian ideology were often identified as the cause of violence in all types of family violence (conjugal, sibling, and elder), as well as in the definition of abuse.

From an ecological perspective, Korean culture is especially permissive to parental punishment of children—a practice deeply rooted in patriarchal family norms in which the view that children belong to their father is dominant. With regard to child abuse, most Koreans do not regard corporal punishment as physical abuse. Moreover, the Constitutional Court of Korea legitimized corporal punishment by teachers for educational purposes (Ham, 2000), following a heated debate on the pros and cons of corporal punishment.

According to a special edition on Korean thoughts by a monthly magazine (e.g., *The Monthly Chosun*, 2000), 14.8% of Koreans think it is okay for a husband to batter his wife and 65.4% think that it is okay for parents to batter their children. Of adolescents who have been battered, 83% think it was caused by their own wrongdoing. However, social recognition of the problems of battered women, sexually abused children, and maltreated elders is increasing in Korean culture, and social devices to prevent violence are under discussion.

To prevent violence within the family, implicit theories of the family need to go beyond traditional morality to a valuing of the fundamental security of human rights for everyone, including women, adolescents, children, and the elderly in families. Family violence does not end at one generation but reproduces a violent society, transmitting "abuser minds" or a "slavery consciousness obedient to violence" to children (Commission on Youth Protection, 1998). Family violence, social violence, and systematic violence have to be exterminated to proceed to a mature society based on communication and persuasion among members.

Family violence cannot be corrected by the effort of one person or one law. Counseling centers, protection facilities, medical institutions, and legal, social and systematic devices should coordinate their efforts to increase understanding of family maltreatment. Further, systematic cooperation structure among these institutions should be directed at the early detection of family violence and efforts to prevent it.

REFERENCES

Academy of Korean Studies. (n.d.). *Common sense on traditional culture.* Available: http://www. ask.ac.kr/trad/trad_hp_view.asp?id=33

Ahn, H. N. (1994). Cultural diversity and the definition of child abuse. In R. Barth, J. D. Berrick, & N. Gillbert (Eds.), *Child Welfare Research Review* (Vol. 1, pp. 28–55). New York: Columbia University Press.

Ahn, Y. J. (2000, December 4). Child abuse hotline 1391. *The Daily Hangyoreh* [online]. Available: http://www.hani.co.kr/section-005000000/2000/005000000200010042157035.html

Cha, K. T. (2002, February 13). Ninety percent of parents want their children to graduate from college. *The Daily Hankyereh* [online]. Available: http://www.hani.co.kr/section-005100006/2002/02/005100006200202131826001.html

Cho-Han, H. J. (1998). *Introspective modernism and feminism.* Seoul: Another culture.

Choi, J. S. (1983). *Study of a history of Korean family system.* Seoul: Iljisa.

Choi, Y. (n.d.). *Family violence.* Available from: Chonnam National University, Child and Adolescent Psychiatric Clinic Web site: http://childpsy.webpd.co.kr/famvio.htm

Chun, J. S. (2000, June 22). Family violence, in Taegu, increased by 71.3% over the previous. *The Daily Sekey* [online]. Available: yearhttp://search.sgt.co.kr/fbin/result.fcgi?search=%B0%A1%C1%A4%C6%F8%B7%C2&dataid=200006231414000083.

Commission on Youth Protection. (1998). *Family violence and adolescent.* Seoul, Korea.

Doe, S. S. (2000). Cultural factors in child maltreatment and domestic violence in Korea. *Children and Youth Services Review, 22,* 231–236.

Ewha Women's Studies. (n.d.). *Formation of patriarchical family* [online]. Available: http://root. re.kr/root/ewha-5.htm

Ham, Y. H. (2000, January 28). Corporal punishment for educational purpose is legitimate according to the Constitutional Court of Korea. *The Daily Kukmin* [online]. Available: http://www.kukminilbo.co.kr/html/kmview/2000/0128/20000128030601631131300.html

Han, I. S. (1998). Domestic violence acts in Korea: Legal construction and policy orientation. *Law, 39* [Electronic version]. Seoul: Seoul National University.

Han, K. H. (1998). *Violence for generations within the family and adolescents.* Seoul, Korea: The Commission on Youth Protection.

Hong, K. E. (1999). *The national survey of child abuse and outcome of abuse* (HMP-99-P-0011). Seoul, Korea: Health and Welfare Committee.

Increased prevalence of family violence following the legislation on domestic violence. (n.d.). *The Weekly Puchon News, 307* [online]. Available: http://www.puchonnews.co.kr/main_news/main307_4.htm

Jang, M., You, H., Malley-Morrison, K., & Mills, R. (1999). Recollections of parental acceptance and control and perceptions of elder abuse: Korean and American college students. *Gerontology and Geriatrics Education, 19,* 67–81.

Kang, M. K. (2000). *Community's recognition and prevention of child abuse* [online]. Available: http://user.chollian.net/~enoch65/s-data/gnikang.html

Kim, K., & Ko, B. (1990). An incidence survey of battered children in two elementary schools of Seoul. *Child Abuse and Neglect, 14,* 273–276.

Kim, S. K., & Cho, A. J. (1998a). The condition and problem of violence toward children in Korean family. In *Seminar by Korean Association for Protecting Children: Vol. 19. On Child Maltreatment within a Family* (pp. 3–34). Seoul, Korea: Korean Association for Protecting Children.

Kim, S. K., & Cho, A. J. (1998b). *The conceptual definition and the actual state of family violence in Korea* (Report 98-04). Seoul, Korea: Institute for Heath and Social Affairs.

Kim, S. Y. (2000). A reiteration of the abolition of the systems of the headship of a family [Electronic version]. *Law, 49.* Pusan: Pusan University.

Korea Legal Aid Center for Family Relations. (2000). *The problems of modern Korean family shown by statistic: Statistical data of counseling by Korea Legal Aid Center For Family Relations during 43 years (1956–1999).* Seoul, Korea: Author.

Korean Institute for Health and Social Affairs. (1998). *The study of the definition establishment and the actual condition of family violence in Korea* [online]. Available: http://www.kihasa.re.kr/data/rm98-04.htm

Korean Institute of Criminology. (1995). *A study on crime and crime damage by the older people.* Seoul, Korea: Author.

Korean marriage and divorce. (2000, January). *The Monthly Chosun* [online]. Available: http://monthly.chosun.com/html/199912/199912310048_7.html

Korean Society for Study of Elder Abuse. (n.d.). *Types of elder abuse* [online]. Available: http://elderabuse.or.kr/index/pattern.htm

Lee, H. J. (1990). Establishment and transformation of Korean patriarchy. In Society for the Study of Korean Women's Society (Ed.), *Korean family theory* (pp. 1–34). Seoul: Kkachi.

Lee, H. S. (n.d.). Dangerous conditions of wife rape. NEWS+. In *The Daily Donga, 160.* Available: http://www.donga.com/doc/magazine/news_plus/news160/np160gg010.html

Lee, K. H. (1990). *An observational study of sibling interaction in preschool children.* Unpublished doctoral dissertation, Yonsei University, Seoul, Korea.

Lee, K. I. (1999, April 13). Husband mistreated by wife: Wife battered by husband. *The Weekly Hankook* [online]. Available: http://hk.co.kr/whan/last/990422/615522.htm

Malley-Morrison, K., You, H., & Mills, R. (2000). Young adult attachment style and perception of elder abuse: A cross-cultural study. *Journal of Cross-Cultural Gerontology, 15,* 163–184.

Mo, S. H. (1999). The elderly and family. In the Center for Future Human Resource (Ed.), *Life of Korean elderly: Diagnoses and prospects* (pp. 83–122). Seoul: Tree of thought.

Park, J. W. (n.d.). *Current condition of child maltreatment* [online]. Available: http://hone.opentown.net/~yurik/abuse.htm

Pusan Women's Hotline. (2001). *The concept of family violence* [online]. Available: http://www.pwhl.or.kr/

Seoul Woman's Hotline. (2001). *Statistical analyses of counseling in 2000* [online]. Available: http://hotline.jinbi.net/infostatistics.html

Society for the Study of Korean Women's Society. (2001). *Family and Korean society* (rev. ed.). Seoul: Kyungmoonsa.

Yang, J. J., & Ahn, J. H. (1996). *The actual condition of family violence expressed through the Korean Legal Aid Center For Family Relations*. Seoul, Korea: Korea Legal Aid Center for Family Relations.

18

Taiwan

Huei-Ping Liu

CAPSULE

Taiwanese society has been going through a huge transition in the past 50 years. Women are still the main victims of marital violence, and many of their children are also maltreated. Some women try to keep their marriage and family together, either believing it is their destiny or better for their children; others have learned how to look for help. Many Taiwanese parents believe they have the right to use corporal discipline on their children, and consider physical punishment an effective way of teaching children to "behave"—which means not only "to have good manners" but also "to reach the parents' expectations" (especially to have high academic achievement). Taiwanese think taking care of elderly parents is the adults' responsibility, so a certain percentage of elderly parents live with their children's families. Sending elders to a nursing home is considered very similar to abandoning them. Conflict between the generations has finally become a common social phenomenon. Siblings might have conflicts, but most Taiwanese do not consider these problems as abuse within families. Other issues that can cause stress in Taiwanese families include culture shock for the wives from other southeast countries, conflicts between daughters-in-law and mothers-in-law, and the responsibility of the eldest son.

THE TAIWAN SAMPLE

There were 90 Taiwanese respondents to our survey—56 females and 34 males, from 16 to 60 years old, with an average age of 28 years. Thirteen percent of the sample identified their ethnicity as Taiwanese, 40% as Yellow or Asian, and 38% as Chinese or Han. (The word "Han," according to Dictio-nary.com, means "A member of the principal ethnic group of China, con-stituting about 93% of the population, especially as distinguished from Manchus, Mongols, Huis, and other minority nationalities.) Half of our par-ticipants said they have no religion; however, most Taiwanese pray and of-fer sacrifices to ancestors, which is not considered a religion but fulfillment of the responsibility to "take care of the family members in another world." About 6% of the sample was Taoist or Buddhist.

Thirty-six respondents (40% of the sample) said they (or someone they know) have had experiences of abuse. Ten respondents mentioned wife or husband abuse, and 13 mentioned child abuse. Twenty-three reported ex-periences of physical abuse, 9 mentioned verbal/mental abuse, 2 talked about parental abandonment, and 3 talked of a parent having an extramar-ital relationship.

Taiwanese Participants' Perspectives on Abuse

In their definitions of abuse within families, 90% of our participants men-tioned physical abuse, 60% mentioned mental abuse, and only 7% and 4% mentioned material abuse and neglect. When asked to give examples of ex-treme abuse, many respondents listed rather violent forms of physical ag-gression such as "killing" or "disabling" family members. Examples in-cluded "hurting them until bleeding—e.g., venting one's anger on family members while drunk" (male, 36 years old); "Life-threatening attacks on other's bodies" (male, 17); "Hurting the other's body until the victim needs medical care—e.g., while quarreling, the husband hits the wife until she gets hurt (including external and internal injury) or slashes the wife with a knife until she gets injured or killed" (female, 21); "using violence, resulting in death—e.g., father kills son, son kills father" (female, 28); "not respecting other as human being. Causing serious mental or physical injuries not easy to recover from in a short time. For example, violence causing injury, words that handicap children's social capability" (male, 32); and "making the vic-tim feel physically and mentally exhausted, and unable to stand. Other peo-ple would feel like killing the abuser" (female, 21).

Examples of extreme abuse also showed concern with the psychologi-cal effects of abuse; "Hurting physically and mentally—e.g., the parents use violence against to the child and cause negative mental effects in his mind" (female, 23); "mental injury, especially which would affect the individual's behavior. Insulting verbally. Financially control. Imprisoning" (male, 24). The few participants who mentioned "sexual aggression" clas-sified it as extreme abuse.

About moderate abuse, many participants mentioned types of mental aggression such as taking control of the victim's life and setting restrictions on the victim's acts—for example, "not allowing others to leave home, and not allowing them to contact other people" (female, 52); "making people feel indelible fear. For example, locking child alone in the bathroom, closet, or cage" (female, 23); "tying the victim and hitting him. Not letting the victim have any chance to escape—e.g., hitting because of tiny mistakes. Not allowing to leave home" (female, 19).

Taiwanese implicit theories concerning abuse showed considerable recognition of the psychological effects of abuse: "Mental abuse causes mental hurts and makes the victim feel not being respected, such as belittling victim" (female, 20). Finally, for mild abuse, most participants mentioned verbal aggression or light physical aggression such as "mocking," "insulting," "hitting the palm," or "quarrelling." However, some of the examples of "mild" abuse could be considered quite severe—"Seldom giving the victim three meals a day. Cruelly beating the victim once in a while—locking the kid in a cage when he is not obedient" (female, 19); "Do not provide the victim enough essential things and take control of the victim's life. For example, do not provide enough food and clothes. Do not let the victim have enough sleep. Not allow the victim to go out" (male, 20).

THE TAIWAN MACROSYSTEM

Socioeconomic Contexts

In the past 50 years, Taiwan has changed rapidly from an agricultural to an industrial society. In 1952, less than 17% of the population had a junior high school education, and only 8% had gone to high school (including 3-year commercial high schools). By the end of 2000, 25% of the population over 15 years had a bachelors degree or higher (2000 Population and Housing Census, 2002). Moreover, education is no longer restricted to men, and the relative educational status of men and women has become quite similar. More and more wives have jobs. In 1998, 42% of Taiwanese families had two incomes, although in more than 90% of these families, the husband's salary was still the main financial source for the family, and wives still did most of the housework. Divorce is legal, but most Taiwanese think that divorced individuals have some serious weakness in their personality that keeps them from getting along with their spouse. Moreover, divorced people are considered not only to be losers in their family life, but also as lacking skill for handling their careers. Compared to Western countries, the divorce rate in Taiwan is quite low: In 2000, only 2.9% of the population over 15 was divorced (2000 Population and Housing Census, 2002).

Family Structure

Family size in Taiwan has decreased from 5.7 people in 1956 to 3.3 in 2000 (Summary of Population and Housing Censuses from 1956 to 2000, n.d.). At the end of 2000, there were 374,000 single-parent families (about 5.8% of all Taiwanese families), and 70.5% of these were composed of the mother and her child(ren). The ratio of marriages arranged by parents dramatically decreased from 62% in the late 1950s to 13% in the early 1980s (Lin, 1994). About 56% of the marriages from 1980 to 1984 were decided by the adult children, although they typically asked for their parents' approval before marriage. Traditionally, a married woman is considered as becoming a member of her husband's family, and most Taiwanese consider marriage a lifetime companionship.

Children's Status

Taiwanese parents strongly value the parent–child relationship and expect children to be respectful and obedient. Taiwanese parents are very concerned with their children's academic achievement, and consider helping children to get high academic achievement a way to love them. When children talk back to their parents or show lack of academic success or effort (including not finishing their homework), parents typically respond with verbal aggression (Chou, 2001).

If there is more than one child in a family, the one with higher scores in school usually has higher status and causes pressure on the other children. Sons usually have higher status than daughters because they will carry on the family name; they are expected to have higher achievement than daughters. The eldest son usually has the highest status among the children, is expected to have the highest achievement, and is pressured to be a perfect role model.

Among the 2,617,000 parents who have children 6 to 12 years old in Taiwan, mothers are still the main caregivers. Nearly all adults under 65 years old think having a child is a necessary part of marriage, but their reasons vary (DGBAS, 1999). About 37% want the child's companionship, 22% want "their own family," 17% want a child to carry on the family name, and 5% want an adult child to take care of them when they are old.

Status of Women

Traditionally, unmarried women are expected to be obedient to their parents, and married women are expected to be obedient to their husbands and their husbands' families. From 1955 to 1959, only 30% of women worked before they got married (Lin, 1994). This ratio increased to 92% in the early 1980s. Employment might seem to provide more opportunities for young women to leave their families and become independent; however, about

75% of unmarried working women gave most of their pay to their parents throughout the period from 1955 to 1984.

In the 1950s and before, Taiwanese women did not have the right to choose their marital partner. About two-thirds of the women who married during the 1950s met their husbands through their parents, relatives, or matchmakers. That ratio has decreased dramatically, and by 1984, 64% of women met their husband in their working place, through friends, and in other places. Nowadays, many Taiwanese women still consider marriage as a must in their lives. In 1990, 96% of women from the 45- to 49-year-old age range were married (Lin, 1994). "To be a good mother and good wife" is still some females' life goal. People who believe in traditional values think females should devote their lives to helping their husband and family. It is not clear how many Taiwanese still hold such traditional values, but one sample of abused wives were very traditional and felt they must devote their lives to their families (G. Chen, 2001).

Elders' Status

It is a common belief in Taiwan that all adult children should care financially for elderly family members and visit them often. The eldest adult son and his family are expected to live with his elderly parents, and the eldest daughter-in-law is expected to be the main caregiver of the elders. It is a moral principle to respect elders, but most elders need their adult children to take care of them. According to the Elder's Welfare Law, promulgated in 1980 and revised as recently as 2002 (Elder's Welfare Law, n.d.), adults are obligated to support their elderly (over 65 years old) parents.

At the end of September 2002, there were 2,013,147 people over 65 in Taiwan (Department of Social Affairs, Ministry of Interior, n.d.), 9% of the total Taiwanese population. According to the Summary of the 1998 Social Development Census (DGBAS, 1999), 33% of parents expect to live with their married sons, and 43% expect their adult sons will financially support them. Only 13% of parents do not want to live with their married sons in the future. In 2000, only 58% of the elders lived with their adult children; 17% lived with their spouse, and 16% lived alone. Over half of the elders were financially supported by their adult children and more than a quarter of them got their living expenses from their own or their spouse's savings or by selling their property.

FAMILY VIOLENCE

In Taiwan, family violence was traditionally thought to be a private matter, not a public issue. There were no laws addressing the problem until the Domestic Violence Prevention Law went into effect in 1998. According to this law, family violence is "the illegal and physical/mental aggression between family members." The Taiwanese government tries to provide complete protection for victims of domestic violence and to integrate all the resources, such as judicial, police, medical, educational, and volunteer service or organizations. The official governmental department with the responsibility of preventing family violence is the Domestic Violence Prevention Committee of the Ministry of Interior, set up in 1999.

In 1999, about one person died of family violence every 3 days in Taiwan, and 26,215 family violence cases were reported to the Committee from July 1999 to July 2000. There were also 79,139 phone calls about family violence to the Committee. From January to August 2001, 10,214 family cases were reported to police offices in Taiwan. Thus, family violence is not just an uncommon news story; however, some Taiwanese still have the bias that family violence happens only in lower class families. Batterers are usually thought of as alcoholics, losers, aggressive to everyone, beset with psychological problems, and unable to control their own aggression. Some victims do not look for help. They just hope the perpetrators will stop hurting them, and may even think violence is acceptable for relieving the batterer's pressures.

Corporal Punishment

Taiwanese generally believe that parents should have the right to discipline their children as they think best. Most of the parents who participated in the 1991 Social Development Census approved of teachers physically punishing their children (Lai, 1999). In 1995, Lin and Wang found that 73% of their interviewees considered it unreasonable to forbid parents to use physical punishment (Lai, 1999). These participants claimed moderate physical punishment at the right moment is good for a young child, and physical punishment by parents and teachers is proper. They believed physical punishment is educative, useful for stopping bad behavior, helpful in encouraging good behavior, and valuable in producing effects immediately. According to the Summary of the 1998 Social Development Census (DGBAS, 1999), 81% of parents with a child between 6 and 12 years old would admonish their children for doing something wrong, and 68% would scold them. About 30% of the parents would hit the children, order them to stand in the corner, and not allow them to do something they like to do. The more educated parents used less physical discipline.

Child Abuse

According to the Frontier Foundation (2002), child abuse and neglect refer to behaviors of parents, guardians, or caregivers that physically or mentally hurt a child under 12 years old or a teenager (12 to 18 years old).

Types of abuse include physical abuse, sexual abuse, mental abuse, and neglect. Neglect takes two forms: not providing necessary care to the child and providing improper things or opportunities to the child (e.g., using the child to commit crimes). Sexual abuse includes physical and oral harassment, providing pornography, and forcing the child to be a prostitute. Mental abuse includes any behavior hurting the child's mental development.

Child maltreatment is not uncommon in Taiwan. From 1990 to 1996, 5,151 child abuse cases were reported to Taiwan's Chinese Children's Fund (CCF; Huang & Wang, 1998). More than 56% of the victims' parents had marital problems, and vented their anger on their children or neglected them; 38% of the batterers lacked knowledge about childrearing; 11% had unrealistic expectations of their children. According to the Department of Social Affairs (n.d.), reported cases of child abuse increased from 1,235 in 1993 to over 4,249 in 1999. In 1998, 1,350 child sexual abuse cases (under 18-years-old) were reported to the police (Chen, 2000)—and many more cases went unreported because of fear of scandal. A 1999 survey of 5,353 children protected by the Child and Youth Protection Center revealed that about half had been physically abused, about 36% neglected, and about 8% abandoned. According to the Children's Bureau (n.d.), 3,933 persons were reported for abusing a total of 3,933 children (2,389 males and 1,544 females) in 2000. Most of the batterers were the victims' parents (1,964 males and 1,211 females).

According to Chi (1999), the estimated number of children living in maritally violent families is between 10,000 and 40,000. Whether these children are abused directly or not, witnessing their parents' marital violence is likely to have negative effects. Lin (2000) cited two studies in Kaohsiung and found that many families with an abused spouse also reported child abuse. Children might be abused because they tried to protect the victimized parent, or because the batterers abused them to control the spouse. Some victims of spousal abuse might also become the batterers of their children—sometimes disciplining their children in front of the batterer, with the goal of saving the children from being more severely battered and injured by the batterer. As a result, many social workers in Taiwan consider child abuse an extension of spouse abuse.

Taiwan Participants' Judgments Concerning Child Abuse

In giving examples of child abuse, approximately 80% of our sample emphasized physical aggression, although more than 50% also gave examples of verbal, emotional, and mental abuse. Among the examples of extreme abuse were "beating a child so badly that scars are left all over his body" (female, 52), "spanking a cranky child with a stick until the child bleeds" (female, 23), "burning a child's hand on the stove because the child stole something" (female, 21), and "cruel beating of the child, for example, tying the child's hands, hanging him on the ceiling, and beating him, when the parents feel angry or depressed. Making the child fearful—putting the child in a bag and taking the bag to the beach, threatening to throw him into the sea. Raping the child" (female, 49). Many of these examples are tied to a child's failing to perform adequately in school or showing disrespect. Another example of extreme child abuse was "an alcoholic mother forcing her daughter (under 18) to prostitute to pay off the mother's debts" (female, 48).

Rather severe behaviors were also listed as examples of moderate abuse—for example, "slapping children 5 times a day" (female, 21), "locking a child in a dark room because the child cried and clamored" (female, 52), "hitting the child because of conflict with a spouse" (female, 26), "yelling, scolding and cruelly beating a kid" (male, 52)—and even of mild abuse (e.g., "hitting or not feeding the kid when he gets bad grades" (female, 19), or "threatening to sell the child if he doesn't listen" (female, 28). At every level of abuse, there is an emphasis on punishing children for failure to live up to parental expectations for academic success.

Woman Abuse

According to the Frontier Foundation's (1999) definition, wife abuse includes physical abuse (with or without a weapon) causing harm or death, sexual abuse, and psychological abuse. Sexual abuse includes forcing the victim to have sex and hurting the victims' reproductive organs. Psychological abuse includes threatening, mental abuse (e.g., humiliating the victim), and controlling the victim's life (e.g., forbidding the victim to have contact with friends). By this definition, someone who controls the spouse's life, hurts the spouse's confidence, and isolates the spouse from society is a batterer.

In the Women's Living Conditions in Taiwan Survey for the Year 1998 (Department of Statistics, 1999), women discussed personal experience with abuse. Nearly 4% said they had encountered family violence, and 3.3% admitted their husbands had violated them. About 3% said family violence is the main problem in their marriages. According to Lee (2001), 18% of married women in Taiwan have been violated by their husbands. The Family Violence and Sexual Violation Prevention Center gets an average of more than 9,000 family violence cases reported each year, and 77% of these are cases of marital violence. The marital violence hotline of Women Rescue Foundation received more than 700 phone calls in 2½ months in 1997. In a 1995 Modern Women's Foundation survey of 7,000 women, 12% admitted being hit by their husbands (Huang, 2000). In 1998, 24% of the women seeking help from the Kaohsiung Lifeline Association had marital violence problems (Huang, 2000). A survey by Feng in 1992 (as cited in Ya, 2001) indicated that 35% of 1,310 participants had been abused by their husband. According to Chi (1999), estimates of wife abuse cases range from 30,000 to 70,000.

According to statistics from the Police Department in Kaohsiung County, 58 family violence cases were reported from January to July 1997. Twenty of the wives who were physically injured did not want to sue their abusers because the abusers were their husbands. These wives considered family violence to be private, and did not want to make it public. Y. Chen (2001) suggested there are many more victims who view their abuse as a private matter and just want to persevere, facing the predicament alone. Even if their husband's and their own family do not blame them for the marital problems, they may feel it is too shameful to tell others their husband is an abuser. Y. Chen's interviews with 10 abused wives revealed that their primary reason for not leaving their husbands was concern for their children. They worried their husband might hit the children if they left, or assumed a two-parent home is better for children than a single-parent one, despite the violence. One woman said "I just do not want my family to be broken."

Despite recent efforts to combat domestic violence, the Women's Living Conditions in Taiwan Survey for the Year 1998 revealed that more than half of the women interviewed were not satisfied with or did not know about family violence prevention services. About 50% of the women thought government should provide more financial aid and employment training for abused women, and 34% believed the government should provide more services, such as prevention for sexual assaults.

Wives From Southeast Asia

Some Taiwanese men join "marriage tour groups" to Southeast Asia (including Vietnam, Indonesia, Thailand, and the Philippines) to buy a bride by giving her family money. Most of these men are of lower socioeconomic status, and dissatisfied with Taiwanese women unwilling to take on a subservient role. Their aim is not love, but a wife to bear their children, take care of their lives, assist their career, and serve their parents. Most of these wives do not speak Mandarin or Taiwanese, and can have serious problems getting used to life in Taiwan. Some are abused by their husbands, but do not know how to seek help. There are no official statistics on the seriousness of the problem, but at the end of 2002, there were 85,194 foreign females married to Taiwanese males and living in Taiwan (Ju, 2003). Over half were from Vietnam and Indonesia.

Taiwan Participants' Perspectives on Wife Abuse

Sixty-two participants mentioned physical abuse in their examples of extreme wife abuse and 53 listed verbal/emotional/mental abuse in examples of mild wife abuse. Severe abuse included "hitting and causing permanent injury" (female, 22), "beating the wife and causing her physical disability or death" (male, 24), and "causing injury. The victim might die" (female, 22). Efforts to control the wife were also seen as extremely abusive; "compel the wife to engage in prostitution. Imprison the wife" (male, 23), "Asking wife for sex all the time" (female, 22).

Several strong themes emerged, cutting across levels of severity of abuse—money, sex, alcohol, and power. Examples of abusive behavior related to money included a "husband who does not provide enough money for his family." Other examples of both severe and moderate abuse were: "Do not have a legal job. Do not financially support the family. Relying on the wife to support the family financially and spending the money only drinking, prostituting, and gambling" (male, 24; severe abuse); "Hitting when losing at gambling. Punching and kicking when the wife does not give him money" (female, 19; moderate abuse). With regard to sex, some responses focused on a presumed extramarital relationship—"Shaving the wife's head to make her embarrassed to go out because the husband suspects the wife has an extramarital relationship" (female, 49). Some other examples were: "Asking for sex whatever the wife agrees or not" (female, 52); "Do not have sex with his wife" (male, 24); and "having an extramarital relationship" (female, 52). The role of alcohol was listed in several examples of both severe and moderate abuse—"Alcoholism. Using violence after drinking" (male, 23; severe abuse), and "Hitting the wife and the kids when drunk" (female, 49; moderate). Responses related to the man's exercise of power in the relationship included "Blaming the child's mistake on his wife" (female, 21); "Believing in male chauvinism deeply" (female, 23); "Taking control of the wife's life" (female, 34); "Do not allow the wife to wear and eat whatever the husband does not want her to wear or eat. The wife needs to wait for the husband's instructions" (male, 24).

Husband Abuse

According to Teng (2000), about one husband in every five couples beat his wife in 1998. From June 24, 1999 to April 30, 2000, 97% of the 960 victims of marital abuse looking for help in Taipei were female (Teng, 2000). There were 17,316 family violence cases reported to the police in 2002, but less than 10% of the victims were male (Lin, 2003). Husband abuse is pretty rare, and all Taiwanese literature on spouse abuse talks about wife abuse. Because many Taiwanese consider "abuse" as "being physically hurt," people do not consider the wife's behavior as abuse unless the husband is physically injured. Nevertheless, many husbands who beat their wives consider themselves as the victim in their marriage. They view their wives as disrespecting them, not taking care of the family, and not listening to them. Sometimes they believe they can earn their wives' respect by hitting them.

Taiwan Participants' Perspectives on Husband Abuse

Compared to their examples of wife abuse, our participants tended to put much greater emphasis on verbal/emotional/mental abuse in their examples of husband abuse. For instance, some participants considered "wasting money" as abusive to a husband. Other participants mentioned "not cooking for the husband" or "not doing the housework" as abusive. Examples of extreme husband abuse sometimes included physical aggression, such as "beating her husband while drunk" (female, 19) and "throwing tableware or kitchenware at the husband while quarreling" (female, 52); emotional hurt such as "threatening her husband by suicide" (female, 23), and "showing improper behavior in the husband's social situation and bringing shame to the husband. Talking about the husband's shortcomings in the husband's social situation to humiliate the husband. Having higher salary or achievement than her husband and not acting humbly" (female, 22); and neglect of the husbands' family, such as "Do not take care of the husband's parents" (female, 36). Other examples of extreme husband abuse included "having an extramarital relationship" (female, 22); "not having children to carry on the husband's family name" (female, 21); and "Having the idea that the husband must earn a lot of money" (male, 17).

About half of our participants described emotional/verbal/mental abuse situations as examples of moderate husband abuse—again, often citing circumstances related to sex, money, or status. These examples included "suspecting her husband of having an extramarital relationship, and asking others to chase him" (female, 26); "Refusing to have sex with her husband. Mocking or belittling the husband's sexual ability. Pretending to be satisfied or having orgasm, but the husband notices her pretending. Complaining the husband's salary is too little. Comparing her husband with another husband" (male, 24); "When the husband does not come back home at night, the wife decides to sleep in separate room" (female, 28); "Leaving home for several days when the husband said something not satisfying to her" (female, 52); "Telling the husband 'you are hopeless' " (female, 22). Examples of mild abuse had similar themes, plus conflict between the wife and the husband's family, such as "When the husband follows his parents' or brothers' opinion, she treats her husband carelessly, ignores her husband, or refuses to have sex with him" (female, 52); "Do not do housework. Do not take care of the child. Do not listen to the parents-in-law" (male, 24).

In the examples of wife abuse compared to husband abuse, some interesting patterns emerged. Younger and single participants often gave identical or similar answers to the two sets of questions. For example, a 21-year-old female gave "hitting" as an example of both forms of extreme spousal abuse, "imprisoning the spouse" for both forms of moderate abuse, and, "mocking the spouse" for both forms of mild abuse. By contrast, older or married participants tended to give different answers for wife abuse than for husband abuse. A 36-year-old female said, "Severely hurting his wife's body" was an extreme form of wife abuse and "Does not take care of the husband's parents" was an extreme form of husband abuse. Two participants said extreme wife abuse was "to rape the wife" or "forcing the wife to have sex with him" whereas three participants mentioned that "refusing to have sex with the husband" was a form of husband abuse.

Elder Abuse

Tsai (1996) classified elder abuse into five forms: (1) physical abuse, including attacking, arresting, sexual abuse, and making the elders starve; (2) mental abuse, including name calling, insulting, and frightening; (3) material abuse—such as, not providing enough necessities for the elders (4) financial abuse—such as, not providing enough financial support and stealing the elder's property; and (5) neglect, including ignoring the elder's needs, refusing to provide medical care (medical abuse), and not taking care of them.

In the traditional patriarchal Taiwanese family, elderly parents are supposed to be the respected advisors of all other family members. Thus, when elder abuse happens, it is hard for victims to admit it. Some elders might blame themselves for not educating their adult children well when the children were young, and consider being abused as evidence of their failure to be good parents. These elders might think being abused is their deserved fate, and choose to bear it. Other abused elders might be too weak physically and mentally to look for help. Still others love their batterers and think bringing their abuse to public attention will ruin their children's honor. Finally, elder abuse does not get as much attention from the public as spouse and child abuse because people do not think it is as common.

There are few official statistics about elder abuse in Taiwan; however, the Old Foundation in Taipei has received more than 5,000 reports about elder abuse since 1995. Most Taiwanese literature on elder abuse appeals to the public to face up to the problem and teaches the medical profession to recognize the symptoms of abuse in elders.

Taiwan Participants' Perspectives on Elder Abuse

Compared to abuse within other family relationships, physical abuse was seldom mentioned and sexual abuse was never mentioned in examples of elder abuse. A typical example of elder abuse was "Any behavior that is not respectful to the elders is serious offense to the elders—for example, do not provide enough food to the elders. Scolding. Defrauding the elders' money and property" (male, 24). Moreover, many participants consider "asking the elders to do house work" and "setting restrictions on their lives" as extremely abusive. Forty-seven participants listed "abandon the parents" or "leave the elders in a nursing home" as severely or moderately abusive. A 36-year-old male said "Treating the elderly parents carelessly. Do not care about them sincerely but only give them food and shelter" is moderately abusive. Other answers include "hitting the elders while the adult is drunk" (female, 52); "leaving the elders at home alone" (female, 23); "refusing to work and asking the elders to support them" (female, 20); and "not having a child" (female, 22). Most participants talked about verbal/mental/emotional abuse and ignoring when asked to give an example of mild elder abuse—for example, "Insulting the elders while depressed. Yelling at the elders by abusive language such as 'why don't you die?' " (female, 23); "Having no patience. Being negligent of the elders' needs" (female, 26); and "The son insults his parents because they cannot financially support him" (female, 21).

Sibling Abuse

"Sibling abuse" is difficult to translate into Chinese. Taiwanese do not consider the conflict between siblings as abuse. Fights between siblings are usually seen as the parents' failure to educate their children properly. Most Taiwanese do not think it is a public issue, and there is no literature or statistics on sibling abuse in Taiwan.

Taiwan Participants' Perceptions on Sibling Abuse

Some participants talked about abuse between adult siblings when they answered these questions, and others talked about abuse between child siblings. The first group of participants mentioned financial abuse such as "fighting for inheritances" more than did the second group, and the second group usually talked about "bullying." Some of the participants in the second group considered conflicts of the parents and the parents' favorite child with the favorite's siblings to be abusive. More than 50 participants talked about physical abuse when giving examples of severe sibling abuse, and 22 mentioned physical injury or death. For example, a 23-year-old female said "To kill brothers for family property. To kidnap brothers" is extreme sibling abuse. Rape (male, 26) is also considered extreme abuse. In the moderate sibling abuse section, the examples included bullying, such as "One sibling asks others to do everything. If the results are not satisfactory, he would complain to the parents. Finally, the one who did the thing would be punished" (female, 19); sexual aggression (female, 52); mocking, such as "The older one mocks the younger sibling when they do something wrong" (female, 21); hostility, such as "Being crafty to siblings. Falsely incriminating the siblings" (female, 21); and material abuse such as "Taking financial advantage of siblings" (male, 32). Examples of mild sibling abuse included: "The older brother thinks the younger siblings are loved, so he hits or pinches the younger kids secretly" (male, 36) and "The dominant sibling bullies the subordinate sibling" (male, 42).

Conflicts Involving Grandparents

Just over 1% of Taiwanese families are composed of grandparents and their unmarried grandchildren. In these families, the relationships between grandparents and grandchildren are very similar to the relationships between parents and children. One of our participants talked about elder abuse by a grandchild: "A grandson locked his grandmother in the refrigerator because he thought she nags constantly" (female, 23; extreme abuse).

Some Taiwanese parents ask their parents to take care of their children. If both parents work, they might ask the grandparents to take care of the children in the daytime and take the children home after work. Some double-income parents might even ask the grandparents to take care of their children for weekdays, and take the children home or visit them on weekends. Some parents work in different cities, and lack job stability. They might ask their parents to raise the children when the children are young, then take the children home when they are old enough to take care of themselves (about the age to enter the elementary school). These children might be much closer to their grandparents than to their parents. One of our participants reported: "Someone raised by his grandmother was not close to his parents. The victim was stubborn and had conflicts with his parents. Finally, the mother would use violence toward to the victim when she was in a bad mood. She would even beat him with hangers, causing injuries. It's extreme abuse" (24-year-old male).

Responsibility of the Eldest Child

Most Taiwanese think the eldest child should be the model for younger siblings. Eldest children experience high expectations and pressure not only from their parents but also from other older relatives. The eldest child is asked to share the responsibility of educating the younger children, and may even be blamed for younger children's faults: "The parents ask the younger one to do some housework. But when the result does not satisfy the parents, they hit the older kid" (female, 19; mild abuse).

Conflicts Between the Wife and Her In-Laws

Su (2000) analyzed the Home and Family page of two popular newspapers from 1988 to 1999 and found that tension between a wife and her mother-in-law is very common. Taiwanese consider the wife as a member of her husband's family, so getting along with the husband's mother and sisters is very important to Taiwanese women, especially it they have to live with their husband's family. Some mothers-in-law and sisters-in-law consider the wife an outsider and may even bully her. Some mothers-in-law feel jealous of their daughters-in-law because their sons pay so much attention to them. In this situation, everyone considers herself as a victim. If the conflict continues, the husband may blame his wife for not being understanding toward his mother, and complain that his wife is generating family problems and bothering him (Teng, 2000).

INTERVENTION AND PREVENTION

The Children's Welfare Law was promulgated in 1973, and revised in 1993 in response to the 1989 U.N. Convention on the Rights of the Child (GIO, 2002). This law protects children from the time they are embryos until they are 12 years old. According to the law, health care professionals, daycare workers, teachers, and the police are required to report cases of child abuse. The Chinese Fund for Children and Families in Taiwan, started in 1987 to provide child protective services, helped 6,014 victims from 1989 to 1998; 43% were cases of neglect, 40% were cases of physical abuse, and 10.5% were cases of improper discipline.

The government has set up a women's protection hotline (GIO, 2002), a Women's Rights Promotion Committee, and a Sexual Violation Prevention program. City governments allocate specific budget items for women's services. Government-sponsored regional coalitions help generate public awareness about gender issues, and have provided medical, legal, psychological, educational, and vocational assistance. Many women's organizations established in the past 15 years seek to help women solve marital problems and to clarify liberalized roles for both men and women. According to the GIO (2002), in 1999, there were 43 comprehensive welfare centers offering counseling, vocational training, seminars, and other services to disadvantaged women. There were also 28 halfway houses and shelters for women with a maximum capacity of 545 in 1999.

There were 745 elder welfare organizations in Taiwan in 2000 (Department of Social Affairs, Ministry of Interior, n.d.). They not only help abused elders but also helped adult children find lost elderly parents. Furthermore, they endeavor to advance elders' welfare and enforce the Elder's Welfare Law (Old People Welfare Advance United Organization, n.d.).

CONCLUSION

After World War II, Taiwan was affected a lot by Western cultures, then speeded up its own modernization and democratization. The government has already found the importance of making the status of male and female equal, advancing children's and elder's welfare, and preventing family violence. Strides have been made on welfare, and domestic laws went into effect when most Taiwanese still thought of domestic violence as only a distant social issue. Sometimes, even when they know they are suffering, they cannot obtain protection for their welfare and rights because they are ignorant of the services provided by government and welfare organizations. The next step for Taiwan is extensive education of the public concerning family violence and abuse.

ACKNOWLEDGMENTS

Thanks to my parents and Li-Ying Hung for collecting data for this chapter.

REFERENCES

1990 Population and Housing Census. (n.d.). Available: http://www.dgbas.gov.tw/census~n/six/lue5/ht4601_2.htm

2000 Population and Housing Census. (2002, November). Available: http://www.dgbas.gov.tw/census~n/six/lue5/census_p&h.htm

Chen, C. (2000). *Knowledge, attitude and behaviors about child sexual abuse: A survey of elementary teachers and parents in Wanhwa, Taipei, Taiwan, R.O.C.* Taipei: Taiwan Normal University.

Chen, G. (2001). My choice: Three abused females' stories. *Family Violence and Sexual Violation Seminar*, 179–205.

Chen, Y. (2001). Research of the abused females' pressure, reaction, and social support in Kaohsiung County and City. *Family Violence and Sexual Violation Seminar*, 63–89.

Chi, Y. (1999). *The relationship between marital violence, attachment, coping strategy and adolescents' well-being*. Taichung: Providence University.

Children's Bureau Ministry of Interior (CBI). (n.d.). Available: http://www.cbi.gov.tw

Chinese Fund for Children and Families/Taiwan (CCF/Taiwan). (n.d.). Available: http://www.ccf.org.tw/

Chou, W. (2001). *The disciplinary scenario when parents use negative verbalization and the children's responding strategies: Retrospective reports of college students*. Taipei: Taiwan University.

Department of Social Affairs, Ministry of the Interior. (n.d.). Available: http://volnet.moi.gov.tw/sowf/index.htm

Department of Statistics, Ministry of the Interior. (1999). *Summary of survey results on women's living conditions in Taiwan for the year of 1998* [online]. Available: http://taiwan.yam.org.tw/womenweb/st/98/status.htm

Department of Statistics, Ministry of the Interior. (2001). *Statistical Yearbook of the Interior, R.O.C.* Taipei: Department of Statistics, Ministry of the Interior.

Directorate-General of Budget, Accounting and Statistics of Executive Yuan. (DGBAS). (1999). *Summary of 1998 Social Development Census* [online]. Available: http://www.dgbas.gov.tw/

Elder's Welfare Law. (n.d.). Available: http://volnet.moi.gov.tw/sowf/04/02/02_1.htm

Frontier Foundation. (1999). Manual of domestic violence prevention. Available: http://www.frontier.org.tw/reports.htm

Government Information Office, Republic of China (GIO). (2002). Available: http://www.roc-taiwan.org/

Huang, M., & Wang, M. (1998). Child abuse causes and prevention. Community Development Journal, 81, 189–196.

Huang, Y. (2000). A research of abused women's help-seeking process in marital violence situation. Taichung: Tunghai University.

Ju, W. (2003). There are about 90,000 foreign wives in Taiwan. China Times [online]. Available: http://news.chinatimes.com/

Lai, H. (1999). The study of coping process of elementary school students who encountered parental improper discipline. Taipei: Chinese Culture University.

Lee, Y. (2001). Perpetrators' psychological process of domestic violence: A phenomenological research. Kaohsiung: National Kaohsiung Normal University.

Lin, H. (1994). Discussion of the marriage and family change in Taiwan, from the angle of the social and economic transformation. Research Development and Evaluation Journal, 18, 12–17.

Lin, L. (2003). Female victims of violence cases are 2.5 times than male victims. UDN News [online]. Available: http://udn.com/

Lin, S. (2000). Whose advantage first—mother or child? The social workers' difficulty in dealing with spouse and child abuse families in Taipei. Taipei: Taiwan University.

Old People Welfare Advance United Organization. (n.d.). Available: http://www.oldpeople.org.tw/indexc.php

Su, F. (2000). A study on content analysis of newspaper in Taiwan: Focused on the concept of family. Taipei: Taiwan Normal University.

Summary of Population and Housing Censuses from 1956 to 2000 [online]. (n.d.). Available: http://www.dgbas.gov.tw/census~n/six/lue5/OTH1.HTM

Teng, C. (2000). Bluebeard shows up—The marital violence treatment program that discloses the mask of batterers. Taipei: Taiwan University.

Tsai, C. (1996). Elder abuse: Its issues and solutions. Community Development Journal, 76, 251–264.

Ya, Y. (2001). Establishing the family violence prevention network—The evaluation of the reaction and effects in police system. Taoyuan: Ministry of Interior.

19

Republika ng pilipinas, the Philippines

Nyryan E-V. Nolido

CAPSULE

The Philippines and her people have persevered for centuries, experiencing both beauty and tragedy. The indigenous Negritos (ancestors of the Aetas of Africa some 30,000 years ago) were followed by migrants and colonizers from Southern China, Tonkin, the Indonesian archipelago, Spain, and the United States (Leinbach & Ulack, 2000). Although strong regionalism exists today, characteristics such as collectivism, patriarchy, adherence to hierarchies based on age and mestizo (Spanish ancestry), and Christianity mixed with animistic beliefs comprise both the greatest strengths and also weaknesses of a Filipino cultural identity. Severe disproportions in power and resources in the family, as well as in the country as a whole, appear to be contributors to family violence.

Although children are highly valued in Philippine culture, corporal punishment is viewed as both acceptable and necessary, and discipline is severe. Sexual abuse, sexual exploitation/trafficking, child labor, and physical maltreatment of women and children emerged as concerns in the 1990s. Generally speaking, Filipinos seem very aware of problems in the family, however, these problems may somehow be rationalized as necessary or dismissed as irresolvable. There are laws against child abuse and a system of mandated reporting. By contrast, there are no laws specifically addressing wife abuse, although the latest antirape law recognizes marital rape. Elders are highly esteemed within the culture, although they also are not free from abuse, including physical abuse. Active efforts are being made to deal with all forms of family violence, although the progress has been greater on paper than in reality.

THE FILIPINO SAMPLE

There were 150 respondents in the Filipino sample (40 male and 110 female). They were primarily middle class, college graduates (ranging from elementary school to a doctoral degree), and Roman Catholic, with an average age of 36 years (ranging from 18 to 77 years). About half were married. The average number of siblings was 3, although some participants had as many as 10. Common occupations included self-employment, teacher, maid, factory/retail worker, physician, nurse, clerk, and laboratory technician. Self-identified culture ranged from Filipino, Asian, Pacific-Islander, Filipino-American, and Malay to regional identifications like Cebuano, Bicolano, Ilocos, Pampanga, Ilonggo, and even "religious." Participants were recruited from universities, churches, and personal contacts. Most were from Luzon, although a few were from Mindanao or were recent immigrants to the United States.

Philippine Respondents' Definitions of Abuse

The major types of maltreatment that emerged include physical, verbal, psychological, sexual, and resource (e.g., pertaining to education, household chores, labor, vices) abuse, neglect/abandonment, and sexual exploitation/trafficking. Common themes included conflicts over the traditional hierarchy of authority in the family (e.g., males over females), interpersonal relationships, and resources. In examples of mild, moderate, and extreme abuse, some form of parent–child abuse was described most by participants, followed by husband–wife. When asked to describe an experience of abuse with which they were familiar, participants were most likely to describe husband–wife abuse. Physical maltreatment was ranked extreme more often than any other type of maltreatment, except in the adult–elder dyad, in which case neglect/abandonment was the typical example of extreme abuse. Some form of verbal/emotional/psychological maltreatment was the most commonly listed type of moderate and mild maltreatment across all dyads.

THE FILIPINO MACROSYSTEM

Historical Context

Filipino culture has been shaped by both pre-Spanish indigenous cultures and Spanish influences stemming from more than three and a half centuries of Spanish colonization, under which Filipinos suffered severely (Root, 1997). Pre-Spanish influences include organization into highly interdependent *barangays* or familial alliances, egalitarian gender roles, and animistic beliefs. Spanish influences include strict adherence to authority, patriarchy, and Roman Catholicism. The Philippines were ceded by Spain to the United States after the Spanish-American War (Leinbach & Ulack, 2000). With the Philippines as a United States "protectorate," the United States benefited greatly from cheap labor, existing oligarchies, strategic military bases, and overall disproportionate economic relations, until Philippine independence in 1946 (Root, 1997). The United States had a significant influence on education, language, and urbanization. For example, although the official language is Filipino (more accurately Tagalog), and there are at least 100 Filipino languages not counting dialects, English is the primary language of education, business, government, and media.

A brutal dictatorship and martial law under Ferdinand Marcos in the 1970s and 1980s was followed by a "People Power Revolution" led by Corizon Aquino in 1986 (Posadas, 1999). From the 1990s to the present, an improving economy was offset by the eruption of Mt. Pinatubo, energy crises, failed land reform, rapid urbanization, an open-door policy toward foreign investment, a rapid switch to an export-oriented industrialization, and the impeachment of President Joseph Estrada (Posadas, 1999).

The Contemporary Socioeconomic Context

In addition to 76% of the total population living below the poverty line in 1996, other bleak statistics include; one-third of people in metropolitan Manila living in squatter or slum areas due to limited job opportunities and limited affordable housing; a net trade deficit in foreign exchange nearly every year since independence; an inflation rate of 6.3% in August 2001; and an unemployment rate of 13.9% and an underemployment rate of 19.6% (NSCB, 2001b). Mass migration to work in metropolitan areas, and overseas employment of approximately 7 million Filipinos (working primarily as service and production/transport workers in countries such as Hong Kong and Saudi Arabia) have been the alternative to the instability of rural life (Leinbach & Ulak, 2000). Although some statistics are positive—for example, a literacy rate of 94%, life expectancies at birth 72 years for females and 67 for males, and an infant mortality of 43 per 1,000 live births—resources remain costly and scarce. For example, there is only one hospital for every 113,040 people and one doctor for every 24,417 (Child Protection, 2002).

The Status of Children

Persons under the age of 18 (32 million) make up 45% of the total Philippine population (NSO, 1998, p. 14). Children, especially sons, are seen as a gift and a sign of the family's prosperity, as well as potential contributors to an elevated family status (Salvador, Omizo, & Kim, 1997). Infants are allowed to mature leisurely until *isip* (literally translated as "thoughts") or the ability to distinguish right and wrong is perceived to have developed (approximately 6 years of age), at which time reprimands such as teasing, shaming, and spanking are acceptable (Tompar-Tiu & Sustento-Seneriches, 1995).

Status of Women

The roles of wives are a mixture of contrasting pre-Spanish and Spanish influences. Prior to colonization, women's rights were more equal to men's; they retained their maiden name, could freely dispose of the property they brought into the marriage, were involved in joint decision making, acted as treasurer for the family, could divorce their husbands, and could assume headship of the barangay (Hunt & Ana-Gatbonton, 2000). Following colonization, Filipino society added Spanish *marianismo* responsibilities to wives, including an emphasis on upholding and elevating the husband's status, diffidence, silent suffering for the good of the family, and sympathy for a husband's past and current frustrations; the rigidity of these norms are only now slowly waning (Hunt & Ana-Gatbonton, 2000).

Status of the Elderly

Within the Philippines, a strong age-based hierarchy prevails, whereby individuals defer to their parents from childhood through adulthood (Blust & Scheidt, 1988). Modernization, including heavy migration to the cities and overseas for work, the imposition of Western values such as materialism and individualism, poverty, and the increasing education of younger generations were cited by participants in a survey on deference to elders as contributors to elder abuse (Ingersoll-Dayton & Saengtienchai, 1999). These factors may weaken extended family relationships, such as filial and sibling loyalty, and leave the elderly more vulnerable to maltreatment as the number of people able to help them decreases. Seeking help for maltreatment outside the family may cause great shame to older persons, which may be why no legislation directly addresses elder abuse. One positive influence from the West may be encouragement of the elderly to remain productive and active rather than dependent on their adult children.

THE FILIPINO MICROSYSTEM

The Filipino family is large and functionally extended. According to Blust and Scheidt (1988), the family is a virtual social security system, providing jobs, old age pensions, scholarships, unemployment benefits, nursery services, credit, land, labor, capital, companionship to the unmarried, care to the sick, homes for the aged, advice for the troubled, love, affection, and emotional sustenance. Perhaps the greatest strength of Filipino culture is interdependence, which is based on core indigenous Filipino values emphasizing inherent human dignity; *kapwa* (shared dignity), *loob* (the source of creativity related to ideas of equality, honor, relatedness to others, God, and Creation), *damdam* (the capacity to feel pity or consideration for another), and *paninindigan* (the ability to stand by what you believe in; Strobel, 2001). These values are echoed in our participants' definitions of abuse; "any acts or words that may debase the dignity of the person" (female, 21 years old); "when you see a person carrying a heavy load or hurting or in pain and you don't care or become insensitive to others' needs" (female, 54). Interdependence can involve sharing a household, pooling resources with one's parents, helping to finance a sibling's education, taking care of a sibling's child so the sibling can work, working in the city to send remittances home, and accompanying a family member to appointments (Pido, 1985). Indeed, the family, and even the *barkada* (close-knit lifelong group of friends) is of the highest value.

Major characteristics of the Filipino family include patriarchy, collectivism, hierarchy based on age, Roman Catholicism mixed with indigenous/animistic beliefs, and bilateralism (lineage traced equally by mother and father). Adherence to various hierarchies reflects the rigidity of structures and roles in the family—including a hierarchy based on Spanish ancestry or *mestizo*. A *mestizo* person with distinct Spanish features such as light skin is looked up to in his/her family, as well as in the community, because such a person will most likely have more opportunities and wealth than others. Many Filipinos believe adherence to these hierarchies is the measure of a civilized and moral person.

Male elders and fathers are revered as the ultimate authorities and representatives of their families, and it is partly the responsibility of wives and children to uphold (and elevate if possible) the ego of husbands and fathers. For example, a wife or child should work to be a good reflection of the husband or father, and never speak badly of them in public. Men are expected to be the breadwinners, although many wives now work, some even as primary earners. Working or not, wives' responsibilities include upholding traditional gender roles through childrearing, maintaining the house, and emotionally supporting their husbands. Complete subordination to parents and other elders is expected from children. Elder parents and grandparents receive the most acts of deference and are valued as role models for and representatives of their families. Extended family members such as uncles/aunts and cousins of all degrees may also play a very large part in the nuclear family.

Perceiving Conflict and Seeking Help

Because mental, medical, family, and other problems are often heavily stig-matized as ill fortune, perhaps from an imbalance in spirits, return for bad behavior, bad blood transmitted through generations, or deviance from group conformity, many families may keep secret or tolerate the worsening of problems (Sue & Morishima, as cited by Tompar-Tiu & Sustento-Seneriches, 1995). Conflict within a family is more likely to be mediated by a family member, close friend, spiritual leader, or indigenous healer than by the generally mistrusted police, hospital, or other service providers. "[A marital conflict] was resolved when [the couple] was connected to Chris-tianity, living a changed life in Jesus Christ" (female, 54). "My husband and I had a disagreement on how we should discipline our children . . . I left him . . . Our kids . . . initiated the reconciliation process" (female, 58).

Several indirect social mechanisms serve to restrain deviant behavior; *pakikisama*, the ability to get along with and sacrifice for the group; *tsismis*, public gossip, especially by friends or neighbors, about someone (who, it is assumed, will correct his/her behavior after hearing what was said); and *bahalana*, the ability to let go of a frustration or trouble by leaving it to fate (Tompar-Tiu & Sustento-Seneriches, 1995). *Tsismis* plays a particularly pow-erful role in influencing behavior and contributing to family violence. For example, a wife who earns more than her husband may be abused by her husband, who may himself feel abused by his wife's violation of his role, and, most importantly abused by the *tsismis* being spread about his capabil-ity and thus status.

FAMILY VIOLENCE IN THE PHILIPPINES

Major features of reported family violence in the Philippines are that most perpetrators are fathers or husbands; most victims are women and chil-dren; alcohol or drugs are involved in one-quarter of cases; and abuse tends to occur in homes with strained marriages, histories of abuse, and ex-treme poverty (although families in the "upper strata" are by no means ex-cluded; UNICEF, as cited in Militante, 1999). Although precolonization laws concerning rape, incest, and the abuse of elders, women, and children ap-peared to have existed, the topic of family violence did not emerge publicly again until the early 1990s (Tompar-Tiu & Sustento-Seneriches, 1995). Al-though abuse in families is acknowledged, it is either seen as necessary and excusable or dismissed as fate, for lack of a better solution.

CHILD ABUSE

One-third of children in a study conducted in schools reported that they had experienced some form of abuse (Hunt & Ana-Gatbonton, 2000). In 2000,

10,749 cases of child maltreatment were serious enough to be reported to the Department Of Social Welfare And Development (DSWD). Of these, there were nearly 10,000 cases of sexual abuse, incest, or rape, nearly 3,500 cases of neglect and abandonment, and 1,575 cases of physical abuse (National Statistical Coordination Board of the Philippines, 2001c).

Sexual maltreatment is the most prevalent reported form of child abuse, and probably very underestimated due to associated stigma. An "average" Filipino victim of sexual abuse has been described as an 11-year-old female and the average perpetrator a 36-year-old father (UNICEF, as cited in Militante, 1999). Familial and nonfamilial perpetrators (e.g., neighbors, acquaintances) appear nearly equally distributed. In January 2001, 14 of 31 men who received the death penalty were convicted of rape (8 of the 14 were fathers), the most prevalent form of sexual abuse against children (Child Protection, 2002). The age of consent in the Philippines is 12; however, sex with someone under age 18 years is considered a crime of "seduction" if the perpetrator is one of authority over the minor (e.g., priest, parent, or teacher). Our participants told many stories of abuse; "a father too possessive with his daughter . . . he wanted his daughter to be his wife . . . she was sexually abused severely." "I know of a couple of girls who were raped by their fathers/stepfathers . . . I was shocked that they didn't report it, but that's how Filipino's are . . . just passive . . . [One girl] still talks about how traumatic that experience was for her and how she felt very insecure and inferior throughout all of her elementary years."

Ideas that men have natural needs and privileges, a child's unquestionable deference to elders or those in authority, and "early" maturation of children may be contributors to sex abuse. It appears that most incest occurs in households where there is an absentee mother, decreased privacy due to living in one-room shanty-type houses, frequent quarreling between husband and wife, economic hardship, and a victim who is home alone in the evening (Molina, 2001). In addition to intimidation by the death penalty, child victims may be reluctant to report maltreatment due to vulnerability in challenging an adult's credibility, fear of being blamed, fear of a father's threats to harm them or other family members, insensitive service providers and legal procedures, inability to survive without the perpetrator, and potential abandonment by one's family (Child Protection, 2002).

Physical abuse cases were the second-most prevalent type of abuse (following sexual abuse) reported to the Philippine National Police in 2000 (Child Protection, 2002). Victims tended to be between the ages of 0 and 3 and perpetrators primarily familial (76%)—with fathers being 39% of familial perpetrators (Ramiro, Madrid, & Amarillo, as cited in Child Protection Unit, 1997). Although corporal punishment is prohibited in the school and penal systems, it is permitted in the home. Discipline is equated with love and good parenting, thus parents may not hesitate to physically discipline their child, even in public (Tompar-Tiu & Sustento-Seneriches, 1995). Children might be disciplined for lying, answering back to a parent, unsatisfactory completion of tasks, or to encourage academic performance. "Father flicks the ears or hits the head of his son who cannot answer questions related to the lessons in school." Our participants viewed spanking as mild abuse, at most: "It's a matter of degrees. Excessive beating is abuse. A spank with hands or belt is NOT abuse. A spank/multiple spanks with a wrench WOULD be abuse." "Most Filipinos have been spanked in childhood, and don't consider it abuse, merely a form of punishment. They will probably also use spanks on their child as punishment too."

Discipline was described as crossing the line into abuse when a parent misused his/her power by disciplining the children in front of others (especially the child's peers), when the reason for discipline was unreasonable or "flimsy," when the disciplinarian was unfair (possibly due to alcohol use), and when the disciplinarian was acting out of his own personal frustrations. Examples given by our participants were "beating," "hitting with an object," "burning with cigarette or iron," "pinching," "kneeling on a pile of salt/mongo beans for a long period of time," "pulling ears/hair," "hanging in a sack," and "locking in a confined space." Explanations included "the mother calls and [the child] doesn't respond to the mom right away . . . and the mom will slap him many times on any part of his body" (female, 46); "extreme abuse usually happens when a father is drunk. A single mistake of a child would result in hitting him by the father" (female, 52); and "a father who burns the ear or palm of his daughter or son—5–10-year-old—with cigarettes, or boxes them when they refuse what the father wants, usually to buy cigarettes."

Psychological Abuse of Children

In a study of 1,000 children in an urban community, 80% reported they had experienced psychological aggression (Ramiro, Madrid & Amarillo, as cited in Child Protection Unit, 1997). Like physical aggression, psychological actions such as scolding, insulting, lecturing, isolating from or embarrassing in front of friends may be utilized by parents for discipline. Although the desired effect is to encourage children to learn obedience and/or to strive for improvement (gratification or gentle verbal direction is thought to hinder such progress), participants described discipline as crossing the line into abuse when the punishment was not appropriate to the mistake, when children were restricted from their social circle, and especially when children could develop feelings of worthlessness, inferiority, and dehumanization as a result. Our participants shared the following; "[Abuse is to] always punish the child for every mistake the child commits. There are no encouraging words or actions for the child" (male, 60). "Parents dislike their kids to answer back. It is abusive to order a kid to keep mum; he/she will grow up inhibited and will be afraid to express whatever he/she feels" (female, 54). Lastly, favoritism emerged as a distinct form of abuse. "[A mother] playing favorites with her children and making this situation known" (female, 54). Indeed, favoritism in a situation where families have limited resources can be quite detrimental to an "unfavored" child.

Child Abuse Related to Resources and Labor

Participants' examples of abuse gave considerable emphasis to situations involving money, labor, and education. Education is viewed as a right of every child; thus, giving priority to boys over girls, was sometimes seen as abuse: "Parents who don't send their children to school, especially the females." (female, 23). Excessive pressure to succeed in school was also an example of abuse. "Parents compel child to study hard and rarely allow him to play. When the child does not meet the expectations of the parents, he is insulted, scolded and embarrassed to others" (female, 48).

The National Statistics Office Survey of Child Laborers in 1995 found 39% of parents wanted their children to work to add to the family income, 28% to take part in the family enterprise, and 20% to appreciate the value of work (NSO, 1998). Most of our participants did not think letting children work, per se, was abusive. In fact, for many children of lower socioeconomic status, work is expected and viewed positively. Child labor was described as crossing the line into abuse when: "Parents consent to their children going to work despite exposure to physical risk or danger because they're both jobless . . . worst scenario is the father gets the money . . . and spends it on vices" (female, 39) and "parents ask the child to do a work that is only for adult. Like asking a child to sell in the streets flowers, etc." (female, 54). "Abuse for me is taking my freedom to choose what kind of life I want to live! I worked since I was 9 years old . . . doing the job of a mature person, physically and mentally. I have no freedom to go out and be with my friends. I always say yes even though it is not my own free will" (female, 43).

SPOUSE ABUSE

From 1991 to 1997, wife abuse reports to the Bureau of Women's Welfare increased rapidly from 850 to 7,850 cases (Tripon, 2000). Current estimates are that 6 out of 10 women are victims of partner abuse (Militante, 1999). Possible contributors to wife abuse appear to be a woman's lack of control over family planning; inability to access medical health care due to stigma, poverty, or the batterer's control; costs of medical/legal help; potential loss of job; lower levels of household wealth; a husband's alcohol/drug use or jealousy; and living in an urban area (Cabaraban & Morales, 1998; Hindin & Adair, 2002; Women's Crisis Center, 2002). Unfortunately, Roman Catholicism may also play a role in the maintenance of wife abuse: "A husband comes home drunk and assaults his wife. She reports that this happens frequently, but doesn't want to leave him because her Catholic faith prohibits divorce." Both physical and psychological abuse can be associated with a woman's perceived inability or unwillingness to fulfill her traditional gender role (Cabaraban & Morales, 1998). "[A] husband is jobless and alcoholic. He kicks and punches his wife when he gets home finding no food on the table even if he knows that he did not provide money" (female, 39).

Physical Abuse of Wives

Of the total 9,480 wife abuse cases reported to the Philippine National Police in 2000, physical injuries were predominant (3,824), followed by rape (1,202; National Statistics Coordination Board, 2001a). Six out of 10 battered women have been abused for more than 5 years, some have been beaten for more than 20 years (Center for Gender and Women Studies, 2002). Predictors of physical wife abuse include jealousy, alcohol, issues related to family planning, accusations of having an affair, refusal to have sex, neglect of children, talking back to or nagging a husband, earning more than a husband, and considering a husband's earning inadequate (Cabaraban & Morales, 1998; Hindin & Adair, 2000; Women's Crisis Center, 2002). In our sample, 83% of the examples of extreme wife abuse were of physical aggression, with "beating" listed most frequently. "Kicking," "boxing," "hitting with an object," "throwing across the room," and even "homicide" were other actions described.

Many Filipino women appear to have an implicit theory of wife beating that makes them reluctant to report abuse. Among the assumptions in their theories are the following: Wife beating is only heard about through neighborhood gossip so perhaps it doesn't exist; the men are drunk and thus their behavior is excusable; it is natural for men to be aggressive, as it is their duty to "maintain and discipline the family"; she must have initiated the violence by nagging, infidelity, or not showing sympathy for the burden her husband bears; the man might still change; she doesn't want a broken family; she doesn't want to be blamed by her parents for the break-up of the family; she can't support the children by herself; he might lose his job if she calls the police (Women's Feature Service, 1993). Moreover, many women may not know they have a right not to be beaten.

Sexual Abuse of Wives

Reports of marital rape have increased from 35% of wife abuse cases in 1995; 60% of survivors were forced into early marriages/live-in arrangements with their assailants; 9 out of 10 battered women have experienced marital rape; 6 out of 10 battered women had unwanted pregnancies; and 4 out of 10 rape victims had been raped at least five times before seeking help (NSCB, 2001a; Women's Crisis Center, 2002). The disproportionate amount of sexual freedom for men in contrast to that of women, the indissolubility of marriage, media images of women as sexual objects and caterers to their husbands' needs, fear of further harm from the perpetrator, an insensitive police force and investigative team, lengthy court trials, and the ultimate control of a husband over his wife may be contributors to marital rape (Hunt & Ana-Gatbonton, 2000; Militante, 1999; Women's Crisis Center, 2002).

Infidelity

Although not identified as a form of spousal abuse as often as wives' infidelity, husband's infidelity was listed as abusive by 14% of our participants—sometimes as a known case of abuse: "A husband with [many] children who married another woman and left the 1st wife to find a living for their many children. When he gets home, he hurts the 1st wife physically and [takes] almost anything the 1st wife earns to the 2nd wife without leaving enough for their many children." Whereas wives' infidelity was typically viewed as severely abusive, husbands' infidelity was generally seen as less serious. One respondent noted that a husband's infidelity would be only mildly abusive "when the behavior doesn't affect the wife at all . . . the victim knows how to handle the situation . . . she knows her husband has another woman but since she is intelligent and smart enough she faces her friends and deals with her colleagues as normally as she can as if nothing is happening behind her back." Conversely, the consequences for a wife's actual or even supposed infidelity are severe and usually include physical maltreatment. "Husband got furious when he learned that his wife is having communication with her ex-boyfriend. He slaps her many times . . ." (female, 49). Indeed, a wife's infidelity is viewed as a direct assault on a husband's status and integrity.

Psychological Abuse of Wives

One participant from the Cabaraban and Morales (1998) study said, "To be called *tanga* (stupid) and *buang* (crazy) is more painful than being hit." In our sample, "name-calling," "fault-finding," "demeaning behaviors done in front of others," "lack of emotional support and consideration," and "isolation" were common examples of wife abuse, especially at the moderate and mild levels: "When the husband utters foul words, attacks the wife's dignity and crushes her self-esteem, even only because of mild disagreements, coupled with physical attacks like beating, slaps." Another participant said,

"[Abuse is] nonrespect for others' rights—e.g., a husband who think he's always right and does not listen to his wife's opinion" (female, 56).

Wife Abuse Related to Resources and Vices

Cabaraban and Morales (1998) found a wife is more likely to experience maltreatment if she earns a living, her husband does traditional female household chores, and she exercises authority in major decisions, or spends large amounts of money without consulting her husband. Many examples of wife abuse in our sample also seemed to reflect challenges to traditional roles; "a husband being dependent on the wife's earnings and thus the mother cannot take her role properly" (male; 26); "a husband [who] wants his wife to stay at home, do all the chores" (female, 52); and "not allowing the wife to have a career and earn." Examples of wife abuse related to resources included a husband "not providing for his family because of spending on vices or his extended family," as well as a husband not providing the opportunity for a wife to perform her uniquely Filipino role as family "treasurer": "a husband's salary is not given fully [to his wife]" (female, 56); "when a husband withholds financial support if he has an argument with his wife" (female, 54). Finally, in our sample there were many allusions to the role of alcohol in domestic violence, followed by gambling and drugs. "[Abuse is] a wife is afraid of the hour her husband comes home from work because she knows he will be drunk and physically hurt her." Wife abuse involving alcohol may be related to the common male practice of "sessions" or drinking with friends primarily after work.

Husband Maltreatment

Although there has been little attention to the possibility of husband abuse, our respondents gave many examples, with a focus on gender role violations and other forms of perceived psychological abuse. Less than half (41%) of respondents gave examples of physical maltreatment of husbands by wives—for example, "hitting a husband in public," "physically aggressing towards a husband because of his inability to provide for the family," and "the use of objects or dangerous liquids." Descriptions of psychological abuse included "humiliation," or "causing a husband to be scorned as under di siya" (literally, "under the skirt")—that is, as under his wife's control.

Some Filipino women may be considered as having "strong blood," a tendency to be assertive presumed to be transferred through the generations. However, many wives may find themselves in a double bind; they suffer when their husbands' earnings are not sufficient or are spent on vices, but may also suffer abuse if they take the initiative to earn money for the family and thereby insult their husband. With regard to decision making, a wife may contribute significantly to the process behind closed doors, despite the maintenance of a subordinate façade in public to her husband, perhaps another example of clashing pre-Spanish and Spanish ideals (Cimmarusti, 1996). In fact, a few of our participants stated, "[It is abusive for a] wife [to leave] all the decision making to the husband" (female, 22). Other participants shared the following sentiment, "[In Filipino culture it is abusive] for a wife to be vocal . . . she is expected to subordinate herself by all means and follow her husband; [but in some cases] the husband or wife whose family is more wealthy from back home is the dominant member of the relationship" (female, 55).

Many Filipino women still consider it their duty to sexually satisfy their husbands (Hunt & Ana-Gatbonton, 2000), and this was reflected in the responses of our participants. One of the most common examples of husband abuse was withholding sex, especially as a tool of manipulation; "a wife depriving husband to sexual pleasure" (female, 52); and "denying [a husband] sex relations for not being able to get what she wants from him in terms of her vanities and personal caprices" (female, 79).

ELDER MALTREATMENT

The eldest or most capable child is expected to take care of the basic needs (food, shelter, care, attention, sense of self-worth) of an aging parent, consistent with the idea of *utang na loob* or eternal indebtedness to one's parents (Blust & Scheidt, 1988). Over 80% of older Filipinos live in extended family households (Williams & Domingo, 1993).

Although no national or published statistics on elder maltreatment were found in the literature search, nearly 49% of our participants gave very specific and personal examples, with an emphasis on neglect and/or abandonment as extreme forms of elder abuse. Not caring for elderly parents can bring shame to a family, especially if the elder is left "to the mercy of other compassionate people in the community" (female, 54). Examples of neglect/abandonment included "ignoring an elder person's financial needs," "controlling/isolating the elderly," and "not letting parent leave the house." The most severely rated abuses were "placing an elderly parent in a home for the elderly," "not visiting regularly or at all after placing them in a home," and "leaving the helpless and elderly parent . . . because he and his family do not want to take care of her because she is no longer helpful to them nor could she contribute to the family's needs" (female, 79).

It is expected that a number of forms of deference will be displayed toward the elderly—respectful language and helpful behavior; tokens such as preparing food, providing living expenses and facilitating the elder's merit making; celebrations focused on the elderly; and accepting the advice of elders on major purchases and family quarrels (Ingersoll-Dayton & Saeng-tienchai, 1999). Behaviors inconsistent with these signs of deference were often listed as examples of moderate or mild elder abuse by our participants. "In the Philippines it is considered to be [extremely] abusive if one answers back to any elder or even tries to reason it out" (female, 58); "when the mother gives an opinion contrary to the opinion of the son, the son orders her to shut up since she is old and does not have an accurate view of things" (female, 48). Ignoring an elder's opinion appears to be growing, as does a so-called "knowledge gap" following from parents encouraging their children to pursue education rather than farming. "Lack of consideration," "ignoring," "isolating," or "not encouraging self-worth" were also examples of elder abuse, along with "Mother not allowed to venture out of home on pretext of security" (female, 58); "Keeping an elderly parent quiet and silent, isolated in a dark bedroom" (female, 54); "Making fun of either of the grandparents because of old age" (female, 50).

Physical Abuse of the Elderly

In our survey, physical abuse was described primarily as a form of extreme abuse, second to abandonment/neglect (37% physical abuse compared to 44% extreme neglect and abandonment). Although physical maltreatment of elderly parents is considered extremely abusive, it appears not uncommon. Examples of known cases of physical maltreatment of elders described by participants included "hitting," "physical harm/hurt," "slapping," and "beating." Several participants described physical abuse occurring as a result of a financial dispute or the influence of alcohol/drugs on the perpetrator—for example, "Most causes of abuse in the elderly are due to over drinking of alcohol . . . [A son] tried to raise a big knife to ward his father because he couldn't have the money he is asking for."

Economic maltreatment was a typical example of mild abuse by our participants (22%). Participants also noted that in addition to "not meeting basic needs," "not funding the requests, social activities, or desires" of the elderly are considered maltreatment in the Philippines, although some participants indicated that this set of societal expectations was not always reasonable. "Most elders expect money from their children even if it is to go on a trip [or] retaining a high social life . . . in terms of the barrio/island—which is beyond reason. For example, having a BIG funeral and feeding practically anyone from the town are necessary or else you're looked down upon by the . . . people in the town you come from" (female, 58). "The projects of the old (which may be church related or civic related activities) have to be financed by the children, otherwise you are not a good child" (female, 55).

Many elders may continue to control the distribution of financial resources without directly contributing by requesting a more successful child to help his/her sibling. "Most often, the elders have favorites among their children and if the eldest sibling is not successful financially—and the younger ones are more successful financially—the elder will try to get the younger child's earnings to give to the eldest child who is unable to be on their own. If you refuse to give in to your elder's wish—you have abused every elder and this creates trouble within the family." An adult child remaining financially dependent on the elderly was considered especially abusive when the child is capable of being self-supporting and when the child manipulates the elderly for a social security check, inheritance, land, or other property, especially if the child has vices. "When an adult child depends on parents financially and is not interested in working" (female, 22); "Getting the inheritance without the elderly knowing it (signing without power of attorney) documents" (female, 56); and "The son has a permanent job and often demands money from his mother to use for gambling . . . The son threatens to sue the mother for withholding his inheritance from his father."

Some elder parents may feel burdensome to their children despite the tradition of filial obligation, because they may coreside with their children out of necessity. "With men, when they lose their work, they become irritable because they perceive themselves as useless, especially if they were the breadwinners all this time" (Williams & Domingo, 1993, p. 420). Many elderly parents may feel that in exchange for a home, they should babysit their grandchildren, cook, do laundry, and clean the house. "Even with our arthritis and rheumatism, their Lolo and I have to dance and play as the occasion and these two angels demand it! Then at sunset, as the younger members of my family arrive, my husband and I supervise the preparation of the evening meal so that our loved ones, who surely are exhausted from their day's work, may find a long welcome for them at home" (Ortega, 2002, p. 1). Many of our participants said that elders, especially grandmothers, may be taken advantage of: "Totally [relying] on an elderly parent to do all the household work 100% without compensation is an abuse; unless the child is helping or has helped in some other way—like plane fare, or gave her some help in return for services—it should be a give and take relationship and not one-sided" (female, 58).

SIBLING MALTREATMENT

Eldest children are expected to receive unquestioned respect from younger siblings, especially when they are assigned primary caretaking roles (Cimmarusti, 1996). Sibling physical, psychological, and sexual maltreatment described by participants seemed to arise primarily from the misuse of authority given to an eldest child or a parent's favorite child. The most common example of sibling abuse was "an eldest child forcing his/her younger sibling to do most or all of the household chores," followed by descriptions of how an older or favorite child might assume superiority over another sibling.

SEXUAL EXPLOITATION AND TRAFFICKING

Although sexual exploitation and trafficking, especially in women and children, is not a new phenomenon, not until the early 1990s was there acknowledgment of such injustices as the sexual enslaving of women from Southeast Asia during World War II (Hunt & Ana-Gatbonton, 2000). The privileged status of men, the daily depiction of sexually exploited women and children in tabloids, and poverty seem to be contributors to this form of abuse—which was exacerbated by the former U.S. military bases. Although this type of abuse is especially taboo, considering the strong influence of the Church, some bleak statistics include; consumers are both Filipinos and foreign nationals; the Philippines ranks fourth in countries with the most prostituted children; 60,000 to 100,000 of the 1.5 million street children are prostituted; and mail-order brides made up as much as 100% of marriages between Filipino women and foreign nationals (ECPAT, as cited in Mission, 2000; Hunt & Ana-Gatbonton, 2000; Intersect, as cited in Child Protection, 2002). Women and children appear to get involved, sometimes knowingly and sometimes through misrepresentations of "legitimate" work, as domestic workers, entertainment workers, street children, overseas employees, and mail-order brides; even husbands and fathers may engage in trafficking (Maceda, 2001). A few of our participants noted such situations as "forced prostitution, [a husband] acting as a pimp for [his] wife" (female, 36), and "a father who is an agent or a pimp for both male and female children" (female, 28).

ARMED CONFLICT

Armed conflict involving rebels fighting against the government primarily for autonomy has plagued the southern island of Mindanao for hundreds of years (UNICEF, 2002). The Armed Forces of the Philippines estimates that 13% of rebels involved in armed conflict are children (UNICEF, 2002). Children may be motivated to participate because of poverty and promises of a better life, intense militarization leading to acts of forced protection, early maturation, family involvement, peer group pressure, and poor monitoring and implementation of CPP and NPA rules concerning children (UNICEF, 2001; UNICEF, 2002).

INTERVENTION AND PREVENTION

Major legislation and programs regarding child abuse emerged in the 1990s and included the 1993 Convention on the Rights of the Child, the Fourth Country Programme of Cooperation of the Filipino government and UNICEF (1994–1998), the Philippine Plan of Action for Children, and the Family Courts Act of 1997 (giving family courts jurisdiction over cases of domestic violence against children; Child Protection Unit, 1997; "Situation of Children and Women in the Philippines," 1997). Many of these programs address such issues as family care and alternative parental arrangements, protection of children in especially difficult circumstances, and fundamental civil rights. The "Special Protection of Children Against Child Abuse, Exploitation and Discrimination Act," enacted in 1991 identified the following as forms of maltreatment; (a) psychological and physical abuse, neglect, cruelty, sexual abuse, and emotional maltreatment, (b) any act by deeds or words which debases, degrades, or demeans the intrinsic worth and dignity of a child as a human being, (c) unreasonable deprivation of basic needs for survival such as food and shelter, and (d) failure to immediately give medical treatment to an injured child resulting in serious impairment of growth and development or in permanent incapacity or death (Philippine National Police, 1999). Also addressed are circumstances endangering the survival and moral development of children, including situations of armed-conflict, hazardous working conditions, indigenous cultural communities, extreme poverty, and man-made or natural disasters or calamities. Implementation and prosecution appears a large problem with a dismal 148 of the 2,311 cases served by the Child Protection Unit filed with a resolution (Child Protection, 2002).

Some programs encouraging the creation and implementation of services for child laborers include the Philippine participation in the International Labor Organization Convention 182 in 1999, the National Program Against Child Labor, and Sagip Batang Manggagawa (UNICEF, 2002). Article X of the 1991 Republic Act 7610 established guidelines for protection of children in situations of armed conflict (UNICEF, 2001).

Policies, programs, and organizations to protect women, which emerged primarily in the 1990s, include the signing of the U.N. Convention on the Elimination of All Forms of Discrimination Against Women, the New Family Code and Sama-samang Inisyatiba ng Kaababaihan sa Pagbabago ng Batas at Lipunan (SIBOL, a women's advocacy group), which address issues of child custody, grounds for legal separation and child support (Women's Feature Service, 1993). Legislation specifically addressing spousal abuse is lacking; however, complaints regarding physical injury can be filed based on provisions of the Penal Code. To file a case of minor physical injury or maltreatment, a person needs to go to the barangay official who, if unable to settle the complaint, is supposed to send the case to court with certification (Women's Feature Service, 1993). Serious physical injuries are the responsibility of the police; a blotted and sworn affidavit must be given and the victim referred by the police to a medico-legal or doctor whose report can then be used in court (Women's Feature Service, 1993). The Anti-Rape Law amended the provisions of the Revised Penal Code on rape to include the recognition of marital rape (Hunt & Ana-Gatbonton, 2000). Specific steps for victims outlined by the Center for Gender and Women's Studies (2002) include calling the nearest Crisis Counseling Office, seeing a medico-legal doctor to prevent pregnancy and treating any injuries. Women's advocacy groups such as SIBOL have been pushing for "The Anti-Abuse of Women in Intimate Relationships Bill," which would specifically define, address, and suggest solutions to abuse within intimate relationships (Mellejor, 2002).

Although several advocacy organizations understandably criticize the government for covering up sexual exploitation, the 1990s saw the following policies, programs, and organizations: the Migrant and Overseas Filipino Act, "The Special Protection of Children Against Child Abuse, Exploitation & Discrimination Act," "The Mail-Order Bride Law," Philippine attendance to the World Congress Against Commercial Sexual Exploitation of Children in Sweden, the Asian Regional Initiative Against Trafficking Meeting with the United States, the U.N. Global Programme Against Trafficking in Human Beings, the Special Project for Women in Especially Difficult Circumstances, End Child Abuse and Prostitution, Child Pornography and the Trafficking of the Children for Sexual purposes (ECPAT), UNICEF and the Preda Foundation (Hunt & Ana-Gatbonton, 2000; Maceda, 2001). These efforts addressed issues of defining victims and perpetrators; cited examples of advertisement, recruitment, establishments, obscene publications, indecent shows, and child trafficking; and shared information and cooperated with agencies of other countries (Abbugao, as cited in Hunt & Ana-Gatbonton, 2000; Maceda, 2001)

Most of the legislation designed in the early 1990s to benefit the elderly focuses on issues of social security, though many still consider social security gravely insufficient. Republic Act 7432 allows persons over 60 years of age, with an income of not more than P60,000 and with a national identification card provided for free by the DSWD, to benefit from a 20% discount on medicines, transportation, hospitals, and so forth.

THE FUTURE

Filipino culture has great strengths, such as feeling obligated to care for and encourage one another, respect for tradition, as well as good intentions for every member of the family. It was evident from our survey that Filipinos have a clear idea of what they consider right and wrong, and a clear view of maltreatment as related to disproportionate roles that benefit a few members and harms others. On a macrosystem level, acknowledging the potential for the government to aid the welfare of her people seems necessary. Indeed, fulfilling basic needs amidst severe economic and social inequality in the family and the country as a whole is a crucial problem. It seems logical that once the basic needs of a family are secure, the family can direct more of its energy to achieving security, and warm and healthy interdependence within the macrosystem.

Exploration and expression of conflict seems a natural next step. It appears from our participants' responses that individual member's opinions and feelings are of high value to other members, although adherence to strict hierarchies based on age and gender, strongly reinforced by a focus on respect and status, have discouraged the depth of such interactions. Women, children, elders, and men each have immense pressures and heartaches, and open expression of these may help in their resolution. Indeed, the use of harmful coping mechanisms such as vices and fatalism may be indicative of traditional inability to express emotions within the family. On a macrosystem level, exploration and acknowledgment of conflict in the family should involve research, education, the development of professionals and professional organizations for aid and advocacy, campaigns, legislation, communication among organizations, and designing ways to reach and educate the organizations most likely to be approached for assistance and possible prevention. The Roman Catholic Church, while traditionally upholding many values that appear to contribute to family violence, is a potentially great source for family violence education and service, because it is one of the most likely places to be utilized early on in a crisis. Media and entertainment, in a culture highly influenced by status and stigma, could help by depicting family situations with potential solutions, replacing its current sensationalization and fatalism with an environment of shared experience and directions for change.

Direct accountability for problems in a culture where these are seen as inconsiderate, lowly, against the grain, and a serious threat to highly valued smooth interpersonal relationships will be very difficult. Although many may fear that confrontation will lead to the "breaking" of the family, a situation where members feel unsafe, taken advantage of, inhibited, worthless, and violated is already broken and awareness of the problems can be a step closer to resolution rather than to disintegration (Tripon, 2000). On a macrosystem level, confrontation and accountability would mean the implementation and general enforcement of policies and programs to aid families in conflict. Specific concerns might include 24-hour emergency services, increased sensitivity and education of service providers such as the police, and better documentation (UNICEF, 1997; as cited in Militante, 1999).

All knowledge and ideas should be available to Filipinos so that they can decide for themselves the best way to proceed with regard to familial relationships. Hopefully, this chapter has presented an accurate description of some conflicts in the family and has offered some interpretations to be considered. The potential of a Filipino family characterized by healthy interdependence is great indeed. It is time that Filipinos, after centuries of coping with, adapting to, and accepting outside imposed hierarchies and values, realize their own unique and great strengths and principles as a people. It is time to eliminate situations such as the following, described by one Filipino participant, "I always say yes even though it is not my own free will" (female, 43).

ACKNOWLEDGMENTS

Many thanks are in order to those who greatly aided me in this journey: KMM, who made this opportunity available; my fellow research group members; my parents, Franklin M. Nolido and Maria C.V. Nolido (the single-most efficient recruiting service); my sister Nathaly A.V. Nolido, D.M.D.; Lyle Lopez, Sam Man Duk Suh Ewing, Lorenz "Peng" Ponce, and Jimmy "Fil" Lee for the encouraging words and candid discussions; Toni Dikit, who deserves special recognition for translating the survey into Tagalog; Evan B. Schuman, for hard and expert work with the qualitative data; and Rouba Youssef and Hariklia K. Kapaniris, for being my human spelling, grammar, and content checks. Special thanks to Ma. Carla V. Lopez, Nelly Perez, Ma. Victoria L. Herrera, M.D., Geraldo Costa, Alpha Paradela, M.D., Father Renee Pinero, Fortunato L. Cristobal, M.D., Cecile Morais, Milagros Fernandez, M.D., and the Maramara and Silvestre families for lending and sending research materials, recruiting participants, collecting and mailing surveys, and contributing comments. Last but not least, thank you to the Filipino survey participants who generously shared their rich, personal, insightful, and articulate thoughts and experiences. I hope I have represented you well.

REFERENCES

Blust, E. P. N., & Scheidt, R. J. (1988). Perceptions of filial responsibility by elderly Filipino widows and their primary care givers. *International Journal of Aging and Human Development, 26*(2), 91–106.

Cabaraban, M. C., & Morales, B. C. (1998). Social and economic consequences of family planning use in Southern Philippines. *Family Health International Women's Studies Project* [online]. Available: http://www.fhi.org

Center for Gender and Women Studies, University of the Philippines Manila. (2002). *Rape is a crime: Know your rights pamphlet*. University Center for Women's Studies, University of the Philippines.

Child Protection. (2002). *The situation of Filipino children* [online]. Available: http://www.childprotection.org.ph

Child Protection Unit. (1997). *A physician's guide to national laws concerning child abuse: The national legal mandate*. Washington, DC: The Advisory Board Foundation.

Cimmarusti, R. A. (1996). Exploring aspects of Filipino-American families. *Journal of Marital and Family Therapy, 22*, 205–217.

Hindin, M. J., & Adair, L. S. (2002). Who's at risk? Factors associated with intimate partner violence in the Philippines. *Social Science & Medicine, 55*, 1385–1399.

Hunt, D. D., & Ana-Gatbonton, C. S. (2000, November). Filipino women and sexual violence: Speaking out and providing services. *Paper presented to the Immigrant Women's Support Service Forum* [online]. Available: http://www.cpcabrisbane.org/CPCA/IWSSForum.htm

Ingersoll-Dayton, B., & Saengtienchai, C. (1999). Respect for the elderly in Asia: Stability and change. *International Journal of Aging and Human Development, 48*(2), 113–130.

Leinbach, T. R., & Ulack, R. (2000). *Southeast Asia: Diversity and development*. Upper Saddle River, NJ: Prentice Hall.

Maceda, C. P. (2001). Trafficking in women and children: Violence against women and humanity. *National Institute of Justice International Center: United Nations Activities* [online]. Available: http://www.ojp.usdoj.gov/nij/international/un_preorehab.html

Mellejor, A. C. (2002). Group pushes bill vs. abuse of women by their partners. *Inquirer News Service* [online]. Available: http://www.inq7.net/reg/2002/mar/18/reg_11-1.htm

Militante, C. (1999). Country experiences: Philippines. In *Changing Lenses—Women's Perspectives on Media* (pp. 102–112). Manila, Philippines: Isis International.

Mission, G. (2000, March 28). Helping children in crisis. *CyberDyaryo* [online]. Available: http://gina.ph/CyberDyaryo/features/f2000_0328_01.htm

Molina, A. (2001). *Towards the development of a treatment approach for children victims of incest* [online]. Available: http://www.childprotection.org/ph/

National Statistical Coordination Board of the Philippines, NCSB. (2001a). *Statistics on violence against women and children* [online]. Available: http://www.nscb.gov.ph/stats/vawc.htm

National Statistical Coordination Board of the Philippines, NCSB. (2001b). *StatWatch* [online]. Available: http://www.nscb.gov.ph/stats/statwatch.htm

National Statistical Coordination Board of the Philippines, NCSB. (2001c). *Victims of child abuse served by the DSWD* [online]. Available: http://www.nscb.gov.ph/factsheet/pdf01/fs1_05.asp.

National Statistics Office, NSO. (1998). *1995 National survey on working children* [online]. Available: http://www.census.gov/ph/data/sectordata/ch95wctx.html.

Ortega, R. P. (2002, February 28). Senior citizen. *INQ7* [Electronic version]. Available: INQ7 Website http://www.inq7.net/opi/2002/feb/08/opi_highblood1-1.htm

Philippine National Police. (1999). *Police handbook: Guidelines and action on child abuse and neglect*. Manila, Philippines: Philippine National Police, Philippine General Hospital and the Advisory Board Foundation.

Pido, A. J. A. (1985). *The Pilipinos in America: Macro/Micro dimensions of immigration and integration*. New York: Center for Migration Studies.

Posadas, B. M. (1999). *The Filipino Americans*. London: Greenwood Press.

Root, M. P. (1997). *Filipino Americans: Transformation and identity*. Thousand Oaks, CA: SAGE.

Salvador, D. S., Omizo, M. M., & Kim, B. S. K. (1997). Bayanihan: Providing effective counseling strategies with children of Filipino ancestry. *Journal of Multicultural Counseling and Development, 25*, 201–209.

Santos, A. F. (2001). *Violence against women in times of war and peace*. Quezon City, Philippines: University Center for Women's Studies University of the Philippines.

Soliman, C. J. (2002, April). Statement by the Philippines at *The second world assembly on ageing Madrid, Spain* [online]. Available: http://www.un.org/ageing/coverage/philippine.htm

Strobel, L. M. (2001). *Coming full circle: The process of decolonization among post-1965 Filipino Americans.* Quezon City, Philippines: Giraffe Books.

Tompar-Tiu, A., & Sustento-Seneriches, J. (1995). *Depression and other mental health issues: The Filipino-American experience.* San Francisco: Jossey-Bass.

Tripon, O. H. (Ed.). (2000). *Body and soul: A forum on divorce and family violence: 'Til death do us part?* Quezon City, Philippines: Women's Feature Services (WFS) Philippines.

Tripon, O. H. (2002). Yes, there is such a thing as marital rape. *Women's Feature Service* [online]. Available: http://www.geocities.com/women_lead/wlead5ART.htm

UNICEF. (1997). *Situation of children and women in the Philippines.* Manila, Philippines: UNICEF.

UNICEF. (2001). *Study focuses on child soldiers* [online]. Available: http://www.unicef.org/philippines/Archive/2001Q4Oct_News06_Child%20soldiers.htm

UNICEF-Philippines. (2002, May 5). The many masks of abuse. *The Daily Tribune* [Electronic version]. Available: http://www.tribune.net.ph/20020505/features/20020505.fea01.html.

Williams, L., & Domingo, L. J. (1993). The social status of elderly women and men within the Filipino family. *Journal of Marriage and the Family, 55,* 415–426.

Women's Crisis Center. (2002). Facts & figures. *Women's Crisis Center Pamphlet.* Quezon City, Philippines: David and Lucile Packard Foundation.

Women's Feature Service. (1993). Domestic violence: Questions and answers. *NCRFW Institutional Strengthening Project* [online]. Available: http://www.salidumay.org/discussions/articles/domestic_violence.htm

20

Australia

Doe West

CAPSULE

Australia is one of the most culturally and linguistically diverse nations in the world. Therein lies both a great strength and a fundamental problem. Its diversity affects both the understanding and ways of responding to the issue of family violence. The fact that Australians come from such divergent cultures creates communication barriers when groups try to agree on basic definitions and proper responses to maltreatment. Additionally, due to its many truly remote settings, the very land itself makes combating family violence difficult. Isolation affects both the genesis of the problems and efforts to respond to individuals seeking relief and protection.

At the very foundation of Australian society lies a painful history and relationship with the ancient cultures of the Aboriginal and Torres Strait Islander people. These original inhabitants of this land suffered some of the worst abuses imaginable from the governing structure that today is attempting to respond to their needs. Historically, that response has created severe crises by its very nature. In one movement, as many as a third of all Aboriginal children were taken from their families in what is now called a "stolen" generation. Continuing mistreatment in the courts reopens old wounds and exacerbates cultural clashes. Although no one disagrees on the need to end family violence, definitions of cultural rights and protections in abusive situations will remain a source of division until or unless the Commonwealth knits these many threads of life into a cohesive pattern of community. That work has begun and will be addressed in this chapter. But there is much work yet to be done and the healing process must never be forgotten or abandoned out of frustration as the process continues.

THE AUSTRALIAN RESPONDENTS

The Australian sample consisted of 41 females and 8 males ranging in age from 20 to 70 years old. Almost half identified themselves as either middle or working class; 21 reported being single, 18 married or partnered, 5 separated, and 4 divorced. Six respondents agreed to personal interviews for follow-up questions. Like the general population of Australia, these respondents showed great diversity in religion. Within this small group, there were members of the following religions; Baptist, Anglican, Methodist, Presbyterian, Catholic, Church of England, United Church, Greek Orthodox, and Christian Hindu. Respondents came from Australia, the United Kingdom, Croatia, England, New Zealand, the United States, Africa, and Scotland, and their parents came from those countries plus Hungary, Ireland, and Switzerland.

Australian Participants' Definitions of Abuse

Australian implicit theories of abuse seem to emphasize harm and/or power and attempts to control, as illustrated in their general definitions of abuse. For example, a 25-year-old female said that abuse is "taking over someone's autonomy—making them participate in something that they may not necessarily want to do—this can be physical—for example, hitting someone without allowing them to say no; sexual—touching someone without allowing them to say no; and mental—telling someone they are worthless. . . ." A 39-year-old woman also referred to power and control, and emphasized the role of cultural values in maintaining abuse:

> Abuse in a relationship occurs when there is a power differential which leads to intimidation, leading to physical, emotional or psychological damage to one party. In Australian society, however, emotional and psychological abuse extending to financial and social abuse are often overlooked and excused and victims are even encouraged to "live with it" by their extended family. The victim is given great physical and emotional support from the extended family to ensure that the family unit remains intact.

In general, respondents' examples of extreme abuse emphasized extent of harm or chronicity of the abuse: "Physical abuse that results in hospitalization, broken limbs, knife wounds, and so forth. Mental, verbal, emotional—drives victim to drastic self-abuse such as suicide" (male, 37 years old); "Ongoing and intense (severe in terms of hurt experienced by the person being abused). Typically, conscious (controlling) and systematic—for example, a wife who constantly belittles her husband in public, and who mentally and physically attacks him at home" (female, 45); "continual, consciously repeated abuse; that which is designed to assert power and dominance and degrade—such as humiliation, physical harm, rape, and so forth, which maintains the victim's sense of powerlessness, fear and lack of control" (female, 43); and "Sexual actions against a non-consenting person. Anything that leaves permanent damage that is difficult to overcome. Physical injury, poor self-esteem affecting ability to function in community" (female, 43). Some of the examples identified a wide range of forms of intimidation—for example, "implied or overt threats of violence, flashing or producing a weapon, euthanasia of pet, separation/isolation from family especially the 'other' parent, failing to report abuse to police" (female, 59).

Almost all of the Australian participants provided examples of abuse that they or someone they knew had experienced. Among these experiences were: "My mother would hit sister and I from frustration with her situation or the world or depression. As a child I would go to school with 'welts' on my legs" (female 52); "A friend of mine was sexually abused by her stepbrother and mentally abused by her stepfather with methods such as calling her a pig and holding her up against a wall and smashing food in her face" (female, 24); "Mother banging back of child's head on brick kitchen wall daily and locking child for hours on end in linen cupboard" (female, 48); "Hitting partner on face. Not so abusive since partner had been abused emotionally by drug-addicted partner for two years and had reached end of tolerance. Mildly abusive" (male, 63). Eleven of the women reported personal experience or knowledge of sexual abuse.

THE AUSTRALIAN MACROSYSTEM

Historical Context[1]

Forty thousand years ago, a group of people walked over a fragile land bridge created during the lowering of the oceans by an ice age into the southern continent of Australia from (most probably) Southeast Asia. The lives of these aboriginal peoples remained quite stable until the arrival of European explorers changed things forever—particularly after Captain James Cook claimed the land for the British Empire in the 1780s and the decision was made to use it as an answer to severe overcrowding in Britain's penal system. There were 750 male and female convicts in the first transport, along with four companies of Royal Marines to control them. They brought supplies for 2 years and spent the next 16 fighting off starvation. The discovery of gold in the 1850s brought a groundswell of people with money, supplies, and a determination to own the land and the gold it produced. Aboriginal people were actively and violently expelled from their tribal lands. New settlers focused on farming and mining to supply the

---

[1]*The World Book Online* (n.d.) was the principal source for the historical information.

needs of England's Industrial Revolution—with such success that the federation of the colonies occurred in 1901.

In the 20th century, wars sparked fears that Australia was seriously underpopulated and consequently vulnerable to attack, leading to a policy of enticing new groups of people to the country. Almost three million people responded to the invitation, with new settlers arriving at a rate of over 100,000 persons a year. In 1974, restrictions were enacted to stem the flow of newcomers, but the recent arrivals had already changed the face of the country. Until the end of WWII, almost all immigrants had come from the British Isles. In the postwar period, less than one third was from Britain; emigrants from Italy (16%), Greece (10%), Germany, the Netherlands, and, most recently, Asia, surged into populated areas. Today, the country faces what some call the "Asianization" of Australia, which is creating new political tensions. Such tensions are multiplied as the population deals with the struggles of its own ancient ancestors. While opening its lands to the refugees, Australia has continued to deny them to the original inhabitants, relegating Aboriginal communities to areas with deplorable conditions.

Aboriginal Families

In 1994, there were over 303,250 Aboriginal and Torres Strait Islander people in Australia. Almost 40% of these were under 15 years of age (compared to 22% of nonindigenous population). Major problems reported by members of these communities include alcohol abuse, low levels of education, and problems with the law, as well as other trauma related to early removal from families (Royal Commission into Aboriginal Deaths in Custody, 1998). Over 10% of the Royal Commission respondents age 25 and older reported having been taken from their natural family. Of the 12,500 people removed from their homes, 32% were raised in non-Aboriginal or Torres Strait Islander families. Approximately 13% of respondents ages 13 and over had been physically attacked or verbally threatened in the 12 months preceding the Royal Commission survey. (Whether these experiences occurred within a family setting was not specified.) When asked how well they thought the police performed their jobs, respondents in rural areas had a more positive perception than did those in urban areas. Over half felt they were treated fairly by police but only 30% said the police did a good job dealing with family violence.

Macrosystem Definitions of Family Violence/Domestic Abuse

Historically, in Australia, there was a general belief that what occurred in the privacy of a home between a man and his wife and children was very much a private affair. As society changed in its perceptions of civil and individual rights in the 20th and 21st centuries, laws were, and are, being passed to redefine those rights, even within the family. However, the implicit theories embodied in laws changes much faster and easier than the perceptions of those called upon to enforce it or live within it.

Under Australian law, use of the term "domestic violence" refers exclusively to violence committed by a heterosexual partner and includes physical injury, intimidation or serious harassment, willful damage to property, indecent behavior without consent, or a threat to commit any of these acts (Alexander, 1993). When the Australian Prime Minister convened a Heads of Government at the National Domestic Violence Summit in 1997, they indicated that "Domestic violence is an abuse of power perpetrated mainly—but not only—by men against women in a relationship or after separation" (http://www.dpmc.gov.au/docs/9-97DV.cfm). Materials put out as a result of this Summit stated that many Aboriginal and Torres Strait Islander communities prefer the term "family violence" to "domestic violence" because family violence "was defined in a broad manner to encapsulate not only the extended nature of indigenous families but also the context of a range of forms of violence occurring frequently between kinspeople in indigenous communities" (http://www.dpmc.gov.au/docs/9-97DV.cfm).

In the Northern Territory, it was not until 1989 that provisions were added to the Justices Act to allow restraining orders to be taken out in spousal relationships. These provisions have allowed police a firmer legal stand to respond from within that complex community/cultural setting; however, even today women are often unwilling to press charges against abusive spouses. According to the Domestic Violence (Family Protection) Act of 1994, domestic violence is a criminal offense and police are bound by law to intervene effectively. As a result, Domestic Violence Units (DVU) have been created within the Northern Territory Police department. These units provide a clear directive that police officers must check on restraining orders, check firearms records, and provide transport or other assistance to victims as needed. The extent to which these units are effective is still in dispute by domestic violence advocates, especially within the Aboriginal communities. In their view, perceptions, language, culture, and community standards continue to work against such innovative programs.

THE AUSTRALIAN MICROSYSTEM

Family Structure

In June, 1992, 84% of the more than four million families identified in Australia contained a couple, and 51% of the couples had dependent children present—indicating that only about 25% of families consisted of a father, mother, and dependent children at home (Australian Bureau of Statistics, 1998). Nine percent of the families were one-parent families, and 53% of the couples with dependents had both persons working outside the home. According to McKay (1993), the current generation of Australians is rapidly becoming the most married and most divorced generation in Australian history, and for the first time in its history, the majority of divorces are being initiated by women.

Some immigrant groups, such as the Vietnamese, are concerned that the new environment in which they live is damaging the stable family structure they knew within their home culture (Lewins & Ly, 1985). For example, whereas extended families once provided the full range of essential support services needed by members of the community, immigrants must now deal with institutions such as day care, a problem that may be intimidating if they have had prior experience with politically run Communist facilities. For financial reasons, parents may need to work; however, leaving their children in the hands of strangers who introduce their children to an alien culture faster than the parents want causes a serious sense of loss of control.

FAMILY VIOLENCE IN AUSTRALIA

In 1996, data put out by the Australian Bureau of Statistics included information on approximately 6,300 Australian women who responded to the Women's Safety Survey. This survey recorded their experience of actual or threatened physical and sexual violence during the preceding 12 months. The findings indicated that over 7% of the women had experienced interpersonal violence; 6% reported a male perpetrator, and 1.6% reported a female perpetrator. Of the women physically assaulted in the previous 12 months, 58% spoke to a friend or neighbor about it; 53% spoke to a family member; 12% spoke to a counselor, and 4.5% spoke to a crisis center. Only 19% reported the incident to the police and 18% never told anyone about it. Extrapolating from data on lifetime experience of violence, the report projected that 2.6 million women (38% of the adult female population) had experienced one or more incidents of physical or sexual violence since the age of 15.

Other relevant statistics come from a national census of the Supported Accommodation Assistance Program (SAAP), which provides accommodations to women escaping domestic violence. The SAAP reported an average of 2,149 women seeking accommodations each night during the 2-week survey in 1994. In that same 2-week period, another 1,956 women sought refuge but could not be accommodated.

Several more localized studies provide further evidence of the pervasiveness of domestic violence. The Women's Domestic Violence Crisis Services of

Victoria received 5,198 calls for information, support, or emergency accommodations in a single 6-month period in 1996. Also in 1995–1996, the Victoria police department received 15,613 reports of incidents of family violence (Department of Justice, 1996). In a 1991 study of hospital patients in Queensland, 23% of the female respondents admitted to a history of domestic violence (Roberts, O'Toole, & Raphael, 1993). Similarly, a survey of general practitioner patients in Melbourne (November 1993–February 1994) revealed that within the prior 12 months, 28% of the women had experienced physical or emotional abuse in their current relationship (Mazza, Dennerstein, & Ryan, 1996). All of these figures are probably underestimates.

Cumberworth (1997) reported several findings specific to Aboriginal communities, including: 1) An estimated 90% of Aboriginal families are faced with family violence; 2) Aboriginal women are 10 times more likely than White women to be killed from family violence; 3) in most states, over 70% of assaults on Aboriginal and Torres Islander women have been carried out by their husbands or boyfriends; 4) over 50% of Aboriginal children are victims of family violence and child abuse; and 5) 79% of chargeable homicides in the Northern Territory in 1987 were Aborigine women. In a graphic example of the issue of Aboriginal rights within the justice system, a state judge ruled in North Queensland that an Aboriginal man's "right to forcible intercourse with an underage girl" was traditional law within their 40,000-year-old practices. The judge in this Northern Territory ruled that the 15-year-old Aboriginal girl "knew what was expected of her and didn't need protection" from the 50-year-old man who raped her. He noted "Expert testimony submitted by an anthropologist in the case called the man's arrangement with the girl 'traditional' and therefore 'morally correct.' " The situation arose from a promise made by the girl's parents at the time of her birth in return for a portion of the man's government allowance. When he came to claim his rights, the girl refused and he was reported to have punched her, put his foot on her neck, and raped her. Several high-ranking government officials approved an appeal judge's decision to uphold the man's defense, acknowledging that while the man knew he was doing "something wrong in the eyes of Western law, his conduct was 'Aboriginal custom' and part of his culture."

Child Abuse

Within the Australian legal system, children are seen as the primary victims of abuse, and children ages 14 and over can apply for their own intervention orders with the permission of the Court. In 1995, amendments were made to the Family Law Act, reinforcing certain areas of concern and protection. These included requiring courts, in the process of custody cases, to consider any evidence not only about violence directly against the children themselves but violence among other family members that the children could witness. They also required family courts to ensure than any order made with respect to children be consistent with any existing family violence order.

Previously, child abuse was seen as a health and welfare issue separate from domestic violence, which was seen as the domain for women's rights and legal advocates. The links between these two forms of family violence are becoming more clearly defined and acknowledged (Ashbury et al., 2000). Hughes (1986) reported an overlap between violence toward women and violence toward children of at least 40%. There is also increasing recognition of vulnerability of children to becoming "secondary victims"—that is, experiencing negative impacts from witnessing violence toward another family member, especially the mother. Although effects vary based on gender, age and stage of development, extent and frequency of violence, role of the child in the family, number of separations and moves, cultural background and personality of the child, there is clear consensus that the impact is significant.

According to a survey done by the Advocates for Survivors of Child Abuse of Australia (n.d.), one in four Australian girls and one in eight Australian boys have been abused, 90% of alcoholics and drug addicts have been abused, 85% of all prisoners were abused, abuse affects more people than illness or accidents, abuse kills more Australians than does any illness, and abuse has reached plague proportions and is the reason behind many suicides. Based on their own survey data, the ASCAA concluded that most abused people are females but many males may be abused but not disclose it; most abusers are males, but females can be perpetrators also; most abuse occurs in the immediate or extended family or by other people known to the victim and not by strangers; very few people report their abuse to the police and only 8% begin court action; multiple forms of abuse are common; the majority of abused children are abused from before the age of 4 years; most people recover memories slowly or have trouble remembering some details of their abuse because of the trauma, guilt, and shame associated with it; and, many abused people turn to someone for help after finding it very difficult to cope by themselves.

Australian Respondents' Perspectives on Child Abuse

In response to our request to provide examples of extreme child abuse, many of our respondents listed examples of sexual abuse. Physical aggression was also a concern, and examples were given of "repeatedly hitting a teenage girl seeking more independence," "hitting a child hard enough to break his legs," and "shaking a baby." Examples of moderate and mild abuse tended to be more psychological—for example, "mental abuse that could scar emotional development for life," "name calling to belittle," "threats to kill, harm, or maim," and "humiliating a child in front of peers." Several participants said there is no such thing as "mild" abuse.

Spouse Abuse

There is evidence that both men and women perpetrate domestic violence in Australia. Bagshaw and Chung (2000) addressed recent findings showing increased reports of women abusing men. Their comparisons of the nature and consequences of men's versus women's violence indicated that; 1) men's violence against women is more severe; 2) women partners are more likely to be killed by current and former male partners than by anyone else; and 3) the main reasons men kill their female partners are desertion, the ending of a relationship, and jealousy. By contrast, studies of wives who kill their husbands reveal a history of marital violence in more than 70% of the cases, and over 50% of the husband killings occur in response to an immediate threat or attack by the husband. Bagshaw and Chung also noted that men's violence is often an attempt to control, coerce, humiliate, or dominate by generating fear and intimidation, whereas women's violence is often an expression of frustration in response to their dependence or stress, or their refusal to accept a less powerful position.

Our respondents gave several examples of abuse of husbands by wives, indicating that their implicit theories encompass husband abuse. Each of the 8 male respondents reported incidents of being personally abused by their wives (almost exclusively emotional/verbal abuse), having their children abused by their wives (physical and emotional/verbal), and/or knowing friends who are abused in their spousal relationships. More abstract examples of husband abuse by both male and female respondents were generally quite similar to the examples of wife abuse—for example, "physical assault requiring medical attention," "sexual abuse," "psychological abuse," and "restriction of freedom." One 35-year-old male respondent, in response to the request for an example of extreme husband abuse, wrote "My culture seems to refuse to accept that women can be abusive." His example of moderate husband abuse was "murder," and his example of mild husband abuse was "attempted murder."

Australian Respondents' Perspectives on Spouse Abuse

In providing examples of severe wife abuse, respondents tended to emphasize both extreme physical violence (e.g., "beating a wife hard enough to cause welts or break the skin because she overcooked the potatoes," or "beating her so hard she sustains injuries") and extreme restriction of her activities (e.g., "tying a wife to a bed while the husband is at work to stop her from seeing other men"). Limiting a wife's freedom was also a strong theme in the examples of moderate wife abuse—for example, "controlling her life, who she is friends with, where she goes, and what she does"; "limiting her freedom or her friends"; and "financial control and social deprivation." Most examples of mild abuse were psychological—for example, "controlling behavior, intimidation, emotional torment, threat of physical harm"; "emotional blackmail"; "continual comments which affect her self esteem"; and "controlling the relationship and making her feel small, worthless and bad about herself."

Elder Abuse

Only recently has the Australian public acknowledged that elder abuse by family members is a problem. It appears to be associated with longer life spans accompanied by serious illness and/or dementia, and the increased demand for family caregiving. Elder maltreatment can be both active abuse (hitting, pushing, financial exploitation) as well as neglect (malnutrition, decubitus ulceration, inappropriate use of medication to oversedate). The more rural the area, and the more family based the community structure, the harder it is to have people admit or accept that there is elder abuse in the community. For recent immigrants from other cultures, such as the Asian, the tradition of elder respect and care can either prevent the problem or hide it when today's generations find themselves unable to deal with the demands of caring for parents.

The available literature indicates that elder abuse is a serious problem. Sadler, Kurrie, and Camerson (1992) found that nearly 5% of people over 65 years presenting to a geriatric service over a one-year period had experienced abuse. Bunt and Livermore (2000) found that more than 5% of referrals to the Central Coast Aged Care Assessment Team (ACAT) indicated they had experienced abuse. In a random community sample of South Australians, 2.5% of the older people ($n = 579$) stated they had experienced spousal abuse since turning 65 years old (Taylor & DelGrande, 1999). Of 55 cases of abuse reported in a Victorian survey, 30 older people were living with dementia (Barron, Cran, & Flitcroft, 1990). Elder abuse was recorded in 1.2% of all referrals to four Aged Care Assessment Teams ($n = 5,246$) from urban and rural areas in three states. Risk factors contributing to the abuse were mental health/alcohol abuse issues of the abuser (30%), dependency of the person experiencing abuse (25%), domestic violence (19%), carer abuse (18%), and financial dependence (8%; Kurrle, Sadler, & Lockwood, 1997).

From 1998 to 1999, 354 people sought assistance from ARAS about abuse of older people by family and friends. Of these, 69% were female, 10% were from a non-English speaking background, 21% had a diagnosis of dementia.

Over 50% had been abuse by their son or daughter, 21% by other family members, 8% by their spouse, 6% by friends, and 11% by multiple family members (Aged Rights Advocacy Service, 1998). Finally, 354 people who sought assistance from ARAS during 1998–1999 reported 658 different types of abuse. Older people reported they often experienced more than one form of abuse at a time from someone close to them. At the time assistance was sought, 35% were experiencing psychological abuse, and 34% were experiencing financial abuse (Sadler, Kurrle, & Camerson, 1992).

Australian Respondents' Perspectives on Elder Abuse

Examples of extreme elder abuse by our respondents included "physical assault," "shooting," and "beating," as well as various forms of restraint (e.g., "not allowing them the independence they deserve"; "forcing them to stay in room because they are incontinent"), and neglect ("ignoring them to point where they are hurt"; "denial of food, shelter and water"). Examples of moderate elder abuse included "shouting angrily," "being rude and demeaning," "restraining to a chair," "assault if not necessary," and "threatening them if they did not hand over money." Mild abuse generally involved psychological abuse or "forcing the elderly into a nursing home."

DOMESTIC VIOLENCE IN IMMIGRANT GROUPS

Groups at high risk for domestic violence include Asian immigrants, especially Asian women who are sponsored by non-Asian men for marriage, and Middle Eastern women brought over in arranged marriage contracts for Middle Eastern men in Australia (Elliott and Shanahan Research, 1988). Both groups of women are especially vulnerable, due to their being displaced from their families and community support and not being fully integrated or accepted into the new community or families. The Victorian Community Council Against Violence issued a report in 1992 stating that over 70% of the migrant women they had contact with had minimal knowledge of the legal rights of persons suffering domestic violence. The impression given was that many of these women did not even know that their husbands' aggression fell under such a label as "domestic violence" rather than simply normal behavior. Police, who are often associated with the military regimes inflicting terror and control in other countries, are not automatically seen as a resource by immigrants. Fear of their potential contact with immigration services only adds to suspicion and concerns of disclosing something "bad" happening in a home.

INDIGENOUS FAMILY VIOLENCE

In 1999, the Aboriginal and Torres Strait Islander Commission noted that "the increasing injuries and fatalities as a result of interpersonal violence have risen to levels which not only impair life but also threaten the continued existence of Australian Indigenous peoples." These levels can be understood only within an ecological framework acknowledging the full historical, political, and sociocultural forces influencing individuals and the communities in which they live. In Australia, colonization was a devastating blow to the immediate and long-term lives of the peoples already inhabiting the land. It is well documented that the use of alcohol and drugs is a major problem within the indigenous communities in Australia, just as it is in the Native American communities in America—and for the same basic reasons. A people were destroyed both externally and internally by the violence perpetrated against them. Violence by outsiders started a cycle of violence that is still being played out. Cawte (1974), whose work is based in a dual role as psychiatrist and anthropologist, has stated that there is "gross stress" within the Indigenous communities that impacts their lives as a form of posttraumatic stress disorder. This "gross stress" creates and continually feeds a sense of loss and bewilderment that manifests as major to mild emotional and behavioral disorders. Even when abused individuals seek respite from their own terror, sense of worthlessness, and questioning whether they somehow "deserve" abusive treatment, the issue of whom to turn to is enmeshed with distrust concerning the institutions that exercise some control in these communities. If the very set of people and agencies that are supposed to help in such crises are ones that have already broken trust and perpetrated their own fear and unjust treatment, how can victims turn to them for help?

In a paper presented at a national forum on men and relationships, Darcy Turgeon (2000; Manager, Aboriginal and Torres Strait Islander Unit, Department of Corrective Services) presented a "routine" psychological report on an Aboriginal prisoner in Brisbane Women's Correctional Center:

> I read with some amazement the General Hospital report which says she was "noted to have a superficial laceration in the right thigh. No other abnormalities noted . . . on examination she was noted to have a multitude of scars on all parts of body. Her chest is deeply scarred from a broken beer bottle; her left forearm and upper arms are extensively scarred from a beer bottle; she has stab wounds to her upper thighs and lower abdomen; a 9–10″ scar just below the breasts from a knife wound; her right eyebrow is scarred from punching; it appears she cannot see out of her left eye due to repeated blows; the back and top of her head has numerous scars from being hit with metal bars and broken bottles." To this Aboriginal woman, violence is part and parcel of her life. She

lives in a violent subculture where jealousies, arguments, and petty disputes are solved by violence. To her, having someone beat you with a metal bar or slash you with a broken beer bottle is anything but extraordinary—it is commonplace. And, as she admits, at times, she gives as good as she receives. It would appear, for this woman, and many of her peers, no other method of dispute settlement comes as naturally as a violent solution.

The Aboriginal people who are working on the issue have defined family violence as a consequence of colonization, forced assimilation, and cultural genocide; the learned negative, cumulative, multigenerational actions, values, beliefs, attitudes, and behavioral patterns practiced by one or more people that weaken or destroy the harmony and well-being of an Aboriginal individual, family, extended family, community or nationhood (Aboriginal Family Healing Joint Steering Committee, 1993, p. 10). The Committee lists many commonly recognized forms of abuse (e.g., physical, psychological, sexual, and financial abuse), but also adds the category of spiritual abuse ("entails the erosion or breaking down of one's cultural or religious belief system"). It is generally not the spiritual abuse of victims and their communities that is being addressed today, but rather the blackened eye or broken nose that finally gets noted.

According to a fact sheet ("An Aboriginal Perspective") from the Australian National Clearinghouse on Family Violence:

> Our Elders and traditional people encouraged us to look at initiating a healing approach rather than continuing to focus on the negative, on the violence. The concepts of healing—rather than merely responding to incidents of violence—and the focus on wellness demand a strategy that is different from the current responses to family violence. There is a contradiction between a solution that seeks harmony and balance, among individuals, family and community, and one that is crisis-oriented, punishes the abuser and separates the family and community. Our approach to wellness includes physical, mental, emotional and spiritual well-being. Throughout our work in addressing family violence, we strive to return our people to a time where everyone had a place in the circle and was valued. Recovering our identity will contribute to healing ourselves: Our healing will require us to rediscover who we are. We cannot look outside for our self-image. We need to rededicate ourselves to understanding our traditional ways. In our songs, ceremonies, language and relationships lay the instructions and directions to recovery. We must avoid a pan-Indian (one size fits all) approach. The issues of violence in our communities are diverse and so are our own cultural ways. It will be a long journey to recovery. The East, South, West and North all must develop our own process of healing—as must urban areas and reserve. This must be done if we are to return once more to a people without violence
> (http://www.hc-sc.gc.ca/hppb/familyviolence/).

ENDING FAMILY VIOLENCE IN AUSTRALIA

Mugford and Nelson (1996) wrote a report for the Australian Institute of Criminology that described 58 projects included in the Australian Violence Prevention Award Program between 1992–1995. A review of the programs offers true hope that Australia is not only taking this problem seriously but is addressing it in meaningful ways. These programs include the Safe Women-Liverpool Project in New South Wales, the Lesbian and Gay Anti-Violence Project in New South Wales, Atunypa Wiru Minyma Uwankaraku (Good Protection for All women) in the Northern Territories, the Joint Churches Domestic Violence Prevention Project in Queensland, the Elder Protection Program in South Australia, Support Help and Empowerment (SHE) in Tasmania, the Men's SHED (Self-Help Ending Domestics) Project in Victoria, and the Aboriginal Alternative Dispute Resolution Service in Western Australia. But what special issues, specific to the Australian culture, will have to be factored in and accommodated if family violence is truly to be dealt with effectively?

Australia's Unique Challenges

When the many blended cultures of Australia are examined, and the associated languages factored in, we see a set of not simply diverse but at times divergent issues facing the immigrant families and the original settlers of this land. Although family violence affects all social strata (age, gender, race, ethnicity, socioeconomic class, religion, etc.), it does not cut cleanly across them. The degree of impact, the degree of societal response, and even the definition of the problem are significantly impacted by the cultures within the Australian macrosystem.

Three fundamental issues were identified via this research in toto and by personal correspondence with some of the respondents from Australia. First, because of the intergenerational transmission of family violence, aggression among family members has become accepted behavior within some communities. Second, when you speak of rural versus urban issues in many countries, you are speaking of towns versus cities but in Australia, "rural" can mean hundreds of miles between small settlements. Social isolation for many farming families supports the agonizing sense of there being no alternative to violence being perpetrated save more violence. Third, the Aboriginal and Torres Strait Islander people experience family violence at a rate unparalleled by any other cultural group within Australia. A huge degree of responsibility for the violence lies within the very nature of the power structure in Australia in relation to this original people. The entire social welfare system is suspect and permeated with a racism that must be addressed before effective outreach can be done.

Allowing that education is a vital first step in combating family violence, we need to ask: Where should we begin the needed education to end family violence in all strata of the Australian culture of the 21st century? In short, the answer is "everywhere." We must continue to educate the personnel and agencies that are the front line of defense, we must do aggressive and comprehensive outreach to the children of this and each successive generation, we must do public education and outreach, with appropriate language and cultural formatting, in all cities and towns, and push to assure it touches the most remote of stations in the farming communities. We must do all this effectively to address the concerns expressed to me in a handwritten note by a woman actively involved in the consumer movement: "As I started to write out a bit more of my experiences for you, I got scared. The reaction of my family to my disclosures (in the past) was so awful that I am scared to speak out."

No voice must be stilled in Australia or anywhere in the world if we are ever to truly end family violence. Fear and silence empowers it; communication and unity empowers us.

ACKNOWLEDGMENTS

First and foremost to those persons who gave the time, caring, and often act of sheer bravery to share their responses and personal insights on our international questionnaire website. Warm thanks go to Bethany Stasiak for her indispensable assistance in recruiting the Australian sample. Special caring notation of appreciation goes to Jen (I will withhold her last name out of respect for the ongoing healing process she is dealing with in her family), who sent me envelopes of recent newspaper clippings to augment my research. Special thanks also go to Pauline Gill, a director of the Advocates for Survivors of Child Abuse, who gave permission for the use of their outstanding data, reprinted with their permission in this chapter; the same level of special thanks to Marilyn Crabtree, Manager Aged Rights Advocacy Service Inc. for their outstanding data, also reprinted with permission. Back in the states, special thanks for research assistance goes to Tania Cornelio for compiling all the responses on a new database after a hard disc crash and her excellent insights from the discussions arising from that work; Jennifer Wells for her compilation of the bibliography out of a box load of books, papers, and printed pages from the Internet and Lori Feldman for her computer research time to track all new ongoing website hits! To all 3 women, beyond these skills and work, I thank them for their care and insight into any and all my projects all the time!! And then—beyond words but requiring the same simple notation in every work done by me—I add the true foundation to my life and times: For you, Beloved.

REFERENCES

Aboriginal Family Healing Joint Steering Committee. (1993). *For generations to come: The is Now—A strategy for Aboriginal family healing.* Ontario, Canada: Author.

Advocates for Survivors of Child Abuse. (n.d.). Facts and figures. Available: http://www.asca.org.au/

Aged Rights Advocacy Service, Adelaide. (1998–99). *Abuse prevention program summary report.* Adelaide, Australia: Author.

Alexander, R. (1993). Wife-battering: An Australian perspective. *Journal of Family Violence, 8,* 229–251.

Ashbury, J., Atkinson, J., Duke, J. E., Easteal, P. L., Kurrie, S. E., Trait, P. R., & Tuner, J. (2000). The impact of domestic violence on individuals. *Medical Journal of Australia, 173,* 427–431.

Australian Bureau of Statistics. (1998). *Marriage and Divorce in Australia, 1998.* (ABS Catalogue 3310.0)

Bagshaw, D., & Chung, D. (2000, November). *Men, women and domestic violence.* Paper presented at the National Forum—Men and Relationships: Partnerships in Progress, Sydney, Australia.

Barron, B., Cran, A., & Flitcroft, J. (1990). *No innocent bystanders: A study of abuse of older people in our community.* Melbourne, Australia: Office of the Public Advocate.

Bunt, R., & Livermore, P. (2000). *Elder abuse amongst clients and carers referred to the Central Coast ACAT—A descriptive analysis.* Unpublished manuscript. (Available from Gosford Hospital ACAT PO Box 361, Gosford New South Wales 2250).

Cawte, J. (1974). *Medicine is the law: Studies of psychiatric anthropology of Aboriginal tribal societies.* Honolulu: University Press of Hawaii.

Cumberworth, A. (1997). Family violence within Australian society: A cross cultural perspective. Student Guild: Public Affairs Council. Available: http://www.gu.uwa.edu.au/councils/pac/sjustice/hb97-9.shtml

Domestic Violence & Incest Resource Centre (DVIRC). *Australian statistics on domestic violence.* Available: http://avoca.vicnet.net.au/~dvirc/Statistics.htm

Domestic violence in regional Australia: A literature review. Available: http://www.padv.dpmc.gov.au/osapdf/dr_regional.pdf

Elliott and Shanahan Research. (1988). *Summary of background research for development of a campaign against domestic violence, conducted for the Office of the Status of Women, Department of Prime Minister, and Cabinet.* Canberra, Australia: Author.

Flood, M. (n.d.). Statistics on violence. Available: http://www.anu.edu.au/~a112465/vstats.html

Hughes, H. (1986). Research with children in shelters: Implications for clinical services. *Children Today, 15*(2), 21–25.

Kurrle, S. E., Sadler, P. M., & Lockwood, K. (1997). Elder abuse: Prevalence, intervention and outcomes in patients referred to four aged care assessment teams. *Medical Journal of Australia, 166,* 119–122.

Lewins, F., & Ly, J. (1985). *The first wave: The settlement of Australia's first Vietnamese refugees.* Sydney: Allen & Unwin.

Mazza, D., Dennerstein, L., & Ryan, V. (1996). Physical, sexual and emotional violence against women: A general practice-based prevalence study. *Medical Journal of Australia, 164,* 14–17.

McKay, M. (1984). *The divorce book.* New Harbinger Publishing.

Mugford, J., & Nelson, D. (1996). *Compilers, violence prevention in practice: Australian award-winning programmes.* Griffith: Australian Institute of Criminology.

National Domestic Violence Summit: Statements of principles agreed by heads of government—Rogers, Blades & Goose—Oakland, New Harbinger 9–7–97. Available: http://www.dpmc.gov.au/docs/9-97DV.cfm

Roberts, G. L., O'Toole, B. I., Lawrence, J. M., & Raphael, B. (1993). Domestic violence victims in a hospital emergency department. *Medical Journal of Australia, 159,* 307–310.

Royal Commission into Aboriginal Deaths in Custody. (1998). Available: http://www.austlii.edu.au/au/other/IndigLRes/rciadic/

Sadler, P., Kurrle, S., & Cameron, I. (1992). Dementia and elder abuse. *Australian Journal of Aging, 14*(1), 36.

Taylor, A., & DelGrande, E. (1999). *South Australian health goals and targets: Violence and abuse health priority area, May 98 (Social Environmental Risk Context Information System [SERCIS] Monograph).* Adelaide, Australia: Department of Human Services.

Turgeon, D. (2000, November). *Ending family violence program for Aboriginal and Torres Strait Islander offenders.* Paper presented at the National Forum—Men and Relationships: Partnerships in Progress, Sydney, Australia.

Victorian Community Council against Violence. (1992). *Public violence: A report of violence in Victoria.* Melbourne, Australia: Author.

World Book Online Americas Edition. (2003). *Australia.* Available: http://www2.worldbook.com

LATIN AMERICA

21

Nicaragua

Kevin Powell

CAPSULE

Like all of the Latin American/Hispanic countries, as well as several of the other countries discussed in this book, family patterns and interactions in Nicaragua have been influenced by a history of colonization and exploitation by other countries. High poverty and unemployment, in a patriarchal culture where machismo and traditional gender roles prevail, put great stress on family relationships. Children are at great risk—from violence, from severe treatment in the penal system, from the necessity to engage in child labor. Abandonment seems to be one of the most likely forms of maltreatment.

THE NICARAGUAN SAMPLE

There were a total of 59 Nicaraguan respondents (38 females, ages 15 to 58, and 21 males, ages 14 to 70), all of whom were living in Nicaragua when they filled out the survey. All respondents reported a religious affiliation; 43 Catholic, and 16 Evangelic. Occupations ranged from unemployed, through positions such as secretary, to university professors.

Nicaraguan Participants' Definitions of Abuse

Most of the Nicaraguan participants indicated that they personally or someone they knew had experienced abuse in the context of the family. Their examples included "your brother takes your wallet and takes your money" (male, 24 years old); "by tricking, seducing a child with motives to violate" (male, 22); "masturbating an underage person" (female, 28); "an adult imposed sexual relations with a child" (female, 40); "forcing another person to be an accomplice" (male, 40); and "father abandoning children for lack of responsibility" (female, 38).

For Nicaraguans, loyalty, reverence, and responsibility to family and relatives are highly valued characteristics that form implicit theories of abuse. In our study, many respondents referred to issues of "abandonment," "neglect," "irresponsibility," and "cheating one's family" as extremely abusive. One female respondent, 17 years old, married, unemployed, and with a ninth-grade education, answered, "abuse is not to abide by the responsibilities, agreements, and rules of the house." She gave as an example of abuse in the family, "to come home later than what was expected." A 27-year-old man wrote that abandonment was the most severe form of abuse in any familial relationship. He noted, for example, that a father is extremely abusive when he "abandons his children because of alcohol addiction." A 29-year-old male gave "irresponsibility to one's family" as an example of extreme abuse. A different perspective comes from a 30-year-old woman, who said that "violation of a minor" and to "disrespect the rights of children" are examples of extreme abuse.

THE NICARAGUAN MACROSYSTEM

Historical Context

Beginning with its independence from Spain in 1821, political instability, civil war, poverty, foreign interventions, and natural disasters have continually afflicted this Central American country. None of the governments since colonial times have been able to achieve stability and sustainable economic growth. This is partly a consequence of the personal corruption and foreign special interests that have generally prevailed over the national interest, but it is also due in part to foreign intervention in Nicaraguan political and economic affairs, especially by the United States. The abusive history endured by Nicaraguans has certainly left its mark. Rampant poverty, high levels of unemployment, and political mistrust are very real wounds resulting from Nicaraguan history. In our survey, many respondents seemed to agree that "to step on others to get what you want" is a form of extreme abuse. Historically, this has been the Nicaraguan experience. As a people who have been repeatedly "stepped on" by successive leaders and foreign powers, it is no wonder that "unjust treatment of people," "not to respect the rights and liberty of humans," and "to step on others to get what you want" are all considered forms of extreme abuse among Nicaraguans.

Poverty

Although the government has made significant attempts at establishing economic programs to provide stability, improve budgetary imbalances, and control inflation in Nicaragua, the annual per capita income is very low—anywhere around US $100.00 (NIC, 2000) to $430.00 (World Bank, 2000; depending on your source), making it virtually impossible for working families to survive. To give these numbers context, Cruickshank pointed out that a professional nurse, who is a fairly advantaged member of Nicaraguan society, earns about $100 a month. For a family of six teenagers and one adult (usually a single mother) to be properly fed, about $250 a month is necessary to purchase local foods that are simple, adequate, and nutritious (Cruickshank, 2000).

A 1985 government study classified 69% of the population as poor because they were unable to satisfy one or more of their basic needs in housing, sanitary services (water, sewage, and garbage collection), education, and employment. The defining standards for this study were set quite low. For example, housing was considered substandard if it was constructed of discarded materials with dirt floors or if it was occupied by more than four persons per room. Today these numbers have improved considerably, although, according to the CIA World Fact Book (2000), 50% of the population still lives below the poverty line. Issues of poverty are compounded by high fertility rates in Nicaragua, which are twice the Latin American standard. On average, three children are born to each woman ("CIA World Fact Book," 2002), a number that increases to seven children per woman in rural areas. With 50% of Nicaragua's population under 17 years of age (World Bank, 2001), creating 84 dependents for every 100 people of productive age (UNFPA), it is no wonder that half the population is impoverished. Of those living in poverty, 70% are in rural areas (World Bank, 2001). Most of the poor are heavily involved in agricultural employment, which creates this paradox: If the poor are sowing the seeds, tending the fields, and harvesting the crops, why are roughly 20% of all children under 5 (and even more of the impoverished children) chronically malnourished (World Bank, 2000)?

According to the CIA World Factbook (2003), Nicaragua is one of the hemisphere's poor countries, with a huge external debt, and one of the most unequal distributions of income on the globe. The enormous international debt translates into harsh economic austerities. Unfortunately, the first expenses eliminated are social programs benefiting the populace as a whole, such as the welfare, public utilities, health, and education (Ramphal, 1999).

Men's and Women's Roles

On the whole, the lives of Nicaraguans are shaped primarily by traditional Hispanic values regarding appropriate sex roles. These roles dictate the proper way men and women should interact with each other, the way they should think, and the opportunities available to them. Although there are a number of factors contributing to interfamily violence in Nicaragua, many workers in the domestic violence field have found that the problem is predominantly cultural (Welsh, 2000, p. 4). For example, *machismo*, a term used to describe the "typical" Nicaraguan male, promotes and condones, among other things, violent attitudes and behaviors in men as evidence of masculinity.

Although there is no single accepted definition of machismo, there is considerable recognition that it represents values and behaviors that are central to the roles, status, rights, responsibilities, influences, and moral positions of men and women in Nicaragua. Consider this definition: "Machismo meant the repudiation of all 'feminine' virtues such as unselfishness, kindness, frankness, and truthfulness. It meant being willing to lie without compunction, to be suspicious, envious, jealous, malicious, vindictive, brutal and finally, to be willing to fight and kill without hesitation to protect one's manly image" (Boye Lafayette De Mente, 1996, p. 83). Machismo thus means that a man cannot let anything take away from his image of himself as a man, regardless of the suffering that resistance and/or retaliation may bring to him and the people around him. The dictionary also states that the proof of every man's manliness is his ability to completely dominate his wife and children, to have sexual relations with any woman he wants, to never let anyone question, deprecate, or attempt to thwart his manhood, and never to reveal his true feelings to anyone lest they somehow take advantage of him (Lafayette De Mente, 1996, p. 83).

This definition, although a Mexican interpretation, indicates well what machismo means in many Central American countries. In our survey, machismo was mentioned explicitly only once, although many of the respondents' answers made direct or indirect references to gender roles (i.e., the "proper" ways in which each sex should act). The one respondent who actually used the term machismo, a 42-year-old housewife, noted that to "perpetuate the machismo of the man during sex" is a form of extreme husband-to-wife abuse. This same respondent's example of wife-to-husband abuse was "to assist the Evangelic church without the husband's consent"; described as a form of mild abuse. This respondent's answers may seem contradictory. On the one hand, machismo during sex is considered abusive, yet on the other hand, doing something without your husband's approval is also seen as abusive. One response seems to condemn machismo, whereas the other condones it.

Status of Children in Nicaragua

Recent data indicated that approximately 46% of the Nicaraguan population is between 0 to 14 years of age; 75% of the under-10 population live in places stricken by poverty; infant mortality is 71.8 per 1,000 live births; 86 of every

1,000 Nicaraguan children between 0 to 6 years of age have no access to either day-care programs or preschool education; and approximately 150,000 children ages 7 to 12 do not attend primary school (Inter-American Commission on Human Rights, 1991).

Under Nicaraguan law, basic education is compulsory and free for all minors up to the end of the primary level (equivalent to sixth grade in the United States). Any guardian (parent or employer) who does not allow a child to receive this basic education is subject by law to penalties, although in practice the law is not enforced. The Government publicly expresses its commitment to children's human rights and welfare, yet does not allocate adequate funding for programs or primary education for children. A constitutional provision known as the "6 Percent Rule" automatically allots 6% of the annual budget to a higher education consortium, often at the expense of funding for primary and secondary education programs ("Area Studies," n.d.). A 1994 UNICEF report revealed that 24% of the children in Nicaragua receive no primary education. In Managua alone, almost 44% of the children between 6 and 9 years old do not know how to read and write (in rural areas the rate is 76%; UNICEF, 1994). Theoretically, all Nicaraguan children should be able to read and write after having received the compulsory primary education; however, 2002 statistics show that 33% of the population is illiterate (Deutsche Presse Agentur, 2002).

With nearly half of its population under 18, and its citizens engulfed in poverty, Nicaragua experiences a high rate of crimes by adolescents. In 1998, the 34,155 reported cases of adolescent crime represented 52% of all criminal cases. The specific offenses included 91 cases of murder (8% of all murders), 2,088 cases of serious assault (13% of all cases), 5,053 cases of theft (18% of all cases), 1,700 cases of breaking and entering (17% of all cases), 105 cases of fraud (5% of all cases), and 119 cases of drug offenses (11% of all cases; INTERPOL, 1998). Despite laws and codes set up to protect children, Nicaragua's penal code does not meet the norms of the United Nations Convention on Children's Rights, ratified by the Nicaraguan Government in 1990, and setting the age of children at 18 and younger. The penal code of Nicaragua considers that a person is an adult from 15 years of age on. Judges make no distinction in judgments of offenses committed by adults and those committed by children. Children are sentenced from 6 months up to 25 years imprisonment depending on the crime. "Lack of special tribunals and codes which take into account the international norms, and the lack of special centers and education programs for youth result in more than 300 minors jailed in the adult penal centers of the country" (Casa Alianza Nicaragua, 2002). A 1997 report (as cited in Casa Alianza Nicaragua, 2002) revealed that 87% of imprisoned youngsters came from marginal neighborhoods with high delinquency; 55% were from one-parent families.

The predominant economic activity in Nicaragua is informal or domestic work, which does not allow families to provide for the basic needs of their children. The priority of these families is survival, and their attention to their children is limited. Families do not have sufficient means for legal defense of their children. Thirty-five percent of criminal cases involving minors had no defense at all, even though official defenders were assigned; 80% of the processed and sentenced adolescents ignored their right of appeal, and 38% of the youngsters showed evidence of having been mistreated by the police when apprehended (Casa Alianza Nicaragua, 2002).

Drug abuse in Nicaragua is a growing problem, affecting the lives of many children. A recent survey carried out by Casa Alianza (1999) revealed that of the 520 children with whom it has daily contact in the streets, 504 children admitted to consuming drugs. The most commonly abused drug is glue, although high rates of crack, alcohol, and marijuana abuse are also found. In the Casa Alianza survey, most children claimed they took drugs to help them forget feelings of depression, sadness, suicide, cold, and hunger. Often times, street children are sexually exploited by adults who offer to buy them drugs in return for sexual favors. In our study, one respondent, a 24-year-old female, stated that "turning them on to drugs—especially the younger ones" is an act of extreme abuse among siblings. A 28-year-old male agrees that "giving drugs to a minor" is an extreme form of abuse.

Child Labor

Pablo and Walter stand outside of the bakery behind the Supermarket La Fe ("The Faith"), begging for money from the middle-class patrons who enter. Their clothes are torn and dirty, and the calluses on their feet testify that they have never owned a pair of shoes. Although they are both ten years old, neither one has ever attended school. However, they consider themselves lucky—they are fortunate enough to have a steady job cleaning the bakery each day for 3.50 cordobas (about 50 cents U.S.). In addition, they receive scraps of food and any money that they can earn begging outside. Pablo confided that in his family of nine, he is the only one who has a steady job. Pablo and Walter are just two of the growing number of Nicaraguan children who have been forced to forego their childhood and prematurely enter the adult reality of hardship and suffering. (Scheid, 1995, ¶ 1)

THE NICARAGUAN MICROSYSTEM

Due to a strong mistrust of government and foreign intervention, the family and kinship system has become for many Nicaraguans the only secure and reliable institution available. As a result, a family's name is used to judge individuals, a family's reputation serves to reserve and advance opportunities, and little stigma is attached to using one's position to advance the interests of relatives. For example, the Somoza Dynasty reigned in Nicaragua, despite their relentless corruption and oppression, for a total of 43 years because they passed down the title of president to family members and kept all other government positions filled by close friends.

Although the size and quality of Nicaraguan homes vary greatly depending on the means of the owner, more than half of Nicaraguan families live in a one-room house. Brick is usually used for the walls, and roofs are typically made of corrugated iron or burnt bricks from clay. Most families are quite large; six to eight people are common. "The Nicaraguan household is typically augmented by the presence of a grandparent, an aunt or uncle, an orphaned relative, a poor godchild, or a daughter with children of her own. Newly married couples sometimes take up residence in the home of one of the parental families" (Library of Congress, n.d.). In the countryside, families are even larger, ranging anywhere from 6 to 15 people, with many peasants taking advantage of the large number of children to help with work. These "typical" living situations are intensified by issues of unemployment, undernourishment, and poverty—creating fertile soil for violence and abuse.

> Daysi Loza lives in the city of Estel in a two-room abode together with her two children. The home has a living room and a kitchen. There is a separate outhouse at the back of the yard. Daysi got running water a year ago and installed a tap and a laundry basin in her yard. Her kitchen has a wood oven built of brick. In the living room there is a bed, two chairs, a table and a sewing machine with treadles. A roof made of corrugated iron protects against rain. Only last year Ms Loza earned her living by mending clothes for local people and washing their clothes. Recently she landed what she regards as a good job in a cigar factory in Estel. In daytime she now rolls cigars and mends clothes in the evening. She earns almost 1000 marks a month [roughly $500.00], which in her opinion is a very good salary. There is one brick wall in Ms Loza's house, two walls made of wood and one of paper still remains. Her savings allowing, she will gradually stock up on brick and cement. A brick wall will eventually replace the paper one.
> (http://www.heureka.fi/main/exhibition/kysy/engvastaus1.html)

The traditional Nicaraguan family structure is patrilineal. The father or corresponding male is the main provider for the family. He is responsible for the economic well-being of the household, and is also the main decision maker in the family. In our survey, for a man "not to administer the family economically" was seen as an act of extreme abuse. However, because of high levels of unemployment, many husbands have no jobs and spend their time drinking alcohol and/or looking for a job. A man who is unable to "control" his family (e.g., provide for them financially) is considered a failure. Thus, with intense societal pressure to be machismo, and a fear of rejection/

failure, it is no wonder that so many Nicaraguan men feel the necessity to exert control and dominance over women. As long as it is seen as extremely abusive for a woman to have "no value for the authority in the house," as one 45-year-old female respondent pointed out, gender and power imbalances will continue to oppress the family, creating an environment of abuse, and men will continue to perpetuate their roles as machistas.

FAMILY VIOLENCE IN NICARAGUA

Wife Abuse

In 1995, intrafamily violence was declared a public health issue in Nicaragua. Data revealed that nearly one-third of Nicaraguan women reported having been physically abused, frequently when their children were present and often during pregnancy. During this time, new laws were passed to prevent and eradicate family violence. For the first time, violence perpetrated by one family member against another was a criminal offense and punishable by a prison sentence. A 1995 research project in the northern city of León revealed that 60% of the women interviewed had been victimized by some type of violence (physical, sexual, or psychological) at least once in their lifetime (Welsh, 2000, p. 1). This research made it abundantly clear that thousands of Nicaraguan women of all ages were being systematically abused and violated by men.

Nicaraguan Participants' Perspectives on Wife Abuse

Interestingly enough, very few Nicaraguan respondents made any reference to physical aggression when giving examples of wife abuse—perhaps because physical abuse was not the most salient problem facing these respondents, or perhaps because physical aggression is so normative that it is not given the status of abuse in their implicit theories. In fact, nearly every example of abuse focused on sexual maltreatment or abandonment or both. Examples of abandonment as a form of extreme abuse included; "to abandon her with 7 children" (female, 30 years old); "Husband leaves the house, running from financial problems" (male, 24); "not to work and to run from one's responsibilities" (male, 29); "abandon your wife for another from Costa Rica" (male, 25); and "abandoning her when she is pregnant" (male, 20). Examples of sexual misconduct as a form of extreme wife abuse included; "Husband demands sex when wife is sick" (male, 15); "Making sexual advances in front of friends" (female, 38); "Tricking wife with sister-in-law (sexually)" (female, 20); and "Presenting a lover at home as a friend—

cheating" (female, 18). Such answers reflect the culture's deep respect for familial ties, and the view that damaging those ties is abusive.

Nicaraguan Respondents' Perspectives on Husband Abuse

For a man to uphold his honor as a "man," it is very important for a woman not to disrespect, humiliate, or wrong him, especially in public. Our respondents indicated that to "publicly cheat on your husband," "confront your partner in front of friends," "talk to your husband rudely," "send him to sleep on the sofa," "talk about his behavior badly in front of his friends," and "not to listen to him when he is drunk," are severe forms of wife-husband abuse—presumably because they are attacks on the man's pride, respect, and honor. When giving examples of extreme wife to husband abuse, respondents never included physically or sexually abusive acts. They appeared to assume that the only way a wife could severely abuse her husband was to use verbal threats or psychologically abuse him by not showing the respect and honor he "deserves" as a man. Even when men are unable to fulfill their responsibility for the family's livelihood, the illusion must be upheld.

Coupled with the fact that 50% of Nicaraguan men are unemployed, and 30% of households are headed by single mothers, it becomes obvious that some aspects of machismo are extremely out of date. Nevertheless, these norms are still a force in the lives of Nicaraguans, and many women continue to accept them. A 50-year-old female respondent listed "not attending to your husband" as a form of extreme abuse. According to other respondents, in order for a woman to attend properly to her husband, she must feed him on schedule, please him sexually, and not bother him with annoying questions. A 20-year-old female secretary stated that "not to feed him the entire day" is a form of extreme abuse—perpetuating the notion that a man is unable to cook or feed himself. Another respondent considered it a form of moderate abuse for a wife "not to have his food ready when he comes home from work."

By traditional Nicaraguan standards, a woman must be sensitive to all of her husband's needs. Women should always please their men sexually, lest they have extramarital affairs. Wives who do "not understand him sexually and neglect him," or who "don't please him sexually," are viewed as failing to fulfill "feminine" obligations adequately. Lastly, women are expected to stay out of the affairs of men. Their role is simply to remain attentive to their husbands and their families. One female respondent believed that "asking him questions like 'what do you do all day?'" was a form of moderate abuse. This same respondent, a 30-year-old female, wrote "infidelity," when asked what would constitute extreme abuse from wife to husband.

Violence Against Children

A Casa Alanza (2001) report revealed that in 2001, 97 children were murdered; 75% of the victims were young men and boys, the other 25% were girls. The most commonly used instrument for murder was a firearm, which took the life of 36 children, followed by some kind of a steel weapon, which took 34 lives. Beating a child to death was the third most commonly used method for murder, accounting for 14 of the deaths. Nearly 50% of the child murders took place in Managua (Casa Alianza, 2001). According to a 1991 UNICEF study, 107,500 children are in a strategy of survival; 1,100 are living and sleeping on the street; 3,500 are victims of abuse and abandonment; 267,000 are victims of the armed conflicts; 182,000 are victims of natural disasters; 113,000 children have specific needs for preventive care. Because the economic and political situation has not improved in the intervening years, it is likely that those numbers have either stayed the same or worse still, have increased.

Nicaraguan Respondents' Perspectives on Child Abuse

By far the most common example of child abuse—particularly of extreme abuse—provided by our Nicaraguan participants was sexual abuse. Among the examples of extreme abuse were "an adult imposes sexual relations on a child" (male, 40); "sexually abusing minors" (female, 35); "to masturbate a minor" (female, 28); "violation of an underage girl by her uncle" (female, 30); "masturbation of a child throughout childhood by a close parent" (female, 35); "stepfather masturbates the stepchild" (female, 24); and "forcing a daughter into prostitution" (same 24-year-old female).

A large proportion of examples of child abuse also focused on the issue of labor, and the related issue of educational deprivation. A 20-year-old male wrote that it is extremely abusive "when a father denies his son to study only because he himself did not study," as is a father "forcing the son to work underage." A 58-year-old mother of eight stated that "abusing the trust of a child" and "forcing a minor to work" are both forms of extreme abuse. "Not to allow children to study" is a form of moderate abuse, according to a 30-year-old mother of two.

The other frequent type of example of child abuse referred to psychological abuse—often in relation to issues of work and school. For example, a 29-year-old father of two stated that telling your children "you are stupid, you aren't worth anything" is moderately abusive. A 45-year-old mother of eight stated that when a father tells his son, "you are a parasite of society," that child is being exposed to a form of extreme abuse.

Nicaraguan Perspectives on Elder Abuse

It proved very difficult to find any information on elder abuse in Nicaragua in the public and research literature. However, almost all of our participants gave examples of behaviors that would be considered forms of elder abuse in Nicaragua. There were no examples of physical or sexual abuse, but a great deal of emphasis on abandonment and some emphasis on financial exploitation and psychological neglect. Nearly a third of the sample said that "sending them into elder homes" was severely abusive. An 18-year-old female was even more inclusive in her example of extreme abuse: "Leaving an elderly parent in a shelter/refuge/institution, forgetting them." Among the examples of financial and material exploitation were the following: "Not to help them economically" (female, 15); "Force them out of their homes" (male, 21); "Take advantage of their lack of mental facilities and keep all of the inheritance" (male, 24); and "Taking the elder father's belongings away from him" (male, 32). Implicit theories of elder abuse also encompassed psychological abuse: "Not to care for them out of a lack of love and caring" (male, 29); "The son allows his father to sleep in the kitchen" (female, 38); "Lack of attention and love" (female, 28). Other forms of neglect included: "Not to care for them in their illness" (female, 30), and "Leave them to die when they need you" (male, 40).

INTERVENTION AND PREVENTION

Reforming Machismo

According to Welsh (2000, p. 1), machismo produces long-term physical and mental health problems in men that she described as "a type of systematic self-inflicted violence." In her view, the socialization practices underlying machismo are dehumanizing to men and lead to chronic health disorders, such as heart disease and cirrhosis of the liver. In Nicaragua, men's life expectancy is lower than women's, and, according to Welsh, these statistics are related to the social construction of male gender identity. If her argument is correct, it appears that transformations in men's perceptions of themselves, in their values, and in the ways they behave will improve not only the quality of women's lives but also their own. Welsh provides examples of several programs developed to combat the pernicious effects of machismo—all of which can be viewed as an effort to change implicit theories as to the appropriate roles for men.

MAVG. The first attempt at reforming machismo in Nicaragua began in 1993 with the creation of the "Men Against Violence Group" (MAVG). One of the major aims of MAVG was to offer a meeting place for men to reflect on the violence in their lives and the effects of machismo on other people and themselves. The group holds the opinion that male values and behavior, including violence, are socially learned and can therefore be unlearned. MAVG has been influential in promoting workshops and seminars all over the country for men to discuss masculinity and violence, putting the issue of machismo on the public agenda. MAVG's message is simple and clear: Violence against women and children is unacceptable, and men must take responsibility for their behavior and contribute to the eradication of domestic violence. (Welsh, 2000, p. 4)

CANTERA. In 1994, the Center for Popular Education and Communications (CANTERA) began to develop a training course for men that asked them to reflect critically on what it means to be male in Nicaraguan society. The course considers men's own life experiences, values, attitudes, ideas, dreams, fears, prejudices, and behaviors as a basis for serious and critical reflection on machismo. As Welsh pointed out, these courses enable men "to discover for themselves to what extent they have incorporated the '*machista* model of masculinity' into their own individual male identity and sincerely analyse the power and violence that they wield in their families, at work and within the community" (Welsh, 2000, p. 4).

Puntos de Encuentro. In 1997, Puntos de Encuentro, a Nicaraguan women's rights association, conducted a research project designed to examine the relationship between violence and male identity, and to identify methods for changing behavior. In 1998, as economic pressures exacerbated problems of domestic violence, Puntos de Encuentro began a campaign in which messages via posters, pamphlets, educational materials, and training for activists, were conveyed to the public. The messages simply stated that men can avoid violent behavior, and that violence against women hinders reconstruction of communities and the nation. Both precampaign and postcampaign surveys were conducted to evaluate its effectiveness. The data collected indicated that the campaign was successful in getting the attention of men and in encouraging them to discuss these messages and begin the process of behavior change (The Communication Initiative, 2000).

AHCV. In 2000, the Asociacion de Hombres Contra la Violencia (AHCV) was founded. Their main goal is to reduce violence against women by developing and implementing ways of working with men on issues of masculinity and violence. They seek to raise men's awareness on issues of gender equity, masculinity, power, and gender-based violence, and to engender changes in patriarchal attitudes, values, and behavior. AHCV has conducted training workshops and courses for male youths, adolescents, and adults, to explore and redefine the ideas of machismo and violence. The association has also participated in TV and radio programs on issues related to masculinity and violence, as well as having published articles for local, national, and international publications. The association is currently developing a program of support and therapy for men who use violence against their partners (AHCV, 2000).

Programs for Children

The Nicaraguan Social Security and Welfare Institute (Instituto Nicaraguense de Seguridad Social y Bienestar; INSSB) is responsible for the care and service programs for minors. Their task is to provide minors up to 15 years of age with the care and attention they need for proper development by means of preventive, protective, and re-educational activities conducted through a national network of centers and Community Work activities (INSSB, 1991). Nicaragua's current population under 15 numbers about 1,790,000 persons, of whom only 56,219 are being cared for by the INSSB under its various programs.

The Nicaraguan constitution contains provisions designed to protect children's rights. It prohibits any child labor that can affect normal childhood development or interfere with the compulsory school year. The Constitution also has provisions intended to protect children from any type of economic or social exploitation. The 1996 Labor Code raised the age at which children may begin working with parental permission from 12 to 14 years. Parental permission to work is also required for 15- and 16-year-old adolescents. The law limits the workday for such children to 6 hours and prohibits night work (Commission on Human Rights, 2000). Labor legislation in Nicaragua prohibits child labor in areas such as mines and garbage dumps, and imposes heavy fines for illegal employment. The Ministry of Labor established an inspection unit to monitor occupational safety and health in the agricultural sector, signed agreements with nightclubs and restaurant owners who pledged to comply with labor laws, and issued a resolution in 1999 prohibiting employment of minors specifically in the free trade zones. However, there have been some exceptions due to most families' need of extra income. The 1996 Labor Code authorizes children to work under certain circumstances, provided they are no younger than 14 years of age and have parental permission (Commission on Human Rights, 2000).

Despite comprehensive legislation prohibiting child labor, structural economic problems have prevented its eradication. The Government has been able to make progress in combating child labor in the formal sector of the economy regulated by the Government, such as factories, construction, restaurants, and nightclubs. However, most of the problems exist in the informal sector of the economy, which is not regulated by the Government. Child workers in the informal sector have no legal employer, often working as street vendors, windshield washers, parking lot attendants, garbage dump scavengers, beggars, prostitutes, and agricultural workers (United States Department of Labor, 2003). The latest official figures regarding the number of working children estimate that approximately 161,000 children between 10 and 19 are presently employed in Nicaragua (U.S. Department of State, 2000). The percentage of participation of children in the labor market runs at 7.4% for boys and at 5.2% for girls (Civil Society on the Rights of Children in Nicaragua, 1999). Over 140,000 children are employed in rural areas at coffee, tobacco, rice, and banana plantations. In Managua alone, over 6,000 children work in the city streets, doing anything from selling merchandise to cleaning automobile windows to begging (U.S. Department of State, 2000).

According to a 2003 United States Department of Labor report, somewhere between 11% and 43% of Nicaraguan children between the ages of 10 and 14 work. In another study, it was concluded that over 161,000 children between 10 and 19 years of age work, including approximately 140,000 employed in rural areas such as coffee, tobacco, rice, and banana plantations, often for less than a dollar a day. The study further revealed that between 4,000 and 5,000 children work in urban areas as beggars, or as self-employed car washers or parking attendants (U.S. Department of Labor, 2003).

Child prostitution in Nicaragua has become a serious problem in recent years. Although national figures are not available, a study conducted in Managua in 1998 found that 40% of the 1,200 prostitutes in the city were under the age of 18. No numbers were available for other cities, but in 1998, UNICEF reported that teenage sexual exploitation had increased in recent years in rural areas, border cities, ports, and in Managua.

The Ministry of Family. The Ministry of Family sponsors several programs that target working minors. These programs, which cover up to 10,000 children nationwide, include childcare services, return-to-school programs, and technical and vocational training. The programs also include training for parents and teachers. The Ministry of the Family, in conjunction with the Ministry of Education, established a program to keep 647 children off city intersections where they wash windshields. The program provides housing for the 75% of these children who are homeless and schooling for the 60% who are school dropouts (Commission on Human Rights, 2000).

Quincho Barrilete. Quincho Barrilete is a recovery program for glue-sniffing boys that began in 1991. The project is named after an 8-year-old boy who lost his parents and his home in an earthquake, yet managed to support himself and his family by selling handmade kites. The program focuses on rehabilitating the boys and helping them reintegrate into society. They receive medical attention, and attend a local school. The founder and director of the program, Zelinda Roccia, claims that the key to the boys' recovery is getting them away from the influence of the subculture associated with the public markets. The project is located on a farm 40 km south of the country's capital, Managua. They currently depend on volunteers and donations to continue their work.

Las Chicas. Las Chicas, a project very similar to Quincho Barrilete, attempts to get girls away from the influence of the glue, yet also teaches them self-sufficiency skills. The girls take classes at a nearby school, or are otherwise tutored at the house. All the girls participate in sewing, ceramic, and baking workshops. The goal of the program is that the girls will acquire a level of self-confidence and skills to build a new life elsewhere.

CONCLUSION

Despite tremendous problems related to poverty, Nicaragua is making tremendous efforts to legislate against violence, and to provide social service programs for citizens at risk. Efforts are being made at both the macrosystem level to address problems of poverty and unemployment, and at the individual level to address machismo, and tolerance for violence in family relationships.

ACKNOWLEDGMENTS

Many thanks go to Elissa McCarthy and Katherine Joseph for helping recruit participants, to Marcia Johnston for typing the survey responses, and to Liana Shelby for assisting with the referencing.

REFERENCES

Area Studies, Nicaragua. (n.d.). Available: http://wrc.lingnet.org/nicaragu.htm

Asociacion de Hombres Contra la Violencia. (2000). *Convoca a primera asamblea general* [Meeting of the first general assembly]. Available: http://www.eurowrc.org/03.network/out_europe/01.out_europe.htm

Casa Alianza—Human Rights—Last Minute News. (1999, October 11). Casa Alianza helping street children quit drugs [online]. Available: http://www.casa-alianza.org/EN/lmn/docs/19991011.00341.html

Casa Alianza Nicaragua. (2001). *Children and youth extra judicially murdered in Nicaragua* [online]. Available: http://www.casa-alianza.org/EN/human-rights/torture-nicaragua/list2001.shtml

Casa Alianza Nicaragua. (2002). *Street children in Nicaragua* [online]. Available: http://www.casa-alianza.org/EN/about/offices/nicaragua/children.shtml

CIA World Fact Book, Nicaragua. (2000). Available: http://www.cia.gov/cia/publications/factbook/geos/nu.html

CIA World Fact Book, Nicaragua. (2002). Available: http://www.cia.gov/cia/publications/factbook/geos/nu.html

CIA World Fact Book, Nicaragua. (2003). Available: http://www.cia.gov/cia/publications/factbook/geos/nu.html

Civil Society on the Rights of Children in Nicaragua. (1999, May–June). *Second Report.* Submitted to the UN Committee on the Rights of Children.

The Communication Initiative. (2000, August 17). Puntos de Enceuntro-Nicaragua. Available: http://www.commitinit.com/pds-08-17-00/sld-yz.html

Cruickshank, C. (2000). Report from Nicaragua: Midwifery and structural adjustment. *Journal of Midwifery & Women's Health, 45*(5), 411–415.

Deutsche Presse Agentur. (2002). *Central America immersed in poverty* [online]. Available: http://www.dpa.de

Inter-American Commission on Human Rights. (1991). Available: http://www.cidh.oas.org/DefaultE.htm

INTERPOL. (1998). *International crime statistics* [online]. Available: http://www.interpol.int/Public/Statistics/ICS/Default.asp

Lafayette De Mente, B. (1996). *The dictionary of Mexican cultural code words.* New York: McGraw Hill/Contemporary Publishing.

Library of Congress. (n.d.). *Country studies: Nicaragua* [online]. Available: http://lcweb2.loc.gov/frd/cs/nitoc.html#ni0004

Nicaraguan Social Security and Welfare Institute [Instituto Nicaraguense de Seguridad Social y Bienestar]. (1991). *Report.* Available: http://www.cidh.oas.org

Ramphal, S. (1999). *Debt has a child's face, UNICEF* [online]. Available: http://www.unicef.org/pon99/pon99_5.pdf

Scheid, A. (1995, January). *The precarious situation of Nicaragua's street children MesoAmerica* [online]. Available: http://pangaea.org/street_children/latin/nicaragu.htm

UNICEF. (1994). *Education commentary* [online]. Available: http://www.unicef.org/pon97/32-39.pdf

U.S. Department of Labor, Bureau of International Labor Affairs. (2003, October 4). Nicaragua. Available: www.dol.gov/ilab/media/reports/iclp/Advancingl/html/nicaragua.htm

U.S. Department of State. (2000). *Country reports on human rights practices.* Available: http://www.globalmarch.org/virtuallibrary/usdepartment/human-rights/latin-america/nicaraqua.htm

Welsh, P. (2000). *Weeping within: Gender work with men in Nicaragua* [online]. Available: http://www.iol.ie/~vmmeurgo/Weeping_Within.html

World Bank. (2000). Appendix 6: Country eligibility for borrowing from the World Bank (as of July 1, 2000). Available: www.worldbank.org/html/extpb/annrep2000/pdf/appndx/ub-a6.pdf

World Bank. (2001). *Nicaragua at a glance* [online]. Available: http://www.worldbank.org/data/countrydata/aag/nic_aag.pdf

22

Brazil

Wilson Bezerra-Flanders

CAPSULE

Brazil has a historical legacy of violence. During the Portuguese colonization, Brazilian Indians, and later African slaves, were punished with lashings, beatings, and death. Throughout the country's history, opponents of the government have been tortured and/or killed. Only during the last decade have Human Rights complaints been addressed. Brazil's relatively recent change from a primarily rural to an urban society has added to strains caused by poverty, as cities struggle to accommodate an influx of immigrants from the countryside. A social war between classes, the power of drug lords and organized crime, and widespread corruption in the justice system, have put Brazilians under siege. Stories of police torture and abuses by guards in prison are frequently on the news. All of these forces have an impact on how families deal with conflict and violence.

Although the new constitution has rigorous protection laws against child maltreatment, domestic violence, and elder abuse, serious violations still take place. Nonprofit organizations, universities, hospitals, and the media are making efforts to educate the public, but ridding Brazil of violent conflict tactics is an ongoing challenge.

THE BRAZIL SAMPLE

The Brazilian survey was filled out by 82 participants (56 female and 26 male), ages 16 to 57, from several regions of the country. Religious affiliations were Catholic (75%), Protestant (14%), Spiritualist (3%), Jewish (1%), and Muslim (1%). Half of the participants were single, followed by married (37%), and divorced (6%). The self-identified social class distribution was upper class (6%), upper middle class (17%), middle class (51%), lower middle class (11%), and poor (16%). Forty percent of the participants had a Bachelors degree, 24% either had a graduate degree or were working on it, 16% had finished high school, 10% had finished middle school, 5% had finished elementary school only, and 4% had only a few years of schooling or no schooling at all. Overall, this means that the majority of participants were quite well educated as compared with the majority of the population. Most of our data were collected over the Internet, but we also interviewed participants. Participation in research is not common in Brazil, and people are wary of talking about family violence to strangers, even through an impersonal means like the Internet. Therefore, the majority of participants can be considered more sophisticated than the average Brazilian, but their perceptions of abuse reflect the culture well.

Brazilian Participants' Examples and Definitions of Abuse

When giving examples of abuse, every respondent mentioned some type of physical aggression (from "hitting lightly" to "throwing objects," to "suffocating" to "killing") as well as some form of verbal abuse (like "calling names," "yelling," or "verbal humiliation"). This can be seen as evidence of a growing awareness in Brazilian society that physical and verbal aggression are abusive. Neglect ("not attending to psychological and physical needs," "ignoring") was also reported by most respondents. Sexual abuse (including "rape") was the least mentioned form of abuse, which may be due both to lack of awareness concerning the prevalence of the problem and the stigma attached to it. "Certain incidents" are talked about only within the family, and sexual abuse is one of them.

THE BRAZILIAN MACROSYSTEM

Historical Context

Originally inhabited solely by indigenous populations, Brazil was claimed by the Portuguese Crown in 1500. The Portuguese colonizers and other Europeans invaders (the French, the Dutch, and the Spanish) either killed the indigenous people or forced them into labor, using torture to subdue any resistance. From 1538 to the late 18th century, millions of Africans were brought to Brazil as slaves. When slavery officially ended, the former slaves were left to fend for themselves on the streets (Page, 1996). The historical legacies of slavery, with its disregard for human life, as well as the rigid divisions between landowner and peasant, employer and worker, and rich and poor, seem to have contributed heavily to the notion that there are inferior beings who count very little in the scale of things (Page, 1996). Historically, women, children, Brazilian natives, and the elderly have been seen as inferior within a patriarchal society with a strong tradition of machismo. These foundation stones of male domination have vested in husbands the right to beat and in some instances to maim or burn their wives. This privilege extends across social boundaries, although wife beating in the upper and middle classes has been less frequently publicized (Martins, 1997).

In 1822, Brazil was made independent from Portugal, and in 1889 it was declared a republic. From the 1940s to the early 1960s, Brazil had a series of populist governments. Then, in 1964, the army took over and instituted a system of state-sponsored torture and murder of opponents. The military coup was followed by a period of intense industrialization and agricultural production—the so-called "Brazilian Miracle," with a yearly growth of 10%. This ended in the 1980s with a debt crisis resulting in the "lost decade" (ActionAid, 2001). In 1985, the Army relinquished control, and a democratic government was elected. In 1988, a new constitution was passed, granting basic universal rights to all citizens and implementing modern environmental protection and market laws.

The Economic Context

Economic changes since the shift from a military dictatorship (1964–1985) to a democratic government have brought a series of transformations to the Brazilian social structure, not all of which have been positive. Unemployment is consistently high, and the economy has been wracked by chronic inflation, with about two thirds of all Brazilians classified as poor (Page, 1996). Brazil's per capita income puts it in the 105th place among all nations, although there is a large disparity between upper and lower classes. According to a 1997 report of the Inter American Commission of Human Rights report, Brazil has one of the most inequitable distributions of income in the world, with 20% of the country's population with the highest incoming receiving 32 times more than the 20% in the lowest bracket between 1981 and 1993. About 8% of the people live in absolute poverty (The World Trade Group, 2001), and about 29% live on less than US$ 1 a day (ActionAid, 2001). Most middle class families live in modest homes, and own televisions and some appliances, with many women and youth working to help support their families. During the past few years, with the closing of the Colombian drug traffic routes, Brazil, with its extensive coast, has seen an increase in the power of drug gangs. Drug lords who run some of the slums in big cities (*favelas*) have sophisticated means of terrorizing the public and confronting the police—for example, from kidnapping to armed robbery, from kids on the streets who steal to buy food and drugs to the so called *arrastão* in tunnels (heavily armed gangs stopping traffic at tunnel entrances and robbing drivers). It is clear that this social war has affected the stress level of the population and people's inclination to resolve disputes with aggression.

Homelessness has been an epidemic in Brazil for the past two decades, with entire families living in the streets of the largest cities. Street children (the so called *pivetes*) are victims of sexual abuse, violence, prostitution, and death (as shown in the films "Pixote" and "Central Station"). In recent years, the Brazilian middle class population has decreased, and the impoverished class has increased. The ever-growing slums in large cities like São Paulo and Rio are filled with millions of destitute, impoverished, and unemployed migrants from other regions of the country. The slums become dens for gangs dealing in drugs, kidnapping, and arms. The crime rate in the metropolitan areas has increased, and Brazil is in the midst of a "social war" between classes, sometimes called "social apartheid" (ActionAid, 2001). Rising crime and overpopulation have made the rich retrench into insulated lives, paying the price of social inequity by armoring and bulletproofing cars and homes to protect themselves from violence.

The tactics of Brazilian police force and unofficial death squads against children living in the streets and against criminals have received international attention. Several factors contribute to the impunity of perpetrators of abuse within the police force, including the lack of political will to prosecute those responsible for violence. The Brazilian government has been immune from punishment for its own excesses for centuries. Its historical use of violence to solve internal problems, the current "social war," lack of job opportunities, media coverage of violence, and violent movies, sports, and computer games, all contribute to a culture in which violence is an intrinsic part of the social fabric.

Due to all these macrosystem problems, numerous obstacles plague Brazil's antidomestic violence movement. Although there are several organizations providing services to victims of family violence, these organizations encounter major difficulties when working under governmental jurisdiction. Humanitarian movements have been producing changes in the way Brazilian society treats and views children, women, and the elderly, but violence continues to permeate society.

The Children Who Live in the Streets of Brazil

Although Brazil's government has signed the United Nations Convention on the Rights of the Child and incorporated the Child and Adolescent Statute into federal law, the problem of street children has not been adequately addressed. Several projects have been implemented by the government and nonprofit organizations to keep poor children out of streets, but there are as many as 7 or 8 million children, ages 5 to 18, living and/or working on the streets of Brazil (Inciardi & Surrat, 1998). Publications on the problem of street children emphasize their roles as victims at risk of poverty, disease, and death squads, or as thieves (De Oliveira, 1997; Drexel, 1994; Monteiro, 1998; Salvador, 1995). The poverty of these children is pervasive, with some children preferring to be on the streets than at home, the street being identified as a place of freedom, stimulation (drug use), and danger (death squads, the police, violence, etc.).

Salvador (1995) identified two main types of Brazilian street children. The first type is characterized by antisocial behavior, no home, no shelter, and no family. The second group consists of children for whom the street is a workplace for their families and themselves; this group returns home at night, most living in shanty homes in favelas (slums) initially formed by freed slaves in the late 19th century. Street children form a society with few protections and many risk factors, aggravated by poverty and lack of attention from families (Salvador, 1995). Widespread use of inhalants, marijuana, cocaine, Rohypnol, and valium is typical of these children (Inciardi & Surrat 1998).

The Status of Women

Until 1962, women in Brazil were in the same legal category as minors and the feeble-minded. Not until 1988 did a new constitution give women and men full equality under the law. Since then, important initiatives have been undertaken to combat discrimination against women. At the international level, the government supported the Declaration of the U.N. World Conference on Human Rights, which condemned violence against women; the declaration on the Elimination of Violence against Women adopted by the UN General Assembly; and the Declaration and Program of Action adopted by the Fourth World Conference on Women's Rights in Beijing, 1995 (Inter-American Commission on Human Rights, 1997).

Despite these signs of change, domestic violence, rape, and incest continue to be common occurrences in the lives of Brazilian women of all classes. International and national media have publicized some of the so-called "crimes of passion" committed by members of the highly educated Brazilian upper class. These crimes illustrate the complexities of the current struggle against individuals fighting to retain the ancient prerogatives of the macho culture (Martins, 1997). These are men who kill women they say they love and are usually acquitted by the court. Certain sexual crimes remain classed as crimes against custom, instead of crimes against the individual, and "honesty" remains a legal requisite for a woman to be characterized as a victim of certain crimes. Marriage between the perpetrator and the victim can still prevent the prosecution of certain crimes. As Freire (1995) has described, social mechanisms in Brazil help victims of oppression coexist with the oppressor by providing them with an illusion of power. For example, Brazilian women, especially the ones living in the countryside, identify with and justify oppressive norms of compliance and obedience to husbands. Incest, infidelity, sexual abuse, and violent behavior are common but not acknowledged, which is typical of collective societies (Dwairy, 2002)—although there are variations in values related to social status, roles, education level, gender, age, profession, and level of individuation.

Until few years ago, it was possible in Brazil for a man to kill his allegedly unfaithful wife and be absolved on the grounds of honor. Rape cases were seldom investigated and rarely prosecuted. Despite new criminal laws, Brazil's justice system still fails frequently to treat violence against women as a crime. Only during the past 25 years has the emergence of women's movements and other liberation and Human Rights movements led to some change in the lives of Brazilian women, children, and the elderly.

THE BRAZILIAN MICROSYSTEM

Brazil is a collectivistic society (Dwairy, 2002), although the younger generations have been struggling to become more individualistic, mainly due to North American influences. Brazilian norms, values, roles, and familial authority directives still predict behavior (Beninca & Gomes, 1998), and individuals rely more on the family than on the government to take care of basic needs. Bribery enables Brazilians to survive within a socially unjust system without confronting the system (Dwairy, 2002). The patriarchal Brazilian culture is also authoritarian, although people can choose the country's president, state governors, and other government representatives.

Generally, the Brazilian household is made up of the husband, the wife, and the children, although other family members such as an elderly parent might live with the nuclear family for a while. Up until the mid-1980s, most families had maids who took take care of the home and sometimes the children. As is typical of most collectivistic societies, most children stay with their families until they marry (Dwairy, 2002; Hofstede, 1997); however, this traditional pattern has also been changing, and more single young adults have been moving out, and either sharing with others, or getting their own place. This is one example of how Brazilian society, especially in large cities, is more and more resembling North American society.

FAMILY VIOLENCE

Obtaining valid information concerning the prevalence of domestic violence and child maltreatment in Brazil, as elsewhere, is complicated by issues of definition. For example, should child neglect be included in the definition of domestic violence and/or child maltreatment? Is it reasonable to accuse a hungry impoverished woman with several children, who lives in a one room shack (a *casa de favela*) and has no social support from family, friends, or the government, of maltreating her children because she cannot feed them? Similarly, should the label of abuse or maltreatment be applied to the case of an elderly woman who is not able to work and who starves because her daughter-in-law does not have enough food to feed her?

Child Abuse and Neglect

Nongovernmental organizations (NGOs) and educational institutions are campaigning to educate Brazilian society about child abuse. One program, called "Spanking is non-educational," was started in 1994 by the Child Studies Laboratory (LACRI) of the Institute of Psychology of the University of São Paulo. Several governmental agencies on the city, state, and federal levels have also set up educational and support programs to help victims of family violence. For example, in 1999, the city of Guaratinguetá started a program called "Centro de Referência a Infância e a Adolescência" (Center for Referrals for Children and Adolescents), initially staffed with two psychologists and a social worker. The objective of the center is to develop prevention projects, research programs, and interventions into domestic violence against children and adolescents. Their homepage on the WWW revealed that out of 81 patients seen at the Center, 53% were victims of sexual violence, 33% of physical violence, and 10% of psychological violence (Center for Referrals, 2003).

Brazilian parents spank children whose behavior is considered "bad." This spanking is considered to be the right way to educate children so that they "don't grow up spoiled." There have been cruel stories in the news of children who were chained to a bed, burned, cut, and severely harmed, or killed. Clearly, the implicit theories of discipline are quite different from those in countries like Sweden that have made it illegal to hit children.

Sexual Abuse. The definition of sexual abuse varies in Brazil as elsewhere; consequently, judgments of the prevalence of this form of abuse are highly variable. Statistics regarding the number of sexually abused children in Brazil are based on cases reported to authorities and on findings from academic research. In São Paulo, Cohen (1993) found that out of the total number of maltreatment victims who reported to the police, nearly 23% were victims of sexual violence by a relative; the perpetrator was the father in 46% of the cases, the stepfather in 21%, uncles in 14%, cousins in 11%, and brothers in 4%. As with any type of domestic abuse, these reported numbers are an underestimate.

In an effort to identity predisposing factors in the families of victims, Flores, Mattos, and Salzano (1998) conducted a study of incest in a southern Brazilian population. Questionnaires were administered at a public school where children had confidence in the staff members, and absolute anonymity was guaranteed. The frequency of incest was reported to be 13%. The strongest predisposing factors were presence of extreme violence in the family environment (74% of the cases) and mental illness in the aggressor (62% of the cases). Flores et al. suggested that incest is far more prevalent than believed, and home is not the safe place is often idealized to be. Mental illness in the aggressor, mother's incapacitating illness, mental retardation of the victim, extreme poverty, social interaction difficulties, complex family problems, and violence were identified as factors making it difficult for adults to form appropriate social ties with their children, and predisposing them to incest and/or other forms of abuse (Flores et al., 1998).

Brazilian Participants' Perspectives on Child Abuse

Physical Violence. Most of the implicit theories of abuse against children reported by our Brazilian respondents identified some form of violent act ranging from "killing a child" to "kicking the child out of the house," and from "breaking the child's bones" to "punishing a child using an iron, piece of wood or hot water." Most respondents referred to physical aggression when giving examples of extreme abuse (65%). A frequent example was "leaving marks of the spanking on the child's body," which demonstrates a change in cultural norms from a greater tolerance of physical abuse. Other typical examples mentioned the use of objects, like "using a piece of wood to hit a child's face when he comes home with a low grade in his report card," "beating a child with a belt," or "hitting a child using a broom or throwing hot water on the child." A 33-year-old respondent reported a case of an 8-year-old child who was "spanked daily by her father with a broom throughout her childhood," and another 35-year-old male reported a case of a father who "used a hot iron to hit his child's buttocks." A 40-year-old respondent admitted the following: "One day I spanked my daughter, more than I should have, because I was overworked that day, and I left the mark of my hand on her face. That was an extreme form of maltreatment." Even when asked for examples of mild forms of maltreatment, 54% of respondents gave examples of physical aggression.

Sexual Abuse. Sexual abuse was mentioned as the most extreme form of child abuse by 15% of our Brazilian respondents. Some examples were "a stepfather who sexually abuses his stepdaughter," "an uncle who sexually abuses nieces and nephews," and "parents who sexually abuse their children." Sexual abuse was always identified as extremely abusive, never as moderate or mild mistreatment. It was the second most frequently named form of abuse, right after physical abuse (65%), and before psychological (13%).

Neglect. Interestingly, only a few participants mentioned any type of neglect in their implicit theories of child abuse; 8% of the sample listed a form of neglect as an example of extreme maltreatment, 4% as an example of moderate maltreatment, and 5% as an example of mild maltreatment. The examples varied from "not feeding the children" to "not changing their diapers." A 21-year-old female gave an example of moderate form of abuse "not to provide the children with some form of childhood activity." A 47-year-old female listed "not caressing" as an extreme form of maltreatment.

Verbal Aggression. Verbal aggression toward a child was given as an example of moderate abuse by 25% of our respondents, and as mild abuse by 17%. "Yelling at the child," "humiliation at home and in public," and "using vulgar language at the child" were some of the examples provided. A 27-year-old female considered "calling their children names," a moderate form of abuse; however, she also commented, "in my culture, this is considered a mild form of maltreatment towards children."

Psychological Maltreatment. Finally, several respondents' implicit theories of abuse encompassed notions of psychological maltreatment. When asked to give examples of extreme abuse, 13% of respondents mentioned some form of psychological abuse—for example, "socially insulating a child" (female, 30), and "parents using addictive drugs in front of their children" (female, 24). When asked to give examples of moderate abuse, the majority of participants (51%) referred to some type of psychological maltreatment—for example, "parents fighting in front of their children" (female, 36).

Domestic Violence

On an international level, Brazil is one of a group of countries that do not yet maintain official statistics about cases of domestic violence. The lack of official statistics and research on violence against women, children, and the elderly contributes to the so-called "plot of silence" that supports implicit theories helping to maintain the violence. Nevertheless, despite some resistance and inertia, several Brazilian universities, research institutes, NGOs, and international agencies have been trying for the past few decades to work closely with the Brazilian government to collect domestic violence data. Human Rights Watch reported that at least one Brazilian woman is battered every 4 minutes (Human Rights Watch, 1995). In Rio de Janeiro, 1,730 incidents of domestic violence were reported in 1990, and 3 years later, 5,595 incidents were recorded (Aboim, 1998). However, as some Brazilian researchers have pointed out, relying on incidence data to draw conclusions about the extent of family maltreatment is looking only at the tip of the iceberg (Azevedo & Guerra, 1998).

There are several logistical difficulties in collecting this type of data. For example, domestic violence and neglect are underreported by Brazilians, who rarely see any kind of punishment being imposed on the perpetrator. This underreporting of family violence and neglect has numerous roots. Oppression by the perpetrator, lack of information, shame, religious beliefs, insufficient resources, and lack of trust in the Brazilian justice system all contribute (Azevedo & Guerra, 1998). Moreover, some acts of violence and neglect are done out of ignorance of the traumatic consequences of such abuses. For example, some types of sibling games using violence can be extremely traumatic, and most caretakers, teachers, children, and adolescents are unaware of it.

Domestic violence—including wife murder, domestic battery, abuse, and rape—is the most common form of violence against women in Brazil (Inter-American Commission on Human Rights, 1997). Studies have shown that Brazilian battered women are often unable to leave their batterers because of religious or cultural pressures, or for personal, social, and economic reasons (Martins, 1997; Mills, 1996). Although the Supreme Court struck down the "honor defense" in 1991, prosecuting and punishing perpetrators of domestic violence is rare (Martins, 1997). Shame, humiliation, lack of social and financial support, and religious beliefs often prevent victims from pursuing legal action against perpetrators, who continue their abuse unpunished.

Brazilian Respondents' Perspectives on Wife Abuse

When asked to give examples of extreme forms of maltreatment from husband to wife, the majority of our Brazilian respondents (83%) mentioned forms of physical aggression—with eight respondents listing "killing his wife." By contrast, a 33-year-old male said that extreme wife abuse was "when he doesn't give her money," moderate abuse was "when he hits her," and mild abuse was "when he cheats on her." Only 8% of respondents listed some form of psychological abuse. For instance, a 47-year-old female said extreme abuse was "When a husband decides everything, and yells when one of the children does something wrong, blaming the wife for it." A 35-year-old woman told this story: "I have a friend who has 3 jobs while her husband studies to be a minister of a church; she serves dinner for her husband and their 4 year-old, and by the time she's able to sit down, both have finished and she eats her dinner alone." Only 4% of the respondents gave examples of sexual abuse and only 2% made any reference to verbal abuse.

A 42-year-old gave the following example of extreme abuse; "when a husband hits his wife and forces her to have sex with him right after," and a 31-year-old female wrote that moderate abuse was "verbal humiliation, ignoring, and not paying attention to the fragility of his wife's body."

Brazilian Participants' Perspectives on Husband Abuse

Interestingly, only half of our participants gave any examples of wives abusing husbands—perhaps because Brazilian implicit theories of family maltreatment do not include women maltreating their husbands as often as they include husband–wife maltreatment. In actuality, cases of women who physically attack their husband are not rare; however, they are seldom prosecuted (Martins, 1997). The majority of examples of extreme abuse (53%) were forms of physical violence. A 22-year-old female gave the following example of extreme abuse; "a wife who cuts her husband's penis off," and a 20-year-old female wrote, "killing the husband."

Forms of psychological abuse were given as examples of extreme maltreatment by 39% of the sample, as examples of moderate abuse by 45%, and as mild by 57%. Interestingly, "cheating" was the most common example of psychological maltreatment, followed by "ignoring the husband." A 33-year-old female gave the example of "my mother maltreating my father when he had cancer, she had no patience with him" as a form of extreme maltreatment. Interesting examples of mild forms of maltreatment were "when a wife is independent" (male, 22) and "not preparing dinner for her husband" (female, 28).

Judgments of Abuse in Other Family Relationships

Maltreatment in other family relationships was also described by respondents. A 33-year-old male said an extreme form of maltreatment was a grandmother who "slaps and pinches the children because she doesn't like her daughter-in-law, and she doesn't give the same type of food, gifts and rights that the other grandchildren have." A 24-year-old female said extreme abuse was a "stepfather who abuses sexually his stepdaughter." Surprisingly, only two respondents mentioned alcohol abuse when describing domestic violence.

Elder Abuse and Neglect in Brazil

According to the Brazilian Statistics Institute, Brazilian women are expected, on average, to live until approximately age 72, and men until age 64 (IBGE, 2001). There are approximately 12 million people in Brazil who are 60 years or older, which is about 15% of the total population (Cabral, 2001). Rio de Janeiro has the largest number of elderly, with 20% of the city older than 60. Only 64% of this population knows how to read and write (IBGE, 2000).

The aging of the population is a new reality in a country that values the young and undervalues the elderly. Elder abuse can be understood as a reflection of the prejudiced way Brazilian society views the elderly (Machado, Gomes, & Xavier, 2001). No studies were published on elder abuse in Brazil until the end of the 1990s (Machado, Gomes, & Xavier, 2001), which reflects not only lack of attention to the subject by the government and academia, but also the lack of "voice" of the elderly in Brazilian society.

The World Health Organization (WHO), the International Network for the Prevention of Elder Abuse (INPEA), and other groups have collected data in Brazil and other countries on perceptions of elder abuse (Machado, Gomes, & Xavier, 2001). Health care workers reported an increase in the deaths of people older than 60 due to accidents (traffic, falls, poisoning, drowning) and intentional deaths (murders, suicides, and others)—and again, these figures are likely to be underestimates.

Because of the close family system in Brazil, only the elderly who do not have family or basic survival conditions live in nursing homes. Brazilian culture is prejudiced against committing elders to nursing home and most are of poor quality of service. As Machado, Gomes, and Xavier (2001) pointed out, financially and emotionally dependent adults have been returning home due to high rates of separation, divorce, and unemployment. Sometimes the stepfamily also moves in with in-laws, due to financial problems. This of course leads to disagreements, which can lead to elder exploitation and other types of abuse, with family conflict being the main complaints of the Brazilian elderly, according to recent statistics.

According to the Brazilian institute of Geography and Statistics (IBGE), in 1996 there were about 110,000 elderly in Rio living in extreme poverty. Reports from Brazilian media and human rights' advocates have pointed out other issues that Brazilian elders must face; physical and sexual abuse, neglect of basic services necessary for the elder's well-being, psychological and emotional abuse, including swearing and calling names with the intention of intimidation, humiliation and teasing; abandoning of the elder in nursing homes and hospitals; and financial exploitation (Cabral, 2001; Machado, Gomes, & Xavier, 2001).

Brazilian Participants' Judgments of Elder Abuse

In our survey, examples of neglect (66%) were the most frequently cited examples of extreme elder abuse, followed by physical (31%) and sexual abuse (3%). "Leaving the elderly in nursing homes" or "abandoning and not visiting them" were clear components of the implicit theories of elder abuse. A 26-year-old female gave this example of extreme elder maltreatment; "when a 50 year-old son leaves his 75 year-old ill father alone at home, without medical care, and yells and complains about his presence in his home as a hindrance." When asked to give examples of moderate forms of maltreatment, examples of neglect were again the most cited (47%), followed by psychological maltreatment (25%). "Forcing an elderly person to eat something that s/he doesn't want to" was an example of moderate abuse from a 20-year-old female. "Financial exploitation" was also a common example of extreme maltreatment. Psychological forms of elder abuse were the most common (40%) examples of mild abuse, followed by neglect (32%), and verbal aggression (25%). A 22-year-old male's example of mild abuse was "not let the father go out dating," and of moderate abuse was "not helping him financially." A 40-year-old female said "being impatient and rude to older parents" was mild abuse and "don't provide medical care and food" was moderate abuse. Another common theme in examples of elder maltreatment was belittlement. A 40-year-old male's example of mild abuse was "making jokes about an elder persons' shortcoming due to his/her age."

INTERVENTION AND PREVENTION PROGRAMS

Legislation Regarding Abuse And Family Violence

Brazil has laws protecting the rights of its citizens in its constitution, but implementing these laws and bringing violators to justice has always been a problem. Additional problems include a slow and antiquated justice system plagued with accusations of bribery; crowded and inhumane conditions in prisons; and the pervasive need for funding for nonprofit and governmental agencies concerned with helping victims of abuse and neglect. Law enforcement agencies lack resources. More personnel, training, and equipment are needed. There are not enough "safe homes" for children and battered women, and more nursing homes are needed for elderly members of society. Finally, the population needs to be educated about abuse and neglect.

The Brazilian government signed the Convention on the Rights of the Child in 1990 (United Nations Press Release, 1997). Although the Convention mandates that ratifying States are legally accountable for their actions toward children, NGOs have noted serious gaps in implementing protections for children. At the end of 1995, the Inter-American Commission on Human Rights, from the Organization of American States (OAS), conducted an on-site mission in Brazil. The published Report on the Situation of Human Rights in Brazil (Inter-American Commission, 1997) concluded that the situation of children in Brazil is extremely serious. The report stated that although there had been undeniable legislative gains, and new institutions had been created to protect children and adolescents, many continue to be the target of various forms of violence varying from summary execution to sexual exploitation.

A number of communities, with some support from city, state, and federal government have been trying new strategies for prevention and intervention programs for street children (De Oliveira, 1997; Inciardi & Surrat, 1998). For example, instead of trying to take these children from the streets abruptly, "open-living houses" have been established where the children can have meals, learn trades, shower, and receive medical and psychological attention.

As a result of changes in public awareness and the political arena, the Women's Special Police Station or "Delegacias de Defesa da Mulher" was created in 1985 (Aboim, 1998). Originally, the Women's Police Station was staffed with policewomen and social workers trained to offer counseling and legal aid to victims of domestic violence in Sao Paulo. There are now more than 350 Women's Police Stations in the country, but they are in fewer than 10% of Brazil's cities. Although more than 2,000 cases of battery or sexual assault were reported to a single Police Station without one perpetrator being sentenced to jail, the Stations have effectively given visibility to the issue of domestic violence in Brazil. These Stations also became a space where women can feel safe in reporting violence.

In November 1997, the Rio de Janeiro State Council for Women's Rights started a local 800 hotline for battered women, and most cities today have this type of hotline. The Justice Department set up a National Council for Women's Rights, which provides guidelines, information, and financial support for State and City councils, which in turn distribute information about discrimination and violence against women to local government and the public. However, there are only a few shelters for battered women and their children in Brazil, mainly in large cities. The absence of such safety nets makes reporting abuse a dangerous undertaking.

Recently, the life of the elderly has improved somewhat in Brazil with the implementation of new laws requiring easier access to public services for older people all over the country. Special teller windows in banks, seats in trains, subways, buses, and free rides in public transportation have also been set up in most cities in Brazil. A special toll-free service called "Disque-Idoso" (Call-Elderly) was set up in most cities during the last decade to provide help and to gather data about elderly abuse and neglect.

Another important step was the creation of a Police Department for the Elderly ("Delegacia da Terceira-Idade") in most large cities and small departments inside the justice department of small towns. The Police Station for the Elderly in Rio received an average of 300 complaints a year by 2001, mostly regarding family disagreements and complaints against nursing homes. Just in Rio, 14 nursing homes were closed by November 2001, due to abuses (Cabral, 2001). The Police Department for the Elderly serves also as a preventive force, making people think twice before abusing the elderly. Reports come mostly from neighbors, distant relatives, and acquaintances of the elderly.

It seems that the solution for elderly abuse and neglect, as well as for any kind of maltreatment, is educating society, preparing people and institutions to deal with aging and the elderly, and organizing the elderly to have more power (Machado, Gomes, & Xavier, 2001). Lately, positive steps have been taken all over the country, with government departments on city and state levels being created, and more financial resources being allocated to develop plans to help the older population. Toll-free numbers for information on activities for the elderly and filing complaints against abuse, special police stations, and legislation guaranteeing special rights for the elderly have been put into place by the federal, state, and city governments. For example, from 1998 to 2000, the special police station that takes complaints of abuse against the elderly in Rio had more than 200 complaints filed and 5 cases were sent to court. Complaints vary from bus drivers who do not respect the law giving free bus rides to the elderly to physical abuse, neglect, and omission of medical assistance (Delegacia de Atendimento ao Idoso, 2002).

Regulations and policies have been adopted to supplement state laws and to establish enforcement systems. In 1996, a federal law established a National Policy for the Elderly, giving the government responsibility to support the elderly when the family cannot. It also set up guidelines to prioritize services in public and private sectors, including free medical care in public hospitals, a retirement pension for people 67 or older even if they have never worked, free legal services, professional training, and leisure centers.

CONCLUSIONS

We cannot disregard the high correlation of poverty with neglect and violence. However, relying on the eradication of poverty to eliminate violence is a flawed solution. Even in the world's richest societies, like the United States, the United Kingdom, Canada, Japan, and Singapore, domestic violence, child neglect, and elder abuse exist. Countries that historically have relied on violence to conquer lands, and/or have resorted to force as a matter of policy are likely to have fostered implicit theories in which violence is seen as an acceptable way of getting problems resolved, both inside and outside the family system. Such views can easily be transmitted from generation to generation, unless there is a paradigm shift in implicit theories concerning the acceptability and justifiability of violence.

Governments promulgating protection laws they do not enforce or lacking the infrastructural means of helping the battered, the neglected, the violated, or the subjected are only repeating the cycle of neglect and abuse they are trying to solve. There are protection laws for women, children, and the elderly in Brazil, but starving Brazilian women send their children out to beg in the streets of Rio, São Paulo, and Beijing. Neither the government nor Brazilian societies have given high priority to enforcement of the laws, nor are perpetrators either detained or educated.

As proposed by Szwarcwald and de Castilho (1998), there is a need to set up programs to prevent the general expansion of firearms not only in large and small cities but also in the countryside. Prevention programs and control of the epidemic of violence need to focus on the multiple aspects of the problem, including the proliferation of firearms among persons involved with international firearm smuggling, increases in criminal activity, expansion of drug trafficking, and exclusion of thousands from social opportunities (Szwarcwald & de Castilho, 1998).

The study of social perception, cognition, and affect can help to refine theoretical views and develop effective planning and interventions at the micro and macro levels of society. Understanding the views of ordinary people in each society regarding violence, abuse, and neglect can play a strong role in bringing about change from within. As Aboim (1998) stated, it is important to provide continuous community education, with the goal of transforming the pervasive mentality that justifies and tolerates domestic violence.

Finally, Azevedo and Guerra (1998) proposed a model of domestic violence that in my view is relevant not just to Brazil but to the international community. Their proposed model takes into consideration political–cultural as well as socioeconomic determinants of domestic violence. This model addresses the living conditions of a society, the associated structuring of society into classes of people with and without power, and the determinants of power relationships. In Azevedo and Guerro's view, power is a product of differences in gender, generation, and ethnicity, and serves as an excuse for domination, oppression, and exploitation of the weak by the strong. Their model also assumes that psychological phenomena are "moments of the social conscience," meaning that they are reflections of the cultural background and its interrelationship with other factors, and that biological bases of behavior need to be taken into consideration.

These and other measures by several groups trying to sensitize and put pressure on the government, especially in the judiciary system, to make sure that children, women, and elderly protection laws are enforced in the country, have brought some changes in the way Brazilian society in general see cases of neglect, domestic violence, and abuse. It is also important to point at that Brazilian society seems to be moving from a collectivistic to a more individualistic society, copying much of North American behavior and values This change may be confusing for many teenagers and young adults, who see themselves as torn between a traditional patriarchal culture and a society where children, women, the elderly, and minorities must be respected and have the same rights as the dominant White male. Brazil is seen as the "sleeping giant" who is slowly waking up. Cultural changes are always slow, especially in a vast country such as Brazil, and it might take one or two more generations for people to recognize the human rights of society's most vulnerable members. We believe that educating the public regarding the consequences of maltreatment is as important as creating laws, and that enforcing the existent laws is also a very important step in assuring the safety and well-being of the population of the "sleeping giant" called Brazil.

ACKNOWLEDGMENTS

My thanks go to: Lillian Bezerra-Willets for helping translating the survey to Portuguese; Ana Cristina Braga Martes, Ph.D., Hillary Burger, Ph.D., Jacqueline Brigagão, Ph.D., and Sylvia DiBiaggi, Ph.D., for their support with this project.

REFERENCES

Aboim, M. L. (1998). *Brazil: Domestic violence and the women's movement* [online]. Available from: Family Violence Prevention Fund, http://fvpf.org/programs/display.php3?DocID=96

ActionAid Brazil. (2001, February). Education can change a life. Poverty in Brazil. Rio de Janeiro, Brazil: ActionAid Publications. Available: www.actionaid.org.br/poverty/e/povinb.htm

Azevedo, M. A., & Guerra, V. N. A. (1998). *Infância e violência fatal em família: Primeiras aproximações ao nível de Brasil* [Violence and death in families and childhood: First approximations in Brazil]. São Paulo: Iglu Editora.

Beninca, C., & Gomes, W. (1998). Mothers' reports about family transformation across 3 generations. *Estudos de Psicologia, 3*, 177–205.

Cabral, S. (2001, November 1). Rio é capital da terceira idade [Rio de Janeiro is the capital city of the elderly]. Caderno da Cidade, *Jornal do Brasil* (Especial), Rio de Janeiro, Brasil.

Centro de Referência a Infancia e Adolescência [Center for Referrals for Children and Adolescents]. Available: from http://www.Criaguaratingueta.hpg.ig.com.br.

Cohen, C. (1993). *O Incesto: Um Desejo* [The incest: A desire]. São Paulo, Brazil: Casa do Psicólogo.

Delegacias de Atendimento ao Idoso [Police Department for the Elderly]. (2002). Available: http://www.pareceresjuridicos.com/3_delegacias.htm

De Mello, S. (1988). *Trabalho e sobrevivência: Mulheres do campo e da periferia de São Paulo* [Work and survival: São Paulo country and suburban women] (p. 138). São Paulo, Brazil: Editora Ática.

De Oliveira, T. C. (1997). Homeless children in Rio de Janeiro: Exploring the meaning of street life. *Child & Youth Care Forum, 26*, 163–174.

Drexel, J. (1994). Human rights of street children in Brazil. *Educational & Child Psychology, 11*, 31–34.

Dwairy, M. (2002). Foundations of psychosocial dynamic personality theory of collective people. *Clinical Psychology Review, 22*, 343–360.

Flores, R., Mattos, L., & Salzano, F. (1998). Incest: Frequency, predisposing factors, and effects in a Brazilian population. *Current Anthropology, 39*, 554–558.

Freire, P. (1995). *Pedagogy of the oppressed.* New York: Continuum.

Hofstede, G. (1997). *Cultures and organizations: The software of the mind.* New York: McGraw-Hill.

Human Rights Watch. (1995). *International Organization of Human Rights* [online]. Available: http://www.hrw.org

IBGE. (2000). *National Census.* Rio de Janeiro, Brazil: Instituto Brasileiro de Geografia e Estatística.

IBGE. (2001). *Sintese the Indicadores Sociais 2000* [Synthesis of Social Indicators 2000]. Rio de Janeiro, Brazil: Instituto Brasileiro de Geografia e Estatística.

Inciardi, J., & Surrat, H. (1998). Children in the streets of Brazil: Drug use, crime, violence and HIV risks. *Substance Use and Misuse, 3*, 1461–1480.

Inter-American Commission on Human Rights. (1997). *Report on the situation of human rights in Brazil.* Available from: Organization of American States, http://www.oas.org/

Machado, L., Gomes, R., & Xavier, E., in conjunction with WHO/INPEA. (2001, September). *Report on elder abuse in Brazil.* Geneva: World Health Organization.

Martins, P. (1997). Passions that hold men in bondage: Violence and intimacy. *Percurso: Revista de Psicanalise, 9*(18), 65–77.

Mills, Linda. (1996). Empowering battered women transnationally: The case for postmodern interventions. *Social Work, 41*, 261–268.

Monteiro, J. (1998). An autophotographic study of poverty, collective orientation, and identity among street children. *The Journal of Social Psychology, 138*, 403–406.

Page, J. A. (1996). *The Brazilians.* Reading, MA: Addison-Wesley.

Salvador, C. (1995). Sociocultural roots of violence: Street children in Brazil. *The Child in the family; The monograph series of the International association for Child and Adolescent Psychiatry and Allied Professions, 11*, 163–170.

Szwarcwald, C., & de Castilho, E. (1998). Mortality by firearms in the state of Rio de Janeiro Brazil: A spatial analysis. *Pan American Journal of Public Health, 4*, 161–170.

United Nations. (1997). Published by Office of the United Nations High Commissioner for Human Rights. Geneva, Switzerland.

The World Trade Group. (2001, July). *World development indicators database.* Washington, DC: World Bank Group.

23

Colombia

Sharon Abramzon

CAPSULE

For many people, Colombia is a mysterious land of cocaine and emeralds, bearing the name of Christopher Columbus, discoverer of the Americas. Known as a land of drug lords and corrupt government, it does not have a very positive international reputation, yet it is a country with a warm and outgoing population. The interesting mélange of the Spanish Catholic culture with the indigenous peoples gave birth to a complex society and way of life. There are implicit rules of behavior that might be undetectable to most observers, yet are ingrained in Colombian views on life, people, and violence. Living in a country plagued by civil war, where guerrillas and paramilitary groups are constantly killing, pillaging, and kidnapping civilians, many Colombians have grown "numb" to violence. After 70 bombs knocked out power in much of Colombia, people boasted that they had gone to bed early and slept soundly (Guillermo-Prieto, 2002).

At a familial level, Colombians are very concerned with privacy and saving face. The culture is still male chauvinistic, accepting traditions such as the man's possession of his spouse and the notion of "marital duties." These traditional chauvinistic values, along with the deeply rooted patriarchal views of society promulgated by the Catholic Church, make for considerable tolerance of violence in Colombian society.

The Colombian family is tightly knit and women are bound to their sacred Catholic marriages. Statistics show these women are severely affected by their husband's violence. Some acts, such as cheating, may be regarded by some peo-

*ple as mildly abusive; however, as Paternostro (1998) explained, by simply be-
ing dutiful wives of cheating husbands having unprotected sex, women risk infection with the AIDS virus. The children in such cases can be severely affected
and in many cases are abandoned on Colombian streets, sniffing glue and
homeless. The elderly are also affected, condemned to geriatric asylums with
poor hygiene and abandoned by their families in the "best case scenario"; in
other cases, they are just left out on the street. Due to the harsh reality of warfare overriding lesser concerns, family violence was previously not a topic of
public discussion. Now, however, human rights groups and NGOs have taken an
interest in human rights violations in Colombia, especially due to the guerilla
warfare, and their attention has extended to family violence.*

THE COLOMBIAN SAMPLE

The Colombian sample consisted of 27 women and 13 men ranging in age
from 18 to 58; 70% of them resided in Colombia at the time they answered
the survey. Sixteen out of the 40 lived with either their parents or grandparents. Their level of education ranged from no formal education to Master's
Degree candidates and a doctoral candidate. Of these, 95% were high
school educated, and 70% had or were pursuing a college or equivalent degree. They represented a diversity of occupations such as housekeepers,
taxi drivers, students, business owners, and scholars. Ninety percent indicated their current religion was Catholicism.

Colombian Participants' Definitions of Abuse

When defining abuse in the context of the family, Colombian respondents
emphasized disrespect and lack of consideration. For example, "abuse
comes in many forms (alcohol, sexual, etc.) but the common denominator
is lack of respect" (male, 26 years old); "abuse is any behavior that is inconsiderate of others' feelings" (male, 29); "[abuse is] not respecting the persons one lives with, physically, verbally, and sexually" (female, 27); "to ignore completely and in an irrational way the desires and choices of others"
(female, 27). There was also a strong tendency among respondents to define abuse in terms of its outcomes; "to frequently corrode somebody's self-
esteem" (female, 26); "any behavior that leaves physical or emotional consequences"; "physical, sexual, or any behavior that can do damage to the
other person—to shout, to hit, etc. for example" (female, 26); "any kind of
behavior that degrades you as a human being" (female, 24). Revealing, perhaps, the influence of Catholic doctrine, a 27-year-old man defined abuse as
"Doing to someone what we wouldn't want to be done to us."

THE COLOMBIAN MACROSYSTEM

Colombia is a fiercely religious country; 90% of the people are Roman Catholic, and a mere 10% are other religions. Catholicism has been the principal religion since the arrival of the Spaniards, and the Catholic clergy have always played an important role in Colombia. Catholicism was one of the tenets of the constitution until its removal in 1993. It is widely accepted that the Catholic Church, with its conservative views on how life should be lived, played an extremely oppressive role in Colombia. The country has also been characterized by an underlying patriarchal social structure, in which women are seen as the keepers of the home, and thus are, in a sense, demoted to second-class citizenship, creating a climate that inhibits the disclosure of family violence.

General Violence

There is a very high rate of violent and criminal attacks in Colombia, accounting for 45% of the deaths of people between 15 and 40 years of age (CIA World Fact Book, n.d.). This high rate of homicide and violent crime is a direct result of the structural problems of poor law enforcement, high levels of social and political violence, and many drug-related criminal activities. These structural problems are exacerbated by a health care system designed to handle "formal" health disorders and not to provide emergency care. Data published by Colombia's government show that in the late 1980s, an estimated 80% of crimes committed were unreported (CIA World Fact Book, n.d.). Of the 20% reported crimes, only 1% resulted in convictions and sentencing. Even this level of response was complicated by an incredibly large number of backlog cases.

Even before the current presidency, the human rights situation in Colombia had deteriorated sharply because of the high level of violence in the land. Political violence is particularly intense in the areas contested by guerrillas. Unfortunately, the most frequent victims of this violence tend to be noncombatant civilians who are forcibly displaced from their homes.

Currently, the largest guerilla group in Colombia is the Revolutionary Armed Forces, known by their Spanish initials as FARC. Along with the ELN, a smaller guerrilla group, they have about 20,000 well-armed members who control about 40% of Colombia. More than 1,800 people have been kidnapped by guerilla units, giving Colombia one of the highest abduction rates in the world, according to Sandra Cameron, who traveled to Colombia on behalf of UNICEF to write about the Children's Movement for Peace, 2002. In 1980, paramilitary groups adopted a policy of brutal warfare against anyone accused of being a guerilla or fraternizing with them. These right-wing paramilitary soldiers have entered villages looking for guerillas and their sympathizers and have slaughtered men, women, and children, in many instances as public executions. In addition to the war between the guerillas and paramilitaries, Colombia has South America's highest rate of homicides (25,000 murdered every year by domestic or other criminal violence). Homicide is the leading cause of death among adults over the age of 15.

It is clear that people in the country are accustomed to this civil war. One young man in an interview with Guillermo-Prieto (2002) stated, "I joined the guerrillas because my family has been in this forever, ever since the days of La Violencia." He went on to say that he made his choice this way, and his family was always divided: "Some of the brothers go into the military, and the other brothers, or the cousins, join the guerrillas. That's just the way it is." As Guillermo-Prieto pointed out, "It is a stupid circle of violence, but for years Colombians on all sides have seem to have been willing to think it is fate . . ." (Guillermo-Prieto, 2002). Interestingly, among our respondents, everyone limited their definitions of abuse and violence entirely to forms of domestic abuse, with no reference to the political violence. In reality, one could argue that domestic violence is associated at least in part with the political war.

Status of Women

Some legal reforms have extended equal civil rights to women. For example, the Inter-American Convention on the Granting of Civil Rights to Women stated that "the majority of the American Republics, inspired by lofty principles of justice, have granted civil rights to women," and that "long before the women of America demanded their rights they were able to carry out nobly all their responsibilities side by side with men" (Inter-American Commission of Women, 1948, ¶ 2 & ¶ 6). Yet, as recently as the year 2000, women received considerably less payment than men for equal work and had considerably less access to political power. Moreover, women accounted for 54% of the population living in poverty, accounted for 60% of the informal sector of the economy, worked long hours, had no job stability, and had no social security coverage (Coomaraswamy, 2002). "Women, who make up 51 per cent of the population, suffer a significantly greater proportion of the effects of violence. Their continuing inequality is manifested in discrimination, social exclusion, disempowerment and chronic social disadvantage in almost every situation they encounter" (Coomaraswamy, 2002, p. 7 of internet print-out).

Status of Children

In part because of high unemployment rates and growing slum areas, children in Colombia are at great risk for maltreatment. In some situations, families too poor to care for their children have abandoned them. These children, left living on the streets and in gutters, sometimes form child communities to keep each other warm and protect themselves. In other cases, children are forced to work on the streets, selling flowers or candy bars to people in cars, many times late at night and in extreme weather conditions.

The Colombia government is making great efforts to change this situation. In 1991, the Change on Behalf of Peace in the National Development Plan was created. Prompted by UNICEF, this participatory governance structure creates partnerships among the local governments, NGOs, and community-based organizations. Topics such as gender equality and children's rights are addressed here. Many municipalities have adopted this program, which has been proven effective in its initial training phase (UNICEF, 1997). In 1998, a similar program initiated in the department of Cauca increased participation in these municipalities by people in government.

THE MICROSYSTEM

Family life in Colombia has undergone considerable change since the 1980s, and there are continuous modifications in the traditional norms and patterns of family life, resulting mostly from a high rate of rural to urban migration. There has been some decline in the classic patriarchal structure due to migration and urbanization, making families a little less cohesive. Women carry the heaviest burden, stemming from displacement due to the armed conflict, since they necessarily assume the role of head of household and breadwinner (Coomaraswamy, 2002). Moreover, traditional elements of mutual dependence among family members persist, and the nuclear family continues to be authoritarian, patriarchal, and patrilineal. When there is a husband living in the home, he is unequivocally considered the head of the household. Similarly, the wife is still generally considered to be the executor of the rules, and the keeper of the household who raises the children and doesn't question the husband's decisions or whereabouts.

Most men in the upper and middle class are paternal, protective, and concerned with sheltering their wives and children from "undesired outside influences." They consider it essential to protect their daughter's virtue and honor. Just as in ancient times, they honor the notion that women are supposed to be pure and virginal until marriage—which is one reason, along with the role of the Catholic Church, why sexual abuse is largely underreported

Women, especially in the lower classes, are allowed to work in the same professions as their male relatives, but are expected to contribute their salary to the family's sustenance and also to work in the fields. Very few communities in Colombia are matriarchal. However, in recent years, there are increasing exceptions in urban society to traditional conceptions of the woman's role, especially since the women of the upper classes are educated and can hold high-ranking jobs in the economy. These Colombian women, who sometimes are very politically active, are considered exceptional. Moreover, most upper class women do not work after marriage; they tend to the household and rearing of the children and remain in the "background" of the family.

VIOLENCE AGAINST WOMEN

As in other South American countries, there is little public discussion of domestic abuse in Colombia. Due to the upsurge in drug-related violence, kidnapping, and other crimes, it is hard for people to recognize and prioritize violence occurring within families. The Human Development Report points out that discrimination against women takes place especially in the form of family violence. Moreover, "In the International trafficking in women, Colombia ranks among the highest in the world" (Coomaraswamy, 2002, pg. 8 internet print-out)

Given the increasing problem of women and children being recruited into the FARC, often forcibly, there has been some effort to learn more about violence experienced by women in the military. Violence occurring inside guerilla camps is inadequately described by the adjective "brutal." Griswold (2002) reported on two women ex-guerrilla fighters living in safe houses in Bogotá, the capital of Colombia. In the article, Griswold described the way young women are brutally forced to join the FARC and trained to kill by age 16. One of these women was taken, as is customary, as a "tax" her family had to pay to spare their lives. By the age of 14, she had already been used as her commandant's lover. At age 15, she was fitted with a mandatory IUD—with her uterus being perforated in the process. These women are forbidden to get pregnant and are required to get an abortion if they do. Promiscuous activity within the guerilla camps leads to chronic gonorrhea, syphilis, and a number of other sexually transmitted diseases (Griswold, 2002). The FARC estimates that around 30% of its fighting force consists of young women (Guillermo-Prieto, 2002), but the tacit male chauvinistic hierarchy prevails; when women get infections due to STDs or any other diseases, they become a burden. As any "good guerilla" knows, this means they may be killed.

In 2001, the paramilitary groups in Colombia warned women who were part of UNIFEM—the women's branch of the UN—that they would be killed if they marched on International Women's day. In response to this threat, the women marched a day early. In turn, the paramilitary group knocked down their office with a bulldozer and declared a "war booty" wherein all women caught during a curfew had their bellies burned. The state of uncertainty created by these tactics is clearly a form of psychological abuse that may be similar to the more severe level of panic and fear experienced in New York City following the terrorist attacks of 9-11-01. Perhaps an even worse form of psychological abuse is the psychological torture of families forced to give their children to the guerrillas or have members kidnapped for ransom.

The focus on violence among Colombia's warring factions, coupled with widespread mistrust of the authorities and the harsh punishment of the church, makes it difficult for people, especially of the poor and working class, to disclose spousal or child abuse. In addition, many sectors lack common health care and risk protection. Under such circumstances, reporting psychological abuse would probably be unthinkable.

Colombian Participants' Perspectives on Domestic Violence

The "machismo" attitude that continues to hold sway in Colombian society can be found in the affluent and the educated population as well as in the masses. When giving definitions of abusive behavior, our respondents seemed to have a different "set of rules," depending on whether the violence was from a husband to his wife or vice-versa. One female respondent stated that an example of mild abuse would be if a husband "neglected economic responsibility" to the home, and an example of an extremely abusive behavior would be if he "hit his wife." When asked about violence toward husbands, this respondent's example of moderate abuse was "not preparing food for the husband when he came home from work" (which is comparable with the "husband neglecting the economic responsibility of paying for food in the home"), yet she didn't think a woman could physically harm her husband. Her implicit theory seems to be that husbands are the only ones who could physically abuse their partner. Another female respondent said that an extremely abusive behavior would be a husband "hitting his wife," a moderately abusive behavior would be "not giving her any money," and a mildly abusive behavior would be "not taking her out." On the other hand, her example of extreme abuse toward a husband was "not having dinner made for him when he gets home from work," moderate abuse was "being in a bad mood around him," and mild abuse was "not being affectionate towards him." Similarly, a male respondent indicated that a wife is being extremely abusive toward her husband when she "comes home late," moderately abusive when she "forgets to do the grocery shopping," and mildly abusive when she "doesn't clean the house." These examples show us that implicit theories of abuse are still informed by traditional chauvinistic family roles.

More than 75% of our respondents gave examples of psychological abuse when defining abuse. For example, one female respondent said that a moderately abusive behavior would be "reprimanding a wife or daughter for expressing an opinion that is different from the father's," whereas another female considered it moderately to extremely abusive to "keep a teenage girl in the home without letting her see her friends."

VIOLENCE AGAINST CHILDREN

As in most cases where there is domestic abuse, violence against children is widespread. According to a report from the Instituto de Bienestar Familiar or National Family Welfare Institute (ICBF), beginning in the year 2000, around 52,000 children were under ICBF protection. This information, however, changes constantly due to the frequent entering and exiting of children. Some of the following are frightening statistics found on the website of the ICBF:

1. According to Legal Medicine, out of 11,790 cases of sexual abuse, 88% are females, and 56% overall are children under 14.
2. There are about 25,000 sexually exploited children, and about 14,400 have been assisted by the ICBF in its different programs throughout the country.
3. It is calculated that 30,000 children are in the streets, almost 6,200 of whom are annually seen to by the ICBF.
4. There may be as many as 1,500,000 children under 18 working in high-risk conditions.
5. According to studies of Profamilia, 11% of women between 15 and 19 have been premature mothers. Sexual relations are starting sooner each day, declining from an average of 19 years old to an average of 14. The ICBF annually assists, in specialized services, almost 500 pregnant adolescents who have been abandoned or maltreated.
6. Twelve percent of the Colombian population (and 6% of children under 18) has some level of disability. The ICBF annually protects almost 10,000 children who were abandoned or in physical or moral danger.
7. The ICBF has under protection almost 24,000 youth who have infringed against Colombian penal law.

Colombian Participants' Perspectives on Child Abuse

The respondents to our survey shared very similar views on the behaviors that constitute child abuse. In general, it appears that within the family structure, violence against children in a Colombian family is tolerated more than in the United States. One of our female respondents gave as an example of extreme abuse "a father punishing his child by sticking his head in a sink full of water." Another female stated that it was extremely abusive "when a father hit his children or exploited them economically." Another stated that extremely abusive behavior would be "when a drunken father hit his daughter or raped her." Examples of mildly abusive behavior from the same respondent were "having your children wait on you," "taking the money they've worked for," and "not permitting a daughter to leave the house." Other examples of mildly abusive behavior included "ignoring your children" or "mocking" them. Unlike in the United States, where citizens may report to authorities when they see abuse from a parent toward his/her child, Colombians tend to keep their business to themselves. This might be another reason why abuse goes unreported and unpunished.

We can see from the ICBF statistics that there are several forms of abuse and violence in Colombia. The underlying hegemonic patriarchal structure, along with the social, economical, and political situations, make the system inadequate and inefficient. The most prevalent forms of maltreatment are negligence and sexual abuse. In some rare instances, women may behave abusively to men, but these cases are rarely reported. The major segment of the population directly affected by violence is women and children.

VIOLENCE AGAINST THE ELDERLY

Crimes against the elderly in Colombia are among the most underreported. There are an estimated 2.5 million elderly people in Colombia, comprising 6.5 % of the total population. According to the PAHO (Pan American Health Organization), 88% of elderly people have no social security protection, and 42% live in extreme poverty. One-third of these people are also illiterate. In 1991, the Colombian Constitution granted universal health care as a right for all citizens. Sadly, not everyone benefits from this care. *Law 100* states that people who do not have health insurance should be covered by public service health facilities. However, hospitals and emergency areas remain woefully underfunded, and often health care is just not feasible.

Although many of the elderly live with their families, the families themselves may abuse them. There also seems to be a cultural stigma against nursing homes. Most of the elderly who end up in homes like Padua in the outskirts of Colombia's capital, Bogotá, are convinced their families have "thrown them away." In many of the cases, this seems to be true, because the families rarely visit their elderly members in nursing homes. This apparent neglect may be due in part to lack of means to take the trip to the nursing homes and a high rate of illiteracy that prevents families from sending and receiving forms of written communication.

Colombian Participants' Perspectives on Elder Abuse

In our survey there were many examples of stories where both women and men physically abused their elderly parents. One 58-year-old man cited an example of extremely abusive behavior where a woman he knew "would tie her 85-year-old mother to a chair and not permit her to use the bathroom or feed her." This same respondent described mildly abusive behavior as "not talking to an elderly relative." A 47-year-old woman stated that extremely abusive behavior would be "to make elderly people work," moderately abusive would be "not to let them sleep," and mildly abusive would be "not to try and spoil them like a child."

PREVENTION AND INTERVENTION

Colombia is a country with an abundance of laws. The problems lie in the execution of those laws and in their application to different sections of the population. The judicial system is inefficient, not sufficiently funded, and in some cases corrupt. Colombia has made a huge effort in the last decade to improve its justice system; however, over 90% of crimes go unpunished (CIA World Fact Book, 2001). As of 2001, Colombia has a new penal code with several laws on carnal access and sexual abuse.

The system to abolish child abuse in Colombia is comprised of NGOs as well as government organizations. The Instituto de Bienestar Familiar or National Family Welfare Institute (ICBF) is the coordinator and integrator of the family welfare service, and all other private or public institutions that contribute directly or indirectly to guaranteeing the services rendered by the family welfare system. The ICBF is one of the most important influences in the country in the creation of abuse legislation. Among its functions, the ICBF can provide legal expertise and ratify approved by-laws. Examples of this are *Law 55*, which is meant to strengthen the family for the sake of the child, and *Law 294*, which prescribes norms to prevent, repair, and punish family violence. In addition, *Law 67*, ratified in August 2001, was created for the prevention of pornography and sexual exploitation of minors, and treatment of problems arising from exploitation.

One of the most important laws addressing violence against women in the new Penal Code is *Law 248 of 1995*, which ratifies the international convention to prevent, punish, and eliminate violence against women. This law applies to any act that takes place in and out of the family and domestic unit, or in any interpersonal relationship, regardless of whether or not the aggressor shares or has shared the same residence as the woman. Rape, torture, forceful prostitution, kidnapping, sexual harassment in the workplace or educational institutions, and sexual abuse all fall under its umbrella.

Law 29 of 1996 in the penal code stipulates that there should be prevention programs for the "more vulnerable" members of the family (mainly women and children), and action taken against those who commit abuse. Previously, intrafamilial violence was not listed as a crime. Although sexual abuse was a crime, there was a belief that in marriage, the body of a woman was a possession of her husband so, by definition, she could not be raped or sexually abused by him. According to Colombia's Constitutional Court, this is no longer true (National and International Legal Framework, n.d.).

In 1996, UNIFEM officially started working in partnership with women's groups, the government, and the entire United Nations system to promote the civil, cultural, economic, political, and social rights of women in Colombia. Its primary function is to achieve the goals of the Convention on the Elimination of All Forms of Discrimination Against Women (CEDAW, 1979). These programs are especially helpful to women in the more rural areas, because few indigenous women have access to information on their rights and lack the means to advocate for them. UNIFEM has sponsored workshops with organizations such as the National Association of Peasant and Indigenous Women of Colombia. Women have slowly begun to exercise their long and torturous journey to exercising their rights (Colombian Penal Code, 1996). On October 31, 2001, the Colombian government invited the United Nations Special Reporter on Violence against Women, Radhika Coomaraswamy, to investigate violence against women in the armed conflict. This report concluded that "human rights have not been given sufficiently high-priority treatment by the Government, nor have international recommendations been followed" (Coomaraswamy, 2002, pg. 10 of internet print-out).

Because of the underlying patriarchal structure of Colombian society, only a few politicians are starting to target the country's tolerance of violence, especially toward women and children. A great example of one politician's courage in addressing the problem was an "experimental" evening in which the mayor of Bogotá, Mr. Antanas Mokus, declared that men would be banned from the streets and only women could go out. This caused great pandemonium; people were not ready for such *experiments*. Nevertheless, it was a brave attempt to get people thinking outside the boundaries of patriarchal thinking.

FUTURE PERSPECTIVES

It is hard to imagine a solution to the male chauvinistic points of views and tolerance of violence in Colombia. Nevertheless, there is increasing recognition in the government and the world of the dire need for revolutionary reforms. It is important for the government and institutions like the ICFB to educate the population on basic human rights and dignity. Programs are being set up with the help of pioneering Human Rights advocates like Shulamit Koening, who works tirelessly with important political figures to create Human Rights cities all over the world. With the help of these educational programs, women can find a voice and understand that they do not need to put up with abusive family situations or to turn a blind eye to their children's abuse.

Currently, many safe houses are sprouting up in Colombia, often for women and children fleeing the armed conflict. Many of these children are seized as young as 9 years old to work as informants, lovers, and soldiers in the rebel army. "Most are between 12- and 17-years-old, but some are as young as nine," according to Juan Manuel Urrutia (Brodzynsky, 2002), director of Colombia's child welfare agency, which runs seven safe houses. The program offers former child combatants vocational training, psychological help, and a chance to resume their education (Brodzynsky, 2002). Other programs include Plan Colombia, a plan set forth by the Colombian Government for "peace, prosperity, and institutional strengthening" (Plan Colombia, 2000). Through this program, the government expects to create an "investment" via projects that benefit less favored Colombians in an efficient way. It also seeks to revive confidence among Colombians "by rescuing basic norms of social coexistence, the promotion of democracy, justice, territorial integrity, the generation of employment conditions, and respect for human rights and the conservation of public order, among other things" (Plan Colombia, 2002). Given the grim situation Colombia faces due to the current economic and social crisis, it is hard to say when and how these issues will be resolved.

REFERENCES

Bermudez, Q. (1993). *El sexo bello: La mujer y la familia Durante el Olimpo Radical* [The beautiful sex: The woman and family during the time of the Olympus.] Bogotá: Ediciones Uniandes.

Brodzynsky, S. (2002, August 7). In Colombia, young warriors drop guns. *St. Petersburg Times Online*. Available: http://www.sptimes.com/2002/08/07/Worldandnation/In_Columbia_young_wa.shtml

CIA World Fact Book Report. (2001). Available: www.odci.gov/cia/publications/factbook/geos.co.html

Convention on the Elimination of All Forms of Discrimination Against Women. (1979). Available: http://www.snvworld.org/gender/themes-and-topics_advocacy_1.htm and from http://www.hri.ca/uninfo/treaties/22.shtml

Coomaraswamy, R. (2002). *Report of the UN High Commissioner for Human Rights on the human rights situation in Colombia* [online]. Available: http://colhrnet.igc.org/newitems/unhrc.report.401.htm

Guillermo-Prieto, A. (2002, May 13). Waiting for war. *The New Yorker*, p. 48.

Griswold, E. (2002, June/July). Fly on the wall. *Jane Magazine*, 102–103.

Instituto De Bienestar Familiar. (n.d.). Available: www.institutodebienestarfamiliar.com

Inter-American Commission of Women. (1948). Inter-American Convention on the Granting of Civil Rights to Women. Available: http://www.oas.org/CIM/english/Convention%20Civil%20Rights.htm

National and international legal framework for women's rights in Colombia. Available: http://www. ilsa.org.co/biblioteca/Informa/Annex6.doc

Paternostro, S. (1998). *In the land Of G-d and man: Confronting our sexual culture.* New York: Dutton.

Plan Colombia. (n.d.). Available: http://www.mamacoca.org/plan_colombia_en.html

UNICEF Colombia. (1997). *Programme: Towards implementing the citizen's mandate for peace, life and liberty* [online]. Available: http://www.unicef.org/programme/girlseducation/peace_ed.htm

NORTH AMERICA

Canada

Indrani J. Dookie

CAPSULE

The Canadian Charter of Rights and Freedoms codifies the requisites of a free and democratic society—including freedom of expression, the right to a democratic government, legal rights of persons accused of crimes, aboriginal peoples' rights, the equality of men and women, and the protection of Canada's multicultural heritage. The Criminal Code of Canada sets out the limits of legal behavior and defenses that may be used to excuse or justify illegal behaviors. In the area of domestic violence, the 1990s saw the addition of criminal harassment or "stalking" to the Code. Victims of domestic violence can invoke a growing variety of civil legislations designed to assist and protect victims immediately and in the longer term. In addition, some provinces and territories have specialized domestic violence courts designed to expedite domestic violence cases for the safety of the victim. These courts have distinct procedures to allow for better coordination of services and support for both victims and the accused in domestic violence cases.

OUR SAMPLE

Requests for participants were posted on Canada-wide listservs, circulated to research centers, and conveyed by word of mouth through personal networks in Ontario and Quebec. In total, 98 women and 49 men completed the survey. In addition to Canada, participants listed 49 other countries, from every continent, as their country of origin. The range of religions included Roman Catholic, Protestant, United Christian, Hindu, Islam, Jewish, Muslim, None, Seventh Day Adventist, Sikh, and United Church of Canada. Approximately 10% of participants identified themselves as gay or lesbian.

Canadian Definitions of Abuse

The implicit theories of family violence of the majority of Canadian participants portrayed abuse as a multifaceted phenomena with physical, emotional, and other aspects; "anything that hurts someone physically or metaphysically, verbally, or nonverbally"; "continual threats, sufficient verbal disrespect so that people feel unwanted, hurt or afraid." Some participants noted that men and women are equally capable of being abusive toward each other, their children, or their elders.

A strong pattern among respondents is that anything causing psychological discomfort is the hallmark of abuse. As one woman put it, abusive situations do not necessarily involve a particular behavior; you know you're in one "when fear becomes a way of life." Many participants defined abuse as "anything intended to dehumanize and hurt another person"—ranging from an act such as "hitting" or "yelling" to an omission such as "neglecting" someone's needs. Participants repeatedly referred to "condescension," "controlling," and "ignoring." Interestingly, some participants said it was abusive "to let children witness parents arguing." Several men and women mentioned "irresponsibility" and "general selfishness" as examples of abuse. Financial abuse was mentioned only in relation to wives and elderly parents—particularly "taking funds without elders' consent" and "restricting income for wives."

A full 10% of participants refused to characterize abusive behaviors into different levels, claiming that " 'mild abuse' is an oxymoron," "there is no range, anything degrading is abuse." In the implicit theories of participants who did respond to the request for examples of severe, moderate, and mild abuse, physical abuse was generally portrayed as extremely abusive, emotional as moderate, and verbal forms as mild. However, one woman listed "verbal attacks" as extreme, "physical attacks" as moderate, and "mild physical attacks" as mild. One participant said, "Severity depends on the recipient," whereas others claimed intentions of the abuser differentiate the level of abuse. Several said that mild abuse can occur "when the perpetrator didn't intend to cause any harm but there was a negative impact on the victim." Some said that criticism is more abusive "when it occurs in public" versus in private, and when it occurs in the absence of support. Most participants considered it abusive to "make family members feel small or criticize them about things they cannot control." Moreover, "a father striking his children because he had a frustrating day at work" was viewed as abusive. Interestingly, some participants judged severity by legal criteria. Extremely abusive behaviors were those meriting prosecution and jail time, moderately abusive behaviors might warrant prosecution or restraint, and mild abuse is annoying but within the bounds of the law.

THE CANADIAN MACROSYSTEM

History

For thousands of years, the Canadian landscape was inhabited by a wide variety of Inuit and First Nations who lived primarily by hunting and gathering. As a group, Aboriginal residents share a deep spiritual relationship with the land and the life supported by nature. Beyond an abiding respect for life in all its forms, there are vast differences among native cultures. "Variations in languages, histories, customs, and values may differentiate [A]boriginal peoples more than the citizens of many European countries"(Gotowiec & Beiser, 1993–1994, p. 7). Contact with European explorers in the 18th and 19th centuries permanently and profoundly changed the lives of indigenous populations. The introduction of firearms and diseases brought devastation to native inhabitants as their population dwindled and, over time, the effects of colonization destabilized and then threatened the very existence of their culture.

Similar to the United States, many Central and South American countries, and Australia, Aboriginal families in Canada continue to suffer the consequences of European colonization—including forced migrations, removal of children from their families and placements into abusive boarding schools, and institutional violence (Robinson, 2001). Among the persistent effects are high rates of suicide, substance abuse, mental health problems, and domestic violence.

Public Attitudes Toward Family Violence

A national public opinion survey of a random sample of 2,053 Canadians ages 16 or older, conducted by EKOS Research Associates between December 2001 and January 2002, found that the majority of Canadians (62%) viewed family violence as a more serious problem in 2002 than it was 10 years earlier, but a majority also stated that family violence does not take place in their community. Over 75% of the respondents indicated that family violence should be an urgent priority for both the federal government (77%) and their community (76%). Although 70% stated that spousal violence is a crime, the majority recommended counseling and treatment as the most appropriate response (62%); 20% recommended time in jail. In cases of child abuse involving a parent kicking or hitting a child with a fist, the most appropriate response, according to 755 respondents, was counseling and treatment. Only 12% believed that jail would be appropriate. Almost two thirds of the survey respondents said the courts treat family violence cases too lightly, and nearly half think the police treat the cases too lightly (EKOS Research Associates, as cited in Canadian Center for Justice Statistics, 2002).

When asked to think about violence in the family, the majority of the EKOS participants identified violence between spouses (67%), followed by violence between parents and children (59%). Violence among siblings was less likely to be mentioned (33%) and abuse of the elderly was rarely stated (1%). Just over 40% of the respondents viewed violence toward children as the greatest cause for concern, whereas 19% cited spousal violence, 10% cited violence toward the elderly or disabled, and 20% indicated that all types of violence are cause for concern.

When asked why violence occurs in some families, Canadians identified both exosystem factors such as stress on the family (e.g., money problems and unemployment; 54%), personal factors such as alcohol and drug abuse (33%), and a history of violence or learned behavior in childhood (23%). The study also revealed that the majority of respondents (61%) knew someone who had experienced family violence. The most recent known incident of family violence was generally toward a spouse (51%) or children (30%) and involved physical and emotional abuse (37%), physical abuse only (31%), or emotional abuse only (22%; EKOS Research Associates, as cited in Canadian Center for Justice Statistics, 2002).

THE CANADIAN MICROSYSTEM

Although the majority of Canadians (84%) live in family settings, this percentage is declining, as is the proportion of married-couple families; at the same time, the number of common-law and single-parent families is increasing (Child Support Team, 2000). In Quebec, in the period of 1993 to 1994, nearly half of all births were out-of-wedlock births. Almost 20% of Canadian children lived in single-parent homes in 1996. Using "low income cutoffs" as an index of poverty, the Child Support Team (2000) estimated that nearly 15% of Canadian families—typically single-parent mothers—fell below the poverty line. According to a governmental Indian and Northern Affairs Report (n.d.), Aboriginal groups reported that more than 50% of their women had never been married (including in common-law marriages), as compared to 38% of non-Aboriginal women. Aboriginal families were much more likely than non-Aboriginal families to have two or more children, and the birth rate for Registered Indians is twice that of the general Canadian population.

CHILD ABUSE

The actual incidence of abuse toward children is difficult to estimate. In addition to smaller, more specialized studies, several national studies of children's lives are currently underway. The National Longitudinal Survey of Children and Youth, which began in 1994/1995 with a sample of 22,000 children and infants, includes items relating to family violence. Other major studies include the Canadian Incidence Study of Reported Child Abuse and Neglect, which includes information on abuse and neglect cases investigated across Canada (Trocmé et al., 2000). The Homicide Survey includes police-reported data on homicides, including infanticide. Beginning in 1997, this report has been expanded to include data on Shaken Baby Syndrome as a cause of death.

Other police reports and victimization surveys are providing a broader and more detailed account of the tragedy of child abuse. Even with all this data, it is estimated that only 11 of every 1,000 cases of maltreatment are reported to police (Bagley & King, 1990). In general, it has been found that rates of physical assaults toward children increase with age through age 17, when physically or sexually assaulted boys tend to be younger than girls at the age of first incident (Locke, 2002), and that maltreated children were shown to have depressive disorders at a rate of 3.4 to 4.5 higher than nonmaltreated children (Brown, Cohen, & Johnson, 1999). It also appears that boys are more often the victim of physical assault whereas girls are more often the victims of sexual assault (Locke, 2002) however, emerging research indicates that male victims of violence have not been well represented in society or in research on child victims (Health Canada, 1996).

Abuse in Aboriginal communities is viewed in a holistic way: Breakdowns in the family unit are seen as breakdowns in the fabric of the community and an affront to the aboriginal way of life. Family violence is seen as "a consequence to colonization, forced assimilation, and cultural genocide; the learned negative, cumulative, multi-generational actions, values, beliefs, attitudes and behavioral patterns practiced by one or more people that weaken or destroy the harmony and well-being of an Aboriginal individual, family, extended family, community or nationhood" (Maracle & Craig, 1993, p. 10). Spiritual abuse, which refers to a range of behaviors that serve to degrade belief systems, prevent people from observing their spiritual practices, or force adherence to another belief system (Health Canada, 1997), has also been identified in research on aboriginal communities.

Canadian Respondents' Perceptions of Child Abuse

Although children and adolescents have considerably more legal protections at the turn of this century than they did 100 years ago, rendering assistance is still hampered by a variety of realities. Implicit theories regarding which behaviors are considered to be abusive or neglectful are widely divergent. Among our sample, participants generally regarded the use of physical force toward children to be more acceptable than toward adults. Legal definitions of acceptable corporal punishment toward children indicate that severe punishment is abusive, but the criteria for levels of abuse are still controversial. Our participants listed "beating with hands or fists," "beating with a weapon," "grabbing," "slapping," and "kicking" as examples of abuse against children and adolescents. However, there was considerable variation regarding whether these behaviors were deemed to be extremely, moderately, or mildly abusive. Moreover, in keeping with legal definitions, several participants regarded hitting a child or adolescent as sometimes necessary.

Participants also listed a variety of forms of emotional or verbal behaviors as examples of abuse. Among these were "ignoring the needs of the child," "criticizing behaviors they cannot control," "punishing different things at different times so the child doesn't know what to expect," "confining to home," "using derogatory language," "uncontrolled yelling," and "put-downs." None of the male participants cited these behaviors as extremely abusive, choosing to label them as moderate or mild, whereas 9% of women designated these behaviors as examples of extreme abuse. "Unwanted sexual contact" was also cited as extremely abusive by 17% of our female participants and 10% of our male participants.

SPOUSAL ABUSE

Abuse of Women

According to the 1999–2000 Transition Home Survey, 96,359 women and children were admitted to 448 of Canada's emergency shelters between April 1, 1999, and March 31, 2000. Women were the vast majority of victims in all categories of spousal violence reported to the police, especially kidnapping/hostage taking (99%) and sexual assault (98%). Over a recent 5-year period, 25% of Aboriginal women were assaulted by a current or former spouse—3 times the rate for non-Aboriginal men and women. In 2000, 75% of criminal harassment reports were initiated by female victims, primarily against ex-spouses and boyfriends. Researchers have noted that in some Northern Communities, it is believed that between 75–90% of women are battered and 40% of children physically abused by a family member (Health Canada, 1997).

Incidence

In 2000, over 28,000 women sought police department intervention relating to family violence—constituting 85% of reports to police for domestic violence interventions. In general, women under the age of 25 and men between the ages of 25–34 are at the highest risk for spousal violence. Homicide risk is also highest for women under the age of 25; separated women in this age group face an even higher risk of being killed by their partner. The most common types of spousal violence are uttering threats (14%), assault with weapon causing bodily harm and aggravated assault (13%), criminal harassment (7%), and other violent offenses (7%).

The Women's Safety Project was a community-based study (Marshall & Vaillancourt, 1993) conducted in Toronto, Ontario, with 420 randomly selected women. In-depth interviews were conducted to examine the prevalence and nature of women's experience of sexual and physical violence in childhood and in mature intimate relationships. Their findings revealed high rates of violence through the lives of women that aren't adequately represented in official reports. Some of their findings included; 1) 27% of the women had experienced a physical assault in an intimate relationship; 2) 50% of the women reporting physical assault experienced sexual assault in the same relationship; and 3) 17% of women reported at least one experience of incest before age 16.

The actual incidence of abuse toward women throughout their lifespan is unknown for a variety of reasons. Fear of reprisal, shame, negative prior experiences reporting abuse, judgmental attitudes by caregivers, and a desire to seek distance from degrading experiences may all hinder women from seeking help and support. Women may also be advised to keep quiet or may not be believed when they begin to seek assistance. Some women in Canada may find themselves dependent or isolated by circumstances they cannot easily change. Women who do not speak the majority language of the area face an uphill battle seeking understanding, let alone assistance, from local services. This situation is compounded for immigrant women seeking refuge from war-torn countries where rape may have been used as a tool of war. For those women, it takes a long time before they become comfortable seeking or accepting assistance from police and other authorities. Immigrants, refugee women, and domestic foreign workers also face restrictions tying them to local employers or their husbands, without information on where to seek help or how to navigate through health care or legal institutions.

Women with disabilities face a broad range of hurdles that may increase their vulnerability to abuse and may hinder help-seeking activities. Women who seek shelter may not have access to emergency accommodations suitable for persons with particular disabilities. In addition, women with "invisible" disabilities such as epilepsy, or with multiple disabilities, may find themselves with limited or inadequate options. Rural women also face limited access to support services and may face extended waits for police intervention in the event of an emergency.

Overall, in the period between 1995 and 2000, reports of spousal violence in Canada increased by 27%. There appear to be several reasons for the growing number of reports. Overall, police have noted an increase in victims' willingness to report to police. There have also been changes in reporting practices to the Canadian Centre for Justice Statistics. In addition, among some groups of women, increased public awareness of domestic violence, a decrease in the social stigma of being a victim, and improved training of police and court support services may have helped lead to an increase in reports of domestic violence among both men and women.

Another indicator of the incidence of familial abuse is the number and occupancy rates of emergency shelters. In the year 2000, there were 508 women's shelters across the country. During the 1980s, the number of emergency shelters open to women and children increased dramatically, with much of this growth between 1989 and 1998 happening in aboriginal communities. The number of shelters in Canada has grown from 18 in 1975 to 508 in 2000, and shelter admissions are increasing dramatically. Between 1991 and 2000, the number of women and children seeking refuge increased by over 20%, and 80% of women housed in emergency shelters were seeking a place of safety from their spouse or ex-spouse.

The most common forms of abuse experienced by women housed in Canada's shelters were psychological abuse (77%), physical abuse (68%), threats (50%), financial abuse (40%), harassment (36%), and sexual assault within their relationship (30%). Recent combined figures for women who chose to remain in their relationship and those who choose to leave indicated that the most common methods of violence reported to police included physical force (72%), threats (15%), and assault with a weapon (11%; Code, as cited in Trainor, Lambert, & Dauvergne, 2002).

Fortunately, while reports of domestic violence have increased, spousal homicide rates have gone down. For women, the rate of spousal homicide dropped by 62% between 1974 and 2000, and for men, their rate dropped by more than half. Several reasons may account for this decline. While youths are in the highest risk group for violence, delaying marriage may serve to reduce the risk of homicide. In addition, increasing labor force participation and rising income levels for women are associated with delayed marriage and improved financial independence. Both of these features may impact on a women's decision to enter or remain in an abusive relationship.

Incidence rates of different crimes vary from province to province. Spousal homicide rates are no different. The provinces are more densely populated than are the territories and tend to have higher numbers of spousal homicides per year. The death toll for women was highest in Manitoba, and for men it was highest in Saskatchewan. In the territories, far higher spousal homicide rates were reported.

The 27-year homicide rate for women in the Northwest Territories was 7 times the national average (77.8 women per million couples) and 4 times the national average in the Yukon (47.3 women per million couples). Similarly, male spousal homicide rates were 14 times higher in the Northwest Territories (48 men per million couples) and 6 times higher in the Yukon (21.5 men per million couples) There have been two spousal homicides in Nunuvut since 1999 (Trainor, Lambert, & Dauvergne, 2002, p. 11).

Canadian Participants' Perspectives on Wife Abuse

A majority of our participants cited physical abuse (74%) as examples of extreme abuse, however, there was a strong gendered difference in descriptions of physical abuse toward wives. Women's descriptions of abuse were far more detailed and broad, whereas men's descriptions tended to fall into the categories of constant assault, punching, leaving marks, and causing bleeding. Frequency and physical consequences seemed to be the salient feature of extreme abuse when reported by men toward wives. When women described extreme physical abuse, they referred to a much broader range of activities such as putting wife in hospital, beating unconscious, constantly breaking bones or battering, physically harming for life (i.e., blinding her), burning, drowning, hitting with a belt or other weapons, beating until causing noticeable injuries, kicking, and slapping.

Women's definitions of physical abuse tended to vary depending on frequency and the antecedent. For example, one 21-year-old woman felt that hitting a wife for no obvious reason is extremely abusive whereas hitting a wife when she disobeys her husband is moderately abusive. When men mentioned grades of physical abuse, none of our participants mentioned intent; instead, they tended to mention degrees of harm physical harm or behavior. Many of our male participants felt that any physical abuse is extremely abusive, however, one 49-year-old man felt that hitting constantly is abusive behavior but occasionally hitting one's wife is moderate and hitting her once in a while constitutes mild abuse. Another 21-year-old man felt that beating one's wife until she loses a lot of blood is extreme, whereas hitting with weapons such as a stick is moderate and hitting without weapons is mildly abusive.

Another area that evidenced divergent views was that of sexual entitlement within a marriage. Across our participants, women were far more likely than men to list rape and any form of sexual assault as extremely abusive. Men were more likely to cite withholding sex as a form of abuse toward husbands whereas women listed rape or other forms of sexual coercion as forms of abuse toward wives. Marital infidelity was cited as extremely abusive by both men toward wives and by women toward their husbands although "adultery" was not cited nearly as often as forms of sexual aggression among marital partners.

Issues relating to household management were also cited for women but not for men. When women cited reasons for abuse to occur, they were often relating to disobeying, failing to keep a clean, orderly house, failing to care for or respect the husband's family, and failing to maintain well-behaved children. For example, one 22-year-old woman believed that a wife not getting along with her mother-in-law is considered to be incorrect behavior that might warrant a husband yelling in front of their children. She felt that this behavior was extremely abusive. The same woman believed that a wife "not keeping children quiet," and "not having dinner ready" for a husband when he arrives home from work constitute moderate and mild forms of abuse respectively. One 26-year-old woman also cited "abuse toward the wife's family" as moderately abusive.

Verbal and emotional abuse was also an area of contrast between our male and female participants. Men tended to list forms of verbal abuse like shouting and put-downs, and emotional cruelty as moderately abusive whereas women cited a far wider range of behaviors. Women in the study reported shouting, "pointing out wife's weak points to others," undermining or "embarrassing her in public," "constant put-downs," "swearing daily," "condescension," "guilt-tripping," "any comment intended to cause emotional harm" and withholding communication ("the silent treatment") as forms of verbal and emotional abuse. Interestingly, although men tended to report acts of commission as forms of abuse, they were also more likely to report acts of omission, or displaced behaviors as abusive. For example, one 22-year-old man cited "misplaced fits of rage i.e. breaking furniture" as less abusive than "disparaging language and verbal abuse" whereas other men reported "passive aggressiveness," "ignoring their wife," and "breaking promises" as mild forms of abuse. When women cited a lack of communication or other omissions they were cited less often but rated as more harsh forms of abuse. Other forms of abuse, like "restricting the wife from social contact and from working outside of the home" were cited by women as forms of wife abuse. None of the men in our sample listed these behaviors as forms of abuse.

Abuse of Men

The issue of husband assault has been highly controversial. Some of our respondents felt that the very idea of husband assault is "absurd," or, when it occurs, amounts to a "non issue." This belief goes against emerging research on husband abuse. According to Trainor, Lambert, and Dauvergne (2002), the one-year rate of spousal violence indicates that an estimated 220,000 women and 177,000 men had been the victim of some form of spousal violence in the past year. Moreover, Statistics Canada findings (Trainor, Lambert, & Dauvergne, 2002b) indicate that men and women are exposed to the risk of violence in almost the same proportions. Assault with a deadly weapon and aggravated assault were more common among male victims of spousal assault than among female victims. Battered men reported similar feelings and offered similar reasons for remaining in their relationships as women who are battered by their husbands.

While men may be vulnerable to more domestic violence than commonly assumed, they are less likely to be hurt and more likely to use severe violence tactics in physical confrontations with their partners (Sommer, 1994, cited in Tutty, 1999). In 2002, women were far more likely to incur an injury that required hospitalization and to require medications when involved in a violent exchange. Although many husbands do not choose to retaliate against abusive wives, some do, and when that happens, the outcome is more likely to halt the escalation of force from the female partner. Given this situation, it appears then that abuse toward husbands may occur in a way that is not fully captured by surveys that catalogue violent acts or by third party reports. Differences in the perceived gradient of harm may also account for some of the difference in official reports.

Case studies of abused men indicate that abuse toward men is a broad phenomenon that has both commonalities and differences with the experience of battered women (Tutty, 1999). The true incidence of battered men may be concealed, in part, because of reluctance to report or bad experiences when men seek assistance. Some men have reported ridicule and disbelief from support or protective services as well as from family members or other confidants. Male victims of violence frequently report that they face laughter and harassment when they seek assistance from friends or support workers. This discourages men from seeking assistance and cuts off an important source of support for a man trying to break free from an abusive relationship. One participant remarked, "If the wife succeeds in physically harming her husband, this would be considered abuse. Otherwise I would think that many people in my culture would find it funny or totally absurd—a woman trying to harm her husband or hurt his feelings."

Canadian Participants' Perspectives on Husband Abuse

As examples of husband abuse, our participants listed "embarrassment" and "disrespect" as often as forms of physical abuse. Ratings of relative harm, however, were marked by great inconsistency. A woman respondent said that extreme abuse is "anything that would bring a victim to tears." One of the men, however, said extremely abusive behavior has occurred "if the victim requires hospitalization," moderate abuse is "abuse requiring medical attention," and mild abuse has occurred "if you still have your senses." Another male participant noted that, in the context of a marriage, "rape" is a mild form of abuse. The vast majority of participants felt that hitting one's spouse was not an acceptable behavior. However, a minority of women did agree that it is sometimes necessary for a wife to hit her husband hard, but drew the line at using weapons.

Within our sample, there appear to be major differences in implicit theories as to appropriate behaviors for men and women in relationships, and the implications of violating norms for the persons involved. One male participant reported that "anything that puts him in a subordinate position" is abusive. Among participants who felt that husband assault was "sometimes necessary," several reported that abusiveness toward husbands could be achieved by attempts to humiliate or subordinate him in any way. For example, "contradicting him in public," "raised voices at any time," and, among some cultures, "disrespect toward his family" were considered abusive. Also listed were a wide range of behaviors from "physical and sexual assault" to "cheating," "public humiliation," "failing to cook," "failing to keep children quiet," "name-calling," and "ignoring." When listing reasons why a woman might abuse her partner, some participants reported that husbands may be abused for "any type of assault," "cheating," "failing to fix things," "failing to provide for the family," or addictive situations like "continual drunkenness." In contrast to a frequent emphasis on preserving traditional sex roles, other participants said that "any behavior that hinders the maintenance of an egalitarian relationship" can be considered a form of wife or husband abuse.

It was interesting to note that behaviors described as abusive were also listed as reasons for a man or woman to be abusive toward the partner. One can see how even in cases not involving physical attacks and self-defense, other forms of abuse can easily become mutual and self-perpetuating. Far more research is needed to develop a fuller understanding of reciprocal abuse, and to develop support services that are accessible, sustainable, and effective for abused men

Abuse in Same-Sex Couples

The violence and other abuses found in gay and lesbian relationships is marked more by similarity to heterosexual patterns than by differences. Clinicians have found that abuse suffered by gay or lesbian couples at the hands of their partners are of the same types suffered by heterosexual couples. Similarly, the way abusive relationships evolve among same-sex couples tends to follow the same cyclic pattern of peacefulness, increasing tension, followed by abusive outbursts. Workers in the field have also found that men and women in both same-sex and opposite-sex relationships tend to suffer from similar emotional and behavioral problems (Health Canada, 1998a, 1998b). Although it is difficult to estimate the actual incidence of abuse in any type of relationship, clinicians' and service workers' reports indicate that members of gay and lesbian couples face domestic abuse in substantial numbers.

In addition to similarities, there are striking differences in the experience of same-sex victims of domestic violence. Gay and lesbian partners face hurdles to accessing services that are not a factor for heterosexual couples. One is the lack of legal standing and protection as a spouse. Although more financial and insurance companies in Canada are recognizing same-sex marriages, the fight for legal recognition continues. In addition, when a member of an abusive relationship does seek assistance, there may be few or no services available that are appropriate. Individuals seeking help may access mainstream services and encounter the same homophobic attitudes prevalent in the rest of their town.

Common myths associated with familial abuse among gay and lesbian couples are: 1) Gay male domestic violence is logical because all men are prone to violence, but lesbian domestic violence does not occur because women are not as prone to violence; 2) because partners are of the same gender, the abuse is mutual, with both partners perpetrating and receiving equally; 3) when abuse occurs in a gay/lesbian relationship, the perpetrator must be the "man" or "butch" and the victim must be the "woman" or "femme," as is presumed to be the case in heterosexual relationships. While several researchers have refuted these myths (e.g., Cook, 1997; Renzetti, 1992), they persist among some legal and health care professionals as well as among members of the general public. One of the most powerful barriers to getting help involves the stigma associated with same-sex lifestyles. For individuals who have not made their orientation public, this information may be used by their partner as blackmail. In many communities, this is a substantial threat, involving potential loss of job, home, family, and friends. Abused partners may also want to keep family abuse quiet to prevent others from having more material to disparage same-sex relationships.

Elder Abuse

In Canada, the elderly are the fastest growing segment of the population—a trend referred to as the "graying" of the Canadian population. Given the social, economic, and physical climate in which the elderly live, abuse against this segment of the population has the potential to become an epidemic in years to come. In addition, all segments of the population are facing shrinking social and health services, and less accessible institutional care. The outcome of these trends is believed to be an increased reliance on care from family members, with an attendant increased risk for domestic abuse. Fortunately, public awareness of this phenomenon is increasing, as are resources for research and intervention.

The most frequent forms of elder maltreatment in Canada are material abuse, followed by chronic verbal aggression, and physical abuse (Podnieks, Pillemer, Nicholson, Shillington, & Frizzel, 1990). Findings indicate that older men are more likely victimized by their adult children, whereas older women are more likely victimized by their spouses; older women are more likely to require hospitalization for maltreatment (20%) than men (5%); and older adults who live with grown children or other caregivers are more likely to be abused than those who live with their spouse.

As with all forms of family violence, underreporting of elder abuse occurs for a variety of reasons. Surveys capture only what victims report. Some self-report difficulties with this group can include underestimating abuse, difficulty recalling incidents, and, in the case of infirm patients, inability to participate in self-report studies. Elderly persons without access to a telephone, institutionalized individuals, those with hearing or other physical impairments, and individuals who are isolated in other ways may not be able to contribute to national data-gathering efforts. Sadly, for those who could be reached via secondary sources, such as doctors or other caregivers, mental or physical impairments may also prevent their situation from being described accurately or fully.

In addition, when elderly individuals are dependent on abusive caretakers, they may fear retaliation from their caretakers or other negative consequences, such as being put into an institution, if they complain. Moreover, when an elderly person tries to report abuse by a caregiver, they may not be believed. Elderly participants in surveys may also underreport for reasons unrelated to intentions or memory. Psychological defenses relating to forgetting or underplaying incidents can also contribute to underreporting just as with other groups of abused individuals. Finally, for some types of maltreatment, like financial abuse, the victim may not be aware that the abuse has taken place.

Canadian researchers have noted a division in caregiving expectations. For men, caregiving is more often perceived as a choice, whereas for women it is an obligation (Chappell & Kuehne, 1998). When no other options exist for male caregivers, they may require significant support. This suggests that services aimed at alleviating caregiver burden and decreasing the risk of family violence should focus not just on the needs of elderly patients, but on support for caregivers thrust into the role against their will. This is an important finding considering the looming demographic shifts in Canada and the apparent expectation among our survey respondents that children and spouses' children should assume substantial caregiving responsibility for their parents.

Canadian Participants' Perspectives on Elder Abuse

When addressing the issue of elder abuse, respondents to our survey almost universally regarded it as unacceptable. They noted that abuse could occur in two directions—from caregiver to elder or elder to caregiver. As examples of abuse that could occur in either direction, participants mentioned "lack of co-operation," and "ignoring the preferences of the other party." For abuse directed specifically toward the elder, however, participants listed "verbally berating," "ignoring," "hitting," and, above all, "neglect."

A strong theme in the treatment of elders is that they should be respected and that violations of an elderly person's sense of dignity constitute a particularly serious form of abuse. On this note, the question of who should attend to the elderly is a culturally sensitive topic. Some respondents noted that it is the responsibility of wives, daughters, and daughters-in-law to attend to the comfort of the elderly. Both men and women participants noted that a woman's failure to care for the elderly parents of both partners constitutes a form of spousal abuse toward husbands. This was a strong theme for some participants, but not for others.

Participants reported behavior such as "withholding necessary care" as mildly abusive, whereas "hitting," "yelling," and "shoving" were considered extremely abusive. This is a shocking finding, given that the consequences of withholding care for the elderly can not only be as extreme as inflicting an injury but may also be less detectable. Thus, data on negative outcomes from withholding care may not be included in prevalence reports on elder abuse. Furthermore, recent research has shown that when spouses reach old age together, abusive tendencies may persist and in fact be exacerbated by the demands of caregiving for an increasingly frail partner. Elders receiving assistance from either family members or other caregivers may also face a range of discriminatory behaviors related to living in an "ageist society." Neglecting and ignoring the needs and emotional lives of the elderly may be compounded by the idea that they are outdated and irrelevant by virtue of being elderly.

Emotional and financial abuse cut across all sociodemographic lines. Both men and women from all income levels and educational backgrounds report incidents of abuse. Characteristics related to this type of abuse include being male, being divorced or separated, having an income between $30,000 and $40,000, or over $60,000, having some postsecondary schooling, and living in a rural area (Pottie Bunge, 2000). This is not a surprising finding, because elders with substantial holdings are less likely to notice shortfalls when others handle their finances, and those living in rural areas are more likely to be isolated. Few participants mentioned financial abuse at all; however, when the elderly have no further productive working years to draw on, the implications of being left impoverished are profound and far-reaching.

"Taking elderly parents' money" or "taking their possessions" was viewed as mildly to moderately abusive by our survey participants. Financial/material abuse can take other forms for the elderly. For example, "pressuring the elderly to perform chores that they are unable or unwilling to do," "pressuring them to make financial decisions that they would not have chosen on their own," or "pressuring them to sign over control of their affairs" were also listed as abusive. The effects of financial abuse are also not a simple matter of becoming impoverished. For the elderly who have experienced financial abuses, they report both a deep sense of betrayal and an intense, pervasive worry about their future.

Almost no participants mentioned "homicide" or "abuse leading to death" in their examples of elder abuse, although several of them did when giving general examples of abuse. Statistics from the year 2000 show that in the majority of elder homicide cases, the perpetrator was a nonfamily member (74%); however, a substantial number were killed by family members. The most likely perpetrators were spouses (39%), adult children (37%), and extended family members (24%). There was a clear gender difference in perpetrators. Over 50% of older women were killed by their spouses, versus 25% of older men. Older men were almost twice as likely as older women to be killed by their adult sons. A gender difference was also apparent in our study where none of the women felt that it was ever necessary to strike an elderly parent. Among men, a minority of our participants agreed that it was sometimes necessary to do so.

How does this situation arise? Findings of the Homicide Survey (Dauvergne, 2002) between 1997 and 2000 indicated that 43% of persons accused of committing homicide against a senior family member had a history of family violence with that victim, whether the victim was male or female. Among strangers, rates of violent crimes tend to decrease as the perpetrator ages, but violence within families may increase, given the unique circumstances of family relatedness. Some of the risk factors for family homicide of an elder member are family obligations to provide care, resentment over previous abuse, lack of support for caregivers, and the overwhelming demands of caring for elders who are seriously impaired.

THE CANADIAN RESPONSE TO FAMILY VIOLENCE

In Canada, there are several official days that focus on the needs and rights of children. November 20th is National Child Day, and marks the adoption of two landmark events for children; the adoption of the United Nations Declaration on the Rights of the Child in 1959 and the adoption of the UN Convention on the right of the Child in 1989. May 25th is National Missing Children's Day, and is intended to raise public awareness of the thousands children who go missing every year (see www.mcsc.ca for The Missing Children's Society of Canada). Finally, National Family Week has been designated since 1985 as the week before Thanksgiving. The focus of this week is to examine ways to ensure that all children are given opportunities, support, and resources they need to grow up as happy healthy contributors to Canadian society.

Over the past 30 years, there have been several major federal studies on violence against women in Canada. In 1970, The Royal Commission on the Status of Women presented 167 recommendations regarding education, employment, and family life. The struggle for information and action for the just treatment of women continued slowly through the next two decades, while the need for action became more and more apparent. In June 1991, a House of Commons subcommittee released their report entitled, "The War Against Women," a distillation of input from antiviolence organizations across the country. Owing, in part, to the recommendation of the War against Women, and to increasing public pressure for the government to act more decisively on this issue, the Canadian Panel on Violence Against Women was founded in August 1991. In its report, the Panel took a community-oriented, nonpartisan, feminist orientation. Over roughly 400 pages, the report considered unique experiences of violence among different groups of women and the experience of violence in Canada's institutions.

Data and public awareness on abuse of the elderly are increasing, and as a consequence, policy changes are becoming evident. For example, among the 467 emergency shelters in Canada, 84% of them now provide programming, outreach, and services designed to address the unique needs of senior women.

A number of useful resources can be found in the appendix at the end of this chapter.

CONCLUSION

Over the past several decades, Canada has shifted emphasis from a "melting pot" mentality of multiculturalism to one of a "cultural mosaic." The new emphasis is on respecting and celebrating the differences among people of different ages, abilities, and backgrounds. This attitude, coupled with increasing cultural prohibitions against violence, has informed recent policies dealing with family violence. Recent publications and policy mandates reveal an interest in developing a flexible approach to dealing with different groups from pubic education programs, through frontline service delivery. Legal and medical strategies are beginning to reflect the differential needs and characteristics of individuals through the lifespan. In addition to that, social mechanisms are also being refined to best cultivate and protect the independence and dignity of individuals affected by family violence throughout the country.

REFERENCES

Bagley, C., & King, K. (1990). *Child sexual abuse: The search for healing.* New York: Routledge.

Brown, J., Cohen, P., & Johnson, J. G. (1999). Childhood abuse and neglect: Specificity of effects on adolescent and young adult depression and suicidality. *Journal of the American Academy of Child and Adolescent Psychiatry, 38*(12), 1490–1496.

Canadian Centre for Justice Statistics. (2002). *Family violence in Canada: A statistical profile, 2002.* Available from Statistics Canada: http://www.statcan.ca/english/freepub/85-224-XIE/85-224-XIE00002.pdf

Chappell, N. L., & Kuehne, V. K. (1998). Congruence among husband and wife caregivers. *12*(3), 239–254.

Child Support Team. (2000). *Selected statistics on Canadian families and family law* (2nd ed.). Available from: Canadian Department of Justice: http://canada.justice.gc.ca/en/ps/sup/pub/rap/SelStats.pdf

Cook, P. (1997). *Abused men: The hidden side of domestic violence.* London: Praeger.

Dauvergne, M. (2002). Family violence against older adults. In *Family violence in Canada: A statistical profile, 2002.* Canadian Centre for Justice Statistics. Catalogue no. 85-224-XIE. Available: http://www.statcan.ca/english/freepub/85-224-XIE/85-224-XIE00002.pdf

Gotowiec, A., & Beiser, M. (1993–1994, winter). Aboriginal children's mental health: Unique challenges. *Canada's Mental Health,* 7–11.

Gregorash, L. (1990). *Family violence: An exploratory study of men who have been abused by their wives.* Unpublished master's thesis, University of Calgary.

Health Canada. (1996). *The invisible boy: Revisioning the victimization of male children and teens* (Cat. No: H72-21/143-1996E). Ottawa: National Clearinghouse on Family Violence.

Health Canada. (1997). *Family violence in Aboriginal communities: An Aboriginal perspective* (Cat. No. H72-21/150-1997E). Ottawa: National Clearinghouse on Family Violence.

Health Canada. (1998a). *Husband abuse: An overview of research and perspectives* (Cat. No. H72-21/157-1998E). Ottawa: National Clearinghouse on Family Violence.

Health Canada. (1998b). *Abuse in lesbian relationships: Information and resources* (Cat. No. H72-21/153-1998). Ottawa: National Clearinghouse on Family Violence.

Indian and Northern Affairs. (n.d.). *Family* [online]. Available: http://www.ainc-inac.gc.ca/pr/sts/awp5_e.html

Locke, D. (2002). *Violence against children and youth* [online]. Available from: Canadian Center for Justice Statistics, *Family violence in Canada: A statistical profile, 2002*: http://www.statcan. ca/english/freepub/85-224-XIE/85-224-XIE00002.pdf

Maracle, S., & Craig, B. (1993). *For generations to come: The time is now: A strategy for Aboriginal family healing.* Ontario: The Aboriginal Family Healing Joint Steering Committee.

Marshall, P. F., & Vaillancourt, M. A. (1993). *Changing the landscape: Ending violence, achieving equality.* Ottawa: The Canadian Panel on Violence Against Women.

Podnieks, E., Pillemer, K., Nicholson, J. P., Shillington, T., & Frizzel, A. (1990). *National survey on abuse of the elderly in Canada.* Toronto: Ryerson Polytechnical Institute.

Pottie Bunge, V. (2000). Spousal violence. In V. Pottie Bunge & D. Locke (Eds.), *Family violence in Canada: A statistical profile* (pp. 11–19). Ottawa: Statistics Canada. Available: http://www.statcan.ca/english/freepub/85-224-XIE/00000085-229-XIE.pdf

Renzetti, C. (1992). *Violent betrayal: Partner abuse in lesbian relationships.* Newbury Park, CA: Sage.

Robinson, B. A. (2001). *Suicide among Canada's native people* [online]. Available from: Ontario Consultants on Religious Tolerance: http://www.religioustolerance.org/sui_nati.htm

Trainor, C., Lambert, M., & Dauvergne, M. (2002a). Consequences and impacts of spousal violence [online]. Available from: Canadian Center for Justice Statistics, *Family violence in Can-*

ada: A statistical profile, 2002: http://www.statcan.ca/english/freepub/85-224-XIE/85-224-XIE00002.pdf

Trainor, C., Lambert, M., & Dauvergne, M. (2002b). Spousal violence. In C. Trainor (Ed.), *Family violence in Canada: A statistical profile, 20002.* National Clearinghouse on Family Violence, Catalogue No: 85-224-XIE. Ottawa: Health Canada.

Trocmé, N. B., et al. (2000). *Canadian incidence study of reported child abuse and neglect* [online]. Available from Statistics Canada: http://www.hc-sc.gc.ca/pphb-dgspsp/publicat/cisfr-ecirf/index.html

Tutty, L. M. (1999). Husband abuse: An overview of research and perspectives. Health Canada, Family Violence Prevention Unit. Available: http://www.hc-sc.gc.ca/hppb/familyviolence/pdfs/husbandenglish.pdf

APPENDIX: RESOURCE LIST

Useful Web-based Canadian Web-based Resources

- Status of Women Canada: www.swc-cfc.gc.ca/iwd
- The National Clearinghouse on Family Violence: www.hc-sc.gc.ca/nc-cn
- The Status of Women in Canada: http://www.swc-cfc.gc.ca/direct.html
- DAWN Canada: The Disabled Women Network: http://www.dawncanada.net/special.htm
- The Canadian Research Institute for the Advancement of Women: http://www.criaw-icref.ca/
- The History of Women in Canada and the Canadian Women's Internet Directory (includes references for Gay/Lesbian, Aboriginal and Differently Abled persons): http://herstory.womenspace.ca
- The Canadian Women's Health Network: www.cwhn.ca
- BC Institute Against Family Violence: www.bciv.org
- 99 Federal Steps to End Violence Against Women—Bibliography: www.casac.ca/99steps/99steps_%20biblio.htm

The United States

Kimberly A. Rapoza

CAPSULE

The United States would seem to have more laws, regulations, and organizations for preventing and intervening in family violence than all the other countries addressed in this book. However, this does not mean that the problem of family violence has been solved in the United States. Substantial numbers of children, wives, husbands, and people over the age of 65 are abused by family members every year. Corporal punishment, which has been rejected as a child-rearing technique in many European countries is still widely defended in the United States. Women tend to be fully employed and have long had equal rights under the law, but they are beaten and murdered at an alarming rate every year. Moreover, men are also subject to abuse by intimate partners, and sibling violence is generally condoned.

THE UNITED STATES SAMPLE

The U.S. sample consisted of 77 women and 33 males ranging in age from 18 to 79 (with a mean age of 34). The majority of the sample (69%) was Caucasian, but there were also 11 African Americans, as well as several Asian Americans, Latinos/Hispanics, and others. Religious affiliations were 40% Christian Protestant, 18% Catholic, 8% Jewish, 2% Buddhist, 2% Pagan/Wiccan, 1% Hindu, 14% Agnostic/Non-Denominational, and 16% none. The

U.S. respondents reported working in a wide variety of occupations, including teacher/instructor, health care professional (e.g., nurse), mental health professional (e.g., social worker), self-employed or freelance, military personnel, and human resources or administrative positions.

U.S. Participants' Definitions of Abuse

When giving definitions of abuse, the U.S. participants almost always made reference to physical or psychological aggression. For example, one 34-year-old self-identified "Caucasian middle-class" male defined abuse in the context of the family as "physical and mental abuse." A 41-year old female self-identified "Republican Southern Baptist" defined it as "verbal— calling someone any name that belittles or subjugates another person (idiot, stupid, bitch . . . etc.)." Some definitions also included references to sexual abuse but rarely was any reference made to neglect. It seems that American implicit theories of abuse within the context of the family lean heavily toward a conceptualization focusing on physical and psychological maltreatment.

Some of the implicit theories forwarded by the U.S. participants conceptualized abuse as damage done to another's self-esteem/self-concept or spirit. For example, a 44-year-old "White Anglo-Saxon" female indicated, "Abuse is when someone is treated in such a way that their self-esteem is affected negatively." Another implicit theory postulated that an action was abusive when it had been done in a deliberate manner or with intentions to cause harm. For instance, a 56-year-old self-identified "WASP" indicated that abuse is "a demeaning act or word leveled against another person with the intent to cause hurt or damage." A third and frequently occurring theme was that something was abusive when it took advantage of another family member, with many participants specifically pinpointing power differentials within a familial relationship. One 42-year-old "Hispanic" female indicated it was abusive "when one person takes mental advantage of another." A 50-year-old self-identified "Jewish American" male indicated that abuse within the family was "taking advantage of a person to that person's detriment . . . scaring someone one has power over (like a parent over a child or a very domineering spouse over a spouse ill-equipped to handle that) . . . or someone using force on someone of weaker physical abilities."

THE U.S. MACROSYSTEM

The United States Constitution was developed in the shadows of colonization. Its emphasis on independence, equality, personal freedom, and limited government interference in the lives of private citizens often influences how the legal system and private citizens view and respond to any given social issue. For instance, Pleck (1989) noted that attempts at enforcing family violence laws in America have often been characterized by a struggle between the public's interest in seeing family violence criminalized and the strongly held notion that matters of the family should be protected or shielded from interventions by the state.

THE MICROSYSTEM

The majority of children in America today grow up in a nuclear family with two working parents. According to Heymann (2001), the majority of working families face long work hours, inflexible employment schedules, and inadequate child-care options. In addition, currently 1 out of 4 working families struggle with providing care for an elderly adult family member. According to the 1995 *Survey on Family Growth* by the CDC, divorce has become more common, as have single-parent homes, stepfamilies, and other "nontraditional" family structures. Although the majority (55%) of children in the United States live in a nuclear family, about 19.7 million children live with an unmarried parent (predominately a female head of household). Additionally, in the 1990s, 39% of out-of wedlock births were to unmarried cohabiting couples.

FAMILY VIOLENCE IN THE UNITED STATES

American society's awareness of the incidence and prevalence of family violence has changed considerably over the past 200 years, as have implicit theories concerning the behaviors that constitute abuse. The first wide scale "discoveries" of child and spouse abuse as social problems in the United States began in the late 1800s. During this time, there were no child labor laws or laws to protect children from physical maltreatment, and beating and whipping children for wrongdoing were the condoned societal norm (McCauley, Schwartz-Kenney, Epstein, & Tucker, 2000). Stemming from media attention in 1875 to the case of "Mary Ellen" (a little girl who had been severely beaten and tortured by her foster parents, but could not legally be removed from their home as there were no laws against cruelty to children), concerned citizens formed the New York Society for the Prevention of Cruelty to Children, the first child protection agency in the country ("The New York Society," n.d.). Around the same time, society started to move away from unequivocally condoning a husband's use of force against his wife (Epstein, 1999). In 1850, the first law against wife beating was passed in Tennessee; however, this, and other early statutes, endorsed an implicit theory that in the absence of serious injury or life threatening violence, the state should avoid intervention in the domestic realm.

The next milestone in public concern over family violence was Kempe, Silverman, Steele, Droegemueller, and Silver's (1962) description of the "battered child syndrome"—injuries such as burns, broken bones, and fractures attributable to parents' maltreatment of their child. By 1967, the explosion of attention generated by this publication resulted in mandatory child abuse reporting laws in all 50 states (Breines & Gordon, 1983). Also, during the 1960s and 1970s, the feminist movement led to the establishment of many battered women's organizations (Fagan, 1995). One of the first battered women's shelters was opened in 1974 in St. Paul, Minnesota, based on a philosophy (implicit theory) reframing wife abuse as a social problem rather than as a private and personal one ("History of the battered women's movement," n.d.).

In the 1980s, high profile media coverage of battered women and the results of the Minneapolis Domestic Violence Experiment drastically changed public opinion and legal approaches to domestic violence cases. This experiment showed that domestic violence recidivism was substantially less for men who were arrested as compared to men who were dealt with using other tactics (Sherman & Berk, 1984). While not all studies have replicated this finding (Tolman & Edleson, 1995), the arresting of batterers and the criminalization of domestic violence was evidence of American society taking more seriously the rights and needs of battered women.

Only recently has elder abuse been recognized as a problem meriting societal concern. Not until the late 1970s and 1980s, after a series of congressional hearings and efforts by individuals involved in the child and spousal abuse movements, did public attention, legislation, and funding begin being directed toward this newly discovered problem (Quinn & Tomita, 1997).

CHILD ABUSE

Many North American cultural values make the prevention of child abuse a challenging and fluctuating venture. The United States has a long history of sanctioning the use of corporal punishment in the upbringing of children. Generally, Americans overwhelmingly believe that parents have a right to physically discipline their children (particularly toddlers) and that corporal punishment should be an option to effectively and reasonably discipline a child (Straus, 2001a). Currently, all 50 states permit the use of corporal punishment by parents (Edwards, 1996). All states, however, also have some form of limitation on this entitlement—for example, indicating that the force used must be reasonable or must not result in serious physical injury (Edwards, 1996). However, the coexistence of these two popular sentiments—that abusing a child is wrong and that parental use of physical force to discipline a child is permissible—often create conflicts over the point at which parental discipline crosses the threshold and becomes child abuse. It is not uncommon for parents to fight a child abuse conviction, even when their actions killed the child, arguing that their conduct was a justifiable attempt to discipline their child (Johnson, 1998).

Our participants seemed concerned with many of these same issues—for example, discipline crossing the line to abuse. For instance, 25% of the examples of extreme abuse, 71% of the examples of moderate abuse, and 22% of the examples of mild abuse described a situation in which, based on the actions of the child, punishment seemed excessive. Some examples are "father hitting his son with a wrench because the child did not choose the screwdriver. Child is not doing what he is told," "parent screaming at a child for an accident, such as spilling drinks," and "yelling or inappropriate punishment (grounding for a month, punishment does not match the crime)."

Characteristics of Child Abuse Victims

While the 1993 National Incidence Study (NIS; Sedlak & Broadhurst, 1996) found that children are vulnerable to sexual abuse from age 3 onward, rates of sexual victimization differed by gender, with girls being sexually abused at 3 times the rate of boys. However, for other forms of abuse (physical and neglect), boys had higher incidence rates than girls. Boys were also more likely to sustain serious injury from their abuse (24% higher). Statistics from Child Protective Services (CPS) (USDHHS, 2002) indicate that younger children have the highest rates of victimization. The role of race in child maltreatment is ambiguous. While the 1993 NIS revealed no race differences in the incidence of child abuse or neglect, African Americans are over-reported in Child Protective Service cases (USDHHS, 2002)—perhaps because of differential attention somewhere during the referral, investigation, and service allocation process (Sedlak & Broadhurst, 1996).

Perpetrators of Child Abuse

In 60% of child abuse cases reported to CPS (USDHHS, 2002) the perpetrator was a female. The 1993 NIS (Sedlak & Broadhurst, 1996) also found children somewhat more likely to be maltreated by a female than by a male (65% vs. 54%). However, the gender of the perpetrator varied with the type of maltreatment committed. Females were more likely than males to perpetrate neglect (78% vs. 43%) and physical abuse (60% vs. 48%), whereas males were the perpetrators of sexual abuse for the overwhelming majority of victims. The 1993 National Incidence Study also revealed that 62% of child abuse incidents and 91% of child neglect incidents were committed by a birth parent; children in single-parent homes were at higher risk, and were over-represented among seriously and moderately injured children. Male dating partners may also be a risk factor for child maltreatment. Police records indicate that since 1991, one in five child homicides in Chicago have been at the hands the mother's boyfriend (Zimmermann, 2002).

Physical Abuse

The 2000 National Child Abuse and Neglect Data Systems study (USDHHS, 2002) reported that about one fifth of substantiated child abuse cases dealt with by Child Protective Services involved physical abuse. The data also indicate that the prevalence of physical child abuse in the United States seems to be rising. Implicit theories of child abuse in our sample indicate that abuse is generally conceptualized as physical; 86% of the participants mentioned physical abuse (or a behavior that could be classified as physically abusive) as an example of extreme abuse, 48% as an example of moderate abuse, and 18% as an example of mild abuse. The most frequently mentioned type of physical abuse was "beating"—for example, "A child is caught stealing and the parent reacts by severely beating the child," "A child comes home with an 'F' on a test and the parent beats the child," and "Beating a child with a belt or wooden spoon." "Hitting" was also frequently listed as an example of abuse, but only rarely did participants' implicit theories of abuse seem to include "slapping" or "spanking." Overwhelmingly, when mentioning a body part in conjunction with an action viewed as abusive, participants mentioned "striking or hitting a child in the face." "Striking a child on the bottom" was listed as only mildly abusive and then only in 4% of examples. The failure of spanking a child on the bottom to fit the criteria for abuse in implicit theories is also reflected in some state statutes. For example, the California statute specifies that child abuse shall not be construed to include reasonable and age-appropriate spanking to the buttocks that does not result in serious physical injury (Edwards, 1996).

The 1995 National Family Violence Survey (Straus, 2001b) found that one out of four U.S. parents reported hitting children with objects (such as belts, paddles, sticks, or hairbrushes) as a form of corporal punishment. Straus (2001b) has noted that the cultural acceptance of these forms of corporal punishment with the intentions of disciplining both toddlers and older children has diminished in very recent years. It would seem that some of our American participants are showing those changing mores, as the use of objects to hit children was listed in 12% of the examples of extreme abuse category and 19% of the examples of moderate abuse.

Psychological/Emotional Abuse

Over the past two decades, rates of emotional abuse, like other forms of child abuse, appear to have increased at an alarming rate. In 1993, the estimated incidence of emotional abuse was 183% higher than in 1986, rising from 188,100 children to 532,200 children (Sedlak & Broadhurst, 1996). In our sample, various types of emotional abuse were given primarily as examples of moderate and mild abuse. The most common forms of emotional abuse mentioned were verbal assault (e.g., "If a child comes home late and the parent yells excessively"), rejection ("Calling a child stupid or in any way inferring they are inferior as a result of perceived failure by the parent"), and ignoring ("Never showing much affection. Never giving the child positive reinforcement"; "Lack of attention from a parent when a child asks for it"). Types of severe emotional abuse were isolating "[I] was not allowed to go to/ have friends over; was not allowed to participate in extracurricular activities"), and terrorizing ("Parent keeps child in fear of punishment at all times").

Neglect

The most common form of substantiated abuse in the United States is child neglect, which accounts for 63% of the substantiated cases (USDHHS, 2002). In addition, 38% of child fatalities linked to child maltreatment were due to neglect (USDHHS, 2002). Considering how prevalent this form of child maltreatment seems to be, it was surprising that comparatively few responses to our survey mentioned neglect. Only 8% of participants listed neglect (or some form of a neglectful behavior) as an example of extreme abuse, 7% as moderate abuse, and 13% as mild abuse. Thus, implicit theories of child abuse within the American public generally conceptualize it in terms of acts of commission rather than omission, although within the Child Protective Services system, it is the neglect cases that are most frequently identified.

Sexual Abuse

Although the prevalence rate of substantiated cases of sexual abuse has been found to be lower than other types of child abuse, 10% of substantiated child abuse cases dealt with by CPS involved the sexual abuse of a child (USDHHS, 2002). Participants in our study seemed aware of the potential for sexual abuse in the parent/child relationship. Eighteen percent of participants mentioned sexual abuse as an example in the extreme abuse.

SPOUSE ABUSE

With regard to cultural values concerning the use of physical force in a marriage, Americans show greater approval for violence perpetrated by a wife toward a husband than by a husband toward a wife (Straus, Kaufman-

Kantor, & Moore, 1997). Whereas approval of a husband slapping a wife decreased from 20% in 1968 to 10% in 1994, approval of a wife slapping a husband remained about constant at 22%. Within our sample, a large number of participants indicated that particular behaviors were abusive when perpetrated by either a husband or a wife; specifically, 40% of the examples of extreme abuse, 40% of the examples of moderate abuse, and 38% of the examples of mild abuse were identical examples for both the husband and wife.

Victims and Perpetrators of Wife Abuse

The 1998 National Crime Victimization Survey (NCVS; Rennison & Welchans, 2000) revealed that a current or former boyfriend/girlfriend or spouse committed about 1 million violent crimes in the United States in 1998; about 85% of the victims were women. Although women of all ethnicities, incomes, and households have been victims of intimate partner violence, the NCVS revealed some ethnic differences in victimization rates, with African-Americans reporting intimate partner violence at a higher rate than their Caucasian and Hispanic counterparts. Women whose family income was in the lowest bracket (less than $7,500) were victimized at 7 times the rate of women in the highest bracket ($75,000 and over). Current trends also show a 21% drop in violent crimes against women from 1993 to 1998, which Straus, Kaufman-Kantor, and Moore (1997) suggested may be a result of shifting cultural values stemming from advocacy groups, educational campaigns, changes in the legal system, and research.

Husband Abuse

Intimate partner violence against males in the United States has been largely ignored—although there is ample evidence that it occurs (e.g., Cook, 1997; Hines & Malley-Morrison, 2001; Steinmetz, 1977). Among our participants, there was a sizable minority who provided personal examples of abuse of men by an intimate partner. One 45-year-old woman noted that a male relative

> was made to feel like he could do nothing right and was constantly berated verbally by his wife. She controlled the money (took his paycheck and gave him $5 a week), the children, where they went, who they spent time with, where they lived. . . . She pulled phones out of the wall, kicked him in the ribs, stuck a lit cigarette in his shoulder, called the police and claimed he was being abusive.

Physical Abuse

The 1998 National Crime Victimization Survey (Rennison & Welchans, 2000) revealed that 81% of victimizations among intimates (spouses, ex-spouses, boyfriends, and girlfriends) were assaults. The National Violence Against

Women's survey (NVAW; Tjaden & Thoennes, 1998) indicated that most assaults against women by an intimate partner involved pushing, grabbing, shoving, slapping, and hitting. Minor physical assault rates were similar across gender, but rates diverged as the severity of the physical attacks increased. Women were 2 to 3 times more likely to report that an intimate partner threw something that could hurt, and 7 to 14 times more likely to report being beat up, choked, and threatened with a gun.

The majority of our respondents gave examples of physical abuse when describing extreme abuse by a husband toward his wife (91% of the examples) and extreme abuse of a wife toward her husband (86% of examples). Typical examples of physical abuse included "hitting" ("One spouse hits the other over anger over paying bills"), and "beating" (especially of a wife—for example, "Wife did not have dinner ready on time and was beaten by the husband"). Less typical examples were "pushing," "shoving," and "punching." "Slapping" and "hitting" were given as examples of abusive behavior from husband to wife and wife to husband at about the same rate, but "punching," "beating," and "kicking" were attributed primarily to husbands.

Emotional/Psychological Abuse

Psychological or emotional abuse has a shorter history of recognition and study in the field of domestic violence than do other forms of abuse (Marshall, 1994); however, it is far from rare. Margolin, John, and Foo (1998) found that 57% of men in their sample admitted using dominating and isolating emotionally abusive behaviors. Kasian and Painter (1992) found that males and females in dating relationships reported high percentages of verbal abuse (55%), withdrawal (60%), attempts to harm self-esteem (38%), and isolation/emotional control (22%) by their partner.

In our sample, overwhelmingly, the most frequently mentioned form of emotional abuse was verbal assault (e.g., "putting down," "swearing at," "belittling," "yelling," "degrading"), which was mostly seen as moderately or mildly abusive, and constituted about 10% of the examples of extreme abuse and about 50% of the examples of moderate and mild wife and husband abuse. Examples of dominance ("bullying," "controlling behavior, not letting the wife lead her own life") were mentioned in 9% of extremely abusive, 26% of moderately abusive, and 9% of mildly abusive examples of abuse from husband to wife, but far fewer examples from wife to husband. Isolation and threats to harm the partner were mentioned infrequently.

Sexual Abuse, Rape, and Sexual Assault

In the United States, rape has been found to be primarily a crime against women (Rennison & Welchans, 2000); however, a sizable minority of men also report experiencing rape or sexual assault (Tjaden & Theonnes, 1998).

In our sample, 19% of participants mentioned a sexually abusive behavior ("sexual abuse," "rape," and "forced sex") by a husband as an example of extreme abuse and 3% as an example of moderate abuse. While 7% of the examples of extreme abuse and 2% of the examples of moderate abuse by wives might be considered forms of sexual abuse, they focused on the withholding of sex (e.g., "not being available for sexual activity as the husband desires," "failure to submit sexually").

In the past, the American legal system has subscribed to the implicit theory that a husband is entitled to sexual relations with his wife and therefore could not be prosecuted for raping his wife. According to Bergen (1999), marriage was presumed to entail a wife's unequivocal consent to sexual relations. She also noted that although marital rape has been a crime in all 50 states since 1993, there are still 33 states that allow spousal exemptions for rape prosecution under certain circumstances. Our own data indicate that America is at a bit of a crossroads in terms of a wife's sexuality and a husband's "entitlement." While defining marital rape as a criminal act has taken some ambiguity out of whether it is "right" or "tolerable" for a husband to force his wife to have sex, many implicit theories still seem to be laced with some traditional suppositions.

ELDER ABUSE

The 1996 National Elder Abuse Incident Study (NEAIS; USAA, 1998) collected data from state and federal reporting agencies, as well as from "sentinels" (people working with the elderly in a variety of settings and not necessarily legally mandated to report abuse). The study found females to be abused at a relatively higher rate than males. The majority of victims were Caucasian (66%), with 19% African American, 10% Hispanic American, and fewer than 1% Asian American or Native American (Tatara & Kuzmeskus, 1996c). The "old" old (80 years and over) were abused and neglected at 2 to 3 times their proportion in the elderly population (NEAIS; USAA, 1998). Nearly all perpetrators were family members, most typically (37%) adult children and perpetrators did not differ by gender (Tatara & Kuzmeskus, 1996b).

Prevalence

National data from Adult Protective Services between the years 1986 and 1996 showed a 150% increase in elder abuse reports (Tatara & Kuzmeskus, 1997); however, the results of the 1996 NEAIS show elder abuse to be largely underreported. Although a total of 449,924 persons age 60 and over were found to be experiencing some form of abuse or neglect in a domestic setting, only 16% of those cases were reported and substantiated by Adult Protective Services. Neglect was the most common form of elder maltreatment

(55% of substantiated reports), followed by physical abuse (14.6% of cases), financial abuse (12.3%), and emotional abuse (7.7%). Sexual abuse of the elderly appeared to be rare (.3% of substantiated cases). Comparatively little attention has been given to the role spousal violence plays in elder abuse. Straus (2001b) noted that partner assault rates tend to drop off as the age of the offender increases. However, 4% of households surveyed with partners in their 70s reported the occurrence of partner violence within the past 12 months.

Physical Abuse

Physical abuse is defined by the National Center on Elder Abuse (NCEA) as "the use of physical force that may result in bodily injury, physical pain, or impairment," and sexual abuse as "non-consensual sexual contact of any kind with an elderly person" (Tatara & Kuzmeskus, 1996a, p. 1). When giving examples of severe and moderate elder abuse, the majority of our participants mentioned some form of physical aggression (69% and 11% respectively). Physical aggression was never given as an example of mild abuse, suggesting that implicit theories of elder abuse conceptualize physical aggression as very abusive. Some of the more frequent examples of physical abuse were "beating" (18%), and "hitting" or "slapping" (36%).

Emotional Abuse

NCEA defined emotional or psychological elder abuse as "the infliction of anguish, pain or distress through verbal or non-verbal acts" (Tatara & Kuzmeskus, 1996a, p. 1). Approximately 17% of our participants mentioned some form of psychological abuse as an example of extreme abuse, 68% as moderate abuse, and 77% as mild abuse. Examples were "screaming at the elder," "put-downs," "infantalizing the elder," and "restricting the elder's activities or freedom." One example given by a 20-year-old female participant was, "An elderly person wants to go outside and take a walk. The adult caregiver thinks this will be too much trouble and only lets the elderly person out of the house for things like doctor appointments." Participants mentioned passive forms of psychological abuse (e.g., "ignoring") in 31% of the emotional abuse examples.

Sexual Abuse

Sexual abuse is recognized by the NCEA as "non-consensual sexual contact of any kind with an elderly person" (Tatara & Kuzmeskus, 1996a, p. 1). Only one of our participants mentioned sexual abuse. This low rate is consistent with empirical data indicating that the prevalence of familial sexual abuse of the elderly is fairly low. Also, cases of elder sexual abuse covered in the media tend to be ones where an elder was sexually abused by nursing home staff. Thus, implicit theories of elder sexual abuse may associate it with institutional, rather than family, settings.

Financial Abuse

Financial or material exploitation is defined by the NCEA as "the illegal or improper use of an elder's funds, property or assets." (Tatara & Kuzmeskus, 1996a, p. 1). Five percent of our participants gave examples of financial/material exploitation in their responses—"stealing assets of the older person," "financially taking advantage of them," and "misuse of power of attorney." Implicit in these responses is the acknowledgment that in the United States, if a person becomes mentally incapacitated, a family member may be granted power of attorney, enabling him/her to make decisions for the elder (Quinn & Tomita, 1997); unfortunately, family members sometimes abuse this power, and there are few protective legal recourses once it has been granted.

Neglect

Neglect is defined as "the refusal or failure to fulfill any part of a person's obligations or duties to an elder," which involves the failure to provide necessary care for the elder. Included in many "official" definitions of elder maltreatment is "self neglect"—behaviors of an elderly person that threaten his or her health or safety (Tatara & Kuzmeskus, 1996a, p. 1). Among our participants, 39% mentioned neglect as an example of extreme abuse, 36% as moderate abuse, and 34% as mild abuse. Many of the examples of physical neglect included "not assisting" with activities of daily living such as providing food, shelter, warmth, baths, and help dressing (27% of neglect responses), medical neglect, such as "not assuring access to health care" (15% of neglect responses), and "not providing social interactions for the elder" (17% of neglect responses). Examples were also given of emotional neglect, such as "ignoring" (31% of emotional neglect responses) and "not visiting" (16% of emotional neglect responses).

Institutional Setting

To date, there are no national statistics available on institutional elder abuse. However, in a sample of 8 states, the Department of Health and Human Services found that 1 to 3% of the nursing home's population surveyed had registered an abuse or neglect complaint (Brown & DeParle, 1999).

Some of our participants seemed to view placing an elder in a nursing home as its own form of elder maltreatment. One 53-year-old female participant felt that it was abusive to "make threats of placement in a nursing home"; another felt that it was extremely abusive "if you put the elderly person in a home for the elderly."

SIBLING VIOLENCE

Whereas other familial relationships in the United States have come under closer scrutiny, Gelles and Cornell (1990) have argued that American society, social service agencies, and researchers have largely ignored the topic of abusive sibling interactions, due in part to their being such a common event. Goodwin and Roscoe (1990) also noted that many American parents view sibling aggression as positive, in that it prepares children to defend themselves or to deal with violent circumstances. In some ways, these perspectives were apparent in our participants' responses. Although 77% of participants gave an example of physical violence in the extremely abusive category, 41% of those responses included caveats that some sort of injury or severe pain to the victim was involved—for example, "any physical violence of an extreme nature resulting in injury," "physical violence resulting in long-term damage," and "siblings fighting to the point where one gets physically hurt." Ewing (1997) noted that there are no legal reporting requirements for physical abuse within sibling relationships. The U.S. legal system, however, is not indifferent to child sexual abuse perpetrated by a sibling. There are a growing number of juvenile sex offender programs in the United States (currently 800 nationally), where a juvenile who is suspected of sexually abusing a sibling (or another child) can be referred (Vieth, 2001).

Characteristics of Victims and Perpetrators

Experiencing sibling abuse seems to vary according to a child's gender and birth order, and the pairing of siblings by gender. Graham-Berman, Cutler, Lintzenberger, and Schwartz (1994) found that females were more likely than males to have experienced abuse from a sibling, and that younger siblings were more likely than older ones to report abuse at the hands of a sibling. Straus (2001b) also found that whereas rates of attacking a sibling were high for both males and female, the rates of attacks by boys were slightly higher. Randall (1992) reported that families who only had sons consistently reported more sibling violence than families with daughters only, and that this difference increased twofold as the children matured into the teen years.

Prevalence

The 1985 National Family Violence Survey revealed that the most violent family relationship is between siblings. The data indicated that 80% of young children committed severe physical acts of violence against a sibling (kicking, choking, punching, hitting with object), with the rate dropping to 64% for teenagers (Straus, 2001b). In a study of adults reporting on childhood experiences, Hardy (2001) found that over 40% of study participants reported being the victim and/or perpetrator of physical aggression in the sibling relationship. Interestingly, only 19–22% of participants considered their sibling's or their own behavior to be abusive. Straus and Gelles (1990) noted that two thirds of teens surveyed reported assaulting a sibling at least once in the past year and one third of them utilized a behavior that had a high probability of causing injury, such as attacking with a knife or gun.

Although sexual abuse and incest have become more generally known to the American public since the late 1970s and early 1980s, most of the focus has been on father–daughter incest or sexual abuse of children by a nonrelative or authority figure. Although it has been noted that sexual abuse by a sibling may be up to 5 times more common than sexual abuse perpetrated by a father (Smith & Israel, 1987), comparatively little is known about sibling sexual abuse. Finkelhor (1980) found that 15% of college females and 10% of college males surveyed reported a sexual experience involving a sibling. Twenty-five percent of those respondents noted that force was used and/or that there was a large age disparity between them and their sibling. Hardy (2001) found 7.4% of her sample reporting some sexual behavior, such as kissing, fondling, or attempted intercourse, between themselves and a sibling; with 20% indicating the behaviors had not been consensual.

U.S. Participants' Perspectives on Sibling Abuse

Nearly 10% of our respondents listed using some type of weapon to attack a sibling as extreme abuse. Seventy-seven percent listed actions classifiable as physical abuse in the extremely abusive category, 44% in the moderately abusive category, and 8% in the mildly abusive category. The most frequently mentioned examples of physical abuse were "hitting," "punching," or "slapping" (31%), followed by "beating up" (18%).

Wiehe (1990) defined emotional abuse between siblings as "verbal comments aimed at ridiculing, insulting, threatening, or belittling ..." (p. 26). Such acts were the most frequently cited of all forms of sibling abuse by our participants. Overall, 20% mentioned behaviors classifiable as emotional abuse in the extreme abuse category, 57% in the moderate abuse category, and 67% in the mild abuse category. Participants overwhelmingly gave examples of verbal abuse—"teasing," "name calling," "put-downs," "swearing at," and "insults." Other examples of direct emotional abuse found were "threatening to do the sibling harm" (17%), "stealing from a sibling" (10%), and "bullying" (6%). Participants also gave examples of more passive and indirect forms of emotional abuse in 33% of responses—"ignoring," "refusal to communicate," "spreading rumors," and "lying about the sibling to someone." Twenty-nine percent of our participants mentioned some form of sexual abuse (e.g., "molestation," "forced sex") always in the extremely abusive category.

INTERVENTION AND PREVENTION

In 1974, Congress enacted the Child Abuse Prevention and Treatment Act (CAPTA), which established the National Center on Child Abuse and Neglect, a government agency that collects and compiles national data on child maltreatment in the United States. CAPTA also established a federal definition of child abuse and neglect and mandatory reporting guidelines (McCauley, Schwartz-Kenney, Epstein, & Tucker, 2000). In all 50 States, certain professionals are required by law to report suspected incidents of child abuse (USDHHS, 2001); however, few states recognize emotional or psychological abuse in their child protection statutes (Shull, 1999). In 1996, Megan's Law was signed into effect, allowing states to register convicted sex offenders and provide notification to the community in which they live ("Megan's Law by State," n.d.). The passage of this law provoked hot debates concerning the balance between the rights of citizens to keep their children safe from harm and the Constitutional rights of all Americans to privacy and protection from additional punishment for a crime beyond what has already been served (Fisher, 2002).

According to Fagan (1995), it has been only since the 1960s that domestic violence was viewed as a criminal activity, with legal attempts to deal with the social problem developing along three tracks—criminal punishment/deterrence, batterer treatment, and legal sanctions. The reauthorized Violence Against Women Act of 2000 (USDJ, 2000) attempts to assist victimized women by enhancing laws against domestic violence, sexual assault and stalking; increasing access to legal assistance for victims of both domestic violence and sexual assault; creating programs to assist with child custody issues for victims of domestic violence; providing funding for programs and training; and improving access to protections for battered immigrant women.

In 1974, legislation under the Social Security Act established a mandate for the creation of Adult Protective Services. Currently in all 50 States, Adult Protective Service agencies have the main responsibility for handling complaints of elder abuse and providing services for elders at risk of abuse (Moskowitz, 1998). In 1987, Congress passed amendments to the Older Americans Act specifically providing for state Agencies on Aging, increasing the standards required for Medicaid/Medicare approved facilities, and outlining the responsibilities of state Long-Term Care Ombudsman Programs to protect residents of institutions from abuse and neglect (Herrington, 1997). Funding for these programs has been left to the individual states, and is often inadequate, leading to a poor response to reports of elder abuse (Moskowitz, 1998).

The United States has a strong history of both public and private advocacy organizations working to end family violence. Although the following list is not intended to be comprehensive, it indicates some of the available resources in the United States:

- The National Domestic Violence Hotline (1-800-799-SAFE in English or Spanish/www.ndvh.org) provides referrals to local programs, crisis intervention, shelter information, and legal advice 24 hours a day, 7 days a week.
- Emerge (www.emergedv.com) provides counseling and education for physically and psychologically abusive men, and referrals to battered women's programs for their spouses.
- The National Child Abuse Hotline (1-800-4-A-Child/1-800-422-4453) provides child abuse reporting information, crisis counseling, and referrals to national, state, and local agencies throughout the United States. The hotline is staffed 24 hours a day, 7 days a week, by mental health professionals.
- The National Elder Abuse Center (www.elderabuse.org/(202) 898-2586) is primarily concerned with elder abuse in domestic settings. It provides educational materials to the public, as well as conducting the National Elder Abuse Incidence Study.
- The National Citizen's Coalition for Nursing Home Reform (www.nursinghomeaction.org/(202) 332-2275) promotes both social and legal advocacy for elderly Americans in long-term institutional care and their families. It also provides contact information for each state's Agency on Aging (the organization that handles institutional abuse complaints).
- Sibling Abuse Survivors' Information and Advocacy Network (www.sasian.org) is an organization geared toward helping the survivors of sibling sexual abuse, but also provides resources/educational materials for victims of physical and emotional abuse.

- The Institute on Domestic Violence in the African-American Community (Toll free 1-877-643-8222/www.dvinstitute.org) provides resources and training geared specifically toward the prevention/reduction of family violence in the African American community.
- The Bureau of Indian Affairs maintains the Indian country Child Abuse Hotline (1-800-663-5155), and provides information on reporting child abuse or neglect in Indian Country. The National Indian Child Welfare Association (503-222-4044/www.nicwa.org) has information culturally relevant to American Indians.
- The National Latino Alliance for the Elimination of Domestic Violence (1-800-216-2404/www.dvalianza.org) and AYAUDA (202-387-2870/www.ayudainc.org) provides information on domestic violence culturally relevant to the Latino community.
- The Asian and Pacific Islander Institute on Domestic Violence (415-954-9964/www.apiahf.org) provides culturally relevant information and resources on domestic violence to the Asian American community.
- Gay and lesbian domestic violence resources, educational materials, and the annual Same Gender Domestic Violence Reports can be found through the Gay and Lesbian Anti-Violence Project (http://www.lambda.org-link under Hate Crimes and Related Incidents).

ACKNOWLEDGMENTS

I would like to thank all the students at Boston University who aided in data collection. In addition, special thanks are given to my loved ones and family, Christine Barie, Thomas and Marie Rapoza, Daniel Rapoza III and Beth Monaghan, Daniel Rapoza and Barbara Manning, and the Mercer's for all their support during this project.

REFERENCES

Bergen, R. K. (1999). *Marital rape* [online]. Available from: The National Resource Center on Domestic Violence, National Electronic Network on Violence Against Women: http://www.vaw.umn.edu/documents/vawnet/mrape

Breines, W., & Gordon, L. (1983). The new scholarship on family violence. *Signs, 8,* 490–531.

Brown, J. G., & DeParle, N. M. (1999, May). *Abuse complaints of nursing home patients.* Available from: Department of Health and Human Services, Office of the Inspector General: http://oig.hhs.gov/oei/reports/oei-06-98-00340.pdf

Center for Disease Control, National Center for Health Statistics. (1995). *Survey on Family Growth.* Washington DC: U.S. Government Printing Office.

Cook, P. W. (1997). *Abused men: The hidden side of domestic violence.* Westport, CT: Greenwood.

Edwards, L. P. (1996). Corporal punishment and the legal system. *Santa Clara Law Review, 36*, 983–1023.

Epstein, D. (1999). Effective intervention in domestic violence cases: Rethinking the roles of prosecutors, judges, and the court system. *Yale Journal of Law and Feminism, 11*, 3–50.

Ewing, C. P. (1997). *Fatal families: The dynamics of intrafamilial homicide.* Thousand Oaks, CA: Sage.

Fagan, J. (1995). *The criminalization of domestic violence: Promises and limits* [online]. Available from: National Institute of Justice, National Criminal Justice Reference Service Information Center: http://www.ncjrs.org/txtfiles/crimdom.txt

Finkelkor, D. (1980). Sex among siblings: A survey on prevalence, variety, and effects. *Archives of Sexual Behavior, 9*(3), 171–194.

Fisher, M. (2002, June 12). Jury is out on Megan's Law. *The Press-Enterprise*, p. A01.

Gelles, R. J., & Cornell, C. P. (1990). *Intimate violence in families* (2nd ed.). Thousand Oaks, CA: Sage.

Goodwin, M. P., & Roscoe, B. (1990). Sibling violence and agonistic interactions among middle adolescents. *Adolescence, 25*, 451–467.

Graham-Bermann, S. A., Cutler, S. E., Lintzenberger, B. W., & Schwartz, W. E. (1994). Perceived conflict and violence in childhood sibling relationships and later emotional adjustment. *Journal of Family Psychology, 8*, 85–97.

Hardy, M. S. (2001). Physical aggression and sexual behavior among siblings: A retrospective study. *Journal of Family Violence, 16*, 255–268.

Herrington, E. B. (1997). Strengthening the Older Americans Act's long-term care protection provisions: A call for further improvement of important State Ombudsman programs. *The Elder Law Journal, 5*, 321–357.

Heymann, J. (2001). *The widening gap: Why America's working families are in jeopardy and what can be done about it.* New York: Basic Books.

Hines, D. A., & Malley-Morrison, K. (2001). Psychological effects of partner abuse against men: A neglected research area. *Psychology of Men & Masculinity, 2*(2), 75–85.

History of the battered women's movement. (n.d.). Available: http://hss.fullerton.edu/womens/bredin/350f99/wmst/history.html

Johnson, K. K. (1998). Crime or punishment: The parental corporal punishment defense: Reasonable and necessary, or excused abuse? *University of Illinois Law Review*, 413–487.

Kasian, M., & Painter, S. L. (1992). Frequency and severity of psychological abuse in a dating population. *Journal of Interpersonal Violence, 7*, 350–364.

Kempe, C., Silverman, F., Steele, B., Droegemueller, W., & Silver, H. (1962). The battered-child syndrome. *Journal of the American Medical Association, 181*, 17–24.

Margolin, G., John, R. S., & Foo, L. (1998). Interactive and unique risk factors for husbands' emotional and physical abuse of their wives. *Journal of Family Violence, 13*, 315–343.

Marshall, L. L. (1994). Physical and psychological abuse. In W. R. Cupach & B. H. Spitzberg (Eds.), *The dark side of interpersonal communication* (pp. 281–311). Hillsdale, NJ: Lawrence Erlbaum Associates.

McCauley, M., Schwartz-Kenney, B. M., Epstein, M. A., & Tucker, E. J. (2000). United States. In B. M. Schwartz-Kenney, M. McCauley, & M. A. Epstein (Eds.), *Child abuse: A global view* (pp. 241–255). Westport, CT: Greenwood.

Megan's law by state. (n.d.). The Klaas Kids Foundation. Available: http://www.klaaskids.org/pg-legmeg.htm

Moskowitz, S. (1998). Saving granny from the wolf: Elder abuse and neglect—the legal framework. *Connecticut Law Review, 31*, 77–204.

Pleck, E. (1989). Criminal approaches to family violence, 1640–1980. In L. Ohlin & M. Tonry (Eds.), *Family violence. Crime and Justice: An annual review of research* (Vol. 11, pp. 19–57). Chicago, IL: University of Chicago Press.

Quinn, M. J., & Tomita, S. K. (1997). *Elder abuse and neglect: Causes, diagnosis, and intervention strategies* (2nd ed.). New York: Springer.

Randall, T. (1992). Adolescents may experience home, school abuse: Their future draws researchers' concern. *Journal of the American Medical Association, 26,* 3127–3131.

Rennison, C. M., & Welchans, S. (2000, May). *Intimate partner violence.* Washington, DC: Bureau of Justice Statistics Special Report.

Sedlak, A. J., & Broadhurst, D. D. (1996). *Executive summary of the third National Incidence Study of Child Abuse and Neglect* [online]. Available from: U.S. Department of Health and Human Services, Washington, D.C. Government Printing Office: http://www.calib.com/nccanch/pubs/statinfo/nis3.cfm

Sherman, L. W., & Berk, R. A. (1984). The specific deterrent effect of arrest for domestic assault. *American Sociological Review, 49,* 261–272.

Shull, J. R. (1999). Emotional and psychological child abuse: Notes on discourse, history and change. *Stanford Law Review, 51,* 1665–1701.

Smith, H., & Israel, E. (1987). Sibling incest: A study of the dynamics of 25 cases. *The International Journal of Child Abuse and Neglect, 11,* 101–108.

Steinmetz, S. K. (1977). The battered husband syndrome. *Victimology, 2*(3–4), 499–509.

Straus, M. A. (2001a). *Beating the devil out of them: Corporal punishment in American families and its effects on children* (2nd ed.). New Brunswick, NJ: Transaction Publishers.

Straus, M. A. (2001b). Physical aggression in the family: Prevalence rates, links to non-family violence, and implications for primary prevention of societal violence. In M. Martnez (Ed.), *Prevention and control of aggression and the impact on its victims* (pp. 1–20). New York: Klewer Academic/Plenum.

Straus, M. A., & Gelles, R. J. (1990). *Family violence in American families: Risk factors and adaptations to violence in 8,145 families.* New Brunswick, NY: Transaction Publishers.

Straus, M. A., Kaufman-Kantor, G., & Moore, D. W. (1997). Change in cultural norms approving marital violence from 1968 to 1994. In G. Kaufman-Kantor & J. L. Jasinski (Eds.), *Out of the darkness: Contemporary perspectives on family violence* (pp. 3–16). Thousand Oaks, CA: Sage.

Tatara, T., & Kuzmeskus, L. M. (1996a). Types of elder abuse in domestic settings. *Elder Abuse Information Series* (No. 1). National Center on Elder Abuse. Washington, DC: U.S. Government Printing Office.

Tatara, T., & Kuzmeskus, L. M. (1996b). Trends in elder abuse in the domestic setting. *Elder Abuse Information Series* (No. 2). National Center on Elder Abuse. Washington, DC: U.S. Government Printing Office.

Tatara, T., & Kuzmeskus, L. M. (1996c). Reporting of elder abuse in the domestic setting. *Elder Abuse Information Series* (No. 3). National Center on Elder Abuse. Washington, DC: U.S. Government Printing Office.

Tatara, T., & Kuzmeskus, L. M. (1997). *Summaries of the statistical data on elder abuse in the domestic setting: An exploratory study of staff statistics for FY 95 and 96.* The National Center on Elder Abuse. Washington, DC: U.S. Government Printing Office.

The New York Society for the Prevention of Cruelty to Children. (n.d.). Available: http://www.nyspcc.org

Tjaden, P., & Thoennes, N. (1998). *Prevalence, incidence, and consequences of violence against women: Findings from the National Violence Against Women Survey.* National Institute of Justice and Centers for Disease Control and Prevention: http://www.ncjrs.org/txtfiles/172837.txt

Tolman, R. M., & Edleson, J. L. (1995). Intervention for men who batter: A review of research. In S. R. Stith & M. A. Straus (Eds.), *Understanding partner violence: Prevalence, causes, consequences and solutions* (pp. 262–273). Minneapolis, MN: National Council on Family Relations.

U.S. Administration on Aging, National Center on Elder Abuse. (1998). *National Elder Abuse Incidence Study.* Washington, DC: US Government Printing Office.

U.S. Department of Health and Human Services, Administration on Children, Youth and Families. (2001). *10 Years of reporting: Child maltreatment 1999.* Washington, DC: U.S. Government Printing Office.

U.S. Department of Health and Human Services, Administration on Children, Youth and Families. (2002). *National child abuse and neglect data system (NCANDS) summary of key findings from calendar year 2000*. Washington, DC: U.S. Government Printing Office. Available: http://www.calib.com/nccanch/pubs

U.S. Department of Justice, Office on Violence Against Women. (n.d.). *The Violence Against Women's Act of 2000*. Washington, DC: U.S. Government Printing Office.

Vieth, V. I. (2001). When the child abuser is a child: Investigating, prosecuting and treating juvenile sex offenders in the new millennium. *Hamline Law Review, 25,* 47–78.

Wiehe, V. R. (1990). *Sibling abuse: Hidden physical, emotional, and sexual trauma*. Lexington, MA: Lexington Books.

Zimmermann, S. (2002, September 1). Keeping children safe from moms' boyfriends. *The Chicago Sun-Times* [online]. Available: http://www.suntimes.com

CONCLUSION

26

Contextualizing Human Rights: A Response to International Family Violence

Marcus D. Patterson

In every country surveyed for this book, abuse within families was found to be present. On the basis of this research and the extensive literature on family violence, it can be confidently asserted that family violence is a global issue. Despite this universality, the prevalence and incidence of the problem are not known with any precision, and conceptions of abuse are poorly understood both domestically and internationally. In this chapter, I argue that a human rights paradigm provides a valuable approach to addressing family violence, but that this approach requires specific local knowledge and adaptation.

Human rights agreements represent a consensus among nations concerning the humane treatment of others and offer a global standard that can serve to counter cultural traditions encouraging or maintaining abusive practices (Melton, 1991). The concept of human rights is, however, limited by its own generality and lack of specificity, which the research presented in this book can help to address. A more precise understanding of cross-national attitudes toward family violence can help to inform human rights approaches by providing culturally specific information utilizable in combating family violence. This book described individual and cultural attitudes toward family violence, and contextual factors influencing the behaviors contributing to this violence. In exposing aspects of family violence that are customarily concealed, it suggests where human rights approaches might be needed and how they might be framed.

Cross-culturally, families are idealized for their ability to protect, nurture, and support family members (Baca Zinn & Eitzen, 1993; Canetto, 1996). Cultures agree in their view of the family as a unified group of individuals, bound together by love, and acting in harmony with each other (Baca Zinn & Eitzen, 1993). This view of the family simplifies the complex dynamics that operate within families and obscures unpleasant truths about behavior within families (Anderson & Sabatelli, 2002). We know, for example, that families are a fundamental source of abuse and that one is more likely to experience violence in the home than anywhere else. As Gelles and Straus (1988) said of their findings on family violence in the United States, "you are more likely to be physically assaulted, beaten, and killed in your own home at the hands of a loved one than any place else, or by anyone else in our society" (p. 18). We also know that family violence is often transmitted across generations (Malley-Morrison & Hines, 2003; Straus, 2001b). According to Levesque (2002), "the study of violence reveals . . . that families constitute a pervasive source of violence and contribute to victimization not usually associated with families" (p. 3).

Family violence is also linked to societal violence in its most extreme and insidious forms. Murder, assault, rape, and torture have all been linked to family violence (e.g., Fineman & Mykitiuk, 1995; Straus, 2001a). Crime statistics include victims of family violence, which often account for the largest percentage of these statistics (e.g., Bureau of Justice Statistics, 1998). Although it is generally considered a family choice or an isolated problem, as evidenced by many of the attitudes in this book, family violence can also be viewed as a public health and even a pandemic problem, because of the deleterious effects it has on society and the considerable contribution it makes to societal violence (Fineman & Mykitiuk, 1995; Voelker, 1992). The universality and sweeping consequences of family violence as revealed by this and previous research necessitates a comprehensive response to it.

A HUMAN RIGHTS RESPONSE TO FAMILY VIOLENCE

The concept of human rights embodies the recognition that certain minimal or basic protections should be available to all people. Human rights do not represent the norms and values of Western countries only, but rather a consensus on general principles among the representatives of hundreds of countries that are signatories to the Universal Declaration of Human Rights (UN, 1983) and subsequent conventions and covenants. Human rights documents represent a sort of "best-practices" approach to the treatment of others; however, because they embody a consensus among numerous nations, the principles are general and abstract in their formulation. Despite their abstractness, these "world-cultural principles" have been found to have the capacity to shape the behavior of states, families, and individuals (Boli & Thomas, 1999).

While human rights principles might seem to have little bearing on the particulars of family violence, there is a small but growing body of literature that suggests that human rights are as applicable to families as to all other social groups (see Levesque, 2001, for review). Further, this work suggests that a human rights perspective may be important and necessary for protecting individuals within the family, particularly when local governments and states have failed to protect them (Hawkins & Humes, 2002; Levesque, 1999).

Human rights were originally treated as universal principles recognized by "States" (members of the United Nations; Levesque, 2001). The original UN Universal Declaration of Human Rights, formulated in response to the Holocaust, formalized the "recognition of the inherent dignity and of the equal and inalienable rights of all members of the human family" (UN, 1983). As it was originally drafted, the general and abstract language of the document made it difficult to determine to whom these principles applied, and did not provide any guidance as to the application and enforcement of human rights (Levesque, 2002). Moreover, the state is not the only source of human rights abuses, as this definition seems to suggest. Despite these limitations, the Universal Declaration has come to be accepted by all UN member nations. The standards it sets forth are not seen simply as aspirational, but also as "customary international law," that can be enforced to change cultural practices (Humphrey, 1976).

Since the ratification of the Universal Declaration, there has been a consistent trend toward increasing recognition by the human rights movement of the most vulnerable groups in society. Significant, substantive protections have been added to the original Declaration to address these groups, which include women, children, the elderly, and the mentally handicapped (see Rosenzweig, 1988, for a review). This trend has meant the growing acknowledgment of the rights of the individual at all levels of society, including within the family.

The Convention on the Elimination of All Forms of Discrimination against Women (CEDAW) required member nations to "pursue a policy of eliminating discrimination against women" (UN, 1996, art. 2). The Convention reaffirmed the equality of human rights for women and men in society and in the family, as suggested in the Universal Declaration. It also obligated states to take action against the social causes of women's inequality, and called for the elimination of laws, stereotypes, practices, and prejudices that impair women's well-being (Berkovitch, 1999). CEDAW directly connected domestic violence against women to human rights, identifying it as a human rights violation (Lockwood, Magraw, Spring, & Strong, 1998). According to CEDAW, it is no longer adequate for the state to do no harm to the individual; rather, it must protect the individual in all domains in which she might be harmed, including the home.

Similarly, the Convention on the Rights of the Child (UN, 1989) stressed the state's obligation to protect children, not as a member of a family, but as individuals (Cohen & Naimark, 1991). The conception of children as individuals entitled to rights separate from the family was seen as an important development in child protection (Cohen, 1990). The Convention placed the responsibility for protecting children on the state if families fail in this capacity (Cohen, 1990).

In the first book of his "Politics," Aristotle theorized that cultures (the city-state) arise organically, as the logical achievement of smaller partnerships (the family and the village). Thus, he thought that all greater political structures derive from the family (Barnes, 1980). Freud's replacement hypothesis (Freud, 1922) reflects a similar viewpoint: that individuals aggregate in larger social and political units to replicate or replace their families. If these visions of human history are true, then human rights are most applicable to families as the proto-political unit. It is ironic that human rights, which appeared first within much larger city-states, are only beginning to be applied to the actions of the family, the initial political unit (Levesque, 2002). The extension of the rights perspective is perhaps a tacit recognition by states of the ancient political power of the family. In any case, the application of a human rights perspective to family violence provides a powerful remedial instrument. A human rights approach conflicts with a view of the family held in many societies. As illustrated in this book, many widely varied societies espouse the privacy of the family and view the home as sacrosanct (see also Baca Zinn & Eitzen, 1993). This special designation is written into political constitutions and legal institutions, influences law enforcement, and is seen as a source of political strength in many countries (Hawkins & Humes, 2002). In some countries, such as the United States, the sacrosanct status of the family is reflected in the separation of church and state; in these countries, the state cannot interfere in the religious affiliations and practices of families. In other countries, such as Saudi Arabia, it is precisely the lack of separation between church and state by which the government upholds the sanctity and inviolability of the family. For example, Article 9 of Saudi Arabia's Basic Law states, "The family is the nucleus of Saudi society," and Article 37 states, "Houses are inviolable." The implicit theories underlying the sanctity or inviolability of the family enhance its privacy, while obscuring much of its behavior.

As shown in this book, implicit theories have consequences for help seeking, interventions, and prevention. For example, an implicit theory that families are inviolable institutions that deal with problems independent of state interference have been associated with lack of intervention into family violence (Segal, 1999). The failure to collect reliable data regarding abuse within the family, in spite of its global prevalence, is an additional index of how deeply ingrained the implicit theories of family privacy are across cultures. By providing a standard for the treatment of family members, a human rights approach can help to transcend social structures that can shield the family from state intervention and encourage family violence (Melton, 1991). In doing so, this approach may begin to break through the arbitrary distinction between public and private that can insulate families, for better or worse.

In spite of the tradition of treating family violence as a private matter, a large number of states have now accepted some responsibility for helping to prevent violence in the home and to prosecute those who violate these principles (Holmes & Humes, 2002). By signing treaties recognizing human rights, member states, such as those described in this book, have already begun to reduce the barrier between public and private. Actual changes in practices, however, vary considerably among states, and in some countries (e.g., Brazil, Nicaragua, Colombia, the Philippines) there are many new laws but limited efforts or ability to enforce them. Thus, there has been a recognition of the applicability of human rights to families both in the language of the human rights policies and in the broad acceptance of these agreements by states, but much remains to be done to change the cultural attitudes and practices that victimize family members.

According to Sen (1999), there have been three basic critiques of the global human rights perspective. One of these, the legitimacy critique, suggests that human beings are not born with human rights but acquire these through legislation and through political structures. This argument can be used to resist the application of human rights to family violence and to protect particular family members, because it implies that family members lacking political representation also lack substantive protections that redound from them. In examining patterns of family violence, it is precisely those individuals with the least political representation who are the most vulnerable to abuse—including children (particularly adoptive or stepchildren), women (particularly unmarried or widowed women), and family members with mental illness (Barnett, 1997). A human rights approach can empower such vulnerable family members by providing a level of political recognition that may not be granted by their own countries, institutions, or families.

In providing alternative norms, human rights principles model alternative social standards and models of treatment for individuals in all societies (Hawkins & Humes, 2002; Melton, 1991). These are particularly powerful alternatives because they are supported by the international community, may even be enforced by the international community, and can ultimately be employed to "socialize" other states around the humane treatment of others

(Melton, 1991). Because of their generality, these principles represent a blanket approach to the issue of family violence, and thereby have certain limitations: they may not protect certain members of a family not specifically mentioned in human rights documents; they may not encompass the unique structure of the family; they may not "speak to" specific cultural or familial practices and values; they may be framed in such a way as to seem foreign or incomprehensible to a particular culture; and they may not offset competing values or norms within the family, such as loyalty, privacy, or respect. However, conceptions of human rights are not static, but represent evolving views among states concerning humane treatment of human beings. As such, they are in a state of constant revision and modification (Rosenzweig, 1988). Further changes should include additional specification and contextualization of human rights to address the limitations noted.

HUMAN RIGHTS IMPLICATIONS OF RESEARCH ON CONCEPTIONS OF ABUSE

Understanding attitudes toward abuse helps to provide a context for a human rights approach to family violence. One must understand specific aspects of family and society before one can begin to think about human rights or minimal protections for individuals within families. Without an appreciation for the structures and attitudes that contribute to the victimization of particular family members, one cannot understand what human rights might mean within these specific contexts. The research in this book, as reviewed below, can help to provide this context.

In its discussion of what is known concerning family violence and abuse in selected countries, this book helps to identify family members at risk for various types of abuse, the manifestations of this abuse, and the cultural norms, attitudes, motivations, expectancies, and justifications behind such abuse. This information has implications for prevention of and intervention into human rights abuses within families. This analysis is not intended to render judgment on particular societies, or to rank order societies by levels of awareness of abusive behavior, but to provide insight into the social structures that place certain family members at risk for violence and to suggest ways in which these individuals might be better protected. Myths or implicit theories about the nature of the family are universal (Baca Zinn & Eitzen, 1993). The human rights paradigm can be considered an emergent implicit theory of the family worthy of the attention of the global community. For it to gain wide acceptance as a way of thinking about relationships and practices characterizing families within their particular cultural contexts, it is important to have psychological research elucidating the relevant views and practices within contemporary cultures and families. Research can be particularly valuable in providing better estimates of prevalence rates, increasing public awareness of the nature of family violence, identifying vulnerable populations, and revealing relevant norms.

PREVALENCE RATES OF FAMILY VIOLENCE

In all of the societies surveyed for this book, family violence is commonly treated as a private matter (also see Hawkins & Humes, 2002). As many of these authors note, privacy can protect families from certain abuses by the state but it can also shield abusive practices within the family from public view. Across all of the societies studied, statistics on the prevalence of family violence are either unreliable or absent. Even in countries that track patterns and prevalence of family violence, such as Canada, the United States, and the United Kingdom, official statistics are believed to significantly underestimate the incidence of all forms of family violence, including incest, marital rape, child abuse, and spousal abuse in both genders (Kendall-Tackett, Williams, & Finkelhor, 2001; Home Office, 1999; Malley-Morrison & Hines, 2003). Thus, it is important to examine other indices that might provide evidence of the extent of abusive family practices within states.

One index that might shed light on the prevalence of family violence is attitudes toward abuse. Individual perspectives on abusive behavior, when aggregated, begin to reveal broader social attitudes toward family violence. The "voices" in this book, while by no means a systematic random sample of the residents in the countries surveyed, are valuable in revealing aspects of family violence that are often obscure or absent cross-culturally. They provide a window into the prevalence of family violence, permitting a somewhat better understanding of the extent of family violence within a particular culture and appropriate targets for intervention.

PUBLIC AWARENESS CONCERNING FAMILY VIOLENCE

Related to determinations of prevalence is the issue of social awareness regarding family violence. As noted earlier, cultures maintain myths about families and these myths are connected to cultural values concerning what is typical, correct, and true of the family (Baca Zinn & Eitzen, 1993). Research on social attitudes can help to counter myths and change implicit theories by raising awareness about the actual nature of family violence. Moreover, research findings may be utilized by the human rights movement to accomplish social change in the direction of more humane treatment of all individuals. It may help to make a society aware of prevailing attitudes toward violence that were not previously evident, help to modify these attitudes, and thereby curb violent behaviors (Straus, Kaufman-Kantor, & Moore, 1997).

This research can also reveal the level of consciousness regarding family violence that prevails in a particular society. Power (2002) discusses the importance of language in both identifying and combating violence. In particular, she traced the history of the word "genocide" and the way that the recognition and use of this word led to greater societal awareness of the phenomenon and contributed to the ability of human rights movements to address it. In developing a survey to capture the voices of people within the countries we were studying, we found that in some languages it was difficult to translate the term *abuse* as it applied to families. In some cases (e.g., Somalia, Turkey), there was no exact word or synonym for abuse. In other cases (e.g., Russia), the term that came closest to the English meaning of abuse connoted, almost exclusively, physical abuse. In still others (e.g., Germany, Iceland), the word closest in meaning was almost exclusively associated with sexual abuse. Related research has found that among the Chinese, the term "abuse" is frequently equated with physical abuse (Lau, Liu, Yu, & Wong, 1999). The human rights movement might be enhanced by greater understanding of differences across states and cultures in levels of public awareness concerning abuse in families, and, based on this understanding, might more effectively provide suggestions on ways to intervene (e.g., by introducing terms that capture these behaviors).

Public awareness is a gradual process that involves changing cultural norms and attitudes. As Rapoza notes in chapter 25, the recognition of family violence has proceeded very slowly in the United States. The term *domestic violence* was not seen as a crime until the 1960s and the concept of *battered child syndrome*, which led to greater recognition of child abuse, also did not arise until then (see Rapoza, chap. 25). Corresponding norms around these behaviors have also changed slowly. Norms related to husbands hitting wives have changed significantly from 1968 to 1994, though norms related to wives hitting husbands appear not to have changed over the same span (Straus, Kaufman-Kantor, & Moore, 1997). Other societies have shown similar patterns. In Japan, child abuse is infrequently identified and even more rarely prosecuted, but awareness does seem to be growing (Kozu, 1999).

There is strong evidence that public awareness can have a salutary effect on family violence. Many of our authors mentioned the importance of public awareness campaigns in countering family violence (e.g., Germany, Italy, and Portugal). State officials in the United States have credited public awareness campaigns with the decline in sexual abuse (Mitchell & Finkelhor, 2001) and individuals who have participated in awareness programs are more likely to report abuse.

POPULATIONS VULNERABLE TO FAMILY VIOLENCE

Finkelhor (1988) argued that building social awareness of family violence requires identifying the likely victims of this violence, and our research has identified additional groups at potential risk in some countries. These included adult children in India; step-siblings and orphans in Brazil; cohabitating partners in the United States; live-in maids and domestic help lacking legal and political recognition in Lebanon, India, and Saudi Arabia; in-laws in Turkey, Italy, Japan, and India; "mail order brides" in the Philippines; grandmothers-in-law and granddaughters-in-law in Korea; wives from other countries, including "mail order brides" in Taiwan, the Philippines, and the United States; and maternal uncles in Somalia. The array of individuals who might be vulnerable to experiencing or perpetrating abuse within the family suggests that human rights protections need to be expanded beyond the specific groups already identified.

FAMILY AND SOCIETAL NORMS REGARDING FAMILY VIOLENCE

Social norms relevant to family violence are not well understood. Norms may influence family violence, but may also conceal its characteristics and rates (Straus, 1999). Social norms are typically implicit and dynamic (Forsyth, 1999); thus, there are rarely reference materials or guidebooks to the norms of a specific society or group. Members of a given society are often unable to articulate the norms of that society, though they are easily able to identify behaviors that deviate from the group norms—i.e., behaviors considered to be "abnormal" (Forsyth, 1999). The implicit nature of group norms is also operative within families, which have "metarules" that direct overall family behavior. Such rules are distinguished both by their ability to shape the behavior of family members and by their invisibility (Laing, 1971). In identifying attitudes toward abuse, the research presented here begins to reveal social norms concerning maltreatment in families and uncloaks the "metarules" behind social behaviors. Identification of these norms can be useful for human rights approaches by revealing implicit structures that contribute to or conceal abuse within families. In doing so, it can suggest ways in which modifications in these norms might enhance the well-being of more members of the family.

MANIFESTATIONS OF FAMILY VIOLENCE

As illustrated throughout this book, family violence takes a variety of forms cross-culturally, and forms of violence that exist in one culture may be unknown in another. Korbin (1995) noted that cross-cultural differences in the forms that family violence takes have been neglected in the study of family violence, and this book helps to address this neglect. Identifying manifestations of family violence is important in raising social awareness (Finkelhor, 1988). Finkelhor and Korbin (1988) argued that an international strategy to combat family violence requires that individual countries identify and prioritize the particular types of abuse that require intervention in their society.

Beyond hitting, kicking, slapping, punching, and spanking, which were almost universal cross-culturally, our research revealed wide variation in practices that were or might be considered abusive. The types of objects used in perpetrating acts of physical aggression varied by country. Sticks, belts, and knives were frequently mentioned, but abuse involving boiling water (e.g., in Brazil, Japan), hot irons, brooms (Brazil), baseball bats (Japan), wooden spoons and hairbrushes (United States), burning on the stove (Taiwan), and burning with cigarettes (Greece, Israel) were also mentioned. Child labor was identified as a common form of child abuse in some countries (e.g., in Portugal, Nicaragua, Turkey), as was neglect and deprivation (e.g., England, Japan, Taiwan, and the United States).

Not every act considered abusive by respondents in the countries studied is necessarily a violation of human rights, and adopting a human rights perspective does not automatically solve all the definitional problems that have plagued the field of family violence. For example, infidelity among women (e.g., in Greece, Portugal, Russia) and, less frequently, men (Russia, Philippines) was seen to be an abusive practice, but so, too, was withholding sex from a partner (e.g., England, Germany, Russia). Criticizing of social roles was identified as a type of abuse suffered by both men and women (e.g., Italy, Russia). Clearly, the extent to which all such behaviors will meet any established or emerging criteria for abuse or for a human rights violation has not been established, but it is important to understand what kinds of practices are considered abusive—and why—if there is to be any hope of an international consensus on human rights within the family.

Sexual abuse, including rape, was mentioned almost universally as a form of abuse likely to be directed at women (e.g., daughters, wives, mothers [particularly in South Africa], sisters, and nieces). There were a number of other forms of abuse directed specifically at women, including genital mutilation (Somalia), Sati (India), and honor killing (Lebanon). Although participants in several countries considered withholding of sex to be a form of abuse directed particularly at men, there were no forms of abuse that consistently involved killing or maiming men. Economic abuse was almost universally cited as a form of abuse most typically directed at the elderly. It was also noted among women, but not men. Interestingly, human rights violations were often cited as examples of abuse (in Saudi Arabia, Somalia, the Philippines).

Because of the considerable variation in forms that abuse is perceived to take cross-culturally, it is important to be aware of cultural differences in what is seen as abuse. Human rights prohibitions against specific forms of maltreatment may not address the most prevalent manifestations of abuse and further empirical and conceptual work is needed to further the global consensus concerning the forms of commission and omission of behaviors in families that should be considered human rights violations. Refinement of the human rights paradigm is an important step in the development of intervention and prevention strategies to reduce unnecessary human suffering occurring in the context of the family.

On the basis of national statistics within the United States, Finkelhor and Dzuiba-Leatherman (1994) found that family violence could be categorized into three groupings. Pandemic victimization were behaviors that affected nearly everyone, such as sibling violence. Acute victimization impacted fewer people, but still a considerable portion of the country; the chief example was physical abuse. Finally, extraordinary victimization, such as infanticide or family homicide, affected a very small percentage of people, but tended to have more catastrophic consequences. Such a classification scheme could be utilized to better understand patterns of family violence within other societies and could help to guide the implementation of human rights programs within these societies.

JUDGMENTS OF FAMILY VIOLENCE

There is strong evidence that judgments of abusive behavior may vary as a function of the gender, age, and status of the individual committing acts of aggression or omitting acts of care. Cross-culturally, as noted by Levesque (2002, p. 45), "each gender expects disparate levels of aggressiveness and victimization and conditions those involved in violence to not even notice coercion." In this book, there was a considerable disparity between the sexes in examples of different levels of abuse; moreover, judgments of severity of abuse depended on who was the abuser and who was the victim. In general, physical abuse directed by wives to husbands was judged to be less abusive than physical abuse from husbands to wives (e.g., Canada, England). Physical punishment of sons by parents was more common and often considered to be less abusive than physical punishment of daughters (e.g., Italy, Israel, Turkey).

Cross-nationally, implicit theories of abuse appeared to have propositions concerning the role of intent and/or justifiability in rendering a behavior abusive. In some countries, the prevailing implicit theories differentiate between child abuse and physical punishment administered for the purpose of instruction (e.g., Saudi Arabia, Japan, Korea, Taiwan, the United States). In regard to violence against women, some respondents (e.g., in Greece, the Philippines) considered infidelity by a wife to be a justification for abuse. Misbehavior by children (e.g., in England, Greece) and disobedience by children (e.g., in Turkey, Iceland, the Philippines) and wives (in Turkey) were sometimes seen as justifications for physical or psychological aggression. In some cultures, acting in anger increased the abusiveness attributed to a behavior (e.g., Taiwan, the Philippines). Justifications for aggression against husbands included male role failure and alcohol use (e.g., in Canada). This orientation is quite disparate from the one embodied in human rights conventions, which indicate, for example, that torture is *never* justifiable.

Whether the abuse occurred in public or whether it was private influenced whether and to what degree particular behaviors were seen as abusive. In general, public aggression against or disparaging of family members was considered more abusive than was private utilization of these behaviors (e.g., in Israel, Turkey, Saudi Arabia, Canada, Korea). Thus, a criterion for judgments of abusiveness in these implicit theories is the extent to which behaviors occur in the public rather than the private domain; aggression in private is judged less abusive. Similarly, physical aggression that left visible marks was often judged to be more abusive (e.g., in Israel, Taiwan), presumably because the physical signs make the private behavior public. These judgments have implications for the human rights approach because they are windows into abusive treatment not labeled as such because it takes place behind closed doors.

EXPECTATIONS ABOUT FAMILY VIOLENCE

Based on generalized implicit theories within societies, certain members of families may accept treatment that would be considered abusive when directed toward other members. In many cultures, children may expect to be physically disciplined by parents (Straus, 2001b), but parents generally do not accept reciprocal treatment from their children. On the basis of our data, women, but not men, often expect to be physically mistreated by their spouse (e.g., in Italy). Our respondents frequently mentioned physical aggression of husbands against wives, but much less commonly mentioned the reverse. It was frequently noted that there was an imbalance between the behaviors that were considered abusive for men versus women. As Donovan (chap. 3) notes, one English respondent said that in England, "withdrawal of sex by wife" would be considered severely abusive, whereas "physical beating of wife by drunken husband" is the comparable level of wife abuse. In many societies (e.g., Brazil) respondents failed to mention any form of husband abuse, and in some countries (e.g., South Africa), some respondents said it was "impossible" for a wife to abuse her husband.

General social orientation (e.g., toward collectivism) may contribute to expectations concerning family violence (Dwairy, 2002). For example, the stronger a society's orientation toward family, the greater the tendency to expect battered wives to change their behavior toward their husbands, assume responsibility for their husbands' violent behavior, and resist seeking help from formal agencies or breaking up the family unit (e.g., Bezerra-Flanders, chap. 22; Haj-Yahia, 2002). As shown in this book, differences in expectations may be used to justify continued abuse and to oppose criticisms of cultural practices from outside groups (e.g., Stathopoulou, chap. 8). On the other hand, it has been argued (e.g., Liu & Chan, 1999) that these expectations may be adaptive within certain environments. In societies in which there is no substantive recourse to forms of maltreatment, enduring violence may be a reasonable coping strategy, rather than expecting help or freedom from abuse. A human rights approach may be a way of changing expectations by offering an alternative standard of treatment, but it will be important to know what the expectations around family violence are for each member and how changes in these expectations might influence coping strategies, particularly in environments in which social support for abused individuals might be lacking (see Nolido, chap. 19).

EXPERIENCE OF FAMILY VIOLENCE

Culture can influence not just implicit theories and expectations, but the way in which maltreatment is experienced, and this influence takes place in a continuous feedback system. Personal experience with a disciplinary event in childhood, in the context of a culture that sanctions this discipline, is associated with a decreased tendency to view that particular form of discipline as inappropriate or abusive (Bower-Russa, 2001). Because of familial influences, many maltreated persons do not view their own experiences as abusive. Rape myths influence the interpretation of dating violence and how society views it (Levesque, 2000); however, not "experiencing" or interpreting a hurtful/harmful act as abuse does not make it acceptable or justifiable. A human rights perspective would counter such an assumption on principle; nevertheless, it is important to know how abuse might be experienced or identified in order to know where such principles might be useful in making these experiences recognizable as abuse.

CONSEQUENCES OF FAMILY VIOLENCE

Many of our respondents judged abuse by its consequences (e.g., whether it resulted in visible marks, broken bones, scars, or physical disability). They also considered the psychological consequences of abuse, including feelings of shame, humiliation, and destruction of character. These implicit theories suggest that abuse should be judged by its specific psychological consequences in individual cases. Because psychological effects are much less visible than physical effects, it is important to disseminate and expand on research findings on the psychological sequellae of family violence.

Although the specific symptoms may vary, one of the most important arguments for addressing international family violence is the fact that it has consequences that are surprisingly consistent and detrimental across cultures, cultural values not withstanding. For example, corporal punishment is associated with experiences of stress and depression (Straus, 2001a; Turner & Finkelhor, 1996). Straus (2001a) has argued that given the prevalence of corporal punishment in the United States, it can be seen as a considerable public health issue, contributing significantly to levels of societal depression. Maltreatment, in general, is found to triple the risk for depressive disorders in children (Brown, Cohen, & Johnson, 1999).

Posttraumatic stress disorder (PTSD) is a frequent consequence of family violence; the likelihood of PTSD increases with both the frequency and severity of the abuse (see Resick, 2001). In general, harm resulting from maltreatment carries a greater risk for the development of PTSD than harm resulting from natural events, such as traffic accidents (Resnick, Kilpatrick, Dansky, Saunders, & Best, 1993). The National Comorbidity Study (Kessler, Sonnega, Bromet, Hughes, & Nelson, 1995) found PTSD rates for women ranged from 20% from child neglect to 49% from child physical abuse. In comparing women who had been abused by a partner to those who had not, Coffey, Leitenberg, Henning, Bennett, and Jankowski, 1996, found significantly greater psychological distress among women who had experienced partner violence. Abuse within families may have even more dire consequences than other forms of violence, because the agent of abuse is a trusted person and the violence is likely to recur (Resick, 2001).

PTSD is manifested similarly across cultures and has similarly detrimental social consequences (Marsella, Friedman, Gerrity, & Scurfield, 1996). Even when victims of physical or sexual abuse do not define their experiences as abusive, the impact of abuse is detrimental (Herman, 1997; Levesque, 2000). Indeed, recognition of abuse in itself may have salutary health and psychological effects (Nabi & Horner, 2001). The consistent, detrimental consequences of family violence are perhaps the most important reason for human rights intervention. Individuals are being harmed and will be harmed by this behavior, even if they and their society are not aware of it.

CONTEXTUALIZING HUMAN RIGHTS: ONE APPROACH TO FAMILY VIOLENCE

A human rights approach to combating family violence in the world's many different cultures and communities requires contextualizing and communicating its abstract principles in a way that is culturally salient. In order to accomplish this, it will be important to identify, within each society:

1. The family structure (i.e., how family is defined within each culture).
2. The organizational structure within the family that influences the treatment of family members, including their roles, norms, attitudes, and values.
3. The specific abuse practices characteristic of each society.
4. Macrosystem factors that might influence family violence.
5. Local or indigenous principles that dovetail with human rights approaches and that might be enlisted in the framing of the human rights message.
6. Local or indigenous movements, including NGOs, that might become the messengers for human rights.
7. Local or indigenous structures and social services that can be enlisted to respond to or help remedy human rights abuses within families.
8. More broadly-based, macrosystem level approaches that might effectively address human rights issues within families in a culturally specific manner.

DEFINING "FAMILY"

Although a definition of family may seem obvious, it is surprisingly difficult to arrive at a universal consensus about what a family is (Anderson & Sabatelli, 2002). The definition of "family" goes beyond kinship bonds, is informed by both cultural and historical factors, and is further complicated by myths or implicit theories about families (Baca Zinn & Eitzen, 1993). The definition of "a normal or healthy family" is similarly influenced by both history and culture (Canetto, 1996). Despite a growing interest in the application of human rights principles to the family, researchers have not reached consensus on how to define and measure family (Rothausen, 1999). This limitation became clear in our own research, when some respondents suggested that we did not specifically address the treatment of many individuals who were considered to be members of families within their society. For example, our survey had no specific questions about attitudes toward abuse of in-laws, adoptive children, nonrelatives including orphans, same-sex couples, adoptees, aunts/uncles, widows, clan or tribe members, and domestic servants. We did, however, have one set of questions on "other relationships" in which abuse might occur, and asked participants to specify what those other relationships might be. Consequently, information regarding family violence in these groups is provided within many chapters. For example, in Nicaragua, a family was likely to include an aunt or uncle, an orphaned relative, and/or a poor godchild (Powell, chap. 21). Maternal uncles (Somalia), domestic help or maids (Saudi Arabia, Lebanon), in-laws

(Turkey, India, Italy), fathers' parents and grandparents (Italy, Japan, Korea), single, divorced, or widowed young women (Russia), and uncles and aunts of both spouses (South Africa) were considered to be part of the family within these societies. If a human rights approach is going to help all vulnerable members of families, it must define family broadly enough to be consistent with the definitions in all societies.

ORGANIZATIONAL STRUCTURE OF THE FAMILY

To be effective a human rights approach to family violence must be both culturally sensitive and culturally specific. What has not been revealed in much of the cross-cultural work are the social forces that contribute to family violence, including political, religious, economic, and geographic forces—both cultural and extracultural forces. Information about all of these forces is essential to a culturally sensitive human rights approach.

Social roles are closely related to definitions of family and to family violence. Our research, like previous research, has shown that family members in roles related to positions of dependency (e.g., dependent elders, children, domestic help, and women) are most vulnerable to abuse. What our research also makes clear is that the behavior of the vulnerable and dependent members of families may itself be labeled abusive when it does not meet the requirements of the more powerful members of the family. The "abusive" behavior of the weaker members is then seen as an excuse for "discipline" or "punishment" by the powerful members, who do not consider their own behavior abusive; moreover, because of generalized implicit theories of appropriate behaviors, the victims themselves and others may also see "punishment" or retaliation as appropriate and justified rather than as abusive.

Cross-culturally, spousal violence has been linked to women's roles within families (Levesque, 2002), and this finding was replicated in our data. In many of the countries surveyed, role failure was frequently identified as abusive. Women not serving dinner or not serving it on time (e.g., in Colombia, the United States), failing to keep a clean house (e.g., in Italy, Japan), not shopping for the family (e.g., in Colombia), or not having children (e.g., in Taiwan) were provided as examples of husband abuse. Familial roles for women also included understanding and meeting husbands' needs, including sexual needs, and failure to do this was sometimes seen as abusive (e.g., in Lebanon, Italy, Greece, South Africa, Korea, the Philippines). Respondents in many countries considered it abusive if women showed disrespect to men, expressed differences of opinion, asserted themselves (e.g., in India), earned more money (e.g., in Taiwan, the Philippines), undermined their husband's sexuality (e.g., in Russia, Taiwan), or did anything that could be seen as undermining the male role (e.g., in Brazil, Italy, Saudi Arabia, the Philippines, Colombia, Portugal, Russia). Additionally, not fulfilling familial roles was generally seen as more abusive for women than for men, and violence was often seen as a justified response to this role failure (e.g., in Lebanon, Portugal, the Philippines). On the other hand, respondents from some countries (e.g., Australia) suggested that serious forms of abuse by wives are more widespread than generally recognized, and traditional sex roles may reinforce some men's desire to hide their own experiences of abuse and may keep them at risk (see Hines & Malley-Morrison, 2001).

Men's failure to fulfill the expected paternal role—through providing for his family—was sometimes seen as a form of abuse (e.g., in Somalia, Nicaragua, Russia, Brazil, Canada, Japan, Taiwan), but men's role failure was seen as abusive far less frequently than was women's. Using alcohol and narcotics, especially if they interfered with role responsibilities (e.g., in Canada, Somalia, South Africa, Russia), and gambling with household money (e.g., in Russia, the Philippines) were also considered abusive, and attributed more to men than to women. A few respondents in several different countries considered it abusive of husbands not to support their wives in their roles (e.g., in Somalia, Russia, Portugal, Saudi Arabia), not to help with domestic work (e.g., in Korea, the Philippines), to withhold sex (e.g., in Germany), and to engage in conflicts with their wives over childrearing (e.g., in Russia, Israel, Greece). Macho roles for men were linked to violence against women in Nicaragua, Brazil, and Portugal.

Dynamics between in-laws were also related to role conflicts and abuse (e.g., in Italy, Lebanon, Turkey, Japan, and India). In particular, the presence of paternal in-laws could make a daughter-in-law vulnerable to family violence (e.g., in India, Turkey, Korea, Taiwan), and a mother-in-law at risk for elder abuse (e.g., in Japan, Korea). There is some suggestion that these phenomena are related—that is, that daughters-in-law are vulnerable at an earlier age and mothers-in-law are vulnerable at a later stage, when they are dependent on family (Jang & Kim, chap. 17). This is similar to the pattern in families in which parents who abused their children are at increased risk for abuse by the grown children in old age (e.g., Donovan, chap. 3). In this context, abuse by mother-in-law was often associated with undermining the daughter-in-law's role in the family, as wife, mother, caretaker (e.g., in Italy, Japan, Korea, India).

In many countries, children have been subjected to normative practices that are now coming to be seen as abusive, at least by the more educated, urbanized members of the society. Such practices include child labor (e.g., in Brazil, the Philippines, Portugal, and Turkey). In the context of sibling relationships, later born siblings may be at risk for abuse by first-born children, when first borns are charged with their care (e.g., in Somalia). First born girls may be at greater risk for abuse, when a younger, later born brother, is granted status over her (e.g., in Portugal). First born siblings may be at greater risk for abuse from parents because of the responsibility placed on them (e.g., in Taiwan).

Power and hierarchy are closely related to these social roles, to violence, and to the recognition of human rights. Imbalances in power are obvious between parent and child, but abuse patterns can be moderated when children are provided with political recognition (Levesque, 2002). Similarly, in numerous cross-cultural studies, imbalances in power between husband and wife, and a lack of legal recourse, have been found to contribute to spousal abuse (see Levinson, 1989, for a review). These power imbalances could be seen in income disparities and differences in treatment. International human rights agreements can be seen as empowering vulnerable members of society, including within the context of their families. Although references to abuse within families as being human rights violations were uncommon within our sample, they did occur, and reflected a particular form of empowerment.

MACROSYSTEM FACTORS AFFECTING FAMILY VIOLENCE

As many of the authors reported, family violence is most commonly viewed in isolation (e.g., as a family problem) cross-culturally. The secrecy surrounding family violence reinforces this view of abuse in families as strictly a family matter. Bolstering this orientation was the implicit theory in many societies that abuse is a problem that besets only poor, dysfunctional, abnormal families (e.g., Germany and Saudi Arabia).

The research reviewed in this book suggests that microsystem incidents of family violence are not simply a series of unique events but are often linked to macrosystem social structures and social attitudes. Identifying the context of familial violence has important implications for intervention. If abusive families act in isolation, and if their behaviors are merely departures from social attitudes and norms, one might combat these abuses by targeting individual offending families. Alternatively, if family violence relates to more pervasive, structural aspects of society, it is important to address these abuses on a macro or societal level. If family violence is related to extrasocietal factors such as war, colonization, or immigration, one will need to address these factors on an international level.

Identifying the macrosystem level factors that influence family violence is important for a human rights approach, because it will help determine the level at which a human rights intervention might be most effective. During times of social and familial stress, violence within families is likely to increase, even in families that do not typically experience family violence (Greenwald, Bank, & Reid, 1997; Straus & Kantor, 1987). Stress has been conceptualized as a sort of feedback system that allows one to assess how successfully (or unsuccessfully) a family is able to adjust to or adapt to stressful situations (Anderson & Sabitelli, 2002). Stress can be family-specific but it can also be related to broader or macrosystems factors (Anderson & Sabatelli, 2002).

Coping strategies, the ways in which families respond to stress, can be more or less adaptive depending on the situation and the response (McCubbin et al., 1980). Cultural patterns in coping strategies can also be more or less adaptive. Family violence has been considered a maladaptive coping strategy utilized by individual families (McCubbin, 1979); it is also a strategy influenced by demographic and cultural factors (Straus & Kantor, 1987). Cross-culturally, there are predicable patterns in the use of violence as a response to stress; specifically, violence as a coping response is disproportionately directed to weaker members. Levesque (2002) noted that when societies experience ecological stress, the three groups most vulnerable to family violence are children, women, and the elderly.

Poverty also affects families differently cross-culturally, as is evident in differing patterns of family violence (Melton & Flood, 1994). Among our participants, poverty was considered a risk factor, particularly for women (e.g., in England, Israel, Greece, and the United States). Moreover, poverty was viewed as contributing to child labor practices seen as harmful to the child (e.g., in Portugal, Brazil, and Nicaragua).

Broad social changes can also have a detrimental impact on families that leads to or exacerbates family violence. Social changes following reunification in Germany may have increased domestic violence in the East. In both the Philippines and India, westernization has been linked to the loss of status and to increases in violence against the elderly (Nolido, chap. 19; Ingersoll-Dayton & Saengtienchai, 1999; Segal, 1999). Even more dramatic changes took place in many of the countries studied following colonization, war, forced assimilation, and apartheid. In this book, violence within families was linked to forced assimilation of indigenous peoples (e.g., in Canada, Australia, Nicaragua, and the United States), apartheid in South Africa, war in Somalia and Israel, and civil war in Lebanon. Social upheaval was linked to the undermining of traditional values emphasizing individual rights and freedom and increases in family violence in Somalia. The feedback system connecting violence in the world community with violence in the family needs to be understood if proponents of peace and human rights are ever to achieve their international goals and if families are to live up to ideals portraying them as a source of respite, love, and support for all members.

Indigenous Principles

As was evident from responses to our survey, many of the principles inhering in the human rights documents are similar to principles within the traditions of individual nations and cultures. This is not surprising given that human rights were themselves drawn from the examples and traditions of the many nations and cultures that helped to draft and frame them. Because of the abstract formulation of human rights, it could be beneficial to identify indigenous principles that reflect a human rights perspective. In what follows, I attempt this task.

Strobel (2001) identified "core values" of Filipino society, which he viewed as providing the strength behind their social institutions. Several of these principles are similar to human rights principles. They are: *Kapwa* (shared identity); *Loob* (shared humanity or dignity); and *Damdam* (the capacity to feel for another). The principle of Loob is closely related to the notion of human rights, and, in chapter 19, Nolido cites two examples from individuals who invoked Loob when defining abuse: 1) "When personal values, interests, needs, wants, desires are unilaterally imposed on a co-member without the latter's permission, as well as total disregard of his rights and welfare—e.g., incest or excessive physical reprimands"; and 2) "When the rights/privileges of a member are transgressed, such as privacy, right to live independently, or overdependence." Thus, these respondents thought of human rights abuses when discussing family violence. The application of human rights to family violence will be more effective and more culturally sensitive and specific if it draws on similar principles within cultures and speaks in their terms.

INDIGENOUS PROTEST MOVEMENTS

Pressure from domestic social groups is an important mechanism for changing norms and behaviors related to family violence (Hawkins & Humes, 2002). Throughout this book, authors have mentioned indigenous protest movements. Most of the societies in this book (e.g., Brazil, Turkey, the United Kingdom, Philippines, Israel, Nicaragua, India) have indigenous movements that seek to protect the rights of vulnerable individuals within families. There are also social networks within cultures to accomplish these goals. Yalcinkaya (chap. 9) talks of the importance of women's networks in promoting women's rights in Turkey. Internationally-approved human rights covenants can help to empower these movements and play a critical role in spreading the message of human rights.

Nongovernmental Organizations (NGOs) have been critical in promoting human rights and have been effective in spurring local changes recognizing these rights (Boli & Thomas, 1999)—a process that is strongly reflected in our survey responses. Although NGOs were originally relief organizations growing out of the missionary movement, they have come to focus on macro-system factors, including social and political issues (Boli & Thomas, 1999). Because of the ineffectiveness of providing relief without changing the structures contributing to these needs, NGOs began to focus on broader systems, including preventive health and community building; their function now includes "catalytic roles," which aim at social change (Korten, 1990). Because of the focus on early charitable work (Fox, 1987), it is not surprising that NGOs have evolved into an important structure for promoting rights within families (Cohen, 1990).

NGOs played a central role in both the drafting of the Convention on the Rights of the Child and its implementation (Cohen, 1990). They have been crucial to the international women's movement, in promoting equal rights for women, and in preventing violence against women (Berkovitch, 1999). Berkovitch (1999) noted "the international women's movement did not only reflect world culture but helped to shape its content and structure" (p. 124). As indicated in this book, NGOs have been important in empowering vulnerable individuals and promoting human rights for women and children in many of the countries we studied (e.g., Brazil, Colombia, Saudi Arabia, South Africa, Turkey).

NGOs are dependent on the social context in which they operate. Hawkins and Humes (2002) found that NGOs are more or less effective depending on social context. In countries where these groups are able to function separately from the state, they are more effective in raising consciousness and increasing pressure for social change. Where they are beholden to the state, their message is often either enlisted in the name of the political power or marginalized. Our research suggests that it will be important not only to work with NGOs to promote human rights within families, but to assess the current or likely role of the NGOs within each country to determine the likely efficacy of working with them. For example, to help indigenous peoples in Australia to combat family violence in their homes, it may be critical to provide assistance that is not associated with the White European power structure that has historically victimized them.

SOCIAL STRUCTURES THAT ADDRESS FAMILY VIOLENCE

A society may dignify the role of parents by encouraging them to recognize their responsibilities in ensuring the rights of their children, as the Convention on the Rights of the Child suggests, but corresponding social structures are needed to address any parental inadequacies. One factor that may contribute to the conspiracy of silence around family violence is the absence of alternatives or responses to such violence (Liu & Chan, 1999). Help seeking is significantly influenced by the availability of social support external to the family (Rickwood & Braithwaite, 1994). In promoting a human rights approach to family violence, it is important that normative changes around rights be accompanied by corresponding institutional changes (Rosenzweig, 1988). The implicit theory of the human rights paradigm assumes that such protections will include the provision of services (Cohen & Naimark, 1991).

In the cultures we examined, it was clear that social services and structures were important for addressing family violence, but also that there was considerable variation in the services available to families. Rape crisis centers, battered women's shelters, and safe houses were available within many cultures, but not necessarily to all people within those cultures—with services often particularly inaccessible to the rural poor (e.g., Greece). A lack of such resources was cited as a reason for less reporting (Bezerra-Flanders, chap. 22). Reporting of family violence was also related to simply being asked (Borrelli & Palumbo, chap. 5; Donovan, chap. 3), indicating a willingness to discuss family violence within a supportive context.

Where such services are not available, family members and friends can be critical to coming to terms with family violence. In many cultures, families seek relief from family violence through friends and family (e.g., in Israel, Turkey, and Saudi Arabia). The presence of supportive family members has been found to decrease wife beating (Counts, Brown, & Campbell, 1992). But culture can also influence help-seeking behavior. In the Middle East, friends and family are often the only individuals who are entrusted with disclosures about family violence (Haj-Yahia & Shor, 1995). Help seeking from external agencies can be seen as a betrayal of the family, which can deter family members from utilizing them (Rabin, Markus, & Voghera, 1999). Thus, a human rights approach must also consider institutions that can respond to family violence and promote their development in concert with its message. It must also understand the indigenous factors, such as economic and social dependence, that might influence utilization of such services.

TAILORING HUMAN RIGHTS INTERVENTIONS

The Commission on Human Rights is the body with the primary responsibility for responding to human rights violations (Steiner & Alston, 1996). Although sanctions often receive the most attention as a means of responding to human rights violations, there are other effective means of accomplishing this goal. In reviewing the implementation strategies of the United Nations, Dinsten (1995) argued that treaties were the most effective means of addressing violations. Treaties are not international law because they do not provide a means of enforcement, but are seen as effective because of their ability to socialize cultures (Cohen, & Naimark, 1991). In what follows, I draw on findings from psychology to suggest some alternative ways in which human rights violations might be addressed within their cultural contexts.

Consciousness raising is an important way in which human rights principles might "intervene" in case of family violence. The history of the human rights movement itself represents a sort of gradual coming to consciousness regarding family violence. This history suggests that protections are provided for the least vulnerable first and then extended to other groups in order of vulnerability (power), with those most vulnerable being recognized last. In a similar vein, Holmes and Holmes (2002) have suggested that states follow developmental stages in their recognition of violence against women, and that the effectiveness of an intervention depends on the developmental stage of the state. In particular, enhancing indigenous women's movements are more effective at an earlier stage of consciousness, whereas socializing on an international scale is effective only at a later stage, when social awareness of domestic violence is greater. The important point is that consciousness of family violence and necessary protections for certain individuals may need to be an evolving process. Societies may have particular blind spots around certain forms of abuse, which are uncovered or recognized gradually. This reality might not change through a direct intervention, but through consciousness raising.

Raising consciousness seems to be locally beneficial. One striking difference in the attitudes of abused versus nonabused women is that abused women are more likely to believe that society gives consent to abusive behavior through its failure to talk about it (Nabi & Horner, 2001). Nabi and Horner (2001) found that abused women believe that talking openly about the problem will make it easier to solve. Moreover, greater recognition of abuse has been linked with less tolerance for abuse. Anglo-American women perceived more types of behavior to be abusive and exhibited less tolerance of wife abuse than Mexican-American women (Torres, 1991).

SHAMING

Human rights have been associated with individualist, as opposed, to collectivistic cultures (Forsyth, 1999). Thus, a human rights approach to family violence may be more effective in cultures in which individualism is valued (Diener, 1995). A response to human rights violations within the family will need to take these different cultural frameworks into account. Braithwaite (2000) argued that shaming is an important supplement to legal structures within communitarian societies, and that shaming can be effective in reintegrating lawbreakers into society without stigmatizing them permanently. As an approach to human rights violations, shaming may be a more effective response to family violence among collectivist cultures than sanctions or prosecution. In Filipino culture, for example, shaming or *hija* is a primary mechanism for social control and is effective in influencing and changing behavior (Enriquez, 1988; Nolido, chap. 19). Similarly, social order in China is more closely tied to moral socialization than to legal deterrence of unwanted behavior (Chen, 2002). According to Braithwaite's theory (1989), shaming can either increase or inhibit criminal behavior, depending on the levels of interdependency within a culture and the way in which shaming is carried out—for example, as stigmatizing or reintegrating. In testing this theory in China, Lu, Zhang, and Miethe (2002) found that interdependency did not affect the ways families approached shaming, but had a significant impact on the way communities practiced it. Thus, interdependency at the level of both the family and neighborhood needs to be considered in efforts to address abuse within families. Human rights interventions may benefit from employing reintegrative shaming to deter family violence within collectivistic cultures.

The effectiveness of a human rights approach depends on other contextual and macrosystem factors, as well. High income and social equality have been associated with valuing of human rights (Diener, 1995). This finding suggests that the success of human rights interventions may depend on a variety of social and economic factors. Addressing these factors directly may enhance the effectiveness of the approach. Conceptualizations of human rights violations also differ across cultures and these differences have been found to be related to beliefs about the relationship between macro and microsystems (Clemence, Devos, & Doise, 2002). A greater understanding of these beliefs can guide approaches to human rights violations.

CONCLUSION

Respondents from the societies surveyed in this book showed widespread agreement that protections are needed for family members at risk for abuse. There was, however, no consensus as to how these protections should be provided. In many cases, families were seen as the appropriate source for intervention, which creates a double bind because it is family members who are carrying out the abuse.

The societies surveyed have signed on to one or more treaties related to human rights. Many of these societies have credited human rights protocols with providing support for vulnerable groups and with consciousness raising regarding family violence. Rights violations and deprivations of freedom were explicitly cited cross-culturally as examples of abuse (Ashy, chap. 10; Hauksdóttir & Gestsdóttir, chap. 2; Nolido, chap. 19; Powell, chap. 21; Scruggs, chap. 13). This suggests that cross-culturally many people are already thinking of family violence in the context of human rights. Psychologists can also use a human rights approach to direct their research toward the protection of family members and the prevention of family violence (Cohen & Naimark, 1991). Given that subjective well-being is closely associated with human rights (Diener, 1995), it will be salutary for nations to promote them.

REFERENCES

Anderson, S. A., & Sabatelli, R. M. (2002). *Family interaction: A multigenerational developmental perspective* (3rd ed.). Boston, MA: Allyn & Bacon.

Baca Zinn, M., & Eitzen, D. S. (1993). *Diversity in families*. New York: HarperCollins.

Barnes, J. (trans.). (1980). *The Complete Works of Aristotle*. Oxford, UK: Oxford University Press.

Barnett, O. W. (1997). *Family violence across the lifespan: An introduction*. Thousand Oaks, CA: Sage.

Berkovitich, N. (1999). The emergence and transformation of the International Women's Movement. In J. Boli & G. M. Thomas (Eds.), *Constructing world culture* (pp. 100–126). Stanford, CA: Stanford University Press.

Boli, J., & Thomas, G. M. (1999). *Constructing world culture: International nongovernmental organizations since 1875*. Stanford, CA: Stanford University Press.

Bower-Russa, M. E. (2001). Disciplinary history, adult disciplinary attitudes, and risk for abusive parenting. *Journal of Community Psychology, 29*, 219–240.

Braithwaite, J. (1989). *Crime, shame and reintegration*. New York: Cambridge University Press.

Braithwaite, J. (2000). Shame and criminal justice. *Canadian Journal of Criminology: Special Issue. Changing punishment at the turn of the century: Finding the common ground, 42*, 281–298.

Brown, J., Cohen, P., Johnson, J. G., & Smailes, E. M. (1999). Childhood abuse and neglect: Specificity of effects on adolescent and young adult depression and suicidality. *Journal of the American Academy of Child and Adolescent Psychiatry, 38*, 1490–1496.

Bureau of Justice Statistics. (1998). *Violence by intimates: Analysis of data on crimes by current or former spouses, boyfriends, and girlfriends* [NCJ-167237]. Washington, DC: U.S. Department of Justice, Office of Justice Programs.

Canetto, S. S. (1996). What is a normal family? Common assumptions and current evidence. *Journal of Primary Prevention, 17*, 31–46.

Chen, X. (2002). The social control in China: Applications of the labeling theory and the reintegrative shaming theory. *International Journal of Offender Therapy & Comparative Criminology, 46*, 45–63.

Clemence, A., Devos, T., & Doise, W. (2002). Social representations of human rights violations: Further evidence. *Swiss Journal of Psychology Schweizerische Zeitschrift fuer Psychologie Revue Suisse de Psychologie, 60*, 89–98.

Coffey, P., Leitenberg, H., Henning, K., Bennett, R. T., & Jankowski, M. K. (1996). Dating violence: The association between methods of coping and women's psychological adjustment. *Violence & Victims, 11*, 227–238.

Cohen, C. P. (1990). Relationship between the child, the family, and the state. In M. D. Bayles, R. C. L. Moffat, & J. Grcic (Eds.), *Perspectives on the family* (pp. 293–316). New York: Edwin Mellen Press.

Cohen, C. P., & Naimark, H. (1991). United Nations Convention on the Rights of the Child: Individual rights concepts and their significance for social scientists. *American Psychologist, 46,* 60–65.

Counts, D. A., Brown, J. K., & Campbell, M. (1992). *Sanctions and sanctuary: Cultural perspectives on the beating of wives.* Boulder, CO: Westview.

Diener, D. (1995). Factors predicting the subjective well-being of nations. *Journal of Personality and Social Psychology, 69,* 851–864.

Dinsten, Y. (1995). Human rights: Implementation through the UN system. *Proceedings of the American Society of International Law, 89,* 242–247.

Dwairy, M. (2002). Foundations of psychosocial dynamic personality theory of collective people. *Clinical Psychology Review, 22,* 343–360.

Enriquez, V. G. (1988). The structure of Philippine social values: Towards integrating indigenous values and appropriate technology. In D. Sinha & H. Kao (Eds.), *Social values and development: Asian perspectives* (pp. 124–148). New Delhi: Sage.

Ferree, M. M. (1991). Feminism and family research. In A. Booth (Ed.), *Contemporary families: Looking forward, looking back* (pp. 103–121). Minneapolis, MN: NCFR Publications.

Fineman, A., & Mykitiuk, D. (1994). *The public nature of private violence.* New York: Routledge.

Finkelhor, D. (1988). *Stopping family violence: Research priorities for the coming decade.* Newbury Park, CA: Sage.

Finkelhor, D., & Korbin, J. (1988). Child abuse as an international issue. *Child Abuse & Neglect, 12,* 3–23.

Finkelhor, D., & Dzuiba-Leatherman, J. (1994). Victimization of children. *American Psychologist, 49,* 173–183.

Forsyth, D. R. (1999). *Group dynamics* (3rd ed.). Belmont, CA: Brooks and Cole.

Fox, T. H. (1987). NGOs in the United States. *World Development, 15,* 11–19.

Freud, S. (1922). *Group psychology and the analysis of ego.* London: International Psychoanalytic Press.

Gelles, R. J., & Straus, M. A. (1988). *Intimate violence.* New York: Simon & Schuster.

Greenwald, R. L., Bank, L., & Reid, J. B. A. (1997). Discipline-mediated model of excessively punitive parenting. *Aggressive Behavior, 23,* 259–280.

Haj-Yahia, M. M. (2002). Attitudes of Arab women toward different patterns of coping with wife abuse. *Journal of Interpersonal Violence, 17,* 721–745.

Haj-Yahia, M. M., & Shor, R. (1995). Child maltreatment as perceived by Arab students of social science in the West Bank. *Child Abuse and Neglect, 19,* 1209–1219.

Hawkins, D., & Humes, M. (2002). Human rights and domestic violence. *Political Science Quarterly, 23,* 231–257.

Herman, J. (1997). *Trauma and recovery.* New York: Basic Books.

Hines, D. A., & Malley-Morrison, K. (2001). Psychological effects of partner abuse against men: A neglected research area. *Psychology of Men & Masculinity, 2,* 75–85.

Holmes, S. T., & Holmes, R. M. (2002). *Sex crimes: Patterns and behaviors* (2nd ed.). Thousand Oaks, CA: Sage.

Home Office. (1999). *The 2000 British Crime Survey.* Retrieved October 31, 2002 from http://www.homeoffice.gov.uk/rds/pdfs/hosb1800.pdf

Humphrey, J. (1976). The International Bill of Rights: Scope and implementation. *William and Mary Law Review, 17,* 527–541.

Ingersoll-Dayton, B., & Saengtienchai, C. (1999). Respect for the elderly in Asia: Stability and change. *International Journal of Aging and Human Development, 48,* 113–130.

Kendall-Tackett, K. A., Williams, L. M., & Finkelhor, D. (2001). Impact of sexual abuse on children: A review and synthesis of recent empirical studies. In R. Bull (Ed.), *Children and the law: The essential readings* (pp. 31–76). Malden, MA: Blackwell.

Kessler, R., Sonnega, A., Bromet, E., Hughes, M., & Nelson, C. (1995). Post-traumatic stress disorder in the National Comorbidity Survey. *Archives of General Psychiatry, 52,* 1048–1060.

Korbin, J. (1995). The intergenerational cycle of violence in child and elder abuse. *Journal of Elder Abuse & Neglect, 7,* 1–15.

Korten, D. C. (1990). *Getting to the 21st century: Voluntary action and the global agenda.* West Harford, CT: Kumarian.

Kozu, J. (1999). Domestic violence in Japan. *American Psychologist, 54,* 50–54.

Laing, R. D. (1971). *The politics of the family.* New York: Random House.

Lau, J. T., Liu, J. L. Y., Yu, A., & Wong, C. K. (1999). Conceptualizing, reporting and underreporting of child abuse in Hong Kong. *Child Abuse and Neglect, 23,* 1159–1174.

Levesque, R. J. R. (1999). *Sexual abuse of children: A human rights perspective.* Washington, DC: American Psychological Association.

Levesque, R. J. R. (2000). *Adolescents, sex, and the law: Preparing adolescents for responsible citizenship.* Washington, DC: American Psychological Association.

Levesque, R. J. R. (2002). *Culture and family violence: Fostering change through human rights law.* Washington, DC: American Psychological Association.

Levinson, D. (1989). *Family violence in cross-cultural perspective.* Newbury Park, CA: Sage.

Liu, M., & Chan, C. (1999). Enduring violence and staying in marriage: Stories of battered women in rural China. *Violence Against Women, 5,* 1469–1492.

Lockwood, C. E., Magraw, D. B., Spring, M. F., & Strong, S. I. (1998). *The International Human Rights Movement of Women.* Washington, DC: American Bar Association.

Lu, H. Z., Zhang, L., & Miethe, T. D. (2002). Interdependency, communitarianism and reintegrative shaming in China. *Social Science Journal, 39,* 189–201.

Malley-Morrison, K., & Hines, D. A. (2003). *Family violence in a cultural perspective: Defining, understanding, and combating abuse.* Thousand Oaks, CA: Sage.

Marsella, A. J., Friedman, M. J., Gerrity, E. T., & Scurfield, R. M. (1996). *Ethnocultural aspects of posttraumatic stress disorder: Issues, research, and clinical applications.* Washington, DC: American Psychological Association.

McCubbin, H. (1979). Integrating coping behavior in family stress theory. *Journal of Marriage and the Family, 41,* 237–244.

McCubbin, H., Joy, C. B., Cauble, A. E., Comeau, J. K., & Needle, R. H. (1980). Family stress and coping: A decade review. *Journal of Marriage and the Family, 42,* 125–142.

Melton, G. B. (1991). Socialization in the global community: Respect for the dignity of children. *American Psychologist, 46,* 66–71.

Melton, G. B., & Flood, M. F. (1994). Research policy and child maltreatment: Developing the scientific foundation for effective protection of children. *Child Abuse & Neglect, 18,* 1–28.

Mitchell, K. J., & Finkelhor, D. (2001). Risk of crime victimization among youth exposed to domestic violence. *Journal of Interpersonal Violence, 16,* 944–964.

Nabi, R. L., & Horner, J. R. (2001). Victims with voices: How abused women conceptualize the problem of spousal abuse and implications for intervention and prevention. *Journal of Family Violence, 16,* 237–253.

Power, S. (2002). *A problem from hell.* New York: Basic Books.

Rabin, B., Markus, B., & Voghera, N. (1999). A comparative study of Jewish and Arab battered women presenting in the emergency room of a general hospital. *Family Violence 29,* 69–84.

Resick, P. A. (2001). *Stress and trauma.* Philadelphia, PA: Psychology Press.

Resnick, H. S., Kilpatrick, D. G., Dansky, B. S., Saunders, B. E., & Best, C. L. (1993). Prevalence of civilian trauma and posttraumatic stress disorder in a representative national sample of women. *Journal of Consulting and Clinical Psychology, 61,* 984–991.

Rickwood, D. J., & Braithwaite, V. A. (1994). Why openness with health inspectors pays. *Social Science & Medicine, 39,* 563–572.

Rosenzweig, M. R. (1988). Psychology and United Nations Human Rights efforts. *American Psychologist, 43,* 79–86.

Rothausen, T. J. (1999). 'Family' in organizational research: A review and comparison of definitions and measures. *Journal of Organizational Behavior, 20,* 817–836.

Segal, U. (1999). Family violence: A focus on India. *Aggression and Violent Behavior, 4*, 213–231.

Sen, A. K. (1999). *Development as freedom*. New York: Knopf.

Straus, M. A. (1999). The controversy over domestic violence by women: A methodological, theoretical, and sociology of science analysis. In X. B. Arriaga & S. Oskamp (Eds.), *Violence in intimate relationships* (pp. 17–44). Thousand Oaks, CA: Sage.

Straus, M. A. (2001a). *Beating the devil out of them: Corporal punishment in American families and its effects on children* (2nd ed.). New Brunswick, NJ: Transaction Publishers.

Straus, M. A. (2001b). Physical aggression in the family: Prevalence rates, links to non-family violence, and implications for primary prevention of societal violence. In M. Martnez (Ed.), *Prevention and control of aggression and the impact on its victims* (pp. 34–56). New York: Kluwer Academic/Plenum.

Straus, M. A., & Kantor, G. K. (1987). Stress and child abuse. In R. E. Helfer & R. S. Kempe (Eds.), *The battered child* (4th rev. & exp. ed., pp. 42–59). Chicago: University of Chicago Press.

Straus, M. A., Kaufmann-Kantor, G. K., & Moore, D. W. (1997). Change in cultural norms approving marital violence from 1968 to 1994. In G. K. Kantor & J. L. Jasinski (Eds.), *Out of darkness: Contemporary perspectives on family violence* (pp. 3–16). Thousand Oaks, CA: Sage.

Steiner, H. J., & Alston, P. (1996). *International human rights in context*. New York: Oxford University Press.

Strobel, L. M. (2001). *Coming full circle: The process of decolonization among post-1965 Filipino Americans*. Quezon City, Philippines: Giraffe Books.

Torres, S. (1991). A comparison of wife abuse between two cultures: Perceptions, attitudes, nature, and extent. *Issues Mental Health Nursing, 12*, 113–131.

Turner, H. A., & Finkelhor, D. (1996). Corporal punishment as a stressor among youth. *Journal of Marriage & the Family, 58*, 155–166.

United Nations. (1983). *Universal Declaration of Human Rights* (U.N. Doc. No. A/41/342). New York: Author.

United Nations. (1989). *Adoption of a Convention on the Rights of the Child* (U.N. Doc. No. A/44/736). New York: Author.

Voelker, R. (1992). Nation begins to see family violence as public health issue. *Journal of the American Medical Association, 267*, 3184–3189.

Author Index

A

Aba-Alrogosh, G., 167, 170, 174, 180, 185, *186*
Abdullahi, M. D., 225, 226, 227, 229, 230, 233, 234, 237, *241*
Aboim, M. L., 406, 410, 412, *413*
Abu-Habib, L., 206, 210, 216, 217, *219*
Abyad, A., 214, *219*
Achieng, J., 238, *241*
Achildieva, Y. F., 121, *128*
Adair, L. S., 348, *359*
Adam, H., 139, 141, *148*
Adami, C., 70, *85*
Adamushkina, M., *128*
Agathonos, H., 131, 139, 141, *148*, *149*
Agathonos-Georgopoulou, H., 135, 139, *148*
Ahmad, O. B., 70, *85*
Ahn, H. N., 307, 308, *317*
Ahn, J. H., 309, *319*
Ahn, Y. J., 305, *317*
Aidid, M. F., 228, 229, 231, 232, 235, *241*
Albishr, K., 167, 170, 174, 180, 185, *186*
Al-Eissa, Y., 168, 178, 183, 184, *186*
Alenezi, H., 167, 170, 174, 180, 185, *186*
Alexander, R., 365, *376*
Al-Gamhoor, H., 181, *186*
Algohar, H., 182, *186*

Allison, A., *298*
Almaghloth, F., 167, 170, 174, 180, 185, *186*
Almokaid, S., 167, 170, 174, 180, 185, *186*
Alnaeem, O., 171, 182, *186*
Al-Namlah, A., 181, *186*
Al Oliyan, 182, 183, *186*
Al-Rashid, N., 182, *186*
Alston, P., 494, *500*
Altshuler, B., 121, *128*
Ana-Gatbonton, C. S., 342, 344, 349, 351, 354, 356, *359*
Anderson, S. A., 474, 487, 491, *497*
Andreu, M. J., *298*
Antonopoulou, C., 136, *148*
Aoalsteinsson, R., 20, *30*
Aprelkov, G., 120, *128*
Arai, M., 113, *128*, 295, *298*
Araújo, Z. A., 53, 54, 59, 60, *66*
Arenson, S., 74, *85*
Ari, M., 159, *163*
Arin, C., 155, 158, 162, *163*
Ásgeirsdóttir, B., 19, *30*
Ashbury, J., 368, *376*
Ashton, V., 9, *12*
Assaf, N., 208, 209, *219*
Assal, A., 209, *219*
Astolfi, P., 73, *85*

Ates, N., 159, 160, *163*
Atkinson, J., 368, *376*
Aushenker, M., 195, *203*
Avni, N., 189, *203*
Azevedo, M. A., 406, 412, *413*

B

Baca Zinn, M., 474, 476, 478, 479, 487, *497*
Bacchus, L., *49*
Badawi, J., 175, 176, *186*
Badawi, M., 234, 236, 238, 239, 240, *242*
Baer, S., 102, *104*
Bagley, C., 435, *448*
Bagshaw, D., 369, *376*
Balding, J., *48*
Balian, S. A., 210, 211, 212, *220*
Bank, L., 491, *498*
Baral, I., 159, 160, *163*
Baras, M., 192, *203*
Barber, M., 37, 38, *50*
Bardi, M., 75, 76, *85*
Bar-Giora, M., 199, *203*
Barker, D., 35, 36, *49*
Barnes, J., 476, *497*
Barnett, O. W., 477, *497*
Barnett, S. Morrison, 7, *13*
Barnow, S., 102, *104*
Barron, B., 370, *376*
Beckmann, S., 103, *105*
Beiser, M., 433, *448*
Belsky, J., 8, *12*
Benediktsdóttir, T., 25, *32*
Beninca, C., 402, *413*
Bennet, L., 192, *203*
Bennett, G., 43, *49*
Bennett, R. T., 486, *497*
Bergen, R. K., 460, *467*
Bergman, S., 199, *203*
Bergmann, C., 92, *104*
Berk, R. A., 454, *469*
Berkovitich, N., 475, 493, *497*
Bermudez, Q., *426*
Bernabei, R., 80, 82, *85*
Berrien, F., 120, *128*
Bertozzo, G., 72, *85*
Best, C. L., 486, *499*
Bewley, S., *49*
Biagini, E., 72, *85*
Biderman, A., 192, *203*

Bilir, S., 159, *163*
Bisharat, B., 192, *203*
Björnsdóttir,, 21, 22, *30*
Björnsson, B., 26, 29, *31*
Blust, E. P. N., 342, 343, 351, *358*
Boli, J., 475, 493, *497*
Borgognoni-Tarli, S. M., 75, 76, *85*
Borkan, Y., 192, *203*
Boukhari, H., 210, *219*
Bower-Russa, M. E., 485, *497*
Bradford, S., 52, *66*
Braithwaite, J., 495, 496, *497*
Braithwaite, V. A., 494, *499*
Branigan, T., 35, *48*
Breines, W., 454, *467*
Broadhurst, D. D., 455, 457, *469*
Brodsky, J., 198, *203*
Brodzynsky, S., *426*
Bromet, E., 486, *498*
Bronfenbrenner, U., 8, *12*
Brooker, S., 37, 38, *48*
Brown, J., 435, *448*, 486, *497*
Brown, J. G., 462, *467*
Brown, J. K., 494, *498*
Browne, K., 43, *49*
Browne, K. D., 139, *148*
Brueckner, M., *104*
Bruno, T., 71, 77, 81, 83, *85*
Bull, A., 71, *85*
Bunt, R., 370, *376*
Bursik, R. J., 9, *12*
Burton, R. F., 228, *242*
Butler, I., 37, 38, *50*
Buzhicheeva, V., 120, *128*
Buzzi, D., 71, *85*
Byron, C., 39, *49*

C

Cabaraban, M. C., 348, 349, 350, *358*
Cabral, S., 407, 408, 410, *413*
Caffo, E., 83, *85*
Cakir, S., 153, *163*
Cameron, I., 370, 371, *377*
Campbell, J. C., 60, *66*
Campbell, M., 494, *498*
Can, D., 159, 160, *163*
Canetto, S. S., 474, 487, *497*
Cantalini, B., 80, *86*
Carbonin, P., 80, 82, *85*

Carollo, G., 82, *85*
Cauble, A. E., 491, *499*
Cavalli, A., 71, *85*
Cawson, P., 37, 38, *48*
Cawte, J., 372, *376*
Çetin, G., 159, 160, *163*
Cha, K. T., 304, *317*
Chan, C., 485, *499*
Chandanos, G., 135, 143, 144, *148*
Chappell, N. L., 444, *448*
Chatzevarnava, E., 135, 143, 144, *148*
Chaya, M., 209, *219*
Chen, C., 327, *336*
Chen, G., 325, *336*
Chen, X., 496, *497*
Chen, Y., 329, *336*
Cheyne, B., 36, *49*
Chi, Y., 327, 329, *336*
Chiu, C., 7, *12*
Cho, A. J., 307, 308, *318*
Cho-Han, H. J., 304, 315, *317*
Choi, J. S., 304, *317*
Choi, Y., 314, *317*
Chou, W., 324, *336*
Chowdhury, A., 272, *279*
Chun, J. S., 305, *317*
Chung, D., 369, *376*
Chung, W., 40, *50*
Church, J., 35, *49*
Cimmarusti, R. A., 351, 353, *359*
Clark, J. D., 225, *242*
Clemence, A., 496, *497*
Clemson, L., 215, *219*
Coffey, P., 486, *497*
Cohen, C., 403, *413*
Cohen, C. P., 476, 493, 494, 495, *497*, *498*
Cohen, P., 435, *448*, 486, *497*
Coid, J., 40, *50*
Comeau, J. K., 491, *499*
Cook, P., 443, *448*
Cook, P. W., 458, *467*
Coomaraswamy, R., 418, 419, 420, 425, *427*
Cooper, B., 94, *104*
Cornell, C. P., 59, *66*, 463, *468*
Costa-Crowell, C. L., 53, 61, *66*
Counts, D. A., 494, *498*
Craig, B., 435, *448*
Cran, A., 370, *376*
Creatsas, G., *148*
Crisina, M., 84, *86*
Cristovam, M. L., 58, *66*
Cruickshank, C., 383, *396*

Cumberworth, A., 367, *376*
Cutler, S. E., 463, *468*

D

Dall'Aria, E., 78, *85*
dal Pozzo, G., 76, *86*
Dannenbeck, C., 94, *105*
Dansky, B. S., 486, *499*
Dasgupta, S., 268, *279*
Dauvergne, M., 438, 439, 440, *448*
de Castilho, E., 412, *414*
De Leo, D., 82, *85*
DelGrande, E., 370, *377*
Dello, B. M., 82, *85*
De Mello, S., *413*
Dennerstein, L., 367, *376*
De Oliveira, T. C., 401, 410, *413*
DeParle, N. M., 462, *467*
Derné, S., 268, 276, *279*
Devos, T., 496, *497*
DeWaal, N., 226, *242*
Diener, D., 495, 496, 497, *498*
DiGiovanni, J., 72, *85*
Dinsten, Y., 494, *498*
Doe, S. S., 307, 311, *317*
Doise, W., 496, *497*
Domingo, L. J., 351, 353, *360*
Donati, C., 215, *219*
Dönmez, N. B., 159, *163*
Doumanis, M., 140, 141, *148*
Drexel, J., 401, *413*
Droegemueller, W., 454, *468*
Duke, J. E., 368, *376*
Dussich, J. P. J., 286, *298*
Dwairy, M., 402, *414*, 484, *498*
Dzuiba-Leatherman, J., 482, *498*

E

Easteal, P. L., 368, *376*
Edelstein, 198, *203*
Edleson, J., 190, *203*
Edleson, J. L., 454, *469*
Edwards, L. P., 454, 455, 456, *468*
Einarsdóttir, T., 24, *30*
Eisikovits, Z., 190, 196, *203*
Eitzen, D. S., 474, 476, 478, 479, 487, *497*
El-Haddad, A., 210, 211, 212, *220*

El-Hassan, K., 218, *219*
Ellertsdóttir, H., 19, *30*
Elliger, T., 97, *106*
Enosh, G., 196, *203*
Enriquez, V. G., 496, *498*
Epivatianos, P., 136, *148*
Epstein, D., 453, *468*
Epstein, M. A., 453, 465, *468*
Erdyneev, A., 113, *128*
Erlendsdóttir, V., 23, *30*
Ersahin, Y., 159, 160, *163*
Esmer, Y., 157, *163*
Euthymiou, G., *148*
Evans, H. H., 10, *12*
Ewing, C. P., 463, *468*

F

Fagan, J., 454, 465, *468*
Fara, G. M., 83, *85*
Fargason, C. A., Jr., 10, *12*
Farhood, L. F., 209, *219*
Farrell, E., 209, *219*
Farrington, D., 39, 40, *49*
Feder, G., 40, *50*
Feghali, E., 208, 210, *219*
Feree, M. M., *498*
Fernandez, M., 273, *279*
Ferreira, M., 258, *260*, *261*
Ferreira da Silva, L., 57, 61, *66*
Figueiredo, E., 60, *66*
Fineman, A., 474, *498*
Finkelhor, D., 464, *468*, 479, 480, 481, 482, 483, 486, *498, 499, 500*
Fisek, G., 154, 156, *163*
Fisher, M., 465, *468*
Fitzgerald, M., 215, *219*
Fleishman, R., 199, *203*
Flitcroft, J., 370, *376*
Flood, M., *376*
Flood, M. F., 491, *499*
Flores, R., 404, *414*
Flynn, C. P., 9, *12*
Fogelman, Y., 192, *203*
Foo, L., 459, *468*
Forsyth, D. R., 481, 495, *498*
Fox, T. H., 493, *498*
Frandsen, K. J., 90, 99, *105*
Frebyberger, H. J., 102, *104*
Freeman, I., 36, *49*

Freire, P., 401, 402, *414*
Freud, S., 476, *498*
Friedman, M. J., 486, *499*
Friðriksdóttir, H., 19, *30*
Fritsche, I., 103, *106*
Frizzel, A., 443, *448*
Fry, D., 35, *49*
Fuchs, D., 75, *85*
Fujihara, T., *298*
Fujii, M., 294, *298*
Fujimaki, K., *299*
Funabashi, K., 286, *298*
Furnham, A., 9, *12*

G

Gambassi, G., 80, 82, *85*
Gardlo, S., 90, 102, *105*
Gaunt, D., 19, *30*
Gelles, R. J., 59, *66*, 463, 464, *468, 469,* 474, *498*
Georgoule, I., 135, 143, 144, *148*
Gerin, D., 77, *86*
Gerrity, E. T., 486, *499*
Gestsdóttir, S., 26, 29, *31*
Ghent, J. S., 189, *203*
Gilleard, C., 43, *49*
Gillham, B., 36, *49*
Giordano, J., 74, 75, *85*
Gíslason, G., 25, *31*
Gíslason, I. V., 25, *31*
Goergen, T., 100, 101, *105*
Golini, A., 80, *86*
Golz, P., 94, *105*
Gomes, R., 408, 411, *414*
Gomes, W., 402, *413*
Gonzo, L., 77, 78, *86*
Goodwin, M. P., 463, *468*
Gordon, L., 192, *203*, 454, *467*
Gotowiec, A., 433, *448*
Graham-Bermann, S. A., 463, *468*
Grasmick, H. G., 9, *12*
Graziano, A. M., 9, *12*
Greenwald, R. L., 491, *498*
Greve, W., 100, *107*
Gries, S., 95, 96, *105*
Griswold, E., 420, *427*
Gross, A., 97, *106*
Grynbaum, 196, *203*
Guerra, V. N. A., 406, 412, *413*

Guillermo-Prieto, A., 415, 418, 420, 421, *427*
Guist, C., 95, 100, *105*
Gülçür, L., 155, 157, 158, 159, *163*
Gurdin, J. E., 26, *31*
Guttman, E., 190, *203*
Guttormsson, L., 20, 21, *31*
Gysi, J., 93, *105*

H

Hada, A., 284, 293, *298*
Haddad, R., 206, 216, *219*
Hafte, B., 90, 99, *105*
Hagemann-White, C., 90, 102, *105*
Haj-Yahia, M., 191, 200, *203*, 485, 494, *498*
Ham, Y. H., *317*
Hampden-Turner, C., 72, 73, 74, *87*
Han, I. S., 306, *318*
Han, K. H., 306, 311, *318*
Hanci, H., 159, 160, *163*
Hanson, D., 75, *86*
Hardy, M. S., 464, *468*
Harris, P. B., 294, *298*
Hawkins, D., 475, 476, 477, 479, 492, 493, *498*
Haworth, A., *49*
Hayashi, I., 288, 289, 291, 297, *298*
Haynes-Taylor, K., 230, 234, *242*
Hegde, R., 268, 272, *279*
Heinsohn-Krug, M., 102, *106*
Henning, K., 486, *497*
Herman, J., 486, *498*
Herman, T., 195, *204*
Hermann, B., 97, *105*
Herrington, E. B., 466, *468*
Herzberger, S. D., 9, 10, *12*
Heymann, J., 453, *468*
Hindin, M. J., 348, *359*
Hines, D. A., 458, *468*, 474, 479, 489, *498, 499*
Hirano, S., *299*
Hobbs, C. J., 46, *49*
Hobbs, G. F., 46, *49*
Hofstede, G., 402, *414*
Holmes, R. M., 477, 495, *498*
Holmes, S. T., 477, 495, *498*
Holt, M., 205, *219*
Holzer, I., 199, *203*
Homer, A., 43, *49*
Hong, K. E., 307, *318*
Hong, Y., 7, *12*
Horne, S., 113, 114, 116, *128*

Horner, J. R., 486, 495, *499*
Houseknecht, S. K., 72, *86*
Huang, M., *337*
Huang, Y., 327, 328, *337*
Hughes, H., 368, *376*
Hughes, M., 486, *498*
Humes, M., 475, 476, 477, 479, 492, 493, *498*
Humphrey, J., 475, *498*
Hunt, D. D., 342, 344, 349, 351, 354, 356, *359*
Huxoll, M., 97, *105*

I

Ikeda, Y., *298*
Ilkkaracan, P., 154, *163*
Impallomeni, M., 83, *86*
Inciardi, J., 401, *414*
Ingersoll-Dayton, B., 342, 352, *359*, 491, *498*
Inoue, M., 70, *85*
Iossifides, M., 140, *148*
Israel, E., 464, *469*
Issa-Salwe, C. M. C., 226, *242*
Itzhaky, H., 200, *203*
Ivanova, T., 120, *128*
Iwata, N., 288, 289, 291, 297, *298, 299*
Izenberg, D., 201, *203*

J

Jacobs, T., 252, *260*
Jang, M., 313, *318*
Jankowski, M. K., 486, *497*
Jewkes, R., 252, *260*
John, R. S., 459, *468*
Johnson, C. F., 288, 289, 290, 291, 297, *298*
Johnson, J. G., 435, *448*, 486, *497*
Johnson, K. K., 455, *468*
Jónsdóttir, G., 23, *31*
Jónsdóttir, N. B., 23, *31*
Jónsson, B., 18, *32*
Joseph, S., 205, 207, 210, 211, 212, 213, 218, *219, 220*
Joy, C. B., 491, *499*
Ju, W., 329, *337*
Júlíusdóttir, S., 19, 20, 21, 25, *31, 32*
Jung-joo, L., 94, *105*

K

Kadman, I., 200, 203
Kagitçibasi, Ç., 156, 160, 161, 163
Kaiser, G., 95, 105
Kandioti, D., 273, 279
Kaneko, Y., 295, 298
Kang, M. K., 307, 318
Kantor, G. K., 491, 500
Kaplan, S., 159, 160, 163
Kapoor, S., 72, 86
Kasahara, Y., 299
Kasian, M., 459, 468
Kattan, H., 167, 168, 178, 182, 183, 184, 185, 186
Kaufman-Kantor, G., 457, 458, 469, 480, 500
Kavemann, B., 103, 105
Keenan, C. K., 210, 211, 212, 220
Keikelame, J., 258, 260
Keiser, S., 94, 105
Kelling, H. W., 91, 92, 105
Kelly, G., 37, 38, 48
Kelly, G. A., 5, 12
Kemp, A. M., 37, 38, 50
Kempe, C., 454, 468
Kendall-Tackett, K. A., 479, 498
Kessler, R., 486, 498
Keyser, J., 235, 242
Khalifah, B., 208, 220
Khweiri, J., 208, 220
Kijima, N., 288, 289, 291, 297, 298
Kilpatrick, D. G., 486, 499
Kim, B. S. K., 342, 359
Kim, K., 307, 318
Kim, S. K., 307, 308, 318
Kim, S. Y., 303, 304, 318
Kimpel, M., 9, 12
Kindergeld, 92, 105
King, K., 435, 448
King, Y., 198, 203
Kitahara, M., 288, 289, 298
Kitai, E., 192, 203
Kitamura, T., 288, 289, 291, 297, 298, 299
Klimenkova, T., 114, 121, 125, 128
Ko, B., 307, 318
Kohyama, T., 298
Kokkevi, A., 139, 148
Kolinksy, E., 93, 94, 95, 106
Kondlyle, D., 135, 143, 144, 148
Kora, K., 159, 160, 163
Korbin, J., 481, 482, 498, 499

Koronaiou, A., 133, 149
Korten, D. C., 493, 499
Kostavara, K., 149
Kouno, A., 288, 289, 290, 291, 297, 298
Kozu, J., 286, 287, 288, 289, 290, 291, 293, 295, 297, 298, 480, 499
Krahe, B., 103, 106
Krispin, O., 192, 204
Kristinsdóttir, G., 22, 31
Kristjánsdóttir, G., 24, 30
Kuehne, V. K., 444, 448
Kumagai, F., 286, 289, 298
Kurrie, S. E., 368, 376
Kurrle, S., 370, 371, 377
Kurrle, S. E., 370, 376
Kushnir, L., 121, 128
Kuzmeskus, L. M., 460, 461, 462, 469
Kuznetsov, B., 116, 117, 128

L

Lafayette De Mente, B., 384, 396
Lai, H., 326, 337
Laing, R. D., 481, 499
Lakkis, S., 212, 218, 220
Lambert, M., 438, 439, 440, 448
Lambie, A., 36, 49
Lau, J. T., 480, 499
Lawrence, J. M., 367, 376
Lee, H. J., 303, 304, 318
Lee, H. S., 305, 311, 318
Lee, K. H., 311, 318
Lee, K. I., 309, 318
Lee, Y., 328, 337
Leinbach, T. R., 339, 341, 359
Leitenberg, H., 486, 497
Lerner, G., 74, 86
Levesque, R. J. R., 474, 475, 476, 483, 485, 486, 488, 490, 491, 499
Levinson, D., 490, 499
Lewins, F., 366, 376
Lewis, I. M., 226, 227, 228, 230, 231, 232, 234, 242
Liedloff, H., 92, 106
Lifshitz, C., 198, 203
Lillo, A., 71, 85
Lin, H., 324, 325, 337
Lin, L., 330, 337
Lin, S., 327, 337
Lintzenberger, B. W., 463, 468

Liu, J. L. Y., 480, *499*
Liu, M., 485, *499*
Livermore, P., 370, *376*
Locke, D., 435, *448*
Lockwood, C. E., 475, *499*
Lockwood, K., 370, *376*
Loizos, P., 53, 60, *67*
Long, S. O., 294, *298*
Lopez, A. D., 70, *85*
Lori, A., 80, *86*
Lowenstein, A., 192, 198, 199, *203*
Lu, H. Z., 496, *499*
Lucht, M., 102, *104*
Ly, J., 366, *376*
Lyons, R. A., 37, 38, *50*

M

Maceda, C. P., 354, 356, *359*
Machado, L., 408, 411, *414*
Magraw, D. B., 475, *499*
Malley-Morrison, K., 26, 29, *31*, 313, *318*, 458, 468, 474, 479, 489, *498, 499*
Mana, A., 254, *260*
Mandela, N., 245, *260*
Mandelson, J., 199, *203*
Manuel, P., 52, *67*
Maracle, S., 435, *448*
Margolin, G., 459, *468*
Markus, B., 197, *203*, 494, *499*
Marques, O. A., 52, *67*
Marsella, A. J., 486, *499*
Marshall, C., 100, *106*
Marshall, L. L., 459, *468*
Marshall, P. F., 437, *448*
Martin, A., 253, *260*
Martins, P., 399, 401, 406, 407, *414*
Mattos, L., 404, *414*
Mazza, D., 367, *376*
McCauley, M., 453, 465, *468*
McClosky, L. A., 76, *86*
McCreadie, C., 44, *49*
McCubbin, H., 491, *499*
McGoldrick, M., 74, *85*
McGowan, R. B., *242*
McIntyre, T. M., 53, *67*
McKay, M., 366, *376*
Mellejor, A. C., 356, *359*
Melton, G. B., 473, 477, 478, 491, *499*
Menon, T., 7, *12*

Mesch, G. S., 196, *203*
Meshefedjian, G., 209, *219*
Meyer, D., 93, *105*
Mezay, G., *49*
Miethe, T. D., 496, *499*
Militante, C., 344, 345, 347, 349, 357, *359*
Mills, L., 406, *414*
Mills, R., 313, *318*
Mingione, E., 80, *86*
Miral, S., 159, 160, *163*
Mirrlees-Black, C., 39, *49*
Mission, G., 354, *359*
Mitchell, K. J., 480, *499*
Mizrahi, G., 199, *203*
Mo, S. H., 304, *318*
Moeller, J., 92, *106*
Mogensen, B., 25, *32*
Molina, A., 345, *359*
Monteiro, J., 401, *414*
Mooney, J., 39, *49*
Moore, D. W., 457, 458, *469*, 480, *500*
Moorey, S., 40, *50*
Morales, B. C., 348, 349, 350, *358*
Morgan, R. J. H., 37, 38, *50*
Morris, I. S., 35, 36, *49*
Morris, M. W., 7, *12*
Mortimer, M., 35, 36, *49*
Mortzou, M., *148*
Mosaval, Y., 258, *261*
Moskowitz, S., 466, *468*
Mueller, E. P., 96, *106*
Mugford, J., 374, *376*
Mullavey-O'Bryne, C., 215, *219*
Munn-Giddings, C., 42, 43, *49*
Mykitiuk, D., 474, *498*

N

Nabi, R. L., 486, 495, *499*
Nadeau, B., 79, *87*
Naimark, H., 476, 494, 495, 497, *498*
Nakou, S., 139, 141, *148*
Namaste, K. A., 9, *12*
Naon, D., 198, *203*
Narita, T., *299*
Nasser, C., 215, *220*
Natarajan, M., 273, *279*
Nauck, B., 93, *106*
Needle, R. H., 491, *499*
Neikrug, S., 198, *203*

Nelson, C., 486, *498*
Nelson, D., 374, *376*
Nicholson, J. P., 443, *448*
Nishioka, K., *299*
Nissen, G., 97, *106*
Noor, M. C., 223, 226, 227, 228, 230, *242*
Nyström, L., 19, *30*

O

Ogg, J., 42, 43, *49*
Ogorodnikova, O., 120, 122, 124, *128*
Ólafsdóttir, H., 23, 25, *32*
Ólafsson, S., *32*
Oliveira, R., 53, 61, *66*
Omizo, M. M., 342, *359*
Opoku-Dapaah, E., *242*
Oral, R., 159, 160, *163*
Ortega, R. P., 353, *359*
O'Toole, B. I., 367, *376*
Owen, R., 74, 78, *86*

P

Page, J. A., 398, 399, *414*
Painter, K., 39, 40, *49*
Painter, S. L., 459, *468*
Panagiotopoulou, V., *148*
Papamichael, S., 133, *149*
Park, J. W., 307, *318*
Paternostro, S., 416, *427*
Patro, A., 272, *279*
Pattnaik, S., 272, *279*
Payne, E. H., 37, 38, *50*
Pepper, T., 79, *87*
Perlitsh, H. D., 113, *128*
Petruckevitch, A., 40, *50*
Pido, A. J. A., 343, *359*
Pillemer, K., 443, *448*
Pina, J., 82, *86*
Pinther, A., 93, *106*
Pitsiou-Darrough, E., 132, 144, 147, 148, *149*
Pleck, E., 453, *468*
Podnieks, E., 443, *448*
Pokroy, J., 254, *261*
Polat, S., 159, 160, *163*
Posadas, B. M., 341, *359*
Potamianou, A., 140, *149*
Power, S., 480, *499*

Prasad, B., 273, 274, *279*
Putnam, D. B., 223, 226, 227, 228, 230, *242*

Q–R

Quinn, M. J., 454, 462, *469*
Rabe, H., 103, *105*
Rabin, B., 197, *203*, 494, *499*
Ramirez, M. J., *298*
Ramphal, S., 383, *396*
Randall, T., 463, 464, *469*
Rao, V., 273, 274, *279*
Raphael, B., 367, *376*
Rapoza, K., 161, *163*
Ravaioli, M., 72, *85*
Reay, A., 43, *49*
Reid, J. B. A., 491, *498*
Rennison, C. M., 458, 459, *469*
Renzetti, C., 443, *448*
Resick, P. A., 486, *499*
Resnick, H. S., 486, *499*
Richardson, J., 40, *50*
Rickwood, D. J., 494, *499*
Riotta-Sirey, A., 75, *85*
Roberts, G. L., 367, *376*
Robinson, B. A., 433, *448*
Rolfe, K., 37, 38, *50*
Romito, P., 77, 84, *86*
Ronen, M., 198, *203*
Rooney, M., 36, *49*
Root, M. P., 340, 341, *359*
Roscoe, B., 463, *468*
Rosendorfer, T., 94, *105*
Rosenzweig, M. R., 475, 478, 494, *499*
Rothausen, T. J., 487, *499*
Ruhela, S. P., 228, 229, 231, 232, 235, *241*
Ryan, V., 367, *376*

S

Saadeh, F., 209, *219*
Sabatelli, R. M., 474, 487, 491, *497*
Sabbadini, L. L., 78, *86*
Sadler, P. M., 370, 371, *376*, *377*
Saengtienchai, C., 342, 352, *359*, 491, *498*
Safilios-Rothschild, C., 140, *149*
Safonova, T. Y., 120, *128*
Saito, I., 7, *13*
Sakado, T., *299*

Salvador, C., 401, *414*
Salvador, D. S., 342, *359*
Salzano, F., 404, *414*
Sant Cassia, P., 73, *86*
Santos, A. F., *359*
Saraceno, C., 72, *86*
Sastry, J., 72, *86*
Sato, T., *299*
Saunders, B. E., 486, *499*
Saurel-Cubizolles, M. J., 84, *86*
Scheid, A., 386, *396*
Scheidt, R. J., 342, 343, 351, *358*
Schein, M., 192, *203*
Schmidt, M. G., 93, *106*
Schmidt, R., 104, *106*
Schneider, N. F., 93, *106*
Schotensack, K., 97, *106*
Schuett, D., 234, *242*
Schutze, S., 103, *106*
Schwartz, P., 71, *86*
Schwartz, W. E., 463, *468*
Schwartz-Kenney, B. M., 453, 465, *468*
Schweikert, B., 102, *104*
Scionti, T., 76, *86*
Scott, I., 35, 36, *49*
Scurfield, R. M., 486, *499*
Sedlak, A. J., 455, 457, *469*
Segal, U., 272, 276, *279*, 477, 491, *500*
Sela-Amit, M., 190, *203*
Sen, A. K., 477, *500*
Senda, Y., 288, 289, 291, 297, *298*
Severny, A., 121, *128*
Sezgin, U., 159, 160, *163*
Sgritta, G., 73, *86*
Shairs, M. S., 295, *298*
Shehadeh, L., 205, 208, 209, 210, 211, 212, *220*
Shenk, D., 211, 214, 215, *220*
Sherman, L. W., 454, *469*
Shillington, T., 443, *448*
Shor, R., 191, 192, 193, 200, *203*, 494, *498*
Shtyleva, L., 124, 125, *129*
Shull, J. R., 465, *469*
Sibert, J. R., 37, 38, *50*
Sidani, T., 209, *219*
Siegel, J., 195, *203*
Sigfúsdóttir, H., 19, *30*
Sigfússon, A., 22, *32*
Sigvaldason, H., 25, *32*
Silva, L., 60, *66*
Silver, H., 454, *468*
Silverman, F., 454, *468*
Smailes, E. M., 486, *497*

Smearman, C. A., 23, 24, 26, 28, *32*
Smith, H., 464, *469*
Snævarr, A., 28, *32*
Sobol, E., 198, *203*
Sodei, T., 295, *299*
Soliman, C. J., *360*
Sonnega, A., 486, *498*
Spiegel, J., 73, *86*
Spinellis, C. D., 132, 144, 147, 148, *149*
Spring, M. F., 475, *499*
Stathacopoulos, N., 131, 141, *149*
Stathakopoulou, G., 139, 141, *148*
Steele, B., 454, *468*
Steiner, H. J., 494, *500*
Steinmetz, D., 192, *203*
Steinmetz, S. K., *469*
Stephan, C. W., 7, *13*
Stephan, W. G., 7, *13*
Sternberg, K. J., 192, *204*
Sternberg, R. J., 5, 10, *13*
Stimmer, F., 97, *106*
Storti, C., 73, *87*
Straus, M. A., *298*, 454, 456, 457, 458, 461, 463, 464, *469*, 474, 480, 481, 484, 486, 491, *498, 500*
Strobel, L. M., 343, *360*, 492, *500*
Strong, S. I., 475, *499*
Sturman, P., 40, *50*
Su, F., 334, 335, *337*
Summerfield, C., 35, *49*
Surrat, H., 401, *414*
Sustento-Seneriches, J., 342, 344, 346, *360*
Svavarsdóttir, E. K., 21, *32*
Swagerty, D., *106*
Symeonidou, c., 135, 143, *149*
Sznaider, N., 200, *204*
Szwarcwald, C., 412, *414*

T

Takahashi, K., 288, 289, 291, 297, *298*
Takayama, H., 79, *87*
Talmud, I., 200, *204*
Tanaka, S., *299*
Tanner, G., 36, *49*
Tatara, T., 460, 461, 462, *469*
Taylor, A., 370, *377*
Teng, C., 330, 335, *337*
Tennen, H., 9, 10, *12*
Tepeli, N., 159, 160, *163*

Terragni, L., 75, 81, *87*
Thiel, S., 79, *87*
Thiessen, R., 102, *106*
Thoennes, N., 459, *469*
Thomas, G. M., 475, 493, *497*
Thorgeirsdóttir, H., 25, *31*
Thorsteinsson, B., 18, *32*
Thyen, U., 102, *106*
Timofeeva, I., 118, *129*
Tinker, A., 44, *49*
Tjaden, P., 459, *469*
Tölke, A., 93, *106*
Tolman, R. M., 454, *469*
Tomita, S. K., 454, 462, *469*
Tomoda, A., *299*
Tompar-Tiu, A., 342, 344, 346, *360*
Torres, S., 495, *500*
Tosi, A., 78, 80, *87*
Trainor, C., 438, 439, 440, *448*
Trait, P. R., 368, *376*
Treviso, M., 76, *86*
Triandis, H. C., 6, *13*
Tripon, O. H., 347, 357, *360*
Trocmé, N. B., 435, *449*
Trompenaars, F., 72, 73, 74, *87*
Tsai, C., 332, *337*
Tsangari, M., 135, *148*
Tsimbal, E. I., 120, 124, *128, 129*
Tucker, E. J., 453, 465, *468*
Tuner, J., 368, *376*
Tung, R. L., 73, *87*
Turan, F., 161, *163*
Turgeon, D., 372, 373, *377*
Turner, H. A., 486, *500*
Tutty, L. M., 441, *449*

U

Uehara, T., *299*
Ulack, R., 339, 341, *359*
Ulizzi, L., 73, *85*

V

Vaillancourt, M. A., 437, *448*
Vasileiadis, A., 136, *148*
Vaz, J. G. M., 60, *67*
Veiga, F. H., 54, *67*
Vieth, V. I., 463, *470*

Ville, R., 78, *87*
Vindhya, U., 269, 271, 273, *279*
Voelker, R., 474, *500*
Voghera, N., 197, *203*, 494, *499*
Voigt, D., 95, 96, *105*

W

Waizenhofer, E., 103, *106*
Walk, D., 199, *203*
Walker, L. E., 75, *87*, *299*
Wall, K., 54, *67*
Wallrabe, D., 96, *106*
Wang, M., *337*
Wattam, C., 37, 38, *48*
Welchans, S., 458, 459, *469*
Welsh, P., 384, 388, 391, 392, *396*
Werczberger, R., 202, *204*
Wetzels, P., 100, *107*
Wiehe, V. R., 464, *470*
Willey, D., 72, *87*
Williams, L., 351, 353, *360*
Williams, L. M., 479, *498*
Wolff, R., 96, 97, *107*
Wong, C. K., 480, *499*
Wynne, J. M., 46, *49*

X–Y

Xavier, E., 408, 411, *414*
Ya, Y., 328, 329, *337*
Yaar, E., 195, *204*
Yalçinkaya, A., 161, *163*
Yamada, Y., 295, *298*
Yamamoto, M., *299*
Yang, J. J., 309, *319*
Yildirim, A., 157, 158, 161, *163*
York, A. S., 200, *203*
Yoshizumi, K., 287, *299*
You, H., 313, *318*
Yu, A., 480, *499*
Yüksel, S., 157, 158, 159, 160, *163*
Yuz, F., 199, *203*

Z

Zahr, L. K., 209, *220*
Zajczyk, F., 80, *86*

Zalzal, M. R., 209, 210, *220*
Zarnari, O., 140, 141, *149*
Zaza, K., 240, *243*
Zhang, L., 496, *499*
Zhmurov, V., 120, *128*

Zimmermann, S., 456, *470*
Zöega, B., 25, *32*
Zonta, L., 73, *85*
Zoumbou, V., 139, *149*
Zuccala, G., 80, 82, *85*
Zurayk, H., 209, *219*

Subject Index

A

Abandonment
  Brazil, 408
  Greece, 144
  Italy, 80, 81
  Korea, 305, 313, 314
  Lebanon, 215
  Nicaragua, 382, 390, 391
  Philippines, 340, 345, 351, 352
  Taiwan, 327, 333
Aboriginal Alternative Dispute Resolution
    Service (Australia), 374
Aboriginal families
  Australia, 364, 367, 372–373
  Canada, 435
Abuse defined
  Australia, 362–363, 364–365, 368, 373
  Brazil, 398, 402–403
  Canada, 432–433
  child abuse, 3, 4–5, 6
  Colombia, 416
  cultural context
    autonomous agents, 7–8
    autonomous units, 7–8
    collectivism, 6–9
    Eastern societies, 6–8
    ecological model, 8, 10
    implicit theories, 7–10
    independent self–view, 6–7
    individualism, 6–9
    interdependent self-view, 6–7
    Western societies, 6–8
  elder abuse, 3, 4–5, 6
  emotional abuse, 3, 4–5
  England, 33–34, 37–38, 43
  extreme abuse, 3, 4–6
  gender influence, 6
  Germany, 90–91, 99
  Greece, 132–133
  Iceland, 18
  implicit theories, 5–6
    abuse judgments, 8–10
    corporal punishment, 9–10
    cultural context, 7–10
    defined, 10
    developmental-ecological context, 8
    developmental-psychological context, 8
    ecological model, 8, 10
    explicit theory distinction, 10
    human rights, 10
    intermediate interactional context, 8
    personal construct theory, 5
  India, 266–267

Abuse defined *(cont.)*
  Israel, 188–189
  Italy, 70–71
  Japan, 285, 289
  Korea, 302–303, 305–306, 315–316
  Lebanon, 206–207, 212, 215–216
  mild abuse, 3, 4, 6
  moderate abuse, 3, 4, 6
  Nicaragua, 381–382
  Philippines, 340
  physical abuse, 3, 4
  research overview, 10–12
    methodology, 11
    objectives, 11–12
    survey development, 11
  Russia, 112
  Saudi Arabia, 168, 174, 178
  Somalia, 224–225
  South Africa, 246
  spousal abuse, 3, 4, 5, 6
  Taiwan, 322, 323, 325–327, 328
  Turkey, 152–153
  United States, 452, 461, 462
  verbal abuse, 3, 4
Act for Child Welfare (2000) (Korea), 306,
    315
Act for Elder Welfare (1980) (Korea), 312
Act for the Prevention and Protection of
    Victims of Domestic Violence (1997)
    (Korea), 305, 312
Act for the Prevention of Child Abuse (1997)
    (Korea), 306
Action on Elder Abuse (England), 43
Act on Maternity/Paternity Leave and
    Parental Leave (2000) (Iceland), 24
Act on the Equal Status and Equal Rights of
    Women and Men (2000) (Iceland), 24
Act on the Punishment of Domestic
    Violence (1997) (Korea), 305, 312, 316
Acute victimization, 483
Adult Protective Services (United States),
    460–461, 466
Advocates for Survivors of Child Abuse of
    Australia, 368
Agency for Child Protection (Iceland), 30
Alcohol consumption
  Australia, 372
  Brazil, 407
  England, 39, 41, 43
  Iceland, 26–27
  India, 266, 274
  Italy, 75

Japan, 293, 294
Korea, 302, 309
Philippines, 346, 348, 350, 352
Russia, 112, 121
South Africa, 246, 250, 251, 252, 253
Taiwan, 330
Turkey, 158
American Academy of Pediatrics, 4
American Psychological Association, 4
Anti-Abuse of Women in Intimate
    Relationships Bill (Philippines), 356
Anti-Rape Law (Philippines), 356
Arab League, 181
Asian and Pacific Islander Institute on
    Domestic Violence (United States),
    467
Asian Regional Initiative Against Trafficking
    Meeting (Philippines-United States),
    356
Asociacion de Hombres contra la Violencia
    (Nicaragua), 392–393
Association to Support Women Candidates
    (Turkey), 162
Australia
  aboriginal families
    alcohol consumption, 372
    child abuse, 367
    ecological model, 372
    family violence, 367, 372–373
    macrosystem, 364
  abuse defined
    child abuse, 368
    cultural context, 362
    domestic violence, 364–365
    emotional abuse, 362–363
    extreme abuse, 362–363
    family violence, 364–365, 373
    implicit theories, 362
    mild abuse, 363
    physical abuse, 362–363
    public humiliation, 362–363
    sexual abuse, 362–363
    verbal abuse, 362
  child abuse
    emotional abuse, 368–369
    extreme abuse, 368
    laws, 367–368
    mild abuse, 368–369
    moderate abuse, 368–369
    perspectives on, 368–369
    physical abuse, 368
    prevalence, 368

public humiliation, 368–369
sexual abuse, 368
domestic violence
defined, 364–365
immigrant groups, 371
marriage, 371
elder abuse
emotional abuse, 371
extreme abuse, 371
financial abuse, 370, 371
individual freedom, 371
mild abuse, 371
moderate abuse, 371
neglect, 370, 371
perspectives on, 371
physical abuse, 370, 371
prevalence, 370
risk factors, 370
verbal abuse, 371
family violence, 366–373
cultural context, 374–375
emotional abuse, 367
human rights paradigm, 489, 491, 493
intervention challenges, 374–375
prevalence, 366–367
services, 374
macrosystem
aboriginal families, 364
domestic violence, 364–365
family violence, 364–365
historical context, 363–364
implicit theories, 365
individual rights, 364–365
laws, 364–365
microsystem
divorce, 366
family structure, 365–366
marriage, 366
research overview
capsule, 361
sample, 362
spousal abuse
emotional abuse, 369, 370
extreme abuse, 369–370
husband abuse, 369
implicit theories, 369
individual freedom, 369–370
mild abuse, 369, 370
moderate abuse, 369, 370
perspectives on, 369–370
physical abuse, 369–370
sexual abuse, 369

verbal abuse, 369
wife abuse, 369
Australian National Clearinghouse on Family
Violence, 373
Australian Violence Prevention Award
Program, 374
Authority for the Advancement of Women
(Israel), 190
Autonomous agents, 7–8
Autonomous units, 7–8

B

Battered child syndrome, 454, 480
Berlin Intervention Project Against Domestic
Violence, 103
Brazil
abuse defined
family violence, 402–403
neglect, 398
physical abuse, 398
sexual abuse, 398
verbal abuse, 398
child abuse
corporal punishment, 403, 404
cultural context, 404
emotional abuse, 403, 405
extreme abuse, 404–405
implicit theories, 403, 404, 405
laws, 400–401, 409–410
mild abuse, 404–405
moderate abuse, 404–405
neglect, 402–403, 405
perspectives on, 404–405
physical abuse, 403, 404, 405
prevalence, 403, 404–405
prostitution, 400
services, 403, 410
sexual abuse, 400, 403–405
street children, 400–401, 410
verbal abuse, 405
domestic violence
alcohol consumption, 407
cultural context, 412–413
individualism, 412–413
intervention agenda, 411–413
laws, 411–412
model of, 412
patriarchal society, 412–413
prevalence, 405–406
rape, 401, 402, 406
services, 412

Brazil *(cont.)*
  elder abuse, 407–409
    abandonment, 408
    cultural context, 408
    elder status, 408
    emotional abuse, 408, 409
    extreme abuse, 408–409
    financial abuse, 408, 409
    implicit theories, 408–409
    laws, 411
    mild abuse, 409
    moderate abuse, 409
    neglect, 408, 409
    perspectives on, 408–409
    physical abuse, 408
    services, 410–411
    sexual abuse, 408
    verbal abuse, 408–409
  family violence, 402–409
    alcohol consumption, 407
    daughter-in-law, 407
    grandmother, 407
    human rights paradigm, 477, 481, 482,
      484, 488–489, 491, 492, 493
    laws, 409–411
    stepfather, 407
  macrosystem
    collectivism, 402
    economic context, 399–400
    gender equality, 401
    historical context, 398–399
    human rights, 402
    machismo, 399
    patriarchal society, 399
    street children, 400–401
    women's movement, 402
    women's status, 399, 401–402
  microsystem, 402
  research overview
    capsule, 397
    conclusion, 411–413
    sample, 397–398
  spousal abuse
    emotional abuse, 406, 407
    extreme abuse, 406, 407
    husband abuse, 407
    implicit theories, 407
    mild abuse, 406, 407
    moderate abuse, 406, 407
    perspectives on, 406–407
    physical abuse, 399, 406, 407
    sexual abuse, 406, 407

    verbal abuse, 406, 407
    wife abuse, 406–407
British Crime Survey (1996), 38–39
British Geriatric Society, 42–43
Bullying
  Japan, 296
  Taiwan, 333–334, 335
  United States, 459

C

Canada
  abuse defined
    emotional abuse, 432
    extreme abuse, 432, 433
    implicit theories, 432–433
    legal criteria, 433
    mild abuse, 432, 433
    moderate abuse, 432, 433
    neglect, 432
    physical abuse, 432–433
    spiritual abuse, 435
    verbal abuse, 432
  child abuse
    aboriginal families, 435
    corporal punishment, 436
    emotional abuse, 434, 436
    extreme abuse, 436
    implicit theories, 435–436
    infanticide, 435
    mild abuse, 436
    moderate abuse, 436
    perspectives on, 435–436
    physical abuse, 434, 435, 436
    prevalence, 434, 435
    public opinion, 434
    sexual abuse, 435
    spiritual abuse, 435
    verbal abuse, 436
  elder abuse
    cultural context, 445
    financial abuse, 445–446
    homicide, 446
    neglect, 445
    perspectives on, 444–446
    physical abuse, 443, 445
    prevalence, 444
    public opinion, 434
    risk factors, 446
    verbal abuse, 443, 445

family violence, 435–446
  cultural context, 447
  human rights paradigm, 479, 483, 484,
    489, 491
  online resources, 449
  public opinion, 433–434
  risk factors, 434
  services, 446–447
  macrosystem, 433–434
    historical context, 433
  microsystem, 434
  research overview
    capsule, 431
    conclusion, 447
    sample, 431–432
  same-sex couples, 442–443
    myths, 443
    services, 443
  sibling abuse, 434
  spousal abuse
    emotional abuse, 434, 438, 440
    extreme abuse, 439, 440, 441
    homicide, 437, 438–439
    husband abuse, 440–442
    kidnapping, 436
    marital rape, 437, 439, 441
    mild abuse, 439, 440, 441
    moderate abuse, 439, 440, 441
    perspectives on, 439–440, 441–442
    physical abuse, 434, 436, 437, 438–439,
      440–442
    prevalence, 434, 436–439, 440
    public humiliation, 440, 441, 442
    public opinion, 433–434
    sexual abuse, 436, 437, 438, 439
    verbal abuse, 437, 440, 442
    wife abuse, 436–440
Canadian Incidence Study of Reported Child
  Abuse and Neglect, 435
Canadian Panel on Violence Against Women
  (1991), 447
Caritas Nunnery Counseling Center for Elder
  Abuse (Korea), 312–313
Center for Abused Women in Greece, 136
Center for Gender and Women's Studies
  (Philippines), 356
Center for Popular Education and
  Communications (Nicaragua), 392
Center for Referrals for Children and
  Adolescents (Brazil), 403
Central Coast Aged Care Assessment Team
  (Australia), 370

Central Institute for Youth Research
  (Germany), 93
Central Region Teachers' Union (Portugal),
  55
Change on Behalf of Peace in the National
  Development Plan (1991) (Colombia),
  419
Child abuse, *see also* Child labor; Child
  maltreatment; Corporal punishment;
  Infanticide; Public humiliation; Street
  children; Trafficking
  abuse defined, 3, 4–5, 6
  Australia, 367–369
  Brazil, 400–401, 403–405, 409–410
  Canada, 434, 435–436
  Colombia, 419, 422–423, 424
  England, 35–38, 44–46
  Germany, 95–98, 101–102
  Greece, 138–143, 146–147
  Iceland, 20–23, 29–30
  India, 271, 272–273
  Israel, 191–195, 200–201
  Italy, 75–77, 81–82, 83–84
  Japan, 288, 289–293, 296–297
  Korea, 305–309, 315, 316
  Lebanon, 209, 211, 213–214, 218
  Nicaragua, 390–391, 393–395
  Philippines, 344–347, 355, 356
  Portugal, 54, 55–59, 63–64
  Russia, 115, 120–124, 127
  Saudi Arabia, 174, 178–179
  Somalia, 235–236
  South Africa, 247–248, 249, 250–251,
    258–259
  Taiwan, 326–328, 335
  Turkey, 154–155, 156, 159–161, 162
  United States, 453, 454–457, 465, 466, 467
Child Abuse Prevention Act (1933) (Japan),
  289
Child Abuse Prevention Act (2000) (Japan),
  289–290
Child Abuse Prevention and Child Relief Act
  (1933) (Japan), 290
Child Abuse Prevention and Treatment Act
  (1974) (United States), 465
Child Abuse Resource Center (South Africa),
  259
Child Advocacy Committee (Saudi Arabia),
  185
Child and Adolescent Statute (Brazil),
  400–401

Child and Youth Protection Center
  (Taiwan), 327
Child Care Amendment Act (South Africa),
  249
Child Justice Alliance (South Africa), 259
Child labor
  Colombia, 419
  India, 272
  Lebanon, 211, 214
  Nicaragua, 386, 390, 393–394
  Philippines, 347, 355
  Portugal, 57–59, 63–64
  Turkey, 156, 160
Childline South Africa, 259
Child maltreatment
  Greece, 146–147
  Israel, 191–193
  Russia, 120
  Saudi Arabia, 178–179
Child Pornography and the Trafficking of
  the Children for Sexual Purposes
  (Philippines), 356
Child Protection Register (England), 46
Child Protective Services (United States),
  455
Children Act (1948) (England), 45
Children Act (1989) (England), 35, 45–46
Children Act (1960) (India), 271
Children's Assessment Center (Iceland), 23
Children's House: Center for Child Sexual
  Abuse (Iceland), 30
Children's Movement for Peace (2002)
  (Colombia), 417
Children's Ombudsman (Iceland), 22
Children's Welfare Law (1973) (Taiwan), 335
Child Support Team (Canada), 434
Child Welfare Act (Iceland), 22
Child Welfare Act (1947) (Japan), 290, 297
Child Welfare (South Africa), 259
China, 480, 496
Chinese Children's Fund (Taiwan), 327
Chinese Fund for Children and Families in
  Taiwan, 335
Climbie, Victoria, 45
Collectivism
  abuse defined, 6–9
  Brazil, 402
  human rights paradigm, 495–496
  India, 267
  Philippines, 343
Colombia
  abuse defined

  emotional abuse, 416
  physical abuse, 416
  sexual abuse, 416
  verbal abuse, 416
child abuse
  child labor, 419
  extreme abuse, 423
  gender equality, 419
  individual rights, 419
  laws, 424
  mild abuse, 423
  neglect, 423
  patriarchal society, 423
  perspectives on, 423
  physical abuse, 423
  rape, 423
  services, 424
  sexual abuse, 422, 423, 424
  street children, 422
  violence statistics, 422
elder abuse, 423–424
  cultural context, 423–424
  extreme abuse, 424
  laws, 423
  mild abuse, 424
  moderate abuse, 424
  neglect, 424
  perspectives on, 424
  physical abuse, 424
family violence, 421–424
  human rights, 426
  human rights paradigm, 477, 488–489,
    493
  individual rights, 425
  intervention agenda, 426
  laws, 424–425
  patriarchal society, 425
  services, 425
  social experiments, 425
  trafficking, 420
macrosystem
  Catholicism, 417
  children's status, 419
  gender equality, 418
  gender inequality, 418
  general violence, 417–418
  human rights, 417
  individual rights, 418
  laws, 418
  women's status, 418
microsystem
  Catholicism, 419–420

family norms, 419–420
  patriarchal society, 419
  patrilineal society, 419
  sexual abuse, 419–420
military violence, 417–418, 420–421
  emotional abuse, 421
  human rights, 425
research overview
  capsule, 415–416
  sample, 416
spousal abuse
  extreme abuse, 421–422
  gender roles, 422
  husband abuse, 421–422
  machismo, 421
  marital rape, 425
  mild abuse, 421–422
  moderate abuse, 421–422
  perspectives on, 421–422
  physical abuse, 421
  wife abuse, 421–422
Committee for the Advancement of Women
    (Israel), 190
Community Care Act (1990) (England), 47
Consciousness raising, 495
Corporal punishment
  Brazil, 403, 404
  Canada, 436
  England, 35, 36, 38
  Germany, 96, 102
  Greece, 140–141, 146
  human rights paradigm, 486
  Iceland, 20–21
  implicit theories, 9–10
  India, 272, 273
  Israel, 192, 193, 201
  Italy, 75–76
  Japan, 292–293
  Korea, 305–306, 307, 308, 316
  Lebanon, 211
  Philippines, 345–346
  Russia, 115, 120, 123, 124
  Saudi Arabia, 174
  Taiwan, 326, 335
  Turkey, 156
  United States, 454–455, 456
Cultural connectivity (Somalia), 237
Culture, *see also* Abuse defined; Family
    norms; Gender roles; Machismo;
    Patriarchal society
  Australia, 366, 367, 370, 373–375
  Brazil, 401–402, 408, 412–413

Canada, 445, 447
Colombia, 423–424
India, 267–268, 273–274
Israel, 190, 198, 200
Italy, 71
Japan, 285, 286–288, 293, 295
Korea, 303–305, 315, 316–317
Lebanon, 210–211, 212–213, 214
Nicaragua, 384, 389
Philippines, 342–345, 351–352, 356–357
Portugal, 53–54
Saudi Arabia, 170–176, 179–180
Somalia, 224, 227, 229, 230–234, 235,
    236–237
South Africa, 248, 251–252, 257
Turkey, 153, 154, 155–156
United States, 452–453, 454

D

Depression, 486
Disciplinary practices, *see* Corporal
    punishment
Divorce
  Australia, 366
  India, 277–279
  Japan, 287
  Philippines, 348
  Somalia, 231, 232, 233
  Taiwan, 323
Domestic violence, *see also* Family violence;
    Same-sex couples
  Australia, 364–365, 371
  Brazil, 405–406, 407, 411–413
  England, 38–40, 41–42, 46
  Germany, 92, 93, 98–99, 102–103
  Greece, 133–134, 135–136, 146
  Iceland, 25–28
  India, 270–271, 277–279
  Israel, 195–198, 201–202
  Italy, 73–74, 75, 77–78, 82–84
  Japan, 289, 293–294
  Korea, 305–306, 310–311, 315–317
  Lebanon, 212, 218
  Portugal, 59–61, 64–65
  Russia, 116–119
  South Africa, 251–252, 253–254, 255, 259,
    260
Domestic Violence Act (1994) (Australia),
    365

Domestic Violence Action and Research
  Group (Japan), 293
Domestic Violence Bill (1998) (South Africa),
  249, 251
Domestic Violence Data Source (2001)
  (England), 39
Domestic Violence Intervention Project
  (Minnesota), 103
Domestic Violence Law (1991) (Israel), 201
Domestic Violence Prevention Law (1998)
  (Taiwan), 325–326
Domestic Violence Units (Australia), 365
Domestic worker abuse
  India, 277
  Lebanon, 216–217
Dowry abuse (India), 270, 273–274
Dowry Prohibition Act (1961) (India), 270

E

Ecological model
  aboriginal families (Australia), 372
  developmental-ecological context, 8
  developmental-psychological context, 8
  implicit theories, 8, 10
  intermediate interactional context, 8
EKOS Research Associates (Canada),
  433–434
Elder abuse, see also Financial abuse;
    Institutional abuse
  abuse defined, 3, 4–5, 6
  Australia, 370–371
  Brazil, 407–409, 410–411
  Canada, 443–446
  Colombia, 423–424
  England, 43–44, 47
  Germany, 92, 100–101, 103–104
  Greece, 143–146, 147–148
  Iceland, 28–29
  India, 276–277
  Israel, 198–199
  Italy, 79–81, 82
  Japan, 294–295, 297
  Korea, 312–314
  Lebanon, 214–215
  Nicaragua, 391
  Philippines, 351–353, 356
  Portugal, 61–63, 65
  Russia, 116, 124–126
  Saudi Arabia, 179–180

Somalia, 237
  South Africa, 256–258, 259–260
  Taiwan, 332, 333, 334, 335
  Turkey, 160–161
  United States, 454, 460–463, 466
Elder Protection Program (Australia), 374
Elder's Welfare Law (Taiwan), 325, 335
Emergency Sexual Assault Ward (Iceland),
  30
Emerge (United States), 466
Emotional abuse, see also Public
    humiliation; Shaming; Verbal abuse
  abuse defined, 3, 4–5
  Australia, 362–363, 367, 368–369, 370, 371
  Brazil, 403, 405, 406, 407, 408, 409
  Canada, 432, 434, 436, 438, 440
  Colombia, 416, 421–422
  England, 33–34, 36, 38, 39, 40, 43–44, 45
  Germany, 90, 91, 95, 96–97, 98, 99, 101, 102
  Greece, 132–133, 134, 137–138, 143, 145,
    146–147
  Iceland, 18, 25, 27
  India, 266
  Israel, 188–189, 191, 192–194, 198–200
  Italy, 70, 73–74, 77, 78, 79, 81
  Japan, 285, 290, 291, 292, 293, 294, 296
  Korea, 302, 306, 307, 309, 311–312, 313–314,
    315
  Lebanon, 206, 215, 216
  Nicaragua, 389, 390
  Philippines, 340, 346–347, 349–350, 353
  Portugal, 52, 63
  Russia, 112, 117, 118, 123, 124, 125–126
  Saudi Arabia, 168, 177, 179, 180
  South Africa, 246, 251, 252, 255, 256, 258
  Taiwan, 322, 323, 326–327, 328, 329, 331,
    333
  Turkey, 153, 158–159, 159, 160
  United States, 452, 457, 459, 460–461,
    464–465
End Child Abuse Prostitution (Philippines),
  356
England
  abuse defined
    child abuse, 37–38
    corporal punishment, 38
    elder abuse, 43
    emotional abuse, 33–34, 38
    extreme abuse, 34
    implicit theories, 33–34
    neglect, 37
    physical abuse, 34, 37

sexual abuse, 34, 37
verbal abuse, 33–34
child abuse
corporal punishment, 35, 36, 38
emotional abuse, 36, 38, 45
extreme abuse, 37, 38
human rights, 35
implicit theories, 38
laws, 35, 44–46
mild abuse, 38
moderate abuse, 38
neglect, 36, 37, 45–46
perspectives on, 37–38
physical abuse, 36–37, 38
prevalence, 36–37
risk factors, 35–36
services, 44–46
sexual abuse, 36, 37, 38, 45
domestic violence
implicit theories, 40
laws, 46
male victims, 41
perspectives on, 39–40
prevalence, 38–39
rape, 39–40
services, 46
elder abuse
alcohol consumption, 43
emotional abuse, 43–44
extreme abuse, 43–44
financial abuse, 43, 44
laws, 47
mild, 43, 44
moderate abuse, 43, 44
neglect, 43, 44
perspectives on, 43–44
physical abuse, 42, 43, 44
prevalence, 43
risk factors, 43
services, 47
sexual abuse, 44
verbal abuse, 43
family violence, 36–44
human rights paradigm, 482, 483, 484, 491
macrosystem
children's status, 35
gender inequality, 34–35
women's status, 34–35
microsystem, 36–38
research overview
capsule, 33

sample, 33
summary, 47–48
spousal abuse
alcohol consumption, 39, 41
emotional abuse, 38, 39, 40
extreme abuse, 38–39, 40, 41, 42
financial abuse, 38
husband abuse, 41–42
implicit theories, 41, 42
laws, 46
marital rape, 39, 40, 41
mild abuse, 40, 41, 42
moderate abuse, 40, 41, 42
perspectives on, 40–42
physical abuse, 38–39, 40, 41, 42
prevalence, 38–39, 40, 41
risk factors, 39
services, 46
sexual abuse, 38, 41–42
verbal abuse, 42
wife abuse, 40–41
Equal Pay and Sex Discrimination Act (1975) (England), 35
Equal Rights for Women Law (2000) (Israel), 202
Eugenic Protection Law (1957) (Japan), 290
European Economic Community (EEC), 53
European Monetary Union (EU), 53
Explicit theories, 10
Extraordinary victimization, 483
Extreme abuse, see also Mild abuse; Moderate abuse
abuse defined, 3, 4–6
Australia, 368, 369–370, 371
Brazil, 404–405, 406, 407, 408–409
Canada, 432, 433, 436, 439, 440, 441
Colombia, 421–422, 423, 424
England, 34, 37, 38–39, 40, 41, 42, 43–44
Germany, 95, 96, 97, 98, 99, 101
Greece, 136–137, 138, 142, 143, 145, 146
Iceland, 18, 22, 26–27, 29
India, 266, 267, 272, 274, 275, 276, 277
Israel, 193, 194, 195, 196, 198, 199
Italy, 70, 75, 76, 79, 80, 81
Japan, 285, 291, 292–293, 294, 295, 296
Korea, 302–303, 309, 311–312, 314, 315
Lebanon, 209, 211, 212–214, 215, 216, 217
Nicaragua, 382, 384, 386, 387–389, 390–391
Philippines, 340, 348, 349, 351, 352
Portugal, 56
Russia, 112, 116, 117, 119, 122, 123, 125, 126
Saudi Arabia, 168, 177, 179, 180

Extreme abuse *(cont.)*
  Somalia, 224, 234, 235, 236
  South Africa, 246, 251, 253, 255, 257–258
  Taiwan, 322, 327–328, 329–330, 331,
    332–333, 334
  Turkey, 153, 156, 160
  United States, 455, 456, 457, 458, 459–460,
    461, 462, 463, 464, 465

F

Family and Child Support Project (Portugal),
    56
Family and Marriage Society of South Africa,
    259
Family Code (1966) (Germany), 94–95
Family Courts Act (1997) (Philippines), 355
Family Law Act (1995) (Australia), 367–368
Family Law Act (1996) (England), 46, 47
Family Law (1975) (Somalia), 238
Family norms, *see also* Gender roles;
    Machismo; Patriarchal society
  Colombia, 419–420
  Germany, 94–95
  Greece, 135, 138, 140, 143
  human rights paradigm, 478, 480, 481
  India, 268–269, 274, 276, 277
  Israel, 190–191, 192, 195
  Italy, 71–72, 73, 74–76, 78, 80, 81
  Japan, 286, 287–288, 295
  Korea, 303–305, 314–315
  Lebanon, 206–207, 210–211, 212, 214–215
  Nicaragua, 384, 387–389
  Philippines, 341–343
  Portugal, 53–54, 55–56, 59–60, 61, 62
  Russia, 113–114, 115, 120, 122, 124–125
  Saudi Arabia, 170, 172, 174, 177, 179–180
  Somalia, 230–234, 235–237
  Taiwan, 324–325, 329, 330, 332, 334
  Turkey, 154–155, 160–161
Family violence, *see also* Child abuse; Elder
    abuse; Human rights paradigm; In-
    laws; Same-sex couples; Sibling
    abuse; Spousal abuse
  Australia, 366–373
  Brazil, 402–409
  Canada, 433–434, 435–446
  Colombia, 421–424
  England, 36–44
  Germany, 95–101
  Greece, 135–146
  Iceland, 20–29
  India, 270–277
  Israel, 190–200
  Italy, 75–81
  Japan, 288–296
  Korea, 306–316
  Lebanon, 212–218
  Nicaragua, 388–391
  Philippines, 344–354
  Portugal, 55–63
  Russia, 113–114, 116–126
  Saudi Arabia, 174–181
  Somalia, 234–237
  South Africa, 249–258
  Taiwan, 325–335
  Turkey, 156–161
  United States, 453–465
Family Violence and Sexual Violation
    Prevention Center (Taiwan), 328
Female genital mutilation (FGM), 238–239
Financial abuse
  Australia, 370, 371
  Brazil, 408, 409
  Canada, 445–446
  England, 38, 43, 44
  Germany, 101
  Greece, 138, 143, 145, 146
  Iceland, 29
  Italy, 78, 80
  Korea, 305, 310, 312, 313, 314, 315
  Lebanon, 215
  Nicaragua, 391
  Philippines, 352–353
  Portugal, 62
  Russia, 125, 126
  Saudi Arabia, 180
  South Africa, 246, 252, 253, 257–258
  Taiwan, 332, 333
  Turkey, 161
  United States, 460–461, 462
Flying Broom (Turkey), 162
Foundation for the Evaluation of Women's
    Labor (Turkey), 162
Fourth Country Programme of Cooperation
    of the Filipino Government and
    UNICEF (1994–1998), 355
Fourth World Conference on Women's
    Rights (1995) (Beijing), 401

G

Gay/lesbian couples, *see* Same-sex couples
Gender equality, *see also* Women's
    movement
  Brazil, 401
  Colombia, 418, 419
  Germany, 91, 92–93, 102
  Greece, 133, 135–136
  human rights paradigm, 493
  Iceland, 23–24
  Israel, 190, 202
  Korea, 303
  Lebanon, 209, 210, 218
  Nicaragua, 392–393
  Philippines, 342
  Portugal, 55, 61
  Russia, 113
  Saudi Arabia, 175–176
  Somalia, 230, 238
  South Africa, 248
  Turkey, 153–154
Gender inequality
  Colombia, 418
  England, 34–35
  human rights paradigm, 475
  India, 268–269, 272, 273, 277–278
  Israel, 189
  Japan, 286–287
  Korea, 303–304
  Lebanon, 210
  Philippines, 347
  South Africa, 248
  Taiwan, 324–325
  Turkey, 155
Gender roles
  Colombia, 422
  Greece, 133, 134, 140
  human rights paradigm, 488–489
  India, 271
  Israel, 189
  Italy, 79
  Japan, 286
  Korea, 310
  Lebanon, 212, 213
  Nicaragua, 383–384, 389, 391
  Philippines, 341, 342, 344, 350–351
  Portugal, 59, 60
  Russia, 113–114, 115, 117–118
  Saudi Arabia, 170–173
  Somalia, 238
  South Africa, 248, 255
  Taiwan, 324

German Children Protection League, 102
German Parliamentary Act, Action Plan 1
    (1999), 98–99
Germany
  abuse defined
    child abuse, 90–91
    domestic violence, 99
    elder abuse, 90
    emotional abuse, 90, 91
    mild abuse, 90
    physical abuse, 90, 91
    sexual abuse, 90
    spousal abuse, 90, 91
    verbal abuse, 90, 91
  child abuse
    corporal punishment, 96, 102
    emotional abuse, 95, 96–97, 98, 102
    extreme abuse, 95, 96, 97, 98
    historical context, 95–96
    individual rights, 101–102
    laws, 92, 101–102
    mild abuse, 98
    moderate abuse, 98
    neglect, 97
    perspectives on, 98
    physical abuse, 95, 96–97, 98
    prevalence, 96–97
    services, 102
    sexual abuse, 97–98
    verbal abuse, 98
  domestic violence
    emotional abuse, 99
    gender equality, 102
    laws, 92, 93, 98–99, 103
    perspectives on, 99
    physical abuse, 99
    policy approach, 102
    rape, 103
    services, 92, 93, 99, 103
    verbal abuse, 99
    women's movement, 102–103
  elder abuse
    emotional abuse, 101
    extreme abuse, 101
    financial abuse, 101
    institutional abuse, 101
    laws, 92, 104
    mild abuse, 101
    moderate abuse, 101
    perspectives, 101
    physical abuse, 101
    prevalence, 100
    services, 100, 103–104

Germany *(cont.)*
  family violence, 95–101
    human rights paradigm, 480, 482, 489,
      490, 491
  macrosystem
    Federal Republic of Germany (FRG),
      91–94
    gender equality, 91, 92–93
    German Democratic Republic (GDR),
      91–94
    government, 92
    historical context, 91–92
    reunification, 91, 93–94
    women's role, 92–93
  microsystem, 94–95
  research overview
    capsule, 89
    conclusion, 104
    sample, 89–90
  spousal abuse
    extreme abuse, 99
    husband abuse, 99
    laws, 103
    marital rape, 103
    mild abuse, 99
    moderate abuse, 99
    perspectives on, 99
    physical abuse, 99
    services, 103
    sexual abuse, 99
    wife abuse, 99
Global Initiative to end all Corporal
      Punishment of Children (2001), 211
Good Protection for All Women (Australia),
      374
Gray Panthers (Germany), 100
Greece
  abuse defined
    emotional abuse, 132–133
    human rights, 132
    individual rights, 132–133
    physical abuse, 132–133
  child abuse
    child maltreatment, 146–147
    corporal punishment, 140–141, 146
    emotional abuse, 143, 146–147
    extreme abuse, 142, 143
    family norms, 140
    financial abuse, 143
    gender roles, 140
    laws, 146–147
    mild abuse, 143

    moderate abuse, 143
    neglect, 138–143, 139, 141, 143, 146–147
    perspectives on, 142–143
    physical abuse, 139, 141, 142, 143
    prevalence, 139, 141
    rape, 147
    research review, 138–142
    risk factors, 139
    sexual abuse, 139, 143, 147
    verbal abuse, 141, 142, 143
  domestic violence
    emotional abuse, 134
    gender equality, 135–136
    laws, 133–134
    physical abuse, 134
    prevalence, 134, 136
    rape, 133–134
    services, 146
  elder abuse
    abandonment, 144
    emotional abuse, 145
    extreme abuse, 145, 146
    family norms, 143
    financial abuse, 145, 146
    laws, 147–148
    mild abuse, 146
    moderate abuse, 145, 146
    neglect, 144, 145
    perspectives on, 145–146
    physical abuse, 144, 145
    prevalence, 144
    verbal abuse, 144, 145, 146
  family violence, 135–146
    human rights paradigm, 482, 483–484,
      488, 489, 491, 494
  macrosystem
    children's status, 134–135
    elder status, 135
    family norms, 135
    gender equality, 133
    gender roles, 133, 134
    media violence, 133
    women's status, 133–134
  microsystem, 135
  research overview
    capsule, 131–132
    conclusion, 148
    sample, 132
  spousal abuse
    emotional abuse, 137–138
    extreme abuse, 136–137, 138
    family norms, 138

financial abuse, 138
gender inequality, 138
husband abuse, 138
implicit theories, 136–138
marital rape, 137
mild abuse, 137, 138
moderate abuse, 137, 138
patriarchal society, 138
perspectives on, 136–138
physical abuse, 136–137, 138
prevalence, 136
sexual abuse, 137
verbal abuse, 138
wife abuse, 136–138
Gulf Cooperation Council (GCC), 181

H

Hague Convention on the Civil Aspects of
    International Child Abduction Act
    (1996), 249
Halt Elder Abuse Line (South Africa),
    259–260
Health Services and Public Health Act (1968)
    (England), 47
Help lines
    Brazil, 410
    Italy, 76, 83
    Japan, 286, 290, 297
    Korea, 315–316
    Lebanon, 212
    South Africa, 259–260
    Taiwan, 335
    United States, 466
HIV/AIDS
    Somalia, 240, 241
    South Africa, 247–248, 254, 256
Home Office Targeted Policing Initiative
    (2001) (England), 41
Homicide Survey (1997) (Canada), 435
Homosexuals, see Same-sex couples
Hotlines, see Help lines
Human rights, see also Individual rights
    Brazil, 402
    Colombia, 417, 425, 426
    England, 35
    Greece, 132
    Iceland, 20, 22
    implicit theories, 10
    Japan, 285, 289

Korea, 304, 308
Portugal, 56
Russia, 127, 128
Saudi Arabia, 181
Somalia, 238
South Africa, 257
Human rights paradigm
    abuse research implications, 478–486
    Australia, 489, 491, 493
    Brazil, 477, 481, 482, 484, 488–489, 491, 492,
        493
    Canada, 479, 483, 484, 489, 491
    China, 480, 496
    Colombia, 477, 488–489, 493
    cultural saliency
        collectivism, 495–496
        consciousness raising, 495
        coping strategies, 491
        economic context, 496
        family defined, 487–488
        family structure, 487, 488–490
        gender equality, 493
        gender roles, 488–489
        implementation strategies, 487, 494–495
        implicit theories, 494
        indigenous principles, 487, 492
        indigenous protest movements, 487,
            492–493
        international treaties, 494–495
        macrosystem factors, 487, 490–491
        microsystem factors, 490
        nongovernmental organizations (NGOs),
            492–493
        poverty, 491
        services, 494
        shaming, 495–496
        social change, 491
        social equality, 496
        social roles, 488–490
        social structures, 487, 493–494
        stress, 490–491
        women's movement, 493, 495
    England, 482, 483, 484, 491
    family violence
        abuse research implications, 478–486
        acute victimization, 483
        consequences of, 485–486
        corporal punishment, 486
        cultural context, 480
        cultural sensitivity, 488
        cultural specificity, 473, 488
        depression, 486

Human rights paradigm *(cont.)*
  family violence *(cont.)*
    expectations about, 484–485
    experience of, 485
    extraordinary victimization, 483
    family context, 474
    family norms, 480, 481
    implicit theories, 478–479, 483–484,
      485–486
    manifestations, 481–483
    pandemic victimization, 483
    perspectives on, 483–484
    posttraumatic stress disorder (PTSD),
      486
    prevalence, 479
    public awareness, 479–480
    social norms, 481
    societal context, 474
    stress, 486
    terminology, 480
    vulnerable populations, 481
  family violence application
    best-practices approach, 474–475
    family norms, 478
    gender inequality, 475
    implicit theories, 476–477
    individual rights, 475–476
    limitations, 477–478
    replacement hypothesis, 476
    universal principles, 474–478
  Germany, 480, 482, 489, 490, 491
  Greece, 482, 483–484, 488, 489, 491, 494
  Iceland, 480, 484
  India, 481, 482, 487–488, 489, 491, 492
  Israel, 482, 483, 484, 489, 491, 492, 494
  Italy, 480, 481, 482, 483, 484, 487–489
  Japan, 480, 481, 482, 483, 487–488, 489
  Korea, 481, 483, 484, 487–488, 489
  Lebanon, 481, 482, 487–488, 489, 491
  Nicaragua, 477, 482, 487, 489, 491, 492
  Philippines, 477, 481, 482, 483–484, 488–489,
    491, 492, 496
  Portugal, 480, 482, 488–489, 490, 491
  research conclusion, 496–497
  Russia, 480, 482, 488–489
  Saudi Arabia, 476, 481, 482, 483, 484,
    487–489, 490, 493, 494
  Somalia, 481, 482, 487–488, 489, 491
  South Africa, 482, 484, 487–488, 489, 491,
    493
  Taiwan, 481, 482, 483, 484, 488–489, 490

  Turkey, 480, 481, 482, 483, 484, 487–488,
    489, 492, 493, 494
  United States, 474, 479, 480, 481, 482, 483,
    486, 488, 491
Human Rights Report (2000), 156

I

Iceland
  abuse defined
    emotional abuse, 18
    extreme abuse, 18
    implicit theories, 18
    individual freedom, 18
    individual rights, 18
    personal independence, 18
    physical abuse, 18
  child abuse
    corporal punishment, 20–21
    extreme abuse, 22
    human rights, 20, 22
    individual freedom, 21–22
    laws, 20, 22, 23
    moderate abuse, 22
    perspectives on, 22
    physical abuse, 22
    Scandinavian method, 20
    services, 22–23, 29–30
    sexual abuse, 22–23
  domestic violence, 25–27
  elder abuse
    extreme abuse, 29
    financial abuse, 29
    mild abuse, 29
    moderate abuse, 29
    perspectives on, 29
    physical abuse, 28, 29
    prevalence, 28–29
  family violence, 20–29
    human rights paradigm, 480, 484
  macrosystem, 18–19
  microsystem, 19–20
  research overview
    capsule, 17
    conclusion, 29–30
    sample, 17–18
  spousal abuse
    alcohol consumption, 26–27
    emotional abuse, 25, 27
    extreme abuse, 26–28

gender equality, 23–24
implicit theories, 26
laws, 24, 27–28
marital rape, 27, 28
perspectives on, 26–28
physical abuse, 23–24, 25, 27–28
prevalence, 25
services, 25, 29–30
sexual abuse, 25, 27, 28
women's movement, 25
Immigrant groups (Australia), 371
Implicit theories, *see also* Abuse defined
Australia, 362, 365, 369
Brazil, 403, 404, 405, 407, 408–409
Canada, 432–433, 435–436
England, 33–34, 38, 40, 41, 42
Greece, 136–138
human rights paradigm, 475, 478–479,
    483–484, 485–486, 494
Iceland, 18, 26
Israel, 193–194, 196
Japan, 285, 292, 294, 296
Korea, 302–303, 308, 314, 317
Lebanon, 212–213, 214
Nicaragua, 382, 388, 391
Philippines, 348
Portugal, 51–52
Russia, 113, 116, 117, 118, 123, 127–128
South Africa, 253
Taiwan, 323
Turkey, 153, 157–158, 159, 161
United States, 452, 454, 457, 460
Independent self-view, 6–7
India
abuse defined
    alcohol consumption, 266
    emotional abuse, 266
    extreme abuse, 266, 267
    maltreatment, 266–267
    mild abuse, 266, 267
    moderate abuse, 267
    neglect, 266
    physical abuse, 266
    sexual abuse, 266
    verbal abuse, 266
child abuse
    child labor, 272
    corporal punishment, 272, 273
    extreme abuse, 272
    female infanticide, 271, 272, 273
    gender inequality, 272, 273
    laws, 271

moderate abuse, 272, 273
neglect, 271
perspectives on, 272–273
physical abuse, 272
prenatal sex selection, 271, 272, 273
domestic violence
    gender inequality, 278
    laws, 277–278
    rape, 270
    services, 277–279
    women's shelters, 278, 280–281
domestic worker abuse
    extreme abuse, 277
    mild abuse, 277
    moderate abuse, 277
    physical abuse, 277
    sexual abuse, 277
    verbal abuse, 277
elder abuse
    elder status, 276, 277
    extreme abuse, 277
    family norms, 276, 277
    father-in-law, 276–277
    neglect, 277
    perspectives on, 276–277
family violence, 270–277
    human rights paradigm, 481, 482,
        487–488, 489, 491, 492
    laws, 270–271
    women's movement, 271
macrosystem
    caste system, 268
    collectivism, 267
    cultural context, 267
    media, 268
    patriarchal society, 267
    patrilineal society, 267
microsystem
    elder status, 269
    family norms, 268–269
    gender inequality, 269
    patrilineal society, 269
research overview
    capsule, 265–266
    sample, 266
spousal abuse
    alcohol consumption, 274
    daughter-in-law, 273–274
    divorce, 277–279
    dowry abuse, 273–274
    dowry death, 270
    extreme abuse, 274, 275, 276

India *(cont.)*
  spousal abuse *(cont.)*
    family norms, 274
    gender roles, 271
    husband abuse, 275–276
    laws, 270–271, 277–278
    marital rape, 275
    mild abuse, 274, 275, 276
    moderate abuse, 274, 275, 276
    mother-in-law, 273
    patriarchal society, 273
    perspectives on, 274–276
    physical abuse, 274, 275–276
    public humiliation, 275
    services, 277–279
    sexual abuse, 275
    wife abuse, 270–271, 273–275, 277–279
Indian Country Child Abuse Hotline (United
    States), 467
Individual freedom
  Australia, 369–370, 371
  Iceland, 18, 21–22
  Italy, 73
  Lebanon, 212–213
  Somalia, 225, 229
  South Africa, 248, 249
Individualism
  abuse defined, 6–9
  Brazil, 412–413
Individual rights, *see also* Gender equality;
    Human rights; Laws; Women's
    movement
  Australia, 364–365
  Colombia, 418, 419, 425
  Germany, 101–102
  Greece, 132–133
  human rights paradigm, 475–476
  Iceland, 18–19
  Italy, 70
  Lebanon, 218
  Nicaragua, 393
  Portugal, 54, 55, 56–57, 62, 63
  Russia, 123
  Somalia, 238
  South Africa, 249–250
Infanticide
  Canada, 435
  India, 271, 272, 273
  Japan, 288
  Saudi Arabia, 178
In-laws
  daughter-in-law

Brazil, 407
India, 273–274
Japan, 295, 296
Korea, 314–315
Taiwan, 334–335
  father-in-law (India), 276–277
  mother-in-law
India, 273
Japan, 295, 296
Korea, 314–315
Lebanon, 217
Taiwan, 334–335
Institute of Support for Children (Portugal),
    63
Institute on Domestic Violence in the
    African-American Community (United
    States), 467
Institutional abuse
  Germany, 101
  Russia, 121–122
  South Africa, 258
  United States, 462–463
Inter-American Commission on Human
    Rights, 409–410
Inter-American Convention on the Granting
    of Civil Rights to Women, 418
Interdepartmental Working Party on
    Domestic Violence (England), 46
Interdependent self-view, 6–7
International Labor Organization, 58
International Labor Organization Convention
    182 (1999), 355
International Monetary Fund, 305
International Network for the Prevention of
    Elder Abuse (INPEA), 408
International Programme on Elimination of
    Child Labour (IPEC), 58, 162
International treaties, 494–495
Internet resources
  Canada, 449
  United States, 466–467
Intervention strategies, *see* Laws; Services
Israel
  abuse defined
    domestic violence, 188–189
    emotional abuse, 188–189
    physical abuse, 188
    sexual abuse, 188
  child abuse
    child maltreatment, 191–193
    corporal punishment, 192, 193, 201
    cultural context, 200

emotional abuse, 191, 192–194
extreme abuse, 193, 194
family norms, 192
implicit theories, 193–194
individual rights, 201
laws, 200–201
mild abuse, 193, 194
moderate abuse, 193, 194
neglect, 191–193, 194
obligatory reporting law, 200
perspectives on, 193–195
physical abuse, 191–193, 194, 200–201
prevalence, 192–193
research review, 191–192
services, 202
sexual abuse, 191–193, 194–195, 200, 201
domestic violence
family norms, 195
gender equality, 202
laws, 201–202
physical abuse, 195, 196–197
prevalence, 195–196
women's shelters, 195, 196, 197–198, 202
elder abuse
emotional abuse, 198–199
extreme abuse, 198
mild abuse, 198
neglect, 198
physical abuse, 198, 199
prevalence, 198
verbal abuse, 199
family violence, 190–200
family norms, 190–191
mild abuse, 191
moderate abuse, 191
religious impact, 190–191, 202
macrosystem
children's status, 190
family norms, 190
gender equality, 190
gender inequality, 189
gender roles, 189
kibbutz, 190
laws, 190
women's status, 189–190
research overview
capsule, 187
conclusion, 202
sample, 187–188
sibling abuse
emotional abuse, 199–200
extreme abuse, 199

mild abuse, 199
moderate abuse, 199
physical abuse, 199
sexual abuse, 199
spousal abuse
extreme abuse, 195, 196
implicit theories, 196
laws, 201–202
marital rape, 195, 196
mild abuse, 196
moderate abuse, 196
physical abuse, 190, 195, 196
services, 202
sexual abuse, 196
wife abuse, 195–198
women's shelters, 202
Italian Institute of Statistics (ISTAT), 77–78
Italian National Health Service, 82
Italy
abuse defined
child abuse, 70
domestic violence, 70
elder abuse, 70
emotional abuse, 70
extreme abuse, 70
family norms, 71
individual rights, 70
machismo, 71
mild abuse, 71
moderate abuse, 71
physical abuse, 70–71
sexual abuse, 70–71
child abuse
corporal punishment, 75–76
extreme abuse, 76
family norms, 75–76
laws, 81–82
mild abuse, 76
moderate abuse, 76
neglect, 76
perspectives on, 76–77
physical abuse, 76–77
prevalence, 76
risk factors, 76
services, 76, 81–82, 83–84
sexual abuse, 76–77, 81–82
domestic violence
alcohol consumption, 75
emotional abuse, 73–74, 77
extreme abuse, 75
family norms, 78
laws, 78, 82–83

Italy *(cont.)*
  domestic violence *(cont.)*
    physical abuse, 75, 77, 78
    prevalence, 77
    services, 73, 78, 82, 83–84
    sexual abuse, 77–78
  elder abuse, 79–81
    abandonment, 80, 81
    emotional abuse, 81
    extreme abuse, 80, 81
    family norms, 80, 81
    financial abuse, 80
    mild abuse, 80, 81
    moderate abuse, 80, 81
    neglect, 80, 81
    perspectives on, 80–81
    physical abuse, 81
    services, 80, 82
    verbal abuse, 81
  family violence, 75–81
    human rights paradigm, 480, 481, 482, 483, 484, 487–489
  macrosystem
    Catholicism, 71–72, 81–82
    cultural context, 71
    family norms, 71–72, 73
    gender inequality, 73
    individual freedom, 73
    laws, 72
    lifestyle, 71
    Mafia, 71–72
    patriarchal society, 72
    women's status, 72–73
  microsystem, 73–75
    family norms, 74–75
    patriarchal society, 74–75
  research overview
    capsule, 69–70
    conclusion, 84
    sample, 70
  same-sex couples, 72
  spousal abuse
    alcohol consumption, 75
    emotional abuse, 74, 78, 79
    extreme abuse, 79
    financial abuse, 78
    gender roles, 79
    husband abuse, 79
    laws, 82
    mild abuse, 74, 78, 79
    moderate abuse, 74, 75, 78, 79
    perspectives on, 78, 79
    physical abuse, 76, 79
    prevalence, 79
    public humiliation, 74
    services, 82
    sexual abuse, 79
    wife abuse, 78

J

Japan
  abuse defined
    cultural context, 285
    emotional abuse, 285
    extreme abuse, 285
    human rights, 285
    implicit theories, 285
    neglect, 285
    physical abuse, 285
    sexual abuse, 285
  child abuse
    bullying, 296
    child trafficking, 288
    corporal punishment, 292–293
    emotional abuse, 290, 291, 292
    extreme abuse, 291, 292–293
    implicit theories, 292
    infanticide, 288, 290
    laws, 289–290, 297
    mild abuse, 292–293
    moderate abuse, 291, 292
    neglect, 290, 291
    perspectives on, 292–293
    physical abuse, 288, 289–290, 291, 292, 293
    prevalence, 290–291
    prostitution, 288
    rape, 289
    services, 286, 290, 296–297
    sexual abuse, 288, 289, 290–291, 292–293
    verbal abuse, 292
  domestic violence
    defined, 289
    rape, 293
    sexual abuse, 293–294
  elder abuse, 294–295
    cultural context, 295
    daughter-in-law, 295
    extreme abuse, 295
    family norms, 295
    laws, 297

mother-in-law, 295
neglect, 295
perspectives on, 295
physical abuse, 295
prevalence, 295
verbal abuse, 295
family violence, 288–296
field emergence, 288–289
human rights, 289
human rights paradigm, 480, 481, 482,
483, 487–488, 489
laws, 289–290
patriarchal society, 288–289
women's movement, 289
macrosystem
cultural context, 285
gender roles, 286
media, 286
rape, 286
microsystem
childhood, 288
Confucianism, 286
cultural context, 287–288
divorce, 287
family norms, 286, 287–288
family status, 287–288
marriage, 286–287
patriarchal society, 286
women's status, 286
mother-in-law, 295, 296
research overview
capsule, 283–284
sample, 284
sibling abuse
emotional abuse, 296
extreme abuse, 296
mild abuse, 296
moderate abuse, 296
perspectives on, 295–296
physical abuse, 296
sexual abuse, 296
spousal abuse
alcohol consumption, 293, 294
emotional abuse, 293, 294
extreme abuse, 294
implicit theories, 294
laws, 297
mild abuse, 294
moderate abuse, 294
perspectives on, 294
physical abuse, 293, 294
services, 297

sexual abuse, 293
verbal abuse, 294
Japanese Institute of Life Insurance, 286–287
Jidou Soudan Center (Japan), 291
Joint Churches Domestic Violence
Prevention Project (Australia), 374
Justices Act (1989) (Australia), 365

K

Kaohsiung Lifeline Association (Taiwan), 328
Kidnapping (Canada), 436
King Faisal Specialist Hospital and Research
Center (Saudi Arabia), 184–185
Korea
abuse defined
alcohol consumption, 302
child abuse, 306–307
Confucianism, 303
domestic violence, 305–306, 315–316
elder abuse, 313
emotional abuse, 302
extreme abuse, 302–303
family norms, 303
implicit theories, 302–303
mild abuse, 303
moderate abuse, 303
patriarchal society, 303
physical abuse, 302
sexual violence, 309
child abuse
child maltreatment, 306–309
Confucianism, 308
corporal punishment, 305–306, 307, 308,
316
emotional abuse, 306, 307, 309
extreme abuse, 309
human rights, 308
implicit theories, 308
laws, 305–306, 315
moderate abuse, 308, 309
neglect, 306, 307
perspectives on, 307–309
physical abuse, 306, 307, 308, 309
prevalence, 305, 307
sexual abuse, 306, 307, 308–309
verbal abuse, 307
domestic violence
abandonment, 305
Confucianism, 316

Korea *(cont.)*
  domestic violence *(cont.)*
    cultural context, 316–317
    emotional abuse, 315
    financial abuse, 315
    implicit theories, 317
    laws, 305–306, 316
    perspectives on, 316–317
    physical abuse, 315
    services, 315–316
    sexual abuse, 315
    spousal abuse, 316
  elder abuse
    abandonment, 313, 314
    emotional abuse, 312, 313–314
    extreme abuse, 314
    family norms, 314
    financial abuse, 313, 314
    implicit theories, 314
    laws, 312
    mild abuse, 314
    neglect, 313
    perspectives on, 313–314
    physical abuse, 312–313
    prevalence, 313
    sexual abuse, 313
    verbal abuse, 312, 313–314
  family violence, 306–316
    human rights paradigm, 481, 483, 484,
      487–488, 489
  macrosystem
    children's roles, 304
    Confucianism, 303–304
    cultural context, 303–305
    family norms, 303–305
    gender equality, 303
    gender inequality, 303–304
    human rights, 304
    laws, 304, 305–306
    patrilineal society, 304
  mother-in-law
    cultural context, 315
    daughter-in-law, 314–315
    extreme abuse, 315
    family norms, 314–315
    moderate abuse, 315
    patriarchal society, 314–315
  research overview
    capsule, 301
    conclusion, 316–317
    sample, 302
  sibling abuse
    emotional abuse, 311–312
    extreme abuse, 311–312
    financial abuse, 312
    mild abuse, 312
    moderate abuse, 312
    perspectives on, 311–312
    physical abuse, 311
    rape, 312
    sexual abuse, 311–312
    verbal abuse, 311–312
  spousal abuse
    alcohol consumption, 309
    extreme abuse, 309, 311
    financial abuse, 305, 310
    gender roles, 310
    marital rape, 305, 306, 309, 310–311
    mild abuse, 310
    moderate abuse, 310, 311
    neglect, 310
    patriarchal society, 310
    perspectives on, 310–311
    physical abuse, 305, 309, 310
    prevalence, 309–310
    services, 315–316
    sexual abuse, 309, 310–311
    verbal abuse, 305, 309, 310
Korean Association for Preventing Child
  Abuse, 306–307
Korean Institute for Health and Social
  Affairs, 307, 309
Korean Legal Aid Center For Family
  Relations, 309, 312
Korean Society for Study of Elder Abuse,
  312, 313
Kouao, Marie-Therese, 45

L

Las Chicas (Nicaragua), 395
Law for the Prevention of Abuse of Minors
  and the Helpless (1989) (Israel),
  200–201
Law of Evidence-Child Protection (1983)
  (Israel), 200
Laws, *see also* Services; *specific legislation*
  Australia, 364–365, 367–368
  Brazil, 400–401, 409–412
  Colombia, 418, 423, 424–425
  England, 35, 44–46, 47
  Germany, 92, 93, 98–99, 101–102, 103, 104

Greece, 133–134, 146–148
Iceland, 20, 22, 23, 24, 27–28
India, 270–271, 277–278
Israel, 190, 200–202
Italy, 72, 78, 81–83
Japan, 289–290, 297
Korea, 304, 305–306, 312, 315, 316
Lebanon, 209, 211, 217, 218
Nicaragua, 388, 393
Philippines, 355–356
Portugal, 56, 59, 61, 62, 63, 64, 65
Russia, 122
Somalia, 238, 239
South Africa, 249–250, 251
Taiwan, 325–326, 335
Turkey, 155, 162
United States, 452–454, 460, 463, 465–466
Lebanon
 abuse defined
  emotional abuse, 206
  family norms, 206–207, 212
  patriarchal society, 206–207
  physical abuse, 206
  sexual abuse, 206
  sibling abuse, 215–216
  verbal abuse, 206
 child abuse
  child labor, 211, 214
  corporal punishment, 211
  extreme abuse, 209, 211, 213–214
  gender equality, 218
  implicit theories, 214
  individual rights, 218
  laws, 211, 218
  mild abuse, 214
  moderate abuse, 214
  neglect, 214
  perspectives on, 213–214
  physical abuse, 214
  rape, 213–214
  services, 218
  sexual abuse, 213–214
 domestic violence
  gender equality, 218
  individual rights, 218
  laws, 218
  services, 218
 domestic worker abuse
  emotional abuse, 216
  extreme abuse, 216, 217
  laws, 217
  mild abuse, 217
  moderate abuse, 217
  physical abuse, 216, 217
  sexual abuse, 216
  verbal abuse, 217
 elder abuse
  abandonment, 215
  emotional abuse, 215
  extreme abuse, 215
  family norms, 214–215
  financial abuse, 215
  mild abuse, 215
  moderate abuse, 215
  neglect, 215
  perspectives on, 215
  physical abuse, 215
  services, 215
  verbal abuse, 215
 extended family
  grandparents, 217
  mother-in-law, 217
  nephews/nieces, 217–218
  uncles/aunts, 217–218
 family violence, 212–218
  human rights paradigm, 481, 482,
   487–488, 489, 491
 macrosystem
  economy, 208–209
  gender equality, 209, 210
  gender inequality, 210
  historical context, 207–208
  laws, 209
  national legal policy, 209
  postwar reconstruction, 209
  religion, 209
  women's status, 209–210
 microsystem
  children's status, 211–212
  cultural context, 210–211
  family norms, 210–211
  patriarchal connectivity, 211
 research overview
  capsule, 205–206
  conclusion, 218
  sample, 206
 same-sex couples, 218
 sibling abuse
  emotional abuse, 216
  extreme abuse, 216
  mild abuse, 216
  moderate abuse, 216
  patriarchal society, 215–216
  physical abuse, 216
  sexual abuse, 216
  verbal abuse, 216

Lebanon *(cont.)*
  spousal abuse
    cultural context, 212–213
    extreme abuse, 212–213
    gender roles, 212, 213
    husband abuse, 214
    implicit theories, 212–213
    individual freedom, 212–213
    mild abuse, 213
    moderate abuse, 213
    patriarchal connectivity, 212–213
    perspectives on, 212–213
    physical abuse, 212–213
    services, 212
    verbal abuse, 212–213
    wife abuse, 212–213
Lesbian and Gay Anti-Violence Project
    (Australia), 374
Lesbian/gay couples, *see* Same-sex couples
LIFELINE (South Africa), 259
Long-Term Care Ombudsman Program
    (United States), 466

M

Machismo
  Brazil, 399
  Colombia, 421
  Italy, 71
  Nicaragua, 384, 387–388, 389, 391–393
  Portugal, 59–60
Mafia (Italy), 71–72
Mail-Order Bride Law (Philippines), 356
Mandatory reporting laws
  Israel, 200
  United States, 454
Manning, Carl, 45
Marital rape
  Canada, 437, 439, 441
  Colombia, 425
  England, 39, 40, 41
  Germany, 103
  Greece, 137
  Iceland, 27, 28
  India, 275
  Israel, 195, 196
  Korea, 305, 306, 309, 310–311
  Philippines, 348–349, 356
  Portugal, 61
  South Africa, 249, 254

  Taiwan, 332
  Turkey, 158–159
  United States, 459–460
Marriage
  Australia, 366, 371
  India, 270, 273–274
  Japan, 286–287
  Philippines, 354
  Somalia, 231–232
  Taiwan, 324, 325
Married Women's Property Act (1874)
    (India), 270
Marxism, 92–93
Marxist-Leninism, 226
Measures Against Domestic Violence Act
    (2001) (Italy), 82
Media
  Greece, 133
  India, 268
  Japan, 286
  Saudi Arabia, 181–183
  United States, 454
Megan's Law (1996) (United States), 465
Men Against Violence Group (Nicaragua),
    392
Migrant and Overseas Filipino Act
    (Philippines), 356
Mild abuse, *see also* Extreme abuse;
    Moderate abuse
  abuse defined, 3, 4, 6
  Australia, 363, 368–369, 370, 371
  Brazil, 404–405, 406, 407, 409
  Canada, 432, 433, 436, 439, 440, 441
  Colombia, 421–422, 423, 424
  England, 38, 40, 41, 42, 43, 44
  Germany, 90, 98, 99, 101
  Greece, 137, 138, 143, 146
  Iceland, 29
  India, 266, 267, 274, 275, 276, 277
  Israel, 191, 193, 194, 196, 198, 199
  Italy, 71, 74, 76, 78, 79, 80, 81
  Japan, 292–293, 294, 296
  Korea, 303, 310, 312, 314
  Lebanon, 214, 215, 216, 217
  Nicaragua, 384
  Philippines, 340, 349, 352
  Russia, 119, 123, 125–126
  Saudi Arabia, 168, 177, 179, 180
  Somalia, 224–225, 235, 236
  South Africa, 246, 251, 253, 256, 258
  Taiwan, 323, 328, 329, 331, 333–334
  Turkey, 156, 160

United States, 455, 456, 457, 458, 459, 461, 462, 464, 465
Military violence
 Colombia, 417–418, 420–421, 425
 Nicaragua, 390
 Philippines, 354
Minimum Guaranteed Income (Portugal), 56
Ministers for Women (England), 46
Ministry for Family, Seniors, Women and Youth (Germany), 100
Ministry of Family (Nicaragua), 394
Minneapolis Domestic Violence Experiment, 454
Moderate abuse, *see also* Extreme abuse; Mild abuse
 abuse defined, 3, 4, 6
 Australia, 368–369, 370, 371
 Brazil, 404–405, 406, 407, 409
 Canada, 432, 433, 436, 439, 440, 441
 Colombia, 421–422, 424
 England, 38, 40, 41, 42, 43, 44
 Germany, 98, 99, 101
 Greece, 137, 138, 143, 145, 146
 Iceland, 22, 29
 Israel, 191, 193, 194, 196, 199
 Italy, 71, 74, 75, 76, 78, 79, 80, 81
 Japan, 291, 292, 294, 296
 Korea, 303, 308, 309, 310, 311, 312, 315
 Lebanon, 213, 214, 215, 216, 217
 Nicaragua, 389–390
 Philippines, 340, 349, 352
 Portugal, 59
 Russia, 112, 115, 116, 117–118, 119, 123, 124, 125
 Saudi Arabia, 168, 177, 179, 180
 Somalia, 224, 235, 236, 237
 South Africa, 246, 251.258, 253, 256
 Taiwan, 323, 326, 328, 330, 331
 Turkey, 153, 160
 United States, 455, 456, 457, 458, 459–460, 461, 462, 464, 465
Modern Women's Foundation (Taiwan), 328
Mother and Child Project (Italy), 81
Mother and Child Protection Act (1937) (Japan), 290

N

National Association of Peasant and Indigenous Women of Colombia, 425

National Center on Child Abuse and Neglect (United States), 465
National Center on Elder Abuse (United States), 461–462
National Child Abuse Hotline (United States), 466
National Child Day (Canada), 446
National Children's Rights Commission (Portugal), 63
National Citizen's Coalition for Nursing Home Reform (United States), 466
National Commission to Combat Child Labour (Portugal), 63
National Committee on Prevention and Management of Child Abuse and Neglect (Saudi Arabia), 184
National Comorbidity Study (United States), 486
National Confederation of Action on Child Labour (Portugal), 63
National Council for the Child (Israel), 201
National Crime Victimization Survey (1998) (United States), 458
National Domestic Violence Hotline (United States), 466
National Elder Abuse Center (United States), 466
National Elder Abuse Incidence Study (1996) (United States), 460
National Family Violence Survey (1995) (United States), 456
National Family Week (Canada), 446–447
National Family Welfare Institute (Colombia), 422, 424
National Health Plan (Italy), 81
National Incidence Study (1993) (United States), 455, 456
National Indian Child Welfare Association (United States), 467
National Institute for Crime and the Rehabilitation of Offenders (South Africa), 259
National Institute of Public Cooperation and Child Development (India), 272
National Latino Alliance for the Elimination of Domestic Violence (United States), 467
National Longitudinal Survey of Children and Youth (1994/1995) (Canada), 435
National Missing Children's Day (Canada), 446

National Network on Violence Against
    Women (South Africa), 259
National Peace Accord Trust (South Africa),
    259
National Policy for the Elderly (Brazil), 411
National Program Against Child Labor
    (Philippines), 355
National Programme Against Poverty
    (Portugal), 56
National Report of Greece, 133–136
National Society for the Prevention of
    Cruelty to Children (England), 44
National Society for the Protection of
    Children (England), 35
National Sovereignty and Children's Day
    (Turkey), 154
National Statistical Service (Greece), 133
National Statistics Office Survey of Child
    Laborers (Philippines), 347
National Violence Against Women (United
    States), 458–459
Neglect
    Australia, 370, 371
    Brazil, 398, 402–403, 405, 408, 409
    Canada, 432, 445
    Colombia, 423, 424
    England, 36, 37, 43, 44, 45–46
    Germany, 97
    Greece, 138–143, 144, 145, 146–147
    India, 266, 277
    Israel, 191–193, 194, 198
    Italy, 76, 80, 81
    Japan, 285, 290, 291, 295
    Korea, 306, 307, 310, 313
    Lebanon, 214, 215
    Nicaragua, 382, 391
    Philippines, 340, 345, 351, 352
    Portugal, 56–57, 61
    Russia, 115, 117, 120, 121–122, 123, 125–126
    Saudi Arabia, 180
    Somalia, 235, 236, 237
    South Africa, 251, 256, 258
    Taiwan, 322, 326–327, 332, 335
    Turkey, 159
    United States, 452, 455–456, 457, 460–461,
        462
New Child Protection Movement (Germany),
    96
New Family Code (Philippines), 355
New York Society for the Prevention of
    Cruelty to Children, 453
Nicaragua

abuse defined, 381–382
    abandonment, 382
    extreme abuse, 382
    implicit theories, 382
    neglect, 382
child abuse
    abandonment, 390
    child labor, 386, 390, 393–394
    emotional abuse, 390
    extreme abuse, 386, 390–391
    individual rights, 393
    laws, 393
    military violence, 390
    moderate abuse, 390
    perspectives on, 390–391
    physical abuse, 390
    prevalence, 390, 394
    prostitution, 394
    services, 393–395
    sexual abuse, 386, 390
    street children, 386, 390
elder abuse
    abandonment, 391
    extreme abuse, 391
    financial abuse, 391
    implicit theories, 391
    neglect, 391
    perspectives on, 391
family violence, 388–391
    gender equality, 392–393
    gender roles, 391
    human rights paradigm, 477, 482, 487,
        489, 491, 492
    implicit theories, 391
    machismo, 391–393
    patriarchal society, 392–393
    services, 391–393
macrosystem
    children's status, 384–386
    cultural context, 384
    gender roles, 383–384
    historical context, 382
    machismo, 384
    poverty, 383
microsystem, 386–388
    family norms, 387–388
    machismo, 387–388
    patrilineal society, 387–388
research overview
    capsule, 381
    conclusion, 395
    sample, 381

spousal abuse
  cultural context, 389
  emotional abuse, 389
  extreme abuse, 384, 388–389, 390
  gender roles, 389
  husband abuse, 389–390
  implicit theories, 388
  laws, 388
  machismo, 389
  mild abuse, 384
  moderate abuse, 389–390
  perspectives on, 384, 388–390
  physical abuse, 388, 389
  prevalence, 388
  public humiliation, 389
  sexual abuse, 384, 388–389
  verbal abuse, 389
  wife, 388–390
Nicaraguan Social Security and Welfare
    Institute, 393
Nongovernmental organizations (NGOs),
    492–493
Nuclear Non Proliferation Treaty, 181

O

Older Americans Act (1987) (United States),
    466
Optional Protocol to the Convention on the
    Rights of the Child on the Sale of
    Children, Child Prostitution, and
    Child Pornography, 56
Organization of Petroleum Exporting
    Countries (OPEC), 181
Organization of the Islamic Conference
    (OIC), 181

P

Pandemic victimization, 483
Patriarchal connectivity (Lebanon), 211,
    212–213
Patriarchal society
  Brazil, 399, 402, 412–413
  Colombia, 419, 423, 425
  Greece, 138
  India, 267, 273
  Italy, 72, 74–75
  Japan, 286, 288–289

Korea, 310, 314–315
Lebanon, 206–207, 211, 212–213, 215–216
Nicaragua, 392–393
Philippines, 331, 341
Somalia, 235
South Africa, 254
Taiwan, 332
Turkey, 153
Patrilineal society
  India, 267, 269
  Korea, 304
  Nicaragua, 387–388
Personal construct theory, 5
Philippine Plan of Action for Children, 355
Philippines
  abuse defined
    abandonment, 340
    child abuse, 340
    emotional abuse, 340
    extreme abuse, 340
    mild abuse, 340
    moderate abuse, 340
    neglect, 340
    physical abuse, 340
    sexual abuse, 340
    spousal abuse, 340
    trafficking, 340
    verbal abuse, 340
  child abuse
    abandonment, 345
    alcohol consumption, 346
    child labor, 347, 355
    corporal punishment, 345–346
    emotional abuse, 346–347
    gender inequality, 347
    laws, 355, 356
    military violence, 354
    neglect, 345
    perspectives on, 346–347
    physical abuse, 345–346
    prevalence, 344–345, 346
    prostitution, 354, 356
    public humiliation, 346, 347
    rape, 345
    services, 355, 356
    sexual abuse, 345
    street children, 354
    trafficking, 354, 356
  elder abuse
    abandonment, 351, 352
    alcohol consumption, 352
    extreme abuse, 351, 352

Philippines *(cont.)*
  elder abuse *(cont.)*
    financial abuse, 352–353
    laws, 356
    mild abuse, 352
    moderate abuse, 352
    neglect, 351, 352
    perspectives on, 351–353
    physical abuse, 352–353
    risk factors, 342
    services, 356
  family violence, 344–354
    alcohol consumption, 344
    cultural context, 356–357
    human rights paradigm, 477, 481, 482, 483–484, 488–489, 491, 492, 496
    intervention agenda, 356–358
    marriage, 354
    religion, 354
  macrosystem
    Catholicism, 341, 357
    children's status, 341–342
    contemporary context, 341
    elder status, 342
    family norms, 341–342
    gender equality, 342
    gender roles, 341, 342
    historical context, 340–341
    patriarchal society, 341
    women's status, 342
  microsystem
    Catholicism, 343
    collectivism, 343
    cultural context, 343
    family conflict resolution, 344
    family norms, 342–343
    gender roles, 344
  research overview
    abuse defined, 340
    capsule, 339
    sample, 340
  sibling abuse
    emotional abuse, 353
    perspectives on, 353–354
    physical abuse, 353
    sexual abuse, 353
  spousal abuse
    alcohol consumption, 348, 350
    Catholicism, 348
    divorce, 348
    emotional abuse, 349–350
    extreme abuse, 348, 349

    gender roles, 350–351
    husband abuse, 350–351
    implicit theories, 348
    infidelity, 349
    laws, 355–356
    marital rape, 348–349, 356
    mild abuse, 349
    moderate abuse, 349
    perspectives on, 348, 349–351
    physical abuse, 348, 349, 350
    prevalence, 347, 348–349
    public humiliation, 349, 350
    risk factors, 347–348, 350
    services, 355–356
    sexual abuse, 348–349, 354
    verbal abuse, 349
    wife abuse, 348–350
Physical abuse, *see also* Corporal punishment
  abuse defined, 3, 4
  Australia, 368, 369–370, 370, 371
  Brazil, 398, 399, 403, 404, 405, 406, 407, 408
  Canada, 432–433, 434, 435, 436, 437, 438–439, 440–442, 443, 445
  Colombia, 416, 421, 423, 424
  England, 34, 36–37, 38–39, 40, 41, 42, 43, 44
  Germany, 90, 91, 95, 96–97, 98, 99, 101
  Greece, 132–133, 134, 136–137, 138, 139, 141, 142, 143, 144, 145
  Iceland, 18, 22, 23–24, 25, 27, 28, 29
  India, 266, 272, 274, 275–276, 277
  Israel, 188, 190, 191–193, 194, 195, 196–197, 199, 200–201
  Italy, 70–71, 75, 76–77, 78, 79, 81
  Japan, 285, 288, 289–290, 291, 292, 293, 294, 295, 296
  Korea, 302, 305, 306, 307, 308, 309, 310, 311, 312–313, 315
  Lebanon, 206, 212–213, 214, 215, 216, 217
  Nicaragua, 388, 389, 390
  Philippines, 340, 345–346, 348, 349, 350, 352–353, 353
  Portugal, 52, 57, 60, 62–63
  Russia, 112, 116, 117, 118, 119, 120–121, 124, 125
  Saudi Arabia, 168, 177, 179, 180
  Somalia, 224, 234, 235
  South Africa, 246, 248, 251, 252, 253, 255, 257–258
  Taiwan, 322, 323, 326–328, 329–330, 331, 332, 333, 334, 335
  Turkey, 152, 156–159, 160

United States, 452, 453–454, 455–456,
  457–459, 460–461, 463, 464
Plan Colombia, 426
Plan on the Elimination of Exploitation of
  Child Labour (Portugal), 64
Police Department for the Elderly (Brazil),
  410–411
Polygamy (Somalia), 225, 232–233
Portugal
  abuse defined
    emotional abuse, 52
    physical abuse, 52
    verbal abuse, 52
  child abuse
    child labor, 57–59, 63–64
    extreme abuse, 56
    family norms, 55–56
    human rights, 56
    individual rights, 54, 56–57, 63
    laws, 56, 59, 63, 64
    neglect, 56–57
    physical abuse, 57
    prevalence, 57
    services, 56–57, 58–59, 63–64
    sexual abuse, 56–57
  domestic violence, 64–65
  elder abuse
    emotional abuse, 63
    family norms, 62
    financial abuse, 62
    individual rights, 62
    laws, 62, 65
    neglect, 61
    physical abuse, 62–63
    services, 65
  family violence, 55–63
    human rights paradigm, 480, 482,
      488–489, 490, 491
  macrosystem
    children's status, 54–55
    cultural context, 53–54
    family norms, 53–54
    historical context, 52–53
    women's status, 55
  research overview
    capsule, 51
    conclusion, 65–66
    implicit theories, 51–52
    sample, 51–52
  spousal abuse
    family norms, 59–60, 61
    gender equality, 55, 61

gender roles, 59, 60
    individual rights, 55
    laws, 61, 64
    machismo, 59–60
    moderate abuse, 59
    perspectives on, 59–60
    physical abuse, 57, 60
    prevalence, 60–61
    services, 64–65
Posttraumatic stress disorder (PTSD), 486
Preda Foundation (UNICEF), 356
Pre-Natal Diagnostic Techniques Act (1994)
  (India), 271
Prenatal sex selection (India), 271, 272, 273
Prevention of Family Violence Act (1993)
  (South Africa), 249
Prevention strategies, see Laws; Services
Project Harmony (Russia), 113–114
Prostitution
  Brazil, 400
  Japan, 288
  Nicaragua, 394
  Philippines, 354, 356
  South Africa, 250–251
Protection from Harassment Act (1997)
  (England), 46
Protection of Children Act (1999) (England),
  45
Psychological abuse, see Emotional abuse
Public Child Guidance Centers (Japan),
  290–291
Public humiliation, see also Shaming
  Australia, 362–363, 368–369
  Canada, 440, 441, 442
  India, 275
  Italy, 74
  Nicaragua, 389
  Philippines, 346, 347, 349, 350
  Russia, 118, 119
  Saudi Arabia, 177
  Somalia, 235, 236
  Taiwan, 331
Puntos de Encuentro (Nicaragua), 392
Pusan Women's Hotline (Korea), 309

Q–R

Quincho Barrilete (Nicaragua), 394–395
Race Relations Act (1976) (England), 47
Rape, see also Marital rape

Brazil, 401, 402, 406
Colombia, 423
England, 39–40
Germany, 103
Greece, 133–134, 147
India, 270
Japan, 286, 289, 293
Korea, 312
Lebanon, 213–214
Philippines, 367
Russia, 116
Somalia, 239–240
South Africa, 247–248, 249, 250, 251–252,
    253–254, 255, 258, 259, 260
Taiwan, 333
Rape Crisis (South Africa), 259
Reform in Marriage and Family Law (1977)
    (Germany), 92
Religion
    Colombia, 417, 419–420
    Israel, 190–191, 202
    Italy, 71–72, 81–82
    Japan, 286
    Korea, 303–304, 308, 316
    Lebanon, 209
    Philippines, 341, 343, 348, 354, 357
    Saudi Arabia, 169, 175–176, 178, 179, 184
    Somalia, 227, 231, 232
Republic Act (1991) (Philippines), 355, 356
Royal Commission on the Status of Women
    (Canada), 447
Russia
    abuse defined
        alcohol consumption, 112
        child abuse, 112
        emotional abuse, 112
        extreme abuse, 112
        moderate abuse, 112
        physical abuse, 112
        verbal abuse, 112
    child abuse
        alcohol consumption, 120, 121
        child maltreatment, 120
        corporal punishment, 115, 120, 123, 124
        emotional abuse, 123
        extreme abuse, 122, 123
        family norms, 120, 122
        implicit theories, 123
        individual rights, 123
        institutional, 121–122
        laws, 122
        mild abuse, 123

        moderate abuse, 115, 123
        neglect, 115, 120, 121, 123
        perspectives on, 123–124
        physical abuse, 120–121
        prevalence, 120–121, 124
        services, 127
        sexual abuse, 120, 124
        social orphanhood, 120, 121–122
    domestic violence
        extreme abuse, 116, 117
        implicit theories, 116
        perspectives on, 117
        physical abuse, 116, 117
        prevalence, 116, 117
        rape, 116
    elder abuse
        emotional abuse, 124, 125–126
        extreme abuse, 125, 126
        family norms, 124–125
        financial abuse, 125, 126
        mild abuse, 125–126
        moderate abuse, 124, 125
        neglect, 125–126
        perspectives on, 125–126
        physical abuse, 124, 125
        prevalence, 116
        verbal abuse, 124, 125
    family violence, 116–126
        human rights, 127, 128
        human rights paradigm, 480, 482,
            488–489
        implicit theories, 113, 127–128
        myths, 113–114
        prevalence, 116–117
        services, 126–128
    macrosystem
        communist theory, 113
        family norms, 113–114
        gender equality, 113
        gender roles, 113–114
    microsystem
        family norms, 115
        family structure, 114–115
        gender roles, 115
    research overview
        capsule, 111–112
        sample, 112
    spousal abuse
        emotional abuse, 117, 118
        extreme abuse, 116, 117, 119
        gender roles, 117–118
        husband abuse, 118–119

implicit theories, 117, 118
mild abuse, 119
moderate abuse, 116, 117–118, 119
neglect, 117
perspectives on, 117–118, 119
physical abuse, 116, 117, 118, 119
prevalence, 116
public humiliation, 118, 119
services, 127
sexual abuse, 119
verbal abuse, 118, 119
wife abuse, 116, 117–118
Russian Association of Crisis Centers for
    Women, 117

S

Safe houses
  Colombia, 426
  England, 46
  Somalia, 234–235
Safe Women-Liverpool Project (Australia),
    374
Same Gender Domestic Violence Reports
    (United States), 467
Same-sex couples
  Australia, 374
  Canada, 442–443
  Italy, 72
  Lebanon, 218
  Somalia, 241
  United States, 467
Saudi Arabia
  abuse defined
    child abuse, 178
    emotional abuse, 168
    extreme abuse, 168
    family violence, 174
    mild abuse, 168
    moderate abuse, 168
    physical abuse, 168
    verbal abuse, 168
  child abuse
    child maltreatment, 178–179
    corporal punishment, 174
    emotional abuse, 179
    extreme abuse, 179
    female infanticide, 178
    Holy Qur'an, 178
    mild abuse, 179

    moderate abuse, 179
    perspectives on, 179
    physical abuse, 179
  elder abuse
    emotional abuse, 180
    extreme abuse, 180
    family norms, 179–180
    financial abuse, 180
    Holy Qur'an, 179
    neglect, 180
    perspectives on, 180
    physical abuse, 180
  family violence, 177–181
    defined, 174
    gender equality, 175–176
    government services, 181
    health services, 184–185
    Holy Qur'an, 175–176
    human rights, 181
    human rights paradigm, 476, 481, 482,
      483, 484, 487–489, 490, 493, 494
    media services, 181–183
    perspectives on, 175–176
    public services, 183–184
    religious services, 184
  macrosystem, 168–169
    Holy Qur'an, 169
  microsystem, 169–174
    Al-Moakasat, 173
    Al-Onosa, 173
    children's role, 173–174
    cultural context, 170–173
    family norms, 170, 172, 174
    family structure, 169–170
    gender roles, 170–173
  research overview
    capsule, 167–168
    conclusion, 185–186
    sample, 168
  sibling abuse, 180–181
    emotional abuse, 180
    extreme abuse, 180
    financial abuse, 180
    mild abuse, 180
    moderate abuse, 180
    physical abuse, 180
  spousal abuse
    emotional abuse, 177
    extreme abuse, 177
    family norms, 177
    husband abuse, 177
    mild abuse, 177

Saudi Arabia *(cont.)*
  spousal abuse *(cont.)*
    moderate abuse, 177
    perspectives on, 177
    physical abuse, 177
    public humiliation, 177
    verbal abuse, 177
    wife abuse, 177
Self-Help Ending Domestics Project
    (Australia), 374
Seoul Women's Hotline, 305, 307
Services, *see also* Help lines; Safe houses;
    Women's shelters
  Australia, 374
  Brazil, 403, 410–411, 412
  Canada, 443, 446–447, 449
  Colombia, 424, 425
  England, 44–46, 47
  Germany, 92, 93, 99, 100, 102, 103–104
  Greece, 146
  human rights paradigm, 494
  Iceland, 22–23, 25, 29–30
  India, 277–279
  Israel, 202
  Italy, 73, 76, 78, 80, 81–82, 83–84
  Japan, 286, 290, 296–297
  Korea, 315–316
  Lebanon, 212, 215, 218
  Nicaragua, 391–395
  Philippines, 355–356
  Portugal, 56–57, 58–59, 63–65
  Russia, 126–128
  Saudi Arabia, 181–185
  Somalia, 234–235, 239, 241
  South Africa, 249, 256, 258–260
  Taiwan, 326, 335
  Turkey, 160, 161–162
  United States, 453, 454, 465–467
Severe abuse, *see* Extreme abuse
Sexual abuse, *see also* Marital rape;
    Prostitution; Rape
  Australia, 368, 369
  Brazil, 398, 400, 403–405, 406, 407, 408
  Canada, 435, 436, 437, 438, 439, 443
  England, 34, 36, 37, 38, 41–42, 44, 45
  Germany, 90, 97–98, 99
  Greece, 137, 139, 143, 147
  Iceland, 22–23, 25, 27, 28
  India, 266, 275, 277
  Israel, 188, 191–193, 194–195, 196, 199, 200,
    201
  Italy, 76–78, 79, 81–82

  Japan, 285, 288, 289, 290–291, 292–294, 296
  Korea, 309, 310–312, 313, 315
  Lebanon, 206, 213–214, 216
  Nicaragua, 384, 386, 388–389, 390
  Philippines, 340, 345, 348–349, 353, 354
  Portugal, 56–57
  Russia, 119, 120, 124
  Somalia, 224
  South Africa, 249, 250–251, 252, 253, 255,
    258
  Taiwan, 322, 327, 328, 329, 330, 332, 333
  Turkey, 153, 159, 160
  United States, 455–456, 457, 459–460,
    461–462, 463, 464, 465
Sexual Abuse Shelter (Iceland), 30
Sexual Harassment Prevention Law (1999)
    (Israel), 201–202
Sexual Violation Prevention (Taiwan), 335
Shaming, *see also* Public humiliation
  China, 496
  human rights paradigm, 487, 495–496
  Philippines, 496
  Turkey, 154–155
Sibling abuse
  Canada, 434
  Israel, 199–200
  Japan, 295–296
  Korea, 311–312
  Lebanon, 215–216
  Philippines, 353–354
  Saudi Arabia, 180–181
  Somalia, 236–237
  Taiwan, 333–334
  United States, 463–465
Sibling Abuse Survivors' Information and
    Advocacy Network (United States),
    466
SIBOL (Philippines), 355
Social orphanhood (Russia), 120, 121–122
Social Welfare Office (Iceland), 30
Somalia
  abuse defined
    cultural context, 224
    extreme abuse, 224
    individual freedom, 225
    mild abuse, 224–225
    moderate abuse, 224
    physical abuse, 224
    polygamy, 225
    sexual abuse, 224
    verbal abuse, 224–225
  child abuse

cultural context, 235, 236
extreme abuse, 235, 236
family norms, 235–236
mild abuse, 236
moderate abuse, 235, 236
neglect, 236
perspectives on, 235–236
physical abuse, 235
public humiliation, 235, 236
verbal abuse, 235, 236
elder abuse
cultural connectivity, 237
family norms, 237
moderate abuse, 237
neglect, 237
perspectives on, 237
family violence, 234–237
human rights paradigm, 481, 482,
487–488, 489, 491
interpersonal abuse
female genital mutilation (FGM),
238–239
gender equality, 238
gender roles, 238
HIV/AIDS, 240, 241
human rights, 238
individual rights, 238
laws, 238, 239
rape, 239–240
services, 239, 241
macrosystem
cultural context, 227, 229
family conflict resolution, 229
historical context, 225–227
individual freedom, 229
religion, 227
Republic of Puntland, 226–227
Republic of Somaliland, 226–227
social structure, 227–229
Somali Republic, 226
microsystem
children's roles, 233–234
cultural context, 233–234
divorce, 231, 232, 233
family norms, 230–231
marriage, 231–232
polygamy, 232–233
religion, 231, 232
research overview
capsule, 223–224
conclusion, 241
sample, 224

same-sex couples, 241
sibling abuse
cultural context, 236–237
family norms, 236–237
spousal abuse
cultural context, 235
extreme abuse, 234, 235
mild abuse, 235
moderate abuse, 235
neglect, 235
patriarchal society, 235
perspectives on, 235
physical abuse, 234, 235
prevalence, 234
services, 234–235
South Africa
abuse defined
alcohol consumption, 246
emotional abuse, 246
extreme abuse, 246
financial abuse, 246
mild abuse, 246
moderate abuse, 246
physical abuse, 246
child abuse
alcohol consumption, 250, 251
emotional abuse, 251
extreme abuse, 251
laws, 249, 251
mild abuse, 251
moderate abuse, 251
neglect, 251
perspectives on, 251
physical abuse, 251
prevalence, 250
prostitution, 250–251
rape, 247–248, 250
services, 258–259
sexual abuse, 249, 250–251
verbal abuse, 251
domestic violence
alcohol consumption, 252, 253
causation factors, 254
cultural context, 251–252
emotional abuse, 252
female abuse, 251–252
financial abuse, 252
gender roles, 255
laws, 249, 251
male abuse, 255, 260
male rape, 255, 260
men's services, 260

South Africa *(cont.)*
  domestic violence *(cont.)*
    men's status, 255
    patriarchal society, 254
    physical abuse, 252
    prevalence, 252, 253
    rape, 251–252, 253–254, 255, 259, 260
    risk factors, 252
    sexual abuse, 252, 253, 255
    verbal abuse, 252
    women's countermeasures, 254–255
    women's services, 259
  elder abuse
    causation factors, 257
    cultural context, 257
    elder status, 256
    emotional abuse, 256, 258
    extreme abuse, 257–258
    financial abuse, 257–258
    human rights, 257
    institutional abuse, 258
    mild abuse, 258
    moderate abuse, 258
    neglect, 256, 258
    perspectives on, 257–258
    physical abuse, 257–258
    prevalence, 256–257
    rape, 258
    services, 256, 259–260
    sexual abuse, 258
    verbal abuse, 258
  family violence, 249–258
    human rights paradigm, 482, 484,
      487–488, 489, 491, 493
    individual freedom, 249
    individual rights, 249–250
    laws, 249–250
    services, 249
  HIV/AIDS, 247–248, 254, 256
  macrosystem
    children's status, 247–248
    cultural context, 248
    gender equality, 248
    gender inequality, 248
    gender roles, 248
    historical context, 246–247
    individual freedom, 248
    women's status, 248
  microsystem, 248–249
  research overview
    capsule, 245
    conclusion, 260

    sample, 245–246
  spousal abuse, 253–255
    emotional abuse, 255
    extreme abuse, 253, 255
    financial abuse, 253
    husband abuse, 255–256
    implicit theories, 253
    laws, 249, 251
    marital rape, 249, 254
    mild abuse, 253, 256
    moderate abuse, 253, 256
    perspectives, 253, 255–256
    physical abuse, 248, 253, 255
    sexual abuse, 248, 253
    verbal abuse, 248, 253, 255
South African Institute for Race Relations,
    250
Spanking in Non-Educational (Brazil), 403
Special Project for Women in Especially
    Difficult Circumstances (Philippines),
    356
Special Protection of Children Against Child
    Abuse, Exploitation and
    Discrimination Act (1991)
    (Philippines), 355, 356
Spiritual abuse (Canada), 432, 435
Spousal abuse, *see also* Domestic violence;
    Family violence; Marital rape; Public
    humiliation; Same-sex couples
  abuse defined, 3, 4, 5, 6
  Australia, 369–370
  Brazil, 399, 406–407
  Canada, 434, 436–442
  Colombia, 421–422, 425
  England, 38–42, 46
  Germany, 99, 103
  Greece, 136–138
  Iceland, 23–28, 29–30
  India, 267, 270–271, 272, 273–275, 274, 275,
    276, 277–279
  Israel, 190, 195–198, 201–202
  Italy, 74, 75, 78–79, 82
  Japan, 293–294, 297
  Korea, 305, 306, 309–311, 315–316
  Lebanon, 212–213, 214
  Nicaragua, 384, 388–390
  Philippines, 347–351, 355–356
  Portugal, 55, 57, 59–61, 64–65
  Russia, 116, 117–119, 127
  Saudi Arabia, 177
  Somalia, 234–235

South Africa, 248, 249, 251, 253, 254, 255–256
Taiwan, 328–332, 335
Turkey, 154–155, 156–159, 161–162
United States, 453–454, 457–460
Street children
  Brazil, 400–401, 410
  Nicaragua, 386
  Philippines, 354
Stress, 486, 490–491
Study Group of Violence from Husbands and Partners (Japan), 289
Supported Accommodation Assistance Program (Australia), 366
Support Help and Empowerment (Australia), 374
Survey on Family Growth (1995) (United States), 453

T

Taiwan
  abuse defined
    child abuse, 326–327
    emotional abuse, 322, 323
    extreme abuse, 322
    family violence, 325–326
    implicit theories, 323
    mild abuse, 323
    moderate abuse, 323
    neglect, 322
    physical abuse, 322, 323
    sexual abuse, 322
    verbal abuse, 322
    wife abuse, 328
  child abuse
    abandonment, 327
    corporal punishment, 326, 335
    emotional abuse, 326–327
    extreme abuse, 327–328
    laws, 335
    mild abuse, 328
    moderate abuse, 326, 328
    neglect, 326–327, 335
    perspectives on, 327–328
    physical abuse, 326–328, 335
    prevalence, 327
    services, 335
    sexual abuse, 327
    verbal abuse, 327
  elder abuse
    abandonment, 333

    emotional abuse, 333
    extreme abuse, 332–333, 334
    family norms, 332
    financial abuse, 332
    grandparents, 334
    laws, 325, 335
    mild abuse, 333
    neglect, 332
    patriarchal society, 332
    perspectives on, 332–333
    physical abuse, 332, 333, 334
    prevalence, 332
    services, 335
    sexual abuse, 332
    verbal abuse, 332, 333
  family violence, 325–335
    family norms, 334
    human rights paradigm, 481, 482, 483, 484, 488–489, 490
    laws, 325–326
    prevalence, 326
    services, 326
  macrosystem
    children's status, 324
    divorce, 323
    elder status, 325
    family norms, 324–325
    family structure, 324
    gender roles, 324
    marriage, 324, 325
    socioeconomic context, 323–324
    women's status, 324–325
  mother-in-law
    bullying, 335
    daughter-in-law, 334–335
  research overview
    capsule, 321
    conclusion, 335–336
    sample, 321–322
  sibling abuse
    bullying, 333–334
    extreme abuse, 333
    financial abuse, 333
    mild abuse, 333–334
    perspectives on, 333–334
    physical abuse, 333
    rape, 333
    sexual abuse, 333
  spousal abuse
    alcohol consumption, 330
    emotional abuse, 328, 329, 331
    extreme abuse, 329–330, 331, 332
    family norms, 329, 330

Taiwan *(cont.)*
  spousal abuse *(cont.)*
    husband abuse, 330–332
    marital rape, 332
    mild abuse, 329, 331
    moderate abuse, 330, 331
    perspectives on, 329–330, 331–332
    physical abuse, 328, 329–330, 331, 332
    prevalence, 328–329, 330
    public humiliation, 331
    services, 335
    sexual abuse, 328, 329, 330
    Southeast Asian wives, 329
    verbal abuse, 329, 331
    wife abuse, 328–330
Telefono Azzurro (Italy), 76, 83
Telefono Rosa (Italy), 83
Trafficking
  Colombia, 420
  Japan, 288
  Philippines, 340, 354, 356
Transition Home Survey (1999–2000)
    (Canada), 436
Turkey
  abuse defined
    child abuse, 152
    cultural context, 153
    emotional abuse, 153
    extreme abuse, 153
    implicit theories, 153
    moderate abuse, 153
    patriarchal society, 153
    physical abuse, 152
    sexual abuse, 153
    spousal abuse, 152
  child abuse
    child labor, 156, 160
    corporal punishment, 156
    emotional abuse, 159, 160
    extreme abuse, 156, 160
    laws, 162
    mild abuse, 156, 160
    moderate abuse, 160
    neglect, 159
    physical abuse, 156, 159, 160
    prevalence, 159
    services, 160, 162
    sexual abuse, 159, 160
    shaming, 154–155
  elder abuse
    family norms, 160–161
    financial abuse, 161

    implicit theories, 161
    women's status, 161
  family violence, 156–161
    human rights paradigm, 480, 481, 482,
      483, 484, 487–488, 489, 492, 493, 494
  macrosystem
    children's status, 155–156
    contemporary context, 154
    family norms, 154–155
    gender equality, 153–154
    gender inequality, 155
    historical context, 153–154
    laws, 155
    women's status, 155, 161
  research overview
    capsule, 151–152
    conclusion, 162
    sample, 152
  spousal abuse
    alcohol consumption, 158
    emotional abuse, 158–159
    husband abuse, 159
    implicit theories, 157–158, 159
    laws, 162
    marital rape, 158–159
    perspectives on, 157–158
    physical abuse, 156–159
    prevalence, 156–157, 158–159
    services, 161–162
    shaming, 154–155
    wife abuse, 156–159
    women's countermeasures, 158
    women's movement, 161–162
    women's shelters, 158
Turkish Women's Union, 162

U

UNICEF, 355, 356, 419
United Nations Commission on Human
    Rights, 305, 494–495
United Nations Committee Meeting on the
    Rights of the Child, 56–57, 212
United Nations Convention on the
    Elimination of All Forms of
    Discrimination Against Women, 82,
    135–136, 355, 401, 425, 475–476
United Nations Convention on the Rights of
    the Child, 10, 20, 22, 35, 45, 63, 162,

181, 201, 211, 218, 305, 335, 355, 400, 409, 446, 476, 493–494
United Nations Declaration of Women's Rights, 181
United Nations Declaration on the Rights of the Child, 446
United Nations Global Programme Against Trafficking in Human Beings, 356
United Nations Human Development Index, 71–72
United Nations Universal Declaration of Human Rights, 181, 401, 474, 475
United States
  abuse defined
    emotional abuse, 452, 461
    financial abuse, 462
    implicit theories, 452
    neglect, 452, 462
    physical abuse, 452, 461
    sexual abuse, 452, 461
    verbal abuse, 452
  child abuse
    battered child syndrome, 454
    corporal punishment, 454–455, 456
    emotional abuse, 457
    extreme abuse, 455, 456, 457
    historical context, 453, 454
    homicide, 456
    implicit theories, 457
    laws, 454, 465
    mild abuse, 455, 456, 457
    moderate abuse, 455, 456, 457
    neglect, 455–456, 457
    perpetrators, 455–456
    perspectives on, 454–455, 456, 457
    physical abuse, 454, 455–456
    prevalence, 455–456, 457
    services, 453, 465, 466, 467
    sexual abuse, 455–456, 457
    verbal abuse, 457
    victim characteristics, 455
  elder abuse
    emotional abuse, 460–461
    extreme abuse, 461, 462, 463
    financial abuse, 460–461, 462
    institutional abuse, 462–463
    laws, 454, 466
    mild abuse, 461, 462
    moderate abuse, 461, 462
    neglect, 460–461, 462
    perspectives on, 461, 462, 463
    physical abuse, 460–461

    prevalence, 460–461, 462
    services, 466
    sexual abuse, 461–462
  family violence, 453–465
    historical context, 453–454
    human rights paradigm, 474, 479, 480, 481, 482, 483, 486, 488, 491
    implicit theories, 453–454
    laws, 452–454, 465–466
    media coverage, 454
    services, 453, 454, 465–467
    women's movement, 454
  macrosystem, 452–453
  microsystem, 453
  research overview
    capsule, 451
    sample, 451–452
  same-sex couples, 467
  sibling abuse
    emotional abuse, 464–465
    extreme abuse, 463, 464, 465
    laws, 463
    mild abuse, 464, 465
    moderate abuse, 464, 465
    perpetrators, 463–464
    perspectives on, 463, 464–465
    physical abuse, 463, 464
    prevalence, 464
    services, 466
    sexual abuse, 463, 464, 465
    verbal abuse, 464–465
    victim characteristics, 463–464
  spousal abuse
    bullying, 459
    cultural context, 457–458
    emotional abuse, 459
    extreme abuse, 458, 459–460
    historical context, 453–454
    husband abuse, 457–458
    implicit theories, 460
    laws, 453–454, 460
    marital rape, 459–460
    mild abuse, 458, 459
    moderate abuse, 458, 459–460
    perpetrators, 458
    perspectives on, 457–458, 459, 460
    physical abuse, 453–454, 457–459
    prevalence, 458–460
    services, 454
    sexual abuse, 459–460
    verbal abuse, 459
    victim characteristics, 458
    wife abuse, 457–458

V

Verbal abuse, *see also* Public humiliation;
   Shaming
 abuse defined, 3, 4
 Australia, 362, 369, 371
 Brazil, 398, 405, 406, 407, 408–409
 Canada, 432, 436, 437, 440, 442, 443, 445
 Colombia, 416
 England, 33–34, 42, 43
 Germany, 90, 91, 98, 99
 Greece, 141, 142, 143, 144, 145, 146
 India, 266, 277
 Israel, 199
 Italy, 81
 Japan, 292, 294, 295
 Korea, 305, 307, 309, 310, 311–312, 313–314
 Lebanon, 206, 212–213, 215, 216, 217
 Nicaragua, 389
 Philippines, 340, 349
 Portugal, 52
 Russia, 112, 118, 119, 124, 125
 Saudi Arabia, 168, 177
 Somalia, 224–225, 235, 236
 South Africa, 248, 251, 252, 253, 255, 258
 Taiwan, 322, 327, 329, 331, 332, 333
 United States, 452, 457, 459, 464–465
Victorian Community Council Against
   Violence (Australia), 371
Violence Against Women Act (2000) (United
   States), 465

W

Wildwasser Groups (Germany), 103
Women for Human Rights (Turkey), 162

Women Rescue Foundation (Taiwan), 328
Women's Domestic Violence Crisis Services
   of Victoria (Australia), 366–367
Women's Hotline (Korea), 315
Women's Living Conditions in Taiwan
   Survey (1998), 328, 329
Women's movement, *see also* Gender
   equality
 Brazil, 402
 Germany, 102–103
 human rights paradigm, 493, 495
 Iceland, 25
 India, 271
 Japan, 289
 Turkey, 161–162
 United States, 454
Women's Rights Promotion Committee
   (Taiwan), 335
Women's Safety Project (Canada), 437
Women's Safety Survey (1996) (Australia),
   366
Women's Shelter (Iceland), 25, 30
Women's shelters
 Canada, 438, 447
 Germany, 103
 India, 278, 280–281
 Israel, 195, 196, 197–198, 202
 Korea, 315
 Turkey, 158
 United States, 454
Women's Special Police Station (Brazil), 410
World Assembly on Aging (1982), 62
World Congress Against Commercial Sexual
   Exploitation of Children (Sweden),
   356
World Gay Pride (2000), 72
World Health Organization (WHO), 408

CPSIA information can be obtained at www.ICGtesting.com
Printed in the USA
LVOW120348081212

310305LV00004B/13/P